D1222052

WISC-IV Advanced Clinical Interpretation

THIS BOOK IS DEDICATED TO

My mother, Audrey..GGW
My parents, Frances and Harold ....DHS
The memory of my parents, Antonio and Maria ....AP
My family, Tina Julia, and Adam ....JAH

WISC-IV
ADVANCED
CLINICAL
INTERPRETATION

LAWRENCE G. WEISS
Harcourt Assessment, Inc.
San Antonio, Texas

DONALD H. SAKLOFSKE
Division of Applied Psychology
University of Calgary
Calgary, Alberta, Canada

AURELIO PRIFITERA
Harcourt Assessment, Inc.
San Antonio, Texas

JAMES A. HOLDNACK
Harcourt Assessment, Inc.
San Antonio, Texas

AMSTERDAM • BOSTON • HEIDELBERG • LONDON
NEW YORK • OXFORD • PARIS • SAN DIEGO
SAN FRANCISCO • SINGAPORE • SYDNEY • TOKYO

ELSEVIER   Academic Press is an imprint of Elsevier

Academic Press is an imprint of Elsevier
30 Corporate Drive, Suite 400, Burlington, MA 01803, USA
525 B Street, Suite 1900, San Diego, California 92101-4495, USA
84 Theobald's Road, London WC1X 8RR, UK

This book is printed on acid-free paper. ∞

Library of Congress Cataloging-in-Publication Data
Weiss, Lawrence G.
WISC-IV advanced clinical interpretation / Lawrence G. Weiss.
    p. cm.
    Includes indexes.
    ISBN 0-12-088763-0 (hardcover : alk. paper)
    1. Wechsler Intelligence Scale for Children. I. Title: Wechsler Intelligence Scale for Children-4
clinical use and interpretation. II. Title: Wechsler Intelligence Scale for Children-four clinical
use and interpretation. III. Title.
    BF432.5.W42W45 2006
    155.4′1393—dc22

                                                                                    2005031694

British Library Cataloguing-in-Publication Data
A catalogue record for this book is available from the British Library.

ISBN 13: 978-0-12-088763-7
ISBN 10: 0-12-088763-0

For information on all Academic Press publications
visit our Web site at www.books.elsevier.com

Printed in the United States of America
06 07 08 09 10   9 8 7 6 5 4 3 2 1

Working together to grow
libraries in developing countries
www.elsevier.com | www.bookaid.org | www.sabre.org

ELSEVIER   BOOK AID
             International   Sabre Foundation

CONTENTS

1

WISC-IV INTERPRETATION IN SOCIETAL CONTEXT

LAWRENCE G. WEISS, JOSETTE G. HARRIS, AURELIO PRIFITERA,
TROY COURVILLE, ERIC ROLFHUS, DONALD H. SAKLOFSKE, AND
JAMES A. HOLDNACK

2

THE ESSENTIALS AND BEYOND

LAWRENCE G. WEISS, AURELIO PRIFITERA, JAMES A. HOLDNACK,
DONALD H. SAKLOFSKE, ERIC ROLFHUS, AND DIANE COALSON

3

ADVANCED INTERPRETIVE ISSUES WITH THE WISC-IV FULL-SCALE IQ AND GENERAL ABILITY INDEX SCORES

DONALD H. SAKLOFSKE, LAWRENCE G. WEISS, SUSAN E. RAIFORD,
AND AURELIO PRIFITERA

4

ADVANCED CLINICAL INTERPRETATION OF WISC-IV INDEX SCORES

LAWRENCE G. WEISS, DONALD H. SAKLOFSKE, DAVID M. SCHWARTZ, AURELIO PRIFITERA, AND TROY COURVILLE

5

ESSENTIALS OF WISC-IV INTEGRATED INTERPRETATION

JAMES A. HOLDNACK, AND LAWRENCE G. WEISS

6

WISC-IV Integrated: Beyond the Essentials
James A. Holdnack, and Lawrence G. Weiss

7

Advanced WISC-IV and WISC-IV Integrated Interpretation in Context with Other Measures
James A. Holdnack, Lawrence G. Weiss, and Peter Entwistle

8

REPORT WRITING: A CHILD-CENTERED APPROACH

VICKI L. SCHWEAN, THOMAS OAKLAND, LAWRENCE G. WEISS,
DONALD H. SAKLOFSKE, JAMES A. HOLDNACK, AND AURELIO PRIFITERA

AUTHORS

Lawrence G. Weiss, Harcourt Assessment, Inc. San Antonio, Texas, 78259.

Donald H. Saklofske, Division of Applied Psychology, University of Calgary, Calgary, Alberta, Canada. T2N 1N4

Aurelio Prifitera, Harcourt Assessment, Inc. San Antonio, Texas, 78259.

James A. Holdnack, Harcourt Assessment, Inc. San Antonio, Texas, 78259.

INVITED CONTRIBUTORS

Diane Coalson, Harcourt Assessment, Inc. San Antonio, Texas, 78259.

Troy Courville, Harcourt Assessment, Inc. San Antonio, Texas, 78259.

Peter Entwistle, Harcourt Assessment, Inc. Pembroke Massachusetts, 02359.

Josette G. Harris, Department of Psychiatry and Neurology, University of Colorado School of Medicine, Denver, Colorado, 80262.

Thomas Oakland, Department of Foundations Education, University of Florida, Gainesville, Florida, 32611.

Susan E. Raiford, Harcourt Assessment, Inc. San Antonio, Texas, 78259.

Eric Rolfhus, Harcourt Assessment, Inc. San Antonio, Texas, 78259.

Vicki L. Schwean, Division of Applied Psychology, University of Calgary, Calgary, Alberta, Canada. T2N 1N4

David M. Schwartz, Harcourt Assessment, Inc. San Antonio, Texas, 78259.

CONTRIBUTORS TO CHAPTERS

Chapter 1 - WISC-IV Interpretation in Societal Context

Lawrence G. Weiss, Josette G. Harris, Aurelio Prifitera, Troy Courville, Eric Rolfhus, Donald H. Saklofske, James A. Holdnack

Chapter 2 - The Essentials and Beyond

Lawrence G. Weiss, Aurelio Prifitera, James A. Holdnack, Donald H. Saklofske, Eric Rolfhus, Diane Coalson

Chapter 3 - Advanced Interpretive Issues with the WISC-IV Full-Scale IQ and General Ability Index Scores

Donald H. Saklofske, Lawrence G. Weiss, Susan E. Raiford, Aurelio Prifitera

Chapter 4 - Advanced Clinical Interpretation of WISC-IV Index Scores

Lawrence G. Weiss, Donald H. Saklofske, David M. Schwartz, Aurelio Prifitera, Troy Courville

Chapter 5 - Essentials of WISC-IV Integrated Interpretation

James A. Holdnack, Lawrence G. Weiss

Chapter 6 - WISC-IV Integrated: Beyond the Essentials

James A. Holdnack, Lawrence G. Weiss

Chapter 7 - Advanced WISC-IV and WISC-IV Integrated Interpretation in Context with Other Measures

James A. Holdnack, Lawrence G. Weiss

Chapter 8 - Report Writing: A Child-Centered Approach

Vicki L. Schwean, Thomas Oakland, Lawrence G. Weiss, Donald H. Saklofske, James A. Holdnack, Aurelio Prifitera

PREFACE

The eight chapters in this book are intended to complement and expand upon our earlier book, *WISC-IV Clinical Use and Interpretation: Scientist-Practitioner Perspectives* (Prifitera, Saklofske, & Weiss, 2005). Psychologists who are proficient with both the administration and scoring of the WISC-IV also require evidence-based interpretation information in order to fully and competently engage in the child-focused assessment process. Our previous book served to both introduce the WISC-IV to psychologists and to examine its clinical use and interpretation when assessing children presenting with a wide range of referral questions. This new book revisits the WISC-IV but takes a much closer and in-depth look at the meaning of test scores, especially the four Index Scores, and how such understanding can be facilitated both by the use of the WISC-IV Integrated and also by considering the context in which children live, learn and develop.

Written for both experienced psychologists and graduate students, this book moves quickly through the essentials of WISC-IV interpretation and onto an insightful analysis of the major cognitive domains assessed by WISC-IV. *It is the intention of the authors to raise the standard of practice in school and applied psychology from an administrative model of "test-label-place" to a functional clinical model of "assessing to understand and intervene".*

In the first chapter, we present a comprehensive array of societal and home environment factors for which there is empirical evidence indicating their impact on the development of children's cognitive abilities, and ultimately their scores on intelligence tests. Subsequent chapters address issues related to the assessment of cognitive abilities that compose "g," with special emphasis on the clinical correlates of working memory and processing speed from both neuropsychological and cognitive information processing perspectives. We have designed the book so that each new chapter builds on material presented in previous chapters and progresses the reader purposefully through deeper levels of understanding of WISC-IV and cognitive assessment in general. Two chapters explicate the processing approach to interpretation, which is the corner stone of the WISC-IV Integrated. A further chapter addresses the interpretation of WISC-IV findings within the context of other instruments as part of a full psychological evaluation. The final chapter provides an extensive case example of how to write psychological evaluation reports from a child-centered rather than a score-centered perspective that can have transforming impact on parents' and teachers' approach to the child.

Together with our complimentary book, we are optimistic that this book on advanced interpretation will also become the standard text and reference for all psychologists who use the WISC-IV in clinical practice.

We are certainly grateful to our colleagues who very generously contributed their expertise as invited co-authors on various chapters throughout this book. It is their knowledge and insights, shared throughout the eight chapters, which will be so instrumental in advancing the clinical use of the WISC-IV. Thanks to Diane Coalson, Troy Courville, Josette Harris, Tom Oakland, Susan Raiford, Eric Rolfhus, Vicki Schwean, and David Schwartz. Thanks also to Kelly Malchow for her work on reference checking and to J.J. Zhu for ensuring the accuracy of various tables throughout the book. We also wish to acknowledge the staff at Academic Press/Elsevier who played a key role in publishing this book. We thank Nikki Levy for her continued support and encouragement of our efforts to promote a best-practices and evidence-based approach to psychological assessment using the Wechsler tests. Barbara Makinster has been instrumental in ensuring the quality of this and our previous book on the WISC-IV. Phil Korn's high standards were applied throughout the editing process and have enhanced the presentation of our book.

Lawrence G. Weiss
Donald H. Saklofske
Aurelio Prifitera
James A. Holdnack

1

WISC-IV

INTERPRETATION IN

SOCIETAL CONTEXT

LAWRENCE G. WEISS, JOSETTE G. HARRIS,
AURELIO PRIFITERA, TROY COURVILLE,
ERIC ROLFHUS, DONALD H. SAKLOFSKE,
AND JAMES A. HOLDNACK

OVERVIEW

We open this book by exploring issues related to interpreting WISC-IV test scores in context with critical aspects of children's backgrounds that influence cognitive development, learning, and the overall expression of intelligent behavior. Experienced psychologists may interpret the same set of test scores in different ways depending on each child's unique background. This is because they strive to obtain and consider all relevant information about an individual child's life and circumstances when interpreting the test results. Experienced psychologists also integrate intelligence test scores with findings from measures of achievement, personality, memory, and executive functions for broader and richer interpretations. Further, the most informative and useful psychological reports describe the child rather than the test scores. This first chapter is intended to position the specific interpretive strategies described in Chapters 2–6 within the context of larger societal and cultural issues that influence the interpretation of test scores. Chapter 7 discusses interpretation of WISC-IV scores within the context of a complete psychological evaluation with other measures. Chapter 8 describes a style of writing psychological evaluations that focuses on the child rather than test scores as the subject of the report.

INTRODUCTION

Children's intelligence is traditionally measured relative to a sample of children the same age that is representative of the national population at large. This helps psychologists answer the question of how the child compares to children across the nation in which he or she will eventually compete. This is important because intelligence has been shown repeatedly to be predictive of a wide variety of important life outcomes (Gottfredson, 1998). However, no child lives in the country as a whole. Children live in neighborhoods that comprise communities, and communities sometimes have unique characteristics that can impact upon the development of cognitive abilities and expression of intelligent behavior in novel ways. Examiners also want to know how the child being tested compares to other children in the same community or culture. This is the essence of *contextual interpretation*. It is contextually informed interpretation of population-based cognitive ability scores in context with salient demographic and environmental variables.

Most chapters written on intelligence test interpretation conclude with a statement such as "The examiner should also take into account other factors such as the child's educational, medical, cultural, and family history, as well as other test scores." This advice has been repeated so frequently that it is often taken for granted, and while most psychologists acknowledge its veracity, not all implement it in practice. With experience, however, many psychologists come to understand that each profile of test scores has a range of meanings depending on the child's history and the context of the evaluation. *In fact, the defining characteristic of an expert psychologist may well be the ability to refine standard, cookbook interpretations of test profiles based on environmental, medical, and other relevant contextual issues.*

Our previous book (Prifitera, Saklofske, & Weiss, 2005) addressed issues related to interpreting WISC-IV scores within specific clinical contexts. This chapter tackles clinical interpretation of WISC-IV test scores within the context of demographic and home environment variables. While this subject is worthy of a book in itself, our modest aim in this chapter is to explore issues and available data regarding the moderating influence of environment and experience on cognitive development and expression of abilities; in applying these discussions to actual clinical work, we provide information that may facilitate the integration of salient cultural and home environmental considerations into routine practice. In doing so, we also attempt to destroy the fallacy that intelligence is a fixed trait unaffected by environmental opportunities and experiences.

BIAS AND FAIRNESS ISSUES IN ASSESSMENT

Prior to beginning our discussion of contextually informed interpretation of cognitive ability test scores, we must devote several pages to the widely held misconception that cultural demographic differences in IQ test scores are due to biases built into the test. Our intent is this section of the chapter is to put aside these issues so that we can focus on contextual mediators of cognitive performance and skill acquisition. We discuss advances in item and method bias research, important societal issues related to the consequences of testing special education samples in which minority children are disproportionately represented, and show that disproportionate representation is not limited to education but is present in many areas of life. We acknowledge a legacy of controversy in these areas and must address it so that we can move forward.

ITEM BIAS AND METHOD BIAS IN COGNITIVE TESTS

Item bias has been studied extensively, and all reputable test developers take special precaution to avoid it. Best practice in test development includes systematic reviews of all items for potential bias by panels of cultural experts. Test developers also collect additional test cases from ethnic minority examinees than the number typically targeted using census percentages so that advanced statistical techniques may be undertaken to detect and replace items that perform differently across ethnic groups. Conceptually, these techniques seek to identify items on which subjects from different demographic groups score differently despite possessing the same overall ability on the particular construct being assessed. However, the reason for any identified differences cannot be determined by these analyses alone. Further, it is common for expert panels to predict that a certain item will be biased because some groups have little direct experience with the content, but then find that various statistical procedures designed to detect bias do not point to that item. At the same time, statistical techniques sometimes point to a particular item as problematic when the expert panel can find no contextual reason. Perhaps this is because the cultural expert panel is never required to provide an evidenced based theory for how culture, as they conceive it, interacts with item content. Moreover, it is not clear that researchers are using the same criteria as the cultural expert panel. For these and other reasons this line of research is no longer referred to as item bias research, but as an analysis of Differential Item Functioning (DIF) because the underlying reasons that items perform differently across groups are not always known In light of the care taken in the development of items for most modern intelligence tests, it seems unlikely that item bias accounts for the bulk of the variance in demographic differences in IQ test scores. However, differential item performance statistics are not very suitable to detect factors that influence entire tests as opposed to single items (Van de Vijver & Bleichrodt, 2001). This is because most DIF studies match respondents from different racial/ethnic groups by using total test scores as the indication of ability or intelligence. If one presumes that dominant culture is inherent to the test, then by matching on test scores, researchers are matching on adherence to some aspect of the dominant culture. This larger issue can be framed as one of possible method bias.

Method bias is more general than item bias and is more difficult to study empirically. According to this view, the formats and frameworks of most major intelligence tests are literacy dependent and middle-class oriented. Further, the testing paradigm itself is a stimulus response set that could be considered a social-communication style specific to western European cultures (Kayser, 1989). The testing paradigm assumes that the test takers will perform to the best of their ability, try to provide relevant answers, respond even when the task does not make sense to them, and feel comfortable answering questions from adults who are strangers to them. In some cultures, individuals are expected to greet unfamiliar events with silence or to be silent in the presence of an adult. Guessing is not encouraged in some cultures and learning takes place through practice rather than explanation. Unfortunately, there are methodological difficulties in determining the amount of variance that may be explained by these factors. No studies have attempted to parse out the extent to which these influences may be ameliorated by the child's experiences within the U.S. educational system where western paradigms are pervasive. Evidence from adult studies suggests that educational experiences may indeed explain variance in performance (Harris, Tulsky, & Schultheis, 2003). Further, there is evidence that the WISC-III taps the same underlying constructs across 16 nations, including such nonwesternized countries as South Korea, Japan, and Taiwan, and that Full-Scale IQ (FSIQ) means for different countries vary systematically with national indicators of affluence and education (Georgas, Weiss, Van de Vivjer, & Saklofske, 2003). Nonetheless, concerns about the fairness of traditional intelligence tests continue to exist in the professional consciousness.

Examining differences in mean scores across groups is a relatively simple but flawed procedure for assessing method or test bias. A somewhat more sophisticated approach is to examine how the relationship of intelligence test scores to important criterion variables differs across groups. The procedure of comparing criterion-test relationships across groups still contains conceptual problems, however, in that it begs the question of what factors or mechanisms underlie differential performance across the groups. Nonetheless, the prediction of achievement from IQ has been studied extensively. Studies have shown a general absence of differential prediction of standardized achievement test scores from IQ scores across racial/ethnic groups for

WISC-R (Poteat & Wuensch, 1988; Reschly & Reschly, 1979, Reschly & Sabers, 1979; Reynolds & Gutkin, 1980; Reynolds & Hartlage,1979) and this finding has been replicated with WISC-III for nationally standardized achievement tests scores in reading, writing, and math (Weiss, Prifitera, & Roid, 1993; Weiss & Prifitera, 1995). Typically, these regression based studies show differences in the intercept but not the slope, and this lack of difference in the slopes is taken as evidence in support of a lack of differential prediction. In other words, IQ scores predict scores on standardized achievement tests equally well for all demographic groups studied. Yet, the possibility exists that this finding is attributable to bias being equally present in both the predictor (i.e., the standardized intelligence test) and the criterion (i.e., the standardized achievement test). This possibility was partially studied by Weiss, Prifitera, and Roid (1993), who used teacher-assigned classroom grades as the criterion rather then standardized achievement test scores. Again, no differential prediction was observed. Although these differential prediction studies have not yet been replicated with WISC-IV, such simplistic questions are no longer being asked.

CONSEQUENCES OF TESTING AND THE FAIRNESS OF TEST USE IN SPECIAL EDUCATION

Some writers have argued that any discussion of test bias is incomplete without commenting on test use, which explicitly involves decisions made about special educational programming based on the test results (Valencia & Suzuki, 2001b); this view is endorsed in the *Standards for Educational and Psychological Testing* (American Education Research Association, American Psychological Association, & National Council on Measurement in Education, 1999). This apparently innocuous statement has some inherent dangers. Clearly, studying the consequences of test use is an important area of research. However, we believe that considering the consequences of test use under the heading of test bias runs the risk of confounding the concept of test bias with possible differential need for services across groups. This is because studies have generally found that low socioeconomic status (SES), minority youth are at greater risk for learning failure (Hall & Barnett, 1991; Reid & Patterson, 1991; Schaefer, 2005; Walker, Greenwood, Hart, & Carta, 1994). *If two groups are truly at differential risk for a particular set of problems, then a test that results in a higher percentage of subjects from the at-risk group receiving services should be considered valid rather than biased.* This is an extremely important but frequently ignored issue. Most state education authorities establish proportionate representation criteria by setting acceptable limits around state census targets without regard to risk status. Fair usage is intended to distinguish individuals in need of differential services from those who have been wrongly referred and would not be aided by remedial services. *Thus, fair usage should be viewed as a person-level rather than a group-level concept.* Much of this chapter concerns taking into account contextual variables in the interpretation of psychological test scores to improve the fairness of individual evaluations. Nonetheless, we continue with a discussion of disproportionate representation of minorities in special educational programs because decisions about entry into these programs lead to claims of unfairness in testing and because the reauthorized IDEA legislation contains important new provisions designed to reduce overrepresentation of minorities in special education programs (IDEA, 2004).

Despite the general lack of evidence for both item bias and differential prediction of achievement, differences in average IQ test scores between demographic groups persist, even when differences in socioeconomic status are taken into account. These differences contribute to disproportionate representation in some special educational programs. First, let us examine programs for learning disabilities (LD). At the national level, the percentage of students in each racial/ethnic group enrolled in LD programs is close to the percentage of each racial/ethnic group enrolled in public school.

According to the U.S. Department of Education's Office of Civil Rights (1997), African Americans (AAs) comprise 17.2% of students in LD programs, as compared to 16.9% of overall school enrollment. When interpreting data related to the AA population, be aware that researchers commonly identify all Black individuals living in the United States as AA, including those who migrated from non-African countries such as Haiti. We use the term AA in this chapter because it is common practice at the time in which we write and because Black individuals from different countries of origin were not recorded separately in the majority of the available data. The reader should keep in mind, however, that the AA samples described herein are likely to be more heterogeneous then the label implies.

Thirteen percent of Hispanics are in LD programs, compared to 12.7% enrolled in school. The percentage of Whites in LD programs is 67.1%, as compared to 65.7% of all students in school. Thus, national data do not support the hypothesis that minorities are overrepresented in LD programs. However, there is considerable variability by state, with minorities vastly overrepresented in some states and substantially underrepresented in other states, as compared to the local census. For example, Hispanics are 14.6% overrepresented in LD programs in New York, but 47.7% underrepresented in Illinois. AAs are 32% underrepresented in LD programs in Illinois, yet 50.7% overrepresented in California, where IQ testing is discouraged by the state courts.

The national picture for both mental retardation (MR) and gifted/talented (GT) programs, however, is not proportionate to the population percentages by racial/ethnic group. At the national level, AAs are substantially overrepresented in MR programs (31.5% as compared to 16.9% enrolled in school), whereas Hispanics and Whites are each somewhat underrepresented. Again, there is wide variation among the states. For example, AAs comprise about one-quarter of the school population in Florida, but nearly half of the state's MR enrollment (U.S. Department of Education, Office of Civil Rights, 1997). Underrepresentation of Hispanics in the MR category may be related to language and immigration status because many practitioners are justifiably reluctant to diagnose mild MR among English language learners who are not yet proficient nor acculturated. Historically, the sparse availability of cognitive ability and adaptive behavior measures in the Spanish language has constrained potential identification of MR in this population, although such measures are now available.

LD and MR enrollment percentages should be considered in relation to each other because mild MR can sometimes be difficult to differentiate from severe or generalized learning disorders. Historically, there has been an inverse relationship between the proportion of students identified as LD versus mild (or, educable) MR, perhaps as funding sources shifted emphasis or as social acceptance of LD classifications changed over time. Controversies also have been raised regarding the lack of use of adaptive behavior measures when diagnosing MR, and it has been observed that about one-third of mild MR students may be diagnosed with no record of an adaptive behavior measure (Reschly & Ward, 1991). The lack of adaptive behavior measures may call into question the validity of many of the mild MR diagnoses. The relationship of LD and mild MR rates, how they cofluctuate over time and vary across states, deserves the attention of future scholars.

In seeking to understand the relationship between rates of LD and MR, it may be instructive to consider mean scores by demographic groups in combination with established rules for determining eligibility for special education services. In many local education agencies, the ability–achievement discrepancy (AAD) criteria have been strictly applied to determine eligibility for LD services over the past decade. In other education agencies, however, the Individual Education Plan (IEP) committee is permitted considerable discretion in determining eligibility, which can lead to a lack of standard criteria for deciding which students receive special education services. Typically, students must have a large (usually 15 points or greater) discrepancy between intelligence and achievement, with achievement being lower, in order to qualify for placement in an LD program. In many school districts, the student must have an IQ score above some minimum level, such as 80, in addition to a significant discrepancy between IQ and achievement. Strict application of AAD criteria may have made LD service less accessible for some low SES AA students whose ability test scores are not above the threshold or whose ability and achievement test scores were both low and thus not discrepant from each other. Although there are no data on the subject, we speculate that IEP committees may have come to view placement in EMR programs as the best available option to obtain much needed assistance for some struggling AA students. The rules for determining eligibility for LD services may begin to change in the next few years, now that the recently reauthorized IDEA legislation no longer requires that the AAD method be used in determining eligibility for LD services. The new legislation encourages local education agencies to consider other methods, such as the student's failure to respond to empirically supported instruction. These methods may qualify some struggling students without AADs, but also may lead to a negative impact on other children with cognitive deficits that are not assessed properly until they fail to respond to multiple interventions. While much is known about response to empirically supported instruction in the acquisition of early reading skills, researchers have a great deal to do to identify more sophisticated procedures for diagnosing and treating reading comprehension disorders in the later grades, as well as other forms of LD (e.g., mathematics, written expression, and oral expression disorders). Thus, the movement away from the AAD model may be slow, at least until other methods are further researched with LD types beyond early reading disorders and the consequences of the newer methods of eligibility determination on proportionate representation are better understood.

When seeking to understand differential rates of LD it is important to examine the larger process of special education eligibility determination, a process in which the IQ test score play only one role, albeit an important one. While the process varies across schools, it is almost always the teacher who first identifies a student as needing assistance to keep up with work in the classroom. In most schools, the teacher is than required to demonstrate that one or more instructional modifications have been attempted and were not effective. At that point, other options are considered, including after-school tutoring, mentoring programs with community volunteers, retention in the same grade, referral for testing, and so on. Researchers and policy advocates are now beginning to examine disproportionate impact in each of the various steps along the way toward placement in LD and MR programs, e.g., possible differential rates of teacher referrals for tutoring versus testing by racial/ethnic group.

It is also important to mention that placement in a special education program can be perceived favorably or unfavorably depending on the perspective of the observer. When a student is placed in a special education program, one can either claim that he or she is receiving the help needed or that the student has been unfairly labeled and segregated. Of students found not eligible for the same special education program, one can argue that they have successfully avoided a stigmatizing label or that they were unfairly denied access to needed services.

The problem of disproportionate representation is large and complex. The present extent of overrepresentation in some areas is so large that it may not be fully accounted for by the differential rates of risk for cognitive and learning problems between racial/ethnic groups. The extent of overrepresentation, which is accounted for by differential risk, needs to be better under-

stood. Given that ethnic minority students who are linguistically diverse and/
or living in low SES environments are at risk for cognitive and learning
problems, we are concerned that enforcing strictly proportionate representation could eventually lead to legal challenges of unfair denial of services.
This could occur if minority children are denied access to special education
because the program has exceeded its quota of minorities. Federal guidelines
are being written to aid state departments of education with implementing
the new IDEA provisions regarding proportional representation, and it is
hoped that these guidelines allow local education agencies to take into
account differential rates of risk by racial/ethnic group when setting acceptable percentages of minorities in special education. Careful attention to these
issues will be important in order to balance both perspectives and ensure that
no child is neither placed inappropriately nor unfairly denied service.

For GT programs, disproportionate representation by racial/ethnic group
is evident at the national level. According to the U.S. Department of Education's Office of Civil Rights (1997), AAs comprise 8.3% of students in GT
programs, as compared to 16.9% of overall school enrollment. The percentage of Hispanics in GT programs is 6.2, compared to 12.7% enrolled in
school. The percentage of Whites in GT programs is 78.7%, while they
comprise only 65.7% of all students enrolled in school. In addition to
Whites, Asian/Pacific Islanders are also overrepresented in GT programs.
Approximately 5.9% of Asian/Pacific Islanders are enrolled in GT programs,
while they comprise only 3.7% of all students. Again, there is great variation
across states. Enrollment of Hispanics in New York is 16.7%, but only 2.8%
of GT students in New York are Hispanic. Similarly, enrollment of AAs
in North Carolina is 32%, but only 9.7% of GT students in North Carolina
are AA.

Whenever any group has a lower mean test score than the national
average, that group will be overrepresented in programs that require low
scores and underrepresented in programs that require high scores on the test.
However, neither MR nor GT determinations should be made based on the
IQ test score alone. As noted earlier, an MR diagnosis requires that intelligence and adaptive functioning test scores are both significantly below
average (by more than two standard deviations), yet there is evidence to
suggest that many MR placements are made without any adaptive behavior
measure. Similarly, IQ should not be the sole requirement for entrance into
GT programs. Starting with Terman (1925), the tendency to equate giftedness solely with high IQ has persisted for several decades and continues to
influence daily practice. Contemporary scholars suggest three general characteristics of giftedness (Renzulli, 1986; Winner, 1996). First, there should be
evidence of precocious ability in general or in some specific area such as
mathematics, guitar, and ballet. Second, a strong task commitment to that
activity should be obvious, or a "rage to master" the skill. Third, creativity
and originality should be evident, or a tendency to "march to one's own

drummer" with respect to the gifted skill. It is in the intersection of these three characteristics that true giftedness resides. While cognitive ability testing has an important role to play in GT determinations, it is not an exclusive role and GT assessments should broaden as our understanding of the concept of giftedness expands.

It is somewhat widely believed that different types of intelligences can be associated with analytical, synthetic, or practical giftedness (Sternberg & Davidson, 1986a; Sternberg, 1997b), and it is possible to consider that giftedness is not a stable trait of the person but an interaction between culturally defined opportunities for action and personal talents that are recognized by the gifted person and acted upon (Csikszentmihalyi & Robinson, 1986). These expansions of the construct of giftedness are more inclusionary and may provide answers to persistent criticisms of the elitist nature of gifted programs (Margolin, 1994).

As with LD and MR programs, understanding disproportionate representation in GT programs requires examination of the larger process. In most cases, teachers nominate students for GT evaluations, although these nominations can be influenced heavily by parent pressure and community expectations. Teachers rely primarily on academic performance, but may include other idiosyncratic criteria. Structured teacher nomination rating scales of observable classroom behavior based on the newer theories of multiple domains of giftedness have been shown to reduce the unreliability inherent in the nomination process and to increase valid identification of gifted and talented students (The Gifted Rating Scales, Pfieffer & Jawarsowik, 2003).

SUMMARY OF BIAS AND FAIRNESS ISSUES

Although the literature on test bias acknowledges the role of socioeconomic status on intelligence test scores, the literature on disproportionate representation in LD, MR, and GT programs has largely ignored the known effects of poverty on learning and cognitive development. This is a serious oversight because poverty is known to be disproportionately represented across racial/ethnic groups. Brosman (1983) found that low SES school districts in California placed twice as many students in LD classes as did high SES school districts and that minority students were overrepresented in the low SES districts. Few researchers have pursued this line of inquiry.

DEMOGRAPHIC DIFFERENCES IN
VARIOUS AREAS OF LIFE

Disproportionate representation of ethnic minorities is not unique to special education, but exists in many important areas of life, including health status, poverty rates, and so on. The next section explores racial/ethnic differences in several important areas of life. We confine this discussion to areas that are theoretically and conceptually related to the development of cognitive abilities, performance, and skill acquisition. Prior to beginning this section, however, we wish to make clear that this discussion is not merely about race or ethnicity. Rather, it is about indirect factors that circumscribe what children and families can accomplish. There has been confusion on this point; because racial/ethnic groups fall into diverse SES categories, people mistakenly believe that they are seeing racial differences when SES related differences are examined.

Disproportionate representation of racial/ethnic groups within the United States has been documented for physical and mental health status, levels of education and high school drop out rate, single versus dual parent family percentages, unemployment rates, median family income, equity of school funding, mean scores on state mandated high school exit exams, equality of schools, and more. Data reported in this section are from a supplemental report of the Surgeon General (U.S. Department of Health and Human Services, 2001), except where otherwise noted.

RACIAL/ETHNIC GROUP DISPARITIES IN MENTAL HEALTH STATUS

We discuss group disparities in mental health status and services for children and adults to show that group differences are not restricted special education services. Further, we presume that parents with significant mental health problems may have fewer resources available to appropriately attend to the cognitive and academic development of their children.

The rates of psychological disorders among AA and Whites appear to be similar after controlling for differences in socioeconomic status, although such conclusions are uncertain because of the disproportionate representation of AAs in high-risk populations that are not readily available to researchers (e.g., homeless, incarcerated). Similarly, there is little basis for firm conclusions about the rate of mental health disorders among AA children, although when present, their mental health needs are less likely to receive treatment than White youths. The proportion of individuals with mental illness is much higher among those who are homeless, incarcerated, or in foster care and AAs are disproportionately represented in these settings. The proportion of the homeless population that is AA is at least 40%, and possibly higher. About 45% of children in foster care are AA, and many of these are victims of abuse or neglect. Although Whites are nearly twice as likely as AAs to commit suicide, this may be due to the very high rate of suicide among older White males. The risk of suicide among young AA men is about the same as that for young White men at present. However, the rate of suicide among AA youth has increased 233% between 1980 and 1995 as compared to 120% for White youth.

The availability of mental health services depends on where one lives and the presence or absence of health insurance. A large percentage of AAs live in areas with diminished access to both physical and mental health care services, and nearly 25% of AAs have no health insurance as compared to approximately 10% of Whites. Medicaid, which subsidizes the poor and uninsured, covers nearly 21% of AAs. The proportion of AAs that do not access mental health services due to the perceived stigma is 2.5 times greater than Whites. Thus, attitudes about mental health disorders among AAs may reduce the utilization of existing services.

With respect to Hispanics, most studies support the lack of difference in rates of mental illness as compared to Whites; however, sample size issues have restricted the generalizability of this finding beyond the Mexican-American (MA) population. Further, this summary statement masks important differences between U.S. and foreign-born Mexican-Americans. The lifetime prevalence of mental disorders is 25% for Mexican immigrants in the United States, but 48% for U.S.-born Mexican-Americans. Also, length of stay in the United States is correlated positively with the increased rate of mental illness for immigrants. Mexican immigrants with less than 13 years of U.S. residence have better mental health than their U.S.-born counterparts and the overall U.S. sample. The picture is different for children, with most studies reporting higher rates of anxiety and depression among Hispanic versus White children and adolescents. Most of these studies are limited, however, by methodological issues with self-reported symptoms. Although the overall rate of suicide among Hispanics (6%) is lower than Whites (13%), Hispanic adolescents in high school report proportionately more suicidal ideation and specific attempts than both Whites and AAs. Similarly, although the overall rate of alcohol use is similar between Hispanics and Whites, there are differences in the rates of alcohol abuse among Mexican-American men (31%) as compared to non-Hispanic White men (21%). The rate of substance abuse is much higher among U.S.-born Mexican-Americans than among Mexican immigrants (7:1 for women and 2:1 for men). Relatively few Hispanics are homeless or in foster care. Hispanic youth are overrepresented (18%) in residential placement facilities for juvenile offenders.

In general, Hispanics underutilize and, in many cases, receive insufficient mental health care services relative to Whites. Approximately 11% of Mexican-Americans with mental disorders access services as compared to 22% of Whites. The rate is even lower among those born in Mexico (5%) as compared to those born in the United States (12%).

Although the overall picture is complicated, the general trend appears to be that new Mexican immigrants have relatively good mental health and maintain this advantage for at least a decade. However, mental health problems are much more prevalent among those that have been in the United States longer, those born in the United States, and for children and adolescents. More studies of Hispanics from other countries of origin are clearly needed. For example, many Hispanics from Central America have historically emigrated to escape civil wars in Nicaragua, El Salvador, and Guatemala. Refugees who have experienced trauma are at high risk for depression and posttraumatic stress disorder. However, the strengths observed in the Mexican immigrant population are noteworthy. One factor may be a tendency of new immigrants to compare their lives in the United States to those of their families in Mexico (typically a positive comparison), whereas those who have been in the United States longer or born here tend to compare their situations to a U.S. standard (more often a negative comparison). Another area of strength involves cultural attitudes toward mental health disorders. At least among Mexicans, views of mental illness do not appear to hold the patient blameworthy and may predispose families to respond supportively to relatives with mental disorders. There appears to be a cultural norm to care for one's ill within the family, regardless of physical or mental illness. This may be reflected in underutilization of mental health services, at least for some illnesses and disorders. The availability of treatment providers who speak Spanish may be an additional factor in treatment access.

RACIAL/ETHNIC GROUP DISPARITIES IN PHYSICAL HEALTH STATUS

We discuss group disparities in the physical health status of both children and adults with the presumption that indirect relationships exist between the physical health of families and the neurocognitive status of children in those families that operate through multiple mechanisms, including prenatal care, well baby checks, and so on. Also, we wish to simply point out that group disparities are not restricted to special education programs or mental health access.

African-Americans have substantially more physical health problems than other groups. One of the more sensitive indicators of a population's health status is infant mortality, and the rate of infant mortality for African-Americans is twice that of Whites. In most population studies, infant mortality tends to decrease with maternal education, yet the rate of infant mortality for even the most educated AA women is higher than the least educated White women. As compared to Whites, AA adults present rates of diabetes more than three times higher, heart disease more than 40% higher, prostate cancer more than double, and HIV/AIDS more than seven times higher. HIV/AIDS is now one of the five top causes of death among AAs.

The high rate of HIV/AIDS is of particular interest to our discussion of cognitive functioning because HIV infection can lead to various mental syndromes, from mild cognitive impairment to clinical dementia, as well as precipitate the onset of mood disorders or psychosis. Overall mental functioning can be gravely compromised in individuals who are HIV positive by the combination of opportunistic infections, substance abuse, and the negative effects of treatment (McDaniel, Purcell, & Farber, 1997). The secondary, environmental effects of parents with HIV-related cognitive impairments on the cognitive development of their children are unknown, which is becoming increasingly important with improved survival rates of the disease.

Another health risk in the AA population is sickle cell disease. We became aware of an important and substantial body of literature on the cognitive effects of this disease when we were asked to supply normal control subjects to a researcher in this area (Steen, Fineberg-Buchner, Hankins, Weiss, Prifitera, & Mulhern, 2005). This study demonstrated that children with hemoglobin SS, the most serious form of sickle cell disease, show evidence of substantial cognitive impairment even when there is no evidence of structural brain abnormality on magnetic resonance imaging. The effect, approximately 12 FSIQ points on WISC-III, was found as compared to a control group matched for age, race, and gender. Although no SES information was collected on the patient group, we also compared the patient sample to controls whose parents did not finish high school. The effect was reduced by about half, but still substantial. In both cases the effect was distributed evenly across verbal and performance scores. In both cases, there was a significant effect for age such that the cognitive effects of the disease appear to worsen over time. Also of interest is the even larger differences observed between controls and the portion of the patient sample that showed abnormalities on magnetic resonance imaging. In interpreting these findings, one should keep in mind that children with active diseases tend to miss considerable numbers of days in school and that the impact of the reduced instruction on cognitive development may be important as a secondary cause of the low test scores observed. While the neurological mechanism responsible for the observed cognitive deficits in children with sickle cell disease is being debated (i.e., stroke, "silent" infarction, or disease-related diffuse brain injury), there is growing evidence for the effect. Although generally thought of as a genetic disorder specific to African or African-American populations, sickle cell disease is actually related to cultures that historically have lived in high malarial environments and has been observed in White populations of Mediterranean descent in the United States. In addition, regions of Mexico such as the Yucatan peninsula are presently considered high malarial areas and many hospitals in the United States do not currently accept blood donations from individuals who have visited that region within the previous year. Based on the studies just cited, we suggest that psychologists consider inquiring about family history of sickle cell disease when evaluating AA children with cognitive or learning delays or any child whose family descends from a high malarial area.

We now turn to a brief overview of the physical health status of the U.S. Hispanic population. The infant mortality rate among Hispanics is less than half that of AA and lower than the rate among Whites. Cuban and Puerto Rican Americans show the expected pattern of lower infant mortality rates with higher levels of maternal education, but the pattern is not so prominent among Mexican-Americans or immigrants from Central America. Compared to Whites, Hispanics have higher rates of diabetes, tuberculosis, high blood pressure, and obesity. Health indicators for Puerto Rican Americans are worse than for Hispanics from other countries of origin.

RACIAL/ETHNIC GROUP DISPARITIES IN EDUCATION

We discuss group differences in education because it is widely known that children's IQ test scores vary sharply and systematically with the level of education achieved by their parents. Overall, the correlation of parental level of education with children's IQ scores is .43. Table 1 shows the mean FSIQ score for children of parents at different levels of educational attainment. Although there is little difference among the two groups that did not complete high school, mean FSIQ scores of children generally increase substantially with each subsequent level of education obtained by their parents. These differences are not trivial. There is a 20 point or greater difference in the mean FSIQ score of children whose parents dropped out of high school as compared to those who completed college. However, these

TABLE 1 Mean FSIQ by Parent Education Level

Parent Educational Level	Children's Mean FSIQ
8th grade or less	88.2 (14.5) $n=47$
9th to 11th grade	87.1 (15.7) $n=113$
High school graduate or GED (12th grade)	94.5 (15.9) $n=292$
Some college (13th–15th years of education)	102.4 (14.4) $n=445$
College graduate (16+ years of education)	108.7 (15.0) $n=305$

differences are not driven only by the group that did not complete high school. The difference in FSIQ of children whose parents graduated from high school is almost a full standard deviation (14.2 points) lower then those whose parents completed college.

Table 2 shows the percentages of each racial/ethnic group that obtained various levels of education based on data from the 2001 U.S. census for parents of children between the ages of 6 and 16 years. Large educational differences are obvious by racial/ethnic group. The percentage of parents with some college or college degrees is 73% for Asians, 67% for Whites, 47% for AAs, and 26% for Hispanics. Thus, there are large differences in the proportion of each group that attended or graduated from college. Conversely, the high school drop out rate is 47% for Hispanics, 19% for AAs, 15% for Asians, and 6% for Whites. Nearly half of AAs attend college, whereas nearly half of Hispanics drop out of high school. Still, the rate of AA's in college is more than 20% lower than that for Whites.

As dramatic as it is, the high school drop out rate for Hispanics does not tell the whole story. There is a large disparity in graduation rates between Hispanics who were born in the United States as compared to those born in other countries. In fact, the drop out rate for foreign born Hispanics is more than twice the dropout rate for U.S.-born Hispanics in the same age range (Kaufman, Kwon, Klein, & Chapman, 1999). This may in part reflect language competency issues with foreign-born Hispanics perhaps experiencing greater difficulties with language mastery, depending on the age of immigration. In addition, socioeconomic factors may force some older children into the workforce at an earlier age, particularly for those already struggling with language and academic mastery.

RACIAL/ETHNIC GROUP DISPARITIES IN INCOME

We discuss group differences in income because the income of parents directly impacts the socioeconomic status of families, which relates to IQ test scores of children through various social and psychological mechanisms,

TABLE 2   Percentage of U.S. Population Ages 6–16 Whose Parents Did Not Complete High School Versus Those Who Entered College (by Racial/Ethnic Group)

	High School Drop Out Rate	College Entrance Rate
White	5.9	67.0
AA	19.3	46.7
Hispanic	47.0	26.0
Asian	15.5	73.3

which are discussed throughout this chapter. Group differences in income is a particularly sensitive topic because there is considerable evidence that African-Americans and Hispanics of color experience discrimination in hiring, which, of course, contributes to lower incomes on average for them relative to Whites. Further, the income statistics do not distinguish new Hispanic immigrants from Hispanics, nor do these data differentiate indigenous African-Americans from recent Black immigrants from Africa, Haiti, or Jamaica. As observed earlier, this latter issue is a problem that is endemic to most research on racial/ethnic group differences. Finally, higher paying occupations often require higher levels of education, which may be less accessible to lower income families. Thus, there are large differences in income between racial/ethnic groups, which may be partially related to a legacy of unfair pay practices in some industries and regions of the country and partially related to differences in occupational opportunity as mediated by educational attainment and, in some cases, English language competencies. As noted previously, educational attainment is substantially different across racial/ethnic groups, which is partly due to accessibility and availability of resources. With these caveats, the following information about income disparities is reviewed here from a 2001 report of the U.S. Surgeon General.

In 1999, 22% of all African-American families had incomes below the poverty line as compared to 10% of all U.S. families. For children, the gap is larger. Approximately 37% of African-American children live in poverty as compared to 20% of all U.S. children. The gap is still larger for those living in severe poverty. Severe poverty is defined as family income more than 50% below the poverty line. The percentage of African-American children living in severe poverty is more than three times larger than White children.

However, household income rose 31% for AAs between 1967 and 1997 much faster than the 18% increase for Whites during the same time period. Further, nearly a quarter of AAs now have annual family incomes greater than $50,000. Thus, the AA community may have become somewhat more diverse in terms of socioeconomic status during the last generation. Still, the proportion of Whites with incomes above $50,000 is vastly higher, and most millionaires are White.

With respect to Hispanics, median family income and educational level vary substantially with country of origin. Median family incomes range from a high of $39,530 for Cubans to a low of $27,883 for Mexicans, with Puerto Ricans at $28,953. The percentage of Hispanics living below the poverty line ranges from 14% of Cubans to 31% of Puerto Ricans, with Mexican-Americans at 27%. These discrepancies reflect real differences in the patterns of immigration from the various Spanish-speaking countries. For example, Mexicans with little education and few job skills tend to immigrate to the United States in search of employment opportunities, whereas political and social issues have motivated many economically successful and more highly educated Cubans to leave their country. Thus, the socioeconomic level of

Hispanics living in the United States systematically varies with country of origin based on differing historical patterns of immigration. The rate of Hispanic children living in poverty is higher than the national average. While 17.1% of all children live below the poverty level in the United States, 30.4% of all Hispanic children living in the United States are below the poverty level (U.S. Census Bureau, 2003).

IMPLICATIONS OF DEMOGRAPHIC DIFFERENCES IN VARIOUS AREAS OF LIFE

Some reviewers will undoubtedly critique our overview of racial/ethnic group disparities in various areas of life as too skimpy to do the topic justice, whereas other readers may wonder why we spent so much time on the topic and how these issues are relevant to intellectual assessment. In many cases the magnitude of the gaps described earlier is shocking and has serious political, legal, and economic implications for our society. Our intention in including this discussion in the current chapter is twofold. First, we wish to make the simple point that discrepancies between racial/ethnic groups have been observed in many important areas of life and are not limited to IQ test scores or special education percentages. We do not imply cause and effect in either direction, but simply note that racial/ethnic group discrepancies are not unique to IQ tests.

Second, and much more importantly for our purposes in this chapter, the differences described earlier suggest, for the most part, that children grow up with differing levels of opportunity for cognitive growth and development depending on their parents level of education, income, mental and physical health, and the resources available in the communities in which they live. Americans are fond of saying that all citizens have an equal opportunity and that any child can grow up to be President of the United States. From a legal point of view this is true (although not for immigrants). Opportunity under the law is equal, although implementation of the law can sometimes vary by jurisdiction for racial/ethnic groups as observed by differential rates of incarceration. However, this is not the kind of opportunity we are talking about. We are talking about opportunity in terms of the development of one's cognitive abilities: the opportunity for a child's mind to grow and expand to its fullest potential. Recall our central tenet that IQ is not an immutable trait, but a basic ability that can be influenced—to some reasonable extent—positively or negatively during development. Cognitive development in children can be influenced by the environment in multiple, interactive and reciprocal ways. We know, for example, that parental education level correlates with children's IQ test scores. While this may be partly due to the inherited level of cognitive ability passed from parent to child, we also know that the level of education obtained by the parents is highly correlated with the parent's occupational status and household income.

This in turn is related to the quality of schools and libraries available in the neighborhoods that are affordable to the parents, the role models present in those neighborhoods, the culturally defined expectations for educational attainment in that context, the expectations for the child's occupational future that surround him or her in the family and community, and the extent to which the young person can pursue academic or other cognitively enriching activities free from concerns about basic survival needs or fears of personal safety that may interfere with learning and development.

In many ways, parent education is a proxy for a host of variables related to the level of cognitive enrichment parents can provide their children. However, it is only a gross indicator replete with numerous exceptions. Certainly, there are many individuals with little formal education who are quite successful in business and society, and their success affords critical opportunities to their offspring that belie expectations based on their own education. Similarly, many readers of this chapter will likely know that even advanced academic credentials do not always equate with financial, marital, or personal success. What is amazing is that this single variable, with all its imperfections, explains so much in the way of children's cognitive development. Next, we expand on the role of home environment, not in terms of fixed demographic characteristics, such as parental education or income, but in terms of specific in-home behaviors that facilitate performance and skill development regardless of educational level or demographic group.

HOME ENVIRONMENT INFLUENCES ON CHILDREN'S COGNITIVE DEVELOPMENT

THEORETICAL CONSIDERATIONS

The family system is the most influential and proximal influence in children's early learning (Bronfenbrenner, 1992). Home environment research findings from developmental psychology have a long history, with roots as far back as Piaget's work in the 1920s. Credited with founding the Chicago school of family environment research, Bloom (1964) concluded that the preschool years were the most important period for children's intellectual stimulation and that family subenvironments should be identified and researched for unique effects on different aspects of cognitive development. These views were elaborated by several of his students, including Wolf (1964), who reported a multiple correlation of .69 between children's measured intelligence and home environment ratings in three subenvironments characterized by the parents' "press" for achievement motivation, language development, and general learning. During the 1970s, a set of international studies based on the Chicago school's approach suggested that ethnicity is a significant variable that should be accounted for in examining the relationship between home environment variables and children's intelligence and achievement and that causal relationships established for one group may not hold for other times, social classes, ethnic groups, or countries (Marjoribanks, 1979; Walberg & Marjoribanks, 1976). In the 1980s, Caldwell and coinvestigators developed the Home Observation for Measurement of the Environment (HOME; Caldwell & Bradley, 1984), which is still the most widely used home environment measure in current research. As summarized by Bradley and Caldwell (1978), HOME scores obtained during the first year of life correlated at low but significant magnitudes with the Mental Development Index of the Bayley Scales of Infant Development at both 6 and 12 months and at moderate to strong levels with Stanford Binet IQ scores at 36 and 54 months, and moderate to high correlations were found between 24-month HOME scores and 36-month Stanford Binet IQ scores.

Children with psychological or psychoeducational disorders provide additional stressors for parents. Although it is common to say that these children need more structure than others, researchers are now systematically studying what this means in terms of home environment. The ability of a family to sustain a daily routine has been shown to be an important factor in the outcome of developmentally delayed children (Weisner, Matheson, Coots, & Bernheimer, 2005). Sustaining meaningful daily routines involves juggling ongoing demands while meeting long-term goals rather than coping with crises and stress. Difficulty sustaining daily routines was more likely to be encountered in single parent families, expanded families, poor families, and multiply troubled families. When family troubles are high and unpredictable, routines are more difficult to sustain. While increasing family resources was associated with higher sustainability, families with low income are often able to create and sustain reasonable daily routines even while struggling with limited resources. These low-income families with sustainable daily routines were found to be troubled by no more than one additional issue beyond caring for a delayed child. However, these researchers also pointed out that the ability of a family to sustain a daily routine is unrelated to the level of stimulation provided the child or family warmth and connectedness. Quality of interaction is as important as the structure.

If home environment is such a powerful predictor of cognitive development, then one must ask how two children from the same family sometimes can be so different from each other in terms of expressed cognitive ability. Writing from another line of research involving behavior genetics, Plomin and Petrill (1997) offered the controversial concept of shared versus nonshared environment to help explain differences between family members. They argued that cognitive development during childhood is largely influenced by aspects of the home environment that are shared by siblings, whereas IQ by the end of adolescence is largely influenced by nonshared aspects of the environment. However, methodological and other issues have been raised regarding this research (Stoolmiller, 1999), and further studies are needed to fully answer this question.

Certainly adolescents are more influenced by peers than children. Thus, even children of the same parents may experience different environments as they enter adolescence a few years apart and come under the influence of different circles of friends. Prior to this period, however, children of the same family may experience different environments as they enter the preschool or preadolescent stages a few years after their older siblings for reasons as varied and normal as changes in job stress, financial security, or marital satisfaction during the intervening years. Finally, even absent environmentally induced changes in the family, parents often interact differently with each child simply because each is different in personality. Speaking purely as parents we are quite sure that each of our respective children experienced different aspects of ourselves as parents, and thus did not fully share the same developmental environment. We prefer to believe that our changing parental behavior was in response to their unique temperaments (rather than some basic flaws in our own personalities). While much of the discussion in this literature is one directional concerning how parental behavior influences children's development, practitioners evaluating children in troubled families should keep in mind that children's approaches to the world around them vary greatly and influence parental responses. Simply put, some children are easier to rear than others.

Expert practitioners spend much time evaluating the ways in which the child's unique characteristics interact with the family systems in the home environment and how these dynamics facilitate or impede the child's unique developmental needs. Many examples exist of children with psychoeducational disorders and/or troubled home environments who turn out to be well adapted. We relate these positive outcomes, in part, to the characteristic of resiliency. Resiliency involves the extent to which a child is sensitive to perceived environmental threats and the speed with which they recover when upset. These characteristics are important to the child's sense of optimism, self-efficacy, and adaptability. While the ability to regulate one's own emotions, attention, and behavior may be related to basic temperament, there are also effective strategies for teaching resilience in children at home and in school (Goldstein & Brooks, 2005). Further, resilience is improved with increases in the child's sense of relatedness to others, which is rooted in basic trust, access to support, social comfort, and tolerance of differences, and these drivers are firmly in the family's domain. A measure of resiliency in children and adolescents has been made available for clinical use (Prince-Embury, 2006).

HOME ENVIRONMENT AND AFRICAN-AMERICAN CHILDREN

Researchers have examined the role of home environment in specific populations. In this way it is possible to explore the hypothesis that the same proximal processes are differentially employed by individuals in different cultures. Several studies correlated home environment and SES ratings with children's measured intelligence and/or academic achievement (Brooks-Gunn, Klebanov, & Duncan, 1996; Bradley & Caldwell, 1981, 1982; Bradley, Caldwell, & Elardo, 1977; Bradley, Caldwell, Rock, Barnard, Gray, Hammond, Mitchell, Siegel, Ramey, Gottfried, & Johnson, 1989; Johnson, Swank, Howie, Baldwin, Owen, & Luttman, 1993; Ramey, Farran, & Campbell, 1979; Trottman, 1977).

Although SES was defined differently across studies, this set of papers generally showed that for AA children the relationship between SES and IQ test scores was not as strong as the relation between home environment and IQ tests scores, nor as strong as the relationship between SES and IQ test scores among White children. This may be because the range of SES within the AA groups was likely truncated, regardless of how it was measured (e.g., parent education, income, occupation). This has led some writers to speculate that historical limitations in educational and employment opportunities lead to more variability in parental behavior within the lower SES AA group then within the lower SES White group. In the studies cited earlier, home environment ratings typically added significant information to the prediction of IQ scores from SES for AA children, and this increment in variance explained was often larger than that for White children.

What this means is that SES, however it is measured, may not be as powerful of a predictor of IQ test scores for AA children as it is for White children. It also means that home environment factors may play a more powerful role in the prediction of IQ test scores for AA than White children.

HOME ENVIRONMENT AND MEXICAN-AMERICAN CHILDREN

Several studies examined the relation of home environment and cognitive ability in Mexican American children (Bradley, Caldwell, Rock, Barnard, Gray, Hammond, Mitchell, Siegel, Ramey, Gottfried, & Johnson, 1989; Henderson, 1972; Henderson, Bergan, & Hurt, 1972; Henderson & Merritt, 1968; Johnson, Breckenridge, & McGowan, 1984; Valencia, Henderson, & Rankin, 1985).

In general, results of these studies support the view that parent's in-home behavior is important to cognitive development and academic performance. It has been shown that low-potential MA children are exposed to a more restricted range of developmental experiences than their high-potential MA counterparts (Henderson & Merritt, 1968). MA parents who demonstrate higher degrees of valuing language (e.g., reading to the child), valuing school-related behavior (e.g., reinforcing good work), and providing a supportive environment for school learning (e.g., helping the child recognize words or letters during the preschool stage) have children who tend to score higher on tests of basic concepts and early achievement (Henderson, Bergan, & Hurt, 1972), and *neither SES nor family size made a significant unique contribution to predicting cognitive ability scores beyond that accounted for by home environment* (Valencia, Henderson, & Rankin, 1985).

We must offer a modest word of caution about generalizing these findings. First, these studies do not address the likely impact of parental language on children's test scores. Perhaps English-speaking parents develop more acculturated children that perform better in American schools and on U.S.-based IQ tests. Further, only MA families were studied and so generalization to Puerto Rican, Cuban, or other Spanish-speaking populations may or may not be valid. As discussed earlier, SES varies systematically with country of origin because of the historical patterns influencing immigration from the various Spanish-speaking nations. The interaction among parent education, home environment, and cognitive development has not been fully studied by language status of the parents or country of origin. *Yet, there is growing evidence that home environment is an important predictor of cognitive development across cultures.*

HOME ENVIRONMENT AND ACADEMIC ACHIEVEMENT

The association of home environment with academic achievement has also been studied. Higher levels of parent involvement in their children's educational experiences at home have been associated with children's higher achievement scores in reading and writing, as well as higher report card grades (Epstein, 1991; Griffith, 1996; Sui-Chu & Williams, 1996; Keith, Keith, Quirk, Sperduto, Santillo, & Killings, 1998). *Research has also shown that parental beliefs and expectations about their children's learning are strongly related to children's beliefs about their own competencies, as well as their achievement* (Galper, Wigfield, & Seefeldt, 1997). Improving the home learning environment has been shown to increase children's motivation and self-efficacy (Dickinson & DeTemple, 1998; Mantzicopoulos, 1997; Parker, Boak, Griffin, Ripple, & Peay, 1999).

Fantuzzo, McWayne, Perry, and Childs (2005) extended the aforementioned finding in a longitudinal study of very low SES AA children in an urban Head Start program, showing that specific in-home behaviors significantly predicted children's receptive vocabulary skills at the end of the school year, as well as motivation, attention/persistence, and lower levels of classroom behavior problems. Homes with high levels of parent involvement in their children's education were characterized by specific behaviors reflecting active promotion of a learning environment at home, e.g., creating space for learning activities at home, providing learning opportunities for the child in the community, supervision and monitoring of class assignments and projects, daily conversations about school, and reading to young children at home.

Home environment influences the learning behaviors demonstrated by children in the classroom, and learning behaviors such as competency motivation, attention, and persistence are important predictors of academic success. The likelihood of specific learning behaviors has been shown to vary with gender, age, ethnicity, urban residence, parent educational level, and special education classification status (Schaefer, 2005). Inattentive classroom behaviors have been found to be significantly higher for AA students than for White or Hispanic students (DuPaul & Eckert, 1997). Researchers have provided data suggesting that differential rates of inattention across racial/ethnic groups may explain as much as 50% of the gap in achievement test scores between AA and White students (Rabiner, Murray, Schmid, & Malone, 2005). Screening learning behaviors in the early grades, combined with functional behavior assessments (e.g., Functional Assessment and Intervention System, Stoiber, 2004) and interventions based on learning styles (e.g., Student Styles Questionnaire, Oakland & Glutting, 1994), may be useful additions to school psychology practice standards.

THE ROLE OF COGNITIVE STIMULATION IN INTELLECTUAL DEVELOPMENT

At this point in the discussion, we elaborate our central thesis: *Enriching, cognitively stimulating environments enhance intellectual development and skill acquisition in children, whereas impoverishing environments inhibit it.* Further, the factors that inhibit cognitive enrichment interact with each other such that the presence of one factor makes others more probable, and the net result is worse than the sum of its parts. Finally, the negative effects of cognitively impoverished environments accumulate over the course of a child's development and the impact worsens with age. As pointed out previously, the IQ gap between AA and White children is substantially larger for teenagers than preadolescent children, and this finding has been consistent across the 12 years that we have studied it in WISC-III (Prifitera, Weiss, & Saklofske, 1998) and WISC-IV (Prifitera, Weiss, Saklofske, & Rolfhus, 2005). The terms enrichment and impoverishment, as used here, are not considered synonymous with the financial conditions of rich and poor. These terms refer to *cognitively* enriching versus impoverishing environments, i.e., environments that encourage growth, exploration, learning, creativity, and self-esteem. While the financial resources available to the family play an important role in children's cognitive development, they map imperfectly to the extent of cognitive stimulation provided for the developing child by his or her family.

Ceci (1996) has proposed a bioecological model of intellectual development that involves (1) the existence of multiple cognitive abilities that develop independently of each other, (2) the interactive and synergistic effect of gene–environment developments, (3) the role of specific types of environmental resources (e.g., proximal behavioral processes and distal family resources) that influence how much of a genotype gets actualized in what type of environment, and (4) the role of motivation in determining how much one's environmental resources aid in the actualization of their potential. According to this model, certain epochs in development can be thought of as sensitive periods during which a unique disposition exists for a specific cognitive ability—called a "cognitive muscle" in Ceci's model—to crystallize in response to its interaction with the environment. Not all cognitive abilities are under maturational control, however, as new synaptic structures may be formed in response to learning that may vary widely among people at different developmental periods. Yet, the sensitive period for many abilities appears to be neurologically determined such that the proper type of environmental stimulation must be present during the critical developmental period, and providing that same stimulation at another time may not have the same impact. In this model, the relative contributions of environment and genetic endowment to intellectual outcome change with the developmental stage of the child. For example, general intelligence at age 7 has been found to be related to key aspects of home environment at ages 1 and 2, but not at ages 3 or 4 (Rice, Fulker, Defries, & Plomin, 1988). This suggests that it may not be possible to fully compensate for an impoverished early environment by enhancing the child's later environment. Where we need more research is in the elucidation of the key paths and the critical developmental timing.

Interestingly, this model does not separate intelligence from achievement because schooling is assumed to elicit certain underlying cognitive potentials. Further, problem solving as operationalized in most intelligence tests relies on some combination of past knowledge and novel insights. We would add that academic learning enhances new synaptic structures and therefore increases intellectual ability directly, in addition to the indirect effect of accumulated knowledge on novel problem solving. Thus, schooling and the quality of education play a powerful role in intellectual development. This is part of the reason that achievement and crystallized knowledge exhibit substantial overlap with reasoning ability in psychometric studies of intelligence tests. Although theoretically distinct, these constructs are reciprocally interactive in real life.

Perhaps most central to our purpose in this chapter is Ceci's elaboration of how proximal processes and distal resources interact to influence the extent to which the developing child's cognitive abilities will be actualized.

He defines proximal processes as reciprocal interactions between the developing child and other significant persons in the child's immediate setting. For maximum benefit, the process must be enduring and lead to progressively more complex forms of behavior. Parental monitoring is an example of an important proximal process. This refers to parents who keep track of their children, know if they are doing their homework, who they associate with after school, where they are when they are out with friends, and so forth. Parents who engage in this form of monitoring tend to have children who obtain higher grades in school (Bronfenbrenner & Ceci, 1994). In the bioecological model, proximal processes are referred to as the engines that drive intellectual development, with higher levels of proximal processes associated with increasing levels of intellectual competence. Practitioners should broaden their scope of clinical inquiry to include an assessment of these proximal, parent–child processes.

The distal environment includes the larger context in which the proximal, parent–child behaviors occur. Perhaps the most important distal resource is SES because it relates to many other distal resources, such as neighborhood safety, school quality, and library access, as well as the education, knowledge, and experience that the parent brings with him or her into the proximal processes. For example, helping the developing child with homework is an effective proximal process that requires that someone in the home know enough about the content of the child's lessons to help them when they study; this background knowledge is part of what is meant by distal environmental resources.

Ceci argues that distal resources can place limits on the efficiency of proximal processes because the distal environment contains the resources that need to be imported into the proximal processes in order for them to work to full advantage and because an adequate distal environment provides the stability necessary for the developing child to receive maximum benefit from the proximal processes over time. While an educated parent may be able to help a child with algebra homework, a parent with little education can still provide a quiet space and regular time for homework and check to see that the assigned work is completed; this monitoring and support can be very beneficial.

At the same time, it is unlikely that there is a universal environment whose presence facilitates performance for all children, or even for all children in the same culture. The likelihood of person by environment interactions suggests that there are different developmental pathways to achievement. School and home environments may be benevolent, malevolent, or null with respect to a variety of dimensions. Practitioners conducting clinical assessments should include an evaluation of distal environmental resources within the family and community and consider how these factors facilitate or inhibit the parent's hopes, dreams, and expectations for their child.

THE ROLE OF THE CHILD IN
COGNITIVE DEVELOPMENT

Without detracting from the critical roles that parents and educators play in the cognitive achievement of children, we believe that one must also examine the role of individual differences in children's approach to the learning environment. Assuming that proper cognitive stimulation is present at the right time, there are noncognitive characteristics of the developing child that mediate the actualization of cognitive potential. The list of possible noncognitive factors is long, but encompasses basic temperament. Some children engage actively with the world around them, drawing inspiration and energy from others, and proactively seeking positive reinforcement from their environment. This stance enhances cognitive development. Others turn inward for energy and insight, passively accommodate to the world around them, and seek only to avoid negative stimulation from the environment. This stance seeks to preserve current status and, if extreme, may inhibit cognitive growth. This *enhancing* versus *preserving* trait is one of the three basic dimensions of Millon's theory of normal personology (Weiss, 1997, 2002). Children that seek out versus shut off stimulation will have different experiences even in the same environment, and their opportunities for cognitive growth will likewise differ. Some children are receptive to new information, continuously revising and refining concepts based on an open exchange of information with the world around them. This curious, open, perceiving stance may facilitate cognitive growth. Other children prefer to systematize new information into known categories as soon as possible and shut off further information as soon as an acceptable classification can be made. While a strong organizational framework can be a positive influence on cognitive development, a closed, judging stance can inhibit intellectual growth if extreme.

Also relevant to cognitive development, learning and the life-long expression of intelligent behavior are general conative (i.e., noncognitive) characteristics such as focus, motivation, and volition. Focus involves directionality of goal. Volition involves intensity toward the goal, or will. Motivation can be proximal or distal. A proximal motivation would be a specific near-term goal. A distal motivation might be a desired state (e.g., to be respected by one's peers) or a core trait (e.g., need for achievement). The list of positive characteristics is long, but includes self-efficacy and self-concept. Self-efficacy is driven by a positive self-concept in combination with learned skill sets. Self-efficacy is task specific whereas self-concept is general. Children who have high self-efficacy with respect to intellectual tasks may have experienced initial successes with similar tasks. They are also likely to learn more from new intellectual activities then other children of similar intelligence, especially if they are intellectually engaged in the task and have a drive to master it. Intellectual engagement and mastery

28 LAWRENCE G. WEISS ET AL.

motivation are critical elements of cognitive growth, along with the ability to self-regulate one's actions toward a goal. The presence of these personal characteristics may enhance cognitive development and the likelihood of success at a variety of life endeavors. However, different factors may be related to success versus failure at intellectual endeavors. After controlling for intellectual level, it may not be simply the absence of positive factors but the presence of specific negative personal factors that are associated with failure to thrive intellectually. Negative predictors may include severe procrastination, extreme perfectionism, excessive rumination, distractibility from goals, rigid categorical thinking, cognitive interference due to social–emotional disorders, or diagnosed psychopathology. Lacking from the psychologist's tool kit is a practical and reliable way to measure these conative factors for individual children. Still, practitioners conducting psychological and educational evaluations would be well advised to broaden the scope of their assessment and inquire into these noncognitive traits as potential moderators of intellectual ability, educational growth, and a successful future for children.

PATTERNS OF IQ AND INDEX SCORE DIFFERENCES ACROSS RACIAL/ETHNIC GROUPS

With the aforementioned discussion on test bias, fairness, and demographic differences in various areas of life as background, we now present mean WISC-IV IQ and index scores by racial/ethnic group in Table 3. Although we have taken care to elaborate the home environmental and other issues that must be considered when interpreting these data, we are nonetheless concerned that some will take this information out of context and interpret it either as evidence of genetically determined differences in intelligence among the races or as proof of test bias. We are convinced that

TABLE 3   Means (and Standard Deviations) of WISC-IV Composite Scores by Racial/Ethnic Group

	White (n=1402)	African American (n=343)	Hispanic (n=335)	Asian (n=92)	Other (n=28)
VCI	102.9 (13.8)	91.9 (15.4)	91.5 (13.4)	102.3 (15.7)	101.1 (15.9)
PRI	102.8 (14.4)	91.4 (15.1)	95.7 (13.0)	107.3 (12.8)	101.0 (11.8)
WMI	101.3 (14.5)	96.1 (15.4)	94.2 (13.7)	102.7 (12.2)	101.4 (10.6)
PSI	101.4 (14.7)	95.0 (15.7)	97.7 (13.4)	107.6 (15.7)	97.7 (14.2)
FSIQ	103.2 (14.5)	91.7 (15.7)	93.1 (12.6)	106.5 (14.2)	101.0 (12.7)

Wechsler Intelligence Scale for Children – Fourth Edition (WISC-IV). Copyright © 2003 by Harcourt Assessment, Inc. Reproduced with permission. All rights reserved.

such interpretations would be scientifically unsound, divisive to society, and harmful to children.

As shown earlier, education levels vary substantially and systematically by racial/ethnic group. This fact has critical implications for the collection of standardization samples when developing intelligence, achievement, and other cognitive tests. The first step in defining an appropriate standardization sample is to identify the variables that account for substantial variance in the construct of interest and stratify the sample to represent the population on those variables. For intelligence tests, these variables have traditionally been socioeconomic status, race/ethnicity, age, gender, and region of the country. These variables may act singly or in complex interactions such that race/ethnicity may be masking other underlying variables. Most test publishers select parent education level as the single indicator of socioeconomic status when developing tests for children because of its high correlation with direct indicators of SES, such as household income and parental occupation, and because it is reported more reliably than income. Given the truncated range of education in the non-White and Hispanic groups resulting from the differential drop out rates and other factors reported earlier, however, parent education may work as a better indicator of indirect SES effects on test scores for Whites than for children of other groups. This hypothesis is addressed by analyses presented later in this chapter.

Current practice in test development is to fully cross all stratification variables with each other, and most major intelligence test publishers follow this practice. Thus, for example, the percentage of Hispanic or African-American children of college-educated parents in the standardization sample will be much less than White children of college-educated parents. While this sampling methodology accurately reflects each population as it exists in society, it exaggerates the difference between the mean IQ scores of these groups because the SES levels of the various racial/ethnic samples are not equal. If test publishers were to use the same national SES percentages for all racial/ethnic groups, the IQ score gap between groups would be smaller, although not eliminated for all groups, as demonstrated later in this chapter. At the same time, however, this alternate sampling procedure would obscure the magnitude of societal differences in the developmental milieu of children across racial/ethnic groups.

As shown in Table 3, the highest mean FSIQ score was obtained by the Asian sample (106.5), followed by the White (103.2), Hispanic (93.1), and African-American (91.7) samples. There largest difference is observed between Asian and AA groups—almost a full standard deviation (14.8 points). The White/AA difference is 11.5 FSIQ points, and the Hispanic/White difference is 10.5 points Recall that these data are based on samples matched to the U.S. census for parent education and region of the country within the racial/ethnic group. Thus, these racial/ethnic samples reflect all the educational and social inequities that exist between these groups in the population, as elaborated earlier. Also noteworthy is that the other group—consisting of Native American Indians, Alaskan Natives, and Pacific Islanders—obtained mean WISC-IV scores very near the population mean of 100.

Several additional points are notable concerning differences in the profile of mean index scores across groups. Asians and Hispanics, traditionally considered to be the two most linguistically diverse groups, exhibit VCI scores 4 to 5 points lower than their mean PRI scores, whereas the AA and White groups show no VCI/PRI differences. This is important in terms of interpreting VCI/PRI discrepancies in a culturally sensitive manner. *It is particularly interesting that the AA sample shows no meaningful VCI /PRI difference because clinical folklore assumes that the verbal subtests are the most biased for AA children due to this group's distance from the dominant culture and use of African-American dialect.* However, data do not support this view. As further evidence in this regard, the percentage of AA children with higher VCI than PRI scores is 52.5%, whereas the percentage with higher PRI than VCI scores is 45.8%. However, no studies to date have examined the linguistic diversity within the group classified as AA, which includes Black immigrants from multiple countries and cultures. While the AA group is traditionally considered monolingual, this assumption may not be valid in all cases. Researchers tend to limit discussion of AA linguistic diversity to dialects. Within the group classified as AA, however, there is the indigenous African-American language (Gullah), as well as French, Spanish, Portuguese, many continental African languages (e.g., Amharic), and Caribbean languages (e.g., Haitian Creole). Because researchers traditionally have assumed that the AA group is monolingual, the influence of language on acculturation and cognitive or achievement test performance has not been investigated adequately.

While the White group presents reasonably consistent mean scores across the four index scores, the Asian group shows lower scores on VCI and WMI as compared to PRI and PSI. This may be due to the linguistic demands of the VCI subtests, as well as secondary verbal demands in the Digit Span and Letter-Number Sequencing subtests that comprise the WMI. If some linguistically diverse children translate letters and numbers from the English presentation of these stimuli to their first language, then these tasks will tax working memory functions more than for those children who do not translate because their first language is English or because they have become sufficiently proficient in English. The Hispanic group shows a similar pattern, although much less pronounced.

For the Hispanic sample, the highest mean score is observed for the PSI. For the AA group, there is a clear pattern of both WMI and PSI scores higher than VCI and PRI. These findings are interesting for a number of reasons. First, clinical folklore assumes that some minority cultures are less attuned to speed of performance and may be penalized by tasks with time limits or time bonuses, yet the PSI score is among the higher of the four index scores for both the Hispanic and the AA groups. To evaluate this issue further, we compared scaled scores on the Block Design Subtest with Time Bonuses (BD) and Block Design with No Time Bonuses (BDN). We found that the mean difference between BD and BDN was approximately one-half of a scaled score point or less for all groups. The percentage of AA children that scored one or more points higher on BDN than BD was 20.0% as compared to 21.1% for Hispanics and 26.9% for Whites. Thus, fewer AA and Hispanic than White children score higher on BD without time bonuses than with them. *These data suggest that common assumptions about the cultural effects of speed and timed performance among AA and Hispanic children may not be supportable by the currently available data.*

It is also worth pointing out that the AA–White gap in FSIQ scores is smaller in WISC-IV than it was in WISC-III. The mean FSIQ score for the AA group increased from 88.6 in WISC-III to 91.7 in WISC-IV, or 3.4 points. At the same time, the White mean remained relatively constant at approximately 103. Thus, the AA/White gap reduced from almost a full standard deviation (14.9 points) in WISC-III to 11.5 points in WISC-IV. While this is positive movement, the gap is still large (effect size = .78). The mean FSIQ score for Hispanics declined by one point from 94.1 to 93.1. The Hispanic/White gap increased slightly, between WISC-III and WISC-IV, by 0.7 points to approximately 10.1 points.

In the early part of the last century, Spearman (1927, cited in Vroon, 1980) hypothesized that group differences in IQ test scores could be explained by innate differences in "g" between the races, and this position continues to rear its ugly head 70 years later (Jensen, 1998; Murray, 2005). Some will likely follow this antique line of reasoning and argue that the AA FSIQ was increased in WISC-IV by increasing the contribution of subtests with lower "g" loadings (e.g., Digit Span and Symbol Search) in the FSIQ, and they could be correct in so far as psychometric studies of "g" are concerned. However, we would point out that many of the subtests purported to be stronger measures of "g" are also those that are influenced more readily by environmental opportunity, such as Vocabulary. Further, the more abstract and fluid reasoning tasks found in the Perceptual scale have also been shown to be susceptible to the effects of changes in environment over time (Flynn, 1984, 1987; Neisser, 1998). In fact, the largest change for AAs was observed between the WISC-III POI (87.5) and the WISC-IV PRI (91.4), a difference of approximately 4 points. Conceptual changes in this index between versions of the tests included a reduction in perceptual organization and an increase in fluid reasoning subtests. Finally, the WM and PS subtests tap basic abilities that are fundamentally neuropsychological.

At this point in our discussion it may be worth stating the obvious: *studies showing between-group differences in IQ test scores say nothing about the source of those differences.* As Sternberg (2005) concluded, the statement that racial differences in IQ or academic achievement are of genetic origin is a "leap of imagination." We have noted repeatedly that race/ethnicity are likely to be proxy variables for a set of active mechanisms that have only been partially identified. In fact, the reason why between-group differences appear to exist may be because the variables that they are substituting for have not been fully identified. Thus, we are not in agreement with Spearman's hypothesis that differences in IQ scores across racial/ethnic groups reflect differences in genotypic ability. We seek to reframe the question in terms of differential opportunity for development of cognitive abilities. Alternatively, cognitively enriched environments may be a synonym for acculturative experiences. Thus, Spearman's hypothesis for IQ score differences across racial/ethnic groups could be reframed in terms of either differential opportunity for cognitive development or differential acculturation experiences. The next section reports results of a series of analyses designed to evaluate the extent to which differences in parent education and income are the source of FSIQ score differences between racial and ethnic groups.

SOCIOECONOMIC STATUS MEDIATORS OF FSIQ DIFFERENCES BETWEEN RACIAL AND ETHNIC GROUPS

This section explores how SES mediates the gap between racial and ethnic groups in intelligence test scores using the WISC-IV standardization oversample. This discussion is not about nature/nurture nor is it about race and IQ. It is about helping people understand why test scores may vary based on contextual factors and using that information to help children.

We applied a regression based methodology recommended by Helms (2005) to examine how much of the variance in test scores attributed to racial/ethnic group is reduced when relevant mediator variables are introduced. Table 4 shows these analyses for the AA/White comparison. In model 1, we regress FSIQ on race. As shown in Table 4, race accounts for 4.7% of the variance in FSIQ score, or 10.4 points (the results in these analyses may differ slightly from the mean FSIQ difference reported earlier based on use of the standardization oversample, which is slightly larger then the standardization sample). In model 2, we introduce parent education (parent education was blocked into four levels as follows: less then 12th grade, high school graduate, some college, and college graduate or higher) as a mediator and examine the reduction in variance accounted for by racial group after controlling for parent education. As shown in Table 4, parent education alone accounts for 18.8% of the variance in FSIQ between AA and White samples, which is substantially larger then the variance accounted for by race alone (4.7%). Controlling for parent education level reduces the

TABLE 4 Regression Analyses of Parent Education Level, Parental Income, and Parental Expectations as Mediators of White/African-American Differences Found in Full-Scale IQ ($n=1032$)

	R^2	R^2	Percentage of White/African-American Effect Mediated	Mean Difference between White and African-American after Mediation
Model 1				
Race	0.047	—	—	10.447
Model 2				
PED	0.188	—	—	—
PED, race	0.214	0.026	44.5%	7.852
Model 3				
PED	0.188	—	—	—
PED, income	0.223	0.035	—	—
PED, income, race	0.239	0.016	65.4%	6.320

Note: PED, parent education level. *Wechsler Intelligence Scale for Children – Fourth Edition (WISC-IV)*. Copyright © 2003 by Harcourt Assessment, Inc. Reproduced with permission. All rights reserved.

amount of variance in FSIQ attributed to race alone by 44.5%, from 4.7 to 2.6%. The remaining mean difference between AA and White samples is 7.8 FSIQ points. As described earlier, parent education is only a rough indicator of SES. Therefore, in model 3 we introduce household income as an additional mediator together with parent education. Parent income explains an additional 3.5% of the variance in FSIQ between groups after controlling for parent education. Together, these two indicators of SES explain 22.3% of the variance in FSIQ scores. Controlling for both parent education and income reduces the variance attributed to race alone by 65.4%. The remaining variance accounted for by racial status is 1.6%. This translates to a mean difference of 6.3 FISQ points between AA and White samples after taking into account parent education and income. Future researchers should use more sophisticated measures of SES (e.g., zip code or block or residence) and study the incremental effects of controlling for additional variables, such as school quality, neighborhood safety, and sickle cell disease.

Table 5 applies the same methodology to the Hispanic and White, non-Hispanic samples. Model 1 shows that ethnic status accounts for 1.4% of the variance in FSIQ scores between groups, which amounts to 6.3 FSIQ points. Model 2 shows that parent education alone accounts for 17.5% of the variance, and controlling for parent education reduces the variance in FSIQ accounted for by ethnic group by 99.0%, leaving a mean difference of essentially zero FSIQ points between Hispanic and White, non-Hispanic samples. In model 3, parent income contributed an additional 3.5% of variance in FSIQ scores, but had no observable effect on the mean difference

TABLE 5   Regression Analyses of Parent Education Level, Parental Income, and Parental Expectations as Mediators of White/Hispanic Differences Found in Full-Scale IQ (n=1046)

	R^2	R^2	Percentage of White/Hispanic Effect Mediated	Mean Difference between White and Hispanic after Mediation
Model 1				
Ethnicity	0.014	—	—	6.340
Model 2				
PED	0.175	—	—	—
PED, ethnicity	0.175	0.000	99.0%	0.553
Model 3				
PED	0.175	—	—	—
PED, income	0.205	0.035	—	—
PED, income, Ethnicity	0.205	0.000	99.0%	0.562

Note: PED, parent education level. *Wechsler Intelligence Scale for Children – Fourth Edition (WISC-IV)*. Copyright © 2003 by Harcourt Assessment, Inc. Reproduced with permission. All rights reserved.

between groups due to rounding. For Hispanic children, parent education explained virtually all of the variance in FSIQ attributed to ethnic group.

We next explored the impact of the number of parents living in the home on children's cognitive ability test scores. Previous research with WISC-III has shown significant FSIQ score differences for children in single versus dual parent families (Granier & O'Donnell 1991). Table 6 shows mean WISC-IV FSIQ scores for children in single versus dual parent families by racial/ethnic group. As anticipated, AA and White children of dual parent families obtain substantially higher mean test scores than single parent families of the same race by 5 to 6 points. The pattern was the same for both VCI and PRI. It may be that single parents simply have less time available to engage in linguistically and cognitively stimulating activities with their children. As noted earlier, single parent families also have more difficulty sustaining daily routines, which has been related to outcome in developmentally delayed children. Further, reduced household income may reduce access to quality schools and other positive environmental influences. Alternatively, recent parental separation or divorce may temporarily depress cognitive functioning for some children who are experiencing emotional distress at the time of testing. To the extent that this familial variable accounts for about one-third of a standard deviation in cognitive ability test scores, then groups that systematically vary on this dimension will show greater FSIQ score differences as a result. Approximately 64% of the AA children in the standardization sample were living in single parent families at the time of testing, as compared to approximately 33% of the Hispanic and 27% of the White

TABLE 6   Mean of WISC-IV FSIQ Scores for Children in Single versus Dual Parent Families by Racial/Ethnic Group

	Single Parent Families	Dual Parent Families
AA	89.4	95.9
Hispanic	92.7	93.3
White	99.3	104.7

Wechsler Intelligence Scale for Children – Fourth Edition (WISC-IV). Copyright © 2003 by Harcourt Assessment, Inc. Reproduced with permission. All rights reserved.

children. Thus, AA children were much less likely to be living in two-parent families than either Hispanics or Whites in the WISC-IV standardization sample. While single/dual parent status was not a control variable for the WISC-IV standardization research project, the principle of randomization would suggest that these percentages may be representative of the general population from which they are drawn. Thus, single versus dual parent family status may be another variable contributing to test score differences between racial/ethnic groups.

Equally interesting is that this same effect is not observed for Hispanic children. Having one or two parents in the home makes no difference in the cognitive test scores of Hispanic children. This finding requires further research to explain. The possible differential role of extended families across groups may be an appropriate focus of investigating to explain this finding.

Next we compared mean WISC-IV scores after matching the groups on the number of parents living in the household, parent education level, geographic region of the country, sex, and age. In this analysis, the AA/White difference reduced from 11.5 points to 8.8 points. The Hispanic/White difference reduced from 10.1 points to 4.8 points. However, the hypothesis that the effects of parental status (single versus dual) are mediated by changes in family income still exists. To test this hypothesis, we applied the mediator analyses given earlier. We found that the number of parents living in the home accounts for 2% of the variance in FSIQ between AA and Whites, reducing the AA/White FSIQ difference by 30%. However, when parent education and income were entered into the model first, the incremental effect of parental status was zero. Thus, it appears that the effect of single versus dual parent family status on the AA/White gap in FSIQ scores is fully accounted for by family income.

Theoretically, if differential opportunity for cognitive enrichment fully explains IQ test score differences between groups, then fully controlling for cognitive enrichment should eliminate the observed score differences. Thus, it is interesting that the effect of parent education fully explains the FSIQ gap between Hispanic and White samples, but not for AA and White samples. Further, including parent income as a mediator adds to the explanation of the AA/White gap, but still does not fully account for it. This suggests that parent education and income may relate to cognitive ability scores in a somewhat different manner for AAs than Hispanics.

Why do some studies still show differences in IQ test scores between AA and White groups even after matching for critical variables such as parent education, income, and the number of parents living in the home? Part of the answer is that these variables exert their effects indirectly and are therefore called distal rather than proximal. Alternatively, unmeasured inequities in societal forces may dampen the positive effects of education and income for AAs.

The indirect nature of the effect, as discussed earlier, means that the relationship is not perfect. These are "proxy" variables. That is, they serve as convenient indicators of other variables that are difficult to measure directly. The level of education attained by the child's parent or parents is a powerful demographic variable influencing cognitive ability scores. Although not perfectly correlated with the financial situation of the family, this variable serves as a reasonable proxy for overall socioeconomic status. Parent education is, in turn, related to a host of important variables, including the parent's employment opportunities, income level, housing, neighborhood, access to prenatal care, adequacy of nutrition during infancy and early development, and the quality of educational experience available to the child. Much of this may have to do with enriched early stimulation and opportunity to learn and grow in a safe and secure environment. Researchers assume that parents with more education have better access to pediatric care, quality schools and safe neighborhoods, but this is not always the case. To date, no matched studies have been accomplished that directly control for all medical, societal, legal, environmental, financial, and educational factors known to account for variance in cognitive development. In addition to being limited by the use of proxy variables, the available studies are typically cross-sectional rather than longitudinal.

More generally, results from scholarly studies (such as those reviewed in this chapter) provide invaluable information that informs psychologists, sociologists, political scientists, and others about group characteristics. However, psychology is unique in its commitment to understanding an individual's differences. Although research studies may provide helpful insights as to qualities that enhance or attenuate cognitive development for groups, psychologists must not assume that group data characterize every individual being assessed. When we uncritically apply group level research findings in our clinical practices we may inadvertently stereotype the very children who were referred to us for help.

It is for all of these reasons that we wish to leave behind the study of racial/ethnic differences in cognitive ability test scores and turn the reader's attention to proximal mediators of children's cognitive development, such as what occurs between parent and child in the home. Our direction is influenced by recent calls from Helms (2005) to cease the use of race as an independent variable in psychological research. This direction is also consistent with recent advances in the study of the humane genome that have led writers from diverse academic disciplines to argue that race is a socially constructed and biologically meaningless concept (Cavalli-Sforza, 2001; Marks, 2002; Schwartz, 2001), whereas others suggest that the division lines between racial/ethnic groups are highly fluid and that most genetic variation exists within genetic groups, not between them (Foster & Sharp, 2002). Further, despite the lightening pace of recent advances in genetics, attempts to establish genes for intelligence have so far found only weak effects, been inconclusive, or failed to replicate (Chorney, Chorney, Seese, Owen, Daniels, & McGuffin, 1998; Hill, Chorney, & Plomin, 2002; Hill, Craig, Asherson, Ball, Eley, & Ninomiya, 1999; Plomin, McLearn, Smith, Skuder, Vignetti, & Chorney, 1995).

At some point in the future researchers will cease using racial/ethnic status groupings because of the fluidity of racial boundaries and the wide variability of culture and language within racial and ethnic groups. Future researchers may wish to study how socially constructed concepts of culture mediate development of the particular cognitive abilities assessed by most major intelligence tests in industrialized countries.

At this point, we leave behind the study of racial/ethnic differences in intelligence and hope that others will do the same. We now turn the proverbial corner and begin a preliminary discussion of home environment variables that enhance children's cognitive development within and across cultural groups. The remainder of this chapter presents initial data regarding home environment and language variables and their impact on cognitive development and cognitive ability test scores.

EFFECTS OF HOME ENVIRONMENT ON WISC-IV SCORES OF ALL CHILDREN

Many of the SES-related variables typically studied in intelligence research are assumed to operate on children's development in two ways. First, there are the distal effects of the environment in terms of school quality, neighborhood safety, medical care, and so on. Many of these are assumed to be captured indirectly by parent education and income level. Second, there are the proximal effects of how parents interact with children in terms of providing linguistically, intellectually, and academically stimulating and encouraging environments. Parent–child interactions may be related to parent education and income. We treat these variables separately because, unlike SES, parents' behaviors and attitudes are more within their immediate control.

Implicit assumptions are often made about how more educated mothers interact with their children in different ways from mothers with less formal education. More educated mothers are assumed to provide increased language stimulation to infants and toddlers, read more often to preschool age children, assist elementary school children more with homework, and generally provide more intellectually stimulating activities throughout childhood and adolescence. This is a broadly sweeping assumption that deserves to be examined in more detail. It is quite possible that there is considerable variability in parenting practices within SES groups and that this variability influences the cognitive development of children.

Recent research with the WPPSI-III suggests that three home environment variables play an important role in the development of verbal abilities among young children. These variables are the number of hours per week that the parents spend reading to the child, that the child spends on the computer, and television. Mean WPPSI-III Verbal IQ (VIQ) scores increased with number of hours spent reading and on the computer and decreased with number of hours watching television. There is also a clear relationship between these variables and parent education. Number of hours spent reading and on the computer systematically increased with parent education, while number of hours spent watching television decreased. Thus, relative to parents with little formal education, more educated parents read to their children more often, discourage television watching, and encourage computer use. Further, children ages 2.5 to 7 who were read to more often, used computers more often, and watched less television had higher VIQ scores on average (Sichi, 2003). Perhaps SES plays a role in the availability of computers in the home and the opportunity to interact with children in cognitively stimulating ways (i.e., reading to them versus allowing excessive television watching) in busy single parent versus dual employment families. At the same time, however, there was substantial variability in the frequency of these behaviors within levels of parent education. *Thus, even among young children whose parents have similar levels of education, spending more time reading and using the computer and less time watching television is associated with higher verbal ability test scores.*

Next, we explore the proximal effects of parental attitudes on school-age children. We selected four items from a larger questionnaire completed by parents of children in the WISC-IV standardization sample ($n=624$) based on exploratory analyses. Review of the subset of parents who completed the questionnaire did not suggest any selection bias in this sample. The four questions selected are shown in Table 7. These four questions clearly relate to parental attitudes and expectations regarding the child's academic success in school. We assume that parents communicate these expectations to children in a multitude of ways, both direct and indirect, during the course of their developmental years.

To analyze the effects of parental expectation on cognitive ability test scores, we return to the mediator analysis methodology described earlier, but with a different focus. The dependent variable is no longer the *gap* in FSIQ scores between groups, but the FSIQ score itself—for the total group of

TABLE 7   Harcourt Parental Expectation of Children's Academic Success Questionnaire

---

How likely is it that your child will accomplish the following:

1. Receive good grades in school?
   (0) Not likely
   (1) Somewhat likely
   (2) Likely
   (3) Very likely

2. Graduate from high school?
   (0) Not likely
   (1) Somewhat likely
   (2) Likely
   (3) Very likely

3. Attend college?
   (0) Not likely
   (1) Somewhat likely
   (2) Likely
   (3) Very likely

4. Graduate from college?
   (0) Not likely
   (1) Somewhat likely
   (2) Likely
   (3) Very likely

---

children combined across all racial and ethnic groups. Thus, we are no longer seeking to explain the gap in FSIQ scores between racial/ethnic groups, but seeking to understand the effect of parental expectations across groups. As shown in Table 8, the combination of parent education and income explains approximately 21% of the variance in FSIQ scores. Parent expectations alone explain approximately 31% of the variance in FSIQ scores across all children. *Thus, parental expectations alone explain more variance in children's FSIQ scores than parent education and income combined.* This is interesting because previous researchers have assumed that the parent level of education has the most powerful effect on cognitive test scores. When all three variables are considered in combination (i.e., parent education, income, and expectations) the model explains approximately 37% of the variance in children's FSIQ scores.

However, are parent expectations simply a function of parent education and income? We examine this hypothesis in models 2 and 3 of Table 8. In this analysis we find that parent education and income explain only 6.5% of the variance in children's FSIQ scores after parental expectations are controlled. This is a 69.5% reduction in explanatory power of parent education and income from 21.3 to 6.5%.

TABLE 8   Regression Analyses of Parent Expectations as a Mediator of the Relationship among Parent Education Level, Parent Income, and Full-Scale IQ Score

	R^2	R^2	Percentage of Effect Mediated
Model 1			
PED, income	.213		
Model 2			
PEX	.307		
PEX, PED, income	.372	.065	69.5%
Model 3			
PED, income	.213		
PED, income, PEX	.372	.159	48.2%

Note: PED, parent education level; PEX, parental expectation level. *Wechsler Intelligence Scale for Children – Fourth Edition (WISC-IV)*. Copyright © 2003 by Harcourt Assessment, Inc. Reproduced with permission. All rights reserved.

Next we examined the reverse question: how much do parental expectations matter after accounting for parent education and income? Here the story is different. As shown in model 3, parental expectations still account for approximately 16% of the variance in children's FSIQ scores after controlling for parent education and income. *Although the explanatory power of parental expectations reduces by about half after controlling for parent education and income, the size of the remaining effect is meaningful.*

We looked still further into these questions by examining parent expectations within each level of parent education. These data are shown in Table 9. We found that parent expectations increase systematically with parent education. Table 10 shows mean FSIQ scores by level parental expectation. The mean FSIQ scores are 78.5 and 107.4 for children whose parents have low versus high expectations for their academic success. Recall Table 1, which shows that the mean FSIQ score for children of parents that did not graduate from high school is 87.4, as compared to 108.7 for parents that completed college. *Thus, a clear progression is obvious such that more edu-*

TABLE 9   Mean Scores on the *Parental Expectations of Children's Academic Success Questionnaire* by Parent Level of Education

Parent Education Level	Parental Expectation Score
Less than high school	9.6
High school	11.6
Some college	13.2
College graduates or higher	13.3

Wechsler Intelligence Scale for Children – Fourth Edition (WISC-IV). Copyright © 2003 by Harcourt Assessment, Inc. Reproduced with permission. All rights reserved.

TABLE 10   Mean WISC-IV FSIQ Scores of Children Whose Parents Have High, Medium, and Low Expectations for Their Child's Academic Success

	FSIQ
Low expectation group	78.5
Medium expectation group	96.5
High expectation group	107.4

Wechsler Intelligence Scale for Children – Fourth Edition (WISC-IV). Copyright © 2003 by Harcourt Assessment, Inc. Reproduced with permission. All rights reserved.

cated parents, and parents that have higher expectations of their children, have children with increasingly higher FSIQ scores. Note that the spread of mean FSIQ scores across the parental expectation level is almost two standard deviations (28.9 points) and larger than the spread of 21.3 points across levels of parent education.

Next, we regressed FSIQ on parent expectations within levels of parent education. We found that parental expectations were significantly related to FSIQ scores at all levels of parent education, but more so among parents with high school educations ($R^2 = .28$) and least among parents who did not graduate from high school ($R^2 = .19$). We interpret these findings in relation to the impact of distal environmental resources on proximal attitudes and behaviors. It may be that real societal and economic factors constrain the power of parent expectations among the lowest SES families. *Still, parent expectations remain a powerful force among all SES groups, just not as powerful among parents who did not graduate from high school. Parent expectations appear most influential among middle SES families where parents have graduated from high school but not attended college.* Although no data exist to explain this finding, we wonder if children in these families may be most on the brink of moving either up or down the SES continuum in adulthood depending on their personal effort, and thus parental expectations are particularly influential.

We then examined the hypothesis that parent expectations operate differently across cultures by examining the effect of parental expectations on the FSIQ gap between racial/ethnic groups after controlling for parent education and income. The remaining variance attributable to parent expectations was approximately 15% for the AA/White FSIQ gap analysis and 18% for the Hispanic/White FSIQ gap analysis, which is very similar to the 16% reported for the entire sample given earlier.

For demonstration purposes, Table 11 shows the percentiles associated with selected FSIQ scores for three different levels of parent education and overall. We considered scores of 6 or below as low. Low scores were only obtained from 10.7% of parents. Scores between 7 and 11 were considered medium and were obtained by 36.1% of parents. Scores of 12 were

TABLE 11   Percentile Ranks Associated with Selected FSIQ Scores by Parental Expectation Level and Overall

		Parental Expectation Level		
FSIQ	Overall	Low	Medium	High
70	2	28	4	0.5
80	9	51	13	3
90	25	77	32	12
100	50	91	54	28
110	75	99	83	57
120	91	>99.9	99	83
130	98	>99.9	>99.9	97
140	99.6	>99.9	>99.9	>99.9

considered high and were obtained by 53.2 % of parents. As shown in Table 11, for the same FSIQ score the associated percentile rank increases for children of parents whose expectations are low and decreases for children whose parents have high expectations. Furthermore, the differences in percentile ranks by the level of parent expectation are quite large. Whereas an FSIQ score of 100 is at the median (i.e., 50th percentile) in the general population, it is at the 91st percentile for children whose parents report low expectations and at the 28th percentile for children whose parents have high expectations for their children's academic performance. The median FSIQ score for children whose parents report low versus high academic expectations is 80 versus 108, respectively. According to this base rate table, a child with a FSIQ score of 90 would have obtained an overall intelligence test score that is above that of 25% of all children of the same age. The same score is above that of 77% of children whose parents that have low academic expectations for them, and above that of only 12% of parents that have high expectations.

To recap, parent education and income combined explain approximately 21% of the variance in children's FSIQ, while parental expectations alone explain approximately 31%. In combination, these three variables explain about 37% of the variability in the measurement of cognitive ability across all children. Further, the effect of parent expectations is only partially accounted for by parent education and income, and the remaining variance attributable to parent expectation is meaningful. Further, parent expectations appear to account for similar amounts of variance in children's FSIQ scores in the AA/White and Hispanic/White comparisons. Available data suggest that while there appear to be systematic differences in parent expectation across levels of parent education, parent expectations still predict substantial variance in the measurement of children's cognitive abilities within each level of parent education.

The explanatory power of this simple parent expectation variable is both surprising and encouraging. The possibility that parental expectations, attitudes, and behaviors can influence the development and measurement of cognitive abilities positively in children of all demographic backgrounds is very exciting, although perhaps a bit naive as well. Do parents express these expectations differently across SES groups? Are there cultural differences in parent expectations that simply mirror differences in standardized test scores? These are all important questions that do not yet have irrefutable data-based answers. However, the analyses given earlier suggest that this may not be the case. Parent's expectations accounted for substantial variance in FSIQ after controlling for two indicators of SES (parent education and income) and a possible indicator of culture (racial/ethnic group). However, racial/ethnic group is not synonymous with culture, and perhaps more sophisticated measures of cultural or familial beliefs and values will identify systematic differences in parent expectations. For now, however, data presented earlier suggest that whatever cultural differences may be captured by simple racial/ethnic group status do not account for substantial differences in parent expectations of children's academic performance.

The psychosocial mechanisms by which parental expectations are translated into specific behaviors in the home, what those behaviors are, whether they vary by culture, and how they increase cognitive ability test scores is an important frontier for potentially fruitful research into contextual interpretation. As Ceci (1996) suggests, these behaviors may differ at different critical stages of cognitive development. Clearly, reading to a preschool child will be more effective than reading to a preadolescent child. Also, playing rhyming games with early elementary children may facilitate the acquisition of phonological awareness, which is critical to the development of early reading skills, but rhyming games with older children who have reading comprehension difficulties may be less effective. When more is known about the timing, and active ingredients of home environment behaviors, and how these may vary across cultures, practitioners will be in a better position to intervene with families of children at risk for cognitive delays or learning disorders.

Still, it is possible that parents know their children's abilities better than anyone and are simply giving realistic estimates of their children's ability based on feedback from schools and other observations when they respond to the parent expectation questionnaire. This is a significant problem with using parent expectations as an independent or classificatory variable in intelligence or achievement research. We have not yet found a way to test the circularity of this argument in the present data. We acknowledge that the effect of parent expectations on children's cognitive abilities is probably not unidirectional, but reciprocally interactive. That is, naturally bright children stimulate their parents toward high expectations of them, which, in turn, motivate the child toward intellectually and academically enriching pursuits that stimulate cognitive development further. At the same time, children with limited intellectual endowment may stimulate their parents to have lower expectations for them, which may steer the child away from intellectual and academic growth activities. Many factors may account for the covariation of parental expectations and FSIQ beyond the parent's education, income, and knowledge of their children's abilities. For example, the parent's motivation for upward mobility or fear of downward mobility is an area for future researchers to investigate. Thus, while parental expectations are worthy of research investigation, at the individual level the reasons for those expectations may be far worthier of clinical exploration.

CONCLUSIONS REGARDING HOME ENVIRONMENT AND COGNITIVE DEVELOPMENT

How parental expectations are translated into parental behaviors and the mechanisms by which these behaviors act on children's cognitive development need further research. However, it seems reasonable to hypothesize that there are both general factors (such as parental monitoring) and specific factors (such as the form of monitoring) that vary by age, developmental level, and familial or cultural context.

In a comprehensive review of intelligence testing and minority students, Valencia and Suzuki (2001a) drew several major conclusions and cautions from the literature on home environment. First, and most importantly, intellectually stimulating and supportive home environments tend to produce bright children. While it is easy to assume that the direction of the effect is from parent to child, Valencia and Suzuki reminds (2001a) us that it is equally possible that bright children capture the attention of parents who respond to them in stimulating ways, which further the child's cognitive growth. Second, measures of home environment are more accurate predictors of children's measured intelligence than SES. While SES is a good global predictor, we are reminded that families within each SES stratum differ considerably in the ways in which the intellectual climate is structured in the home and in the amounts of stimulation provided. Third, most of the research on minority families has demonstrated significantly positive correlations between home environment and children's intellectual performance. While there probably are some commonalities in what constitutes a cognitively enriching environment, the specific expression of these characteristics may vary across cultures. Fourth, these studies can be taken together to debunk the view that low SES families can not raise intelligent children. Clearly, specific in-home behaviors are as important, if not more important, than the parents income, occupation, or education. Stated succinctly, *what parents do is more important than what they are.* This is critical because SES can be difficult for families to change. However, as shown in a series of field studies more than a quarter century ago, low SES minority parents can be trained effectively to teach specific intellectual skills to their children and to influence their motivation toward academic activities (Henderson & Garcia, 1973; Henderson & Swanson, 1974; Swanson & Henderson, 1976). Such intervention programs, however, must be sensitive to cultural differences in the specific expression of cognitively stimulating behaviors and the ways in which these are taught and reinforced. The same home environment factors may interact in differing ways in school systems outside the United States or when measured by other methods. We also must be cognizant of Ceci's (1996) caution that distal environmental resources can limit the effectiveness of these proximal processes in the home environment. In other words, severely impoverished environments may constrain the influence of parent expectations, but does not eliminate it.

The WISC-IV findings reported in this chapter are important and have significant implications for practice. While SES (as estimated by parent education and income) explains considerable variance in IQ test scores at the group level, these finding suggest that children born into low SES families are not predetermined to have a lower cognitive ability and that parents can play an important role in enhancing their children's cognitive development, thus improving their educational and occupational opportunities as young adults. Understanding the types of parental behaviors that enrich or stimulate cognitive development as compared to those that inhibit or stifle intellectual growth is a critical activity for scholars and practitioners alike. However, identifying these behaviors is only the first step. The timing of these behaviors within critical developmental periods must also be understood. Further, developing culturally sensitive models for communicating these findings to parents of different backgrounds and cultures and for training parents to implement these ideas effectively in their homes is essential.

These are not new ideas. Most elementary school teachers can easily distinguish students whose parents work with them at home from those who do not. Also, teachers will readily empathize with the difficulty of changing parental behavior relating to academic monitoring of children. However, these findings suggest that the benefits for children can be large enough to warrant sustained effort. We strongly encourage psychologists and teachers to speak directly with parents about these in-home behaviors and the benefits of them for their children, to do so at the earliest possible ages, and to follow up regularly. Available research suggests that it can be influential to engage parents in conversations about what they do at home to monitor their children's homework and class projects, encouraging quiet time for reading together or independently, limiting time spent watching television, encouraging computer use (at the local library if necessary), and positively communicating expectations for academic success.

Overall, this is a very positive message for the fields of psychology and education, consistent with the trend toward positive psychology espoused by Seligman (1998). Initially, we had been concerned that reporting IQ differences between groups of children based on static demographic characteristics such as parent education or income could inhibit the potential of individual children in these groups by reducing expectations for them. However, the variability within these groups, combined with the finding that parents' interactions with children in the home can ameliorate the impact of low SES and other relatively fixed demographic characteristics, encourages us to give voice to hope. If readers remember only one sentence from this chapter, we would want them to remember this: *Demographics are not destiny*. This is the main contribution of our chapter.

While we have attempted to make a strong case in favor of interpreting cognitive ability scores in context with home environment variables, we also believe it is possible to take such interpretations too far. Mercer (1978) developed adjusted IQ scores for the WISC-R based on a myriad of variables, including income, urban versus rural status, family size, and parent education. Thus, children from families with different incomes and numbers of children would be given "IQ" scores that were different despite answering the same number of questions correctly. While noble in its intent, this effort served to confuse interpretation of IQ test scores, and researchers did not offer these types of adjustments for WISC-III. Our approach with WISC-IV is to retain a population-based reference group for the IQ and index scores, while simultaneously providing supplemental base rate information that allows the IQ score to be interpreted within the context of specific factors that reflect the child's unique home environment more closely.

WISC-IV AND ACCULTURATION AMONG U.S. SPANISH-SPEAKING CHILDREN

The WISC-IV Spanish (Wechsler, 2005) is an adaptation of WISC-IV for use with Spanish-speaking children in the United States and Puerto Rico. Verbal subtest items that could be translated into Spanish with the same level of difficulty as the corresponding English item were retained and existing items were modified or new items were developed. Linguistic differences between Hispanics from various countries of origin were addressed carefully in the adaptation of instructions, verbal items, and acceptable responses. The WISC-IV Spanish yields scores that have been calibrated to the WISC-IV (U.S. edition). The calibration sample closely represents the demographics of the population of U.S. Hispanic children by country of origin, parent education level, and region of residence within the United States and Puerto Rico.

Because the scores are calibrated to the WISC-IV, the WISC-IV Spanish yields IQ and index scores that are referenced to the full population of children the same age in the United States. Thus, the WISC-IV Spanish IQ and index scores have the same meaning as the WISC-IV scores. This allows the examiner to compare the child's performance against all children the same age in the United States regardless of racial/ethnic group or language spoken. This reference group represents the cohort with which the child will compete for grades, college entrance, and/or job and career opportunities.

At the same time, data analyses of the calibration sample revealed significant differences for some index scores by the number of years the child has been in the U.S. educational system relative to his or her total education. As shown in Table 12, there is only a 2.2 point difference in the WISC-IV Spanish mean FSIQ score of Spanish-speaking children with little educational experience in the United States as compared with children whose educational experience is largely in the United States. However, large mean differences of approximately 10 points each are observed on the PRI and PSI. These findings suggest that adaptation, as estimated by the amount of experience in U.S. schools, increases scores on perceptual reasoning and processing speed tasks once the impact of language differences is neutralized by testing in the student's primary language. This is an interesting finding because it is widely assumed that lack of adaptation and acculturation primarily affects crystallized knowledge and processing speed tasks.

When percentage of U.S. educational experience is combined with parent education level and blocked into five categories, the differences are much larger. Table 13 presents these data. As shown in Table 13, the mean FSIQ difference on WISCIV Spanish is about 18 points between Spanish-speaking children who have little U.S. educational experience and whose parents have limited formal education as compared to those who have most of their education in the United States and whose parents have additional formal education. Again, the largest difference is on the PRI (22.7 points). The smallest difference is on the WMI (15.9 points).

Based on these findings, we decided to offer supplemental base rate tables in the test manual by the percentage of the child's education obtained in the United States combined with parent education level. Thus, an 8-year-old Hispanic child with an FSIQ score of 109 is at the 73rd percentile compared to all children in the United States. When compared to other Hispanic immigrants in their first year of U.S. public school and whose parents did

TABLE 12   Mean WISC-IV Spanish Scores by Percentage of Education in the United States

% U.S. Education	FSIQ	VCI	PRI	WMI	PSI
Minimal (<30%)	92.9	92.9	89.3	96.1	87.5
Most (30 to 99%)	92.9	92.6	94.2	97.2	92.5
All (100%)	95.1	95.1	99.3	96.7	97.6

Wechsler Intelligence Scale for Children – Fourth Edition (WISC-IV). Copyright © 2003 by Harcourt Assessment, Inc. Reproduced with permission. All rights reserved.

TABLE 13   WISC-IV Spanish Scores by Combined Levels of Parent Education and Percentage of Education in the United States

	FSIQ	VCI	PRI	WMI	PSI
Level I	80.9	85.4	82.5	89.9	82.0
Level II	89.0	90.9	89.7	95.0	89.9
Level III	95.5	95.8	96.8	99.0	93.7
Level IV	100.4	97.5	102.0	101.1	100.0
Level V	105.0	103.3	105.2	105.8	99.1

Wechsler Intelligence Scale for Children – Fourth Edition (WISC-IV). Copyright © 2003 by Harcourt Assessment, Inc. Reproduced with permission. All rights reserved.

not graduate from high school, however, she would be in the 97th percentile. This same child would be in the 60th percentile compared to Hispanic immigrants that had already completed 1 full year of education in the United States and whose parents graduated from college. Although acculturation was not measured directly, we believe that these two variables may be thought of as proxies for adaptation and perhaps acculturation in that children who have received a greater percentage of their education within the U.S. educational system have been exposed more to U.S. culture, academic content, and expectations. Further, children of higher SES families live more often in neighborhoods that provide more resources and greater opportunity for learning and academic development and achievement.

The combination of population-based IQ and index scores with percentiles based on distal resources and support provides the psychologist greater information with which to interpret the child's current level of intellectual performance from multiple points of reference while retaining the meaning of the IQ test score as a comparison to the larger population of all children in the United States.

Even when the child is tested in his or her first language, however, practitioners should consider a third variable: the language of the community. Primarily Spanish-speaking children may live in neighborhoods that are either primarily Spanish or English speaking or bilingual. Further, educational instruction may be in either or both languages. The child's first language and the language environment of the community may interact in as yet unknown ways on the acculturation process as well as the development and expression of both language skills and cognitive abilities. However, little is known about this issue. In what language should parent's work with their children at home? Is it necessary for these activities to occur in the language of the dominant culture in which the child attends school and will be tested or is it sufficient to work with them in the language with which the parent is most familiar? These are important questions that do not yet have answers.

These issues are not unique to Hispanic immigrants in the United States. Many Canadian children whose first language is French live in primarily

English-speaking communities such as Toronto, whereas others live in primarily French-speaking communities such as Montreal. The issue is compounded in Europe where national and linguistic borders do not necessarily coincide.

TESTING IMMIGRANT CHILDREN

The global population is increasingly mobile. Psychologists around the world are trying to learn new cultures to keep up with ever-changing patterns of immigration in different regions. They wonder how to fairly test recently arrived immigrant children who are struggling in new schools, countries, and languages. Our international work has shown us that there are currently issues with appropriately testing Jamaican children in Toronto, Asian children in British Columbia, Iranian children in Paris, Turkish children in The Netherlands, Moroccan children in Belgium, southeast Asian children in Australia, Russian children in Lithuania, and more. In the United States, most large urban school districts serve children that speak many different languages. While Spanish is clearly the most widely spoken second language in the United States, the number and variety of languages spoken in U.S. public schools are overwhelming for school officials and parent advocacy groups alike. In New York City (NYC), 43% of children attending public school live in homes where English is not the primary language spoken, and a recent survey identified 24 different languages spoken by NYC public school children (Advocates for Children of New York, May 2003). This is just the tip of the iceberg. Psychologists and educational diagnosticians in medium and small size school districts throughout the United States struggle with the same problems as their big city and international colleagues. For example, the Web site for the North Clackamas School District in Oregon, where the local population is 102,000, reports that children there speak 20 different languages in that district.

There is a strong need to be able to differentiate learning problems or developmental delay among immigrant children from language acquisition and cultural adaptation issues in order to ensure appropriate placement and programming. While testing immigrant children is an emerging area of research around the world, we are not aware of any tests that have been standardized entirely on immigrant populations

An acceptable answer to this problem is to administer a nonverbal cognitive assessment. There are several well-established nonverbal tests available (Bracken, 1998; Naglieri, 2003, Raven, 1998, Roid, 1997) and the new Wechsler Nonverbal Scales of Ability (WNV; Naglieri, 2006). Practitioners should keep in mind that these tests differ in the format of instructions (verbal, pantomime, pictorial) when selecting an appropriate instrument. All of these assessments are good measures of psychometric "g," and each author would argue that these tasks provide valid assessments of general cognitive ability using nonverbal methods. The inclusion in WNV of nonverbal tasks that are typically verbally mediated, such as picture arrangement, may further increase construct coverage of the various domains of intelligence measured nonverbally.

Practitioners in the United States are generally unaware that the WISC-III is available to them in more than two dozen languages, with norms available in 16 languages and countries. Practitioners can access test materials and norms tables to assess recently arrived immigrants from Austria, Belgium, Canada, France, Greece, Japan, Lithuania, Slovenia, South Korea, Sweden, Switzerland, Taiwan, and The Netherlands. Translations and adaptations are available without normative data in many other languages. Despite the release of WISC-IV in the United States in 2003, the WISC-III is still the most recently standardized IQ test in most of the world. The WISC-IV has been adapted and standardized only in the United Kingdom, Canada, Australia, and France to date, and the German project is under way.

The best practice in the use of international editions of tests requires a trained bilingual examiner fluent in the child's first language and culture to administer a version standardized in that country. This is often not possible. The second best practice is to train a trusted member of the local community to appropriately administer a standardized version. This "surrogate" examiner should be a bilingual professional individual such as a teacher or nurse, who is not a relative of the child. The surrogate should successfully complete practice administrations of an English language version of the measure with the supervising psychologist, followed by practice administrations of the alternate language test. Unethical practices include asking the child's mother to translate the questions during the testing session or attempting to administer the test in a language the examiner only studied in high school.

When interpreting scores obtained using international adaptations, consider that the reference group consists of children in the examinee's country of origin and provides no information about how the child compares to other children in the United States. At present, there is no way to equate IQ scores obtained on international versions to the U.S. population. Be sure to state clearly in the report that the normative group consisted of children in the examinee's country of origin. Evaluations conducted in this manner are essential to rule out linguistic issues in MR and LD determinations, but keep in mind that the psychological stressors involved when children immigrate can also depress intellectual functioning in their first language until they adjust. While always true, this is critical when the reasons for immigration involve escape from famine, war, or natural disasters that can precipitate post-traumatic stress disorders. Unfortunately, there are not good answers for how to evaluate a child's cognitive functioning in these terrible situations. However, one thing seems clear to us: no matter how reliable and psychometrically valid they may be, test scores cannot substitute for a careful clinical interview and multiple sources of observation over time. In some situations, the child's culture is so different from the testing culture that even language adaptations of the directions and test items are insufficient and children must first be acculturated to the process of a question–answer testing paradigm with adults before valid assessment results can be obtained. This may be the case, for example, with children from nonindustrialized cultures such as Aboriginal children in western Australia or First Nations children in northern Canada. In such situations, a dynamic assessment approach may be considered in which the examiner takes several sessions to acculturate the child to the testing demands by first playing question and answer board games. The approach holds promise, but further research is needed.

SUMMARY

This chapter laid the foundation for a model of contextual interpretation. We argue that an evaluation of socio-cultural-economic context should be part of the nuts and bolts of a general practice model of clinical assessment. Practitioners should pay attention to context in order to test cognitive hypotheses for referral problems in relation to the child's family and community and to differentiate effective intervention strategies.

We have made a case that while racial/ethnic differences in cognitive ability tests exist, they are not due to item or test bias, nor are they unique with respect to many other areas of life. Further, racial/ethnic differences are likely a proxy for a multitude of other variables that we are just beginning to identify and study. Still, these differences have important implications for individual students in need of educational assistance as well as contribute— along with variability in prereferral methods and funding mechanisms across local and state education authorities—to disproportionate representation of minorities in special education programs. We make the point that disproportionate representation in special education may partially reflect the disproportionate risk experienced by ethnic minority children living in low SES environments. We argue that intelligence tests do not measure pure intelligence, but some combination of innate ability and learning based on interaction with the environment and that environments vary on critical dimensions that differentially enhance or attenuate cognitive development. Perhaps most important, we argue that cognitive growth is malleable, within limits, based on environmental opportunities for cognitive development. We have shown that SES, as estimated by parent education and income, accounts for a large portion of the variance in children's intelligence test scores between racial/ethnic groups. More importantly, we have shown that substantial variability in cognitive test scores can be explained by home environment behaviors such as parental expectations of children's academic success, even after controlling for parent education and income. While low SES environments place children at risk for cognitive delay and many other health factors, the negative cognitive effects of low SES can be mitigated by the expectations that parents have for their children's success, how they interact with children in the home with regard to providing language and cognitive stimulation, reading to children, monitoring schoolwork and learning, and more. It is for these reasons that we offer a voice of hope and encourage practitioners to involve families in the treatment of children at risk for cognitive delays and learning disorders. Similarly, we suggest that researchers systematically study the critical development periods in which specific types of cognitive stimulation are applied most effectively by parents and teachers and how such interventions may need to be modified for diverse cultural styles. Therein lays a meaningful life's work!

ACKNOWLEDGMENTS

The authors gratefully acknowledge Janet E. Helms for her extensive and insightful comments on earlier drafts of this manuscript. We also thank Susana Urbina, Debra Crocket, and Donald Barfield for their helpful reviews.

REFERENCES

Advocates for Children of New York (May, 2004). *From translation to participation: A survey of parent coordinators in New York City and their ability to assist non-English speaking parents.* New York: New York Immigration Coalition.

American Education Research Association, American Psychological Association, & National Council on Measurement in Education (1999). *The standards for educational and psychological testing.* Washington, DC: American Psychological Association.

American Psychological Corporation (2003). Guidelines on multicultural education, training, research, practice, and organizational change for psychologists. *American Psychologist, 58,* 377–402.

Bloom, B. S. (1964). *Stability and change in human characteristics.* New York: John Wiley.

Bonham, V., Warshauer-Baker, E., & Collins, F. (2005). Genes, race, and psychology in the genome era. *American Psychologist, 60,* 5–8.

Bracken, B. A., & McCallum, R. S. (1998). *Universal nonverbal intelligence test.* Itasca, IL: Riverside.

Bradley, R. H., & Caldwell, B. M. (1978). Screening the environment. *American Journal of Orthopsychiatry, 48,* 114–130.

Bradley, R. H., & Caldwell, B. M. (1981). The HOME inventory: A validation of the preschool for Black children. *Child Development, 53,* 708–710.

Bradley, R. H., & Caldwell, B. M. (1982). The consistency of the home environment and its relation to child development. *International Journal of Behavioral Development, 5,* 445–465.

Bradley, R. H., Caldwell, B. M., & Elardo, R. (1977). Home environment, social status, and mental test performance. *Journal of Educational Psychology*, 69, 697–701.

Bradley, R. H., Caldwell, B. M., Rock, S., Barnard, K., Gray, C., Hammond, M., Mitchell, S., Siegel, L., Ramey, C., Gottfried, A. W., & Johnson, D. L. (1989). Home environment and cognitive development in the first three years of life: A collaborative study involving six sites and three ethnic groups in North America. *Developmental Psychology*, 28, 217–235.

Bronfenbrenner, U. (1992). Ecological systems theory. In R. Vasta (Ed.), *Six theories of child development: Revised formulations and current issues* (pp. 187–249). Ithaca, NY: Cornell University Department of Human Development and Family Studies.

Bronfenbrenner, U., & Ceci, S. J. (1994). Nature–nurture reconceptualized in developmental perspective: A bio-ecological model. *Psychological Review, 101*, 568–586.

Brooks-Gunn, J., Klebanov, P. K., & Duncan, G. J. (1996). Ethnic differences in children's intelligence test scores: Role of economic deprivation, home environment, and maternal characteristics. *Child Development, 67*, 396–408.

Brosman, F. L. (1983). Overrepresentation of low-socioeconomic minority students in special education programs in California. *Learning Disability Quarterly, 6*, 517–525.

Caldwell, B. M., & Bradley, R. (1984). *Home Observation for the Measurement of the Environment*. Little Rock, AR: Authors.

Cavalli-Sforza, L. L. (2001). *Genes, peoples, and languages*. Berkeley: University of California Press.

Ceci, S. J. (1996). *On Intelligence: A bioecological treatise on intellectual development* (expanded Ed.). Cambridge, MA: Harvard University Press.

Chorney, M. J., Chorney, K., Seese, N., Owen, M. J., Daniels, J., McGuffin, P., et al. (1998). A quantitative trait locus associated with cognitive ability in children. *Psychological Science, 9*, 159–166.

Csikszentmihalyi, M., & Robinson, R. E. (1986). Culture, time, and the development of talent. In R.J. Sternberg & J.E. Davidson (Eds.), *Conceptions of giftedness* (pp. 264–284). New York: Cambridge University Press.

Dickinson, D. K., & DeTemple, J. (1998). Putting parents in the picture: Maternal reports of preschoolers' literacy as a predictor of early reading. *Early Childhood Research Quarterly, 13*, 241–261.

DuPaul, G. J., & Eckert, T. L. (1997). The effects of school-based interventions for Attention Deficit Hyperactivity Disorder: A meta-analysis. *School Psychology Review, 26*, 5–27.

Ellis, A. P. J., & Ryan, A. M. (2003). Race and cognitive–ability test performance: The mediating effects of tests preparation, test-taking strategy use and self-efficacy. *Journal of Applied Social Psychology, 33*, 2607–2629.

Epstein, J. L. (1991). Effects on student achievement of teachers' practices of parent involvement. In S.B. Silvern (Ed.) *Advances in reading/language research: Vol. 5. Literacy through family, community, and school interaction* (pp. 61–276). Greenwich, CT: JAI Press.

Fantuzzo, J., McWayne, C., Perry, M. A., & Childs, S. (2004). Multiple dimensions of family involvement and their relations to behavioral and learning competencies for urban, low-income children. *School Psychology Review, 33*, 467–480.

Flynn, J. R. (1984). The mean IQ of Americans: Massive gains 1932 to 1978. *Psychological Bulletin, 95*, 29–51.

Flynn, J. R. (1987). Massive IQ gains in 14 nations. *Psychological Bulletin, 101*, 171–191.

Foster, M. W., & Sharp, R. R. (2002). Race, ethnicity, and genomics: Social classifications as proxies of biological heterogeneity. *Genome Research, 12*, 844–850.

Galper, A., Wigfield, A., & Seefeldt, C. (1997). Head Start parents' beliefs about their children's abilities, task values, and performances on different activities. *Child Development, 68*, 897–907.

Georgas, J., Weiss, L. G., Van de Vijver, F. J. R., & Saklofske, D. H. (Eds.) (2003). *Culture and children's intelligence: Cross cultural analysis of the WISC–III*. San Diego, CA: Academic Press.

Goldstein, S., & Brooks, R. B. (2005). *Handbook of resilience in children*. New York: Kluwer Academic / Plenum Publishers.

Gottfredson, L. S. (1998).The general intelligence factor. Scientific American, November, 1–10. Retrieved February 5, 2002 from http://www.scientificamerican.com/specialissues/1198 intelligence/1198gottfred.html

Granier, M., & O'Donnell, L. (1991). Children's WISI-III Scores: Impact of Parent Education and Home Environment. Paper presented at the annual meeting of the American Psychological Association; San Francisco.

Griffith, J. (1996). Relation of parental involvement, empowerment, and school traits to student academic performance. *Journal of Educational Research, 90*, 33–41.

Hall, J. D., & Barnett, D. W. (1991). Classification of risk status in preschool screening: A comparison of alternative measures. *Journal of Psychoeducational Assessment, 9*, 152–159.

Harris, J.G., Tulsky, D.S., & Schultheis, M.T. (2003). Assessment of the non-native English speaker: Assimilating history and research findings to guide practice. In D.S. Tulsky, D.H. Saklofske, G.J. Chelune, R.K. Keaton, R.J. Ivnik, R. Ornstein, A. Prifitera, & D. Ledbetter (Eds.), *Clinical interpretation of the WAIS-III and WMS-III*. San Diego: Elsevier Science.

Helms, J. E., Jernigan, M., & Mascher, J. (2005). The meaning of race in psychology and how to change it: A methodological perspective. *American Psychologist, 60*, 27–36.

Hill, L., Chorney, M. C., & Plomin, R. (2002). A quantitative trait locus (not) associated with cognitive ability? *Psychological Science, 13*, 561–562.

Hill, L., Craig, I. W., Asherson, P., Ball, D., Eley, T., Ninomiya, T., et al. (1999). DNA pooling and dense marker maps: A systematic search for genes for cognitive ability. *NeuroReport, 10*, 843–848.

Henderson, R. W. (1972). Environmental predictors of academic performance of disadvantaged Mexican-American children. *Journal of Consulting and Clinical Psychology, 38*, 297.

Henderson, R. W., Bergan, J. R., & Hurt, M. Jr. (1972). Development and validation of the Henderson Environmental Learning Process Scale. *Journal of Social Psychology, 88*, 185–196.

Henderson, R. W., & Garcia, A. B. (1973). The effects of a parent training program on the question-asking behavior of Mexican-American children. *American Educational Research Journal, 10*, 193–201.

Henderson, R. W., & Merritt, C. B. (1968). Environmental background of Mexican-American children with different potentials for school success. *Journal of Social Psychology, 75*, 101–106.

Henderson, R. W., & Swanson, R. A. (1974). Application of social learning principles in a field study. *Exceptional Children, 40*, 53–55.

Individuals with Disabilities Education Improvement Act of 2004, Pub. L. No. 108–446, 118 Stat. 2647 (2004).

Jensen, A.R. (1998). *The g factor: The science of mental ability*. Westport, CT: Praeger.

Johnson, D. L., Breckenridge, J., & McGowan, R. (1984). Home environment and early cognitive development in Mexican-American children. In A.W. Gottfried (Ed.), *Home environment and early cognitive development: Longitudinal research* (pp. 151–195). Orlando, FL: Academic Press.

Johnson, D. L., Swank, P., Howie, V. M., Baldwin, C. D., Owen, M., & Luttman, D. (1993). Does HOME add to the prediction of child intelligence over and above SES? *Journal of Genetic Psychology, 154*, 33–40.

Kaufman, P., Kwon, J. Y., Klein, S., & Chapman, C. D. (1999). Dropout rates in the United States: 1998. Statistical Analysis Report (NCES Report No. 2000–022). Retrieved July 25, 2001, from http://nces.ed.gov/pubs2000/2000022.pdf.

Kayser, H. (1989). Speech and language assessment of Spanish–English speaking children. *Language, Speech, & Hearing Services in Schools, 20*, 226–244.

Keith,T. Z., Keith, P. B.,Quirk, K. J., Sperduto, J., Santillo, S., & Killings, S. (1998). Longitudinal effects of parent involvement on high school grades: Similarities and differences across
gender and ethnic groups. *Journal of School Psychology, 36*, 335–363.

Mantzicopoulos, P. Y. (1997). The relationship of family variables to Head Start's children's
preacademic competence. *Early Education & Development, 8*, 357–375.

Margolin, L. (1994). *Goodness Personified: The emergence of gifted children.* New York: Aldine
de Gruyter.

Marjoribanks, K. (1979). *Families and their learning environments: An empirical analysis.* London: Routledge & Kegan Paul.

Marks, J. (2002). *Folk heredity.* In J. M. Fish (Ed.) *Race and Intelligence: Separating science
from myth.* (pp. 95–112). Mahwah, NJ: Erlbaum.

McDaniel, J. S., Purcell, D. W., & Farber, E.W. (1997). Severe mental illness and HIV-related
medical and neuropsychiatric sequelae. *Clinical Psychology Review, 17*, 311–325.

Mercer, J. R., & Lewis, J. F. (1978). *System of multicultural pluralistic assessment: Technical
Manual.* San Antonio, TX: The Psychological Corporation.

Murray, C. (2005). "The inequality taboo." Commentary, September, pp. 13–22.

Naglieri, J. A. (2003). *Naglieri nonverbal ability test–Individual administration.* San Antonio, TX:
The Psychological Corporation.

Naglieri, J. A. (2006). *Wechsler nonverbal scales of ability.* San Antonio, TX: Harcourt Assessment, Inc.

Neisser, U. (1998). Introduction: Rising test scores and what they mean. In U. Neisser (Ed.), *The
rising curve: Long term gains in IQ and related measures* (pp. 3–22). Washington, DC:
American Psychological Association.

Oakland, T., Glutting, J., & Horton, C. (1996). *Student styles questionnaire.* San Antonio, TX:
The Psychological Corporation

Osborne, J. W. (2001). Testing stereotype threat: Does anxiety explain race and sex differences
in achievement? *Contemporary Educational Psychology, 26*, 291–310.

Parker, F. L., Boak, A. Y., Griffin, K. W., Ripple, C., & Peay, L. (1999). Parent–child
relationship, home learning environment, and school readiness. *School Psychology Review,
28*, 413–425.

Pfeiffer, S., & Jarosewich, T. (2003). *Gifted rating scale.* San Antonio, TX: Harcourt Assessment, Inc.

Plomin, R., Mclearn, G. E., Smith, D. L., Skuder, P., Vignetti, S., Chorney, M. J., et al. (1995).
Allelic associations between 100 DNA markers and high versus low IQ. *Intelligence, 21*,
31–48.

Plomin, R., & Petrill, S. A. (1997). Genetics and intelligence: What's new? *Intelligence, 24*,
53–77.

Poteat, G. M., Wuensch, K. L., & Gregg, N. B. (1988). An investigation of differential
prediction with the WISC–R. *Journal of School Psychology, 26*, 59–68.8.

Prifitera, A., Saklofske, D. H., & Weiss, L. (2005). *WISC–IV clinical use and interpretation:
Scientist–practitioner perspectives.* San Diego, CA: Elsevier Science.

Prifitera, A., & Saklofske, D. H. (1998). *WISC–III clinical use and interpretation: Scientist–
practitioner perspectives.* San Diego, CA: Academic Press.

Prince-Embury, S. (2006). *Resiliency scales for children and adolescents.* San Antonio, TX:
Harcourt Assessment, Inc.

Rabiner, D. L., Murray, D., Schmid, L., & Malone, P. (2004). An exploration of the relationship between ethnicity, attention problems and academic achievement. *School Psychology
Review, 33*, 498–600.

Ramey, C., Farran, D. C., & Campbell, F. A. (1979). Predicting IQ from mother–child
interactions. *Child Development, 50*, 804–814.

Raven, J., Raven, J. C., & Court, J. H. (1998). *Manual for Raven's progressive matrices and
vocabulary scales.* Oxford, United Kingdom: Oxford Psychologists Press.

Reid, J. B., & Patterson, G. R. (1991). Early prevention and intervention with conduct problems: A social interactional model for the integration of research and practice. In G. Stoner, M. R. Shinn, & H. M. Walker (Eds.), *Interventions for achievement and behavior problems* (pp. 715–739). Bethesda, MD: National Association of School Psychologists.

Renzulli, J. S. (1986). The three-ring conception of giftedness: A developmental model for creative productivity. In R. J. Sternberg & J. E. Davidson (Eds.) *Conceptions of giftedness* (pp. 53–92). New York: Cambridge University Press.

Reschly, D. J., & Reschly, J. E. (1979). Validity of WISC–R factor scores in predicting achievement and attention for four sociocultural groups. *Journal of School Psychology, 17,* 355–361.

Reschly, D. J., & Saber, D. L. (1979). Analysis of test bias in four groups with the regression definition. *Journal of Educational Measurement, 16,* 1–9.

Reschly, D. J., & Ward, S. M. (1991). Uses of adaptive behavior measures and overrepresentation of Black students in programs for students with mild mental retardation. *American Journal on Mental Retardation, 96,* 257–268.

Reynolds, C. R., & Gutkin, T. B. (1980). Stability of the WISC–R factor structure across sex at two age levels. *Journal of Clinical Psychology, 36,* 775–777.

Reynolds, C. R., & Hartlage, L. C. (1979). Comparison of WISC and WISC–R regression lines for academic prediction with black and white referred children. *Journal of Consulting and Clinical Psychology, 47,* 589–591.

Rice, T., Fulker, D.W., Defries, J. C., & Plomin, R. (1988). Path analysis of IQ during infancy and early childhood and the index of the home environment in the Colorado adoption project. *Behavior Genetics, 16,* 107–125.

Roid, G. H., & Miller, L. J. (1997). *Leiter International Performance Scale–Revised.* Wood Dale, IL: Stoelting.

Schaefer, B. (2004). A demographic survey of learning behaviors among American students. *School Psychology Review, 33,* 481–497.

Schwartz, R. S. (2001). Racial profiling in medical research. *New England Journal of Medicine, 344,* 1392–1393.

Seligman, M. E. (1998). *Learned optimism.* New York: A.A. Knopf, Inc.

Sichi, M. (2003, Nov.). *Influence of free–time activities on children's verbal IQ: A look at how the hours a child spends reading, using the computer, and watching TV may affect verbal skills.* Poster session presented at the Texas Psychological Association conference, San Antonio, TX.

Spearman, C. (1927). *The abilities of man.* New York: Macmillan.

Steele, C. M. (1992). Race and the schooling of black Americans. *The Atlantic, 269,* 68–72.

Steele, C. M. (1997). A threat in the air: How stereotypes shape intellectual identity and performance. *American Psychologist, 52,* 613–629.

Steen, R. G., Fineberg-Buchner, C., Hankins, G., Weiss, L., Prifitera, A., & Mulhern, R. K. (2005). Cognitive deficits in children with sickle cell disease. *Journal of Child Neurology, 20*(2), 102–107.

Sternberg, R. J. (1997b). A triarchic view of giftedness: Theory and practice. In N. Colangelo & G. A. Davis (Eds.), *Handbook of gifted education* (2nd ed., pp. 43–53). Boston: Allyn & Bacon.

Sternberg, R. J., & Davidson, J. E. (Eds.) (1986a). *Conceptions of giftedness.* New York: Cambridge University Press.

Sternberg, R. J., Grigorenko, E. L., & Kidd, K. (2005). Intelligence, race, and genetics. *American Psychologist, 60,* 46–57.

Stoiber, K. (2004). *Functional assessment and intervention system.* San Antonio, TX: Harcourt Assessment, Inc.

Stoolmiller, M. (1999). Implications of the restricted range of family environments for estimates of heritability and nonshared environment in behavioral genetic adoption studies. *Psychological Bulletin, 125*, 392–409.

Swanson, R. A., & Henderson, R. W. (1976). Achieving home–school continuities in the socialization of an academic motive. *Journal of Experimental Education, 44*, 38–44.

Sui–Chu, E., & Williams, J. D. (1996). Effects of parental involvement on eighth-grade achievement. *Sociology of Education, 69*, 126–141.

Terman, L. M. (1925). *Genetic Studies of genius: Vol. 1. Mental and physical traits of a thousand gifted children.* Stanford, CA: Stanford University Press.

Trotman, F. K. (1977). Race, IQ, and the middle class. *Journal of Educational Psychology, 69*, 266–273.

U.S. Department of Education, Office for Civil Rights (1997). *Fall 1994 elementary and secondary school civil rights compliance report.* Washington, DC: Author.

U.S. Department of Health and Human Services (2001). *Head Start FACES: Longitudinal findings on program performance. Third progress report.* Washington, DC: Author.

Valencia, R. R., & Suzuki, L. A. (2001a). *Intelligence testing and minority students: Foundations, performance factors, and assessment issues* (pp. 108–110). Thousand Oaks: Sage Publications, Inc.

Valencia, R. R., & Suzuki, L. A. (2001b). *Intelligence testing and minority students: Foundations, performance factors, and assessment issues* (p. 145).Thousand Oaks: Sage Publications, Inc.

Valencia, R. R., Henderson, R. W., & Rankin, R. J. (1985). Family status, family constellation, and home environmental variables as predictors of cognitive performance of Mexican-American children. *Journal of Educational Psychology, 77*, 323–331.

van de Vijver, F. J. R., & Bleichrodt, N. (2001). Conclusions. In N. Bleichrodt & F. J. R. van de Vijver (Eds.), *Diagnosing immigrants: Possibilities and limitations of psychological tests* (pp. 237–243). Lisse, The Netherlands: Swets.

Vroon, P. A. (1980). *Intelligence on myths and measurement.* In G.E. Stelmach (Ed.), *Advances in psychology 3* (pp. 27–44). New York: North-Holland.

Walberg, H. J., & Marjoribanks, K. (1976). Family environment and cognitive models. *Review of Educational Research, 76*, 527–551.

Walker, D., Greenwood, C., Hart, B., & Carta, J. (1994). Prediction of school outcomes based on early language production and socioeconomic factors. *Child Development, 65*, 606–621.

Wechsler, D. (2005). *Wechsler Intelligence Scale for Children–Fourth Edition–Spanish.* San Antonio, TX: Harcourt Assessment, Inc.

Weisner, T. S., Matheson, C., Coots, J., & Bernheimer, L. P. (2005). Sustainability of daily routines as a family outcome. In A. E. Maynard & M. I. Martini (Eds.), *Learning in cultural context: Family, peers, and school.* New York: Kluwer Academic/Plenum.

Weiss, L. G. (2002). Essentials of MIPS Assessment. In S. Strack (Ed.), *Essentials of Millon Inventories Assessment* (2nd Ed.). New York: John Wiley & Sons, Inc.

Weiss, L.G. (1997). The MIPS: Gauging the dimensions of normality. In T. Millon (Ed.), *The Millon Inventories: Clinical and personality assessment.* New York: The Guilford Press.

Weiss, L.G., & Prifitera, A. (1995). An evaluation of differential prediction of WIAT achievement scores from WISC-III FSIQ across ethnic and gender groups. *Journal of School Psychology, 33*, 297–304.

Weiss, L. G., Prifitera, A., & Roid, G. (1993). The WISC–III and the fairness of predicting achievement across ethnic and gender groups. *Journal of Psychoeducational Assessment* (monograph series, Advances in Psychological Assessment, Wechsler Intelligence Scale for Children–Third Edition), pp. 35–42.

Winner, E. (1996). *Gifted children: Myths and realities.* New York: Basic Books.

Wolf, R. M. (1964). *The identification and measurement of environmental variables related to intelligence.* Unpublished doctoral dissertation, University of Chicago.

2

THE ESSENTIALS AND

BEYOND

LAWRENCE G. WEISS, AURELIO PRIFITERA, JAMES A. HOLDNACK, DONALD H. SAKLOFSKE, ERIC ROLFHUS, AND DIANE COALSON

OVERVIEW

This chapter briefly presents the rationale for standardized test administration and then introduces WISC-IV interpretive strategies. Although this chapter covers much of the basics of WISC-IV interpretation, it also should be read by experienced users because it includes several unique contributions to the basic interpretive processes. In the section titled "Suggested Procedures for Basic Profile Analysis," we argue that the Index scores should be considered as the primary level of clinical interpretation, and an improved method of Index score discrepancy analyses is presented. A set of theory-based cluster scores are presented, with interpretive recommendations. Suggestions are made for how to streamline all discrepancy analysis procedures. Finally, the notion that Full-scale (FSIQ) is rendered invalid by large profile discrepancies is challenged, and the proper role of the FSIQ as a summary score is discussed.

STANDARDIZED TEST ADMINISTRATION

RATIONALE

Valid and clinically useful psychological assessment results depend, in part, on adherence to standardized test administration procedures, including use of the proper test environment and establishing and maintaining rapport, yet accommodations for individual differences are sometimes required. There are two major ideas behind the proper test-taking environment for which standard test administration procedures are designed. First, standard administration procedures represent a controlled psychological experiment. Second, they provide an environment that facilitates maximal performance.

A standard administration of the WISC-IV is a controlled psychological experiment designed to replicate the conditions under which the instrument was standardized. During development, the instructions and prompts for each subtest were optimized to reduce differences in the child's performance due to misunderstanding by the examiner of the subtest instructions, the use of varying and different approaches to presenting the test questions and establishing the assessment environment, or idiosyncratic strategies employed in the scoring of each subtest, that in turn, may undermine the meaning of the resulting scaled score. In other words the standardized instructions and prompts serve to minimize variance in test scores due to differences in potential examiners and testing environments.

Like most standardized assessments, a WISC-IV administration is a maximal-performance environment—within the bounds of enabling a standard environment without performance feedback. Children are encouraged, prompted, and instructed and an environment is created with few distractions. Contrast this with school grades, that are measures of *typical* intellectual performance over time, or parent ratings of behavior, where children's performances are summarized over time from behavior in a naturalistic environment.

Thus a standard administration is a compromise between a desire to tap the child's best intellectual performance and to allow comparability under standard conditions. Some children may perform even better if a parent were present to provide encouragement, but as this is a source of variance that cannot be controlled easily across children, it threatens comparability with a normative population.

1. A standard administration is a controlled psychological experiment.
   • Norms generalize to those assessed under the same conditions
   • Every instruction, prompt, and query are necessarily scripted
2. This testing environment should facilitate maximal performance.
   • Maximal vs typical distinction
   • Prompts/queries intentionally designed to facilitate maximum performance

THE TESTING ENVIRONMENT

The recommended testing environment should have a number of standard attributes, exactly as those requested of the standardization examiners. Testing should occur in a quiet well-lit room, without glare, in a space free from distractions. These distractions may include a view from a window, a clock, or the test materials themselves. Sitting across or at right angles from the child is desired. The child should be seated comfortably on a chair and at a table of the proper height As discussed later, the writing surface of the record form should be obscured at all times. Materials not in use should be easily accessible to the examiner and out of sight of the child, perhaps on a chair on the opposite side from the child in an open briefcase. Few things can be more distracting than blocks within reach of a young or impulsive child who is attempting to solve a difficult Matrix Reasoning problem! Materials in use must be readily visible to you and within reach at all times. Of course materials the child is using must be within close, comfortable, and easy reach of the child. If the writing surface is uneven, place a hard smooth surface under test booklets.

In practice the absence of an appropriate testing environment sometimes requires psychologists to test in inappropriate spaces, such as a partially cleared custodial storeroom with no windows, poor ventilation, and dim lighting! These situations should be avoided if at all possible. If the testing environment may have interfered with a child's maximal performance on the test, it should be noted in the written report.

ESTABLISHING AND MAINTAINING RAPPORT

Establishing a good rapport with the child is of utmost importance, to encourage maximum effort, while not breaking standard administration procedures. In order to create an ordered but nonstressful environment it is important to be familiar and confident with the testing materials and procedures. This will not only allow the child to be comfortable and confident with you and the testing environment, but will save time. Fatigued individuals will not of course give a maximum performance. Teenagers who have questionable relationships with authority figures may be less invested if you appear uncertain and inefficient.

Of particular help is a good knowledge of the verbal subtest scoring and query rules, as well as facility with handling the stopwatch and recording responses simultaneously. Note that efficiency in administration is not worth an incomplete or sloppy recording of the child's responses. Often a single word can change the point value of a verbal item score. Simple errors in recording completion time can change Block Design item scores. Carefully record verbal responses verbatim, including notations such as (Q).

Encouragement should be used to facilitate maximum engagement without providing feedback about the child's actual performance. Neutral statements such as *I appreciate how hard you're working, some of these are easy and some very hard*, or *just do your best* are acceptable. Feedbacks such as *that's right* or *almost got that one* are not allowed. Your clinical judgment must be used as to how much verbal encouragement is required to keep the child engaged without ever giving performance feedback beyond what is in the manual instructions for specific subtests. This injunction also applies to the Record Form and Stimulus Book, where it can be obvious when the child was discontinued and not administered all items. Prevent the child from viewing the Record Form by employing a clipboard and tilting it away from the child's view when scoring or recording responses. Also, minimize opportunities for the child to see that some items were not administered.

Except under exceptional circumstances parents and guardians should not be allowed in the testing session. If required for purposes of making the child sufficiently comfortable to assess, these adults should not be allowed to speak, restate questions or answers, encourage the child, or disrupt the test session in any way and should remain seated behind the child so that the child cannot see their expressions or mannerisms. The presence of a parent or guardian during testing should be noted in the report, along with the reason it was considered necessary. A session in which the parent, guardian, or other observer is a vocal participant is not a standard administration and should be stated in the report.

Specific transition phrases between subtests have been provided in the manual; these can be eliminated or modified for purposes of rapport, but statements specific to each subtest may not be modified except as noted within the instructions for that subtest.

It is recommended that the WISC-IV administration be completed in one session. Short breaks within a session may be given in order to minimize fatigue, but these should be used sparingly and only granted between subtests, never during a subtest. If a second testing session is required, it should be completed within 1 week.

INDIVIDUAL DIFFERENCES

Children bring their personal experiences and background into the testing session. It is important for the examiner to pay attention to individual differences that may affect motivation and orientation toward the session. For any number of reasons a child's performance may not represent their best. These include such factors as when the child is not in agreement with the reason for testing, when the child transfers poor rapport with other adults to the examiner, cultural influences regarding how to relate to adults, familiarity with the testing paradigm, test performance anxiety, and clinical depression. Such factors may require additional time and effort to establish a cooperative environment that induces maximal performance. These factors should be noted in the report when present, along with any steps taken by the examiner to address them. For example, we once observed a very experienced psychiatrist attempt to interview a highly resistant preteen boy. Upon introduction, the boy gave a socially inappropriate response to the psychiatrist who replied in a calm tone of voice, "Don't give me that nonsense. I asked you a normal question, now why don't you give me a normal answer." After a walk to the facilities snack bar for a soda and 10 minutes of conversation about sports, the psychiatrist was able to obtain a valid interview. The degree and character of the rapport should always be noted in the report, and extraordinary efforts to obtain rapport should be described in detail.

TESTING CHILDREN WITH CLINICAL SYNDROMES

The WISC-IV is designed to achieve efficient and reliable estimates of cognitive ability using start and discontinue rules that minimize the number of items a child must attempt in order to reduce fatigue and possible frustration. Specific rules for administering each subtest are fully detailed in the test manual and are not repeated here. However, children with some clinical conditions present unique challenges for standardized testing. Many clinically relevant and helpful descriptions for assessing children with special needs (e.g., hearing impaired, ADHD, LD) with the WISC-IV are presented in Prifitera, Saklofske, and Weiss (2005) and in the WISC-IV Administration Manual. When assessing children referred for cognitive or academic problems, we must recognize that while we are testing their cognitive ability and potential, it is sometimes the very symptoms and effects of the clinical syndrome that will impact the child's test behavior, test scores, and resulting interpretation. We are reminded of one psychologist who complained that the Cancellation subtest was biased because her ADHD children could not perform that type of task. However, that is precisely the point of the evaluation. Certain cognitive abilities are impaired in certain disorders, and these impairments are reflected in a proper clinical assessment.

TESTING CHILDREN WITH SPECIAL NEEDS

Children with special physical needs, such as physical, language, or sensory limitations, are frequently referred for psychological evaluations. With such children, it is important not to attribute low performance on a cognitive test to low intellectual ability when, in fact, it may be attributable to physical, language, or sensory difficulties. Depending on the nature of the difficulty and the test administered, the child's performance may result in scores that underestimate intellectual capacity if the test is administered in the standard fashion. For example, a child with fine motor impairment would most likely obtain low scores on the WISC-IV subtests that require fine motor abilities or manipulation of test materials under time constraints (e.g., Block Design, Coding) Similarly, a child with hearing, language, or speech impairment may be at a disadvantage on the verbal comprehension subtests.

Prior to testing a child with physical, language, or sensory difficulties, become familiar with the child's limitations and preferred mode of communication, both of which may necessitate deviations from standard procedures. Some flexibility may be necessary to balance the needs of the particular child with the need to maintain standard procedures. For example, a child with physical delays may be at a disadvantage on tasks that require even simple motor skills (i.e., Picture Concepts, Matrix Reasoning, and Coding). Cancellation, which requires less fine motor skill than coding, may be substituted for Coding in deriving the PSI. In cases of severe physical impairment, the Verbal Comprehension scores may be used as estimates of children's cognitive abilities. Other tests, designed for such populations, may be used to supplement the WISC-IV, such as the Wechsler Nonverbal Scales of Ability (WNV; Naglieri, 2006), Naglieri Nonverbal Ability Test–Individual Administration (NNAT-I; Naglieri, 2003), Ravens Progressive Matrixes (Ravens, 1998), Universal Nonverbal Intelligence Test (UNIT; Bracken & McCallum, 1998), or Leiter International Performance Scale–Revised (Roid & Miller, 1997).

Similar challenges may arise when English language learners are referred for evaluation. In addition to the nonverbal tests just mentioned, the WISC-IV Spanish may be used with children in the United States whose primary language is Spanish. Issues related assessing immigrant children in other languages are addressed in Chapter 1.

Any and all modifications from the standardized administration and scoring instructions need to be documented on the WISC-IV Record Form, described in the report, and considered when interpreting test results. Professionals who evaluate the child's functioning will need to rely on clinical judgment to evaluate the effects of such modified procedures on the test scores. Despite the fact that some modifications invalidate the use of the norms, such testing of limits often provides very valuable qualitative as well as quantitative information about the child's strengths and weaknesses in intellectual functioning.

TESTING CHILDREN WHO ARE DEAF OR HARD OF HEARING

As stated in the test manual, the WISC-IV contains subtests that facilitate the measurement of cognitive abilities in many special populations, including children who are deaf or hard of hearing (see Braden, 2005; Braden & Hannah, 1998). To obtain reliable, valid, and clinically useful results, examiners must accommodate the child while minimizing modifications to standard administration procedures. This process is complex and warrants expanded discussion and guidelines.

Examiners administering the WISC-IV to members of the deaf and hard of hearing population must be aware that a significant percentage of children classified as deaf, hard of hearing, or hearing impaired may also present with additional disabilities. Results from annual demographic studies indicate that approximately 32% of this population is reported to have one or more additional disabilities, such as behavioral, emotional, cognitive, learning, and physical disabilities (Gallaudet Research Institute, 1998). Many individuals classified as multiply handicapped or impaired may also present with a hearing impairment.

While the standardized instructions for the WISC-IV permit pointing and gestures, these types of responses on the WISC-III have been reported to be ambiguous for children who are deaf (Blennerhassett & Traxler, 1999) and may be a source of potential error in scoring and interpretation. Other researchers report conflicting information on the appropriate selection and use of intelligence tests with deaf individuals (for an overview, see Maller, 2003). When assessing children who are deaf or hard of hearing, examiners should consider diversity issues and educational placement, as well as such issues as the use of special group norms, the lack of standardized sign translations, the appropriateness of verbal scales, and the limitations of profile analysis. It is clear that further psychometric studies are needed to establish empirically derived standards for use of the WISC-IV with a variety of deaf and hard of hearing individuals. These guidelines are provided as a step toward the goal of a more standard WISC-IV administration with children who are deaf or hard of hearing.

MODES OF COMMUNICATION

When selecting instruments or subtests and planning accommodations for children who have a significant hearing disability, the child's primary language(s) or preferred mode(s) of communication should be considered the most critical issue, as opposed to the type or degree of hearing ability or inability. The communication method used to administer the WISC-IV to a given child may differ across different languages and modalities (e.g., between manually signed American Sign Language and spoken English) with gradations, combinations, and systems in between. Items on the WISC-IV may be conveyed differently depending on the signs and sign language(s) used. A child may use one or any combination of the following modes of communication, which have been grouped into four broad categories.

AMERICAN SIGN LANGUAGE (ASL)

American Sign Language is a complete visual–spatial language with its own grammar, idioms, semantics, syntax, and pragmatics. ASL incorporates facial expressions as well as various hand shapes, dynamic movements, various locations on or near the body, and differing orientations of the palm. Some signs require two hands whereas others require a single hand.

ASL can also be used in a tactile format with children who are deaf–blind, but may need to be modified to convey visually based linguistic information. Examiners should also be aware that there are regional variations in signs.

SIMULTANEOUS COMMUNICATION (SIM-COM)

Simultaneous communication, which can include Manually Coded English (MCE), is the use of signs in English word order. Users of Sim-Com may include parts of spoken language that do not exist in ASL, with simultaneous use of spoken English. MCE systems include sign systems, which may be referred to as signed exact English and Pidgin Signed English (PSE).

CUED SPEECH

Cued speech is a sound-based visual communication system that tries to make all the phonemes of spoken language (including English) visually accessible. It combines eight hand shapes in four different locations on or near the face with the natural mouth movements of speech.

AURAL/ORAL

Aural/oral is the use of spoken languages without signs or gestures, usually aided by some form of auditory amplification or assistive listening device such as FM systems, hearing aids, or cochlear implants. Children who use this system may rely upon the amplified auditory input along with visual cues from speech reading or primarily depend on their residual/amplified hearing skills without any visual or speech reading cues.

WISC-IV SUBTEST ADMINISTRATION ACROSS COMMUNICATION MODALITIES

Table 1 provides general appropriateness ratings for administration of WISC-IV subtests and scales for the four general modes of communication. These ratings were developed by Steven Hardy-Braz, who served as the primary consultant on issues of assessment with children who are deaf or hard of hearing. In addition, trained, experienced specialists in the assessment of children who are deaf or hard of hearing shared their impressions and experiences following administration of the WISC–IV to a limited sample of individuals in each communication subgroup. Appropriateness ratings are based on the assumption that the child has been deemed fluent in or able to use the identified system or language as appropriate for their age and developmental level. Note that the numerical ratings range from 1 to 6; a

TABLE 1 Subtest and Scale Appropriateness Ratings for the Deaf and Hard of Hearing by Mode of Communication

	ASL	Sim-Com	Cued	Aural/oral
Subtest				
Block Design	6 T	6 T	6 T	6 T
Similarities	2	2	5	5
Digit Span	3 M	3 M	5 M	5
Picture Concepts	6	6	6	6
Coding	6 T	6 T	6 T	6 T
Vocabulary	2	2	5	5
Letter–Number	1 M	2 M	5 M	5
Matrix Reasoning	6	6	6	6
Comprehension	2	2	5	5
Symbol Search	6 T	6 T	6 T	6 T
Picture Completion	4 P	4 P	6 P	6 P
Cancellation	6 T	6 T	6 T	6 T
Information	2 A	2 A	5	5
Arithmetic	3 B	4 B	5	5
Word Reasoning	2	4	5	5
Scale				
Verbal Comprehension	2	2	5	5
Perceptual Reasoning	6	6	6	6
Working Memory	1	2	3	3
Processing Speed	3 T	3 T	3 T	3 T
Full Scale	1	2	3	3

1. Administration is not recommended
2. Administration is possible but may be problematic
3. Administration is possible but interpretation may be difficult
4. Administration is possible with caveats for some items due to linguistic issues
5. Administration is possible with caveats due to pronunciation demands on the child
6. Administration is possible with little or no modification
A. Less difficult items may require additional modification
B. More difficult items may require additional modification
M. Modification by modality may affect performance and interpretation
T. Timed nature may affect performance and interpretation
P. Pointing responses may be ambiguous
Wechsler Intelligence Scale for Children – Fourth Edition (WISC-IV). Copyright © 2003 by Harcourt Assessment, Inc. Reproduced with permission. All rights reserved.

rating of 1 indicates that use of the subtest or scale with that group is not recommended, and a rating of 6 indicates that use of the subtest or scale is possible with few or no accommodations or modifications.

Because items within a single subtest are typically presented in order of increasing difficulty, appropriateness ratings may vary across the subtest item set. For example, the examiner needs to be aware that the less difficult arithmetic items are administered readily using signed language, but the more difficult items must often be signed in an iconic fashion. If the appropriateness of subtest administration varies with the item set administered, the appropriateness rating includes the letter A (i.e., less difficult items may require additional modification) or B (i.e., more difficult items may require additional modification).

Although subtest administration may be possible in a particular communication modality, use of that modality may alter the cognitive task demands or deviate from standardized procedures used in the collection of the normative sample. For example, when administering timed items, examiners should be aware of additional time needed for interpreters to transmit messages and of some individuals' need to visually process while speechreading the examiner. Subtests that may be susceptible to altered cognitive task demands include the letters M (i.e., modification by modality may affect performance and interpretation), T (i.e., timed nature may affect performance and interpretation), or P (i.e., pointing responses may be ambiguous) in the appropriateness rating.

Generally, aural/oral children whose amplified hearing is determined to be normal or near normal should be able to take all of the subtests according to standardized procedures. The transliteration of instructions via cued speech does not alter the linguistic content of the message, and children who are knowledgeable in that system should also be able to have the subtests administered to them without significant modifications. However, administration in either modality may be affected by the child's ability to respond and/or speak clearly and fluently. The ability to hear does not clearly predict one's ability to speak, nor does the ability to speak clearly predict one's ability to hear.

Examiners must remain cognizant of the fact that an inability to hear clearly, regardless of communication modality, may result in environmental conditions that impede incidental learning. For example, compared to a child of normal hearing, a child who is deaf has more limited learning opportunities from everyday exposure to orally presented information. It is important to distinguish between performance related to cognitive functioning and those aspects of performance that may reflect the unique environment of children who are deaf or hard of hearing.

Any accommodation for children who are deaf or hard of hearing may significantly modify the functioning of the item and/or subtest and introduce undesired amounts of construct-irrelevant variance. Table 2 provides general caveats (i.e., cautions) for the administration of WISC-IV subtests to children who are deaf or hard of hearing. Readers are again referred to the very practical chapter written by Braden (2005). However, the ultimate selection of subtests, administration accommodations, and interpretation of results are the responsibility of the individual examiner, as well as judgments regarding the reliability and validity of results. Due to the extremely diverse nature of this population, these suggestions are intended primarily as a guide.

TABLE 2   General Subtest Caveats for the Deaf and Hard of Hearing

Subtest	General Caveat
BD	While differences in communication modalities do not appear to alter the administration of this subtest substantially, examiners should be aware that this is a timed subtest in which the items are displayed as the directions are explained. This may be a disadvantage for children who must view the examiner's signs, cues, or lips instead of listening and simultaneously viewing the displayed items.
SI	Examiners should be aware that the English vocabulary demands of this subtest and the translation of several items in signs or finger spelling modify items significantly and introduce some amount of construct-irrelevant variance.
DS	Administering the items in this subtest in a primarily visual format alters the cognitive demands of the subtest from one that taps into auditory memory to one that taps into visual memory. Examiners should consider visual communication accommodations as resulting in significant modifications to the cognitive demands of this subtest.
PCn	Differences in communication modalities do not appear to alter the administration of this subtest significantly. Appropriate accommodations should provide access to the cognitive demands of this subtest.
CD	While differences in communication modalities do not appear to alter the administration of this subtest substantially, examiners should be aware that this is a timed subtest in which the items are displayed as the directions are explained. This may be a disadvantage for children who must view the examiner's signs, cues, or lips instead of listening and simultaneously viewing the displayed items.
VC	Examiners should be aware that the English vocabulary demands of this subtest and the translation of several items in signs or finger spelling modify items significantly and introduce some amount of construct-irrelevant variance. Some signs may provide unintended cues for children.
LN	Like Digit Span, administering the items in this subtest in a primarily visual format alters the cognitive demands of the subtest from one that taps into auditory memory to one that taps into visual memory. Due to the overlapping similarities between the hand shapes used to communicate several letters and numbers, administration of this subtest may introduce additional confounds. Examiners should consider visual communication accommodations as resulting in significant modifications to the cognitive demands of this subtest.
MR	Differences in communication modalities do not appear to alter the administration of this subtest significantly. Appropriate accommodations should provide access to the task demands of this subtest.
CO	Examiners should be aware that the English vocabulary demands of this subtest and the translation of several items in signs or finger spelling modify items significantly and introduce some amount of construct-irrelevant variance.
SS	While differences in communication modalities do not appear to alter the administration of this subtest substantially, examiners should be aware that this is a timed subtest in which the items are displayed as the directions are explained. This may be a disadvantage for children who must view the examiner's signs, cues, or lips instead of listening and simultaneously viewing the displayed items.
PCm	Pointing responses on the WISC-III have been reported to be ambiguous for this subtest. While administration is possible, examiners need to be aware of the similar nature of some signs and the missing components in the pictures.

(Continues)

TABLE 2 *(Continued)*

Subtest	General Caveat
CA	While differences in communication modalities do not appear to alter the administration of this subtest substantially, examiners should be aware that this is a timed subtest in which the items are displayed as the directions may be explained. This may be a disadvantage for children who must view the examiner's signs, cues, or lips instead of listening and simultaneously viewing the displayed items.
IN	Examiners should be aware that the English vocabulary demands of this subtest and the translation of several items in signs or finger spelling modify items significantly and introduce some amount of construct-irrelevant variance. Some of the less difficult items may be confounded by signed or gestured responses that merely mimic or replicate the examiner's instructions.
AR	While differences in communication modalities do not appear to alter the administration of this subtest substantially for less difficult items, the examiner needs to be aware that more difficult items are often signed in an iconic fashion and thus may modify the item difficulty.
WR	Examiners should be aware that the English vocabulary demands of this subtest and the translation of clues into signs or finger spelling modify items significantly and introduce some amount of construct-irrelevant variance.

LEGAL ISSUES

The reader should consider how his or her practice would be affected if it were discovered that many of the children who were being assessed had been coached on the questions and answers of the tests they routinely administer. While it is unethical for psychologists to coach children on the answers to intelligence or other tests, the only way to prevent this from happening by well-meaning parents or an attorney is to control the security of the test questions and answers. This is why the sale of intelligence and other psychological tests is restricted to professionally qualified individuals and why photocopying, recording, or videotaping are prohibited.

The privacy rule of the Health Insurance Portability and Accountability Act (HIPAA) provides that individuals have a qualified right of access to individually identifiable health information maintained by health care providers covered by HIPAA. Widespread dissemination of record forms, however, may disclose test questions and answers and would render test instruments invalid and therefore useless to professional psychologists and to the public at large. For these and other reasons, test questions and answers are classified as trade secrets. It is important to note that HIPAA does not require any person to disclose any trade secret materials. Therefore, all restrictions on the dissemination of test record forms and protocols remain in effect.

Even in a school setting, the release of copies of test questions or protocols in any form is not required under federal law. The applicable U.S. statute is the Family Education Rights and Privacy Act (FERPA). This establishes the right of parents "to inspect and review the education records of their children" (20 U.S.C. § 1232G(a)(1)(A)). It requires schools to establish procedures that enable parents to review their children's records within a reasonable time after a request is made.

The regulations implementing this section define "the right to inspect and review education records" as including "(1) the right to a response from the [school] to reasonable requests for explanations and interpretations of the records; and (2) the right to obtain copies of the records from the [school] where failure of the [school] to provide the copies would effectively prevent a parent or eligible student from exercising the right to inspect and review the education records" (34 C.F.R. § 99.11(b)).

The import of this section is that only where failure to provide copies would deny the exercise of this right will schools be obliged to provide copies. In all other cases, inspection alone would presumably suffice. If a parent requests an inspection of a child's record, once the school agrees to review the content of the child's test record with the parent, it is most unlikely that a court would find that exercise of the right to review educational records had been denied.

We encourage professionals to review test results with parents, including, if the psychologist deems appropriate, review of responses to individual items. This may involve showing a test protocol or answer contained in test booklets to parents in order to facilitate discussion. However, we strongly oppose the release of copies of protocols for the reasons just noted. The tests are extremely valuable instruments, which are widely used throughout the world. Impairment of their security could threaten the validity of the tests and, therefore, their value as a measurement tool. Disclosure of the test threatens the ongoing validity of the test results and, therefore, the clinical value of the test.

In some cases, parents may wish to consult a second professional regarding a child's test scores. In these situations, a copy of the completed test protocol may be sent to another professional for the purposes of review; however, the materials should pass directly from professional to professional and not through the hands of the parents or their attorney.

Should litigation in which a psychologist is involved reach the stage where a court considers ordering the release of proprietary test materials to nonprofessionals such as counsel, we suggest that the psychologist request that the court issue a protective order prohibiting parties from making copies of the materials; requiring that the materials be returned to the professional at the conclusion of the proceedings; and requiring that the materials not be publicly available as part of the record of the case, whether this is done by sealing part of the record or by not including the materials in the record at all.

In addition, testimony regarding the items, particularly that which makes clear the content of the items, should be sealed and again not be included in the record. Pleadings and other documents filed by the parties should not, unless absolutely necessary, make specific reference to the content of or responses to any item, and any portion of any document that does so should be sealed. Finally, the psychologist should request that the judge's opinion, including both findings of fact and conclusions of law, not include descriptions or quotations of the items or responses.

In other countries where the WISC-IV or any of the Wechsler intelligence scales are used (in their present or in an adapted form), we encourage psychologists to be fully aware of the legal and ethical issues, as well as professional standards, related to test administration, scoring, interpretation, and report writing.

BASIC ISSUES IN TEST INTERPRETATION

This section reviews basic issues in test interpretation, including the meaning of standard scores, ranges of classification, and problems with the use of test age equivalents.

REPORTING AND DESCRIBING PERFORMANCE

The number of items answered correctly on any test tells us nothing about the child's level of skill relative to others. Once we know the average score on the test and the average spread of scores across a larger group, then we can begin to understand the meaning of the child's score. The conversion of raw scores into standard scores enables practitioners to compare scores within the WISC-IV and between the WISC-IV and other related measures. The use of age-corrected standard scores allows the practitioner to compare each child's cognitive functioning with children of similar age. Standard scores provide the most accurate description of test data. However, for individuals who are unfamiliar with test interpretation, standard scores may be difficult to understand in isolation. Other information, such as percentile ranks, confidence intervals, descriptive classifications, and test-age equivalents, is often used in conjunction with standard scores to describe a child's performance relative to others.

Standard Scores

Two types of age-corrected standard scores are provided in the WISC-IV: scaled subtest scores and composite scores. Scaled subtest scores represent a child's performance relative to his or her same-age peers. They are derived from the total raw scores on each of the 15 subtests and are scaled to a metric with a mean of 10 and a standard deviation of 3. A subtest scaled score of 10 reflects the average performance of a given age group. Scores of 7 and 13 are 1 SD below and above the mean, respectively, and scaled scores of 4 and 16 deviate 2 SDs

TABLE 3   Relation of Scaled Scores to Standard Deviations from Mean and Percentile Rank Equivalents

Scaled Scores	Number of SDs from the Mean	Percentile Rank Equivalent
19	+3	99.9
18	+2 2/3	99.6
17	+2 1/3	99
16	+2	98
15	+1 2/3	95
14	+1 1/3	91
13	+1	84
12	+ 2/3	75
11	+ 1/3	63
10	0	50
9	− 1/3	37
8	− 2/3	25
7	−1	16
6	−1 1/3	9
5	−1 2/3	5
4	−2	2
3	−2 1/3	1
2	−2 2/3	0.4
1	−3	0.1

Note: Percentile ranks are theoretical values for a normal distribution. *Wechsler Intelligence Scale for Children – Fourth Edition (WISC-IV)*. Copyright © 2003 by Harcourt Assessment, Inc. Reproduced with permission. All rights reserved.

from the mean. Note that the scaled score equivalents of five process scores (i.e., BDN, DSF, DSB, CAR, and CAS) are derived in the same manner as the subtest scaled scores. Table 3 presents the relation of WISC-IV-scaled scores to standard deviations from mean and percentile rank equivalents.

WISC-IV composite scores (i.e., VCI, PRI, WMI, PSI, and FSIQ) are standard scores based on various sums of subtest-scaled scores. The composite scores are scaled to a metric with a mean of 100 and a standard deviation of 15. A score of 100 on any of the composites defines the average performance of children similar in age, and scores of 85 and 115 are 1 SD below and above the mean, respectively. Scores of 70 and 130 are 2 SDs below and above the mean, respectively. About 68% of all children obtain composite scores between 85 and 115, about 96% score in the 70–130 range, and nearly all children (about 99.8%) obtain scores between 55 and 145 (3 SDs on either side of the mean). The relation of WISC-IV composite scores to deviations from the mean and associated percentile rank equivalents are presented in Table 4.

Percentile Ranks

The WISC-IV provides age-based percentile ranks for subtest-scaled scores and composite scores that indicate a child's standing relative to

TABLE 4   Relation of Composite Scores to Standard Deviations from Mean and Percentile
Rank Equivalents

Composite Scores	Number of SDs from the Mean	Percentile Rank Equivalent
145	+3	99.9
140	+2 2/3	99.6
135	+2 1/3	99
130	+2	98
125	+1 2/3	95
120	+1 1/3	91
115	+1	84
110	+ 2/3	75
105	+ 1/3	63
100	0	50
95	− 1/3	37
90	− 2/3	25
85	−1	16
80	−1 1/3	9
75	−1 2/3	5
70	−2	2
65	−2 1/3	1
60	−2 2/3	0.4
55	−3	0.1

Note: Percentile ranks are theoretical values for a normal distribution. *Wechsler Intelligence Scale for Children – Fourth Edition (WISC-IV)*. Copyright © 2003 by Harcourt Assessment, Inc. Reproduced with permission. All rights reserved.

other children of the same age. Percentile ranks reflect points on a scale below which a given percentage of scores lie based on the standardization sample. Percentile ranks typically range from 1 to 99, with 50 as the mean and median. For example, children with a percentile rank of 15 perform as high or higher than 15% of other children the same age (or perform at or lower than 85% of other children the same age).

Although easy to understand and useful for explaining a child's performance relative to that of others, percentile ranks have various limitations. Percentile ranks do not have equal intervals. Percentile ranks in a normal distribution, such as the FSIQ, tend to cluster near the median, the 50th percentile. Consequently, for children who score within the average range on the WISC-IV, a change of 1 or 2 total raw score points may produce a large change in their percentile ranks. However, for those children with more extreme scores, a change of 1 or 2 raw score points is not likely to produce a sizable change in their percentile ranks.

Standard Errors of Measurement and Confidence Intervals

Observed scores on measures of cognitive ability are based on observational data and represent *estimates* of a child's true scores. They reflect a child's true abilities combined with some degree of measurement error. A child's true score is represented more accurately by establishing a confidence interval of the true score: a band of scores in which the true score is likely to lie. Confidence intervals provide another means of expressing score precision and serve as a reminder that measurement error is inherent in all test scores. Scores that are less reliable have a broader band, whereas those that are more reliable have a narrower band. Practitioners are encouraged to report confidence intervals around the WISC-IV composite scores and to use this information to ensure greater accuracy when interpreting the test scores.

Norms found in the *WISC-IV Administration and Scoring Manual* provide confidence intervals of the WISC-IV composite scores using SEE and estimated true scores. Note that confidence intervals calculated with SEM are centered around the observed scores, whereas confidence intervals calculated with SEE are centered around the estimated true scores corrected for regression toward the mean.

Descriptive Classifications

Composite scores are often described in more qualitative terms according to the child's level of performance. Table 5 lists the descriptive classifications of WISC-IV composite scores (i.e., VCI, PRI, WMI, PSI, and FSIQ). In place of the term *intellectually deficient* used in the WISC-III, the WISC-IV uses the term *extremely low*. This practice avoids the implication that a very low IQ score is sufficient evidence for the diagnosis of "mental retardation." It does, however, reflect that the child's obtained score on the WISC-IV is much lower than the average level of functioning and may be indicative of a deficit in cognitive functioning. Test results can be described in a manner similar to the following example:

> Relative to children of comparable age, this child is currently functioning within the [Insert appropriate descriptive classification] range of intelligence on a standardized measure of intellectual ability.

TABLE 5 Qualitative Descriptions of Composite Scores

Composite Score	Classification	Theoretical Normal Curve
130 and above	Very superior	2.2
120–129	Superior	6.7
110–119	High average	16.1
90–109	Average	50
80–89	Low average	16.1
70–79	Borderline	6.7
69 and below	Extremely low	2.2

Test-Age Equivalents

Test-age equivalents represent the average age in years and months at which a given total raw score is typical. For example, a total raw score of 21 on the comprehension subtest corresponds to a test-age equivalent of 9 years 10 months. Test-age equivalents of the WISC-IV are provided in the *WISC-IV Administration and Scoring Manual* (Wechsler, 2003).

Although test-age equivalents are useful for describing a child's cognitive functioning in comparison to median or typical functioning for children of various ages, there are limitations to their use. First, test-age equivalents provide little information about a child's standing relative to his or her same-age peers. A child who obtains an apparently meaningful test-age equivalent may be in the average range compared to other children of the same age. For example, Nathan, aged 12 years 10 months, obtained a test-age equivalent of 10 years 10 months on the Vocabulary subtest. Although Nathan may appear to be performing poorly on this subtest, his raw score of 35 is in the average range of functioning for other children his age.

Second, small raw score changes may result in large changes in test-age equivalents. Notable differences between test-age equivalents and a child's chronological age may be obtained, but interpretation of the child's cognitive functioning as being far below or above average for his or her age may be unwarranted. This is because the range of average scores overlaps at adjacent age groups. For example, Maria and Katie are both 7 years 2 months old and were administered the Picture Concepts subtest. Maria earned a total raw score of 10 points and a test-age equivalent of 6 years 6 months. Katie earned a total raw score of 13 points and a test-age equivalent of 7 years 6 months. This does not necessarily mean that Katie's skill is significantly more advanced than Maria's. In fact, the scaled scores of Maria and Katie are 9 and 11, both in the average range compared with their age peers.

Third, test-age equivalents may not be comparable across subtests (e.g., a child's percentile ranks for two subtests with the same test-age equivalents may differ substantially). For example, if a child age 12 years 9 months obtains a test-age equivalent of 15 years 10 months on both the Digit Span and Coding subtests, the respective percentile ranks for these subtests are 63 and 91%, respectively.

Finally, an extreme test-age equivalent does not signify that the child's cognitive functioning resembles that of the extreme age group in every way. In addition, test-age equivalents at the most extreme ends of the age range are particularly difficult to interpret because they may only be reported as *under 6:2* or *over 16:10* (or as *under 8:2* or *over 7:10* for the Coding and Symbol Search subtests).

Due to these limitations, test-age equivalents are not recommended as the primary scores and should be interpreted with caution. *Standard scores or percentile ranks must be used to compare a child's performance to other children the same age.* Clinical decisions should be made from a review of the child's standard scores and other background and qualitative informa-tion. Placement decisions or diagnosis should never be based only on test-age equivalents or any one type of score.

INTERPRETIVE STRATEGIES

The remainder of this chapter focuses on basic interpretive procedures. Although much of this information is contained in the *WISC-IV Technical and Interpretation Manual* (Wechsler, 2003), we add new information about an improved method for determining index score differences (see also Prifi-tera, Saklofske, & Weiss, 2005) and make the case that the index scores are the primary level of clinical interpretation. This is not to discount the importance of the FSIQ score, that will be extensively discussed in the next chapter. The FSIQ is the most reliable and psychometrically sound score in the WISC-IV. It is also the best predictor of a wide variety of real life outcomes from school achievement to job performance (Gottfredson, 1998). Because FSIQ is composed of several related but different domains of cognition, however, clinical interpretation is more meaningful when each of these domains is considered separately. Thus, while the best overall psychometric value is found in the FSIQ, the best clinical value is found in the index scores, that are further detailed in Chapter 4. We discuss the proper role of FSIQ as a summary score rather than the main focus of intellectual evaluation. In addition, we describe six theory-based cluster scores and their interpretation. Further, we suggest a streamlined process for profile analysis that skips the determination of statistical significance and focuses on the base rate of particular profile discrepancies.

SUGGESTED PROCEDURES FOR BASIC
PROFILE ANALYSIS

A child's performance on the WISC-IV can be evaluated in terms of his or her patterns of composite and subtest scaled scores. Profile analysis can occur from both an intraindividual and an interindividual perspective by comparing the child's score patterns across subtests or by comparing his or her score patterns to the appropriate normative reference group. These ability comparisons can help the practitioner identify potentially meaningful patterns of strengths and weaknesses, which is important in describing functional impairment and for designing and preparing educational plans.

Criticisms of subtest profile analysis have been offered (e.g., McDermott, Fantuzzo, & Glutting, 1990), yet appropriate practice includes the generation and testing of hypotheses based on the referral question that are, in turn, either corroborated or refuted by the score pattern, other evaluation results, background information, or direct behavioral observations (Kamphaus,

2001). Although the WISC-IV Record Form is designed to assist the practitioner with profile analysis, interpretation of these findings must be made with consideration of information from other sources. Practitioners should always attempt to obtain as much collaborative data as possible, including information about the child's birth and development, medical history, familial and cultural background, social and educational history, and previous assessments. The additional information should be compared or integrated with the WISC-IV results.

The following approach outlines the mechanics of basic profile analysis, but meaningful interpretation requires integration of these data with the full clinical picture by a knowledgeable professional. This is the subject of many of the following chapters in this book.

PERFORMING THE PROFILE ANALYSIS

Step 1. Report and Describe the Four Index Scores

The four WISC-IV index scores are considered the primary level of clinical interpretation. Constructs measured by the Verbal Conceptualization Index (VCI), Perceptual Reasoning Index (PRI), Working Memory Index (WMI), and Processing Speed Index (PSI) contribute to general intelligence in important ways as described fully in Chapter 3. Table 6 lists the subtests that compose each index and the domains of intelligence assessed by each subtest.

The WISC-IV VCI is primarily a measure of *verbal concept formation and reasoning, and also incorporates knowledge acquired from one's environment.* The VCI is composed of Vocabulary, Similarities, and Comprehension subtests. Word Reasoning and Information are supplemental VCI subtests that can be administered for additional information or if one of the core subtests is spoiled during administration.

The PRI is primarily a measure of *reasoning with visual stimuli and also includes elements of spatial processing and visual–motor integration.* Reasoning with visual stimuli is also referred to as perceptual reasoning, and sometimes as fluid reasoning. The core PRI subtests are Block Design, Matrix Reasoning, and Picture Concepts. The supplemental subtest is Picture Completion.

The WMI provides a measure of the child's working memory abilities. Tasks that require working memory require the *ability to temporarily retain information in memory, perform some operation or manipulation with it, and produce a result.* Working memory involves attention, concentration, mental control, and reasoning. Contemporary research indicates that working memory is an essential component of other higher order cognitive processes, as well as being closely related to achievement and learning (see Chapter 4). Letter Number Sequencing and Digit Span are the core WMI subtests, with Arithmetic as optional.

TABLE 6   WISC-IV Index Scores, Domain Definitions, and Member Subtests

---

Verbal Comprehension Index (VCI)
  Primary Domain: Reasoning with verbal stimuli and verbal concept formation
  Secondary construct involved: Some items and subtests may require previously acquired
    knowledge of verbal constructs
  Core subtests: Vocabulary (VO), Similarities (SI), and Comprehension (CO)
  Supplemental subtests: Information (IN) and Word Reasoning (WR)

Perceptual Reasoning Index (PRI)
  Primary domain: Reasoning with visual stimuli
  Secondary constructs involved: Some items and subtests require spatial reasoning and visual-
    motor integration
  Core subtests: Block Design (BD), Matrix Reasoning (MR), and Picture Concepts (PCn)
  Supplemental subtest: Picture Completion (PCm)

Working memory index (WMI)
  Primary Domain: Ability to briefly retain information in memory while performing some
    operation or manipulation with it
  Secondary constructs involved: Attention, concentration, mental control, and some reasoning.
  Core subtests: Digit Span (DS) and Letter Number Sequencing (LN)
  Supplemental subtest: Arithmetic (AR)

Processing speed index (PSI)
  Primary Domain: Ability to process visual stimuli quickly and accurately
  Secondary constructs involved: Attention, short-term visual memory, visual discrimination,
    and visual-motor coordination
  Core subtests: Coding (CD) and Symbol Search (SS)
  Supplemental subtest: Cancellation (CA)

The PSI provides a measure of the child's *ability to scan, sequence, or discriminate simple visual information quickly and correctly*. Faster processing of information may conserve working memory resources. This composite also involves short-term visual memory, attention, and visual–motor coordination. Research indicates a significant correlation between processing speed and general cognitive ability, and the sensitivity of such measures to such clinical conditions as ADHD, learning disability, and traumatic brain injury (see Chapter 3 Chapter 4). Coding and Symbol Search are the core processing speed subtests, and the new Cancellation subtest serves as the supplemental processing speed subtest.

Each of the four index scores should be reported with an appropriate confidence interval and percentile rank and classified in relation to the level of performance (e.g., average, high average, etc.). This is the nomothetic phase of interpretation, i.e., comparison of the child's performance to the average group performance of his or her peers.

Step 2. Index-Level Discrepancy Comparisons

The next step is an intraindividual (or ideographic) comparison among the index scores. This means that the child's scores on the four index scores are compared to each other (rather then to other children's scores) in order to identify possible patterns of strengths and weaknesses. This is an intra-individual analysis, sometimes referred to as a personal analysis, of strengths and weaknesses as opposed to the normative (i.e., nomothetic) analysis undertaken in step 1.

This section goes beyond the test manual to suggest an improved method for evaluating strengths and weaknesses among the four index scores that were introduced in our earlier book (Prifitera, Saklofske, & Weiss, 2005). The best method for comparing Indexes is to calculate the mean of the four index scores and compare each index to the mean. This method is preferred to evaluation of all possible comparisons among the index scores because it reduces the possibility of spurious findings by reducing the number of comparisons from six to four. To find the average index score, add the VCI, PRI, WMI, and PSI and then divide by four.

Discrepancy analyses typically follow a two-step process of (a) determining if the discrepancy is statistically significant and (b) determining if the discrepancy is large enough to be rare among nonclinical children. While the first part of the process tests if the discrepancy is mathematically significant, the second part of the process reveals if the finding is clinically significant. Thus, the second step is the more important one. This two-step process was first recommended at a time in our field when clinical interpretations were being made based on statistical significance alone. Researchers then pointed out that it was possible for a discrepancy to be statistically significant, yet not uncommon in the general population. In fact, when conducting profile analyses of WISC-R, WISC-III, and WISC-IV composites, minimum statistically significant discrepancies could be identified in roughly one-quarter to one-third of the standardization sample. Thus, it became important to check statistically significant findings against base rates to determine if the finding was rare and potentially clinically meaningful. There are two reasons that a discrepancy may be statistically significant but not uncommon. First, statistical significance is related, in part, to sample size. The WISC standardization sample sizes are large enough to have sufficient statistical power to detect relatively small differences between scores as significant. Second, flat profiles with little subtest or composite scatter are not as common among normally developing children as once believed. The variability in functioning across domains of cognitive ability for normal children is fairly wide. For all of these reasons, we hereby break with tradition and suggest that the first step may be skipped. It is not always necessary to first determine if a discrepancy is statistically significant before evaluating the frequency of occurrence of a discrepancy of that magnitude. For most types of discrepancy analyses, the examiner can streamline the interpretive analysis of score differences and proceed directly to the base rate tables.

To further our point, Table 7 shows the minimum difference between each index standard score and the child's average index standard score that

TABLE 7   Minimum Difference between Each Index Standard Score and the Examinee's Average Index Standard Score Required for Statistical Significance (with Bonferroni adjustments) and Percentages at Selected Base Rates

	P<.05	P<.01	1%	2%	5%	10%	25%
VCI	8.6	10.4	22.3	20.7	16.7	14.0	9.7
PRI	9.2	11.1	21.1	19.2	16.2	13.5	9.5
WMI	9.3	11.3	25.0	22.5	18.7	15.0	10.2
PSI	10.7	13.0	25.6	23.2	20.0	17.0	11.7

Wechsler Intelligence Scale for Children – Fourth Edition (WISC-IV). Copyright © 2003 by Harcourt Assessment, Inc. Reproduced with permission. All rights reserved.

would be required for statistical significance. For example, a difference between PRI and the mean index score of 9.5 points or more would be statistically significant at the $p<.05$ level. As also shown in Table 7, a difference of 9.5 points or more between PRI and the mean of the Index scores was obtained by 25% of the sample. Inspection of the remainder of Table 7 will reveal similar findings for the other index scores. We would remind the reader that tables that allow for the comparison of each index score to the mean are also presented for 3 different age bands (6–7, 8–13, 14–16 years) in Prifitera et al. (2005; p. 68). There are some small differences between the scores required for significance included in Table 7 for the total standardization sample versus the three age groupings; however we again would contend that it is the base rate data that are most critical.

Thus, we recommend that practitioners skip the step of determining if the discrepancy is statistically significant and proceed directly to the full base rate comparisons shown in Table 8 when comparing index scores to the average index score. If examiners do not have Table 8 handy when interpreting a profile, we suggest that an 11- or 12-point discrepancy is a good rule of thumb for most comparisons of index scores to the average index score, but that PSI comparisons to the average index score should be slightly higher at 14 points.

If rare, then the finding is interpreted as a relative strength or weakness (depending on the direction of the difference from the mean). However, such interpretation must also be sensitive to the nomothetic interpretation of that index score as well. For example, an intellectually deficient child may have an ideographic strength on PSI, but it would be misleading to report this finding as an unqualified strength. The examiner might write, for example, "In designing instructional modifications for Chobe, his teachers may take advantage of the relative strength in processing speed compared to his other cognitive abilities, but should keep in mind that his processing speed ability is still much lower than that of other children his age."

TABLE 8 Cumulative Percentages of Comparisons of Each Index Score to the Average Index Score by Direction

	Overall Sample								
	VCI-AVG		PRI-AVG		WMI-AVG		PSI-AVG		
Amount of Discrepancy	VCI< AVG (−)	VCI> AVG (+)	PRI< AVG (−)	PRI> AVG (+)	WMI< AVG (−)	WMI> AVG (+)	PSI< AVG (−)	PSI> AVG (+)	Amount of Discrepancy
40	0.0	0.0	0.0	0.0	0.0	0.0	0.0	0.0	40
39	0.0	0.0	0.0	0.0	0.0	0.0	0.0	0.0	39
38	0.0	0.0	0.0	0.0	0.0	0.0	0.0	0.0	38
37	0.0	0.0	0.0	0.0	0.0	0.0	0.0	0.0	37
36	0.0	0.0	0.0	0.0	0.0	0.0	0.0	0.0	36
35	0.0	0.0	0.0	0.0	0.0	0.0	0.1	0.0	35
34	0.0	0.0	0.0	0.0	0.0	0.0	0.1	0.0	34
33	0.0	0.0	0.0	0.0	0.0	0.0	0.1	0.0	33
32	0.0	0.0	0.0	0.0	0.1	0.0	0.1	0.0	32
31	0.0	0.0	0.0	0.0	0.2	0.1	0.1	0.0	31
30	0.0	0.1	0.0	0.0	0.2	0.2	0.2	0.0	30
29	0.0	0.1	0.0	0.0	0.2	0.2	0.3	0.2	29
28	0.1	0.1	0.0	0.0	0.3	0.3	0.4	0.3	28
27	0.2	0.1	0.1	0.0	0.4	0.4	0.4	0.4	27
26	0.3	0.1	0.1	0.0	0.5	0.4	0.6	0.5	26
25	0.3	0.2	0.1	0.1	0.6	0.5	0.7	0.6	25
24	0.4	0.2	0.1	0.3	0.7	0.7	0.9	0.9	24
23	0.6	0.3	0.2	0.4	1.0	1.0	1.1	1.3	23
22	0.9	0.5	0.3	0.5	1.5	1.3	1.5	1.6	22
21	1.2	0.9	0.4	0.8	2.0	1.6	2.1	2.0	21
20	1.5	1.2	0.7	1.0	2.4	2.0	2.7	2.7	20
19	1.9	1.6	1.2	1.4	2.8	2.5	3.1	3.6	19
18	2.2	2.1	1.5	2.0	3.6	3.1	4.0	4.5	18
17	2.8	2.8	2.2	2.5	4.3	3.5	5.2	5.8	17
16	3.8	3.5	2.9	3.1	5.0	4.4	6.1	7.0	16
15	5.2	4.1	3.5	4.2	6.0	5.0	7.7	8.0	15
14	6.3	4.9	4.6	5.4	7.7	6.1	9.1	9.2	14
13	7.7	6.0	5.7	6.8	8.8	7.4	10.7	11.3	13
12	9.3	8.0	7.5	8.4	10.8	9.5	12.5	13.4	12
11	11.7	9.7	9.1	10.3	12.5	11.0	14.6	16.3	11
10	14.6	12.3	11.5	13.0	15.4	13.4	17.2	19.0	10
9	17.2	15.0	13.9	15.2	18.0	15.8	19.6	21.8	9
8	20.0	18.0	17.0	18.3	21.0	18.5	22.1	24.0	8
7	23.6	21.1	20.5	21.8	25.5	21.9	25.4	27.0	7
6	27.7	24.9	24.7	26.4	29.3	25.6	28.4	30.1	6
5	31.7	28.1	29.4	30.2	33.2	29.2	31.0	33.5	5
4	36.0	31.1	33.2	34.5	37.0	33.6	35.2	37.0	4
3	40.2	35.0	37.5	39.0	40.7	37.6	39.6	40.0	3
2	44.7	39.5	42.0	44.0	45.3	41.5	44.1	43.7	2
1	50.5	44.0	46.8	48.4	49.7	46.1	47.9	47.5	1
Means	7.2	7.2	6.8	7.0	7.8	7.5	8.3	8.7	Means
SD	5.2	5.1	4.7	4.9	5.7	5.6	6.1	6.0	SD
Median	6.0	6.0	6.0	6.0	7.0	6.0	7.0	8.0	Median

In some cases, the examiner may have an a priori hypothesis about a specific relationship between two index scores based on the referral question, medical history, or classroom observation. In this case, the examiner may skip the general comparison among the four index scores and proceed directly to a planned, pairwise comparison. Again, it is possible to skip the statistical comparison of these scores and proceed directly to the base rate analysis. Table B.2 of the *Administration and Scoring Manual* provides the cumulative frequency of discrepancies among the various index scores in the WISC-IV standardization sample (base rates). The frequency of occurrence in the standardization sample provides a basis for estimating the rarity or commonness of a child's obtained score difference compared to the general population. Note that Table B.2 of the *Administration and Scoring Manual* provides base rate data by overall normative sample and by ability level. This is because data analysis revealed that the frequency of WISC-IV index score discrepancies differs significantly across various levels of general intellectual ability. For example, among the children whose FSIQ is 120 points or higher, about 13.7% obtained VCI scores that are 15 or more points higher than their PRI scores. Among the children whose FSIQ is 79 points or less, about 10.2% obtained such a discrepancy. Table B.2 of the *Administration and Scoring Manual* also provides base rate data separately for two directions of the discrepancies (such as VCI < PRI and VCI > PRI). This is because the direction of the difference between scores influences interpretation and, given the same absolute value, the base rate for the two directions may be quite different (Sattler & Dumont, 2004). For example, among the children whose FSIQ is 79 points or less, about 10.2% obtained VCI scores that are 15 or more points higher than their PRI scores, whereas 16.7% obtained PRI scores that are 15 or more points higher than their VCI scores.

One of the questions asked frequently by practitioners is what level of occurrence can be considered rare: 15 , 10 , 5 , or 1%? Clinical judgment and factors such as the child's cultural background and medical or physical condition should be considered when determining the rarity of a discrepancy score. Sattler et al. (2004) suggested that differences between scores that occur in less than 10 to 15% of the standardization sample should be judged as unusual.

Practitioners should note that composite scores are estimates of overall functioning in a particular cognitive domain or content area. As such, composite scores should always be evaluated in the context of those subtests that contribute to that composite score. Extreme variability within a composite score indicates that the score represents a summary of diverse abilities. The practitioner should closely examine the child's relative performance on subtests comprising the composite when interpreting these scores. Table B.6 of the WISC-IV *Administration and Scoring Manual* provides information about the cumulative percentages of intersubtest scatter within the various composite scores. When significant and unusual differences are noted, interpretation of comparisons to the composite scores must take this variability in subtest performance into account.

Step 3. Planned Comparisons among Clusters of Subtests Using the CHC Theory

Several theoretically based clusters of conceptually related WISC-IV subtests have been described by Flanagan and Kaufman (2004) based on CHC theory (Carroll, 1993). This is one model of how WISC-IV subtests may cluster, but not the only model. Many shared abilities among clusters of WISC subtests have been proposed over the years (Kaufman, 1979, 1994).

Step 3 is optional and further, it is *not* recommended that examiners calculate all clusters for all children. Examiners should plan which comparisons they will conduct, if any, based on hypotheses about specific skills based on referral questions in combination with background information and observations during administration.

The subtests that compose each cluster are shown in Table 9, and the norms for each cluster are provided in Table 10. We examined the minimum values required for statistically significant differences between each pair of cluster scores in relation to the base rates of these discrepancies and again determined that it is safe to skip the statistical comparison and proceed directly to the base rate analysis. Table 11 shows the cumulative percentages of cluster score discrepancies by direction in the standardization sample. Fifteen points is a good rule of thumb; however, we encourage practitioners to consult the tables and identify the specific base rates for each comparison by direction.

First, we describe the visual–spatial ability and fluid-reasoning clusters. The MR, PCn, BD, and PCm subtests all load on the perceptual reasoning factor in factor analyses of WISC-IV subtests; however, there are subtle differences in the constructs tapped by each. While all involve a strong dose of both visual–spatial organization and reasoning ability to successfully complete, the BD and PCm subtests are believed to be more visual–spatial than reasoning, whereas the MR and PCn tasks may tap more reasoning

TABLE 9   Theoretical Clusters of WISC-IV Subtests

Visual Spatial Reasoning (Gv). Block Design (BD) + Picture Completion (PCm)

Fluid Reasoning (Gf). Matrix Reasoning (MR) + Picture Concepts (PCn)

Gf – Verbal. Similarities (SI) + Word Reasoning (WR)

Lexical Knowledge (VL). Word Reasoning (WR) + Vocabulary (VO)

General Knowledge (KO). Comprehension (CO) + Information (IN)

Long-Term Memory (LTM). Vocabulary (VO) + Information (IN)

2. THE ESSENTIALS AND BEYOND

TABLE 1 O   Cluster Norms: Sums of Subtest-Scaled Scores (SSS) to Cluster Standard Score
Transformations for Six Theory-Based Clusters of WISC-IV Subtests

SSS	Gv	Gf	Gf-Verbal	VL	KO	LTM	SSS
2	50	50	50	50	50	50	2
3	53	53	52	53	53	54	3
4	56	55	55	56	56	57	4
5	59	58	58	59	59	60	5
6	62	61	61	62	62	63	6
7	65	64	63	65	65	66	7
8	67	67	66	68	68	69	8
9	70	69	69	71	71	72	9
10	72	71	72	74	73	74	10
11	75	74	75	76	76	77	11
12	78	77	78	79	78	79	12
13	80	79	81	81	81	81	13
14	83	82	84	84	83	84	14
15	86	85	86	86	85	87	15
16	88	88	89	89	88	89	16
17	91	91	92	91	91	91	17
18	94	94	94	94	94	94	18
19	97	97	97	96	97	97	19
20	100	100	100	99	99	99	20
21	103	103	102	102	102	102	21
22	106	106	105	105	105	105	22
23	108	109	108	108	108	108	23
24	111	112	111	110	111	111	24
25	114	115	113	113	114	113	25
26	117	118	116	116	117	116	26
27	120	121	120	120	120	119	27
28	123	124	123	123	123	122	28
29	126	127	126	126	126	125	29
30	130	130	129	129	129	127	30
31	133	133	132	132	131	130	31
32	135	135	135	135	133	133	32
33	138	138	137	137	136	136	33
34	140	140	140	140	139	138	34
35	143	143	142	142	142	141	35
36	145	145	145	145	145	144	36
37	148	148	147	147	148	147	37
38	150	150	150	150	150	150	38

than visual–spatial skill. Thus, the BD and PCm cluster can be thought of as
primarily visual spatial reasoning (Gv), whereas the MR and PCn cluster
could be thought of as primarily perceptual fluid reasoning (Gf). It should be
recognized that it may not be possible to measure pure fluid reasoning absent
of some influencing context such as perceptual or verbal stimuli. However, it

TABLE 11 Cumulative Percentages of Cluster Score Discrepancies, by direction.

Discrepancy	Gv <Gf	Gv >Gf	Gv <Gf2	Gv >Gf2	Gfv <Gf	Gfv >Gf	VL <KO	VL >KO	ILTM <WM	ILTM >WM	ILTM <WM2	ILTM >WM2	ILTM <Gfv	ILTM >Gfv	Gf <VCWM	GF >VCWM
40	0.1	0.2	0.1	0.1	0.3	0.2	0.0	0.0	0.3	0.3	0.3	0.5	0.0	0.0	0.5	0.2
39	0.2	0.2	0.1	0.1	0.4	0.3	0.0	0.0	0.4	0.5	0.4	0.5	0.0	0.0	0.7	0.4
38	0.2	0.2	0.1	0.1	0.4	0.5	0.0	0.0	0.4	0.5	0.5	0.5	0.0	0.0	0.8	0.4
37	0.2	0.3	0.1	0.1	0.5	0.5	0.0	0.0	0.4	0.6	0.7	0.8	0.0	0.0	0.8	0.4
36	0.3	0.3	0.1	0.1	0.6	0.5	0.0	0.0	0.6	0.8	0.9	0.9	0.0	0.0	0.9	0.4
35	0.4	0.4	0.3	0.1	0.6	0.6	0.0	0.0	0.7	0.8	0.9	1.0	0.0	0.0	1.0	0.5
34	0.5	0.6	0.4	0.1	0.9	0.8	0.0	0.0	0.8	1.1	1.0	1.5	0.0	0.0	1.0	0.5
33	0.7	0.6	0.6	0.3	1.0	0.8	0.0	0.0	1.0	1.4	1.2	1.5	0.0	0.1	1.2	0.9
32	1.1	1.1	0.7	0.6	1.2	1.2	0.0	0.0	1.2	1.4	1.4	1.9	0.0	0.1	1.4	1.0
31	1.2	1.2	0.9	0.7	1.7	1.6	0.0	0.0	1.3	2.0	1.6	2.1	0.0	0.1	1.4	1.2
30	1.5	1.3	0.9	0.9	1.9	1.6	0.1	0.1	1.5	2.3	2.0	2.3	0.0	0.1	1.8	1.7
29	1.8	2.3	1.0	1.1	2.0	2.5	0.1	0.3	2.0	2.4	2.2	2.7	0.0	0.2	1.8	2.1
28	2.1	2.3	1.3	1.4	2.6	2.8	0.1	0.3	2.1	3.2	3.0	3.2	0.0	0.3	1.9	2.3
27	2.7	2.4	1.6	1.5	3.0	2.8	0.1	0.4	2.4	3.4	3.4	3.5	0.1	0.3	2.8	2.8
26	3.0	3.6	2.4	1.8	3.5	3.7	0.3	0.5	3.1	3.9	3.6	4.1	0.2	0.3	2.9	3.1
25	3.5	3.7	2.7	1.8	4.3	4.2	0.3	0.8	3.5	5.1	4.4	5.0	0.3	0.6	3.0	3.5
24	4.7	4.2	3.1	2.5	4.8	4.2	0.5	1.2	4.0	5.1	4.7	5.2	0.4	0.7	4.3	4.3
23	5.1	5.5	3.9	3.1	5.3	5.9	0.7	1.3	5.2	6.0	5.3	6.9	0.5	0.9	4.4	4.8
22	5.7	5.5	4.6	3.7	6.4	6.3	0.8	1.7	5.9	7.2	6.4	7.0	0.7	1.1	4.5	5.4
21	7.0	6.0	5.1	4.1	7.0	6.5	1.5	2.0	6.8	7.4	7.5	7.9	1.4	1.6	7.2	7.0
20	7.9	7.8	6.0	5.0	7.7	8.5	2.0	2.3	7.7	8.8	8.5	10.1	1.6	2.1	7.4	7.5
19	8.2	7.9	6.9	5.7	9.4	9.1	2.4	2.9	8.6	9.8	9.7	10.4	2.1	3.0	7.5	8.5
18	10.0	9.0	8.4	6.5	10.4	9.7	3.5	3.6	9.9	10.6	11.9	11.6	3.1	3.4	10.4	10.5
17	10.9	11.0	9.2	7.7	11.5	12.0	4.0	4.3	10.8	12.9	13.0	13.7	3.9	4.3	11.3	11.3
16	11.7	11.0	10.9	9.0	13.5	12.6	5.1	5.2	12.7	13.6	14.2	14.3	5.2	5.0	11.3	11.3
15	14.9	13.3	12.7	10.2	14.6	14.0	6.7	6.4	14.4	14.4	16.6	16.4	6.3	5.3	14.3	16.0
14	16.0	16.0	14.7	12.3	15.7	16.7	7.5	8.2	15.7	18.2	17.7	17.9	7.7	7.4	15.5	16.8

13	17.2	16.1	16.1	13.8	18.5	17.6	9.4	8.9	18.6	18.9	19.5	19.2	9.5	9.2	15.6	18.5
12	20.9	18.9	18.6	15.7	20.0	18.8	11.4	10.2	19.6	21.2	21.8	22.3	10.6	9.7	20.1	22.2
11	22.0	22.1	20.0	18.3	22.1	22.2	13.3	13.7	21.5	23.9	22.9	23.5	12.9	13.3	22.0	22.9
10	23.5	22.1	21.8	20.3	25.4	23.9	16.0	14.2	23.9	24.5	25.3	25.0	14.8	15.3	22.0	24.0
9	27.6	26.5	24.6	23.0	27.4	25.6	19.6	16.7	24.9	28.2	27.8	28.9	17.2	17.2	27.7	28.1
8	28.7	29.7	27.7	26.0	29.5	28.7	21.9	22.9	28.3	30.4	29.5	29.4	21.3	22.0	29.1	28.7
7	31.3	30.0	30.2	28.3	32.6	31.0	24.6	23.0	30.8	31.7	33.1	32.1	23.6	23.5	29.1	30.5
6	35.8	34.7	33.8	31.5	34.8	32.8	29.5	27.9	31.5	35.6	34.7	35.0	27.6	26.8	35.2	36.0
5	37.2	37.4	36.8	34.3	37.5	36.1	32.1	32.8	36.1	38.0	38.1	36.4	32.1	32.7	36.9	36.9
4	39.9	38.2	39.5	36.9	41.0	39.3	34.9	33.3	37.7	40.4	41.5	39.4	33.2	33.5	37.3	38.8
3	44.9	42.5	42.7	39.7	43.0	41.7	41.6	40.0	40.3	45.8	43.4	41.6	41.8	40.2	42.9	44.9
2	46.3	44.7	46.1	43.5	45.7	45.9	43.6	44.5	44.5	47.0	46.3	45.1	44.0	44.1	44.5	45.8
1	49.2	46.0	49.3	46.4	50.0	48.3	47.0	46.4	45.3	50.6	49.6	48.4	47.1	45.1	45.3	47.3
mean	11.1	11.5	10.3	9.9	11.2	11.2	8.1	8.1	11.6	11.5	11.6	12.0	7.8	8.2	11.7	11.7
sd	8.0	8.0	7.5	7.2	8.5	8.5	5.5	5.8	8.3	8.8	8.6	9.1	5.4	5.6	8.3	8.0
median	9.0	9.0	8.0	8.0	10.0	9.0	7.0	6.0	10.0	9.0	10.0	10.0	7.0	7.0	9.0	10.0

Wechsler Intelligence Scale for Children – Fourth Edition (WISC-IV).

may be useful to compare Gv to Gf, especially when the examiner hypothesizes that the child has a visual–spatial weakness that is interfering with his performance on the PRI. This comparison requires completion of the supplemental PCm subtest. If Gv is very low relative to Gf, it may suggest that the child's capacity to demonstrate his or her reasoning abilities with perceptual stimuli is impaired by a possible deficiency in visual–spatial organization. In this case, a follow-up with neuropsychological tests may be indicated.

Because both Gf and Gv clusters involve visual–spatial organization in varying degrees, the Gf cluster can also be thought of as a visual–conceptual cluster that does not involve significant motor skills, whereas the Gv does, due primarily to BD. Another subtest that involves both visual spatial skills and motor skill is SS. Thus, Gf can be compared to *VC-no motor* to determine the extent to which motor skills may impair the expression of visual–spatial reasoning skills. This is especially useful when the examiner hypothesizes that a motor problem is influencing the child's performance on PRI. If the VC-no motor cluster score is far below Gf, the finding may be used to support the examiner's observation that fine or gross motor skills are interfering with the child's ability to express intelligence on the test. A referral to an occupational therapist or neuropsychologist may be indicated.

As noted earlier, fluid reasoning can apply equally to the Perceptual or Verbal domain but must be assessed within some domain. After all, one cannot reason about nothing. Thus, the Gf cluster may also be compared to a combination of SI and WR, which is believed to represent fluid reasoning in the verbal domain, or Gf-verbal. This planned comparison requires administration of the supplemental WR subtest. This may be useful when the examiner suspects that auditory processing or other linguistic abilities are involved. If Gf-verbal is far below Gf, it may suggest that the requirements of processing verbal, semantic, or linguistic stimuli interfere with the child's capacity to express his reasoning ability in the verbal domain. However, one must be careful to evaluate language proficiency as well as general fund of information before making this interpretation.

Lexical knowledge (VL) is believed to be tapped by the WR and VO cluster, whereas general fund of information (KO) may be tapped by IN and CO. This comparison requires administration of two supplemental subtests: WR and IN. This planned comparison is useful when the examiner hypothesizes that an environmentally based deficiency in crystallized knowledge is the cause of a low VCI score and that verbal reasoning may be intact.

The VO and IN subtests require the examinee to access information from long-term storage. Thus, this cluster is referred to as long-term memory (LTM). The LN and DS subtests involve different memory structures than VO and IN. The DS and LN subtests involve short-term and working memory. Important differences between short-term and working memory are discussed in Chapter 4. Of course, the LN and DS composite is the WMI. This comparison requires administration of the supplemental IN subtest. This planned comparison may be useful when teachers and parents report that the child seems to be able to accurately recall distant information but seems unable to recall, for example, where he left his homework.

Note that the interpretation of VO and IN as LTM assumes that the child was exposed previously to the requested information and has encoded that information successfully into long-term storage. This assumption is discussed further in Chapters 4 and 5, and methods for clinically evaluating the assumption are described.

The LTM cluster (VO and IN) can also be thought of as general knowledge without a requirement for reasoning, whereas the Gf-verbal cluster (SI and WR) can also be thought of as general knowledge with a requirement for reasoning. If Gf-verbal is much lower than LTM, it may suggest that the child is dependent on his or her recall of facts and that he or she may have less ability for novel uses of those facts. If LTM is much lower than Gf-verbal, it may suggest that the child has not been exposed to the required knowledge, did not encode that knowledge when exposed, or has difficulty accessing it from long-term storage. Again, methods for evaluating these hypotheses are discussed in Chapters 4 and 5.

Step 4. Evaluate Single Subtest Strengths and Weaknesses

Most children have areas of relative cognitive strengths and weaknesses. It is, in fact, very uncommon for the average person to function at the same level in every ability area. Practitioners should have a clear reason for calculating a difference score, and that reason should be based on the child's history, the referral question, behavioral observations, and other test results. It should also be remembered that a difference between two scores may be clinically meaningful for one child, but not for another child. The best practice is to begin with a hypothesis based on a referral question and then test that hypothesis by evaluating score discrepancies and other related clinical information (Kamphaus, 2001).

Table B.5 of the *Administration and Scoring Manual* provides minimum differences between a single subtest and the average of several subtest-scaled scores required for statistical significance; however, this table also provides base rate data for these difference analyses. We recommend that the practitioner proceed directly to the base rate section of the table to determine how rare an observed discrepancy is in the normative sample.

The WISC-IV Record Form provides a section for determining the child's strengths and weaknesses at the subtest level. The practitioner must choose whether to use the mean score of the 10 subtests used to calculate the FSIQ or the mean scores of the verbal comprehension and perceptual reasoning subtests separately. If the latter method is used, the mean score of the three administered verbal comprehension subtests is the base against which each verbal comprehension subtest score is compared, and the mean score of three administered perceptual reasoning subtests is the base against which each perceptual reasoning subtest score is compared. *In general, if there is not a rare discrepancy among the index scores, the mean of 10 core subtests should be used for the strength and weakness analysis.* If separate verbal comprehension and perceptual reasoning mean scores are chosen as a basis for comparison, evaluation of the processing speed and working memory subtests as strengths or weaknesses is not possible.

Step 5. Comparing Two Subtests

For most situations, the examiner skips to step 6 regarding the evaluation of patterns of item responses within subtests. However, occasionally there are reasons to compare two subtest scores to confirm or refute a specific priori hypothesis. In such cases, step 4 may be skipped and the examiner can proceed directly to this planned comparison among two subtests to evaluate the specific hypothesis. Table B.4 in the *Administration and Scoring Manual* provides the percentage of the standardization sample that obtained various subtest-scaled score discrepancies. The Record Form provides space for noting specific pairwise comparisons that may be of particular interest to the practitioner. For example, comparison of performance on the Picture Concepts and Similarities subtests provides useful information regarding the possible influence of verbal expression demands on the measurement of a child's categorical reasoning ability.

Step 6. Evaluate the Pattern of Scores within Subtests

To analyze a child's profile further, the practitioner should consider the pattern of scores within a subtest. For example, the child who achieves a scaled score of 10 on a subtest by getting 20 items correct and then meeting the discontinue criteria is quite different from the child who gets the same number of items correct but does so with a lot of item scatter (e.g., misses easy items but passes harder ones). The child with an uneven pattern of scores on several subtests may have certain problems related to attention or language that need to be evaluated further or may be a very bright child who is bored with the test. Pay particular attention to unusual or bizarre responses and to the child's overall response pattern. Unusual responses can often be very revealing of clinical conditions that may be affecting the child's current level of cognitive functioning.

Step 7. Performing the Process Analysis

The final step in profile analysis, prior to summarizing overall perform-ance, is examination of the response processes the child used to solve the test problems and answer the test questions. It is useful to examine the process by which a child arrived at a correct response or the reasons for an incorrect response. The *process approach* to interpretation advocated by Kaplan (1988) was designed to help the practitioner determine the nature of errors that were committed on standard tests. Although each subtest of an intelli-gence scale is designed primarily to measure a specific cognitive process, other cognitive processes can also be invoked during the performance of the task. A score of 0 points on an item may occur for various reasons. For example, children may fail a Block Design item because they did not perceive the design correctly, are not able to analyze the configuration of the design, or ran out of time.

The WISC-IV includes process scores that are designed to provide more detailed information on the cognitive abilities that contribute to a child's subtest performance. Process analysis can occur from an interindividual perspective by comparing the child's process scores to those obtained by the appropriate normative reference group. Intraindividual analysis of pro-cess scores is performed by evaluating the child's process scores in relation to other subtest or process scores obtained by the same child. The process analysis can assist the practitioner in the evaluation of the child's specific information-processing styles, which can be important when describing cognitive strengths and weaknesses or making diagnoses.

Block Design

The Block Design No Time Bonus (BDN) process score is based on the child's performance on the Block Design (BD) subtest *without* additional time bonus points for rapid completion of items. The reduced emphasis on speed of performance reflected in this score may be particularly useful when a child's physical limitations, problem-solving strategies, or personality characteristics are believed to affect performance on timed tasks.

Like the subtest-scaled scores, the BDN process score is scaled to a metric with a mean of 10 and a standard deviation of 3. Thus, scores of 7 and 13 are 1 SD below and above the mean, respectively, and scaled scores of 4 and 16 deviate 2 SDs from the mean. Approximately 68% of children obtain scaled scores between 7 and 13, and about 96% score in the 4–16 range. At the intraindividual level of process analysis, the discrepancy between the child's BD and BDN scores provides information on the relative contributions of speed and accuracy to the child's performance on the Block Design subtest. Base rates among all process analysis difference scores are provided in Appendix B of the *Administration and Scoring Manual*. For most children, there is very little difference between BD and BDN scaled scores.

Digit Span

The Digit Span Forward (DSF) and Digit Span Backward (DSB) process scores are also scaled scores and are derived from the total raw scores for the corresponding Digit Span tasks. Although both of these tasks require storage and retrieval of information through immediate auditory recall, the Digit Span Backward task places additional demands on the child's attentional and working memory abilities. The discrepancy between DSF and DSB process scores reflects the child's differential performance on a relatively simple and more complex memory task.

Because a child with variable performance (i.e., intrasubtest scatter) on the Digit Span Forward and Digit Span Backward tasks may obtain similar DSF and DSB scores, two additional process scores were included to further evaluate the child's differential performance: LDSF and LDSB. LDSF and LDSB scores are raw scores reflecting the number of digits recalled on the last trial scored 1 point in the corresponding Digit Span task. Base rates in the standardization sample are provided for LDSF and LDSB raw scores, as well as for the discrepancy between the two scores.

Cancellation

Cancellation Random (CAR) and Cancellation Structured (CAS) process scores provide measures of the child's visual selective attention and processing speed in two different modes of visual presentation: random and structured. Cancellation tasks have been used extensively in neuropsychological settings as measures of visual neglect, response inhibition, and motor perseveration.

CAR and CAS process scores are scaled scores derived from total raw scores for items 1 and 2 of the Cancellation subtest, respectively. Comparison of these scores provides information regarding the child's differential performance on a task requiring the child to scan random arrangements of visual stimuli and a similar task with structured arrangements of visual stimuli.

Step 8. Summarize Overall Intelligence

The Full-Scale IQ is usually considered to be the score that is most representative of *g*, or general intellectual functioning. While the FSIQ and its relevance in clinical assessment will be elaborated in the following chapter, there are several key points that must be made in the context of this current discussion. The FSIQ is the most reliable score obtained on the WISC-IV and is traditionally the first score to be considered in the interpretation of the profile. *This chapter breaks with tradition and suggests that reporting the FSIQ score be reserved for the final section of the psychological report, as it represents the best summary of overall performance that can be obtained in a single score.* FSIQ should always be reported with the corresponding percentile rank, confidence interval, and ability range.

The FSIQ provides important summary information regarding a child's *current* level of cognitive functioning. Note the use of the word "current" in the previous sentence. Many parents and teachers believe that IQ is a fixed trait that can be measured precisely and does not change over time. While the precision of measurement is quite reliable and valid, intelligence is malleable at the individual level, within limits. (The factors that influence cognitive development in children, both positively and negatively, are discussed in Chapter 1) While examiners attempt to elicit maximal performance on standardized intelligence tests, both individual difference and environmental factors impinge on children's ability to perform, especially for children who have emotional problems or are in difficult life circumstances. For example, children with emotional problems may not be functioning at their full cognitive potential. When the emotional problems are treated, cognitive ability scores may increase. Also, immigrant children in transition may show increases in cognitive functioning as stress reduces with adaptation to new circumstances. This is why FSIQ must be interpreted relative to clinical, environmental, and societal contexts and always reported as an estimate of *current level of functioning.*

Interpretation of the FSIQ score will also depend on the extent of any discrepancies among the four index scores. It has become common practice for psychologists to state that the FSIQ is *invalid* if a significant discrepancy is observed between the VCI and the PRI, or any other pair of Index scores. This is an overstatement. It is known, for example, that significant discrepancies are common among normal children in the standardization sample. Further, FSIQ correlates very highly with achievement in the standardization sample, even though large numbers of subjects with so-called invalid profiles are included. Further, this correlation is among the highest known relationships between any two variables in the field of psychology. To demonstrate this point, we examined the correlation of FSIQ with the WIAT-II Total Achievement score for subjects in the WISC-IV/WIAT-II linking sample with VCI–PRI discrepancies of 15 points or more as compared to those with less than 15-point VCI-PRI differences. The correlation of FSIQ with WIAT-II total achievement is between .87 and .89 for subjects with 15-point V>P discrepancies, 15-point P>V discrepancies, subjects with less than 15-point V-P differences, and all subjects combined.

We further examined these data by academic area. Table 12 shows correlations of FSIQ with the WIAT-II Mathematics, Oral Language, Reading, and Writing composites for each of the groups described earlier. As shown in Table 12, the correlation of FSIQ with achievement is *higher* for subjects with large VCI-PRI discrepancies (15 or more points) than for subjects without large VCI-PRI differences, and this finding holds for all academic areas assessed. *These data strongly suggest that FSIQ is valid for*

TABLE 12   Correlations of WISC-IV FSIQ with WIAT-II Composite Scores for Subjects
with 15-Point V>P and P>V Discrepancies and No V-P Discrepancies

	Mathematics	Oral Language	Reading	Writing
V > P by 15 or more points	.83 (n=54)	.77 (n=53)	.86 (n=53)	.79 (n=50)
P > V by 15 or more points	.82 (n=61)	.89 (n=59)	.80 (n=58)	.79 (n=51)
Less than 15 point V-P split	.78 (n=548)	.75 (n=544)	.78 (n=547)	.77 (n=531)

predicting achievement among subjects with large verbal–perceptual discrepancies. For these reasons, we suggest that practitioners cease referring to FSIQ as invalid when large discrepancies are found.

At the same time, it is also clear that cognitive ability is a multidimensional construct and that the various dimensions of cognition may not develop evenly for every child. For many children, there are important strengths and weaknesses among the various domains of intelligence that are masked by any single summary score. The presence of discrepancies in the development of various cognitive dimensions makes that individual child's profile rich with potentially useful clinical information. This is why we advocate that the primary focus of interpretation be index scores, which represent the four major domains of cognitive ability as measured by the WISC-IV, and these be addressed first in written reports.

The FSIQ should still be reported when significant discrepancies are observed, although further explanation is required. For example, the summary section might begin:

> Drew's current level of intellectual functioning is in the average range. He obtained a FSIQ score of 100 (90% confidence interval 95–105), which is at the 50th percentile compared to other children his age. Drew's overall intellectual ability is difficult to summarize in a single score, however, because his nonverbal reasoning ability is much better developed then his verbal reasoning ability. To fully understand Drew, one must consider his verbal and nonverbal skills separately. Drew functions in the high average range when reasoning with nonverbal material and in the low average range when reasoning with verbal material. These test findings are consistent with the teacher's observation that Drew looks forward to math and art classes, but is below grade level in reading.

In some evaluations the FSIQ is described as invalid as justification for the use of either the VCI or the PRI in an ability-achievement discrepancy (AAD) analysis designed to determine eligibility to receive special education services in a public school setting. Often the PRI is higher than the VCI in children referred for learning problems, and the use of the higher of the two ability scores increases the chances of finding a significant discrepancy between ability and low achievement, thus making the student eligible for special assistance. General issues related to the use of AAD analysis are addressed in the following chapter. However, the decision to report and describe FSIQ can be independent of the decision to use VCI or PRI in an AAD analysis. The usual rules (e.g., 15+ point discrepancy between composites) can be used to make this determination.

Practitioners should also realize that the FSIQ is not the mathematical average of the four index scores, but is normed separately based on the sum of the 10 subtest-scaled scores. Because of a statistical phenomenon known as regression to the mean, each of the four index scores can all be closer to the mean of 100 than the FSIQ score. For example, a child who obtains a standard score of 60 on all four indexes would have a FSIQ score much lower than 60. A child who obtains a standard score of 120 on all four indexes would have a FSIQ much higher than 120. The further the child's scores from the mean, the more pronounced the effect. This is because each index is considered a separate estimate of overall ability and repeated estimates of the same phenomenon should theoretically regress toward the population mean. When this does not occur, the FSIQ score moves further away from the mean. This can be a very difficult concept to communicate to parents and teachers. Such questions are usually not asked with respect to high-functioning students because higher scores are almost always considered better. Perhaps the simplest explanation for parents of low functioning students is that children usually score higher on one or two of the indexes, which is why the summary score is lower. However, the focus of interpretive feedback should remain on the index scores.

The General Ability Index (GAI) is an alternate way of summarizing performance, which is composed of the six core VCI (Vocabulary, Similarities, and Comprehension) and PRI (Block Design, Matrix Reasoning, and Picture Concepts) subtests, excluding the WMI and PSI subtests. Some practitioners find GAI useful because it organizes the more highly g-loaded subtests into a single summary score and allows one to evaluate them separately from those subtests with relatively lower g loadings (e.g., Letter-Number Sequencing, Digit Span, Coding, and Symbol Search). A full discussion of the relative merits of FSIQ and GAI can be found in the following chapter of this book.

SUMMARY AND PREVIEW OF OTHER CHAPTERS

This chapter briefly described the basic rationale for standardized administration procedures and then outlined basic interpretation processes. This chapter is important because it goes beyond the test manual by providing an improved method of evaluating index score discrepancies and several planned pairwise comparisons between theory-based clusters of subtests. Unique to this chapter is the suggestion that in most cases, practitioners can skip the statistical analysis of discrepancy scores and proceed directly to base rate comparisons to determine the clinical significance of the finding. Also, novel, this chapter suggested that psychological reports begin the section on cognitive functioning with a discussion of the index scores, which are considered to be the primary level of interpretation, and reserve discussion of the FSIQ for the summary section of the report.

Chapter 3 expands on the powerful role of FSIQ as an overall indicator of *g* and discusses the relative merits of GAI as compared to FSIQ. Chapter 4 goes into depth regarding clinical, theoretical, and research issues related to interpretation of the index scores. Chapters 5 and 6 expand on the process analyses proposed in step 7 shown earlier by presenting basic (Chapter 5) and advanced (Chapter 6) interpretive strategies for the WISC-IV Integrated. Chapter 7 discusses the interpretation of WISC-IV and WISC-IV Integrated in context with other measures often given in a complete psychological or neuropsychological evaluation. Finally, Chapter 8 explains why influential psychological reports deemphasize test scores, and provides examples of how to write reports that are child centered rather than score centered.

REFERENCES

Blennerhassett. L., & Traxler, C. (1999). *WISC-III utilization with deaf and hard of hearing students (99–1)*. Washington, DC: Gallaudet Research Institute.

Bracken, B. A., & McCallum, R. S. (1998). *Universal nonverbal intelligence test*. Itasca, IL: Riverside.

Braden, J. P., & Hannah, J. M. (1998). Assessment of hearing-impaired and deaf children with the WISC-III. In A. Prifitera & D. Saklofske (Eds.), *WISC-III clinical use and interpretation: Scientist-practitioner perspectives* (pp. 175–201). San Diego, CA: Academic Press.

Carroll, J. B. (1993). *Human cognitive abilities: A survey of factor-analytic studies*. Cambridge, England: Cambridge University Press.

Flanagan, D. P., & Kaufman, A. S. (2004). *Essentials of WISC–IV assessment*. Hoboken, NJ: Wiley.

Gallaudet Research Institute (1998, November). Results of the 1996–1997 Annual Survey of Deaf and Hard of Hearing Students. Unpublished raw data. Washington, DC: Author.

Gottfredson, L. S. (1998). The general intelligence factor. Scientific American, November, 1–10.

Kamphaus, R. W. (2001). *Clinical assessment of child and adolescent intelligence* (2nd ed.). Needham Heights, MA: Allyn & Bacon.

Kaplan, E. (1988). A process approach to neuropsychological assessment. In T.J. Boll & B.K. Bryant (Eds.), *Clinical neuropsychology and brain function: Research, measurement, and practice* (pp. 129–167). Washington, DC: American Psychological Association.

Kaufman, A. S. (1994). *Intelligent testing with the WISC-R*. New York: Wiley.

Kaufman, A. S. (1979). *Intelligent testing with the WISC-III*. New York: Wiley.

Maller, S. (2003). Intellectual assessment of deaf people: A critical review of core concepts and issues. In M. Marschark & P. E. Spencer (Eds.), *Oxford handbook of deaf studies, language, and education*. New York: Oxford University Press.

McDermott, P. A., Fantuzzo, J. W., & Glutting, J. J. (1990). Just say no to subtest analysis: A critique on Wechsler theory and practice. *Journal of Psychoeducational Assessment 8*(3), 290–302.

Naglieri, J. A. (2003). *Naglieri nonverbal ability test: Individual administration*. San Antonio, TX: The Psychological Corporation.

Naglieri, J. A. (2006). *Wechsler nonverbal scales of ability*. San Antonio, TX: Harcourt Assessment, Inc.

Prifitera, A., Saklofske, D. H., & Weiss, L. (2005). *WISC-IV clinical use and interpretation: Scientist–practitioner perspectives*. San Diego, CA: Elsevier Science.

Raven, J., Raven, J. C. & Court, J. H. (1998). *Manual for Raven's progressive matrices and vocabulary scales*. Oxford, United Kingdom: Oxford Psychologists Press.

Roid, G. H., & Miller, L. J. (1997). *Leiter international performance scale–Revised*. Wood Dale, IL: Stoelting.

Sattler, J. M., & Dumont, R. (2004). *Assessment of children: WISC–IV and WPPSI–III Supplement*. San Diego, CA: Author.

Wechsler, D. (2003). *Wechsler intelligence scale for children–Fourth Edition Administration and Scoring Manual*. San Antonio, TX: The Psychological Corporation.

3

ADVANCED INTERPRETIVE ISSUES WITH THE WISC-IV FULL-SCALE IQ AND GENERAL ABILITY INDEX SCORES

DONALD H. SAKLOFSKE, LAWRENCE G. WEISS,
SUSAN E. RAIFORD, AND AURELIO PRIFITERA

INTRODUCTION

- *Robert's WISC-IV full-scale IQ (FSIQ) of 71 strongly suggests that he does not have the cognitive capabilities to plan and carry out complex delinquent and criminal acts. Rather it is likely that he is more of a "pawn" in this gang-based delinquent activity.*
- *Beth's inconsistency in school achievement may be related to difficulties with working memory. Her FSIQ of 105 is in the average range. However, while Beth's short-term auditory memory score as assessed by her immediate recall of digits forward (Digit Span subtest) is average, she experienced much greater difficulty when required to mentally manipulate this information for digits repeated backwards. This was also confirmed with the Letter–Number Sequencing subtest where she was observed to have considerable difficulty holding even short sequences in memory and rearranging the content.*
- *Ruth's WISC-IV FSIQ of 128 appears to be both a reliable and a valid indication of her current intellectual abilities. Her very superior ability to think and reason with words is complemented by superior scores on*

tasks assessing nonverbal spatial reasoning and working memory. While relatively lower than her other scores, Ruth's speed of mental processing is in the high average range and does not appear to place any limitations or strain on her other well-developed abilities or on her school achievement. In part, these lower scores may reflect a motivational aspect as the tasks tapping processing speed are relatively simple. Ruth's speed and attention appeared to vary shortly after beginning both subtests, and she stated that she did not find them very interesting. The WISC-IV FSIQ score is in line with her outstanding achievement in school and in other pursuits.

The focus of WISC-IV (Wechsler, 2003c) interpretation now rests solidly on the four factor-analytically based and clinically meaningful index scores (see Weiss, Saklofske, & Prifitera, 2003, 2005; see also chapter 2 and chapter 4 of this book). While some psychologists still lament the loss of the Verbal IQ (VIQ) and Performance IQ (PIQ) scores, the use of a dual system of IQ and index scores did not add to the clinical utility of the Wechsler Intelligence Scale for Children–Third Edition (WISC-III; Wechsler, 1991) and might even have led to some confusion among teachers and parents reading psychological reports. As described in the previous chapter, changes have been made to both items and subtests comprising the Verbal Comprehension Index (VCI) and the renamed Perceptual Reasoning Index (PRI). In addition, only three subtests are now required to derive each of these index scores. The addition of two new Perceptual Reasoning (PR) subtests (i.e., Picture Concepts and Matrix Reasoning) enhanced the integrity of the factor structure, clarified the cognitive abilities being assessed, and resulted in the change in nomenclature (from perceptual organization to PR). Increasing importance has also been placed on the Working Memory (WM) and Processing Speed (PS) factors. These formerly so-called minor or small factors now comprise 40% of the WISC-IV FSIQ. Their potential utility in clinical and psychoeducational assessment is more important, as psychologists have come to expect a closer link between cognitive assessment and treatment. These factors have also undergone some change in nomenclature as well, with the factor previously labeled Freedom from Distractibility now being referred to as WM. Letter–Number Sequencing complements the Digit Span subtest as a measure of auditory working memory, and Arithmetic is now a supplementary, albeit still very important, subtest for addressing particular clinical questions.

- *Rick's WISC–IV FSIQ of 108 suggests overall average ability. However, this summary score does not reflect the variability in Rick's abilities assessed by the separate index scores. He appears to have well developed (high average range) nonverbal spatial reasoning ability in contrast to low average verbal knowledge and reasoning scores. These differences are seen infrequently in children (less than 5% of children show this score discrepancy). This may certainly help explain Rick's inconsistent work in school.*

Somewhat more controversial in certain professional circles, such as clinical neuropsychology, is the retention and relevance of the FSIQ. There is no question that a general mental ability factor is invariably found when a number of cognitively complex tasks are examined, whether these be the full range of subtests included in such comprehensive tests as the Stanford Binet–Fifth Edition (Roid, 2003), the Woodcock Johnson–III (Woodcock, McGrew, & Mather, 2001), or the Cognitive Assessment System (Naglieri & Das, 1997). Most convincing from a purely psychometric perspective are the findings from Carroll's (1993) factor analysis of more than 400 intelligence data sets. However, the question is whether or not a composite or summary estimate of intelligence reflected in an FSIQ has much clinical relevance and usefulness in contemporary assessment practices.

The focus of the present chapter is the WISC-IV FSIQ and its complement, the general ability index (GAI). The next chapter reviews the WISC-IV factor structure and the relevance of the four index scores to the assessment process. Taken together, these two chapters set the stage for the chapters to follow that focus on the process approach to WISC-IV interpretation. More specifically, this chapter

- *Summarizes the role of intelligence in assessment*
- *Revisits the relevance of the WISC–IV FSIQ in clinical assessment*
- *Presents a description of and tables for calculating the GAI, first described for the WISC-III (Prifitera, Weiss, & Saklofske, 1998)*
- *Provides tables that link the GAI with the Wechsler Individual Achievement Test–Second Edition (WIAT-II; Harcourt Assessment, Inc., 2002).*

INTELLIGENCE AND ASSESSMENT

- *I don't want my child tested and labeled with an IQ score. My child is special, unique, and needs to be respected as an individual.*

This section begins with some general comments about the assessment of intelligence. The field of psychology widely recognizes the importance of intelligence in describing human behavior and individual differences (see Deary, 2001; Neisser, Boodoo, Bouchard, Boykin, Brody, Ceci, Halpern, Loehlin, Perloff, Sternberg, & Urbina, 1996). However, no other construct, in theory or in practice (i.e., measuring and reporting intelligence), has created such controversy, even to the present day. Although the WISC-IV and other current intelligence tests meet the highest psychometric standards and draw on an extensive theory, research, and clinical base (e.g., Georgas, Weiss, van de Vivjer, & Saklofske, 2003; Prifitera, Saklofske, & Weiss, 2005), there are many detractors to their use in general, particularly to their use in schools. Current concerns include disproportionate identification of children from minority groups (presenting with different linguistic and cultural backgrounds) with special education needs. In the area of learning disability assessment, the exclusive use of a simple ability–achievement discrepancy (AAD) as the sole basis for diagnosis has rightly been called into question (e.g., Fletcher & Reschly, 2005; Siegel, 2003). Critics also point to the lack of a direct link between assessment, diagnosis, and treatment.

Some of the criticisms of tests and test use are justified even today, but much remains a reflection of past practices. The current "look" of intelligence tests and their use in assessment are in contrast with the early years of intelligence tests and testing (see Tulsky, Saklofske, & Richer, 2003; Harris, Tulsky, & Schultheis, 2003). The foundation of the ongoing controversy surrounding intelligence tests may rest in large part in a "clash of beliefs." The Hegelian dialectic reflecting an egalitarian vs elitist perspective has implications for both the construct and the assessment of intelligence. However, the philosophical and societal contexts in which intelligence tests can provide relevant and important information have changed from one of simply measuring IQ and determining school placement or making some other key decision to one that is cast within public, educational and social policies such as the Individuals with Disabilities Education Act (IDEA) and "No Child Left Behind." How often have we also heard that it is not intelligence tests that make decisions, label children, or place them in a limited or restricted learning environment? To paraphrase from the general field of measurement and evaluation literature, "tests don't make decisions, we do." The "we" who make the decisions about how to use the results of intelligence tests include psychologists, teachers, administrators, politicians, lobbyist groups, and the public in general.

CURRENT ASSESSMENT PRACTICES

Psychology has matured as both a science and a practice, and psychologists are committed to the scientist–practitioner model. Furthermore, psychological practice is placed squarely in the context of ethical codes and best practices standards, which certainly reflect societies' views of the rights and dignity of the individual and the expectation of quality from psychology service providers. From a best practices perspective, Meyer and colleagues (2001) concluded: "formal assessment is a vital element in psychology's professional heritage and a central part of professional practice today" (p. 155). On a positive note, it seems fair to say that

The comprehensive training of school and clinical child psychologists in assessment, including the use of intelligence tests, the carefully crafted and clearly articulated practice standards and codes of ethics relating to psychological practice in general and assessment more specifically, together with the significant advances in the study of human intelligence and its measurement have done much to quell some of the IQ test controversy (Saklofske, Prifitera, Weiss, Rolfhus, & Zhu, 2005, p. 36).

Current assessment practices have progressed from being primarily test driven, especially single test driven, to a multimethod and even multidisciplinary process that produces a comprehensive description and understanding of the individual. Furthermore, intelligence tests have been integrated into these models rather than being seen as stand-alone and "do-it-all" tests. An excellent example of current assessment methodology and practice has been articulated by Berninger, Dunn, and Alper (2005). Their integrated multilevel model of tier one and two assessment practices includes branching, instructional, and profile assessment. A comprehensive psychological assessment (1) comprises a collection of information from different sources (e.g., parents, teachers, child) (2) through the use of different methods (e.g., tests, observations, interviews) that (3) reflect characteristics of the child (e.g., intelligence, personality, motivation) and (4) the child's environment (e.g., home, school). These four pillars of assessment, including formal and informal assessment, interviews and observations (Sattler, 2001), extol the psychologist to employ multiple methods that will provide even more potentially valuable information of relevance to most diagnostic decision needs and to formulating prevention and intervention strategies. Chapter 7 discusses use of the WISC-IV in context with information from other measures, and Chapter 1, of course, has already discussed interpreting WISC-IV results in context of the child's environment.

- *An enriched and accelerated program would certainly appear to be appropriate for Jori. Her WISC-IV index scores are all in the 95–99 percentile and the CMS results attest to an exceptionally well-developed memory. WIAT-II scores in the broad areas of reading and math are congruent with both current and past school achievement. Over the past 2 years, Jori's teachers have supported her placement in this program. Results from the Gifted Rating Scale completed by her current teacher lend additional support to this recommendation.*

In contrast to intelligence tests of the past, which were largely "unconnected," at least psychometrically, with measures of achievement and self-concept, the WISC-IV now belongs to a much larger family of standardized measurement instruments ranging from a suite of linked or equated intelligence tests (the Wechsler Preschool and Primary Scale of Intelligence–Third Edition [WPPSI-III; Wechsler, 2002], the Wechsler Adult Intelligence Scale [WAIS-III; Wechsler, 1997], and the Wechsler Abbreviated Scale of Intelligence [WASI; Wechsler, 1999]), and linked measures of cognitive processes (the WISC-IV Integrated; Wechsler et al., 2004), achievement (WIAT-II), memory (Children's Memory Scale [CMS; Cohen, 1997]), giftedness (Gifted Rating Scales [GRS; Pfeiffer & Jarosewich, 2003]), adaptive behavior (Adaptive Behavior Assessment System–Second Edition [ABAS-II; Harrison & Oakland, 2003]) and emotional intelligence (BarOn Emotional Quotient–Inventory [Bar-On EQ; Bar–On, 1997]). These linking studies add important data beyond the single test and provide additional data that support and contribute to the convergent validity but also the incremental validity of two or more measures (see Hunsley, 2003). A case in point is the concurrent use of the WISC-IV and WISC-IV Integrated to facilitate the understanding of how and why a child obtains particular scores on subtests such as Vocabulary (McCloskey & Maerlender, 2005; see Chapters 5 and 6 in this book). Although rightfully challenged as an exclusive approach to assessing learning disabilities, ability-achievement discrepancy (AAD) analysis is relevant to both a priori and a posteriori hypothesis testing. More to the point, and as argued later in this chapter, the WISC-IV is very important in the assessment of learning disabilities (Berninger & O'Donnell, 2005).

There is still much that needs to be learned about intelligence, but there is also much that we know and can use in our descriptions and understanding of children (Deary, 2001; Neisser et al., 1996; Saklofske, 1996). The practicing psychologist, like the physician or psychiatrist who must also diagnose complex conditions and prescribe treatments from a potentially large pool (e.g., the various pharmacological and psychotherapies for depression), must keep abreast of the current literature if they are to use the WISC-IV "intelligently" (Prifitera, Saklofske, & Weiss, 2005).

GENERAL INTELLIGENCE (FSIQ) AND THE WISC–IV

- *Barry's current FSIQ of 66 is in contrast to his average performance in his first 5 years of school and at least one group ability test, suggesting average to high-average ability. The massive head injury sustained in the car accident last year, taken together with the cranial surgery required to save his life, has resulted in significant loss of both general and specific cognitive abilities.*
- *How can an IQ score be useful; is it not just the average of lots of different abilities? The children in my classroom are all in the average ability range but there are such wide differences in everything from achievement to skills, talents, and interests. There are three boys with identical FSIQ scores but they are so different in their classroom performance.*

Wechsler defined intelligence as an aggregate or global capacity "of the individual to act purposefully, to think rationally, and to deal effectively with his environment (Wechsler, 1944, p. 3). While the notion of a VIQ and PIQ was central to the success of early Wechsler tests, the preschool, child, and adult versions of these tests have always been firmly grounded in the tradition of "g" or general mental ability. A long history or tradition does not necessarily make something scientifically correct; however, longevity can certainly contribute to either accumulating a scientific base of facts and findings or alternatively, over time may reinforce nonempirically validated ideologies and beliefs!

There are essentially two views on the relevance of the FSIQ in clinical assessment and diagnosis. School psychologists contend that the FSIQ is useful because of its history for classification purposes and its relevance in AAD analysis. However, neuropsychologists argue that a composite IQ score is less than meaningful because of its lack of sensitivity and specificity in differential diagnosis, treatment planning, and prognosis.

The FSIQ was retained in the WISC-IV because of evidence supporting a general mental ability factor and its wide use in research and assessment. From a purely psychometric perspective, a general factor tends to emerge in studies of intelligence (Carroll, 1993) and is found in almost all intelligence tests that tap a cognitively complex array of abilities. *The WISC-IV Technical and Interpretive Manual* (Wechsler, 2003b) provides statistical support (e.g., subtest and index score correlations, factor analysis) for a general factor that retains the FSIQ label. While this makes a psychometrically compelling case for the calculation of the FSIQ, the question of clinical usefulness must still be addressed.

The research literature has clearly demonstrated the significance of general mental ability as a key individual-differences variable and a predictor of a vast array of human behaviors. Again, however, the issues confronting psychologists are the relevance and meaning of the FSIQ in assessment practices. As described elsewhere (Prifitera, Saklofske, & Weiss, 2005), there is considerable ecological and criterion validity for measuring general intelligence (Gottfredson, 1997, 1998; Kuncel & Hezlett, 2004). The FSIQ is of central importance in operationally defining and identifying children with mental retardation, intellectual giftedness, low achievement, and learning disabilities. It is also a useful summary score when there is little subtest or index score variability and remains one of the best predictors we have of school achievement in heterogeneous groups of elementary school children. In relation to other tests linked with the WISC-IV, the FSIQ in almost all instances shows the highest correlation with subtests tapping both achievement and memory. The FSIQ also correlates more highly with the Gifted Rating Scale–School-Age Form (GRS–S; Pfeiffer & Jarosewich, 2003) than any of the index scores. In the final analysis, the psychologist must decide if the FSIQ is both accurate and relevant to describing the intelligence of the child being assessed, and in turn using this information to serve the best interests of the child.

In part, the way in which we have used the FSIQ when examined in the context of today's psychometric and clinical knowledge underlies calls from certain quarters that its use be abandoned in assessment. The history of intelligence and intelligence testing (e.g., Boake, 2002; Tulsky, Saklofske, & Ricker, 2003) and the literature related to psychological assessment in general document progressive growth in our knowledge of these individual differences variables, our increasing psychometric sophistication regarding their measurement, and the use of this information in a "best practices" framework that has evolved over the past 100 years and especially in the past 10 or so years. However, the relevance of the FSIQ has again come to the foreground in large part because of differing opinions surrounding its use in the assessment of learning disabilities in children. This issue is discussed briefly here in the context of the WISC-IV FSIQ and further reviewed later in this chapter and Chapter 4.

A CURRENT CONTROVERSY: ABILITY (FSIQ)–ACHIEVEMENT DISCREPANCY (AAD) ANALYSIS IN THE ASSESSMENT OF LEARNING DISABILITIES

- *If a child is achieving below his measured ability, does that mean he has a learning disability? Our school uses IQ and achievement tests to determine if a student has a learning disability.*

For some time, the primary vehicle used by school psychologists for obtaining assistance for children with low achievement has been to identify a significant discrepancy between the FSIQ on a recognized intelligence test such as the WISC-III or the WISC-IV and some standardized measure of achievement in core areas, including reading and arithmetic, such as the WIAT-II. The use of AAD became federally legislated under the Individuals with Disabilities Act (IDEA: Public Law 101–476, 1990; IDEA '97, Public Law 105–17, 1997) and was adopted by virtually all school districts in the United States. However, criticism of using this two-test discrepancy score as the only approach for identifying children with learning disabilities has increased (e.g., Francis, Fletcher, Stuebing, Lyon, Shaywitz, & Shaywitz, 2005; Siegel, 2003). First, it seems quite logical that an IQ–achievement discrepancy could reflect something other than a learning disability; certainly, there can be many other reasons for such score discrepancies. Furthermore, a learning disability is a much more complex condition than can be fully assessed and identified psychometrically by an intelligence test such as the WISC-IV and an achievement test (e.g., WIAT-II). Third, there is no single agreed-upon method for determining severe discrepancies that could include, for example, the use of simple or regression-based comparisons. Even more problematic is the combination of different ability measures (e.g., WISC–IV, Woodcock Johnson–Third Edition [Woodcock, McGrew, & Mather, 2001],

Stanford-Binet–Fifth Edition [Roid, 2003], Das-Naglieri Cognitive Assessment System [Naglieri & Das, 1997], Differential Ability Scales [Elliot, 1990]) and achievement scales (e.g., WIAT–II, Woodcock-Johnson–III, Wide Range Achievement Test–III [Wilkinson, 1993], Kaufman Test of Educational Achievement, Second Edition [Kaufman & Kaufman, 1998]) that leaves it almost impossible to imagine, let alone create, "equivalency" tables to meet a particular discrepancy standard. Whereas any set of tables can be created within and between tests, more to the point is whether ability–achievement (e.g., WISC-IV/WIAT-II) tables and "preset" discrepancy cutoffs are diagnostic of learning disabilities.

Nor are we convinced that simply saying that children in the bottom 25% of the class are those who are learning disabled is an acceptable solution. There are likely as many—if not more—reasons for low achievement alone as for "significant" FSIQ–achievement discrepancies. Francis and colleagues (2005) reported data suggesting that neither method is valid for such diagnostic decision-making. However, in partial defense of the use of both intelligence tests and IQ–achievement discrepancies in the identification of children with learning "difficulties," we would argue that a significant discrepancy that is also not a high-frequency occurrence (low base rate) has value for either a priori or a posteriori hypothesis testing or generation. If this is, perhaps, the third or fourth finding that supports a learning disability diagnosis, then convergent support from multiple sources and methods exists. If such a finding emerges at the onset of the assessment process, then it serves to alert the professional to look for an explanation that may lead to a diagnosis of learning disability.

In relation to the WISC-IV, there is compelling support for its relevance in learning disabilities assessment, not again as a stand-alone test but rather one that can contribute a significant amount of information to understanding a child's cognitive abilities. Learning disability is recognized as a condition impacting the acquisition, retention, understanding, organization, and use of verbal and nonverbal information. Impairments are indicated in one or more psychological processes related to learning, including, for example, visual–spatial and perceptual-motor processing, memory and attention, executive functions, and phonological and language processing. Furthermore, learning disability is associated with specific rather than global impairments and with average ability (or at least low average ability and higher). An examination of the WISC-IV scores, including FSIQ, index scores, and subtest scores, clearly shows the relevance of this test in the assessment of learning disabilities. The AAD analysis is a method of examining further the relationships between cognition and intelligence on the one hand and specific educational skills and tasks on the other that may be compromised by a learning disability. Certainly the exclusive reliance on a "test criterion" approach to identifying children with learning disabilities is overly simple and neither diagnostic nor prescriptive. Now under review, it is likely that the AAD model will be only one method among others (e.g., documenting responsiveness to empirically supported classroom interventions; clinical evaluations of deficits in core cognitive processes that underlie specific disorders) for determining eligibility for special education services. This discussion continues at the end of the next chapter, as it serves as a basis for describing how the assessment role of the WISC-IV has been extended by the introduction of the WISC-IV Integrated.

USE OF THE FSIQ IN ASSESSMENT

- *Lukas is a very bright child. His WISC-IV FSIQ is in the 138–147 range, which places him in the top 1% of the ability range relative to other children his age.*
- *Ken's current difficulties in grade 4 have also been reported by his teachers since he entered grade 1 and would appear to be related to his lower cognitive abilities. His FSIQ on the WISC-IV corroborates earlier findings from the WISC-III that he is functioning in the borderline range. This will continue to place challenges on his efforts to achieve in school and he will likely require a modified educational program.*

The FSIQ is a composite measure and for that reason will not provide the kind of detail that the "parts" (i.e., indexes) of the test might convey in the assessment context, even though the FSIQ is the most reliable and valid score. Certainly when all of the subtest and index scores are uniformly high or low, the FSIQ aids in the identification of children with intellectual giftedness or mental retardation. Creating a composite score when there is not significant variability in the lower order test scores is not dissimilar to calculating a grade point average (GPA) based on a range of similar grades or having your doctor say that all of your test results suggest that you are in good health for someone your age.

It is common practice to begin reports of children's intellectual functioning with a discussion of the most global score and then to proceed in successive discussion to less global, more specific scores (e.g., Kaufman, 1994). The suggested basic profile analysis described in the *WISC-IV Technical and Interpretive Manual* (Wechsler, 2003b) recommends beginning with the FSIQ; this same procedure is also recommended for the WISC-III (Kaufman, 1994; Sattler & Saklofske, 2001).

Whereas the structure of the WISC-IV might suggest a top-down approach to test score interpretation beginning with the FSIQ, this is not strictly or always the strategy employed. In fact we suggested in chapter 2 that the psychologist begin with an examination of the index scores and proceed through various profile analyses ending with the FSIQ. The FSIQ is a very useful way to communicate overall ability when there is little score variation between and within the index scores. However, a factor at any level is deemed to "fracture" when the parts that comprise it break from the expected relationship among scores. Large differences between index scores may limit the communicative value of the FSIQ as a summary score. Base rate tables for discrepancy comparisons contained in Appendix B.1–B.6 of the *WISC–IV Administration and Scoring Manual* (Wechsler, 2003a) should be consulted to determine the appropriateness of combining subtests to yield both index scores and the FSIQ. These tables should serve as guideposts for determining if it is meaningful to use the FSIQ to communicate overall performance on the test. Thus substantial score variation may lead to statements such as the following:

- *It is difficult to summarize Lucy's abilities with a single score. Her nonverbal reasoning abilities are much better developed than her verbal comprehension and reasoning abilities and this is likely to be noticeable in the variability of her performance across classroom and other activities that depend on these abilities.*
- *Wally's WISC-IV test results showed exceptionally large subtest score differences within both the VCI and the WMI and between the four index scores. These results do not support the calculation of an FSIQ but rather reflect Wally's unique pattern of cognitive abilities.*

A key question concerns the magnitude of discrepancy needed to downplay the FSIQ as the most meaningful summary of performance for an individual child. As a general rule of thumb, we might suggest that a 20-point VCI–PRI discrepancy should certainly raise "red flags" in the examiner's mind. VCI < PRI and VCI > PRI discrepancies of 20 points or greater were obtained by 6.1 and 6.7% of the standardization sample, respectively. This frequency varies depending on the index score comparisons being made and the base rate for the population of which the individual is a member.

This does not necessarily reduce the relevance of the FSIQ score. As noted in Chapter 2, the FSIQ is equally predictive of achievement with and without large verbal–perceptual discrepancies. The task of the psychologist, if such discrepancies were expected as a function of earlier diagnosis, is to use this information in a confirmatory way rather than being concerned about the factor structure of the WISC-IV. If the results were unexpected, the psychologist can continue the search to better understand both why such score discrepancies occurred and what they mean to the functioning of the particular child.

It is not uncommon to find children with some variation in FSIQ to be achieving at similar levels in school. As psychologists we might be more accurate in some of our predictions about academic achievement if we were more inclined to consider score ranges rather than specific scores. While the WISC-IV is among the most reliable measures of its kind, the question of validity is another issue. Thus the cognitive differences between a child with an FSIQ score of 104 and another with an FSIQ score of 107 are difficult enough to distinguish (given also measurement error) and are not likely to play a significant role in the differential prediction of achievement between two children. Furthermore, it is common knowledge among teachers and psychologists that several children, all with FSIQ scores of 100, may perform quite differently in the classroom and other real-world contexts. One child shows little variability on the WISC-IV subtests and index scores and is an average student. The second child has a similar pattern of index scores but a slightly more variable pattern of subtest scores (ranging from low average scaled scores of 7 to high average scores of 13), is not motivated, has a poor academic self-concept, and is somewhat test anxious, all resulting in poor classroom achievement. The third child has high average scores on the PRI, average on the VCI and PSI, but borderline scores on the WMI and an inconsistent pattern of achievement. Thus the FSIQ may at times be too gross a measure because FSIQs of 100 for all three children would predict similar achievement results.

For all of these reasons, we suggest that practitioners report the FSIQ score only in the summary section of the evaluation rather than the common practice of reporting FSIQ as the first score in the body of the report. The exception might be for those cases in which all index scores are very close to each other and it becomes redundant to describe each index separately in the report. *We believe that obtaining the FSIQ should not be the sole purpose of a WISC-IV administration.* Rather, in most situations, children are better served when practitioners utilize the index scores as the primary level of clinical interpretation. While the FSIQ is the most reliable single score and has the highest psychometric value of any score on the test, index scores have the highest clinical value and are the most useful for understanding children's cognitive abilities. Chapter 4 continues and deepens the discussion of index score interpretation begun in Chapter 2 and here.

ESTIMATING FSIQ: THE GENERAL ABILITY INDEX (GAI)

- *In comparing Larry's WISC-IV FSIQ and GAI, his much slower PS subtest scores and average WM subtest scores do have an impact on his overall ability assessment. His GAI is 101 in contrast to his FSIQ of 92.*
- *I have so many referrals and sometimes I just don't have the time to complete a full WISC-IV. At other times I really just want an estimate of a child's overall intelligence and really don't need the results of a full WISC-IV administration.*

The search for a brief and accurate estimate of FSIQ has followed the publication of each of the Wechsler intelligence tests for children. Sattler and Saklofske (2001a) described the various short forms of the WISC-III. More recently, Sattler and Dumont (2004) have provided tables listing the most frequently used WISC-IV short forms. In general the "best" short forms have very good validity coefficients, ranging from .8 for two-subtest forms to .90 or higher for four- and five-subtest short forms. At the same time, short forms are not without their limitations (Sattler & Saklofske, 2001).

Beginning with the WISC-III, Prifitera, Weiss, and Saklofske (1998) proposed an alternative composite score, the General Ability Index (GAI), derived from subtests that entered the VCI and the POI (Perceptual Organization Index). The GAI and the WISC-III FSIQ correlated .98 in the Canadian standardization sample (Weiss, Saklofske, Prifitera, Chen, & Hildebrand, 1999). The GAI has been recommended for use with the WAIS-III where the VCI and the POI comprise only three subtests each (Tulsky, Saklofske, Wilkins, & Weiss, 2001; Saklofske, Gorsuch, Weiss, Zhu, & Patterson, 2005). Again, with correlations of .96 between the FSIQ and the GAI, both measures appear to provide excellent estimates of general mental ability.

The WM and PS subtests account for 40% of the subtest contribution to the WISC-IV FSIQ. Their important role in describing the cognitive abilities of children suggests there may be considerable clinical utility in determining or parsing out their effects on the expression of intelligent behavior. In fact we alert readers at this point that a Cognitive Proficiency Index, comprised of the WMI and PSI, is presented in Chapter 4 and further examined in relation to the GAI. Recall also that the WISC-IV has reduced the emphasis on timed performance on the perceptual reasoning subtests. Thus, the GAI has two possible roles to play. First, the FSIQ may, when compared to the GAI, provide an indication of the effects of depressed (or elevated) WM and PS subtest scores. Second, as long as school districts continue to employ AADs as a major criterion for special education services eligibility, the FSIQ that is decreased by low WM and PS subtest scores may reduce this ability–achievement difference. It has never been our intention, however, that the GAI serve as a short form of the WISC-IV because we believe that variabilities in working memory and processing speed are not only essential components of effective intellectual functioning, but are particularly germane to many cognitive disorders. Only among intact, nonreferred samples is GAI likely to be a valid short form for assessing overall intelligence.

What follows is a description of the WISC-IV GAI with all necessary tables for calculating the GAI using the American standardization sample (Raiford, Weiss, Rolfhus, & Coalson, 2005). We further include the full set of tables for examining GAI–WIAT-II discrepancies. This text and tables may also be found on the Harcourt Assessment Web site. The Harcourt Assessment Web site in Canada has tables for the GAI and GAI–WIAT-II discrepancy comparison using Canadian norms (Saklofske, Zhu, Raiford, Weiss, Rolfhus, & Coalson, 2005).

AN ALTERNATE APPROACH TO
SUMMARIZING GENERAL
INTELLECTUAL ABILITY: THE
GENERAL ABILITY INDEX

OVERVIEW

The technical report available on the Harcourt Web site (reprinted here) is the fourth in a series intended to introduce the WISC-IV. Technical Report #1 (Williams, Weiss, & Rolfhus, 2003a) presented the theoretical structure and test blueprint for the WISC-IV, as well as subtest changes from the WISC-III. Technical Report #2 (Williams, Weiss, & Rolfhus, 2003b) presented the psychometric properties of the WISC-IV. Technical Report #3 (Williams, Weiss, & Rolfhus, 2003c) addressed the instrument's clinical validity.

This report provides information about the derivation and uses of the GAI. The GAI is a composite score that is based on three verbal comprehension and three perceptual reasoning subtests and does not include the WM or PS subtests included in the FSIQ. Detailed information about the GAI is also available in Prifitera, Saklofske, and Weiss (2005).

BACKGROUND AND HISTORY OF THE WECHSLER
COMPOSITES AND THE GAI

The original *Wechsler Intelligence Scale for Children* (WISC; Wechsler, 1949), the *Wechsler Intelligence Scale for Children–Revised* (WISC-R; Wechsler, 1974), and the WISC-III included an FSIQ as well as a VIQ and PIQ. The WISC-III introduced four index scores to represent more narrow domains of cognitive function: the VCI, the POI, the Freedom from Distractibility Index (FDI), and the PSI. With the introduction of these index scores, a total of seven composite scores could be derived with the WISC-III: the FSIQ, VIQ, PIQ, VCI, POI, FDI, and PSI.

Introduction of the index scores gave practitioners the ability to select the composite scores that best described verbal and perceptual ability based on the outcome of the assessment. When necessary to aid in interpretation, the practitioner could describe verbal abilities using the VCI in place of the VIQ and describe perceptual abilities using the POI in place of the PIQ. This flexibility was particularly useful when scores for certain subtests contributing to the VIQ or PIQ were discrepant at a significant and unusual level. In particular, the index scores were preferable for cases in which the VIQ was considered less descriptive of verbal ability than the VCI because Arithmetic—a subtest from the working memory domain—was discrepant from the verbal comprehension subtests at a level that was unusual in the standardization sample and for cases in which the PIQ was considered less descriptive of perceptual ability than the

POI because Coding—a subtest drawn from the processing speed domain—was discrepant from the perceptual organization subtests at a level that was unusual in the standardization sample. The GAI was first developed for use with the WISC-III by Prifitera, Weiss, and Saklofske (1998) to offer additional flexibility in describing broad intellectual ability. The WISC-III GAI provided a measure of general cognitive ability that did not include the influence of Arithmetic or Coding on FSIQ. The WISC-III GAI was based on the sum of scaled scores for all subtests that contributed to the traditional 10 subtest FSIQ, with the exception of Arithmetic and Coding. The eight contributing subtests were all drawn from the Verbal Comprehension and Perceptual Organization domains and included Picture Completion, Information, Similarities, Picture Arrangement, Block Design, Vocabulary, Object Assembly, and Comprehension. The WISC-III GAI was recommended as a useful composite to estimate overall ability if a great deal of variability existed within VIQ and/or PIQ due to low scores on Arithmetic and/or Coding (Prifitera et al., 1998). The GAI was subsequently applied for use with the WISC-III using Canadian norms (Weiss et al., 1999), the WAIS-III (Tulsky et al., 2001), and the WAIS-III using Canadian norms (Saklofske et al., 2005).

The WISC-IV provides an FSIQ and a four-index framework similar to that of the WISC-III. The framework is based on theory and supported by clinical research and factor-analytic results. As noted in the *WISC-IV Technical and Interpretive Manual* (Wechsler, 2003b) and in Technical Report #1 (Williams et al., 2003a), the POI was renamed the Perceptual Reasoning Index (PRI) to reflect more accurately the increased emphasis on fluid reasoning abilities in this index, and the FDI was renamed the Working Memory Index (WMI), which describes more accurately the abilities measured. In addition, the dual IQ and index score structure was no longer utilized. The elimination of the dual structure reduced concerns about the influence of working memory and processing speed when summarizing verbal comprehension and perceptual reasoning abilities, respectively. The WISC-IV FSIQ, however, includes (to a greater extent than the WISC-III FSIQ) the influence of working memory and processing speed to reflect research that suggests both working memory and processing speed are important factors that contribute to overall intellectual functioning (Engle, Laughlin, Tuholski, & Conway, 1999; Fry & Hale, 1996, 2000; Heinz-Martin, Oberauer, Wittmann, Wilhelm, & Schulze, 2002; Miller & Vernon, 1996; Vigil-Colet & Codorniu-Raga, 2002). Recent research continues to confirm the importance of working memory and processing speed to cognitive ability and to refine knowledge about the nature of these relations (Colom, Rebollo, Palacios, Juan-Espinosa, & Kyllonen, 2004; Mackintosh & Bennett, 2003; Schweizer & Moosbrugger, 2004).

The FSIQ is used most frequently to describe an underlying, global aspect of general intelligence, or *g*. The FSIQ is utilized for a number of purposes in clinical practice. The FSIQ can serve as a summary of performance across a number of specific cognitive ability domains (i.e., verbal comprehension, perceptual reasoning, working memory, and processing speed). It is used most often in conjunction with other information as part of a diagnostic evaluation in clinics and hospital settings, to determine eligibility to receive special education services in public school settings, or to make decisions about level of care and placement in residential settings.

The FSIQ is an aggregate score that summarizes performance across multiple cognitive abilities in a single number. When unusual variability is observed within the set of subtests that comprise the FSIQ, clinical interpretation should characterize this diversity of abilities in order to be most useful for parents, teachers, and other professionals.

INTRODUCTION TO THE WISC-IV GAI

As with the WISC-III GAI and WAIS-III GAI, the WISC-IV GAI provides the practitioner a summary score that is less sensitive to the influence of working memory and processing speed. For children with neuropsychological issues such as learning disorders, attention-deficit/ hyperactivity disorder, and other similar issues, difficulties with working memory and processing speed may result in lower FSIQ scores (Wechsler, 2003b). In children with intact neuropsychological functioning, the GAI may provide a comparable approximation of overall intellectual ability as represented by the FSIQ (Prifitera et al., 2005; Weiss et al., 1999).

The GAI can be used as a substitute for the FSIQ to determine eligibility for special education services and placement classification. The GAI increases flexibility in this respect because it is sensitive to cases in which working memory performance is discrepant from verbal comprehension performance and/or processing speed performance is discrepant from perceptual reasoning performance at an unusual level. It can also be compared to the FSIQ to assess the effects of working memory and processing speed on the expression of cognitive ability.

Various sources for GAI tables are available; however, those sources differ according to the method by which they were created. Four such sources are (a) this technical report, (b) Prifitera et al. (2005), (c) Flanagan and Kaufman (2004), and (d) Dumont and Willis (2004). The GAI tables provided in this technical report and in Prifitera et al. (2005) are the only GAI tables supported by Harcourt Assessment, Inc. (formerly known as The Psychological Corporation). These tables were created using the actual WISC-IV standardization sample ($n=2200$), whereas the GAI tables provided in other sources were created using statistical approximation. The calculations in Flanagan and Kaufman (2004) and Dumont and Willis (2004) were based on a statistical technique for linear equating that was developed by Tellegen and Briggs (1967, Formula 4), which allowed the GAI to be calculated based on intercorrelations between the VCI and the PRI. In contrast, tables in this technical report provide values for the GAI based on the standardization sample and the sum of subtest scaled scores that contribute to the index. The Tellegen and Briggs formula underestimates scores in the upper portion of the distribution and overestimates scores in the lower portion of the distribution. On average, this difference is approximately two to three points, but can be as much as six points for some children with mental retardation or some gifted children. The Tellegen and Briggs formula is appropriate for use if actual standardization data are not available: The tables provided by Flanagan and Kaufman (2004) and by Dumont and Willis (2004) were generated while practitioners were waiting for the tables based on the standardization sample to be created. As the tables based on the standardization sample are now available, those GAI tables should be considered out of date. Thus, practitioners are advised to use the GAI tables in this chapter (and the technical report it reprints), which are the same (within rounding variance) as the tables in Prifitera et al. (2005). Canadian readers are encouraged to consult the Canadian Harcourt Web site where they will find an equivalent technical report and tables (Saklofske et al., 2005) for the WISC-IV GAI and WIAT-II based on Canadian norms.

THE ROLE OF ABILITY IN DETERMINING ELIGIBILITY FOR SPECIAL EDUCATION SERVICES AS LEARNING DISABLED

The WISC-IV Integrated Technical and Interpretive Manual (Wechsler et al., 2004) outlines a number of concerns with the isolated use of the AAD model for identifying learning disabilities. An AAD indicates that some problem exists, as achievement is not at a level commensurate with cognitive ability. Established practice currently includes the use of AADs as general screeners for nonspecific learning problems. The general finding of such a discrepancy should be followed with additional assessment before a formal diagnosis is rendered. A determination that a learning disability is present requires evidence of impairment in the core cognitive processes underlying the specific academic skill of concern, but an AAD alone is often sufficient evidence to obtain special education services in most public school settings. Although several new models for evaluating learning disorders and learning disabilities have been proposed (Berninger, Dunn, & Alper, 2005; Berninger & O'Donnell, 2005), diagnostic markers generally have yet to be established clearly in the literature. Some progress has been made in this area, however. For example, pseudoword decoding and rapid automatized naming appear to predict early reading disorders.

The progression toward utilizing a number of approaches to assess learning disabilities is evident in federal legislation. The new Individuals with Disabilities Education Improvement Act of 2004 indicates that local education agencies should ensure that a variety of assessment tools and strategies are used to gather relevant functional, developmental, and academic information that may assist in determining whether the child has a learning disability. The Individuals with Disabilities Education Improvement Act of 2004 further states that, in general, a local educational agency is *not required* to take into consideration whether a child has a severe AAD in determining whether a child has a specific learning disability. Local education agencies may continue to use the AAD method if desired or may incorporate or transition to a process that determines if the child responds to intervention as a part of the evaluation (Individuals with Disabilities Education Improvement Act of 2004; Public Law 108–446). Proponents of the response-to-intervention model advocate that eligibility for special education services be determined solely on the basis of the student's low achievement and failure to respond to empirically supported educational instruction, regardless of the results of cognitive evaluations (Fletcher & Reschly, 2005). Others have defended the role of cognitive assessment in the evaluation of individuals with brain-based learning disorders, while not necessarily advocating strict adherence to AAD as the only method for classification (Hale, Naglieri, Kaufman, & Kavale, 2004; Scruggs & Mastropieri, 2002).

USE OF THE GENERAL ABILITY INDEX

Presently, most school district policies continue to require evidence of an AAD in order to obtain special education services, and it was largely for this reason that the GAI was first developed. For some children with learning disabilities, attentional problems, or other neuropsychological issues, concomitant working memory and processing speed deficiencies lower the FSIQ. This is evident in Table 4, which shows that FSIQ < GAI profiles were obtained by more than 70% of children in the following WISC-IV special group samples: reading disorder ($N=56$), reading and written expression disorders ($N=35$), reading, written expression, and mathematics disorders ($N=42$), and learning disorder and attention-deficit/hyperactivity disorder ($N=45$). While potentially clinically meaningful, this reduction in the FSIQ may decrease the magnitude of the AAD for some children with learning disabilities and make them less likely to be found eligible for special education services in educational systems that do not allow consideration of other methods of eligibility determination.

It also may be clinically informative in a number of additional situations to compare the FSIQ and the GAI to assess the impact of reducing the emphasis on working memory and processing speed on the estimate of general cognitive ability for children with difficulty in those areas due to traumatic brain injury or other neuropsychological difficulties. This comparison may inform rehabilitation programs and/or educational intervention planning.

It is important for practitioners to recognize that the GAI is not necessarily a more valid estimate of overall cognitive ability than the FSIQ. Working memory and processing speed are vital to the comprehensive evaluation of cognitive ability, and excluding these abilities from the evaluation can be misleading. The classroom performance of two children with the same GAI score but very different WMI/PSI scores will likely be quite different. In educational situations where evidence of a significant AAD is required to obtain services, the GAI may be used as the ability score; however, the WMI and PSI should still be reported and interpreted. Refer to Prifitera et al. (2005) for additional discussion.

The practitioner may wish to consider using the GAI in a number of clinical situations, not limited to, but including the following.

1. A significant and unusual discrepancy exists between VCI and WMI.
2. A significant and unusual discrepancy exists between PRI and PSI.
3. A significant and unusual discrepancy exists between WMI and PSI.
4. Significant and unusual intersubtest scatter exists within WMI and/or PSI.

To review index discrepancies, consult the discrepancy comparison critical value and base rate tables B.1–B.6 of the *WISC-IV Administration and Scoring Manual* (Wechsler, 2003a) using the procedures outlined in chapter 2 of the manual. The analysis page of the WISC-IV Record Form provides space for these pairwise discrepancy comparisons in the discrepancy comparisons table. A statistically significant difference between index scores, however, may not indicate that there is a clinically significant difference: The frequency of occurrence in the standardization sample (base rate), not just the critical value, should be considered. Consult Table B.2 in the *WISC-IV Administration and Scoring Manual* (Wechsler, 2003a) to obtain the base rate for a given discrepancy. Sattler (2001) suggests that differences between scores that occur in less than 10 to 15% of the standardization sample be judged as unusual. Subtest scatter can be examined within the FSIQ, and within the VCI and PRI, using Table B.6 of the *WISC-IV Administration and Scoring Manual* (Wechsler, 2003a).

STEPS TO CALCULATING AND USING THE GAI

The following steps are provided as a guide for calculating the GAI and comparing it to the FSIQ to obtain more information about a child's cognitive ability.

Calculate the General Ability sum of scaled scores. If you have determined that the GAI is important to consider in interpretation, calculate the general ability sum of scaled scores. The general ability sum of scaled scores is the sum of scaled scores for three Verbal Comprehension subtests (i.e., Vocabulary, Comprehension, and Similarities) and three Perceptual

Reasoning subtests (i.e., Block Design, Matrix Reasoning, and Picture Concepts). Record the general ability sum of scaled scores.

In some situations, you may choose to substitute a supplemental subtest for a core subtest that contributes to the GAI. Follow the same subtest substitution rules that are outlined in the *WISC-IV Administration and Scoring Manual* (Wechsler, 2003a) for the FSIQ if you choose to substitute a supplemental subtest for a core subtest that contributes to the GAI. Follow the standard administration order of subtests listed in chapter 2 of the *WISC-IV Administration and Scoring Manual* (Wechsler, 2003a) even when you expect to substitute a supplemental subtest for a core subtest.

Determine the GAI composite score. Locate the general ability sum of scaled scores in the extreme left column of Table 1. Read across the row to determine the GAI composite score. Continue to read across the row to find the corresponding percentile rank and confidence intervals. Record the composite score, the percentile rank, and the confidence interval (90 or 95%).

Analyze the FSIQ-GAI discrepancy. Calculate the difference between the FSIQ and the GAI by subtracting the GAI composite score from the FSIQ composite score. Record this value. Table 2 provides the required differences between the FSIQ and the GAI to attain statistical significance (critical values) at the .15 and .05 levels for each age group. Select the desired level of statistical significance and note it for your records. Using Table 2, find the age group of the child and the desired level of significance. Read across the row to the appropriate column to determine the critical value and record this critical value. The absolute value of the child's difference score must equal or exceed that critical value to be statistically significant. Determine whether the absolute value of the child's difference score equals or exceeds the corresponding critical value.

Table 3 provides the percentage of children in the WISC-IV standardization sample that obtained the same or greater discrepancy between the FSIQ and the GAI (base rate). Values reported in Table 3 are provided for the overall standardization sample and by ability level and are separated into "−" and "+" columns based on the direction of the difference. Locate the absolute value of the child's difference score in the amount of discrepancy column to the extreme left or right and read across the row to the column that corresponds to the direction of the difference score (e.g., FSIQ < GAI) either by the overall sample or by ability level, if desired. Record this value.

In some situations, practitioners may wish to determine how unusual the same or greater FSIQ–GAI discrepancy was in a particular special group sample (e.g., children identified as intellectually gifted, children diagnosed with mental retardation, children diagnosed with various learning disorders) that is relevant to the child being evaluated. Table 4 provides the percentage of children from various special groups described in the *WISC-IV Technical and Interpretive Manual* (Wechsler, 2003b) who obtained the same or greater

TABLE 1   GAI Equivalents of Sums of Scaled Scores

Sum of Scaled Scores	GAI	Percentile Rank	Confidence Level 90%	Confidence Level 95%	Sum of Scaled Scores	GAI	Percentile Rank	Confidence Level 90%	Confidence Level 95%
6	40	<0.1	38–47	37–48	50	90	25	86–95	85–96
7	40	<0.1	38–47	37–48	51	91	27	87–96	86–97
8	40	<0.1	38–47	37–48	52	92	30	88–97	87–98
9	40	<0.1	38–47	37–48	53	93	32	89–98	88–99
10	40	<0.1	38–47	37–48	54	94	34	90–99	89–100
11	40	<0.1	38–47	37–48	55	95	37	90–100	90–101
12	41	<0.1	39–48	38–49	56	96	39	91–101	91–102
13	42	<0.1	40–49	39–50	57	97	42	92–102	91–103
14	43	<0.1	41–50	40–51	58	98	45	93–103	92–104
15	44	<0.1	42–51	41–52	59	99	47	94–104	93–105
16	45	<0.1	42–52	42–53	60	100	50	95–105	94–106
17	46	<0.1	43–53	43–54	61	101	53	96–106	95–107
18	47	<0.1	44–54	43–55	62	102	55	97–107	96–108
19	49	<0.1	46–56	45–57	63	103	58	98–108	97–109
20	51	0.1	48–58	47–59	64	104	61	99–109	98–109
21	52	0.1	49–59	48–60	65	105	63	100–110	99–110
22	53	0.1	50–60	49–61	66	106	66	101–110	100–111
23	55	0.1	52–62	51–62	67	107	68	102–111	101–112
24	57	0.2	54–63	53–64	68	108	70	103–112	102–113
25	58	0.3	55–64	54–65	69	110	75	105–114	104–115
26	59	0.3	56–65	55–66	70	111	77	106–115	105–116
27	61	0.5	58–67	57–68	71	112	79	107–116	106–117
28	63	1	60–69	59–70	72	113	81	108–117	107–118
29	64	1	61–70	60–71	73	115	84	110–119	109–120
30	65	1	62–71	61–72	74	116	86	111–120	110–121
31	67	1	64–73	63–74	75	117	87	112–121	111–122
32	69	2	66–75	65–76	76	119	90	114–123	113–124
33	70	2	66–76	66–77	77	120	91	114–124	114–125
34	71	3	67–77	67–78	78	121	92	115–125	115–126
35	73	4	69–79	68–80	79	122	93	116–126	115–127
36	74	4	70–80	69–81	80	123	94	117–127	116–128
37	75	5	71–81	70–82	81	124	95	118–128	117–129
38	77	6	73–83	72–84	82	126	96	120–130	119–131
39	78	7	74–84	73–85	83	127	96	121–131	120–132
40	79	8	75–85	74–85	84	128	97	122–132	121–133
41	81	10	77–86	76–87	85	129	97	123–133	122–133
42	82	12	78–87	77–88	86	130	98	124–134	123–134
43	83	13	79–88	78–89	87	132	98	126–135	125–136
44	84	14	80–89	79–90	88	133	99	127–136	126–137
45	85	16	81–90	80–91	89	135	99	129–138	128–139
46	86	18	82–91	81–92	90	136	99	130–139	129–140
47	87	19	83–92	82–93	91	138	99	132–141	131–142
48	88	21	84–93	83–94	92	139	99.5	133–142	132–143
49	89	23	85–94	84–95	93	140	99.6	134–143	133–144

(Continues)

120

DONALD H. SAKLOFSKE ET AL.

TABLE 1   *(Continued)*

Sum of Scaled Scores	GAI	Percentile Rank	Confidence Level 90%	95%	Sum of Scaled Scores	GAI	Percentile Rank	Confidence Level 90%	95%
94	142	99.7	136–145	135–146	104	155	>99.9	148–158	147–158
95	143	99.8	137–146	136–147	105	156	>99.9	149–158	148–159
96	144	99.8	138–147	137–148	106	157	>99.9	150–159	149–160
97	146	99.9	139–149	139–150	107	158	>99.9	151–160	150–161
98	147	99.9	140–150	139–151	108	159	>99.9	152–161	151–162
99	148	99.9	141–151	140–152	109	160	>99.9	153–162	152–163
100	150	>99.9	143–153	142–154	110	160	>99.9	153–162	152–163
101	151	>99.9	144–154	143–155	111	160	>99.9	153–162	152–163
102	153	>99.9	146–156	145–157	112	160	>99.9	153–162	152–163
103	154	>99.9	147–157	146–157	113	160	>99.9	153–162	152–163
					114	160	>99.9	153–162	152–163

Wechsler Intelligence Scale for Children – Fourth Edition (WISC-IV). Copyright © 2003 by Harcourt Assessment, Inc. Reproduced with permission. All rights reserved.

discrepancy between the FSIQ and the GAI (base rate). Values are provided for children identified as Intellectually Gifted, children with Mild or Moderate Mental Retardation, children with various Learning Disorders, children with a Learning Disorder and Attention-Deficit/Hyperactivity Disorder, children with Attention-Deficit/Hyperactivity Disorder, children with Expressive Language Disorder, children with Mixed Receptive-Expressive Language Disorder, children with Traumatic Brain Injury, children with Autistic Disorder, children with Asperger's Disorder, and children with Motor Impairment.

TABLE 2   Differences between FSIQ and GAI Scores Required for Statistical Significance (Critical Values) by Age Group and Overall Standardization Sample

Age Group	Level of Significance	Composite Pair FSIQ–GAI
6:0–11:11	.15	6
	.05	8
12:0–16:11	.15	6
	.05	8
All ages	.15	6
	.05	8

Note. Differences required for statistical significance are based on the standard errors of measurement of each composite for each age group and are calculated with the following formula:
Critical value of difference score $= Z\sqrt{SEM_a^2 + SEM_b^2}$
where Z is the normal curve value associated with the desired two-tailed significance level and SEM_a and SEM_b are the standard errors of measurement for the two composites.
Wechsler Intelligence Scale for Children – Fourth Edition (WISC-IV). Copyright © 2003 by Harcourt Assessment, Inc. Reproduced with permission. All rights reserved.

TABLE 3 Cumulative Percentages of Standardization Sample (Base Rates) Obtaining Various FSIQ-GAI Score Discrepancies, by Overall Sample and Ability Level

Amount of Discrepancy	Overall Sample		GAI ≤ 79		80 ≤ GAI ≤ 89		90 ≤ GAI ≤ 109		110 ≤ GAI ≤ 119		GAI ≥ 120		Amount of Discrepancy
	FSIQ<GAI (−)	FSIQ>GAI (+)	FSIQ<GAI (−)	FSIQ>GAI (+)	FSIQ<GAI (−)	FSIQ>GAI (+)	FSIQ<GAI (−)	FSIQ>GAI (+)	FSIQ<GAI (−)	FSIQ>GAI (+)	FSIQ<GAI (−)	FSIQ>GAI (+)	
18	0.0	0.0	0.0	0.0	0.0	0.0	0.0	0.0	0.3	0.0	0.0	0.0	18
17	0.0	0.0	0.0	0.0	0.0	0.0	0.0	0.0	0.3	0.0	0.0	0.0	17
16	0.1	0.0	0.0	0.0	0.0	0.0	0.0	0.0	0.3	0.3	0.4	0.0	16
15	0.2	0.0	0.0	0.0	0.0	0.0	0.2	0.0	0.3	0.3	0.9	0.0	15
14	0.5	0.3	0.0	1.2	0.7	0.3	0.4	0.2	0.3	0.5	2.2	0.0	14
13	0.9	0.5	0.0	1.2	1.4	0.3	0.4	0.4	0.3	0.5	4.5	0.4	13
12	1.4	0.8	0.0	2.9	2.1	0.3	0.8	0.7	0.5	0.5	6.3	0.4	12
11	2.3	1.2	0.0	4.1	2.8	0.3	1.6	1.4	1.8	2.4	7.6	0.4	11
10	3.4	2.2	0.6	5.8	4.5	1.4	2.6	2.2	2.9	3.9	9.4	0.4	10
9	5.4	3.7	0.6	8.2	6.6	2.1	4.7	3.9	5.0	4.7	12.1	0.9	9
8	7.9	5.4	2.3	9.4	8.7	3.1	6.8	6.3	8.1	6.8	16.1	1.8	8
7	11.0	8.2	5.3	16.4	12.2	4.9	9.2	9.3	13.6	8.1	18.8	3.1	7
6	14.5	11.6	8.8	24.0	16.0	8.7	12.1	13.0	17.0	11.8	25.1	4.9	6
5	19.8	16.9	13.5	31.0	21.2	13.2	17.3	19.5	23.6	18.1	29.6	6.7	5
4	25.6	22.7	16.4	36.3	26.0	18.1	23.0	26.1	30.6	25.1	36.8	9.0	4
3	32.6	28.3	20.5	45.6	30.6	23.6	29.5	31.1	39.3	32.7	49.3	12.1	3
2	39.9	35.5	28.1	50.9	39.2	30.9	36.1	38.7	47.1	41.1	57.0	18.4	2
1	48.7	43.3	33.3	58.5	51.0	38.2	44.7	46.9	54.2		68.2	23.8	1
Mean	4.4	4.2	3.9	5.1	4.4	3.8	4.2	4.3	4.5	3.8	5.1	3.5	Mean
SD	3.0	2.8	2.3	3.1	3.3	2.5	2.9	2.7	2.8	2.8	3.7	2.6	SD
Median	4.0	4.0	3.0	5.0	4.0	3.0	4.0	4.0	4.0	3.0	4.0	3.0	Median

Wechsler Intelligence Scale for Children – Fourth Edition (WISC-IV). Copyright © 2003 by Harcourt Assessment, Inc.

Careful review of base rate data presented in Table 4 reveals clinically interesting patterns of FSIQ/GAI discrepancies across a variety of diagnostic groups. Notably, 40% of children in the intellectually gifted group obtained GAI scores that were five or more points greater than their FSIQ scores. Similar results were noted in all of the learning disorder groups, as well as the ADHD groups, language disorder groups, head injury groups, and motor impairment group: Fully a third to over half the group in these samples obtained GAI scores that were five or more points greater than their FSIQ scores. As the FSIQ includes scores from processing speed subtests (and all WISC-IV processing speed subtests require motor responses from the child), the GAI may be particularly useful with children with motor impairment, for whom 55% of children obtained GAI scores five or more points greater than their FSIQ scores. The groups of children with autistic disorder and children with Asperger's disorder produced even more robust results: Approximately 50% of children in these groups obtained GAI scores eight or more points greater than their FSIQ scores.

The values reported in Table 4 are separated by special group and into "−" and "+" columns for each special group based on the direction of the difference. Locate the absolute value of the child's difference score in the amount of discrepancy column to the extreme left or right and read across the row to the column that corresponds to the desired special group of comparison and to the direction of the difference score (e.g., FSIQ < GAI). Record this value.

STEPS TO REPORTING AND DESCRIBING THE GAI

Standard Score

The GAI is an age-corrected standard score. It can be interpreted similarly to other composite scores, as outlined in Wechsler (2003b).

Percentile Rank

Age-based percentile ranks are provided for the GAI that indicate a child's standing relative to other children the same age. Percentile ranks reflect points on a scale at or below which a given percentage of scores lies based on the standardization sample. The percentile ranks for the GAI are interpreted as are other percentile ranks, as described in Wechsler (2003b).

Standard Error of Measurement and Confidence Interval

Scores on measures of cognitive ability are based on observational data and represent estimates of a child's true scores. They reflect a child's true abilities combined with some degree of measurement error. Confidence intervals provide another means of expressing score precision and serve as a reminder that measurement error is inherent in all scores. Refer to

TABLE 4   Cumulative Percentages of Various Special Group Samples (Base Rates) Obtaining Various FSIQ–GAI Score Discrepancies

	Clinical Group																
	GT (N = 63)		MR Mild (N = 63)		MR Mod (N = 57)		RD (N = 56)		RWD (N = 35)		MD (N = 33)		RWMD (N = 42)		LD/ADHD (N = 45)		
Amount of Discrepancy	FSIQ< GAI (−)	FSIQ> GAI (+)	FSIQ< GAI (−)	FSIQ> GAI (+)	FSIQ< GAI (−)	FSIQ> GAI (+)	FSIQ< GAI (−)	FSIQ> GAI (+)	FSIQ< GAI (−)	FSIQ> GAI (+)	FSIQ< GAI (−)	FSIQ> GAI (+)	FSIQ< GAI (−)	FSIQ> GAI (+)	FSIQ< GAI (−)	FSIQ> GAI (+)	Amount of Discrepancy
18	0.0	0.0	0.0	0.0	0.0	0.0	0.0	0.0	0.0	0.0	0.0	0.0	0.0	0.0	0.0	0.0	18
17	1.7	0.0	0.0	0.0	0.0	0.0	0.0	0.0	0.0	0.0	0.0	0.0	0.0	0.0	0.0	0.0	17
16	3.3	0.0	0.0	0.0	0.0	0.0	0.0	0.0	0.0	0.0	0.0	0.0	0.0	0.0	0.0	0.0	16
15	3.3	0.0	0.0	0.0	0.0	0.0	0.0	0.0	0.0	0.0	0.0	0.0	0.0	0.0	0.0	0.0	15
14	3.3	0.0	0.0	0.0	0.0	0.0	3.8	1.9	0.0	0.0	0.0	0.0	0.0	0.0	4.9	0.0	14
13	3.3	0.0	0.0	0.0	2.1	0.0	3.8	1.9	0.0	0.0	0.0	0.0	0.0	2.6	7.3	0.0	13
12	5.0	0.0	0.0	0.0	2.1	0.0	3.8	1.9	9.4	0.0	0.0	0.0	0.0	2.6	17.1	0.0	12
11	8.3	0.0	0.0	0.0	2.1	0.0	5.7	1.9	9.4	0.0	0.0	0.0	0.0	2.6	22.0	0.0	11
10	13.3	0.0	1.8	0.0	2.1	2.1	7.5	1.9	9.4	0.0	0.0	0.0	2.6	2.6	24.4	0.0	10
9	15.0	0.0	3.6	0.0	2.1	4.2	9.4	1.9	18.8	0.0	3.3	0.0	10.5	2.6	24.4	2.4	9
8	20.0	0.0	7.1	3.6	2.1	6.3	22.6	3.8	21.9	0.0	13.3	0.0	15.8	2.6	31.7	2.4	8
7	25.0	0.0	10.7	7.1	2.1	8.3	37.7	5.7	28.1	0.0	20.0	0.0	18.4	2.6	34.1	4.9	7
6	31.7	0.0	14.3	17.9	2.1	14.6	47.2	5.7	43.8	0.0	26.7	3.3	26.3	2.6	41.5	7.3	6
5	40.0	0.0	16.1	25.0	2.1	22.9	50.9	7.5	53.1	3.1	33.3	6.7	39.5	5.3	43.9	9.8	5
4	43.3	6.7	17.9	33.9	2.1	25.0	56.6	9.4	65.6	6.3	36.7	10.0	44.7	10.5	46.3	9.8	4
3	53.3	13.3	25.0	50.0	4.2	29.2	64.2	13.2	68.8	6.3	46.7	16.7	55.3	15.8	61.0	14.6	3
2	65.0	20.0	33.9	51.8	4.2	39.6	66.0	15.1	71.9	9.4	53.3	23.3	65.8	15.8	68.3	17.1	2
1	68.3	25.0	37.5	57.1	6.3	54.2	75.5	17.0	84.4	12.5	56.7	30.0	71.1	26.3	73.2	22.0	1
Mean	5.9	2.6	4.5	4.3	5.7	3.8	6.0	5.1	5.7	3.0	5.1	3.0	4.9	3.5	6.8	4.1	Mean
SD	3.9	1.1	2.8	1.9	6.4	2.7	3.2	3.7	3.3	1.8	2.5	1.7	2.7	3.3	4.3	2.8	SD
Median	5.0	3.0	3.0	4.0	3.0	3.0	6.5	4.0	6.0	3.0	5.0	3.0	5.0	3.0	6.0	3.0	Median

Note: GT = Intellectually Gifted; MR Mild = Mental Retardation-Mild Severity; MR Mod = Mental Retardation-Moderate Severity; RD = Reading Disorder; RWD = Reading and Written Expression Disorders; MD = Mathematics Disorder; RWMD = Reading, Written Expression, and Mathematics Disorders; LD/ADHD = Learning Disorder and Attention-Deficit/Hyperactivity Disorder. *Wechsler Intelligence Scale for Children – Fourth Edition (WISC-IV)*. Copyright © 2003 by Harcourt Assessment, Inc. Reproduced with permission. All rights reserved.

(*Continues*)

TABLE 4 (Continued)

Clinical Group

Amount of Discrepancy	ADHD (N = 89) FSIQ<GAI (−)	ADHD FSIQ>GAI (+)	ELD (N = 27) FSIQ<GAI (−)	ELD FSIQ>GAI (+)	RELD (N = 41) FSIQ<GAI (−)	RELD FSIQ>GAI (+)	OHI (N = 16) FSIQ<GAI (−)	OHI FSIQ>GAI (+)	CHI (N = 27) FSIQ<GAI (−)	CHI FSIQ>GAI (+)	AUT (N = 19) FSIQ<GAI (−)	AUT FSIQ>GAI (+)	ASP (N = 27) FSIQ<GAI (−)	ASP FSIQ>GAI (+)	MI (N = 21) FSIQ<GAI (−)	MI FSIQ>GAI (+)	Amount of Discrepancy
18	0.0	0.0	0.0	0.0	0.0	0.0	0.0	0.0	0.0	0.0	0.0	0.0	8.3	0.0	0.0	0.0	18
17	0.0	0.0	0.0	0.0	0.0	0.0	0.0	0.0	0.0	0.0	0.0	0.0	8.3	0.0	0.0	0.0	17
16	0.0	0.0	0.0	0.0	0.0	0.0	0.0	0.0	0.0	0.0	0.0	0.0	8.3	0.0	0.0	0.0	16
15	0.0	0.0	0.0	0.0	0.0	0.0	0.0	0.0	0.0	0.0	5.9	0.0	12.5	0.0	0.0	0.0	15
14	1.2	0.0	0.0	0.0	0.0	0.0	0.0	0.0	0.0	0.0	17.6	0.0	12.5	0.0	0.0	0.0	14
13	1.2	1.2	0.0	0.0	2.6	0.0	7.1	0.0	0.0	0.0	17.6	0.0	16.7	0.0	0.0	0.0	13
12	1.2	1.2	0.0	0.0	7.9	0.0	7.1	0.0	0.0	0.0	17.6	0.0	29.2	0.0	5.6	0.0	12
11	2.4	1.2	0.0	0.0	7.9	0.0	7.1	0.0	0.0	0.0	29.4	0.0	29.2	4.2	5.6	0.0	11
10	6.1	1.2	0.0	0.0	7.9	0.0	14.3	0.0	4.0	0.0	29.4	0.0	37.5	4.2	5.6	0.0	10
9	9.8	1.2	4.5	0.0	18.4	0.0	14.3	0.0	4.0	0.0	47.1	0.0	41.7	4.2	11.1	0.0	9
8	17.1	1.2	9.1	0.0	23.7	0.0	21.4	0.0	8.0	0.0	52.9	0.0	45.8	4.2	22.2	0.0	8
7	19.5	1.2	9.1	0.0	28.9	2.6	28.6	0.0	8.0	0.0	58.8	0.0	58.3	4.2	27.8	0.0	7
6	30.5	4.9	18.2	0.0	34.2	5.3	42.9	0.0	32.0	0.0	58.8	0.0	58.3	8.3	33.3	0.0	6
5	35.4	4.9	31.8	0.0	44.7	10.5	42.9	0.0	40.0	0.0	64.7	0.0	62.5	12.5	55.6	0.0	5
4	39.0	7.3	50.0	9.1	50.0	10.5	50.0	0.0	48.0	4.0	70.6	0.0	70.8	12.5	55.6	0.0	4
3	45.1	9.8	54.5	9.1	60.5	15.8	50.0	0.0	52.0	4.0	76.5	0.0	79.2	12.5	72.2	5.6	3
2	54.9	17.1	68.2	13.6	65.8	21.1	57.1	0.0	64.0	8.0	76.5	5.9	79.2	12.5	88.9	5.6	2
1	65.9	20.7	77.3	13.6	71.1	23.7	71.4	0.0	72.0	12.0	76.5		87.5	12.5	88.9	11.1	1
Mean	5.0	3.5	4.2	3.3	6.0	3.8	5.8		4.6	2.3	9.2	1.0	8.5	7.3	5.3	2.0	Mean
SD	3.2	3.0	2.3	1.2	3.4	2.0	3.9		2.5	1.5	3.8		5.1	3.2	2.9	1.4	SD
Median	5.0	2.0	4.0	4.0	5.0	3.0	6.0		5.0	2.0	9.0	1.0	8.0	6.0	5.0	2.0	Median

Wechsler (2003b) for additional information about confidence intervals and their use in interpretation.

Of note is that the average GAI reliability, computed using Fisher's z transformations for ages 6–11 is $r=.95$ and for ages 12–16 is $r=.96$. The respective standard errors of measurement are 3.3 and 3.0 standard score points, respectively. The associated 95% confidence intervals are $\pm$ 6.6 and $\pm$ 5.9, respectively.

Descriptive Classification

Composite scores, including the GAI, can be described in qualitative terms according to the child's level of performance. Refer to Wechsler (2003b) for qualitative descriptions of the WISC-IV composite scores, which also may be used to describe the GAI.

SUGGESTED PROCEDURE FOR BASIC INTERPRETATION OF THE GAI

Note that this procedure is supplemental and does not replace any portion of the 10-step procedure outlined in Wechsler (2003b).

Evaluate the Overall Composite Scores

The FSIQ and the GAI are composite scores that should always be evaluated in the context of the subtests that contribute to that composite score. Extreme variability within the subtests that comprise the FSIQ or the GAI indicates that the score represents a summary of diverse abilities. Practitioners should examine closely the relative performance on subtests that contribute to the composite score when interpreting that score. Part of the decision to use the GAI also typically involves reviewing the discrepancies among the four index scores.

Evaluate the FSIQ–GAI Discrepancy

The first step in performing a pairwise comparison is aimed at determining whether the absolute value of the score difference is significant. Table 2 provides the minimum differences between the FSIQ and the GAI required for statistical significance (critical values) at the .15 and .05 levels of confidence by age group. When the absolute value of the obtained difference between the FSIQ and the GAI is equal to or larger than the critical value, the difference is considered a true difference rather than a difference due to measurement error or random fluctuation. If the two scores are not significantly different, this implies that reducing the influence of working memory and processing speed on the estimate of overall ability resulted in little difference.

If comparison of the FSIQ and the GAI indicates a significant difference, the practitioner should then judge how rare the difference is in the general population. Table 3 provides the cumulative frequency of discrepancies between the FSIQ and the GAI in the WISC-IV standardization sample (base rates). The base rate provides a basis for estimating how rare or common a child's obtained score difference is compared to the general population. Table 4 provides the cumulative frequency of discrepancies between the FSIQ and the GAI in various WISC-IV special group samples. Refer to Wechsler (2003b) for additional information.

ABILITY–ACHIEVEMENT DISCREPANCY

When an AAD criterion is part of the learning disability determination process, practitioners must select one of two methods for comparing intellectual ability and academic achievement: the predicted-difference method and the simple-difference method. Although both methods are used, the predicted-difference method is generally preferred because the formula accounts for the reliabilities and the correlations between the two measures. Use of the predicted-difference method requires that the ability and achievement measures were co-normed on the same national sample. The predicted-difference method uses the ability score to predict an achievement score and then compares the predicted and observed achievement scores. The simple-difference method merely compares the observed ability and achievement scores. The *WIAT-II Examiner's Manual* (Harcourt Assessment, Inc., 2002) provides additional details related to the rationale for choosing these methods and the statistical procedures involved.

PREDICTED-DIFFERENCE METHOD

Table 5 provides WIAT-II subtest and composite scores predicted from WISC-IV GAI scores. Locate the GAI score in the extreme left or right column and read across the row to obtain the child's predicted WIAT-II subtest and composite scores. Record the predicted scores. For each subtest or composite, subtract the child's predicted score from the obtained score to obtain the difference score. Record these difference scores.

The practitioner must take into account the statistical significance and the base rate of the difference scores. Table 6 provides the required differences between the predicted and obtained WIAT-II subtest and composite scores to attain statistical significance (critical values) at the .05 and .01 levels for two age groups (ages 6:0–11:11 and ages 12:0–16:11). Select the desired level of statistical significance and note it for your records. Using Table 6, find the age group of the child and the desired level of significance. For each subtest or composite, read across the row to the appropriate column to determine the critical value and record it. The absolute value of the child's difference

TABLE 5   WIAT–II Subtest and Composite Scores Predicted from WISC–IV GAI Scores

WISC-IV GAI	WIAT-II														WISC-IV GAI
	Subtest Scores									Composite Scores					
	WR	NO	RC	SP	PD	MR	WE	LC	OE	RD	MA	WL	OL	TA	
40	56	60	55	59	64	54	60	52	66	54	55	57	54	49	40
41	56	60	56	59	65	55	61	53	67	55	56	58	55	50	41
42	57	61	57	60	65	56	62	54	68	55	57	58	55	51	42
43	58	62	57	61	66	57	62	54	68	56	57	59	56	52	43
44	59	62	58	61	66	57	63	55	69	57	58	60	57	52	44
45	59	63	59	62	67	58	64	56	69	58	59	60	58	53	45
46	60	64	60	63	68	59	64	57	70	58	60	61	58	54	46
47	61	64	60	63	68	60	65	58	70	59	60	62	59	55	47
48	62	65	61	64	69	60	66	58	71	60	61	63	60	56	48
49	62	66	62	65	69	61	66	59	71	61	62	63	61	57	49
50	63	67	63	66	70	62	67	60	72	62	63	64	62	58	50
51	64	67	63	66	71	63	68	61	73	62	63	65	62	58	51
52	64	68	64	67	71	64	68	62	73	63	64	65	63	59	52
53	65	69	65	68	72	64	69	62	74	64	65	66	64	60	53
54	66	69	66	68	72	65	70	63	74	65	66	67	65	61	54
55	67	70	66	69	73	66	70	64	75	65	66	68	65	62	55
56	67	71	67	70	74	67	71	65	75	66	67	68	66	63	56
57	68	71	68	70	74	67	72	66	76	67	68	69	67	63	57
58	69	72	69	71	75	68	72	66	76	68	69	70	68	64	58
59	70	73	69	72	75	69	73	67	77	68	69	70	68	65	59
60	70	73	70	72	76	70	74	68	78	69	70	71	69	66	60
61	71	74	71	73	77	70	74	69	78	70	71	72	70	67	61
62	72	75	72	74	77	71	75	70	79	71	72	73	71	68	62
63	73	75	72	74	78	72	76	70	79	72	72	73	72	69	63
64	73	76	73	75	78	73	76	71	80	72	73	74	72	69	64
65	74	77	74	76	79	73	77	72	80	73	74	75	73	70	65
66	75	77	75	77	80	74	78	73	81	74	75	76	74	71	66
67	76	78	75	77	80	75	78	74	82	75	75	76	75	72	67
68	76	79	76	78	81	76	79	74	82	75	76	77	75	73	68
69	77	79	77	79	81	76	80	75	83	76	77	78	76	74	69
70	78	80	78	79	82	77	80	76	83	77	78	78	77	75	70
71	79	81	78	80	83	78	81	77	84	78	78	79	78	75	71
72	79	81	79	81	83	79	82	78	84	78	79	80	78	76	72
73	80	82	80	81	84	79	82	78	85	79	80	81	79	77	73
74	81	83	81	82	84	80	83	79	85	80	81	81	80	78	74
75	82	83	81	83	85	81	84	80	86	81	81	82	81	79	75
76	82	84	82	83	86	82	84	81	87	82	82	83	82	80	76
77	83	85	83	84	86	83	85	82	87	82	83	83	82	80	77
78	84	85	84	85	87	83	85	82	88	83	84	84	83	81	78
79	84	86	84	86	87	84	86	83	88	84	84	85	84	82	79
80	85	87	85	86	88	85	87	84	89	85	85	86	85	83	80

(Continues)

TABLE 5   *(Continued)*

	WIAT-II														
	Subtest Scores									Composite Scores					
WISC-IV GAI	WR	NO	RC	SP	PD	MR	WE	LC	OE	RD	MA	WL	OL	TA	WISC-IV GAI
81	86	87	86	87	89	86	87	85	89	85	86	86	85	84	81
82	87	88	87	88	89	86	88	86	90	86	87	87	86	85	82
83	87	89	87	88	90	87	89	86	90	87	87	88	87	86	83
84	88	89	88	89	90	88	89	87	91	88	88	88	88	86	84
85	89	90	89	90	91	89	90	88	92	88	89	89	88	87	85
86	90	91	90	90	92	89	91	89	92	89	90	90	89	88	86
87	90	91	90	91	92	90	91	90	93	90	90	91	90	89	87
88	91	92	91	92	93	91	92	90	93	91	91	91	91	90	88
89	92	93	92	92	93	92	93	91	94	92	92	92	92	91	89
90	93	93	93	93	94	92	93	92	94	92	93	93	92	92	90
91	93	94	93	94	95	93	94	93	95	93	93	94	93	92	91
92	94	95	94	94	95	94	95	94	96	94	94	94	94	93	92
93	95	95	95	95	96	95	95	94	96	95	95	95	95	94	93
94	96	96	96	96	96	95	96	95	97	95	96	96	95	95	94
95	96	97	96	97	97	96	97	96	97	96	96	96	96	96	95
96	97	97	97	97	98	97	97	97	98	97	97	97	97	97	96
97	98	98	98	98	98	98	98	98	98	98	98	98	98	97	97
98	99	99	99	99	99	98	99	98	99	98	99	99	98	98	98
99	99	99	99	99	99	99	99	99	99	99	99	99	99	99	99
100	100	100	100	100	100	100	100	100	100	100	100	100	100	100	100
101	101	101	101	101	101	101	101	101	101	101	101	101	101	101	101
102	101	101	102	101	101	102	101	102	101	102	102	101	102	102	102
103	102	102	102	102	102	102	102	102	102	102	102	102	102	103	103
104	103	103	103	103	102	103	103	103	102	103	103	103	103	103	104
105	104	103	104	103	103	104	103	104	103	104	104	104	104	104	105
106	104	104	105	104	104	105	104	105	103	105	105	104	105	105	106
107	105	105	105	105	104	105	105	106	104	105	105	105	105	106	107
108	106	105	106	106	105	106	105	106	104	106	106	106	106	107	108
109	107	106	107	106	105	107	106	107	105	107	107	106	107	108	109
110	107	107	108	107	106	108	107	108	106	108	108	107	108	109	110
111	108	107	108	108	107	108	107	109	106	108	108	108	108	109	111
112	109	108	109	108	107	109	108	110	107	109	109	109	109	110	112
113	110	109	110	109	108	110	109	110	107	110	110	109	110	111	113
114	110	109	111	110	108	111	109	111	108	111	111	110	111	112	114
115	111	110	111	110	109	111	110	112	108	112	111	111	112	113	115
116	112	111	112	111	110	112	111	113	109	112	112	112	112	114	116
117	113	111	113	112	110	113	111	114	110	113	113	112	113	114	117
118	113	112	114	112	111	114	112	114	110	114	114	113	114	115	118
119	114	113	114	113	111	114	113	115	111	115	114	114	115	116	119
120	115	113	115	114	112	115	113	116	111	115	115	114	115	117	120
121	116	114	116	114	113	116	114	117	112	116	116	115	116	118	121
122	116	115	117	115	113	117	115	118	112	117	117	116	117	119	122
123	117	115	117	116	114	117	115	118	113	118	117	117	118	120	123

(Continues)

TABLE 5 *(Continued)*

WIAT-II

WISC-IV GAI	WR	NO	RC	SP	PD	MR	WE	LC	OE	RD	MA	WL	OL	TA	WISC-IV GAI
124	118	116	118	117	114	118	116	119	113	118	118	117	118	120	124
125	119	117	119	117	115	119	117	120	114	119	119	118	119	121	125
126	119	117	120	118	116	120	117	121	115	120	120	119	120	122	126
127	120	118	120	119	116	121	118	122	115	121	120	119	121	123	127
128	121	119	121	119	117	121	118	122	116	122	121	120	122	124	128
129	121	119	122	120	117	122	119	123	116	122	122	121	122	125	129
130	122	120	123	121	118	123	120	124	117	123	123	122	123	126	130
131	123	121	123	121	119	124	120	125	117	124	123	122	124	126	131
132	124	121	124	122	119	124	121	126	118	125	124	123	125	127	132
133	124	122	125	123	120	125	122	126	118	125	125	124	125	128	133
134	125	123	126	123	120	126	122	127	119	126	126	124	126	129	134
135	126	123	126	124	121	127	123	128	120	127	126	125	127	130	135
136	127	124	127	125	122	127	124	129	120	128	127	126	128	131	136
137	127	125	128	126	122	128	124	130	121	128	128	127	128	131	137
138	128	125	129	126	123	129	125	130	121	129	129	127	129	132	138
139	129	126	129	127	123	130	126	131	122	130	129	128	130	133	139
140	130	127	130	128	124	130	126	132	122	131	130	129	131	134	140
141	130	127	131	128	125	131	127	133	123	132	131	130	132	135	141
142	131	128	132	129	125	132	128	134	124	132	132	130	132	136	142
143	132	129	132	130	126	133	128	134	124	133	132	131	133	137	143
144	133	129	133	130	126	133	129	135	125	134	133	132	134	137	144
145	133	130	134	131	127	134	130	136	125	135	134	132	135	138	145
146	134	131	135	132	128	135	130	137	126	135	135	133	135	139	146
147	135	131	135	132	128	136	131	138	126	136	135	134	136	140	147
148	136	132	136	133	129	136	132	138	127	137	136	135	137	141	148
149	136	133	137	134	129	137	132	139	127	138	137	135	138	142	149
150	137	134	138	135	130	138	133	140	128	139	138	136	139	143	150
151	138	134	138	135	131	139	134	141	129	139	138	137	139	143	151
152	138	135	139	136	131	140	134	142	129	140	139	137	140	144	152
153	139	136	140	137	132	140	135	142	130	141	140	138	141	145	153
154	140	136	141	137	132	141	136	143	130	142	141	139	142	146	154
155	141	137	141	138	133	142	136	144	131	142	141	140	142	147	155
156	141	138	142	139	134	143	137	145	131	143	142	140	143	148	156
157	142	138	143	139	134	143	138	146	132	144	143	141	144	148	157
158	143	139	144	140	135	144	138	146	132	145	144	142	145	149	158
159	144	140	144	141	135	145	139	147	133	145	144	142	145	150	159
160	144	140	145	141	136	146	140	148	134	146	145	143	146	151	160

Note. WR = Word Reading; NO = Numerical Operations; RC = Reading Comprehension; SP = Spelling; PD = Pseudoword Decoding; MR = Math Reasoning; WE = Written Expression; LC = Listening Comprehension; OE = Oral Expression; RD = Reading; MA = Mathematics; WL = Written Language; OL = Oral Language; TA = Total Achievement. *Wechsler Intelligence Scale for Children – Fourth Edition (WISC-IV).* Copyright © 2003 by Harcourt Assessment, Inc. Reproduced with permission. All rights reserved.

score must equal or exceed that critical value to be statistically significant. Determine whether the absolute value of the child's difference score equals or exceeds the corresponding critical value.

If comparison of the predicted and obtained WIAT-II subtest and composite scores indicates a significant difference, the practitioner should then judge how rare the difference is in the general population. Table 7 provides the cumulative frequency of discrepancies between predicted and obtained WIAT-II subtest and composite scores in the WISC-IV standardization sample (base rate). Locate the subtest or composite of interest in the extreme left column and read across the row to locate the child's difference score. The column header above the child's difference score indicates the percentage of the theoretical normal distribution (base rates) that represents the percent-

TABLE 6   Differences between Predicted and Obtained WIAT-II Subtest and Composite Scores Required for Statistical Significance (Critical Values): Predicted-Difference Method Using WISC-IV GAI

Subtest/Composite	Significance Level	Ages 6–11	Ages 12–16
Word Reading	.05	5	7
	.01	6	9
Numerical Operations	.05	12	9
	.01	16	11
Reading Comprehension	.05	7	8
	.01	9	10
Spelling	.05	8	8
	.01	11	11
Pseudoword Decoding	.05	5	6
	.01	7	8
Math Reasoning	.05	9	9
	.01	12	12
Written Expression	.05	11	12
	.01	15	15
Listening Comprehension	.05	13	13
	.01	17	18
Oral Expression	.05	10	12
	.01	13	15
Reading	.05	5	6
	.01	7	7
Mathematics	.05	9	7
	.01	12	9
Written Language	.05	8	11
	.01	11	14
Oral Language	.05	10	9
	.01	13	11
Total	.05	6	6
	.01	8	8

TABLE 7   Differences between Predicted and Obtained WIAT-II Subtest and Composite Scores for Various Percentages of the Theoretical Normal Distribution (Base Rates): Predicted-Difference Method Using WISC-IV GAI

	Percentage of Theoretical Normal Distribution (Base Rates)								
Subtest/Composite	25	20	15	10	5	4	3	2	1
Word Reading	7	9	11	13	17	18	19	21	24
Numerical Operations	8	10	12	15	19	20	21	23	26
Reading Comprehension	7	9	11	13	17	18	19	21	24
Spelling	8	10	12	14	18	20	21	23	26
Pseudoword Decoding	9	11	13	16	20	22	23	25	28
Math Reasoning	7	9	11	13	17	18	19	21	23
Written Expression	8	10	12	15	19	20	22	24	27
Listening Comprehension	7	8	10	12	15	16	17	19	21
Oral Expression	9	11	13	16	21	22	24	26	29
Reading	7	9	10	13	16	17	19	20	23
Mathematics	7	9	11	13	17	18	19	21	24
Written Language	8	9	11	14	18	19	20	22	25
Oral Language	7	9	10	13	16	17	19	20	23
Total	6	7	9	11	13	14	15	17	19

Note. Percentages represent the theoretical proportion of WIAT-II scores lower than WISC-IV GAI scores by the specified amount or more. *Wechsler Intelligence Scale for Children – Fourth Edition (WISC-IV).* Copyright © 2003 by Harcourt Assessment, Inc. Reproduced with permission. All rights reserved.

age of the sample that obtained WIAT-II scores lower than their WISC-IV GAI scores by the specified amount or more.

SIMPLE-DIFFERENCE METHOD

Table 8 provides the required differences between WISC-IV GAI scores and WIAT-II subtest and composite scores to attain statistical significance (critical values) at the .05 and .01 levels for two age groups (ages 6:0–11:11 and ages 12:0–16:11). Select the desired level of statistical significance and note it for your records. Using Table 8, find the age group of the child and the desired level of significance. For each subtest or composite, read across the row to the appropriate column to determine the critical value and record it. The absolute value of the child's difference score must equal or exceed that critical value to be statistically significant. Determine whether the absolute value of the child's difference score equals or exceeds the corresponding critical value.

If comparison of the WISC-IV GAI score and the WIAT-II subtest and composite scores indicates a significant difference, the practitioner should then judge how rare the difference is in the general population. Table 9

TABLE 8   Differences between WISC-IV GAI Scores and WIAT-II Subtest and Composite Scores Required for Statistical Significance (Critical Values): Simple-Difference Method by Age Group

Subtest/Composite	Significance Level	Ages 6–11 GAI	Ages 12–16 GAI
Word Reading	.05	7	8
	.01	9	11
Numerical Operations	.05	13	10
	.01	17	13
Reading Comprehension	.05	8	9
	.01	11	12
Spelling	.05	10	10
	.01	13	13
Pseudoword Decoding	.05	8	8
	.01	10	10
Math Reasoning	.05	10	10
	.01	13	13
Written Expression	.05	12	12
	.01	16	16
Listening Comprehension	.05	14	14
	.01	18	19
Oral Expression	.05	12	13
	.01	15	17
Reading	.05	7	7
	.01	9	9
Mathematics	.05	10	8
	.01	13	11
Written Language	.05	10	12
	.01	13	15
Oral Language	.05	11	10
	.01	14	13
Total	.05	8	7
	.01	10	9

Wechsler Intelligence Scale for Children – Fourth Edition (WISC-IV). Copyright © 2003 by Harcourt Assessment, Inc. Reproduced with permission. All rights reserved.

provides the cumulative frequency of discrepancies between WISC-IV GAI and WIAT-II subtest and composite scores in the WISC-IV standardization sample (base rates). Locate the subtest or composite of interest in the extreme left column and read across the row to locate the child's difference score. The column header above the child's difference score indicates the percentage of the theoretical normal distribution (base rate) that represents the percentage of the sample that obtained WIAT-II scores lower than their WISC-IV GAI scores by the specified amount or more.

SUMMARY AND CONCLUSIONS

This chapter presented evidence for the robustness of "g" as an organizing theme in intellectual assessments, describing a long history of empirical

TABLE 9   Differences between WISC-IV GAI Scores and WIAT-II Subtest and Composite Scores for Various Percentages of the Theoretical Normal Distribution (Base Rates): Simple-Difference Method

Subtest/Composite	Percentage of Theoretical Normal Distribution (Base Rates)								
	25	20	15	10	5	4	3	2	1
Word Reading	8	10	12	14	18	19	21	23	26
Numerical Operations	9	11	13	16	21	22	23	26	29
Reading Comprehension	8	9	11	14	18	19	20	22	25
Spelling	8	10	13	16	20	21	23	25	28
Pseudoword Decoding	10	12	14	18	23	24	26	28	32
Math Reasoning	8	9	11	14	18	19	20	22	25
Written Expression	9	11	13	16	21	22	24	26	29
Listening Comprehension	7	8	10	13	16	17	18	20	23
Oral Expression	10	12	15	19	24	25	27	29	33
Reading	7	9	11	14	17	18	20	21	24
Mathematics	8	9	11	14	18	19	20	22	25
Written Language	8	10	12	15	19	20	22	24	27
Oral Language	7	9	11	14	17	18	20	21	24
Total	6	7	9	11	14	15	16	17	20

Note. Percentages represent the theoretical proportion of WIAT-II scores lower than WISC-IV GAI scores by the specified amount or more. *Wechsler Intelligence Scale for Children – Fourth Edition (WISC-IV).* Copyright © 2003 by Harcourt Assessment, Inc. Reproduced with permission. All rights reserved.

support in terms of factor analytic research and in predicting a variety of important life outcomes, including success in many academic and occupational endeavors. With the introduction of additional working memory and processing speed tasks into the WISC-IV, the clinical sensitivity of the FSIQ to psychoeducational and neuropsychological conditions has increased. At the same time, the discrepancy between overall ability and achievement may decrease when assessing children with various learning disorders precisely as a result of this increased psychodiagnostic utility. For these reasons, the GAI was introduced as an alternative summary score that excludes the working memory and processing speed subtests. A brief history of the GAI derived from the WISC-III and WISC-IV was described. We have reprinted normative tables for determining the GAI and also tables for use of the WISC-IV GAI with WIAT-II in AAD analyses. However, practitioners are cautioned not to consider GAI as a short form of WISC-IV because it omits essential components of effective cognitive functioning (i.e., working memory and processing speed).

Controversies in the use of the AAD model are also considered. The presence of a significant AAD signals that some problem is likely present (e.g., slow learning, inadequate instruction, learning disability, or other behavioral/emotional problems affecting academic performance negatively). While AAD alone is not sufficient to diagnose the nature of the problem, it is presently sufficient to qualify the student to receive special educational assistance in almost all school districts. Much of the remainder of this book is devoted to going beyond a single number—whether that is the FSIQ or GAI—toward more clinically sophisticated methodologies of assessment, including interpretive considerations of the four index scores and the process approach incorporated into the WISC-IV Integrated. The next chapter delves deeper into the clinical meaning of the four WISC-IV index scores, with particular emphasis on the WMI and the PSI.

REFERENCES

Bar–On, R. (1997). *BarOn Emotional Quotient–Inventory*. San Antonio, TX: Harcourt Assessment, Inc.

Berninger, V. W., & O'Donnell, L. (2005). Research-supported differential diagnosis of specific learning disabilities. In A. Prifitera, D. H. Saklofske, & L. G. Weiss (Eds.), *WISC-IV clinical use and interpretation: Scientist-practitioner perspectives* (pp. 189–233). San Diego, CA: Elsevier.

Berninger, V. W., Dunn, A., & Alper, T. (2005). Integrated multilevel model for branching assessment, instructional assessment, and profile assessment. In A. Prifitera, D. H. Saklofske, & L. G. Weiss (Eds.), *WISC-IV clinical use and interpretation: Scientist-practitioner perspectives* (pp. 151–185). San Diego, CA: Elsevier.

Boake, C. (2002). From the Binet-Simon to the Wechsler–Bellevue: Tracing the history of intelligence testing. *Journal of Clinical and Experimental Neuropsychology, 24,* 383–405.

Carroll, J. B. (1993). *Human cognitive abilities: A survey of factor-analytic studies*. New York: Cambridge University Press

Cohen, M. (1997). *Children's Memory Scale*. San Antonio, TX: Harcourt Assessment, Inc.

Colom, R., Rebollo, I., Palacios, A., Juan-Espinosa, M., & Kyllonen, P. C. (2004). Working memory is (almost) perfectly predicted by g. *Intelligence, 32,* 277–296.

Deary, I. J. (2001). *Intelligence: A very short introduction*. Oxford: Oxford University Press.

Dumont, R., & Willis, J. (2004). *Use of the Tellegen and Briggs formula to determine the Dumont-Willis Indexes for the WISC–IV*. Retrieved December 1, 2004 from http://alpha.fdu.edu/psychology/WISCIV_DWI.htm

Elliot, C. D. (1990). *Differential ability scales*. San Antonio, TX: Harcourt Assessment, Inc.

Engle, R. W., Laughlin, J. E., Tuholski, S. W., & Conway, A. R. A. (1999). Working memory, short-term memory, and general fluid intelligence: A latent-variable approach. *Journal of Experimental Psychology: General, 128,* 309–331.

Flanagan, D. P., & Kaufman, A. S. (2004). *Essentials of WISC–IV assessment*. Hoboken, NJ: Wiley.

Fletcher, J. M., & Reschly, D. J. (2005). Changing procedures for identifying learning disabilities: The danger of perpetuating old ideas. *The School Psychologist, 59,* 10–15.

Francis, D. J., Fletcher, J. M., Steubing, K. K., Lyon, G. R., Shaywitz, B. A., & Shaywitz, S. E. (2005). Psychometric approaches to the identification of LD. *Journal of Learning Disabilities, 38,* 98–108.

Fry, A. F., & Hale, S. (1996). Processing speed, working memory, and fluid intelligence: Evidence for a developmental cascade. *Psychological Science, 7,* 237–241.

Fry, A. F., & Hale, S. (2000). Relationships among processing speed, working memory, and fluid intelligence in children. *Biological Psychology, 54,* 1–34.

Georgas, J. Weiss, L. G., van de Vijver, F., & Saklofske, D. H. (2003). *Culture and children's intelligence: A cross-cultural analysis of the WISC–III.* Amsterdam: Elsevier Science.

Gottfredson, L. S. (1997). Why *g* matters: The complexity of everyday life. *Intelligence, 24,* 79–132.

Gottfredson, L. S. (1998). The general intelligence factor. *Scientific American Presents, 9,* 24–29.

Hale, J. B., Naglieri, J. A., Kaufman, A. S., & Kavale, K. A. (2004). Specific learning disability classification in the new Individuals with Disabilities Education Act: The danger of good ideas. *The School Psychologist, 58,* 6–13, 29.

Harcourt Assessment Inc. (2002). *Wechsler individual achievement test–Second edition.* San Antonio, TX: Author.

Harris, J. G., Tulsky, D. S., & Schultheis, M. T. (2003). Assessment of the non-native English speaker: Assimilating history and research findings to guide clinical practice. In D.S Tulsky et al. (Eds.), *Clinical interpretation of the WAIS-III and WMS-III.* (pp. 343–390). San Diego: Academic Press.

Harrison, P. L., & Oakland, T. (2003). *Adaptive behavior assessment system–Second edition.* San Antonio, TX: Harcourt Assessment, Inc.

Heinz-Martin, S., Oberauer, K., Wittmann, W. W., Wilhelm, O., & Schulze, R. (2002). Working-memory capacity explains reasoning ability—and a little bit more. *Intelligence, 30,* 261–288.

Hunsley (2003). Introduction to the special section on incremental validity and utility in clinical assessment. *Psychological Assessment, 15,* 443–445.

Individuals with Disabilities Education Act Amendments of 1991, Pub. L. No. 102–150, 105, Sta. 587 (1992).

Individuals with Disabilities Education Act Amendments of 1997, 20 U.S.C. 1400 *et seq.* (Fed. Reg. 64, 1999).

Individuals with Disabilities Education Improvement Act of 2004, Pub. L. No. 108–446, 118 Stat. 328 (2004).

Ives, B. (2003). Effect size use in studies of learning disabilities. *Journal of Learning Disabilities, 36,* 490–504.

Kaufman, A. S. (1994). *Intelligent testing with the WISC-III.* New York: Wiley.

Kaufman, A. S., & Kaufman, N. (1998). *Kaufman test of educational achievement– Second edition.* Circle Pines, MN: American Guidance Service, Inc.

Kuncel, N. R., & Hezlett, S. A. (2004). Academic performance, career potential, creativity, and job performance: Can one construct predict them all? *Journal of Personality and Social Psychology, 86,* 148–161.

Mackintosh, N. J., & Bennett, E. S. (2003). The fractionation of working memory maps onto different components of intelligence. *Intelligence, 31,* 519–531.

McCloskey, G., & Maerlender, A. (2005). The WISC-IV Integrated. In A. Prifitera, D. H. Saklofske, & L. G. Weiss (Eds.), *WISC-IV clinical use and interpretation: Scientist-practitioner perspectives* (pp. 102–150). San Diego, CA: Elsevier.

Meyer, G. J., Finn, S. E., Eyde, L. D., Kay, G. G. Moreland, K. L., Dies, R. R., Eisman, E. J., Kubiszyn, T. W., & Reed, G. M. (2001). Psychological testing and psychological assessment: A review of evidence and issues. *American Psychologist, 56,* 128–165.

Miller, L. T., & Vernon, P. A. (1996). Intelligence, reaction time, and working memory in 4- to 6-year-old children. *Intelligence, 22,* 155–190.

Naglieri , J. A., & Das, J. P. (1997). *Cognitive assessment system.* Itasca, IL: Riverside.

Neisser, U., Boodoo, G., Bouchard, T. J., Jr., Boykin, A. W., Brody, N., Ceci, S. J., Halpern, D. F., Loehlin, J.C. Perloff, R., Sternberg, R. J., & Urbina, S. (1996). Intelligence: Knowns and unknowns. *American Psychologist, 51,* 77–101.

Pfeiffer, S., & Jarosewich, T. (2003a). *Gifted rating scales*. San Antonio, TX: Harcourt Assessment, Inc.

Pfeiffer, S., & Jarosewich, T. (2003b). *Gifted rating scales: School-age form*. San Antonio, TX: Harcourt Assessment, Inc.

Prifitera, A., Saklofske, D. H., & Weiss, L. G. (Eds.) (2005). *WISC-IV clinical use and interpretation: Scientist–practitioner perspectives*. San Diego, CA: Elsevier.

Prifitera, A., Weiss, L. G., & Saklofske, D. H. (1998). The WISC-III in context. In A. Prifitera & D. H. Saklofske (Eds.), *WISC-III clinical use and interpretation: Scientist–practitioner perspectives* (pp. 1–38). New York: Academic Press.

Raiford, S. E., Weiss, L. G., Rolfhus, E., & Coalson, D. (2005). *General ability index* (WISC–IV Technical Report No. 4). Retrieved July 5, 2005, from http://harcourtassessment.com/ hai/ Images/pdf/wisciv/ WISCIVTechReport4.pdf

Roid, G. H. (2003). *Stanford-Binet Intelligence Scales–Fifth edition*. Itasca, IL: Riverside.

Saklofske, D. H. (1996). Using WISC-III Canadian study results in academic research. In D. Wechsler (Ed.), *WISC–III manual Canadian supplement* (pp. 5–13). Toronto, ON: The Psychological Corporation.

Saklofske, D. H., Gorsuch, R. L., Weiss, L. G., Zhu, J. J., & Patterson, C. A. (2005). General ability index for the WAIS–III: Canadian norms. *Canadian Journal of Behavioural Science, 37*, 44–48.

Saklofske, D. H., Prifitera, A., Weiss, L. G., Rolfhus, E., & Zhu, J. (2005). Clinical interpretation of the WISC–IV FSIQ and GAI. In A. Prifitera, D. H. Saklofske, & L. G. Weiss (Eds.), *WISC-IV clinical use and interpretation: Scientist–practitioner perspectives* (pp. 33–65). San Diego, CA: Elsevier.

Saklofske, D. H., Zhu, J., Raiford, S. E., Weiss, L. G., Rolfhus, E., & Coalson, D. (2005). *General ability index: Canadian norms* (WISC–IV Technical Report No. 4.1). Retrieved July 5, 2005, from http://harcourtassessment.com/hai/Images/pdf/wisciv/ WISC-IV_4.1_Re1.pdf

Sattler J. M. (2001). *Assessment of children: Cognitive applications* (4th ed.). San Diego, CA: Author.

Sattler, J. M., & Dumont, R. (2004). *Assessment of children: WISC-IV and WPPSI-III Supplement*. San Diego, CA: Author.

Sattler, J. M., & Saklofske, D. H. (2001a). Wechsler intelligence scale for children–III (WISC-III): Description. In J. M. Sattler (Ed.), *Assessment of children: Cognitive applications* (4th ed.) (pp. 220–265). San Diego, CA: Author.

Sattler, J. M., & Saklofske, D. H. (2001b). Interpreting the WISC–III. In J. M. Sattler (Ed.), *Assessment of children: Cognitive applications* (4th ed.) (pp. 298–334). San Diego, CA: Author

Schweizer, K., & Moosbrugger, H. (2004). Attention and working memory as predictors of intelligence. *Intelligence, 32*, 329–347.

Scruggs, T. E., & Mastropieri, M. A. (2002). On babies and bathwater: Addressing the problems of identification of learning disabilities. *Learning Disability Quarterly, 25*, 155–168.

Siegel, L. S. (2003). IQ–discrepancy definitions and the diagnosis of LD: Introduction to the special issue. *Journal of Learning Disabilities, 31*, 2–3.

Tellegen, A., & Briggs, P. (1967). Old wine in new skins: Grouping Wechsler subtests into new scales. *Journal of Consulting Psychology, 31*, 499–506.

The Psychological Corporation. (2001) *Manual for the Wechsler individual achievement test– Second edition*. San Antonio, TX: Author.

Tulsky, D. S., Saklofske, D. H., Wilkins, C., & Weiss, L. G. (2001). Development of a general ability index for the Wechsler Adult Intelligence Scale–Third edition. *Psychological Assessment, 13*, 566–571.

Tulsky, D. S., Saklofske, D. H., & Ricker, J. H. (2003). Historical overview of intelligence and memory: Factors influencing the Wechsler scales. In D. S. Tulsky D. H. Saklofske et al.

(Eds.), *Clinical interpretation of the WAIS-III and WMS-III* (pp. 7–41). San Diego, CA: Elsevier.

Vigil-Colet, A., & Codorniu-Raga, M. J. (2002). How inspection time and paper and pencil measures of processing speed are related to intelligence. *Personality and Individual Differences, 33*, 1149–1161.

Wechsler, D. (1944). *The measurement of adult intelligence.* Baltimore: Williams & Wilkins.

Wechsler, D. (1949). *Wechsler intelligence scale for children.* New York: The Psychological Corporation.

Wechsler, D. (1974). *Wechsler intelligence scale for children–Revised.* San Antonio, TX: The Psychological Corporation.

Wechsler, D. (1991). *Wechsler intelligence scale for children–Third edition.* San Antonio, TX: The Psychological Corporation.

Wechsler, D. (1997). *Technical manual for the Wechsler adult intelligence scale–Third edition and the Wechsler memory scale–Third edition.* San Antonio, TX: Harcourt Assessment, Inc.

Wechsler, D. (1999). *Wechsler abbreviated scale of intelligence.* San Antonio, TX: Harcourt Assessment, Inc.

Wechsler, D. (2002). *Wechsler preschool and primary scale of intelligence–Third edition.* San Antonio, TX: Harcourt Assessment, Inc.

Wechsler, D. (2003a). *Administration and scoring manual for the Wechsler intelligence scale for children–Fourth edition.* San Antonio, TX: Harcourt Assessment, Inc.

Wechsler, D. (2003b). *Technical and interpretive manual for the Wechsler intelligence scale for children–Fourth edition.* San Antonio, TX: Harcourt Assessment, Inc.

Wechsler, D. (2003c). *Wechsler intelligence scale for children–Fourth edition.* San Antonio, TX: Harcourt Assessment, Inc.

Wechsler, D., Kaplan, E., Fein, D., Kramer, J., Delis, D., & Morris, R. (1999). *Manual for the Wechsler intelligence scale for children–Third edition as a process instrument.* San Antonio, TX: The Psychological Corporation.

Wechsler, D., Kaplan, E., Fein, D., Kramer, J., Morris, R., Delis, D., & Maerlender, A. (2004a). *Wechsler intelligence scale for children–Fourth edition integrated technical and interpretative manual.* San Antonio, TX: Harcourt Assessment, Inc.

Wechsler, D., Kaplan, E., Fein, D., Kramer, J., Morris, R., Delis, D., & Maerlender, A. (2004b). *Wechsler intelligence scale for children–Fourth edition–integrated.* San Antonio, TX: Harcourt Assessment, Inc.

Weiss, L. G., Prifitera, A., & Dersh, J. (1995). *Base rates of WISC-III verbal-performance discrepancies in Hispanic and African American children.* Unpublished manuscript.

Weiss, L. G., Saklofske, D. H., Prifitera, A., Chen, H. Y., & Hildebrand, D. K. (1999). The calculation of the WISC-III general ability index using Canadian norms. *The Canadian Journal of School Psychology, 14*, 1–9.

Weiss, L. G., Saklofske, D. H., & Prifitera, A. (2003). Clinical interpretation of the WISC-III factor scores. In C. R. Reynolds & R. W Kamphaus (Eds.), *Handbook of psychological and educational assessment of children: Intelligence and achievement (2nd ed.).* New York: Guilford Press.

Weiss, L. G., Saklofske, D. H., & Prifitera, A. (2005). Interpreting the WISC-IV index scores. In A. Prifitera, D. H. Saklofske, & L. G. Weiss (Eds.), *WISC-IV clinical use and interpretation: Scientist–practitioner perspectives* (pp. 72–100). San Diego, CA: Elsevier.

Wilkinson, G. S. (1993). *Wide range achievement test–Third edition.* Lutz, FL: Psychological Assessment Resources, Inc.

Williams, P. E., Weiss, L. G., & Rolfhus, E. (2003a). *Theoretical model and test blueprint* (WISC–IV Technical Report No. 1). Retrieved July 5, 2005, from http://harcourtassessment.com/hai/Images/pdf/wisciv/WISCIVTechReport1.pdf

Williams, P. E., Weiss, L. G., & Rolfhus, E. (2003b). *Psychometric properties* (WISC-IV Technical Report No. 2). Retrieved July 5, 2005, from http://harcourtassessment.com/hai/Images/pdf/wisciv/WISCIVTechReport2.pdf

Williams, P. E., Weiss, L. G., & Rolfhus, E. (2003c). *Clinical validity* (WISC–IV Technical Report No. 3). Retrieved July 5, 2005, from http://harcourtassessment.com/hai/Images/pdf/wisciv/WISCIVTechReport3.pdf

Woodcock, R. W., McGrew, K. S., & Mather, N. (2001). *The Woodcock-Johnson–Third edition.* Itasca, IL: Riverside.

4

ADVANCED CLINICAL INTERPRETATION OF WISC-IV INDEX SCORES

LAWRENCE G. WEISS, DONALD H. SAKLOFSKE,
DAVID M. SCHWARTZ, AURELIO PRIFITERA,
AND TROY COURVILLE

- *Tracey's WISC-IV profile is very scattered. There were significant differences among three of the index scores that call into question the meaningfulness of the full-scale IQ (FSIQ). However, our director says that this score is needed in order to secure additional funding for this student.*
- *Wally's teachers have commented on his variable performance across school subjects since entering school 3 years ago. While some earlier test results reporting a summary IQ score indicated that he may have the overall cognitive ability to cope with a regular program, results of the current assessment suggest that the more relevant focus of his school learning and achievement difficulties may be found in the significant and rarely occurring score differences among his high average Verbal Comprehension Index (VCI), low average Perceptual Reasoning Index (PRI) and Working Memory Index (WMI), and borderline scores on the Processing Speed Index (PSI).*

While the traditional procedure for investigating and reporting a child's WISC-IV profile may begin at the full-scale level and then proceed with an analysis of the index and subtest scores, invariably there are times when this is not the "best practice" to follow. In Chapter 2, we argued that the index scores should be regarded as the primary level of interpretation. In fact, in some, if not many, referral cases, extreme discrepancies among scores are the more common finding and may thus render less useful a higher level interpretation such as the FSIQ. In large part this is a psychometric question that can best be addressed by employing the various tables in the WISC-IV manual to determine the cohesiveness or disparity within score groupings at the subtest, index, and FSIQ (GAI) levels. To determine if the FSIQ and GAI scores are good summaries of general mental ability, the investigation should begin concurrently at both the subtest and the index score level and build up to the global interpretations. For example and as discussed in Chapter 2, index score discrepancies of 20 or more points may render the FSIQ less meaningful as an overall summary of intellectual ability. In this case, the FSIQ does not meaningfully communicate the full range of the child's cognitive abilities.

This chapter focuses on the role of the four WISC-IV index scores in understanding the cognitive abilities of children referred for clinical evaluation. It also describes the interactive nature of the index scores and considers the clinical richness of the subtests that comprise them. Finally, we shall return to an issue initially raised in Chapter 2 that examines the controversial area of the relevance of intelligence tests in the assessment of learning disabilities.

FLAT VS DISCREPANT WISC-IV INDEX PROFILES

The large and uncommon discrepancies among index scores may provide the most clinically interesting and useful information of relevance to the assessment protocol. In cases of intellectual giftedness or moderate to severe mental retardation, we can expect more of a relatively flat profile and a summary or FSIQ score can certainly be used to describe this finding. As well, similar subtest and index scores of a child with a FSIQ of 107 certainly allows the psychologist to describe this child as having average ability and further manifesting average VCI, PRI, WMI, and PSI. This would then shift the hypotheses related to poor school performance to other noncognitive factors such as work and study skills, personality, motivation, learning style, and the teaching–learning–social environment of the classroom. However, in other cases, such as recent lateralized brain trauma, the presence of a large discrepancy between, for example, VCI and PRI may be very meaningful and should be the focus for interpreting cognitive abilities.

Thus it is prudent to take the position that the presence of large discrepancies makes interpretation of the child's intellectual functioning more difficult and complex (Saklofske, Prifitera, Weiss, Rolfhus, & Zhu, 2005). This occurrence then points to the need to shift test interpretation to the index score level where the most clinically relevant information is more likely to be found. Clearly this is a strength of the WISC-IV. Similarly though, any factor-based score such as the PSI essentially "disintegrates" when, for example, a scaled score of 15 is obtained for Symbol Search versus 7 for Coding. This is more likely to be an issue with WMI and PSI because there are only two subtests that define each index. Significant score differences among all three of the VCI or PRI subtests or between the subtests and the mean for that scale are clear indicators that the composite measure does not provide an "average" indication of the child's ability in that domain. Instead of focusing on a less meaningful summary score, efforts should be directed to determining the clinical relevance of the subtest findings using the clinical clusters described in Chapter 2 and also the process analyses described in Chapters 5 and 6, assuming the test was administered and scored properly, the testing conditions were adequate, and the examinee was both motivated and seemed to understand the task demands. Lower scores on Block Design (BD) versus Matrix Reasoning (MR) might result from differences in the task demands. In contrast to MR, which is not unlike a multiple choice question, BD requires the actual construction of simple to complex two-dimensional designs using three-dimensional blocks. Once the investigation is accomplished in this detailed, bottom-up manner, the report may then be written in the more traditional top-down manner, whether it begins with the FSIQ or index scores.

- *Mary completed the Block Design and Matrix Reasoning tasks quickly and efficiently in contrast to teacher reports describing her disorganization and confusion with new tasks and her inability to form and use effective problem-solving strategies.*
- *Given his serious hearing impairment since an early age, I would "hypothesize" that Tom's verbal test scores will likely be lower than his nonverbal scores and that the best description of his cognitive abilities is to present these scores separately.*

Before moving on to a discussion of the index scores, we should like to revisit a point strongly reflected throughout our earlier book (Prifitera, Saklofske, & Weiss, 2005) and in Chapter 1 of this book. While the psychometric properties (e.g., reliability, validity, test standardization and norms) of the WISC-IV should give us confidence in the scores as numerical descriptions of intelligence, the clinical relevance of the scores must be determined by the psychologist who examines these scores "in context". Investigation of WISC-IV scores, at all levels, should be conducted within an ecological context. Interpretations of score patterns may vary depending on the sociocultural background (Georgas, Weiss, van de Vijver, & Saklofske, 2003; Harris & Llorente, 2005; Weiss et al., Chapter 1), family values, pattern of academic strengths and weaknesses, motivation, and psychiatric and medical history or even due to behaviors that occur and can be observed during the test session (Sattler, 2001; Oakland, Glutting, & Watkins, 2005). A common mistake is to offer stock interpretations of WISC-IV score patterns while ignoring the effects of these mediating influences (see Kamphaus, 1998). Thus while an FSIQ of 112 by itself suggests high average ability, an ADHD child with clearly observable hyperactivity and impulsivity and with a superior VCI and low average WMI will certainly present differently in the classroom than another "typical" child with a flat profile of subtest and index scores yielding an FSIQ of 110. As well, all psychologists have had numerous opportunities to observe children perform contrary to expectations on the WISC-IV; in fact this is the basis for conducting ability–achievement discrepancy analyses. Not only will interpretations differ in relation to the examinees' personal context and history, but the examiners' expectations of the likeliness of finding certain patterns will be influenced by the referral information.

The top-down and bottom-up approach can be used in an interactive or reciprocal way to explore various clinical interpretations. Thus while the FSIQ can be a clinically meaningful summary of a child's overall cognitive functioning, an examination of the "parts" can also provide meaning and insight to the assessment process. For example, Arithmetic (AR) is now a supplemental test on the WMI, but it may be very useful in assessing the effects or impact of more basic working memory difficulties. Both Digit Span Backward and Letter-Number Sequencing (LNS) are excellent measures of auditory working memory but are relatively artificial tasks. However, the AR subtest has an element of authentic assessment or ecological validity because it is one of the common essential learnings in elementary school and has everyday practical utility in the real world. Thus if a child has low scores on all three WM subtests, this may be further evidence that WM is a significant factor underlying his poor school performance rather than a specific arithmetic/mathematics difficulty as we might observe if DS and LNS were in the 10–12 range but the AR score was 6. Kamphaus (2001) stated that an anticipated or hypothesized pattern of strengths and weaknesses based on such factors, which are subsequently observed in test data, leads to a more meaningful and valid interpretation than the same pattern identified through a "buckshot" approach of comparing all possible test scores.

There has clearly been a change in emphasis in the Wechsler tests from measuring FSIQ to one that focuses on the key index scores of VC, PR, WM, and PS. This change brings the WISC-IV more in line with the psychologist's current need for a test that has implications for description, diagnosis, and prescription. The next sections focus on the WISC-IV index scores, expanding on Weiss, Saklofske, and Prifitera (2005).

WISC-IV INDEX SCORES

- *While Peter's FSIQ does tend to suggest borderline ability, his PSI and PRI scores fall in the average range, with some subtests comprising these factors, suggesting high average ability. Thus Peter would appear to have both average ability and relative strengths in nonverbal visual spatial and perceptual reasoning. In contrast, verbal comprehension and working memory appear to be less well developed. He did not appear to have well-automatized verbal skills and demonstrated much less interest and effort toward those subtests that required a verbal response or that reflected crystallized knowledge and language development.*

A major shift from the WISC-III to the WISC-IV is that the index scores have become the primary level of clinical interpretation. The domains measured by the four indices are robust clinical constructs with strong psychometric properties. As well, both similarities and differences among the factor-based index scores are clinically important and worthy of study. While the interpretation of subtest scores and the qualitative analysis of the unique response patterns the child utilizes in approaching each task are important, they are addressed more directly in the next two chapters focusing on the WISC-IV Integrated (Wechsler, Kaplan, Fein, Kramer, Delis, Morris, & Maerlender, 2004).

Interpretation begins by comparing each index score with averages of the four index scores to determine relative strengths and weaknesses, as described in Chapter 2. If background and referral information lead the examiner to an a priori hypothesis about the relationship between two particular indexes, then this planned comparison may be conducted directly using tables found in appendix B of the *WISC-IV Administration and Scoring Manual.*

What follows is a basic description focusing on the interpretation of the WISC-IV index scores. Since so much more has been written on the VCI and PRI (POI) beginning with WISC-III and WAIS-III (e.g., Weiss, Saklofske, & Prifitera, 2003; Sattler & Dumont, 2004), we give greater coverage to the WMI and PSI. We again remind psychologists that while an understanding of the abilities being tapped by the index and subtest scores is fundamental to using this test, these scores must also be placed in the larger context of each child and their "world."

INTERPRETING THE WISC-IV VERBAL COMPREHENSION INDEX

- *Tim appears to have a sizable vocabulary and can recite learned facts but does not appear to reason effectively using words and language. This is also quite obvious in more authentic and everyday tasks that require, for example, comprehending the meaning of stories read in class and in analogical thinking. This is corroborated further by his WISC-IV subtest scores for Vocabulary (12) and Information (11) in contrast to Similarities (6), Comprehension (9), and Word Reasoning (8).*

"The VCI is composed of subtests measuring verbal abilities utilizing reasoning, comprehension, and conceptualization..." (Wechsler, 2003, p. 6). To determine if the VCI should be interpreted as a single index score, the basic strategy is to compare each VCI subtest-scaled score to the mean of the child's VCI subtest-scaled scores and evaluate the significance and frequency of any observed differences using Table B.5 in the *WISC-IV Administration and Scoring Manual*. To understand the complexity but also the common elements of the VCI, we turn to a brief description of the subtests that comprise it. Readers are also referred to Sattler and Dumont (2004) and Flanagan and Kaufman (2004).

The Information (IN) subtest, primarily a measure of crystallized knowledge, is now supplemental, and a new supplemental subtest called Word Reasoning (WR) was created to assess reasoning with words. However, reasoning with verbal material almost always involves some level of crystallized knowledge as a prerequisite. The Vocabulary (VOC) subtest requires that the meaning of a word was learned, can be recalled, and expressed coherently. There is no apparent demand to reason in this subtest; it is essentially the case that one "knows" the word. However, VOC is one of the highest "g" loaded subtests and one of the best predictors of overall intelligence. Perhaps this is because higher order thinking requires that more pieces of related information are chunked into a coherent whole for quicker processing. Individuals with larger vocabularies can chunk larger concepts into a single word and while they may also have enjoyed a more enriched cognitive environment, they must also be able to apply their knowledge appropriately. Use of advanced vocabulary words in conversation also requires the individual to comprehend nuances of the situation accurately, which requires a higher level of abstract reasoning. However, the conventional view is that a strong vocabulary is simply an indication of a high degree of crystallized knowledge. While word recognition and semantic understanding, memory and retrieval, as well as expressive language skills, are all involved, the VOC and IN subtests draw primarily from the child's knowledge base.

The Similarities (SI) subtest asks how two words representing objects or concepts are alike. The concepts must have been acquired and stored in long-term memory and the child must be able to access that knowledge from semantic memory upon demand. Once these words are recalled, the child can begin the reasoning process to determine how they are similar. This reasoning process appears to take place within a transitory working memory space, and the ability to reason may be related to working memory capacity and the efficiency with which ideas are processed in working memory before the trace fades (see later). Similar issues are at play with WR and Comprehension (CO).

The SI, CO, and WR subtests require a higher level of reasoning for successful performance than the VOC and IN subtests. Children with deficits in crystallized knowledge and/or retrieval from long-term memory of previously acquired information may score higher on SM, CO, and WR than on VC and IN if they have adequate verbal reasoning ability. Conversely, children with an age-appropriate knowledge base that is readily accessible but who have deficits in higher order categorization of abstract verbal concepts may show the reverse score pattern. In these cases, it may then also be instructive to compare performance on SM with Picture Concepts (PCn). Both subtests require categorization of abstract verbal concepts, but PCn does not require that the child explain his or her thinking verbally. Thus, children with good abstract reasoning skills but poor verbal expression may perform better on PCn than on SM.

Recall that a low score on an intelligence test such as the WISC-IV may reflect low ability, a lack of opportunity to develop particular abilities, or some kind of "interference" that compromises the acquisition or expression of particular abilities (e.g., a learning disability, ADHD, auditory or visual impairment). Prior to making an interpretation of low verbal ability, the psychologist should also ask if the knowledge was encoded but cannot now be recalled (for several possible reasons) or was it never acquired in the first place? The methodology for addressing this issue is the "recognition paradigm." All of the WISC-IV VC subtests involve free recall, which is a much more difficult cognitive task than cued recognition. The WISC-IV Integrated, described in Chapters 5 and 6, provides a recognition format (i.e., multiple choice versions) of the core WISC-IV Verbal Comprehension subtests. Children who answered incorrectly because they could not retrieve the information from long-term storage will recognize the correct information in the multiple choice paradigm more readily. In this way, the examiner can explore if the incorrect responses were a function of lack of knowledge or lack of access to knowledge learned and stored previously in the semantic lexicon. Clearly, this makes a critical difference in interpretation. The first author clearly recalls a young girl who was referred because initial assessments and poor school performance suggested mental retardation (initial WISC-III FSIQ in the 50–60 range). Upon retesting, her VOC score was 3, but on the Integrated, her multiple choice VC score was 8 and her picture vocabulary score was 12. Together with other clinical data, it became clear that mental retardation was not the basis for her poor classroom achievement.

INTERPRETING THE WISC-IV
PERCEPTUAL REASONING INDEX

- *Tracey has a history of a somewhat variable pattern of school achievement. A recently administered WISC-IV shows that VC, PS, and WM scores were all in the average range but that she obtained a superior score of 129 on PRI.*

The construct measured by the PRI composite has changed from primarily perceptual organization with some fluid reasoning in WISC-III to primarily fluid reasoning with some perceptual organization in WISC-IV (Wechsler, 2003). Picture Arrangement (PA) and Object Assembly (OA) were removed from the test to make room for the new fluid reasoning subtests, and Picture Completion (PCm) was made supplemental. Along with BD, two new subtests were added, MR and Picture Concepts (PCn), which primarily tap fluid reasoning. BD and MR also involve an element of perceptual organization, whereas PCn requires little perceptual organization. Overall, this composite invokes less visual spatial skills and more nonverbal fluid reasoning, although PCn may invoke verbal mediation.

Comparison of each PRI subtest to the child's mean subtest score can be accomplished with Table B.5 of the *WISC-IV Administration and Scoring Manual*. When neither the VCI subtests nor the PRI subtests are significant strengths or weaknesses in the profile of index scores, comparison of the VCI and PRI subtests should be against the mean of the 10 core subtests. If either VCI or PRI is significantly different from the mean of the four index scores and the magnitude of the difference is rare, then the comparison of VCI and PRI subtests should be conducted with the relevant VCI and PRI means. Again, basic interpretations of individual PR subtests have been well documented elsewhere (Sattler & Dumont, 2004; Flanagan & Kaufman, 2004) and are not repeated here.

Users of the WISC-III and WISC-R will recall the major role that speed played in determining a child's PIQ. While speed of processing has been identified as a most important component of intelligence, this does present a problem for psychologists when the tests that they use "confound" speed and some other factor such as perceptual reasoning. Does a lower score mean that the child is lacking in, say, nonverbal spatial reasoning or is it because the child is able to "solve" the problems (e.g., BD) but does so more methodically and with a lot of checking of responses? One of the authors recalls an old high school friend who seldom ever finished a test in math or chemistry. Usually the friend would get through 80–90 % of the test but always got a mark that was 80–90! In contrast, the author would finish the test in record time, but his marks shall remain a secret. Let us just say that the author seldom earned more than 80–90%!

Concerns have been raised in the past about the negative impact of time bonuses on performance subtests with gifted and talented students and with various minority populations. Changes to the WISC-IV relative to time have reduced this concern. PA and OA, both timed subtests, have been omitted from the WISC-IV. The BD subtest may now be scored with and without time bonuses. Only the score with time bonuses is used in the calculation of PRI and FSIQ. The impact of speed on the child's performance can be determined by comparing performance in these two conditions. Contrary to popular belief, there is very little difference in children's scaled scores on BD with and without time bonuses. As shown in Table B.10 of the *WISC-IV Administration and Scoring Manual*, even a difference of two scaled score points between BD with and without time bonuses occurred in less then 10% of the standardization sample.

Again, the WISC-IV Integrated, discussed in Chapters 5 and 6, is likely to prove most useful to psychologists in their efforts to "understand" atypical WISC-IV PRI scores. The Integrated includes a multiple choice version of the BD subtest to help parse out those children whose low BD scores are due to the possible influence of motor demands on the children's performance. For children with BD < BDMC discrepancies, it is possible that performance on block design was limited by the children's ability to construct the design rather than difficulties with perceptual integration. Higher scores on BD than BDMC (i.e., BD > BDMC) may occur for a number of reasons. Children with visual discrimination problems may fail to appreciate subtle differences among the distracters within the response options. There are no such competing visual stimuli in the Block Design subtest. Impulsive children may select a response without fully considering or scanning all response options.

This is an opportune spot to briefly mention the relationship of other cognitive functions on WISC-IV scores and again to link the WISC-IV and WISC-IV Integrated. Organization, planning, and other executive functions can impact performance on various WISC-IV subtests. Executive functions are a domain of cognitive skills that comprise many discrete abilities that influence higher order reasoning. Elithorn Mazes (EM) focus narrowly on immediate planning, self-monitoring, and ability to inhibit impulsive responding, thus allowing for a preliminary evaluation of some of these important executive functioning influences. The child's performance on MR and BDMC may be compared directly to EM. The BDMC–EM comparison enables clinicians to rule out deficits in basic visual identification and discrimination that may impact performance on Elithorn mazes. EM < BDMC may indicate that visual–perceptual processes do not account for poor performance on EM and may indicate that poor spatial planning is affecting performance. Visual scanning and processing speed may also account for this disparate performance and need to be evaluated further. EM > BDMC may indicate intact planning ability despite difficulties with visual discrimination and integration. EM < MR suggests better developed visual discrimination and reasoning abilities than spatial planning. Difficulties with motor control and processing speed may also account for this difference and need to be investigated directly. EM > MR suggests well-developed spatial planning abilities, visual–spatial sequencing, and execution; however, difficulties with detailed visual discrimination and reasoning may be present.

INTERPRETING THE WISC-IV WORKING MEMORY INDEX

- *Mary has such difficulty remembering things that we have been working on in class. I know she is paying attention and her records show that she has earned average scores on group intelligence tests. She just can't seem to keep the information in her mind long enough to use it.*

- *Barry's teacher reports that he seems confused when engaging in more complex mental tasks. For example, he can solve a printed arithmetic problem, especially if he is using paper and pencil, but if the same question is presented to him orally, he appears to forget parts, asks questions about what he should be doing, and generally just gets lost. Of interest is that his score on the WMI was significantly lower than the average of the four WISC-IV index scores. Furthermore, Barry required additional repetition and asked for clarification, especially on VCI subtests that placed increasing cognitive demands on his short- and long-term memory and included a required reasoning in comparison to recall (e.g., Similarities, Comprehension).*

The WMI is "composed of subtests measuring attention, concentration, and working memory" (Wechsler, 2003, p. 6). This composite is composed of Digit Span and letter-number sequencing, with arithmetic as supplemental. The debate over the retention of the arithmetic subtest has subsided to some extent because subtle changes to the word problems have reduced the auditory processing component of the task and its verbal factor loadings. Working memory is the ability to hold information in mind temporarily (storage buffers) while performing some operation or manipulation (e.g., rehearsal processes) with that information or engaging in an interfering task and then reproducing the information accurately or acting on it correctly. Working memory can be thought of as mental control (executive processes) involving reasonably higher order tasks (rather than rote tasks), and it presumes attention and concentration. Thus, the WMI measures the complex ability or latent trait relevant to sustaining attention, concentration, and exerting mental control. "Working memory is a system that can store a small amount of information briefly, keeping that information quickly accessible and available for transformation by rule and strategies, while updating it frequently" (Jonides, Lacey, & Nee, 2005, p. 2).

Baddeley (2003) developed a model that is seminal in the area of working memory. He proposes a phonological loop and a visual–spatial sketch pad in which verbal and visual stimuli, respectively, are stored and refreshed and a central executive that controls attention is directed toward these sources. A fourth component of the model known as the *episodic buffer* has also been included in this model. This buffer is assumed to be controlled attentionally by the central executive and to be accessible to conscious awareness. Baddeley (2003) regards the episodic buffer as a crucial feature of the capacity of working memory to act as a global workspace that is accessed by conscious awareness. When working memory requires information from long-term storage, it may be "downloaded" into the episodic buffer rather than simply activated within long-term memory.

Models of working memory and their neural underpinnings (Jonides, Lacey, & Nee, 2005) are still being actively researched and refined, and the associated terminology will continue to evolve for some time. The term *registration* is used to convey the process by which stimuli are taken in and maintained in immediate memory. The capacity for registering information in immediate memory can be measured by the length of the person's immediate forward span. *Mental manipulation* implies a transformation of information active in immediate memory, involving higher order cognitive resources. The precise point in this process at which working memory resources are invoked is debatable. While attending to, storing, and repeating a license plate number may appear to only involve short-term visual (or auditory) memory, the role of working memory may enter the picture when there is interference from other sources, when a mnemonic is employed to assist in remembering the content and order, or when the observer is also now asked to describe the car, the direction it was going, and so on. Thus these processes may be more of a continuum, as the point at which one moves from passive registration of auditory stimuli to active strategies for maintenance is not always clear, as shown next.

DS and LNS are the two primary WISC-IV tasks designed to tap working memory. An advantage of the WISC-IV is that DS may be treated as a composite score but also as two separate scores when examining both short-term auditory memory and auditory working memory. Digit Span Forward (DSF) requires initial registration of the verbal stimuli—a prerequisite for mental manipulation of the stimuli. In some cases, DSF also requires auditory rehearsal to maintain the memory trace until the item presentation is concluded. To the extent that longer spans of digits require the application of a method for maintaining the trace, such as rehearsal or chunking, then some degree of mental manipulation of the stimuli is also involved. The point in the DSF item set at which this is required will vary as a function of age and ability level and the response processes utilized by the examinee. In Digit Span Backward (DSB), the child must hold a string of numbers in short-term memory (STM) store while reversing the given sequence and then reproduce the numbers in the new order correctly. This is a clear example of mental manipulation. However again, developmental level and other cognitive factors, such as general mental ability and processing speed, may vary the role played by working memory. For example, short spans of digits backward may tax working memory resources only marginally in older or brighter children. Again, the point at which these children substantially invoke working memory resources on DSB will vary by age and ability. Tables B.7 and B.8 of the *WISC-IV Administration and Scoring Manual* provide base rate comparisons for DSF and DSB by age.

INCLUDING ARITHMETIC IN THE ASSESSMENT OF WM

The Arithmetic (AR) subtest is a more ecologically valid working memory task than digit span backward. We are frequently called upon to mentally calculate arithmetic problems in real life situations. Some examples include estimating driving time, halving a cake recipe, and changing U.S. to Canadian dollars to Mexican pesos. For students who have not learned grade level skills related to arithmetic calculation and mathematical operations or students with a primary mathematical disability, the AR subtest may not be an accurate indication of working memory. The AR subtest assesses a complex set of cognitive skills and abilities, and a low score may have several appropriate interpretations depending on the clinical context. For example, a child with low scores on all three subtests (DS, LN, AR) is more likely to have a problem with WM than the child who earns average or above scores on DS and LN but below average scores on AR. In the latter instance, the issue may be more one of not having learned the arithmetic skills called for or having a specific learning difficulty related to arithmetic and mathematics. Alternatively, a child who earns a higher score on Arithmetic than either or both of the compulsory WM subtests may also find the Arithmetic task to be more grounded in real life, e.g., " I do arithmetic everyday in school" (McCloskey & Maerlender, 2005). For this reason, we encourage psychologists to administer the three WM subtests if there is a question about either WM or arithmetic skills. In anticipation of the next two chapters, it will become clear that the WISC-IV integrated is intended to assist the clinician in determining the role of WM in lower performance on these subtests. Variations in the presentation format (i.e., process approach) for AR but also LN should assist the psychologist in diagnosing problems of WM.

PSYCHOMETRIC CONSIDERATIONS IN INTERPRETING THE WMI

As alluded to elsewhere in this chapter, FSIQ is a meaningful summary of the test results when the child's various cognitive abilities are intact and the profile is essentially flat. However, many referred children exhibit substantial variation across the domains of cognitive ability tapped by the WISC-IV. When large discrepancies occur between index scores, the profile is clinically rich with potentially meaningful interpretations.

Similarly, interpretation of the WMI, like all other WISC-IV index scores, presumes that it reflects an intact construct for the child being evaluated. If the DS and LNS subtest-scaled scores are very different from each other, then the WMI score can only represent the "arithmetic average" of two widely divergent sets of abilities and would therefore have little intrinsic or clinical meaning as a composite score. These two subtests load on the same factor in factor analyses of the WISC-IV, yet correlate only moderately ($r=.49$ across ages). As a result, divergent scores are certainly possible and a difference may signal that there are potentially meaningful interpretations at the subtest level. Table B.4 of the *WISC-IV Administration and Scoring Manual* shows percentages of the standardization sample obtaining various DS–LN discrepancies. Less then 10% of the sample obtained a five-point difference or greater in either direction. Further, it would be clinically inappropriate to report that a child's working memory is in the average range when the DS and LN subtest-scaled scores are 12 and 7, respectively, a difference of five points. A five or more point difference between DS and LN subtests strongly suggests that these subtests should be interpreted independently.

WMI AND DIAGNOSIS

Do low WM scores in the presence of average VC and PR scores suggest that the child has an LD or ADHD?

Clearly, a serious deficit in working memory can have major implications in the academic life of a student and create difficulties in daily life functioning as well as in many vocational settings. The role of WM has been implicated in learning and attention disorders. Groups of children diagnosed with LD or ADHD are more likely to obtain lower average scores on working memory. Schwean and Saklofske (2005) summarized the results of several studies of children with ADHD suggesting that these children tended to earn their lowest scores on the WM composite. This finding was also replicated in clinical group studies reported in the WISC-III and WISC-IV technical manuals (Wechsler, 1991, 2003). Similar results are noted for children with LD, and the robustness of this finding has been extended to the Canadian WISC-IV with WM producing the largest mean difference (i.e., effect size) between LD and matched control groups. However, caution must always be applied when using group data to make inferences about individuals. The WISC-IV was never intended to be diagnostic of ADHD or LD nor can it be, given their complexity. Such nomothetic descriptions should rather be used as another "indicator" supporting or not the eventual diagnosis of LD or any other condition in which cognition is implicated. Thus we are clearly advocating that diagnosis is of an individual and that test score findings from the WISC-IV or any other assessment battery be demonstrated to be relevant to each individual rather than being assumed to apply to all children with a particular diagnosis or being used as a diagnostic "marker" (see Kaufman, 1994).

Children with serious deficits in working memory are challenged academically, but not necessarily because of lower intelligence. A weakness in working memory may make the processing of complex information more time-consuming and tax the student's mental energies more quickly compared to other children of the same age, perhaps contributing to more frequent errors on a variety of learning tasks. Executive function system deficits in planning, organization, and the ability to shift cognitive sets should also be evaluated with these children. In addition, examiners should be alert to the social and behavioral consequences of mental fatigue and school failure that can ensue from these disorders and assess the level of parental support and emotional resiliency possessed by the child carefully.

EXPANDING THE ASSESSMENT OF WM USING A PROCESS APPROACH

Working memory does not involve only numbers, as reflected in the arithmetic subtest of DS. Other examples include writing the main points of a teacher's lecture in a notebook while continuing to attend to the lecture or keeping in mind the next points you want to make in a conversation while explaining your first point. It should also be remembered that all three of the WM subtests described earlier tap only verbal (auditory) working memory and not spatial or visual working memory. The WISC-IV Integrated also includes a Spatial Span subtest. This is a working memory task in the visual domain. It includes both registration (forward immediate span) and mental manipulation (backward span). Score differences between Spatial Span and Digit Span, Letter-Number Sequencing, or Arithmetic may reflect individual differences in visual versus auditory working memory abilities. The Spatial Span subtests are described more fully elsewhere in this book.

Another variation of a WISC-IV WM subtest is the WISC-IV Integrated LNS processing approach (LNPA) subtest. It is a variation of the core letter–number sequencing subtest in which the scored trials contain embedded words in the presented sequence of letters and numbers. Children with well-developed executive control processes and adequate orthographic abilities are likely to perceive the embedded words and use this knowledge to focus additional working memory resources on the sorting and reordering of numbers and letters. Cognitively rigid children may experience difficulty disassociating the letters from the word, which is often required to reorder the letters properly. Low LNPA scores may be related to difficulties with auditory working memory, registration, discrimination, attention, sequencing, spelling ability, or material specific weaknesses in auditory encoding, either numeric or alphabetic (Weiss, Saklofske, & Prifitera, 2005). Finally, the WISC-IV Integrated process approach may assist the psychologist in parsing out low performance in AR by systematically reducing the working memory load. Variations include presenting the items with the word problem remaining in view and in allowing the use of a pencil and paper. Working memory demand is reduced further by examining performance on these process approach tasks with and without time bonuses. Finally, the child may be given a set of number (not word) problems to solve with paper and pencil to determine the extent of any deficits in numerical skills. Thus, the examiner has a range of observed behaviors from which to generate meaningful recommendations about teacher-generated modifications to lesson and test formats that may facilitate academic performance in the classroom.

INTERPRETING THE WISC-IV
PROCESSING SPEED INDEX

- *Bryan is a relatively bright child but appears to be an underachiever because of a lack of environmental stimulation and early learning opportunities. His lowest scores on the VC subtests reflect limitations in crystallized abilities, including acquired knowledge, in contrast to his average scores on PS and WM. Most outstanding were his scores on the PS subtests, suggesting that his speed of mental operations, especially for tasks requiring visual–motor coordination and discrimination, as well as short-term visual memory, is very well developed and a strength relative to his peer group and his own personal abilities.*

The PSI is "composed of subtests measuring the speed of mental and graphomotor processing" (Wechsler, 2003, p. 6). These three subtests provide a good sampling of a factor that has more recently been clearly implicated in a description of intelligence. Horn's (1998) intelligence model includes two (of nine) factors labeled decision speed and processing speed, whereas Carroll's factor analyses of a huge volume of intelligence data show two second stratum factors similarly labeled broad cognitive speediness and processing or decision speed. The significant role of mental speed has been implicated in studies of cognition and aging. Salthouse (1996a,b, 2000a,b) argued that the decline observed in general mental ability with age is, in the main, due to a slowing of mental processing speed. In fact, removing the effects of mental speed on intelligence test scores also removes the largest effects that have been linked to age. Thus speed of mental processing would appear to be more than simply doing a task at a faster or slower rate but in itself is a key cognitive and individual differences variable.

In contrast to reaction time measures, the PSI subtests included in tests such as the WISC-IV are relatively simple visual scanning tasks for most children. However, it would be a mistake to think of the PSI as a measure of simple clerical functions that are not relevant or related to intelligence. While PSI is listed last in representations of Wechsler factor structures as a matter of convention, it actually emerges third in most factor analyses and accounts for greater variance in intelligence than the working memory factor. Consistent evidence shows that both simple and choice reaction times correlate about .20 or slightly higher with scores from intelligence tests, whereas inspection time (hypothesized by some to be a measure of the rate that information is processed) correlates about .40 with intelligence test scores (see Deary, 2001; Deary & Stough, 1996).

As defined operationally on the WISC-IV, the PSI is an indication of the rapidity with which a child processes simple or routine information without making errors of either omission or commission. Many learning tasks involve information processing that is both routine (such as reading) and complex (such as reasoning). Slowness in the speed of processing routine information may make the task of comprehending novel information more time-consuming and consequently more difficult. A weakness in simple visual scanning and tracking may leave a child less time and mental energy for the complex task of understanding new material. Thus processing speed interacts in a critical way with other higher order cognitive functions and may impact general cognitive functioning and everyday learning and performance (Weiss, Saklofske, & Prifitera, 2005).

The Coding (CD), Symbol Search (SS), and Cancellation (CA) subtests at first glance would appear to be little more than simple visual scanning and tracking tasks. A direct test of speed and accuracy, the CD subtest assesses the child's ability to scan and sequence simple visual information quickly and correctly. Performance on this subtest may also be influenced by short-term visual memory, attention, or visual–motor coordination. Thus while a low score does raise the question of processing speed, it may also be influenced by motor problems. Children presenting with spastic muscles in the hand and arm or who hold a pencil in a rigid and tense way will likely complete fewer items on the CD subtest, but this does imply a problem with processing speed. However, a very perfectionistic and obsessive-compulsive child may also earn lower scores on CD, again not due to a processing speed deficit but rather because of a personality disposition.

The SS subtest requires the student to inspect several sets of symbols and indicate if special target symbols appeared in each set. It is also a direct test of speed and accuracy and assesses scanning speed and sequential tracking of simple visual information. Performance on this subtest may be influenced by visual discrimination and visual–motor coordination. Here again we caution the psychologist to use their observation skills and also ensure that the findings from the WISC-IV corroborate or are supported by other "clinically relevant" findings. For example, an ADHD child who rushes through this task will likely make sufficient errors that will lower the SS score. Again this is not due to processing speed but rather impulsivity. The new supplemental Cancellation subtest also requires these skills and a minor degree of decision-making. Examinees must decide if each stimulus is a member of the target class of stimuli (e.g., animals). While the decisions are generally simple, the psychologist must again take care not to underestimate the cognitive load for the youngest children, especially those without preschool experience or who are developmentally delayed.

It has been observed that processing speed abilities more often tend to be lower than reasoning abilities among students who are experiencing academic difficulties in the classroom (Wechsler, 1991, 2003). Schwean and

Saklofske (2005) have summarized research studies with the WISC-III, indicating that children with ADHD earn their lowest scores on the PSI. This finding was replicated with WISC-IV clinical studies showing that ADHD and comorbid ADHD-LD children tend to score relatively lower on PS than VC or PR. It may be hypothesized that children with processing speed deficits may learn less material in the same amount of time or take longer to learn the same amount of material compared to those without processing speed deficits. These children may also mentally tire more easily because of the additional cognitive effort required to perform routine tasks. In other words, slow PS taxes the entire cognitive network, especially when there are time constraints imposed, such as 45–minute classes. In turn, this could lead to more frequent errors, less time spent studying, and possible expressions of frustration. When speed of processing information is at least in the average range or a relative strength for a child, this may facilitate the acquisition of new information.

PSYCHOMETRIC ISSUES IN INTERPRETING THE PSI

- *Wayne's WISC-IV profile does not allow the calculation and meaningful interpretation of the PSI. While he earned an above average score of 12 on SS, his CD score of 6 was well below average and significantly lower than his SS.*

A major issue for psychologists that comes to the fore on both PS and WM factors is the problem of "fractured" factors. Using only two subtests to define a factor is certainly parsimonious and does show, as is also the case with the three subtest VC and PR index scores, how psychometrically sophisticated we have become in measuring such complex cognitive constructs. However, when there are only two subtests and they differ significantly, the psychologist must look deeper than the index score to apply meaning to the results. Thus, if the CD and SS subtest-scaled scores are very different from each other, then the PSI score may have little intrinsic meaning and should not be interpreted as a unitary construct reflecting speed of processing. In fact it would not be informative or accurate to report a summary score. Published tables (see Sattler & Dumont, 2005) portray the common and unique "parts" shared by various subtests. It becomes clear that even subtests comprising a single factor have considerable unique or nonshared variance and may therefore show considerable score differences because of this. For example, SS is a relatively simple visual scan test that requires a minimum of graphomotor demand in relation to CD, which has more demanding visual search, memory, and copying components that could be significant factors in understanding score differences. It should not come as a great surprise that any "small" factor (i.e., composed of only two subtests) may not hold together. While there are various noncognitive reasons why two subtests that load on and define a factor may differ, the very fact that CD and SS correlate moderately ($r=.53$) suggests a shared processing speed component and also some unique variance. Table B.4 of the *WISC-IV Administration and Scoring Manual* shows percentages of the standardization sample obtaining various Coding–Symbol Search discrepancies. As before, we continue to recommend that a difference of 5 or more points between CD and SS should raise strong concerns about interpreting the PSI as a unitary construct. Only 11.2% of the sample obtained a 5-point difference or greater in either direction. A difference between these two subtests of only 3.5 points is significant at the $p<.05$ level (see Table B.3 of the *WISC-IV Administration and Scoring Manual*). If the difference between Coding and Symbol Search is 5 points or greater, then these two subtests are best interpreted separately.

Because CA is a new task but also supplementary, it may be less well understood with respect to its role in more in-depth interpretation of the processing speed tasks. Cancellation Random (CAR) and Cancellation Structured (CAS) process scores represent the child's ability to scan both a random and a structured arrangement of visual stimuli for target objects (i.e., animals). Cancellation tasks have been used extensively in neuro-psychological settings as measures of visual selective attention, visual neg-lect, response inhibition, and motor perseveration (Adair et al., 1998; Lezak, 1995; Na, Adair, Kang, Chung, Lee, & Heilman, 1999). In contrast to other versions, the WISC-IV Cancellation subtest requires the child to determine if visual stimuli belong to a target category (i.e., animals). Thus, the child may also employ visual–lexical associations to discriminate between target and distracter stimuli.

Children with high CAR and CAS process scores are likely to demon-strate rapid visual scanning ability, effective response inhibition, and organ-ized visual search patterns. Low CAR and CAS process scores may be related to slow visual scanning or visual–motor abilities, poor response inhibition, disorganized search patterns, or difficulties with visual discrim-ination. In addition the child's visual–lexical associations (i.e., ability to categorize objects correctly) may be slow or incorrect. For both random and structured cancellation tasks, some children naturally invoke a search strategy to organize their visual scanning of the page. Presumably, an organized strategy allows for more efficient identification of target objects. The structured condition lends itself to an organized search strategy more readily than the random condition. Many children will follow the inherent structure of the rows to search for targets; however, some children will engage in a disorganized search despite the inherent task structure.

The CAR and CAS process scores should assist in characterizing the child's search strategy. For each score, the psychologist assigns a letter (i.e., A, B, C, or D) to describe and classify the child's search strategy into one of four categories. Search strategy A is characterized by a search pattern that remains organized throughout item administration. Strategy B represents a pattern that began organized, but became disorganized as the child progressed. Conversely, beginning the task using a disorganized search pattern and then adopting an organized pattern would reflect search strategy C. Visual search patterns that remain disorganized throughout item administration are assigned search strategy D. Examples of each search strategy are provided in the scoring instructions for the Cancellation subtest in the *WISC-IV Integrated Administration and Scoring Manual*. Table D.23 of the *WISC-IV Integrated Administration and Scoring Manual* provides base rate information from the standardization sample by age group. As data from this table indicate, the use of search strategy A increases with age, whereas the use of search strategy D decreases with age. A majority of children in most age groups have some degree of disorganization in their search pattern; the most common search pattern in the standardization sample was search strategy C. Comparison of the CAR and CAS process scores provides information about how the child's performance on Cancellation varies with the arrangement of visual stimuli. A CAR < CAS discrepancy suggests that the child benefits from the structured presentation format. The child's search strategies could also be examined to provide additional information to confirm or refute hypotheses regarding the influence of structure on cancellation performance.

Clinical studies reported in the *WISC-IV Technical and Interpretive Manual* suggest that subjects in the ADHD sample may have benefited from the structure in the CAS because they obtained higher scaled scores on CAS than CAR. In contrast, children with mental retardation may have been unable to benefit from the additional structure provided in CAS to the same degree as their peers, and therefore obtained lower scores on CAS than CAR. The gifted sample scored essentially the same on CAR and CAS, suggesting that they may be able to apply an effective search strategy regardless of the condition. Thus the relevance of structure in relation to processing speed may certainly vary across groups of children defined by both general cognitive ability and clinical conditions.

SYNERGIES AMONG COGNITIVE ABILITIES

- *Tom's weakness in working memory may make the processing of complex information more time-consuming, draining his mental energies more quickly compared to other children his age, perhaps resulting in more frequent errors on a variety of learning tasks.*

Prifitera et al. (2005) described the interaction and relationship between WM and PS index scores on the WISC-IV, which are now discussed.

The VC and PR subtests have the highest "g" loadings on the WISC-IV and on all of the Wechsler intelligence tests. While the "g" loadings for the WM and PS subtests are lower, they represent abilities that play a critical role in overall intellectual functioning, including the acquisition of new learning and the ability to utilize encoded (crystallized) knowledge to solve new problems. WM and PS should then be considered central to Wechsler's definition of intelligence as the ability to learn and adapt to a changing environment. From his first test, David Wechsler included tasks that tap these abilities (DS, CD, AR), although the terminology has changed over time as understanding of the underlying constructs continues to evolve (Tulsky, Saklofske, & Ricker, 2003; Tulsky, Saklofske, & Zhu, 2003).

Evidence in support of working memory and processing speed in a description of intelligence is increasingly convincing. For example, Jonides et al. (2005) stated that "without working memory, people would not be able to reason, solve problems, speak and understand language, and engage in other activities associated with intelligent life" (p. 2). There are large and obvious age-related trends in processing speed that are accompanied by age-related changes in the number of transient connections to the central nervous system and increases in myelination. Several investigators have found that measures of infant processing speed predict later IQ scores (e.g., Dougherty & Haith, 1997), and WISC-IV PSI scores have been shown to be potentially sensitive to neurological disorders such as epilepsy (Wechsler, 1991). As described earlier, studies of aging have shown that processing speed may be a central factor in the cognitive changes associated with aging (Salthouse, 2000).

The interrelationship between WM and PS was described earlier by Kyllonen and Christal (1990). High correlations were reported between these working memory research tasks and traditional measures of intelligence believed to tap reasoning ability. High scores on these reasoning tasks were differentially sensitive to the extent of a person's previous knowledge, whereas successful performance on pure working memory tasks was more dependent on the person's ability to process information rapidly. The interrelatedness among working memory, reasoning, prior knowledge, and processing speed led Kyllonen and Christal (1990) to conclude that reasoning ability is little more than working memory capacity. In this regard, Baddeley's (2003) proposal for an episodic buffer in which crystallized knowledge is downloaded from long-term storage for further manipulation is rather intriguing for the study of reasoning ability.

The relevance of this interactive and dynamic view of intelligence has considerable implications for the practicing psychologist engaged in the process of differential diagnosis. Thus while the steps for analyzing the WISC-IV presented earlier in this book might, on the surface, suggest a simple sequential approach, we have already indicated that a top-down and bottom-up approach is necessary. Further, each subtest, as well as the index scores, assesses cognitively complex traits. It is impossible to think of a child's performance on, say, the similarities subtest without also thinking of the role of working memory and speed of processing in the acquisition of these "facts" or knowledge, in retrieval, and in the service of engaging in this reasoning task. Fry and Hale (1996) administered measures of processing speed, working memory, and fluid intelligence to children and adolescents between 7 and 19 years of age. Age-related increases in speed of processing were associated with increases in working memory capacity, which, in turn, were associated with higher scores on measures of fluid reasoning. This study suggests that as children develop normally, more rapid processing of information results in more effective use of working memory space, which enhances performance on many reasoning tasks. Kail (2000) concluded that "Processing speed is not simply one of many different independent factors that contribute to intelligence; instead processing speed is thought to be linked causally to other elements of intelligence."

A number of studies have indicated that WMI contributes the second largest amount of variance, after VCI, to the prediction of reading, writing, and mathematics scores on the WIAT and other measures of achievement (Konold, 1999; Hale, Fiorello, Kavanagh, Hoeppner, & Gaither, 2001). High correlations between working memory and reading comprehension have been replicated numerous times (see Daneman & Merikle, 1996). Similar findings have been observed for a range of other academic tasks, including spelling (Ormrod & Cochran, 1988), the acquisition of logic (Kyllonen & Stephens, 1990), note taking (Kiewra & Benton, 1988), and following directions (Engle, Carullo, & Collins, 1991). Generally, the magnitude of these correlations is near .50 (Baddeley, 2003), suggesting a moderate relationship between working memory and various academic outcomes.

THE RELATIONSHIP OF WM AND PS TO FLUID INTELLIGENCE

The precise mechanisms by which working memory is related to fluid reasoning are complex, and likely multiply determined. The original resource sharing model (Daneman & Carpenter, 1980) emphasizes a trade-off between storage and processing demands such that working memory span is a function of the amount of resources one has available for storage after the processing demands of the task are met. However, other researchers postulate that working memory space itself may not be limited, but its use is limited by the efficiency of various processes that control it. For example, the efficiency with which one can perform the processing component of a particular span task affects the duration for which the target items need to be retained in memory (Hitch, Towse, & Hutton, 2001). Thus, working memory capacity will appear larger when processing proceeds efficiently, regardless of the size of the working memory space. Processing can proceed efficiently when the task invokes a crystallized base of knowledge that is readily retrieved from long-term storage, activated in short-term storage, and easily chunked into large and meaningful units based on the individual's prior experience and expertise with the material. Thus, there are few pure working memory tasks, and any pure task that could be created would artificially separate the various reciprocal processes that operate together to form the working memory system. Good working memory tasks bring all of these influences together in the same way as the natural world.

The role of the central executive is critical to the relationship between working memory and fluid reasoning. The central executive controls attention to the target task in the face of interfering or distracting stimuli (Kane, Bleckley, Conway, & Engle, 2001). The more efficiently attention is focused, the more effectively working memory is utilized, regardless of working memory capacity. Similarly, the ability to inhibit irrelevant information, or degree to which working memory is "clutter free," may also influence efficient cognitive performance regardless of the size of the working memory space (Lustig, May, & Hasher, 2001). Thus, individual differences in performance on working memory tasks may reflect primarily differences in various executive functions, such as the ability to sustain focused attention and inhibit competing responses rather than the size of one's working memory space, particularly in real life situations outside of the research laboratory where interference and distraction are commonplace. Current research suggests that the central executive component of WM may account for the strong relationship between WM and fluid reasoning tasks, through the mechanism of controlled attention (Engle, Tuholski, Laughlin, & Conway, 1999).

Together with the central executive, short-term memory plays a role in the efficient processing of information in working memory. As the source of controlled attention, the central executive activates long-term memory traces through controlled retrieval and maintains them in short-term storage systems, such as the visual spatial sketch pad or the phonological loop. For any given individual, there are obvious differences in the long-term traces that can be activated in STM based on prior knowledge and familiarity with the task at hand. The more prior knowledge the person brings to a WM problem, the less fluid reasoning is required to respond correctly. Thus, what is clearly a WM task for some participants might be primarily an STM task for others. This is likely true not just at different levels of task difficulty, but also among individuals at different stages of development depending on intellectual ability, skill, familiarity, and practice with the task. If STM and WM are interrelated in this way, then it makes clinical sense to consider STM tasks (such as DSF) and WM tasks (such as DSB) together and separately. Although DS forward and backward tasks are usually thought of as STM and WM tasks, respectively, this may not always be the case for all individuals. Easy DSB items may invoke no real processing and require only passive registration of stimuli into STM. More difficult DSF items may require some type of processing, such as rehearsal or chunking, thus activating WM systems. The precise point in the items sets where these response processes shift will vary by individual depending on ability and familiarity with the task. Although closely associated with each other, STM and WM relate differently to fluid reasoning. WM is highly correlated with fluid reasoning whereas STM is not.

Perceptual processing speed is another important cognitive ability that influences the efficiency of working memory functions. Fry and Hale (1996) stated that as children age and mature, the changes that occur in processing speed lead to changes in working memory and "in turn, lead to changes in performance on tests of fluid intelligence" (p. 237). Although moderately correlated with each other, working memory and perceptual processing speed are differentially related to fluid reasoning. Working memory correlates moderately, whereas perceptual processing speed correlates weakly with fluid reasoning ability as measured by Ravens progressive matrices (Ackerman, Beier, & Boyle, 2002). It appears that processing speed exerts its effect on fluid reasoning indirectly through its facilitation of working memory. While working memory ability may be related primarily to one's capacity for controlled attention, the relationship between working memory and fluid reasoning also appears to be mediated by processing speed.

A synergistic model of cognitive information processing suggests that language and reading impairments that interfere with the rapid processing of information may burden the working memory structures and reduce the student's capacity for comprehension and new learning. Learning-disabled and attention-deficit samples had lower PSI and WMI scores compared to their VCI and PRI scores (e.g., Schwean & Saklofske, 2005) and scores of the standardization sample (Wechsler, 2003).

Research in this area is still unfolding. However, practitioners should keep in mind that scores on factor-based indexes are not necessarily orthogonal; multiple reciprocal interactions are expected among these neurocognitive pathways. Understanding the clinical correlates of these synergistic effects is critical to meaningful interpretation of psychometric test scores.

ISSUES SURROUNDING THE USE OF COGNITIVE TESTS IN LD ASSESSMENT

We now turn to an area of controversy that challenges the role and relevance of intelligence tests such as the WISC-IV in the assessment and diagnosis of LD. Chapter 3 commented briefly on this debate, but this section examines more extensively some of the key issues here as they relate to the use of intelligence tests in LD assessment. By placing the WISC-IV in the context of the current controversy surrounding psychometric approaches for assessing and identifying learning disabilities, it is hoped that the reader will be better able to appreciate both the limitations and the strengths of the WISC-IV. This section examines the core issues raised by the major proponents of the two current opposing views and sets the stage for an alternative approach that runs through the next three chapters of this book.

The WISC-IV, like most major intellectual tests over the past 5 years, has become increasingly differentiated in terms of the constructs it assesses. Yet, LD assessments in most school-based settings continue to rely on a single IQ score compared to achievement. This ability–achievement discrepancy approach has come under increasing criticism on the grounds that the AAD model may delay intervention for some children, that the presence of an AAD is not a pure marker of learning disability, that the cut points used do not result in the identification of stable groups, and that a one-time AAD assessment also does not produce a reliable and valid diagnosis of LD (e.g., Francis et al., 2005). While the AAD model has its conceptual problems, some have further argued that ability tests should not be included in LD evaluations (Siegel, 2003). While intelligence tests have always had their share of critics, it has very much come to the fore in recent debates surrounding the diagnosis of learning disabilities, especially the use of the AAD.

ABILITY–ACHIEVEMENT DISCREPANCY

There is presently much controversy surrounding the use of the ability–achievement discrepancy (AAD) model to determine eligibility for special education services as learning disabled. In fact, the discussion tends to reflect an operational dilemma in the identification of children who do not achieve in the classroom. It is not unusual for the school psychologist to identify a child with poor performance on measures of both ability and achievement who does not obtain a large enough discrepancy between the two scores to be determined eligible for services. However, the supervisors and administrators require some easily quantifiable measures to determine eligibility. This helps ensure that the eligibility requirements are applied fairly and equitably across all students.

An additional complication is the lack of consistent values and rules for the discrepancy across districts, counties, and states. For example, one state requires a difference of 16 points for eligibility determination. Another sets the discrepancy value based on the student's age. A third requires 30 points for the discrepancy. This last value may seem high, but it represents two standard deviations from the mean, a relatively consensual point of agreement for significance. In some instances, there are differences between districts in the same state. Theoretically, one could argue that a way to "cure" a learning disability or decrease the number of students receiving services would be to move students from the first state mentioned earlier to the last state mentioned earlier, with the point being that it makes no sense that a child would be deemed disabled in one state but not another.

Further complicating the discussion is the requirement of some districts to use the full-scale IQ score as opposed to index scores or a partial score. For example, suppose a child achieved an FSIQ of 100 with a VCI of 101 and a PRI of 99 and another child has an FSIQ of 100 with a VCI of 120 and a PRI of 80. Both children have an FSIQ of 100, but those "100's" are not equal. The significant discrepancy in abilities evidenced by the second child will be minimized if the FSIQ is required as part of the discrepancy determination. The clinician must move beyond the global scores and utilize additional process analyses at the index and subtest level.

Just as the global scores may not be reflective of a child's actual ability and skills, there is a need to carefully consider the scores at the index and subtest level. This can be illustrated with the following examples at the subtest level. If a child takes 1 second longer than the time limit on a Block Design trial, they will receive a score of "0." If a second child places the blocks in their mouth for the entire time limit, they too receive a "0." Quantitatively, these zeroes are equal and contribute to the total at the bottom of the page the same way. However, qualitatively they could not be more different in their implications and linkage to interventions.

A similar illustration can be seen in the following vocabulary example. Suppose a child was asked the meaning of the word "repair." If the child was to respond to the request with, "You repair a broken toy or a flat tire," the response would likely receive a "0." Teachers often mark a child wrong when they use a word to define the same word. However, it appears obvious from the child's response that the child understands the meaning of the word by using it correctly in context. The child may have a problem with articulating their knowledge verbally. Therefore, the intervention should focus on developing strategies for articulating knowledge rather than treating this as a lack of knowledge. In fact, research by Chall (1996) found that at the end of third grade, the average child had between 5000 and 10,000 words in their listening vocabulary. However, they could only formally define 300 to 500 of those words. This finding has significant implications for how we utilize the scores.

One solution to this confound is to consider the utilization of additional procedures designed to focus on assessing the knowledge, skills, and abilities of the child from multiple perspectives. The WISC-IV Integrated provides standardized procedures designed to quantify the testing of limits to address these types of problems. A more comprehensive discussion of the WISC-IV Integrated and its related procedures can be found in Chapters 5 and 6.

Finally, a practical example of the difficulties related to reliance on a discrepancy approach to identification of a learning disability or determination of eligibility is illustrated by the Connecticut Longitudinal Study (Shaywitz, Fletcher, Holahan, Schneider, Marchione, Steubing, Francis, & Shaywitz, 1999). In that study, children were followed from kindergarten through grade 12. Teachers identified those children who were not making appropriate progress in preliteracy and literacy skills. Once identified, those children were tested. Those children were divided into two groups. One group demonstrated a significant AAD in reading and were identified as reading disabled according to a discrepancy between IQ and reading achievement. The second group was identified as low reading achievement with no discrepancy. Both of these groups were followed throughout their education. Their respective growth curves in reading were virtually indistinguishable. The difference between their growth curves and that of the not reading impaired (NRI) group was evident well before grade 3, when many children are referred for initial assessment. Neither group caught up to the NRI group anywhere between kindergarten and grade 12.

This study illustrates two key principles. First, the AAD may not identify the child early enough in their education to make significant improvements with early interventions. This model sometimes results in a delay until the child scores sufficiently low on achievement to demonstrate a significant discrepancy between ability and achievement. At that point the child is typically "staffed" and referred for comprehensive evaluation. There is a reliance on an AAD for diagnosis, eligibility, and ultimately services. Unfortunately, as the study suggests, the delays are critical and may have a negative impact on a child's educational progress. The next important principle that this example illustrates is that relying on an AAD to identify a learning disability often results in missing an entire population of children with significant learning difficulties. This is one of the more significant arguments made against reliance on the AAD model. At the same time, it is unclear which of these children have genuine learning disabilities, which lacked adequate preparation or instruction to learn, and which are low achievers.

RESPONSE TO INTERVENTION

Currently, there is much discussion of alternative strategies for identifying learning disabilities. This most commonly cited alternative is referred to as the response to intervention (RTI) model. RTI typically consists of a multi-level approach to students whose academic performance is below grade level in the classroom. They are initially provided interventions in the general education classroom. A central theme of RTI is that these educational interventions would be research based, scientifically sound, and empirically supported. Ongoing progress monitoring provides data on the effectiveness of the intervention and, when necessary, the need for modification or additional interventions and services. The goal is to keep the student in the least restrictive educational environment. This is within the intent, scope, and spirit of Public Law 94–142 (Education of All Handicapped Children Act) and now codified as the Individuals with Disabilities Education Improvement Act or IDEA 2004.

If a child responds to the interventions, they will continue in the general education classroom. If a child does not respond to the interventions, they are usually referred for more comprehensive evaluations and services. Theoretically, those children who fail to respond to the interventions will be identified as learning disabled and eligible for special education services.

On the surface, RTI approaches address significant issues presented by the ability–achievement discrepancy. RTI does not rely on a discrepancy for identification for need for services. A child having difficulty in a general education classroom can begin receiving empirically based interventions as soon as the difficulties are demonstrated and identified.

The time line for intervention and action is significantly shorter. The child does not need to wait until the child study team or student support team meets to discuss the problems, consider alternatives, decide on a course of action, implement the plan, and then meet again to discuss the results and plan interventions. It is not uncommon for the traditional process to take up to 2 to 3 months during the school year. A child with academic delays who is already behind in skill and knowledge acquisition may fall further behind their peers over time unless proper interventions are implemented. RTI potentially shortens the cycle to days and weeks rather than weeks and months.

The language of the Individuals with Disabilities Educational Improvement Act no longer requires a severe discrepancy between achievement and intellectual ability and permits the use of an RTI approach as an alternative. The specific language of this section of IDEA 2004 is listed here.

(6) SPECIFIC LEARNING DISABILITIES

(A) IN GENERAL. Notwithstanding section 607(b), when determining whether a child has a specific learning disability as defined in section 602, a local educational agency shall not be required to take into consideration whether a child has a severe discrepancy between achievement and intellectual ability in oral expression, listening comprehension, written expression, basic reading skill, reading comprehension, mathematical calculation, or mathematical reasoning.

(B) ADDITIONAL AUTHORITY. In determining whether a child has a specific learning disability, a local educational agency may use a process that determines if the child responds to scientific, research-based intervention as a part of the evaluation procedures described in paragraphs (2) and (3).

RTI and Unresolved Issues

On the surface, RTI may seem like the ideal alternative to the ability–achievement discrepancy approach. However, on closer examination, RTI also has some significant limitations. Mastropieri (2003), responding to Reschly's (2003) four-tier model, posed several poignant questions during the National Research Center on Learning Disabilities Symposium on Responsiveness-to-Intervention (2003) that highlight some of the difficulties presented by RTI approaches. Some of the more challenging questions are as follows.

- *Who prepares all general education teachers to deliver instruction using this scientifically based approach?*
- *Does this happen in university teacher preparation programs? Will school districts provide extensive in-service education to all current teachers?*
- *Does the general educator provide Tier I, Tier II, Tier III instruction simultaneously within a single classroom?*
- *What are the curriculum materials and instructional methods at each of the four tiers that have scientific evidence supporting their efficacy?*
- *Who monitors whether general educators teach this way?*
- *How long will students remain in a tier?*
- *What are the "tests" teachers will use to determine whether a student remains in a tier?*
- *How is the "nonresponsiveness" to intervention determination made (e.g., will all teachers use a standard cutoff score on classroom tests)?*
- *What is the record-keeping system teachers use?*
- *Who has the ultimate decision-making power to move students up and down the tier system?*
- *What exactly are special educators doing and when?*
- *What do teachers do about the child that learns but requires a very slow pace of instruction with additional practice activities and multiple exemplars before moving to the next new concept?*

In addition, we would point out that failure to respond to intervention has not been shown to be a clinical marker of learning disability. This is an administrative criteria designed to reduce the number of children that require special education funding by intervening earlier and, hopefully, raising their academic achievement scores to grade level. The thinking is that many children receiving special education services are not truly LD but are in need of better instruction. By providing empirically supported instruction early in the academic career of these students as part of the regular education process, it is thought that most will not require special education, thus reducing funding requirements for special education programs. *As laudable as its goals may be, it should be recognized that RTI is ultimately an administrative response to a clinical problem.* While the goal of intervening earlier is clearly worthwhile, it is also true that children whose cognitive disabilities are not readily observable will most likely wait until they have failed to respond to multiple educational interventions before an appropriate psychological assessment is offered.

Further, the impact of the RTI model on fairness of assessment issues and the social consequences of assessment policies have not been investigated. It is not known if system-wide implementation of the RTI model will increase or reduce disproportionate representation of racial/ethnic groups in special education programs—a problem that the IDEA specifically directs state and local education authorities to resolve. Thus, resolution of one administrative problem may inadvertently create other administrative problems.

In some ways, RTI represents a "buckshot approach" to interventions. Because RTI does not require the identification of a weakness or deficit based on a specific evaluation procedure, an educator would likely "load their gun" with all of the interventions they know for a specific area and "fire" at the student. The intent would be that one or more of the interventions will address the problems successfully and the child would improve.

There are two areas that should be emphasized. First, it would require the educator to know and be able to identify the actual underlying causes for a child's failure to learn and progress. Second, and a much more important issue, is that the educator will utilize all of the interventions *that they know*. Thus professional development and training become critical. Schools have not had the luxury of time nor the funds necessary for focusing on the skills required by *No Child Left Behind* legislation for developing and enhancing core competencies in teachers.

Another issue with a "pure" RTI approach is the lack of empirically supported interventions outside the domain of reading. In fact, even within the reading domain, research-based interventions are limited to the acquisition of early reading skills. The scientific literature includes multiple studies with very small populations or single case reports. There is difficulty translating this to wider applications. What would the lack of specific research-based interventions mean for children with math difficulties or problems with the critical thinking requirements in science, social studies, and other curricular areas?

Many proponents of an RTI approach dismiss the efficacy of comprehensive evaluations in service of the goal of linking assessment to intervention. Similarly, many proponents of a comprehensive evaluation approach fail to recognize the importance of the ultimate goal of the assessment, which is to identify specific efficacious interventions that address the problems identified by the evaluation.

It is unclear why an either/or approach is necessary. In order to be effective, school psychologists must identify the specific underlying cause(s) of an academic problem and target that problem. A "cognitive hypothesis testing" approach (Hale & Fiorello, 2004) to assessment fits with this goal. This model starts with research-based hypotheses as possible explanations for the observed academic difficulties and selects specific tests or subtests across batteries to confirm or refute the hypothesis. The cognitive hypothesis testing approach could result in the modified use of a test, as opposed to the entire test. This would require some cognitive shifts in the thinking of school psychologists accustomed to administering complete batteries. Is it possible that a customized battery of subtests may best address the referral problem? Is it possible that the selection of appropriate subtests and supplemental procedures provided from the WISC-IV integrated would result in the necessary information to identify problem areas and link to specific research-based interventions that target those problem areas?

A case must be made for the importance of linking assessment to interventions. Consider the following math example. A child demonstrates significant difficulty with multiplication. The teacher notes that a child routinely gets multidigit multiplication problems incorrect. A "process-oriented" approach to the assessment might identify that the child does multiply correctly. However, the child fails to move over one column when multiplying by the digit in the "tens" column, and so on. Without the "process-oriented" approach, a teacher might focus on multiplication knowledge as opposed to multiplication procedures. Ultimately, this would assist the teacher in discriminating between lack of knowledge or understanding and the inability to articulate or demonstrate that knowledge functionally.

Can These Two Approaches Be Combined in the Assessment of LD?

In consideration of the relative strengths and weaknesses of the multiple approaches to identification, Fuchs and Fuchs (1998) have proposed a "dual discrepancy" approach that incorporates the concept of discrepancy and the use of an RTI model. The discrepancy that is required is that a child's achievement is below that of their peers *and* learning is at a slower rate than that of their peers (Bradley et al., 2002).

To clarify the concept of the "dual discrepancy" model, consider the presentation by McMaster and colleagues at the National Research Center on Learning Disabilities Symposium on Responsiveness-to-Intervention (2003). McMaster presented the findings of a study entitled *Responding to Nonresponders: An Experimental Field Trial of Identification and Intervention Methods*. In this study, the "dual discrepancy" approach was used to identify children were unresponsive to peer-assisted learning strategies, also known as PALS. During this study, "dual discrepancy" was determined by slopes and levels >.5 SD below average on the Dolch and/or nonword fluency measures. Percentile rank was determined by scores below the 30th percentile on the WRMT-R Word Identification and/or Word Attack subtests. The criterion level was determined by < 40 correct words per minute on the near-transfer and/or far-transfer fluency measures. No growth was determined by a gain of 0 words (or less) on Word Identification and/or Word Attack. Limited growth was determined by a gain of 10 words or less on Word Identification and/or a gain of 5 words or less on Word Attack. The findings of this study revealed that "the dual discrepancy approach reliably distinguished among unresponsive at-risk, and average-performing readers" (p. 1). McMaster and colleagues further concluded that "dual discrepancy holds promise as a better method of identification than performance-level-only and growth-rate-only approaches" (p. 21).

As can be seen from this study, a specific criterion was set for determination of the first requirement, which is that the student's achievement be below that of their peers. That was operationalized in the McMaster and coworker study as poor performance on Dolch and/or nonword fluency measures. The second requirement is that the rate of learning be slower than that of their peers. This, too, was operationalized as growth measures. In practice then, the child is manifesting difficulty with both the attainment and the rate of acquisition of important academic skills.

The model requires verification of adequate classroom instruction prior to the discrepancies noted earlier. If the initial requirements are met, the child would receive initial interventions in the general education classroom prior to a formal referral. The child would remain at this level for a designated period of time and be monitored for improvement. Ongoing progress monitoring is critical here. If the student fails to respond to interventions, the child is referred for a more comprehensive evaluation. This is an ongoing process over time (i.e., 8 weeks), after which the team would determine the need for formal identification and services/placement.

The key point here is that neither an AAD model nor a pure RTI model is likely to be sufficient. Integrated problem-solving models are in place (i.e., Iowa) and under development (i.e., Volusia County, Florida). These models integrate some degree of norm-referenced measurements with direct behavioral observation, functional behavior analysis, and RTI approaches. These multilevel, phased models are being implemented in Reading First and Non-Reading First Schools. They are implemented in poor-performing as well as high-performing schools. Assessment instruments that can be used in concert with other approaches to enhance the identification of specific learning difficulties have the greatest value. For example, the WISC-IV can be used with the *Early Reading Success Inventory* (ERSI; The Psychological Corporation, 2003) to provide additional diagnostic information related to reading and to provide risk estimates for specific WISC-IV subtests. Similarly, utilization of the *Process Assessment of the Learner* (Berninger, 2001), in conjunction with the WISC-IV, will provide depth to the assessment of cognitive processes involved with reading and writing.

Dual LD Criteria: Low Achievement with Processing Deficits

As noted earlier, there are many possible reasons why a child may present with lower achievement than expected given her or his intellectual capacity. Possible reasons include inadequate classroom instruction, linguistic diversity, low motivation, environment not conducive to studying, attention disorders, memory disorders, executive function disorders, cognitive interference due to familial distress, emotional disorders, and posttraumatic stress disorder. Proper evaluation of children referred for possible learning disabilities involves ruling out differential diagnoses and assessing the relevance of contributing conditions. *When a child is not achieving up to his or her potential, it is a clear signal that something is wrong.* This statement passes the "reasonableness test" in that almost every parent and teacher would agree that a problem exists if a child is not achieving up to potential. It is therefore ironic that not every psychologist agrees with that statement. However, the analysis of the child's achievement problem should not stop at this point, as it frequently does, and end with a referral to special education. *The next step is for the psychologist to sift through the various possible reasons the child may be underachieving in systematic fashion.* This is similar to how pediatricians practice when a parent brings their child for examination due to a high fever. Elevated body temperature is not diagnostic of any particular disorder. Possible reasons range from the flu to leukemia, and almost everything in between. However, high fever is a clear sign that something is wrong with the child's health, and it is the role of the physician to rule out possibilities and determine why the child's temperature is elevated. Similarly, the psychologist must determine why the child is not achieving at the same rate as his or her peers, given that he or she has the intellectual capacity to do so. Thus, substantial underachievement relative to ability might best be considered as a necessary but not sufficient condition for the diagnosis of a learning disability.

Dumont and Willis (2001) recommend that practitioners examine a new composite based on a combination of the WISC-IV WMI and PSI. We refer to this composite as the Cognitive Proficiency Index (CPI) because it assesses a set of diverse functions whose common element can best be described as the proficiency with which one processes certain types of cognitive information. The CPI combines two basic psychological processes—working memory and processing speed—into a single score based on the four core subtests in these indexes. Proficient processing, through quick visual speed and good mental control, facilitates fluid reasoning and the acquisition of new material by reducing the cognitive demands of novel tasks, as described earlier.

To investigate the utility of this new index, we examined the discrepancy between the CPI and the GAI in each of the clinical groups collected with the WISC-IV standardization research project. (GAI is a composite of VCI and PRI, and GAI norms are presented in Chapter 3.) First, we created norms for the CPI and then computed base rate comparisons of CPI–GAI discrepancies in the normative sample. Table 1 shows the CPI equivalents of sums of scaled scores. Table 2 shows the cumulative percentages of the standardization sample obtaining each CPI–GAI score discrepancy by direction. The CPI norms presented in Table 1 are based on actual standardization data and are therefore preferred to those presented by Dumont and Willis (2001), which are a statistical approximation of data.

For each clinical group, we then identified a sample of nonclinical subjects matched on all relevant demographic variables and examined the sensitivity (true positive rate) and specificity (true negative rate) for classifying these conditions at various cut scores. We selected 60% as the minimum acceptable rate for both sensitivity and specificity. For 9 of the 12 clinical groups studied, we found that it was not possible to identify an adequate cut score for the discrepancy between CPI and GAI that correctly identified an acceptable percentage of both clinical and nonclinical subjects. Minimally acceptable results were obtained for four clinical groups. Children receiving special education services for learning disabilities in reading and writing were identified with a sensitivity of 66% and a specificity of 63% when CPI was 5 or more points less than GAI. Children diagnosed with closed, traumatic brain injuries were identified with a sensitivity of 65% and a specificity of 61% when CPI was 4 or more points lower than GAI. By way of comparison, children with open, traumatic brain injuries were identified with a sensitivity of 67% and a specificity of 62% when CPI was 4 or more points lower than GAI. Asperger's clients were identified with a sensitivity of 68% and a specificity of 63% when CPI was 11 or more points lower than GAI.

These data suggest that while an AAD alone is not sufficient evidence to diagnose LD, neither is a GAI–CPI discrepancy. Next we examined the base rates of large ability-achievement and GAI-CPI discrepancies in the nonclinical sample separately and in combination. We defined a large discrepancy as 15 or more points. For the GAI–CPI comparison, we only considered discrepancies in the hypothesized direction of CPI < GAI. Of the 516 nonclinical subjects administered both WISC-IV and WIAT-II, 21% had a large difference between ability and achievement, but not between GAI and CPI. Clearly, this percentage is much higher than the base rate of LD in the general population and reflects all of the other reasons that an AAD may occur, as noted earlier. Approximately 9% of this sample had a large CPI < GAI discrepancy, but not a large AAD. Only 2% met the dual criteria (i.e., only 2% of normal children obtained a large CPI < GAI difference in combination with a large AAD).

Finally, we examined the frequency of these dual criteria in the reading disorder, writing disorder, combined reading and writing disorder, and mathematics disorder samples reported in the *WISC-IV Technical and Interpretive Manual*. The percentage of children receiving LD services that met both criteria ranged between 45 and 50% in the various reading and writing disorder samples, but less than 1% in the math disorder sample. This suggests that these combined criteria may hold promise in the identification of children with learning disabilities in reading or writing, but not math.

However, many of these children were first identified as eligible for special education services based on a large AAD using the WISC-III, WIAT-II, SB-V, WJ-III, KABC, or other standardized measures of intelligence and achievement. Because all of these children were originally identified based solely on the presence of an AAD, many may have been underachieving relative to their cognitive potential for reasons other than a learning

TABLE 1　CPI Equivalents of Sums of Scaled Scores

Sum of Scaled Scores	DWI	Confidence Interval 90% CI	95% CI	Percentile Rank	Sum of Scaled Scores	DWI	Confidence Interval 90% CI	95% CI	Percentile Rank
4	40	38–50	37–51	<0.1	41	101	95–107	94–108	53
5	42	40–52	39–53	<0.1	42	102	96–108	95–109	56
6	44	42–54	41–55	<0.1	43	104	98–110	97–111	62
7	46	44–56	43–57	<0.1	44	106	99–111	98–112	65
8	48	46–58	44–59	<0.1	45	107	101–113	100–114	69
9	50	47–60	46–61	<0.1	46	109	102–114	101–116	73
10	52	49–61	48–63	0.1	47	112	105–117	104–118	79
11	54	51–63	50–64	0.1	48	113	106–118	105–120	81
12	56	53–65	52–66	0.2	49	116	108–121	107–122	85
13	58	55–67	54–68	0.3	50	117	110–122	109–123	87
14	60	57–69	56–70	0.4	51	119	112–124	111–125	90
15	62	59–71	57–72	1	52	121	113–125	112–126	92
16	63	60–72	58–73	1	53	123	115–127	114–128	93
17	65	61–74	60–75	1	54	125	117–129	116–130	95
18	67	63–75	62–77	1	55	127	119–131	118–132	96
19	68	64–76	63–77	2	56	129	121–133	120–134	97
20	70	66–78	65–79	2	57	131	123–135	122–136	98
21	71	67–79	66–80	3	58	133	125–137	124–138	99
22	72	68–80	67–81	3	59	136	127–140	126–141	99
23	73	69–81	68–82	4	60	138	129–141	128–143	99
24	75	71–83	70–84	5	61	140	131–143	130–144	99.6
25	76	72–84	70–85	5	62	142	133–145	132–146	99.7
26	77	73–85	72–86	7	63	144	135–147	134–148	99.8
27	79	74–87	73–88	8	64	146	137–149	136–150	99.9
28	80	75–87	74–89	9	65	148	139–151	137–152	99.9
29	81	76–88	75–90	10	66	150	140–153	139–154	>99.9
30	83	78–90	77–91	12	67	152	142–154	141–156	>99.9
31	84	79–91	78–92	14	68	154	144–156	143–157	>99.9
32	86	81–93	80–94	18	69	156	146–158	145–159	>99.9
33	87	82–94	81–96	20	70	158	148–160	147–161	>99.9
34	89	83–95	82–97	22	71	160	150–162	149–163	>99.9
35	91	86–98	84–99	28	72	160	150–162	149–163	>99.9
36	93	87–99	86–100	31	73	160	150–162	149–163	>99.9
37	94	88–100	87–102	34	74	160	150–162	149–163	>99.9
38	96	90–102	89–104	39	75	160	150–162	149–163	>99.9
39	98	92–104	91–105	44	76	160	150–162	149–163	>99.9
40	100	94–106	93–107	50					

TABLE 2   Cumulative Percentages of Standardization Sample (Base Rates) Obtaining GAI–CPI Score Discrepancies by Direction

	GAI–DWI		
Amount of Discrepancy	GAI>DWI (−)	GAI<DWI (+)	Amount of Discrepancy
40	0.0	0.1	40
39	0.1	0.1	39
38	0.1	0.2	38
37	0.1	0.3	37
36	0.3	0.4	36
35	0.3	0.5	35
34	0.3	0.6	34
33	0.4	0.7	33
32	0.6	0.7	32
31	0.7	0.8	31
30	0.8	0.8	30
29	1.0	1.1	29
28	1.3	1.4	28
27	1.4	1.6	27
26	1.7	2.0	26
25	2.1	2.5	25
24	2.5	2.9	24
23	3.1	3.5	23
22	3.8	4.3	22
21	4.4	5.0	21
20	5.2	6.0	20
19	6.3	7.2	19
18	7.3	8.3	18
17	8.7	9.5	17
16	10.1	11.0	16
15	11.2	12.5	15
14	12.5	14.1	14
13	14.0	16.8	13
12	16.5	18.5	12
11	18.3	20.6	11
10	20.7	22.9	10
9	22.9	25.0	9
8	25.2	27.7	8
7	27.7	30.8	7
6	30.8	33.7	6
5	33.5	37.0	5
4	37.0	40.7	4
3	40.0	43.6	3
2	43.1	46.8	2
1	47.1	50.1	1
Mean	9.8	10.2	Mean
SD	7.4	7.5	SD
Median	8.0	8.0	Median

disability. The fact that AAD was the method used to identify these samples partially confounds the results, but also points out the difficulty identifying pure criterion groups. After all, what set of test results would unambiguously confirm a diagnosis of LD apart from the administrative rules used to determine eligibility for special education services in public schools? Until this question can be answered, LD research will continue to be a murky area.

Based on the aforementioned results and rationale, *we suggest that the presence of a deficiency in a basic psychological process in combination with an ability–achievement discrepancy may be more convincing evidence of a genuine learning disability than either an AAD or processing deficit alone, or a singular failure to respond in interventions.* Within a framework of dual criteria for LD evaluations, RTI may be best utilized to monitor the progress of LD children receiving research-based educational interventions and to determine when formulative assessments are necessary to guide more intensive interventions. There are many other types of psychological processing deficits, however, and Chapters 5 and 6 expand on the use of the process approach in the analysis of basic psychological and cognitive processes.

COMMENTS ON COGNITIVE TESTS IN LD ASSESSMENTS

It is worth recalling that the AAD model was mandated by IDEA at a time in our professional history when little was known about the etiology, diagnostic criteria, prevalence, or treatment of learning disabilities. Congressional committees formulating the legislation were concerned about committing federal and state government funds for an undetermined number of children with an unknown cost of treatment. Statistics associated with the normal curve allowed administrators to set specific ability–achievement discrepancy criteria that controlled the number of students that would require services, thus limiting the financial liability of various governmental agencies. *After decades of using the AAD model, the field appears to have confused administrative evaluations to determine eligibility for services with clinical assessment.* They are not the same! This confusion continues with the RTI model.

While AAD is not a clinical model of assessment, neither is RTI. Only a valid clinical assessment affirms the child's uniqueness and examines individual differences in a way that leads to an effective use of strengths to accommodate weaknesses. Our approach provides a clinical model of assessment that best utilizes information from both intellectual and achievement tests to evaluate specific cognitive hypotheses using a process-oriented approach that incorporates the discrepancy score as a necessary condition in the evaluation, but not the determining factor. We suggest that when children underachieve relative to potential and also demonstrate deficits in related domains of cognition, then an LD diagnosis *may* be warranted. Otherwise, they are likely to be underachieving for other reasons that may be related to being unprepared to enter school, linguistically diverse, slow learners, inadequately instructed, and so on.

Compelling data that have been presented in various studies leave little question about the limitations of both AAD and RTI approaches in the identification of LD. And yet there are still a few voices that may be heard calling for the total exclusion of cognitive assessment with tests such as the WISC-IV and the responsible use of other psychometrically sound tests. This would not make either the assessment or the development of educational prescriptions for children with LD, AD/HD, and any other neurocognitively based difficulty any easier; in fact, it would be taking away a powerful information base. As noted in Chapter 3, the current definition of LD includes an examination of the very cognitive constructs included in the WISC-IV (e.g., the links among WM, PS, and LD). Francis et al. (2005) stated that "the identification of children as having LD based solely on individual test scores not linked to specific behavioral criteria leads to invalid decisions about individual children.... If we accept the premise of multiple classes of low achievers, then we must develop identification systems that are valid and abandon systems whose only merits are their historical precedence and convenience" (p. 98). Again this does not preclude the use of the WISC-IV. Rather the description of LD and the latent traits measured by the WISC-IV are in many ways complementary from both an a priori and a posteriori hypothesis testing. To observe a child with a history of achievement and learning problems but who has an FSIQ of 118, or who has a 26-point VCI-PRI discrepancy, or who manifests very slow PS that further appears to be placing an extra burden on WM tasks is clearly of significance to the psychologist searching for not only an understanding and description of what the child can and cannot do but also help to explain why. In the context of a multimethod and continuous approach to assessment, the WISC-IV can certainly contribute to a better understanding of the child from a cognitive perspective.

SUMMARY

This chapter focused on the relevance of the WISC-IV index scores in clinical assessment in general and in the assessment of students with cognitive disorders such as LD and AD/HD that impair psychological and educational functioning. In particular we focused on advanced clinical interpretive issues related to how working memory and processing speed interact to facilitate fluid reasoning and the learning of new material. The next two chapters elaborate on selecting specific WISC-IV Integrated Process Approach subtests to test cognitive hypotheses derived from the child's observed performance on WISC-IV and presenting problems. Chapter 5 explores empirically how WISC-IV index scores and WISC-IV Integrated process approach subtests join together with other assessments to further confirm or refute hypotheses about specific cognitive functions. Knowledge of how these assessments are designed to work together will provide practitioners with tools needed to conduct clinically useful psychoeducational assessments regardless of the administrative framework used to determine eligibility for services.

REFERENCES

Ackerman, P. L., Geier, M. E., & Boyle, M. O. (2002). Individual differences in working memory within a nomological network of cognitive and perceptual speed abilities. *Journal of Experimental Psychology: General, 131*(4), 567–589.

Adair, J. C., Na, D. L., Schwartz, R. L., & Heilman, K. M. (1998). Analysis of primary and secondary influences on spatial neglect. *Brain and Cognition, 37*(3), 351–367.

Baddeley, A. (2003). Working memory: Looking back and looking forward. *Nature Reviews/ Neuroscience, 4,* 829–839.

Berninger, V. (2001). *Process assessment of the learner: Test battery for reading and writing.* San Antonio, TX: The Psychological Corporation.

Bradley, R., Danielson, L., & Hallahan, D. P. (2002). Specific learning disabilities: Building consensus for identification and classification. In R. Bradley, L. Danielson, & D. P. Hallahan (Eds.), *Identification of learning disabilities: Research to practice* (pp. 791–804). Mahwah, NJ: Lawrence Erlbaum.

Carroll, J. B., (1993). *Human cognitive abilities: A survey of factor-analytic studies.* New York: Cambridge University Press.

Chall, J. S. (1996). *Stages of reading development* (2nd ed.). Orlando, FL: Harcourt Brace.

Daneman, M., & Carpenter, P. A. (1980). Individual differences in working memory and reading. *Journal of Verbal Learning and Verbal Behavior, 19,* 450–466.

Daneman, M., & Merikle, M. (1996). Working memory and language comprehension: A meta-analysis. *Psychonomic Bulletin Review, 3,* 422–433.

Deary, I. J. (2001). *Intelligence: A very short introduction.* Oxford: Oxford University Press.

Deary, I. J., & Stough, C. (1996). Intelligence and inspection time: Achievements, prospects, and problems. *American Psychologist, 51,* 599–608.

Dougherty, T. M., & Haith, M. M. (1997). Infant expectations and reaction times as predictors of childhood speed of processing and IQ. *Developmental Psychology 33*(1), 146–155.

Dumont, R., & Willis, J. (2001). Use of the Tellegen & Briggs formula to determine the Dumont–Willis Indexes (DWI-1 & DWI-2) for the WISC-IV. http://alpha.fdu.edu/psychology/

Engle, R. W., Carullo, J. J., & Collins, K. W. (1991). Individual differences in working memory for comprehension and following directions. *Journal of Educational Research, 84,* 253–262.

Engle, R. W., Tuholski, S. W., Laughlin, J. E., & Conway, A. R. A. (1999). Working memory, short term memory, and general fluid intelligence: A latent variable approach. *Journal of Experimental Psychology: General, 128*(3), 309–331.

Flanagan, D. P., & Kaufman, A.S. (2004). *Essentials of WISC-IV assessment.* New York: Wiley.

Francis, D. J., Fletcher, J. M., Stuebing, K. K., Lyon, R. G., Shaywitz, B. A., & Shaywitz, S. E. (2005). Psychometric approaches to the identification of LD: IQ and achievement scores are not enough. *Journal of Learning Disabilities, 38,* 98–108.

Fry, A. F., & Hale, S. (1996). Processing speed, working memory, and fluid intelligence: Evidence for a developmental cascade. *Psychological Science, 7*(4), 237–241.

Fuchs, L., & Fuchs, D. (1998). Treatment validity: A unifying concept for reconceptualizing the identification of learning disabilities. *Learning Disabilities Research & Practice, 13,* 204–219.

Georgas, J., Weiss, L. G., van de Vijver, F. J. R., & Saklofske, D.H. (2003). *Culture and children's intelligence: Cross-cultural analyses of the WISC-III.* San Diego, CA: Academic Press.

Hale, J. B., & Fiorello, C. A. (2004). *School neuropsychology: A practitioner's handbook.* New York: Guilford.

Hale, J. B., Fiorello, C. A., Kavanagh, J. A., Hoeppner, & Gaither (2001). WISC –III predictors of academic achievement for children with learning disabilities: Are global and factor scores comparable? *School Psychology Quarterly Special Issue 16(1),* 31–55.

Harris, J. G., & Llorente, A. M. (2005). Cultural considerations in the use of the WISC-IV. In A. Prifitera, D. H. Saklofske, & L. G. Weiss (Eds.), *WISC-IV clinical use and interpretation: Scientist–practitioner perspectives* (pp. 381–413). San Diego, CA: Elsevier.

Hitch, G. J., Towse, J. N., & Hutton, U. (2001). What limits children's working memory span? Theoretical accounts and applications for scholastic development. *Journal of Experimental Psychology: General, 130,* 184–198.

Horn, J. L. (1998). A basis for research on age differences in cognitive capabilities. In J. J. McArdle & R. W. Woodcock (Eds.), *Human cognitive abilities in theory and practice* (pp. 57–87). Mahwah, NJ:. Erlbaum.

Jonides, J. Lacey, S.C., & Nee, D.E. (2005). Process of working memory in mind and brain. *Current Directions in Psychological Science, 14,* 2–5.

Kail, R. (2000). Speed of information processing: Developmental change and links to intelligence. *Journal of Psychology Special Issue: Developmental perspectives in intelligence 38(1),* 51–61.

Kamphaus, R. W. (1998). Intelligence test interpretation: Acting in the absence of evidence. In A. Prifitera,, D. H. Saklofske, & L. G. Weiss (Eds.), *WISC-III clinical use and interpretation: Scientist–practitioner perspectives* (pp. 39–57). San Diego, CA: Academic Press.

Kamphaus, R. W. (2001). Clinical assessment of child and adolescent intelligence (2nd ed.). Needham Heights, MA: Allyn & Bacon.

Kane, M. J., Bleckley, M. K., Conway, A. R. A., & Engle, R. W. (2001). A controlled attention view of working memory capacity. *Journal of Experimental Psychology: General. 130,* 169–183.

Kaufman, A. S. (1994). *Intelligent testing with the WISC–III.* New York: Wiley.

Kiewra, K. A., & Benton, S.L. (1988). The relationship between information processing ability and note taking. *Contemporary Educational Psychology, 13,* 3–44.

Konold, T. R. (1999). Evaluating discrepancy analysis with the WISC–III and WIAT. *Journal of Psychoeducational Assessment, 17,* 24–35.

Kyllonen, P. C., & Christal, R. E. (1990). Reasoning ability is (little more than) working memory capacity. *Intelligence, 14,* 389–433.

Kyllonen, P. C., & Stephens, D. L. (1990). Cognitive abilities as the determinant of success in acquiring logic skills. *Learning and Individual Differences, 2,* 129–160.

Lezak, M. D. (1995). *Neuropsychological assessment* (3rd ed.). New York: Oxford University Press.

Longman, R. S. (2005). Tables to compare WISC-IV index scores against overall means. In A. Prifitera, D. H. Saklofske, & L. G. Weiss (Eds.), *WISC-III clinical use and interpretation: Scientist–practitioner perspectives* (pp. 66–69). San Diego, CA: Elsevier.

Lustig, C., May, C. P., & Hasher, L. (2001). Working memory span and the role of proactive interference. *Journal of Experimental Psychology: General 130,* 199–207.

Mastropieri, M. A. (2003). *Feasibility and consequences of response to intervention (RtI): Examination of the issues and scientific evidence as a model for the identification of individuals with learning disabilities.* Paper presented at the National Research Center on Learning Disabilities Responsiveness-to-Intervention Symposium, Kansas City, MO.

McCloskey, G., & Maerlender, A. (2005). The WISC-IV Integrated. In A. Prifitera, D. H. Saklofske, & L. G. Weiss (Eds.), *WISC-III clinical use and interpretation: Scientist–practitioner perspectives* (pp. 101–149). San Diego, CA: Elsevier.

McMaster, K. L., Fuchs, D., Fuchs, L. S., & Compton, D. L. (2003). *Responding to nonresponders: An experimental field trial of identification and intervention methods.* Paper presented at the National Research Center on Learning Disabilities Responsiveness-to-Intervention Symposium, Kansas City, MO.

Na, D. L., Adair, J. C., Kang, Y., Chung, C. S., Lee, K. H., & Heilmand, K. M. (1999). Motor perseverative behavior on a line cancellation task. *Neurology, 52*(8), 1569–1576.

Oakland, T., Glutting, J., & Watkins, M. W. (2005). Assessment of test behaviors with the WISC-IV. In A. Prifitera, D. H. Saklofske, & L. G. Weiss (Eds.), *WISC-III clinical use and interpretation: Scientist–practitioner perspectives* (pp. 435–463). San Diego, CA: Elsevier.

Ormrod, J. E., & Cochran, K. F. (1988). Relationship of verbal ability and working memory to spelling achievement and learning to spell. *Reading Research Instruction, 28,* 33–43.

Prifitera, A., Saklofske, D. H., & Weiss, L. G. (2005). *WISC-III clinical use and interpretation: Scientist–practitioner perspectives.* San Diego, CA: Elsevier.

Reschly, R. J. (2003). *What if LD identification changed to reflect research findings?* Paper presented at the National Research Center on Learning Disabilities Responsiveness-to-Intervention Symposium, Kansas City, MO.

Saklofske, D. H., Prifitera, A., Weiss, L. G., Rolfhus, E., & Zhu, J. (2005). Clinical interpretation of the WISC-IV FSIQ and GAI. In A. Prifitera, D. H. Saklofske, & L.G. Weiss (Eds.), *WISC-III clinical use and interpretation: Scientist–practitioner perspectives* (pp. 33–65) San Diego, CA: Elsevier.

Salthouse, T. A. (1996a). Constraints on theories of cognitive aging. *Psychonomic Bulletin and Review, 3,* 287–299

Salthouse, T. A. (1996b). The processing speed theory of adult age differences in cognition. *Psychological Review, 103,* 403–428.

Salthouse, T. A. (2000a). Pressing issues in cognitive aging. In D. C. Park & N. Schwarz (Eds.), *Cognitive aging: A primer* (pp. 43–54). Philadelphia: Psychology Press.

Salthouse, T. A. (2000b). Steps toward the explanation of adult age differences in cognition. In T. J. Perfect & E. A. Maylor (Eds.), *Models of cognitive aging* (pp. 19–49). New York: Oxford University Press.

Sattler, J. M. (2001). *Assessment of children: Cognitive applications* (4th ed). San Diego: Author.

Sattler, J. M., & Dumont, R. (2004). *Assessment of children: WISC-IV and WPPSI-III Supplement.* San Diego: Author.

Schwean, V. L., & Saklofske, D. H. (2005). Assessment of attention deficit hyperactivity disorder with the WISC-IV. In A. Prifitera, D. H. Saklofske, & L. G Weiss (Eds.), *WISC-IV clinical use and interpretation: Scientist–practitioner perspectives* (pp. 235–280). San Diego, CA: Elsevier.

Shaywitz, S. E., Fletcher, J. M., Holahan, J. M., Schneider, A. E., Marchione, K. E., Steubing, K. K., Francis, D. J., & Shaywitz, B. A. (1999). Persistence of dyslexia: The Connecticut Longitudinal Study at Adolescence. *Pediatrics, 104,* 1351–1359.

Siegel, L. S. (2003). IQ-discrepancy definitions and the diagnosis of LD: Introduction to the special issue. *Journal of Learning Disabilities. 31,* 2–3.

The Psychological Corporation (2003). *Manual for the Early Reading Success Indicator.* San Antonio, TX: Author.

Tulsky, D. S., Saklofske, D. H., & Ricker, J. H. (2003). Historical overview of intelligence and memory: Factors influencing the Wechsler scales. In D. S. Tulsky, D. H. Saklofske, G. J. Chelune, R. J. Ivnik, A. Prifitera, R. K. Heaton, R. Bornstein, & M. F. Ledbetter (Eds.), *Clinical interpretation of the WAIS-III and WMS-III* (pp. 7–41). San Diego, CA: Academic Press.

Tulsky, D. S., Saklofske, D. H., & Zhu, J. (2003). Revising a standard: An evaluation of the origin and development of the WAIS-III. In D. S. Tulsky, D. H. Saklofske, G. J. Chelune, R. J. Ivnik, A. Prifitera, R. K. Heaton, R. Bornstein, & M. F. Ledbetter (Eds.), *Clinical interpretation of the WAIS-III and WMS-III* (pp. 43–92). San Diego, CA: Academic Press.

Wechsler, D. (1991). *Wechsler intelligence scale for children–Third Edition.* San Antonio, TX: The Psychological Corporation.

Wechsler, D. (1997). *Manual for the Wechsler adult intelligence scale–Third edition.* San Antonio, TX: The Psychological Corporation.

Wechsler, D. (2003) *Manual for the Wechsler Intelligence Scale for Children–Fourth edition.* San Antonio, TX: The Psychological Corporation.

Wechsler, D., Kaplan, E., Fein, D., Kramer, J., Delis, D., Morris, R., & Maerlender, A. (2004). *Wechsler intelligence scale for children–4th edition: Integrated.* San Antonio, TX: Harcourt Assessment, Inc.

Weiss, L. G., Saklofske, D. H., & Prifitera, A. (2003). Clinical interpretation of the WISC-III factor scores. In C.R. Reynolds & R.W Kamphaus (Eds.), *Handbook of psychological and educational assessment of children: Intelligence and achievement* (2nd ed.). New York: Guilford Press.

Weiss, L. G., Saklofske, D. H., & Prifitera, A. (2005). Interpreting the WISC-IV index scores. In A. Prifitera, D. H. Saklofske, & L. G. Weiss (Eds.), *WISC-III clinical use and interpretation: Scientist–practitioner perspectives* (pp. 71–100). San Diego, CA: Elsevier.

5

ESSENTIALS OF WISC-IV
INTEGRATED
INTERPRETATION

JAMES A. HOLDNACK AND LAWRENCE G. WEISS

The intent of any psychological or psychoeducational assessment is to make sound clinical decisions about an individual child or adolescent. Mostly, these clinical decisions relate to eligibility determination, diagnosis, and recommendations for accommodations. Many clinicians use a specific set of cognitive and psychological tests when assessing children due to limited time to perform assessments (Cashel, 2002). In general, most clinicians are familiar with the Wechsler Intelligence Scales for Children (Cashel, 2002; Lally, 2003; Rabin, Barr & Burton, 2005). Past revisions of these scales typically did not have dramatic changes to the content and procedures from previous editions. Subsequently, most clinicians found it easy to adjust to the latest edition.

The fourth revision of the Wechsler Intelligence Scale for Children (WISC-IV: Wechsler, 2003) involved the most pronounced changes to the content and procedures of any previous WISC revision. The changes reflect the goal of focusing the interpretation of the scale away from FSIQ or "g" to cognitive domain scores (index scores). The factor composition was slightly modified from the WISC-III (Wechsler, 1991) in terms of their description; however, more dramatic changes occurred at the subtest level. The subtest level changes were designed to reduce competing hypotheses when interpreting factor scores (i.e., reducing processing speed demands of perceptual organization). These changes are discussed in more detail elsewhere in this book.

The WISC-IV revision successfully eliminated a number of competing hypotheses when describing why a child may have performed poorly on a specific index. Subsequent to the initial publication of the WISC-IV, additional improvements were made to the existing WISC-IV to help the

WISC-IV Advanced Clinical Interpretation

181

Copyright © 2006 by Elsevier. All rights reserved.

clinician better understand and communicate about the child's performance. The WISC-IV Integrated (Wechsler, Kaplan, Fein, Kramer, Delis, Morris, & Maerlender, 2004) provides an additional set of tools for understanding low scores obtained on the standard WISC-IV subtests. The procedures allow for the quantitative and qualitative analysis of the examinee's performance.

This chapter is designed to provide clinicians with the basic application of the additional subtests. This includes when to use the additional procedures, basic interpretation of the results, and recommendations for "how to get started" using these measures. The chapter is divided into sections based on the four WISC-IV Integrated domains: Verbal, Perceptual, Working Memory, and Processing Speed. The Integrated subtests are designed to test specific hypotheses about performance within these domains.

STRUCTURE OF THE WISC-IV INTEGRATED

The WISC-IV Integrated is composed of core, supplemental, and process subtests. The core subtests are used to derive the index scores: Verbal Comprehension, Perceptual Reasoning, Working Memory, and Processing Speed. The supplemental subtests will often be used when the examiner has spoiled the administration of a core subtest. The examiner may use the supplemental score to obtain the index level score and Full-Scale IQ (FSIQ), provided they follow the specific guidelines outlined in the *WISC-IV Integrated Administration and Scoring Manual* (Wechsler et al., 2004). Additionally, the examiner may administer a supplemental subtest to obtain additional information regarding the child's performance within a specific domain. The process subtests are new to the Wechsler intelligence scale but were published previously as the *Wechsler Intelligence Scale for Children*–3rd Edition as a Process Instrument (WISC-III PI; Kaplan, Fein, Kramer, Delis, & Morris, 1999). Users familiar with that battery will find many similarities to the WISC-IV Integrated. *The process subtests are designed to be used individually (i.e., it would be highly unusual to administer more than a couple of these subtests for any single child).* For the core subtests and the process subtests, there are additional scores referred to as process scores. These are described briefly here and discussed in more detail in Chapter 6.

WHEN TO USE PROCESS SUBTESTS

The decision to use specific process subtests is determined by the hypotheses the clinician wants to explore for that particular child. These hypotheses may be driven by clinical questions such as "Does this child's history of motor coordination impairments interfere with their performance on Block Design?" This question might be known at the time of referral (i.e., history of treatment in occupational therapy or teacher's observation of poor printing skills), whereas at other times an observation of the child made during the course of testing (i.e., labored or clumsy responses on motor tasks) may prompt the administration of additional tests. It may be an accommodation question (i.e., does the child benefit from more time on tests?) that prompts the use of specific scores or tests. There are no hard and fast rules for deciding to use a particular subtest. There will be some subtests that are used frequently while others are used rarely. As part of this chapter, the concept of when to use the process subtest is discussed, but all possibilities cannot be presented. The clinician should be aware of the multidimensional nature of the core subtests and how conclusions that may be drawn from administering these subtests are informed by the child's performance on the associated processing subtests.

VERBAL DOMAIN SCORES

The WISC-IV Verbal Comprehension domain is composed of subtests that measure the child's capacity to solve verbal problems. These skills often require the expression of knowledge obtained through formal and informal training or personal experiences. Additionally, skills such as conceptual and abstract reasoning, long-term verbal memory, deductive reasoning, and understanding social conventions are invoked. The composite of these skills is often referred to as "crystallized" intellectual abilities. These tests require the child to express themselves verbally and require at least some degree of information retrieval from memory. It would be impossible for any person to correctly state the meaning of a word they have never heard before or to relate two words they had never come across. Therefore, the information has to be in their memory (i.e., even if it is an incomplete or inaccurate form of knowledge) and the child must be able to "retrieve" that information.

WHEN TO USE VERBAL PROCESS
SCORES

The primary interpretation of low scores on VCI is low verbal intelligence. However, some children score low on one or more core verbal subtests for other reasons such as difficulties with verbal expression, difficulties recalling semantic information from long-term storage, or a lack of acquired verbal knowledge. The verbal process scores are designed to evaluate these types of difficulties associated with the core and supplementary

WISC-IV Integrated verbal subtests. One hypothesis is associated with poor expressive language skills with intact receptive knowledge. Another hypothesis relates to poor memory retrieval skills. The clinician may have information prior to the evaluation that would enable them to decide before seeing the child that they may need to use one or more of the process subtests. If the child has a history of speech articulation problems that interfere with communication, then it would be prudent to use at least one of the verbal process subtests.

Children with an expressive language disorder do not necessarily show improved performance on process subtests, as children with an expressive language disorder will often have some deficits in aspects of comprehension or auditory working memory. In many cases, it will not be clear if a child that has a history of language delays will have had an expressive language disorder, a mixed expressive-receptive language disorder, or language delays that will resolve. Therefore, in children with known language delays, it is good practice to administer at least one or two verbal process subtests.

Children that have a history of acquired brain injury due to head injury or a neurological condition may have difficulty retrieving information from memory. In particular, older children and adolescents that have experienced an extended period of normal development prior to injury or onset of their neurological condition may have an established knowledge base but experience difficulty retrieving that knowledge. In children experiencing head injury at a young age, language impairments are likely to be more pervasive (Ewing-Cobb & Barnes, 2002) and using process measures is not likely to yield differences from the core subtests.

Pre-referral information is often too vague or inadequate to make a priori decisions about which subtests to administer. Teachers' observations such as limited language production, poor memory, or "does not work to ability" can provide some clues about potential weaknesses in expressing knowledge. More often than not, the decision to administer additional verbal subtests will be made based on observed behaviors or test scores. Observations of low language production, significant articulation problems, or excessive verbal production resulting in spoiled responses signal problems with control of language that could interfere with performance on core verbal subtests. If the child expresses difficulties accessing knowledge (i.e., "I know that, why can't I remember it") or remembering information in general, completing verbal process subtests will yield important clinical information.

Alternately, the decision to perform additional verbal process subtests will occur after the verbal subtests have been scored. For children with significantly low Verbal Comprehension Index or Working Memory Index scores, the verbal process scores provide information about the degree to which language production and/or auditory working memory problems have affected performance. In some cases, a specific core verbal subtest will be significantly lower than all the rest of the subtests in the domain.

The process subtest that corresponds to that core subtest can be administered to determine if there is a specific weakness in that content area or if the examinee had problems expressing knowledge for that subtest. Administration of a process subtest is indicated if the child displays inconsistent or atypical performance within a specific core subtest (i.e., misses easier items and then receives full credit on more difficult items or consistently provides one-point responses). In these situations, the scaled score for the core subtest may not be particularly low but the inconsistency in performance signals difficulties expressing or accessing knowledge.

VERBAL PROCESS SUBTESTS

The process subtests in the verbal domain are multiple-choice adaptations of the corresponding Verbal domain subtests: Similarities Multiple Choice, Vocabulary Multiple Choice, Picture Vocabulary Multiple Choice, Comprehension Multiple Choice, and Information Multiple Choice. The multiple choice version should be used when a child obtains a low score on a corresponding verbal comprehension subtest (i.e., Similarities, Vocabulary, Comprehension, or Information). While the response options are presented visually, the examiner can read the options to the child. Therefore, children who have difficulty reading the stimulus words and response options for the multiple-choice adaptations of the Verbal Comprehension subtests will still be able to demonstrate their reasoning and concept formation abilities if they have adequately developed listening comprehension and auditory working memory. The Verbal domain process subtests items are scored 0-point, 1-point, or 2-points based on scoring studies of the standardization data. In order to have only two responses per item worth points, some multiple-choice responses that would receive 1-point credit on the core subtest were intentionally changed to a 0-point value. These were marginal responses that were rarely picked by children of high ability. Changing these assigned point values reduced the potential for achieving points by guessing.

The multiple-choice subtests were not developed to assess giftedness or reading ability. *The examiner should never substitute a multiple-choice subtest for a core subtest to obtain an index level score, even if the core subtest was spoiled during administration.* These subtests were also not designed to assess the child's reading ability. The examiner should not administer the test having the child reading the possible responses and using this score to determine if reading the choices results in a lower score. The multiple-choice subtest should be used only to determine if articulation, expressive language, or memory retrieval problems are interfering with the expression of intellectual abilities.

SIMILARITIES MULTIPLE CHOICE

The Similarities Multiple Choice subtest should be used when the examiner believes that low scores on the core Similarities subtest were lower than expected. The examiner may have observed many one-point responses or inconsistency in responding (i.e., misses easy items but achieves points on harder items). If the Similarities subtest is the lowest score among verbal comprehension items and the examiner believes the child understands the conceptual relationships between words but had difficulty expressing these relationships, then the multiple-choice version should be administered. The results of this subtest are interpreted as the child's ability to identify the best conceptual relationship between words and ideas.

VOCABULARY MULTIPLE CHOICE

The Vocabulary Multiple Choice subtest is used when the examiner believes that the child's score on the core version of the Vocabulary subtest does not fully represent the child's knowledge base. This subtest should also be used when the examiner knows the child has a history of language delays, speech–language therapy, or poor verbal expression as observed by parents or teachers. The Vocabulary subtest is an important indicator of the child's current knowledge base, and low scores must be analyzed for global knowledge deficits versus expression or access to that knowledge. This subtest is interpreted as an indication of the child's ability to recognize correct definitions of stimulus words and estimates the extent of the foundation of their semantic knowledge.

PICTURE VOCABULARY

The Picture Vocabulary Multiple Choice subtest measures the child's semantic knowledge through pictures. This subtest was designed specifically to significantly reduce the listening comprehension and auditory working memory demands associated with the multiple-choice version of Vocabulary. Examiners familiar with the Peabody Picture Vocabulary Test (Dunn & Dunn, 1997) will quickly understand the administration, scoring, and interpretation of this subtest. The Picture Vocabulary subtest evaluates the child's semantic knowledge base in isolation of other language comprehension or reading abilities. This subtest is easy to administer and score, making it ideal for use in most clinical evaluations. This subtest, in conjunction with the Vocabulary Multiple Choice subtest, should be used when evaluating a child that has a history of language delays or impairments. Also, this test should be used when evaluating children for potential reading disorder, as stimuli are not affected by reading, working memory, or listening abilities. This subtest is interpreted as an indication of the child's ability to identify the visual representation of a word's definition. It provides an estimation of their semantic knowledge.

COMPREHENSION MULTIPLE CHOICE

The Comprehension Multiple Choice subtest evaluates the child's ability to recognize best responses to social conventions without the free recall response demands of the standard Comprehension subtest. The standard version of the Comprehension subtest makes significant demands on sustained language production, more than other verbal subtests. Sometimes the child is required to make more than one response per item, unlike other verbal domain subtests. This subtest should be used when the child is observed to have low verbal production (i.e., frequently uses one-word responses or does not engage in conversation readily) or when the core Comprehension subtest is significantly lower than all other verbal scores. For children who can recognize, but not articulate, descriptions of the reasons for, or consequences of, the conventions and general principles underlying personal social situations and organized societies, the multiple-choice version will show their understanding of these concepts.

INFORMATION MULTIPLE CHOICE

The Information Multiple Choice assesses the extent to which the child has acquired, stored, and recognizes facts about a wide range of topics. Performance on this task is a good estimate of the child's general fund of knowledge. The multiple-choice version allows the child that has intact knowledge but inability to access and retrieve that information the opportunity to demonstrate their knowledge. Since the standard version of this subtest is optional, the multiple-choice version is used infrequently. It should be utilized when Information scores are unexpectedly low in light of other verbal comprehension subtests.

RECOMMENDED APPLICATION OF VERBAL PROCESS SCORES

- *Clinicians will find the multiple-choice subtests easy to administer, score, and interpret and can be used readily by most clinicians familiar with the Wechsler scales.*

- *Administration time prohibits the use of all five subtests on a regular basis.*
- *The Picture Vocabulary subtest could be used routinely, especially for learning disability evaluations, children with language delays or working memory deficits, or in children with observed low verbal production/ expression.*
- *The Vocabulary Multiple Choice subtest should be used when evaluating children with a history of language delays or observed expressive language difficulties.*
- *The Comprehension Multiple Choice should be used when the examinee has low verbal production or when Comprehension is unexpectedly lower than other verbal subtests.*
- *Similarities and Information Multiple Choice should be used when low scores are obtained or the parallel core/supplemental verbal subtest is unexpectedly low.*
- *These tests do not diagnose language disorder, reading disorder, expressive language problems, memory impairment, or working memory deficits.*
- *These tests cannot be used to measure giftedness and should not be used to compute VCI or FSIQ.*
- *These tests may inform about accommodations related to the use of open-ended versus multiple choice questions and to the child's capacity to respond to questions during class with or without prompts or cues.*
- *The subtest scores are presented as age-corrected scaled scores and performance is interpreted the same as core and supplemental subtests.*

PERCEPTUAL-REASONING DOMAIN SCORES

The WISC-IV Perceptual Reasoning domain is composed of subtests that measure the child's capacity to solve problems presented visually. In previous versions of the WISC, the assessment of these skills relied heavily on processing speed, executive, and motor control in addition to the primary assessment of visual–perceptual abilities. The WISC-IV was designed to create a relatively pure visual-reasoning factor, reducing the impact of motor control and processing speed. While the visual processing speed and motor control are reduced significantly in the most recent version, the Block Design subtest requires, to some degree, adequate processing speed, construction, executive functioning, and motor control. Low scores on this subtest, particularly when other visual reasoning tasks are significantly higher, may signal difficulties with factors other than visual–perceptual functioning. The process subtests were designed to explicitly test the hypothesis that speed, motor control, or executive functioning may be influencing Block Design performance.

WHEN TO USE PERCEPTUAL-REASONING PROCESS SCORES

The Perceptual Reasoning Process subtests described in this chapter are designed to assess two primary hypotheses associated with performance on core and supplemental perceptual-reasoning subtests (particularly Block Design). The first hypothesis is that the child has low Block Design scores due to motor control impairments that affect both accuracy and speed of performance. The second hypothesis is that low perceptual reasoning scores are due to impulsivity (i.e., tries to complete design quickly and loses points due to small errors from not checking work for accuracy) or a haphazard problem-solving style (i.e., trial-and-error approach). Children having obvious motor impairment (i.e., cerebral palsy) or executive functioning impairment (i.e., Traumatic Brain Injury) may do poorly on visual-reasoning tasks for reasons not due to poor visual–perceptual ability.

Children with gross or fine motor delays score low on visual–perceptual tasks due to the motor demands. This is not to say that they do not have visual-reasoning deficits, but determining the source of their poor performance becomes confounded when using tasks that require rapid motor control. Children having a history of acquired brain injury may have significant difficulties with processing speed and executive functioning. Executive functioning is an important component of performing the Block Design task. Children with minor difficulties with behavioral control and regulation may miss a few items because they failed to recheck their work, worked too quickly, or did not employ an effective strategy to complete the task. Individuals diagnosed with attention deficit disorder, hyperactive impulsive type, and combined type may show minor difficulties on Block Design due to executive functioning or processing speed deficits. More significant deficits on Block Design would be observed in children with significant motor, processing speed, and/or executive functioning deficits. Children with neurological conditions are at risk for having impaired performance on this subtest due to a number of factors.

In cases where pre-referral information is inadequate to know if potential motor, executive functioning, or processing speed difficulties may be present, teacher's reports of slow work habits, poor handwriting, drawing, or copying skills, or impulsive behavior will enable the clinician to make a decision to administer the perceptual-reasoning process subtests before seeing the child. Frequently, the decision to administer additional perceptual-reasoning process subtests is based on observation of the child's behavior while completing the block design and other subtests. Obvious difficulties with motor control, such as dropping blocks or labored attempts to keep blocks together, indicate a need to administer the process subtests.

The decision to administer one or more perceptual reasoning subtests can be determined after administration of the three core perceptual reasoning subtests. Because these subtests are scored easily, the age-correct scale can be calculated after administration of the core WISC-IV. If the Block Design subtest is significantly lower than Matrix Reasoning or Picture Concepts, then the examiner should administer one or both of the process subtests.

VISUAL–PERCEPTUAL PROCESSING AND EXECUTIVE FUNCTIONING

Executive functioning is a category of cognition composed of many specific cognitive abilities. These are higher order skills that influence performance on other cognitive tasks. One executive function capacity is the efficient organization of information used to solve problems systematically. The proposed abilities subsumed under the rubric of executive functioning include, but are not limited to, organization, planning, flexibility, self-monitoring, information retrieval, productivity, impulse control, and controlling motor programs. Executive functioning, as measured by WISC-IV Integrated, measures immediate planning, self-monitoring, and impulse control. Self-monitoring indicates the capacity to evaluate one's own behavior for adherence to task rules, limiting and correcting erroneous responses, and maintaining task focus to achieve task goals.

PERCEPTUAL-REASONING PROCESS SUBTESTS

The Perceptual-Reasoning Process subtests are Block Design Multiple Choice (BDMC), Block Design Process Approach, and Elithorn Mazes. This chapter covers the Block Design Multiple Choice and Elithorn Mazes subtests. The Block Design Multiple Choice should be administered to children with obvious motor difficulties and those scoring low on the Block Design subtest compared to other core and supplemental perceptual-reasoning subtests. Children demonstrating an impulsive response style on any of the perceptual-reasoning subtests can be a reason to administer the Elithorn Mazes subtest. Both of these subtests are scored with or without time bonuses. In children with both slow processing speed and poor motor control, it is advisable to report the score that does not include time bonuses.

BLOCK DESIGN MULTIPLE-CHOICE SUBTEST

The BDMC subtest is designed to assess a child's visual-integration and mental construction abilities without the influence of motor planning and execution. The subtest contains two types of items. The first 18 items use two-dimensional representations for the child to complete. With the exception of 1 item, there is no content overlap with the core Block Design subtest. Items 20–25 have three-dimensional stimuli and the examinee must consider the appearance of more than one side of the figure when completing the task. The first 18 items may be completed successfully by comparing individual blocks from the target to each possible solution. These items are a good measure of visual matching and discrimination. They also require some capacity to understand angles. The degree of difficulty is considerably less for these items than for the standard version of Block Design. The three-dimensional items were added to increase difficulty. These items require adequate visual matching and discrimination but also tap the ability to perceive angles, mentally rotate objects, and construct a whole design from its parts. This subtest is used to test the hypothesis that low scores on the core Block Design subtest are due to motor or executive functioning impairments rather than a deficit in visual construction abilities. For children with concurrently low scores on processing speed, the no time bonus score should be reported for this subtest.

ELITHORN MAZES SUBTEST

The Elithorn Mazes subtest assesses immediate spatial planning skills, rapid visual–perceptual processing, spatial working memory, and ability to follow task rules and inhibit impulsive responses. There is an opportunity for the child to learn from their mistakes on this subtest. If an error is made on the first trial of the item, the child is allowed to try again. The inability to benefit from feedback (i.e., seeing their first mistake) could indicate significant problems with cognitive flexibility and behavioral control. For children with processing speed deficits, the no time bonus score should be reported. Low scores on this test suggest poor planning ability and impulsive responding.

This test should be used when evaluating children having obvious difficulties with self-control as evidenced by impulsivity, emotional outbursts, and hyperactivity. Children with mild degree impulsivity may do well on this test, particularly on the second trial. Poor performance, especially overtly impulsive performance (i.e., quick responses with numerous errors and rule violations) strongly implicate poor executive control of behavior.

RECOMMENDED APPLICATION
OF PERCEPTUAL REASONING
PROCESS SCORES

- *Clinicians will find administration of the Block Design Multiple-Choice subtest somewhat easier than Elithorn Mazes. The latter may take some practice administrations prior to using with clinical cases.*
- *Administration time prohibits using all of the perceptual reasoning process subtests routinely. Clinicians may decide to use Block Design Multiple Choice frequently, given its ease of use and utility as pure visual–perceptual/spatial task without motor contributions.*
- *Block Design Multiple Choice should be used when evaluating children with a history of motor delays or a history of occupational therapy services.*
- *Block Design Multiple Choice should be used when Block Design is significantly lower than other measures within the perceptual reasoning domain and there are indications of motor control problems.*
- *It is recommended that the examiner administer the Elithorn Mazes subtest if the child has a history of very impulsive behavior and if impulsive behavior appears to have impacted their WISC-IV performance negatively, particularly the child that impulsively picks responses on matrix reasoning and picture concepts.*
- *Block Design Multiple Choice is not designed to diagnose motor problems but enables the clinician to reduce the impact of motor problems on test performance.*
- *Elithorn Mazes performance does not diagnose or rule out attention deficit disorder. It may provide some support for that diagnosis but does not make the diagnosis.*
- *These tests cannot be used to measure giftedness and should not be used to compute PRI or FSIQ.*
- *These tests may inform about accommodations associated with providing additional time for testing or need for accommodations (i.e., pencil grips) to improve motor control of writing.*
- *Subtest scores are presented as age-corrected scaled scores and performance is interpreted the same as core and supplemental subtests.*

WORKING MEMORY DOMAIN

The WISC-IV Integrated Working Memory domain contains tests that measure components of registration and mental manipulation. The core and supplemental subtests in the working memory domain measure working memory for auditory numeric, letter, and math stimuli. The process subtests expand the assessment of working memory to include visual stimuli and procedures that enable the clinician to better understand performance deficits observed on the standard and supplemental subtests. Subtest performance in this domain is described by the terms *registration* and *working memory*. The term registration is applied to scores that relate to the child's capacity to temporarily make information accessible in conscious awareness. The information is not manipulated but is simply repeated. Working memory, as used in the WISC-IV Integrated, refers to any process that requires both the registration of information in conscious awareness and subsequent mental manipulation of that information. The term working memory does not imply equivalence in the difficulty of the mental operations used in the manipulation, only that some type of mental transformation of that information has occurred. The operations utilized are resequencing, storage of multiple stimulus types, and math computations.

WHEN TO USE WORKING MEMORY PROCESS SCORES

The Working Memory Process subtests enable the clinician to test four primary hypotheses. The first hypothesis asks "does the child have global deficits in registration and working memory or are they restricted to a specific modality?" The second use of the process subtests is to determine if the child has difficulty with performing working memory tasks related to a specific stimulus type (i.e., numbers versus letters or spatial versus numbers and letters). The third reason for using the process subtests is to identify if the child has difficulty on the mental operations that need to be performed on the stimuli. This last reason could be poor math skills or an inability to hold two types of stimuli (i.e., numbers and letters) simultaneously.

The decision to use the additional process subtests will likely be made during the observation of the child's performance. There are, however, some background characteristics that will prompt the examiner to employ some of the process subtests prior to the evaluation. The linguistic background of the child is important. In other words, any child with a history of impoverished linguistic environment, bilingual, English as a second language, learning disability, central auditory processing disorder, or language disorder should be administered the visual registration and working memory subtests. This will help the clinician determine if low scores on the working memory index reflect global deficits or relate specifically to auditory tasks. When testing children with known math difficulties, it is prudent to use process subtests to discern if low working memory subtest scores are due to poor number skills (i.e., sequencing) and math computation ability. Children with reading problems may have poor letter knowledge; additional measures differentiating letter and number recall abilities will be helpful in determining if difficulties are content specific or more general.

Teacher observations of the child may be useful in making a priori decisions about additional subtests. If the teacher notes significant language problems or inattentiveness, then the examiner will want to administer some additional working memory tasks. Also, the teacher may note memory problems and describe the child as "forgetful." Often times, forgetfulness refers to working memory problems rather than long-term storage deficits. Therefore, understanding the nature of the memory problem may facilitate the development of appropriate accommodations or modifications for the child.

The decision to use additional working memory subtests is likely to occur during the evaluation. Observed difficulties with auditory processing and language functioning will clue the examiner to complete visual process measures. Poor math skills, as evident in achievement testing, will inform the examiner that number and computation weaknesses will affect other test results. Specific low scores on Digit Span, Letter–Number Sequencing, or Arithmetic will prompt the examiner to administer at least one visual working memory task. Given that there are no visual working memory tasks among the core subtests, the decision to use the visual working memory subtests may also be prompted by significantly low Perceptual Reasoning Index scores. This would test the hypothesis that visual–perceptual difficulties are more global and that poor visual working memory contributes to low perceptual-reasoning scores.

WORKING MEMORY PROCESS SUBTESTS

The working memory process subtests are Spatial Span, Visual Digit Span, Letter Span, Letter–Number Sequencing Process Approach, Arithmetic Process Approach Parts A and B, and Written Arithmetic. The visual working memory measures are Visual Digit Span and Spatial Span. These can be used in cases where a child demonstrates poor auditory working memory skills or low perceptual reasoning scores. Letter Span is an additional subtest used to determine the extent of content deficits in auditory working memory. The Letter–Number Sequencing Processing Approach can be used when a child has a significantly low score on Letter–Number Sequencing compared to Digit Span. The Arithmetic subtests can be used to test hypotheses about working memory and math skills as well as potential accommodations.

SPATIAL SPAN

The Spatial Span subtest requires the child to tap blocks in spatial sequences of increasing length. In the first part of the subtest, the child repeats the sequence in the same order as the examiner. In the second part, the examinee must tap the blocks in backward sequence. This is a spatial analog to digits forward and backward. The Spatial Span Forward component represents immediate spatial registration as the child must temporally hold the visual sequence in mind before executing the sequence themselves. In the backward task, the child must mentally reorder the sequence of taps and execute the sequence in reverse order. This requires both registration and manipulation of the information. Additional skills impact performance on this test, which are discussed in more detail in the next chapter.

The Spatial Span subtest is a useful measure for determining the extent of working memory deficits. This is the only subtest that does not use verbally meaningful stimuli. In individuals with significant difficulties encoding and processing auditory/verbal information, all working memory subtests may be low, including visually presented digits. It is recommended that this test be used for children with low verbal ability, low auditory working memory, or a history of language problems. Also, an isolated deficit in perceptual reasoning may warrant investigation of the impact of visual working memory on these abilities.

While the administration of this subtest is straightforward, the response coding requires some practice. Most clinicians will find that one or two practice administrations are sufficient to use the test effectively. Scaled scores for forward and backward conditions are provided. In some cases, the examiner may wish to only administer the forward condition as a means of screening for visual working memory problems. This requires only a brief administration time, which makes it easier for routine use.

VISUAL DIGIT SPAN

In the Visual Digit Span subtest, the examinee sees a string of numbers and must remember the numbers in the same order as they are presented. This subtest has a forward condition only. The examiner may wish to compare this score to Digit Span Forward to determine if visual presentation improves performance. This subtest is useful in cases where the examinee has low auditory Digit Span or Digit Span Forward. The subtests are not completely comparable because on Visual Digit Span the examinee is exposed to all the items at once, whereas in standard Digit Span the digits are presented one at a time. Clinicians will likely find this subtest useful intermittently. This subtest is helpful in determining if visually presenting information may help the child's registration functioning.

LETTER SPAN

The Letter Span subtest uses letters instead of numbers using the same administration method as Digit Span Forward. This subtest provides a direct assessment of auditory registration for letters. The subtest is composed of trials that have rhyming letters and nonrhyming letters. Scaled scores are provided for both rhyming and nonrhyming items. This separation of scores enables the clinician to assess the impact of phonological distinctiveness on registration. The Letter Span subtest is used primarily to determine if registration deficits are content specific (i.e., due to poor number skills). It is recommended that clinicians use this subtest when the examinee has very poor math skills or evidence of poor numeric processing difficulties during testing. Also, in cases of low scores on Letter-Number Sequencing compared to Digit Span, the examiner may wish to assess Letter Span to ascertain if poor letter registration has influenced performance on that task. Clinicians will find Letter Span easy to administer and score.

LETTER–NUMBER SEQUENCING PROCESS APPROACH

The Letter–Number Sequencing Process Approach subtest is a variation of the core Letter–Number Sequencing subtest. This version of the subtest contains embedded words in the presented sequence of letters and numbers. The embedded words potentially reduce the working memory load of the letters. The letters can be recalled as a single unit, which is the embedded word; however, the child must recognize that the letters spell a word in order to take advantage of the reduced memory load. Examiners use this subtest to determine if working memory functions can be enhanced by reducing the load on registration.

ARITHMETIC PROCESSING APPROACH AND WRITTEN ARITHMETIC

In cases where the clinician has administered the Arithmetic subtest and found the score to be significantly lower than other auditory working memory measures, the Arithmetic Process Approach subtest may be administered to determine the degree to which poor math skills or impaired working memory produced the low scores. The Arithmetic Process Approach Part A allows the child to read all items missed on the standard version. This reduces the registration demands but still requires the examinee to perform the math operations mentally. The examiner can determine if poor Arithmetic performance was due to excessive auditory processing demands.

The Arithmetic Process Approach Part B allows the examinee to use pencil and paper to solve the problems not performed correctly in Part A. This eliminates all the registration and mental manipulation demands and directly tests the child's ability to solve math word problems. This information is useful particularly for making classroom accommodations. Some children are able to solve the problem when writing it down, but unable to respond correctly when hearing it or seeing it. These children may have problems responding to teacher questions in class and appear to know less than they actually do.

The Written Arithmetic procedure is not a working memory test. It is a measure designed to determine if the child is able to perform the math operations required in the Arithmetic subtest. In this measure, the child solves the mathematical representation of the arithmetic items. Children that do not understand math symbols will have difficulty completing these items. Clinicians may want to use this measure when the child appears to have problems with the computational aspects of the Arithmetic subtest.

RECOMMENDED APPLICATION OF WORKING MEMORY PROCESS SCORES

- *Clinicians will find administration of the auditory process subtests similar to the standard procedure. Examiners may wish to practice administration of visual subtests*
- *Administration time prohibits routine use of all of the working memory process subtests. Clinicians may wish to use Spatial Span Forward on a regular basis as a screen for adequate visual registration skills.*
- *Visual working memory subtests, particularly Spatial Span, should be used when low scores on auditory working memory measures are observed. These subtests should be used when assessing children with poor language skills.*
- *Letter Span should be used to determine if low scores on Letter–Number Sequencing are due to specific problems with registration of letters. The Letter Span test also enables the clinician to determine if the distinctiveness of the auditory input affects registration capacity.*
- *The Letter–Number Sequencing Process Approach should be used if the child has very low scores on Letter–Number Sequencing.*
- *The Arithmetic Process Approach subtest and Written Arithmetic are used infrequently because the Arithmetic subtest is a supplemental rather than core measure. When low scores on Arithmetic are obtained, it is important to determine if these are due to working memory deficits or computational difficulties.*
- *These tests cannot be used to measure giftedness and should not be used to compute WMI or FSIQ.*
- *The subtest scores are presented as age-corrected scaled scores and performance is interpreted the same as core and supplemental subtests.*

PROCESSING SPEED DOMAIN

Processing speed tasks require the rapid integration of multiple cognitive skills. There are few additional procedures developed for this domain beyond the core and supplemental subtests (i.e., Coding, Symbol Search, and Cancellation). The only specific subtest in the Process domain is Coding Copy. The Coding Copy subtest is designed specifically to determine how quickly the child is able to write the symbols from the Coding subtest. This subtest eliminates additional cognitive components of incidental learning (i.e., Learning Number–Symbol associations) and the visual scanning from the bottom to the top of the page. This subtest is a good indicator of direct copying speed.

WHEN TO USE CODING COPY

Coding Copy is useful for testing two hypotheses. The first relates to low Coding scores. If the examiner suspects that the child's low scores on coding reflect simple slow copying speed, they will administer the Coding Copy condition. In this case, the hypothesis is that lower level cognitive skills are interfering with the expression of higher order abilities and concurrent low scores on Coding Copy would confirm this hypothesis. The second hypothesis is that the child has adequate copying speed but has poor incidental learning and visual scanning, which slows down performance on the Coding subtest. In this case, high scores would confirm intact basic copying skills but problems with higher order scanning abilities.

This subtest should be used in children that have a history of fine motor difficulties or required occupational therapy services. The examiner may wish to use this subtest when the teacher or parent needs feedback regarding the child's ability to copy information off the board quickly and accurately or to be physically capable of completing homework assignments in a reasonable amount of time. In terms of accommodations, this subtest is a good indicator of if the child may need time extensions for written tests that are independent of the cognitive aspects of writing. This subtest may also be useful if the teacher is considering having another child help the examinee with note taking or wishes to know if they need to provide the child with more written materials.

The Coding Copy subtest was not designed to measure giftedness and cannot be used as a replacement subtest for the core Coding subtest. This subset was not designed to diagnose motor impairment or writing disorder. It yields information that is useful in making accommodations and interventions for children with motor difficulties.

SUMMARY

This chapter is designed for clinicians that have no previous experience or familiarity with the WISC-III as a Process Instrument and who wish to get started using the WISC-IV Integrated. This chapter described the basic uses of the WISC-IV Integrated Process subtests. Clinicians will rarely use all or even many of the process subtests with any individual child. This chapter provided guidelines for when to use specific subtests and the rationale for using that subtest. The rationale for using the subtest is based on the history of presenting problems, teacher referral questions and observations, observed behaviors during testing, and profile of scores. Basic interpretation of the subtest focused on the clinical questions the subtest was designed to answer. Recommendations were provided for the routine use of several subtests, including Picture Vocabulary and Spatial Span Forward. Caveats for use and interpretation were also provided. The next chapter expands on this basic approach to the WISC-IV Integrated subtests and reviews additional process measures and planned comparisons.

REFERENCES

Cashel, M. L. (2002). Child and adolescent psychological assessment: Current clinical practices and the impact of managed care. *Professional Psychology: Research and Practice, 33*, 446–453.

Dunn, L. M., & Dunn, L. M. (1997). *Examiner's manual for the Peabody picture vocabulary test–third edition*. Circle Pines, MN: American Guidance Services.

Ewing-Cobbs & Barnes, M. (2002). Linguistic outcomes following traumatic brain injury in children. *Seminars in Pediatric Neurology, 9*, 209–217.

Kaplan, E., Fein, D., Kramer, J., Delis, D., & Morris, R. (1999). *Wechsler intelligence scale for children–3rd edition*. San Antonio, TX: The Psychological Corporation.

Lally, S. (2003). What tests are acceptable for use in forensic evaluations? A survey of experts. *Professional Psychology: Research and Practice, 34*, 491–498.

Rabin, L. A., Barr, W. B., & Burton, L. A. (2005). Assessment practices of clinical neuropsychologists in the United States and Canada: A survey of INS, NAN, and APA division 40 members. *Archives of Clinical Neuropsychology, 20*, 33–65.

Wechsler, D. (1991). *Wechsler intelligence scale for children–third edition*. San Antonio, TX: The Psychological Corporation.

Wechsler, D. (2003). *Wechsler intelligence scale for children–fourth edition*. San Antonio, TX: Harcourt Assessment, Inc.

Wechsler, D., Kaplan, E., Fein, D., Kramer, J., Delis, D., Morris, R., & Maerlender, A. (2004). *Wechsler Intelligence Scale for Children–fourth edition*. San Antonio, Texas: Harcourt Assessment, Inc.

6

WISC-IV INTEGRATED: BEYOND THE ESSENTIALS

JAMES A. HOLDNACK AND LAWRENCE G. WEISS

This chapter applies neuropsychological concepts to the interpretation of the WISC-IV Integrated. A number of approaches exist to aid the clinician in interpreting subtest profiles of Wechsler scales. These approaches focus on the subtest content and the statistical relationships among measures (Kaufmann, 1994; Sattler, 2001). The utility of these approaches is not discussed here; rather an alternative approach to understanding composite and subtest variability is presented. The conceptual framework underlying this chapter has commonalities with the "hypothesis testing approach" proposed by Fiorello and Hale (2003) and the process approach (Kaplan, 1988; Kaplan, Fein, Kramer, Delis, & Morris, 1999). The chapter incorporates pragmatic issues of test development in understanding the variability in performance among clinical groups. The chapter provides information necessary to effectively utilize the WISC-IV Integrated in clinical practice.

COMPLEXITIES OF MEASURING INTELLIGENCE

A primary tenet of the "process approach" is that performance on intelligence tests requires the integration of multiple cognitive skills, as opposed to the position that a single ability accounts for all of the variability in the construct referred to as "intelligence" (Kaplan et al., 1999). A distinction must be articulated between the integration of multiple cognitive skills and the conceptualization of multiple intelligences. The postulation of multiple intellectual abilities presumes that the skills in question have a normal distribution within the general population. Therefore these skills can be measured using basic principles of test design. However, the types of cognitive skills of interest in this chapter are not likely to be distributed normally within the general population. A very simple example of the distribution of such skills is visual acuity. Most people have 20/20 vision with only a small number of people having above 20/20. A substantial minority of people have vision worse than 20/20 with varying degrees of severity. The resultant distribution is skewed with most people at or near 20/20 and a long tail of frequencies of people having acuity that is less than average. More basic cognitive processes will have similar distributions with most people having an adequate ability in the domain and a subgroup of people being below average to varying degrees.

This conceptualization has a direct impact on interpreting factors associated with subtest variability. If the clinician believes that subtests and composites separate intellectual abilities, then variations in test performance relate only to the specific ability tapped by the anomalous subtest or composite. If, however, the clinician believes that the integration of multiple cognitive skills is necessary to complete subtests on intelligence tests, then poor capacity in a particular cognitive skill will affect performance on a number of subtests but to differing degrees. Fluctuations occur across subtests to the degree that the specific skill is necessary to complete that particular task. Variability in task performance is not explained as variability in intelligent behavior. Rather, variability is examined to determine if factors related to characteristics of the test and the cognitive skill set of the examinee affect their capacity to express intelligent behavior.

WHAT DO INTELLIGENCE TESTS MEASURE?

One important goal in the development of intelligence tests is to obtain normal or roughly normal distributions at the subtest level. Obtaining normal distributions is necessary to create sufficient variance to measure a broad range of capacities (i.e., mental deficiency to genius levels). Subsequently, the examiner can differentiate performance at multiple skill levels. As part of the development process, it is imperative to select tasks that can be made into a normal distribution. For instance, the use of vocabulary to measure intellectual function is nearly ubiquitous across tests. Vocabulary lends itself well to creating normal distributions and controlling item difficulty levels across a diverse age range. It is possible to make vocabulary tests that are not distributed normally and therefore not measures of intelligence. Simple criterion referenced vocabulary tests developed to assess mastery of academic progress are not measures of general intelligence.

Many skills could effectively be made into measures of intelligence. For instance, the Benton Face Recognition Test (Benton, Hamsher, Varney, &

Spreen, 1983) measures the ability to identify novel faces. The test does not measure intelligence, but item difficulty level is controlled by the introduction of other abilities, such as presenting the faces at angles (i.e., introduces the ability to identify visual information presented at angles that may not be specific to faces). Item difficulty could be increased further by adding a registration component to the test. The examinee would be required to hold the information in their mind before being able to solve the problem. Adding cognitive skills tests the limits of the individual's capacity to complete the subset of skills in question (i.e., face recognition), but that process introduces confounding factors that need to be considered when interpreting test scores. Therefore, there are pros and cons to testing the limits of a particular skill. Not only does increasing item difficulty require adding a different set of cognitive abilities, but these skills must be *integrated* effectively with the specific cognitive demands created by the test content in order for successful task completion. Some researchers (Glutting, McDermott, Konold, Snelbaker, & Watkins, 1998; McDermott, Fantuzzo, & Glutting, 1990; Watkins, 2000) imply by focusing only on the interpretation of "g" that these factors are measurement error. Other researchers use this information to gain a better appreciation of the underlying difficulties impeding a child's performance (Hale, Fiorello, Kavanagh, Hoeppner, & Gaither, 2001).

Intelligence is a construct that we attempt to measure based on the hypothesis that highly intelligent people possess the ability to solve complex problems across a variety of tasks. The test itself is not intelligence, but intelligent behavior is manifest in test performance. Intelligent behavior is necessarily restricted by the context in which the behavior occurs. The opportunity to express intelligent behavior when lost in a barren desert is different from the opportunities available if one is working in a complex job with multiple problems to solve and a range of resources available to put into place. Since intelligent behavior exists within a context, the context itself will have an impact on the degree to which intelligent behavior may be expressed. In other words, the nature of the test will "pull" and/or "limit" the expression of intelligence. Differing results obtained between measures of intelligence are in part a reflection of the contextual aspects of the tests themselves.

This chapter focuses on cognitive skills that impact performance on WISC-IV Integrated subtests. The stimuli and the rules and requirements of examinee responses affect the types of skills needed to perform well on specific subtests. For instance, a test that requires verbal responding (setting one aspect of the context of the test) to answer the item will require expressive language abilities, the capacity to retrieve information from memory stores, and the ability to monitor one's mental search and response for accuracy. Low scores occur due to expressive language limitations, weak executive functioning, or low intelligence. A number of hypotheses need to be evaluated to understand low scores. This chapter is designed to help clinicians formulate hypotheses when interpreting low scores on the WISC-IV Integrated. The first part of this chapter reviews some of the common cognitive skills that impact scores on measures of intellectual functioning. The remainder of the chapter reviews the WISC-IV Integrated subtests and discusses the skills measured by the test and alternate hypotheses that need to be considered when understanding performance on these subtests.

COGNITIVE SKILLS THAT MAY IMPACT TEST PERFORMANCE

The reader should be acquainted with basic cognitive skills described by neuropsychologists. These skills provide a means for describing and understanding behavior. This section reviews some cognitive skills referred to when describing hypotheses regarding WISC-IV Integrated subtest performance. This review is not intended to include all possible cognitive skills nor all possible conceptualizations of neuropsychological skills. This section is divided by specific domains of cognitive functioning: attention; executive functioning; auditory/language skills; visual and visual–perceptual processing; and sensory and motor processing. The reader is referred to neuropsychological texts such as Feinberg and Farah (1997) and Kolb and Wishow (1990) for review of basic neuropsychological contructs, neuroanatomy and neurobehavioral conditions.

ATTENTION

Attention is a basic cognitive skill that contributes to effective performance across most environments. Deficits in attention do not imply an absence of attention; rather deficits reflect greater than expected inconsistency in control of attention within a context or across contexts. Attention is not a unitary construct and multiple forms of attention have been hypothesized to exist (Mirsky, Anthony, Duncan, Ahearn, & Kellam, 1991).

Sustained Attention/Vigilance

Often people understand attention as the capacity to maintain focus on a task for an extended period of time. This type of attention is called sustained attention or vigilance. Children, whose minds wander in class, who have difficulty listening or watching for extended periods, exhibit difficulties with sustained attention. Distractibility reflects a breakdown in sustained attention. The child is unable to sustain attention in the presence of other environmental information.

Visual/Auditory Scanning

Visual/auditory scanning refers to the ability to engage in an active search for salient information by examining the environment carefully. Systematic deficits in visual scanning (i.e., in a particular visual field) may reflect a syndrome called "neglect" in which the person does not have full awareness of their environment. The most common problem associated with skill is inconsistency in identifying salient information across visual fields.

Divided Attention

Divided attention is the ability to register and attend to multiple bits of information simultaneously. This skill is manifest in the ability to listen to the teacher talk while simultaneously copying notes off the chalkboard. Some children will show adequate sustained attention but falter when divided attention is required. They may be able to listen to the teacher lecture or write down what the teacher writes on the board but cannot do both simultaneously.

Shifting Attention

Appropriately changing focus of attention from one source of information to another (when the salience of the information changes) is an important skill that relates to executive control of attention (i.e., self-regulation). Some children become hyperfocused on a single task or object. It is nearly impossible for them to shift their focus to another task or object. These children will ignore all other informational sources within the context. This is different from cognitive flexibility, which occurs at the ideational level, whereas attention shift occurs at the stimulus level.

Registration/Brief Focused Attention

Registration refers to the capacity to briefly hold and repeat/copy information. The capacity to pay attention to a specific stimulus for a brief period without distraction is an important component of registration. Severe attention disturbance may affect the capacity to maintain attention for even short periods of time.

Focus/Execute

The ability to initiate and execute a search for important information is an important skill. This reflects early stages of problem solving in which the examinee must search for salient information to solve a problem.

EXECUTIVE FUNCTIONING

This term generally refers to higher order cognitive processes that enable the individual to successfully manage/regulate their behavior in complex environments over the course of time (see Barkley [1996] for a conceptual review and Delis, Kaplan, and Kramer [2001] for a review of executive functions). The broad category of executive functioning refers to multiple component skills described here.

Cognitive Flexibility

Cognitive flexibility describes the capacity to change one's behavior to meet the changing demands of the environment. The capacity to change problem-solving behavior, when provided corrective feedback or when the rules of the task or environment change, characterizes behavioral manifestations of cognitive flexibility. The propensity to engage in nonfunctional repeated behaviors (perseverations) reflects deficits in cognitive flexibility. Some manifestations of deficits in cognitive flexibility in children include continued engagement in negative or off-task behaviors despite frequent corrective interventions; difficulty adapting to changes in routine or schedules; or repeated errors on academic tasks. Cognitive flexibility is one component of creative thinking.

Planning

Planning skills are manifest in the setting of short- or long-term goals and the establishment of a behavioral routine (strategy) for accomplishing these goals. Planning requires an initial period of inspection time (analysis of the problem at hand), strategy development, implementation of the strategy, and strategy modification if there is evidence that the strategy will not result in goal attainment. Poor planning behavior is evidenced by a lack of initial inspection time (jumping into a problem without thinking about it), failing to set goals, or failure to consider factors that would interfere with goal attainment. Impulsivity, inefficiency, and trial-and-error problem solving are hallmark signs of poor planning.

Organization

Organization is observed in the capacity to effectively assemble materials needed to complete a task, scheduling activities to meet specific task goals or deadlines, storing materials systematically for easy retrieval and away from interfering with work flow, and keeping work space (or living space) free of excess clutter. Children with organization problems frequently do not have the materials needed to complete a task accessible, such as a specific book they need to do homework, or will have messy, cluttered work areas (or bedrooms). They have difficulty locating materials needed to complete tasks. As a result of their disorganization, they often will waste time in preparation efforts, which then limits their resources (i.e., time and energy) for actually completing the task at hand.

Self-Monitoring

Self-monitoring is to the capacity to "watch" one's own behavior for the purpose of making adjustments and corrections as needed. The purpose of self-monitoring is to ensure that one's behavior will accomplish the goals set by the individual or that one's behavior conforms to the "rules" of the situation/environment. Frequent rule violations despite accurate knowledge of the rules or engagement in activities that interfere with goal attainment represents a breakdown in self-monitoring.

Inhibitory Control

The ability to resist an urge to engage in a highly enticing behavior and the capacity to stop oneself from engaging in "automatic" behaviors represent functions of inhibitory control mechanisms. Some behaviors are prepotent; they have a high probability of occurring and occur automatically (i.e., without conscious decision). These behaviors are "pulled" by elements in the environment, as exemplified by a child in a toy store wanting to touch and play with the toys on the shelf. The capacity to stop one's behavior despite wanting to touch, grab, or talk reflects a higher level cognitive capacity. This skill represents the signature deficit in children diagnosed with attention deficit disorder (Barkley, 2003).

Abstract Reasoning

Abstract reasoning reflects the capacity to think about a problem, object, or situation beyond its immediate physical manifestations or presence. A poor ability to understand figurative language and difficulties understanding relationships among objects, ideas, or events beyond immediate physical features or tangible elements are manifestations of poor abstract reasoning. Abstract reasoning is an important component of creative thinking and is a critical component of intellectual functioning.

Initiation and Maintenance

The capacity to engage in problem-solving behavior (i.e., not get mentally stuck, to get started) and to maintain that behavior over time (i.e., sustaining effort, avoiding distraction, maintaining memory search) is an important component of executive functioning. The inability to initiate behavior (i.e., generating ideas, strategizing) is observed in children that appear unmotivated, cannot direct their own behavior, or need frequent prompting to start or continue working. Problems maintaining behavior over time are reflected in children that "run out of ideas" quickly.

Rule Learning/Set Formation and Maintenance

Some aspects of rule learning occur automatically, such as rote learning or procedural learning (i.e., repeated motor tasks). Other rule learning conditions require more cognitive effort, and following the rules may involve multiple complex cognitive processes. Task rules are very important in influencing performance on the particular task. For example, if the child is required to use language accurately, using appropriate sentence structure and word use, on a vocabulary task, their performance may be very different compared to a vocabulary task that requires only the ability to communicate the general meaning of the word. On verbal fluency tasks, test results would differ if the child may use "slang" or "product names." The rules create the cognitive set for the task. The "set" is the frame of reference the child must use when responding to the test items. On language tests, the set is accurate use of language, whereas on IQ tests the set is the ability to express knowledge without deductions for language errors. Subtle differences in rules between tests may have a big impact on outcomes. Differences between task rules must be considered when comparing results between tests that purportedly measure the same construct. Some children have difficulty establishing the cognitive set of the task and become confused when multiple rules must be followed to solve the problem. Some children will lose the cognitive set of the test during the course of administration. They may focus on one aspect of the rules but not be able to complete the task while following all of the rules of the task.

AUDITORY PROCESSING AND LANGUAGE SKILLS

The capacity to effectively use and understand age-appropriate language significantly influences performance on most cognitive tests. The degree to which language skills influence test results relates not only the complexity of the task instructions and linguistic stimuli, but also the degree to which the test requires accurate use of language and rapid mental processing of linguistic concepts. There are a number of components involved in language processing; those relevant to assessment of intellectual functioning are reviewed here [see Semel, Wiig and Secord, 2003, for review of language functions].

Auditory Decoding

Auditory decoding refers to the capacity to identify the auditory structure of an individual word. A child that has difficulty decoding the auditory structure of individual words will misunderstand what has been said to them. These children will misidentify words (i.e., they hear "big" when the spoken word was "pig") and their responses will be based on what they believe was said, not what was actually said. If they have intact semantic knowledge, they may ask for a repetition because the misunderstood word results in an illogical semantic construction (i.e., "The big is in the barn"); otherwise, they may say "don't know" or make no response.

Semantic Decoding

Semantic decoding refers to the ability to link auditory input with appropriate knowledge structures. A child with poorly developed semantic knowledge will have limited understanding of the meaning of specific words. Often times, children with significant comprehension problems will not respond or will respond with "don't know." Some children with milder semantic deficits will make responses that are inaccurate or partially correct, depending on the degree to which contextual information enables them to make an educated guess. Semantic weaknesses limit the child's knowledge for the multiple meanings that an individual word has depending on the context in which it is used.

Syntactic Decoding

Syntactic decoding relates to the child's skill in breaking down sequences of words into appropriate meaning structures. Identifying the subject, verb, and appropriately linking modifiers within a linguistic stream are important skills that promote general language comprehension. Deficits in syntactic processing are most evident when complex linguistic structures are presented to the child (i.e., multiple clauses).

Speed and Capacity for Language Processing

Rapid decoding of the auditory, semantic, and syntactic features of spoken language facilitates overall comprehension. The amount of language that the child is able to process and maintain in conscious awareness (working memory for language) will affect their ability to respond accurately to increasingly longer strings of verbal information. Speed and capacity for language processing relate to the automaticity of the underlying decoding skills, as well as the general integrity of processing speed and working memory functions.

Decoding Language Sequence

Decoding language sequences describes the capacity to understand time and event order references of spoken language. The best example of this skill is the ability to follow multistep commands. This is not a purely linguistic task in that it integrates information about time knowledge (i.e., "when" do you do something), time and order reference (i.e., "when" you do something is linked in time and sequence to another event), and other cognitive skills (i.e., "what" you need to do). Consider the example of a teacher saying "I want you to take out your spelling books, turn to page 53, and complete all the odd items before the end of class today." Within this phrase are a number of sequence references [i.e., (1) get book out, (2) turn to page 53, and (3) complete odd items], time references [i.e., (1) now (implied) and (2) before the end of class], and numeric knowledge structures (i.e., number sequences "53" and "odd" pages). In this example, the sequence of tasks is logical and overlearned (i.e., taking books out of desk always proceeds opening them and working on a task), but in many cases the sequence information will be novel (i.e., learning regrouping procedures in mathematics). A limited capacity for decoding language sequences and time referents creates significant problems with learning new skills when the information is presented primarily in an oral, linguistic format. This problem may also lead to incomplete work or incorrectly performed work when a task is performed out of sequence. Understanding of key sequence words (i.e., first, last, then, now, before, after) is important for correct interpretation of verbal commands.

Articulation

Articulation refers to the capacity to link acoustic knowledge with motor programs that control speech production. Poor articulation may signal problems with auditory/acoustic process or reflect some deficit in motor control of speech process (i.e., speech apraxia). Poor articulation exists often in the absence of any significant impairment in language processing. Articulation problems, particularly severe problems, may result in miscommunication of the child's actual knowledge.

Language Production

Language production refers to the amount of verbal information produced by the child irrespective of accuracy. Children with low productivity may give only single word responses or very short, simple responses. Other children may have excessively high rates of production that do not necessarily reflect superior knowledge or integrity of the language system.

Repetition

Repetition is the ability to repeat exactly what has been said. Intact repetition should not be considered an indicator of intact language comprehension or production. The ability to repeat information does not necessarily indicate that the information has been decoded accurately, although repetition is facilitated by intact semantic decoding. Children with very good language processing speed and verbal working memory may be very good at repeating information without necessarily understanding it.

Semantic and Syntactic Production

The accuracy of the semantic and syntactic aspects of spoken language likely reflects underlying decoding skills in these domains. Semantic and syntactic errors in many cases reflect some deficit in linkage between auditory and knowledge structures. In some cases, errors occur only in the production of language. This reflects the inability to locate specific knowledge structures during speech production but not during decoding. Similarly, syntactic impairments may occur at the production level only. Effective language production requires the capacity to organize information into meaningful units. The use of novel and complex linguistic structures requires mental flexibility. A significant interaction between language production and executive functioning exists. Executive functioning modifies the individual's expressive language abilities.

VISUAL AND VISUAL–PERCEPTUAL PROCESSING

It has been proposed that the visual system is divided into two primary visual pathways (for review, see Cytowic, 1996). The "ventral stream of vision" processes visual elements into meaningful visual structures. This is the "what is it" component of visual processing. This ventral stream of vision encompasses aspects of the occipital and temporal lobes. The "dorsal stream of vision" is purported to decipher the location of objects in space. This is the "where is it" visual processing system and is processed via the occipital and parietal lobes. It has also been proposed that the left hemisphere specializes in decoding of "local" details of visual information, whereas the right hemisphere deciphers the "global" organization or gestalt of visual information [see Kaplan et al., 1999, for review]. Different types of behavioral deficits occur when processing impairments within the visual system exist depending on the visual systems involved. The visual system is complex and requires the integration of smaller units of visual information increasingly integrated at higher levels. A majority of visual processing occurs subconsciously and these processes influence the accuracy of perception of the perceptual features (i.e., color, size, shading) and the acuity of the visual image.

Visual Field Deficits

Although rare in children, difficulties with processing information from a particular region within the visual field may result in incomplete acquisition of visual knowledge. In many cases, the deficit is not self-evident so the person will not adjust their head position in order to acquire the missing information. This is referred to as "visual neglect." In some cases, children will constantly be adjusting their head or body position in order to better "see" a visual input. This problem may be linked to a problem coordinating the oculomotor system resulting in a convergence disorder. In this case, a referral to a vision specialist (i.e., ophthalmologist or optometrist) may be helpful.

Visual Discrimination

Visual discrimination refers to the capacity to recognize all relevant visual information. Poor visual discrimination will result in problems with visual matching/comparison between two objects. Visual discrimination is a precursor skill for higher visual–perceptual abilities. Poor visual discrimination is not necessarily caused by poor visual acuity but is due to a variety of low-level visual processing and organization functions.

Local Processing

Children with weaknesses in the local processing of visual information will show an intact capacity to imitate or create specific general shapes but they may confuse specific detailed elements within that object. On visual tasks such as Block Design, they would be able to create the square shape using the block but may align details within the design incorrectly. On puzzles tasks, they will try to put together objects by shape rather than aligning the visual details contained on the puzzle piece. Drawings will reflect limited visual detail and/or disorganization of detail, but the overall gestalt of the object will be intact.

Global Processing

Poor global processing is reflected in problems organizing information into meaningful wholes. There is an overfocus on the parts of the object, resulting in constructions that lack accurate representation of the general shape and relationship of objects. On tasks such as Block Design they may lose the general configuration that the final object is a square because they are focused on lining up the blocks to best mimic the details of the design. Breaks in configuration on this test may be a sign of difficulties with global processing. Tasks such as Matrix Reasoning, though, may be performed well as these tend to focus on detailed aspects of design with stability of shapes within items.

Spatial Processing

Spatial processing reflects the capacity to understand the orientation of visual information in two- and three-dimensional space. At the highest level, this skill enables a person to visualize a mental map of elements in three dimensions, estimate distances of objects, and mentally rotate and/ or construct objects in three-dimensional space. Difficulties in spatial processing may result in problems with pattern analysis, construction (i.e., drawing), judging distance and orientation of objects in the environment, and route learning (i.e., learning directions to get from one point to another).

MEMORY AND LEARNING

The capacity to acquire new knowledge, retain it, and access new information is a critical component to the development of intellectual capacity. A discussion of the intricacies of memory functioning is well beyond the scope of this chapter. The reader is referred to Budson and Price (2005), Squire and Butters (1984), Kapur (1994), and Stringer (1996) for reviews of memory functions and clinical implications. For the purposes of this chapter, *learning* refers to the acquisition of new information or skills. *Memory* is the retention of new information. The term learning as used here is more general than is applied to learning disability in that it is not limited to the acquisition of new academic skills.

Declarative Memory

Declarative memory refers to the process for intentional, explicit storage and recall of information. This information could be general knowledge and facts that are not encoded with reference to a specific time or event, *semantic memory*. The information could be associated with a specific event, time, person, or place, *episodic memory*. The purpose of declarative memory skills is to build knowledge that may be retrieved at a later time, whereas working memory focuses on storage of information for only immediate use and is not to be remembered at a later time. *Long-term memory* refers to information that is stored for retrieval at some later time, be it minutes, hours, days, weeks, or years later. Amnesia is a severe impairment in declarative memory.

Incidental Learning

Incidental learning refers to a change in behavior or knowledge that occurs as a function of interacting with the environment and occurs without conscious effort (e.g., child learns the names of children in their class after the teacher has role call every day). *Procedural learning* is one type of incidental learning and indicated by improved performance on a task or skill after exposure to the task. Procedural learning may be incidental (i.e., performs a skill better without trying to learn to do it better) or as a function of repeated trials (e.g., child learns to swim better after taking lessons or writing improves with practice).

Encoding

Encoding refers to the process of getting information into long-term memory stores. Memory encoding can be facilitated by efficient organization and association with existing knowledge stores. An encoding deficit refers to problems getting information into long-term memory stores.

Retrieval

Retrieval refers to the process of extracting information from long-term memory. This process is facilitated by the use of organized memory search strategies. *Free recall* is the retrieval of information from memory without any external hints or clues being provided (e.g., "What did you eat for breakfast yesterday?"). *Cued recall* is recall from memory that is aided by an external hint or clue that restricts the range of possible solutions and is related to the information to be retrieved (e.g., "When you ate breakfast, did you need to use a bowl for the food?"). *Recognition memory* is the ability to identify the correct answer without producing it independently (e.g., "Did you eat eggs for breakfast yesterday?"). An *intrusion* is the free recall of incorrect information. A *false positive* is the endorsement of erroneous information during recognition memory. A retrieval deficit refers to the inability to access information during free recall but normal ability to recognize the correct information.

Rote Learning

Rote learning refers to the ability to memorize new information or a new skill through repeated exposure. Rote learning often focuses on accurate verbatim performance without regard for understanding the content or skill being learned.

Automaticity

Hasher and Zacks (1979) described the impact of automaticity and effortfulness on memory performance. *Automaticity* refers to overlearned material that does not require any or any significant conscious awareness to retrieve. This information processing occurs automatically (e.g., word reading in skilled readers occurs whenever presented with a real word). *Effortful* processing refers to information retrieval processes that require conscious effort and control. Effortful processing is very important in the early phases of learning a new skill or piece of information. The quality of learning and subsequent automaticity will depend on the degree to which the child can engage in active, effortful processing. Automaticity and procedural learning are important skills for establishing fluent performance of a particular cognitive or motor skill.

Material-Specific Memory

Material-specific memory refers to the ability to recall modality-specific stimuli (i.e., visual versus auditory) and content-specific stimuli (i.e., faces versus designs). Recall by modality and content can vary within individuals and is subserved by overlapping and distinct neuropathways.

SENSORY AND MOTOR PROCESSING

Interpretation of simple and complex sensory inputs affects development of knowledge about the environment and behavioral response and control. Sensory mechanisms provide important information about social relations (i.e., understanding a soft gentle touch versus rough grabbing), potential harm (i.e., knowledge of hot, cold, sharp, hard), localization of self in space (i.e., sitting, standing, moving), and internal feedback about one's own motor activity (i.e., am I throwing this object with force or lightly). Impairments in sensory processes may result in subtle or not so subtle behavioral disturbances that may be attributed to psychological traits or motivation. Sensory impairments, beyond those typically considered (i.e., hard of hearing or poor visual acuity), have an impact on test performance and should be considered when interpreting test results and making causal inferences regarding behavior and motivation.

The term motor skills will be limited here to refer to lower level coordination skills. The capacity to control the movements of muscles and extremities quickly, smoothly, and efficiently is required to engage in visuomotor activities such as writing, drawing, and throwing. Visuomotor integration requires the coordination of visual input or mental imagery into a motor output. While most components of motor control occur subconsciously, executive functioning skills such as planning, estimation, initiation, and productivity play a role in the quality of motor output. Poor motor control has implications for test performance (i.e., speeded motor task may be performed slowly and less accurately). Behaviorally, poor motor control has social implications, as the child may appear awkward and clumsy.

WISC-IV INTEGRATED PROCESS ANALYSIS

The WISC-IV Integrated provides a wealth of information regarding a child's current cognitive functioning. This part of the chapter provides a detailed assessment of WISC-IV Integrated subtests and process measures. This section provides the examiner with more information about the skills measured by the subtests and is divided into sections referring to the four cognitive domains measured by the WISC-IV Integrated: Verbal, Perceptual Reasoning, Working Memory, and Processing Speed.

VERBAL COMPREHENSION DOMAIN

In the verbal domain, poor test performance may occur for a number of reasons. Previously, a number of language skills were reviewed. A deficit in one or more of these language skills will produce attenuated scores on verbal subtests. The key hypotheses that should be explored when low verbal index scores are obtained include delayed language development, language disorder, difficulties retrieving knowledge (i.e., low ability versus access to knowledge), reading disability, impaired auditory attention or working memory, or impaired executive functioning. At the subtest level, the demands for specific language skills such as auditory decoding, semantic decoding and productivity, articulation, and decoding language sequences vary. The subtest content and task demands affect the impact that language skills have on performance. Interpretation of subtest variability should consider the degree that language demands are present.

Vocabulary, Vocabulary Multiple Choice, and Picture Vocabulary

The standard administration of the Vocabulary has subtest a very long history in the use of psychology and is a strong indicator of verbal intelligence. The examinee defines words using as much or as little language (i.e., production) as necessary to communicate their knowledge. The scoring system requires the examinee to define the word but does not require precise use of language (i.e., the cognitive set is knowledge, not linguistic accuracy). Errors in syntax and nominal semantic errors are ignored. The examinee may even provide a general definition that would apply to many words (i.e., dog is an animal). As the items get more difficult, general semantic knowledge is inadequate and more specific word knowledge or usage is required. The examinee is not required to know multiple meanings of the same word. The difficulty level is associated with the frequency at which the word is used in the predominant cultural environment and complexity (i.e., abstractness) of the concept represented by the word. Environmental factors, such as education and vocabulary exposure in the home environment, play a role in performance in this task.

The examinee must have accurate auditory decoding, adequate but not precise semantic decoding, and adequate semantic production. The test is designed as a measure of word knowledge so semantics is a critical component to performance. Limited capacity for language production may interfere with the examinee's communication of their knowledge. Therefore, multiple-choice versions of the vocabulary subtest were developed to reduce emphasis on language production. The vocabulary multiple choice subtest presents the child with several possible meanings for the word and the child picks the correct choice. While the demands for production are reduced, the semantic and syntactic decoding and speed and capacity of language processing demands are increased. The child is required to decode long strings of auditory information and compare the semantic structure to determine the best representation of the target word. The increased verbal demands require rapid decoding and comparison skills that may be poorly developed in children with language disorders.

The Picture Vocabulary subtest was developed to further reduce the nonspecific language demands of the Vocabulary test. On this task, the child must associate the target word with one of four pictures that represents the core meaning of the word. The reduction in language production demands is substantial. Additional cognitive skills are introduced in this task, however. The child must have the capacity to interpret pictures into their semantic representation. They must attend to the salient components of the picture and correctly interpret the visual representation of the action or object.

For the Vocabulary subtests, there are a number of hypotheses to test when the examinee receives a low score. These clinical questions include the following: Are low scores due to impaired auditory or semantic decoding, semantic productivity, access to semantic knowledge and/or executive functioning, or limited auditory working memory capacity? Some of these questions can be answered by comparing performance between the different versions of the subtest.

Correlations, mean differences, and base rates for scores differing by three or more standard deviations for select clinical groups and the standardization sample for all verbal domain scores are presented in Table 1. In the standardization sample, Vocabulary has a high correlation with Vocabulary Multiple Choice, the mean of zero indicates that one score is not higher than the other in general, and most children score within two scaled-score points on these measures. In general, the clinical groups exhibit moderate to high correlations between the two subtests with the lowest correlation in the Reading Disorder and ADD groups. Average performance differences between the two versions were relatively small for most clinical groups, with the largest differences observed in the ADD, math disorder and Traumatic Brain Injury (TBI) groups. The TBI group benefited from the multiple-choice format, whereas the ADD and Math Disorder groups performed worse. Vocabulary Multiple Choice is negatively affected by impulsive responding but helps children that have difficulty retrieving information from memory.

The correlation between Picture Vocabulary and Vocabulary was consistently smaller than Vocabulary Multiple Choice and Vocabulary. There is greater variability in performance between these two versions. While in the standardization and most clinical groups there is little or no performance difference between the two versions, this is not the case for the autistic and the expressive language disorder groups. For both groups, they display better vocabulary knowledge on the Picture Vocabulary subtest compared to the standard version.

These results indicate that the Picture Vocabulary enables children with expressive language difficulties to demonstrate their knowledge.

TABLE 1 Correlation coefficients, average differences and rate of discrepancy for WISC-IV Verbal Domain Core and Supplemental versus Process Subtests

	Vocabulary Multiple-Choice				Picture Vocabulary			
	r	Mean (SD)	% VC > VCMC	% VC < VCMC	r	Mean (SD)	% VC > PV	% VC < PV
Standardization Sample	0.71	.03 (2.3)	12.8	11.2	0.67	−.02 (2.4)	13.1	12.6
ADD	0.52	.49 (2.4)	16.3	16.3	0.68	−.04 (2.1)	10.2	12.2
Autistic	0.71	−.31 (2.2)	12.5	18.8	0.56	−1.5 (3.5)	6.2	31.2
Expressive Language Disorder	0.71	−.13 (2.1)	6.5	15.2	0.46	−.65 (2.7)	6.5	28.3
Receptive-Expressive Language Disorder	0.65	−.13 (2.3)	10.9	17.4	0.50	−.35 (2.4)	10.0	19.6
Math Disorder	0.60	.44 (2.0)	9.3	9.3	0.31	−.11 (2.8)	13.9	18.6
Reading Disorder	0.53	.27 (2.4)	16.1	11.3	0.66	−.18 (1.8)	3.2	8.1
Traumatic Brain Injury	0.76	−.58 (1.9)	5.3	18.4	0.63	−.21 (2.5)	7.9	15.8

	Similarities Multiple-Choice				Comprehension Multiple-Choice			
	r	Mean (SD)	% SI > SIMC	% SI < SIMC	r	Mean (SD)	% VC > PV	% VC < PV
Standardization Sample	0.60	.03 (2.6)	19.0	16.3	0.52	−.01 (2.9)	17.7	19.2
ADD	0.66	.35 (2.6)	20.4	12.2	0.53	−.18 (2.8)	18.4	22.4
Autistic	0.65	−1.4 (2.9)	12.5	37.5	0.84	.38 (2.2)	25.0	6.2
Expressive Language Disorder	0.55	.30 (2.6)	23.9	17.4	0.53	−.13 (3.0)	19.6	17.4
Receptive-Expressive Language Disorder	0.34	.26 (2.8)	19.6	15.2	0.36	−.10 (2.8)	23.9	21.7
Math Disorder	0.23	−.18 (2.6)	18.6	25.6	0.20	.58 (3.0)	25.6	18.6
Reading Disorder	0.42	.04 (2.8)	16.1	17.7	0.25	.24 (2.8)	14.5	9.6
Traumatic Brain Injury	0.58	.60 (2.9)	26.3	18.5	0.39	.65 (3.4)	26.3	15.8

(Continues)

TABLE 1 *(Continued)*

		Information Multiple Choice		
	r	Mean (SD)	% IN > INMC	% IN < INMC
Standardization Sample	0.75	.04 (2.1)	10.4	11.1
ADD	0.61	.26 (2.1)	8.2	14.3
Autistic	0.70	−.56 (2.6)	12.5	12.5
Expressive Language Disorder	0.83	.02 (1.6)	2.2	10.9
Receptive-Expressive Language Disorder	0.70	.10 (2.0)	4.4	10.9
Math Disorder	0.56	.60 (1.9)	11.6	7.0
Reading Disorder	0.52	.24 (2.0)	9.6	11.3
Traumatic Brain Injury	0.77	−.13 (2.0)	7.9	13.2

Note: Listwise deletion used for all measures resulting in the following sample sizes—standardization (712), ADD (49), Autistic (16), Expressive Language Disorder (46), Receptive-Expressive Language Disorder (46), Math Disorder (43), Reading Disorder (62), and Traumatic Brain Injury (36). All comparisons are computed as core or supplemental minus process subtest. *Wechsler Intelligence Scale for Children – Fourth Edition Integrated.* Copyright © 2004 by Harcourt Assessment, Inc. Reproduced with permission. All rights reserved.

Similarities and Similarities Multiple Choice

Similarities have a long history of use as a measure of verbal intellectual ability. The test requires the capacity to semantically decode individual words and to compare the semantic structure of two words for commonalities that may be directly associated with the meaning of the word (i.e., cat and mouse are both mammals) or a common referential element (i.e., flood and drought have different semantics but both refer to weather/climate conditions associated with water). Because the stimulus words used in the task tend to be those learned at an early age, the type of semantic knowledge tested varies from the Vocabulary subtest and requires more abstract reasoning ability. On Similarities, the examinee must know multiple meanings and concepts that are associated with the word. It taps the ability to categorize concepts into higher order categories. These links are not likely to have been taught explicitly.

The degree of language production is less than Vocabulary as many of the concepts can be expressed with only a few words. There are still significant demands on language production. The Similarities Multiple-Choice subtest was designed to reduce the demands for language production and to focus on semantic decoding and abstract reasoning skills. The multiple-choice version introduces similar decoding demands as mentioned for the Vocabulary Multiple-Choice task. Education and environmental influences while present are not as influential as on vocabulary, as by design most of the words should be within the vocabulary of the examinee. For the Similarities subtest, hypotheses to be tested when low scores are obtained include difficulties with language production, poor semantic knowledge, impaired executive functioning (i.e., cognitive flexibility), or limited auditory working memory. Because the multiple-choice version requires almost no language production and working memory demands are reduced, the impact of these skills on Similarities performance can be answered by comparing the two versions.

In Table 1, the correlation between Similarities and Similarities Multiple Choice is moderate for the standardization sample and for most clinical groups. The correlation was low in the Math Disorder and Receptive-Expressive Language Disorder groups. The average difference is near zero for the standardization sample and for most clinical groups except the Autistic and TBI groups. The Autistic group had better scores on the multiple-choice version, whereas the TBI group had the opposite pattern of results. The group characterized by pragmatic language and social deficits benefited from the multiple-choice format. The multiple-choice format did not aid retrieval in the TBI group and resulted in more errors. Perhaps they were drawn into choosing highly salient but more concrete responses they had not considered during the free response administration.

Comprehension and Comprehension Multiple Choice

The Comprehension subtest measures the examinee's ability to articulate knowledge and understanding of social conventions and problem solving about specific life events (i.e., if there was a fire). Of all of the verbal subtests, Comprehension places the most demands on verbal production skills. The higher level of production is due to the amount of information required to complete a response satisfactorily. The examinee must decode long linguistic streams, placing significant demands on auditory and semantic decoding skills. Concurrently, the length of the stimulus and response creates additional demands on auditory working memory. The capacity to inhibit inappropriate responses (i.e., an executive function) also plays a role on this test. The multiple-choice version enables the clinician to address language production issues; however, the child with poor language decoding skills or slow language processing may not benefit from the multiple-choice format. For Comprehension, low scores may be due to a number of factors that may relate to the specific content (i.e., knowledge of social rules and conventions) or the linguistic demands. On this subtest, the hypotheses to be tested include deficits in language production and decoding, access to knowledge, low auditory working memory, and impulsivity. Comparing the two versions enables the clinician to determine if production, access, or working memory problems affected performance on the Comprehension subtest.

The standard and multiple-choice versions are moderately correlated in the standardization sample. For many clinical groups, the correlation between the two versions is low with the exception of the Autistic sample, which showed a high degree of consistency between versions. In general, clinicians should expect more dissociation when the correlation is low between two test versions. In most cases, the groups had very small mean differences between versions. Having similar mean performance with lower correlation suggests that score differences between versions will be observed equally in both directions. The math disorder and traumatic brain injury groups had the biggest differences, which were in favor of the standard version. These children could have been drawn into overly concrete responses due to impulsivity or from failing to detect the better abstract reasoning of the correct response.

Information and Information Multiple Choice

The Information subtest measures the child's knowledge in a number of domains, such as history, science, calendar facts, quantitative knowledge, and literature. Some children may have weaknesses related to the specific content of the subtest. This subtest assesses the child's general fund of knowledge. Subsequently, the impact of education and environmental influences needs to be considered when evaluating low scores. The language production demands on this subtest are less than the aforementioned verbal subtests. Some children do not access knowledge efficiently. They know the information but have difficulty finding it on free recall. For those children, the multiple-choice version enables them to express their knowledge more effectively. As with all verbal subtests, auditory and language decoding skills are always important to consider. For the information subtest, low scores need to be evaluated for content-specific weaknesses, language production and decoding weaknesses, auditory working memory, and executive functioning skills (i.e., ability to search memory stores for information).

Information and Information Multiple Choice were highly correlated in most groups and large differences between these scores were unusual. The Autistic and Math Disorder groups had the biggest discrepancies in performance between the two versions. Children with Autism benefited from the multiple-choice presentation, whereas the Math Disorder group did worse on that version.

INTERPRETING STANDARD FORM VS PROCESS VERSION DIFFERENCES

When evaluating process-level difference score comparisons, a number of hypotheses could account for observed differences. If the scaled scores for the multiple-choice version are significantly higher than the free-recall version, support is provided for the hypothesis that the child may have difficulty with access or retrieval of verbal concepts if external prompts or cues are not present. Oral expression difficulties impede obtainment of full credit responses on standard versions of the verbal subtest. If the scaled score for the multiple-choice adaptation is significantly lower than the scaled score on the corresponding verbal comprehension subtest, the child may have difficulty rejecting salient but conceptually lower level distracters or impulsively choose responses without careful consideration of options. When interpreting score differences, additional information from other sources should be used to corroborate the findings.

Interpretation of difference scores should account for the results presented in Table 1. There is much more variability in specific comparisons, even among children not diagnosed with a clinical condition (i.e., Similarities and Comprehension). When analyzing differences on these measures, more stringent criteria for interpreting the differences as meaningful should be employed (i.e., four or five scaled score point differences). The specific pairwise comparisons yield somewhat different results across clinical groups. Children with Autistic Disorder appeared to benefit the most from recognition trials, suggesting that inconsistent language functioning and pragmatics (social aspects of language use) may interfere with performance on the standard versions of the verbal domain subtests.

The Picture Vocabulary subtest aided children with expressive and social/pragmatic language problems to demonstrate their knowledge. Children with TBI and, to lesser degrees, children with Math Disorder often did more poorly on the multiple-choice versions. Perhaps this is due to poor executive functioning, such as being drawn into more concrete responses. The TBI group did benefit from the Vocabulary Multiple-Choice subtests; perhaps this subtest improves retrieval better than other multiple-choice measures. Impulsivity (i.e., ADD) did not have a large effect on performance, although this group may have too mild deficits for these effects to emerge. The findings here do not inform about the impact of process measures in children with speech-related disorders (i.e., articulation disorder and stuttering), which reflect oral motor programming more than language-based deficits.

GENERAL ISSUES TO CONSIDER WHEN USING VERBAL MULTIPLE-CHOICE SUBTESTS

Although the modified format of the process subtests is designed to reduce some of the cognitive demands required in the free-recall format, several nonlinguistic cognitive processes also contribute to a child's performance on the multiple-choice adaptations. The presentation of multiple response options requires the child to engage in a comparative evaluation to determine the "best" response. This evaluation of options may not have been present during the free-recall condition. The child is presented with highly salient alternative responses that they had not considered previously. Consider the Comprehension item, "Why do cars have seatbelts?" and the foil in Comprehension Multiple Choice "It's the law." During free recall, the child may provide a high-level response that references the safety aspect of wearing seatbelts but provides the conceptually lower level response of "It's the law" when presented with this highly salient (especially in states that have public service advertisements about their seatbelt laws) alternate response option. An illustration of this point is found in a study of verbal memory functioning in children with a reading disorder. In this study, the authors reported that the reading disorder group made more recognition memory errors than controls when the distracters were related semantically to the target word; the rate of errors was the same in both groups for semantically unrelated distracters (Kramer, Knee, & Delis, 2000). Highly salient alternate responses (i.e., responses belonging to the same semantic category) were selected more frequently by the Reading Disorder group than distracters that were from categories that were semantically different from the target words.

Some of the distracter response options (i.e., response options with lower point values) were designed purposely to be phonetically similar to the target word or key phrases to pull for "stimulus-bound" responses. This type of distracter is typically more difficult to reject for those children who have difficulty disassociating acoustic or visual features from semantic or abstract characteristics of the stimuli. Impulsive children may also select phonetically similar items due to a failure to consider all available options. An example of such a response can be found in the Vocabulary Multiple-Choice subtest. For the target word "precise," one of the foils is "precious" and is the only response that is orthographically similar to the target. To select this response, the examinee would only be considering the orthographic (similar spelling) and not the semantic (knowledge) features of the word. In older children, this may represent an overapplication of standard rules of morphology in that word segments themselves have specific meanings and that words with similar morphology have semantic similarity. In some children, there will be a "pull" to respond to that item as it "looks" the most correct based on its stimulus feature. In this case, other evidence of stimulus-bound behavior would likely be present in other contexts as well.

GOING BEYOND THE NUMBERS

There are some behavioral observations that may be made across domains. A few of these behaviors that have social and communication implications are covered here. These observations are useful for making inferences about children with poor language functioning. Poor language functioning creates a risk for impairments in social relationships that may manifest in a number of observable behaviors.

Don't Know Responding

In many instances, responding "I don't know" is appropriate and results in overall performance that is efficient and has fewer errors. If the child is encouraged to take guesses saying "I don't know," it could indicate initiation, retrieval, responses comparison (i.e., multiple-choice options), cooperation, or memory search problems. Rates of saying "don't know" vary by content, suggesting that the skill itself will pull for more or less responses of this nature. Base rate tables enable the clinician to determine if "don't know" responding appears to be excessive. The examiner will need to use sound clinical judgment when making inferences about the possible reasons for "don't know" responses. This should include a review of other test results and information from other sources.

No Response

No response from a child may indicate a number of problems. Importantly, it provides a means for estimating the degree the child is able to engage in the process of the assessment. The "no response" has a very different implication than the "don't know" response. Socially, a response is expected when another individual requests information or asks for task completion. Consistent failure to engage in the minimal requirement of a response may signal significant problems in psychosocial functioning. In particular, the examiner should note if the child responds to their own name and if they are able to establish and maintain eye contact. "No response" does not mean the child is being oppositional, although that may certainly occur; rather the child lacks the social skills or confidence to state that they don't know the answer or to make an effort to make a response of any kind. Children with very severe anxiety, impaired social relatedness, or impaired language skills may engage in this behavior. Having a "no response" is generally rare for most subtests; having multiple "no responses" on a single task is very atypical and may signal problems with the content area being assessed. If the child fails to respond across tests and domains, a more general problem engaging in the assessment process may be present. Intellectual, social, and language development need to be considered when making inferences regarding why a child is not responding to questions.

Self-Corrections

In most cases, self-correction of behavior should not be interpreted as a pathological finding. The ability to self-correct reflects an intact ability to monitor one's behavior for accuracy and relevance. Very high rates of self-correction, however, indicate that the child's information search and expression are error filled. In some impulsive children, they will blurt out a response and once they hear it, they are able to reflect upon it and make a self-correction. Self-corrections are generally rare but are more common on the multiple-choice tests. On these tests, the child has several available options presented directly before them and they may be more inclined to reconsider a response with salient distracters present. The clinician will wish to confirm high rates of self-corrections with other sources before deciding if the problem is pervasive or restricted to the current context.

Requested Repetition

The observation of "requests for repetitions" signals the child has awareness that they did not comprehend or process all the information presented to them. The occasional request for repetition represents good engagement in the assessment process and a desire to do well. Very high rates of requesting repetition of responses may signal problems regulating brief focused attention, auditory processing and decoding problems, or poor language processing. Some very anxious children may request repetitions out of fear they have misunderstood and need reassurance that their understanding is accurate. Requests for repetitions are unusual but are more likely to be observed on the multiple-choice subtests. Multiple requests for repetition are unusual and indicate difficulties with attention or language processing. The source of these problems needs to be verified by outside data or on observed test scores.

Prompts

The frequent need to prompt a child for a response is cognitively associated with the "no response" observation. Poor behavioral initiation results in children not responding without having an external cue to get them started. Highly distractible children need to be prompted to maintain their task focus. Having a very high rate of behavioral prompts may signal that the child is not fully engaged in the process and is distracted by internal or external events. Children with slow cognitive processing may need more time to initiate problem solving. Oppositional children need to be prompted to comply with the process as they will try to resist whenever possible. Interpreting the need for prompts must account for intellectual limitations, slow processing speed, and executive functioning impairments.

GENERAL OBSERVATIONS/INTERPRETATIONS

While psychometric data are an important aspect of clinical and school evaluations, observational data provide insight into potential sources of cognitive strengths and limitations. Based on data presented in this section, it is evident that intact language-processing skills are essential for completing verbal intellectual tasks. Close observation of communication skills will yield important insight into poor scores on verbal intellectual functioning.

Children requiring frequent prompting to start responding (initiation of search/problem-solving behavior) or responding with only a few words and saying "I can't think of anything else" (maintenance of search/problem solving behavior) may have an underlying language disorder or may have impairment in executive control of language functions. If the problem is restricted to executive control of language functions or problems with on-line processing of linguistic information and not impaired semantics, the children may benefit from prompting, cueing, or presenting information in a multiple-choice format. Socially, children with low rates of verbal production may be perceived as "slow," "ignorant," or "shy and quiet."

Children can have significant language problems but have normal rates of language production or even excessive rates of production. In some cases, children with impaired naming skills will produce a large amount of verbal output that describes features about an object or concept "in general" but lacks precision or never quite finds the correct word or expression (circumlocution). Underlying semantic difficulties are likely to be observed in these children but they do not have difficulties with initiation and maintenance of linguistic behavior. Naming errors and use of neologisms likely reflect problems with underlying language functioning and may be observed concurrently with circumlocution. Some children will have a high rate of word use errors, which may be environmental (i.e., exposed to incorrect use of words) or may signal one or more underlying problems with semantic knowledge, self-monitoring of information recall for accuracy, or impulsivity. Socially, children that have high rates of language production but significant deficits in semantic abilities or monitor their verbal output poorly may be perceived by others as "odd or strange," "impulsive," "chatty," or "hard working but not intelligent."

Children that have problems with on-line processing of language due to poor auditory working memory or slow language processing speed may ask for information to be repeated. If this occurs in light of relatively intact semantic knowledge, they will be able to respond appropriately after one or more repetitions. In some cases, the children will learn to not ask for repetitions all the time because others get annoyed when they do it. Rather than ask for a repetition, they will attempt the task based on limited information. Their responses will be inaccurate or incomplete. Socially, those with generally intact auditory attention but difficulties processing language quickly and accurately will appear "inattentive," whereas those with global auditory attention problems will be viewed as both "inattentive and forgetful." More global attention problems will result in inattention to details during conversation but also problems tracking what they are doing. They may forget what they were talking about or forget something they were about to do. Children that have very good auditory decoding and good auditory working memory skills but have underlying language decoding problems will be able to repeat what they hear verbatim yet not understand what has been said to them. These children may show initiation problems (don't initiate because they don't know what they are supposed to do) or ask for repetitions but fail to act correctly on the repetitions. This situation is aggravating to people working with the child because they appear to understand what is said to them but are not following directions. These children often do not act upon verbal requests or do so in a haphazard manner. Socially, this can be misinterpreted as "passive-aggressive," "defiance," "not cooperative," or "oppositional" behavior.

Clinicians using the WISC-IV Integrated will find the base rates for specific observed verbal behaviors useful in assessing some of the behaviors noted earlier. The manual provides percentages of cases saying "don't know," "asks for repetitions," and "no response." The clinician's observations regarding the child's behavior provide a wealth of data that can be shared with teachers, parents, and staff working with the child to improve their understanding and interventions with the child.

A qualitative evaluation of item content can be particularly useful for subtests in the verbal domain. This type of analysis may signal academic areas that require remediation or social situations to which the child has had limited exposure. For example, the information and information multiple-choice items can be grouped into the following content categories: those that require a quantitative response (items 4, 5, 6, 11, 13, and 31), those that require recall of calendar information (items 7, 9, 11, 12, 17, and 18), those that reflect knowledge of science (items 10, 14, 15, 19, 20, 23, 24, 26, 29, 30, 32, and 33) and historical/literary figures (items 16, 27, and 28), and those that assess knowledge of geography or directions (items 22, 25, and 31). The child's item-level performance can be evaluated qualitatively to determine if his or her performance varies across such content areas.

Many of the Verbal Comprehension Multiple-Choice items were developed with particular types of distracters. For example, the range of incorrect choices often includes a correct but more concrete alternative, a phonetically similar word, and a completely incorrect response. Examiners may wish to consider the type of distracters generally chosen on incorrect items to further understand the examinee's performance.

PERCEPTUAL REASONING
DOMAIN

In the Perceptual Reasoning domain, poor test performance may occur for a number of reasons. Previously, a number of visual–perceptual skills were reviewed and a deficit in one or a number of these areas may produce inefficient/attenuated scores on perceptual reasoning subtests. The main hypotheses to consider when low Perceptual Reasoning Index scores are obtained include visual–spatial development, visual discrimination, visual scanning (visual fields)/attention, visual working memory, global versus local processing, executive functioning, processing speed, and motor skills. At the subtest level, the demands for specific visual–perceptual skills such as visual–spatial development, visual discrimination, visual scanning (visual fields)/attention, visual working memory, and global versus local processing will vary. The subtest content and task demands will affect the degree to which intact visual–perceptual skills are required. Interpretation of subtest variability should consider the degree to which the visual–perceptual demands of the task affect performance.

VISUAL–PERCEPTUAL DEMANDS OF WISC-IV
INTEGRATED PERCEPTUAL REASONING SUBTESTS

The visual–perceptual subtests on the WISC-IV Integrated require a number of lower level skills as well as intellectual abilities (i.e., fluid reasoning, conceptual reasoning, visual–spatial integration, and construction). A number of these skills were reviewed earlier in the chapter. There are a number of hypotheses that need to be tested when low perceptual reasoning scores are obtained. Clinicians should be concerned with the child's visual discrimination, visual attention and working memory, global versus local visual–perceptual processing, processing speed, motor skills, and executive functioning. At the subtest level, the demands for specific visual–perceptual skills will vary. The subtest content and task demands will affect the degree to which intact visual–perceptual skills are requisite to task performance. Interpretation of subtest variability should consider the degree to which the visual–perceptual demands of the task affect performance.

The visual–perceptual subtests on the WISC-IV Integrated are Block Design, Block Design No Time Bonus, Block Design Multiple Choice, Block Design Multiple Choice No Time Bonus, Block Design Process Approach Parts A and B, Picture Concepts, Matrix Reasoning, Elithorn Mazes, and Elithorn Mazes No Time Bonus. This section discusses the degree to which these subtests require intact visual processing skills. Changes made to the subtest composition of the Perceptual Reasoning Index from the WISC-III Perceptual Organization Index were designed to reduce the impact of motor ability and processing speed on performance. This was accomplished, in part, by replacing Object Assembly and Picture Completion with Matrix Reasoning and Picture Concepts as core subtests in this Index. Although the emphasis on motor control and processing speed has been reduced at the index level, these factors may still influence performance on the Block Design subtest.

Block Design, Block Design Multiple Choice, and Block Design Process Approach

The Block Design subtest has a long history of use as part of intellectual batteries. The task requires the examinee to construct a two-dimensional design using three-dimensional blocks. The designs increase with difficulty. Difficulty is associated with the number of blocks used in the design, the proportion of the blocks that are colored half red and half white, the orientation of the half-shaded blocks, and the presence or absence of grid lines. All the items have time limits and in the standard form bonus points for fast (accurate) performance. This task requires adequate visual discrimination skills, visual attention, rapid visual processing, motor control, and execution. The Block Design No Time Bonus score provides a measure of constructional accuracy without emphasizing rapid performance. There are still time limits, so very slow processors will still lose points because they cannot complete the item in time. Both scores demand motor execution, and a problem with motor control may result in a loss of points due to an inability to place the blocks together quickly and efficiently.

The Block Design Multiple Choice subtest was designed to eliminate the motor demand present on the standard version of the test. The examinee mentally completes the design and identifies the correct answer out of four choices. There are two- and three-dimensional constructions in this subtest. This task requires intact visual discrimination, visual scanning, and visual attention. Timed and untimed scores are available for this subtest.

The Block Design Process Approach subtest enables the clinician to segment the visual–perceptual processes to determine the source of poor Block Design performance. This subtest differentiates visual–perceptual processing deficits associated with integration of the overall gestalt of the design, "global" features, versus difficulties determining the specific features (i.e., coloration and orientation of individual blocks), "local" features of the design. Children having intact "global" processing but poor "local" processing will be able to reproduce the external shape of the design correctly (i.e., 2×2, 3×3) but will place individual blocks incorrectly in terms of their orientation and coloring. Conversely, the child with intact "local" processing but deficient global processing will try to re-create features of the design with individual blocks, but they will violate the design's overall shape and structure. Having intact local versus global processing does not mean that the child will be better at placing individual blocks but that they will focus on specific details as a means to solving the overall problem. These children have higher rates of configuration breaks (i.e., a figure that is not 2×2 or 3×3) during (on route) and at the completion (final) of the design and will be more likely to use extra blocks. This indicates difficulties integrating parts into a whole (Kramer, Kaplan, Share, & Huckeba, 1999). They will, however, benefit from the placement of the grid overlay on the design. When the grid is placed on the design, the placement of the individual blocks is highlighted.

Children having difficulties processing the whole design configuration as well as details of the individual blocks will benefit only modestly from the use of the grid overlay. This represents a more pervasive deficit in visual–perceptual processing. Some children are able to recognize the global pattern but have significant difficulties with mental rotation and are not able to align the orientation of the block correctly. Observationally, these children will have many rotations of individual blocks and/or of the total design. Their total scores will be affected by the number of half red and half white blocks required by the design, as all white or red blocks cannot be rotated incorrectly (on these items look for whole design rotations). The examiner may wish to use extended time limits and evaluate partial credit by item for children with apparent difficulties with block orientation.

To facilitate the clinician's understanding of the child's performance, three types of observational data are recorded during administration: en route breaks in configuration, breaks in final configuration, and use of extra blocks. En Route Breaks in Configuration occur when the child, in the process of trying to figure out the design, creates a block pattern that does not follow the expected 2×2 or 3×3 shape. The break in final configuration is when the child's final solution contains a response that does not adhere to the 2 × 2 or 3×3 shape.

Extra block errors occur when the child uses more than four or nine blocks in the final solution. The child that frequently breaks configuration en route to the final solution but does not make many breaks in the final solution may have some mild difficulties with global processing of visual stimuli. More serious problems are evident by frequent configuration breaks in the final solution. The child is unable to recognize that the produced pattern does not match the target design in overall shape. Local details may be correct in some cases and the inability to integrate the local information with the whole gestalt is present. Other children with more severe visual–perceptual problems have errors in configuration as well as poorly placed local detail (orientation and color of individual blocks). Problems in visual–perceptual processing specifically associated with local or global processing may indicate the integrity of left (local) versus right (global) hemisphere processing of visual information. Breaks in configuration en route to the final solution are not uncommon and are usually corrected by children from nonclinical samples. Breaks in configuration have been linked to possible perceptual bias toward local detail versus global processing and are related to lower total Block Design scores.

Additional scoring procedures are available if the clinician chooses to use the extended time per item procedure. Partial credit is awarded for each block that is placed correctly. In cases of youth that are inattentive or impulsive, they may obtain a zero score using standard scoring based on the misorientation or color placement of a single block. Over several items, this may drastically reduce the overall score that they obtain. Partial credit scores enable the clinician to determine the severity of performance deficits and make better judgments about impairments due to careless or inattentive performance versus those due to more severe visual perceptual processing problems. Partial scores are also a good mechanism for assessing improvement to functioning related in intervention and progress monitoring. While total designs may still be difficult for impaired children to complete, they may have better local processing due to intervention and be able to place individual blocks correctly. In other words, overall abilities are improved but continued difficulties with visual–perceptual processing or inattention (i.e., neglect or brief focused attention) may limit the number of total designs improved over time, despite effective treatment and improved abilities. The partial credit score also enables the child to continue working past the traditional time limits. Some children may benefit from having extended time to work on the items. Their partial credit score will be higher due to the extended testing time.

All versions of the Block Design subtest require intact visual discrimination, visual scanning, and visual attention. Processing speed demands are varied by the use of time bonus versus no time bonus or in the process approach version extended time limits. The impact of motor skill deficits is controlled through the use of the multiple-choice procedure. Executive functioning (i.e., initiation of behavior, productivity, self-monitoring, planning) impacts performance on all of the Block Design subtests. When low scores are achieved on the standard version of Block Design, the hypotheses to consider beyond low intellectual functioning are deficits in visual discrimination, visual scanning, visual attention, visual processing speed, motor execution, and executive functioning.

Correlations in Table 2 show the relationship of Block Design, Block Design No Time Bonus, and Block Design Multiple Choice. The correlation between Block Design and Block Design No Time Bonus is very high in both clinical and standardization samples. Large differences in scores are very rare and the clinical groups did not exhibit any large differences between versions. There is a moderate correlation between the multiple choice and the standard version of Block Design that is consistent across groups. Among the clinical groups, the Math Disorder groups had better performance on the multiple-choice version. This group may have some difficulty executing the solution to the Block Design problem in its standard form.

Matrix Reasoning

The Matrix Reasoning subtest assesses the child's ability to determine logical associations among visual designs. This subtest is new to the WISC scales for the 4th edition, but the matrix paradigm has a long history of use in psychology and assessment of intellectual abilities. The test uses a multiple-choice response format, which minimizes the effects of motor control and processing speed. Visual discrimination, attention to detail, and visual scanning skills are important underlying skills for this subtest. Executive functioning as the capacity to consider all possible options rather than respond impulsively to designs that are nearly correct is important.

Some children can verbalize, either overtly or mentally, the associations among the visual elements. Using language can facilitate performance on this subtest, but it is not a required element to complete the task. Because some children use a linguistic strategy to facilitate their performance, children with language difficulties could potentially score lower compared to normative data on this subtest. When interpreting low scores on this subtest, alternate hypotheses regarding the impact of visual discrimination, attention and scanning, and impulsivity should be considered.

Picture Concepts

The Picture Concepts subtest was new to the Wechsler family of intellectual assessments for the *Wechsler Preschool and Primary Scale of Intelligence*–3rd edition (WPPSI; Wechsler, 2002). The child must identify key visual features among an array of objects that associates two or three of the objects. The association among the objects is identified by visual processes and no verbal response is required, but concepts linking the objects are semantic. This subtest requires adequate visual scanning, attention to visual details, visual discrimination, and adequate semantic knowledge. Motor skills and visual processing speed and executive functioning, such as inhibitory

TABLE 2 Correlation coefficients, average differences and rate of discrepancy for WISC-IV Perceptual Reasoning Subtests

	Block Design Versus Block Design No Time Bonus				Block Design Versus Block Design Multiple Choice			
	r	Mean (SD) Difference	BD > BD no Time	BD < BD no Time	r	Mean (SD) Difference	BD > BDMC	BD < BDMC
Standardization Sample	0.95	−.10 (0.9)	0.6	1.3	0.63	−.04 (2.6)	16.5	16.2
ADD	0.96	0.02 (0.7)	0	0	0.52	−.19 (3.0)	18.8	24.5
Autistic	0.98	0.13 (0.8)	0	0	0.63	−.20 (3.7)	26.7	33.3
Expressive Language Disorder	0.97	−.10 (0.8)	0	0	0.51	−20 (3.1)	13.8	27.6
Receptive-Expressive Language Disorder	0.98	−.11 (.7)	0	0	0.62	0 (2.7)	11.1	16.7
Math Disorder	0.98	−.11 (0.7)	0	0	0.66	−1.02 (2.4)	4.6	32.6
Reading Disorder	0.95	0.0 (0.8)	0	1.6	0.50	.43 (2.4)	21	12.9
Traumatic Brain Injury	0.94	−.04 (0.9)	0	0	0.65	−.03 (2.4)	13.9	8.3

	Block Design Multiple Choice Versus Elithorn Mazes				Cancellation Versus Elithorn Mazes			
	r	Mean (SD) Difference	BDMC > EM	BDMC < EM	r	Mean (SD) Difference	CA > EM	CA < EM
Standardization Sample	0.41	0.06 (3.3)	23.6	23.1	0.14	−.05 (4.0)	26.9	27.6
ADD	0.13	−.28 (4.1)	18.8	34	−0.05	−.74 (4.5)	18.9	30.2
Autistic	0.26	2.3 (4.7)	66.7	13.3	0.28	.73 (3.9)	33.3	26.7
Expressive Language Disorder	0.18	−.45 (4.2)	20.7	31	0.24	−.28 (3.7)	20.7	24.1
Receptive-Expressive Language Disorder	0.39	.75 (3.6)	36.1	16.7	0.22	.97 (4.1)	30.6	16.7
Math Disorder	0.41	−.12 (3.6)	32.6	27.9	−0.04	.44 (4.7)	34.9	16.3
Reading Disorder	0.14	−.32 (3.2)	21	25.8	0.24	.82 (3.5)	29	16.1
Traumatic Brain Injury	0.48	−.42 (3.3)	22.2	25	0.44	−.91 (3.8)	13.9	36.1

(Continues)

TABLE 2 (Continued)

	Matrix Reasoning Versus Elithorn Mazes				Elithorn Mazes Versus Elithorn Mazes with No Time Bonus			
	r	Mean (SD) Difference	MR > EM	MR < EM	r	Mean (SD) Difference	EM > No Time	EM > No Time
Standardization Sample	0.37	−.10 (3.4)	21.5	25.6	0.90	−.05 (1.3)	2.9	3.2
ADD	0.16	−.58 (3.7)	24.5	34	0.90	.13 (1.3)	7.6	0
Autistic	0.48	.93 (3.0)	26.7	13.3	0.92	−.13 (1.0)	6.7	0
Expressive Language Disorder	0.47	−1.14 (3.5)	13.8	34.5	0.92	.10 (1.3)	3.4	0
Receptive-Expressive Language Disorder	0.36	−.11 (3.6)	25	25	0.94	.03 (1.2)	2.8	0
Math Disorder	0.24	−.77 (3.6)	20.9	25.6	0.97	.14 (0.9)	0	0
Reading Disorder	0.41	−.35 (2.8)	16.1	27.4	0.91	−.11 (1.1)	1.6	1.6
Traumatic Brain Injury	0.53	.19 (2.9)	25	22	0.86	−.08 (1.7)	5.6	0

Note: Listwise deletion used for all measures resulting in the following sample sizes—standardization (624), ADD (53), Autistic (15), Expressive Language Disorder (29), Receptive-Expressive Language Disorder (36), Math Disorder (36), Reading Disorder (43), and Traumatic Brain Injury (36). All comparisons are computed as core or supplemental minus process subtest. *Wechsler Intelligence Scale for Children – Fourth Edition Integrated.* Copyright © 2004 by Harcourt Assessment, Inc. Reproduced with permission. All rights reserved.

control and self-monitoring, could influence performance on this test. Underlying requisite skills should be considered when interpreting low scores on this subtest.

Picture Completion

The Picture Completion subtest has a long history of use in the Wechsler family of intellectual assessments. On this subtest, the child must identify key visual features that are missing from an object. The examinee responds verbally but pointing responses may be accepted. This subtest requires significant demands on attention to visual detail and visual scanning. Some verbal responding is involved and, to that extent, intact verbal productivity and naming skills are important. The Picture Completion subtest is a supplemental test for this version of the WISC.

EXECUTIVE FUNCTIONING

Executive functioning is a category of cognitive processes composed of many discrete abilities. This domain of cognitive skills reflects higher order processes that influence performance on other cognitive tasks. For instance, the ability to efficiently organize information and solve problems in a systemic manner will affect performance on language, visual perceptual, memory, and other tasks. The proposed abilities subsumed under the rubric of executive functioning include, but are not limited to, organization, planning, flexibility, self-monitoring, information retrieval, productivity, freedom from impulsivity, and executing the motor programs necessary to accomplish the task (i.e., verbalize thought or draw design).

Executive functioning, as measured by WISC-IV Integrated, focuses primarily on immediate planning, self-monitoring, and freedom from impulsive responding. Self-monitoring reflects self-awareness as related to solving specific problems. This includes the ability to evaluate one's own performance for adherence to task rules, freedom from making erroneous responses, and maintaining task focus to achieve task goals. Executive functioning abilities are necessary for all complex tasks, such as most of the subtests of the WISC-IV Integrated. In most cases, these skills are not measured explicitly; however, these abilities may underlie superior or deficient performances.

Elithorn Mazes

The Elithorn Mazes subtest is a relatively simple visual–perceptual task made more complex with demands for spatial planning ability. This measure is a process subtest of the WISC-IV Integrated. This subtest measures executive functioning effects on visual–perceptual processes. It requires intact visual scanning, discrimination and attention, spatial working memory, visual processing speed, and visual–perceptual reasoning. More specifically, the Elithorn Mazes subtest assesses the child's immediate spatial planning, inhibitory control, cognitive flexibility, and ability to follow task rules. Clinicians may wish to administer this test when they suspect that low scores in the perceptual-reasoning domain are due to executive functioning difficulties, particularly impulsivity and poor self-monitoring.

The Elithorn Mazes task affords the child an opportunity to benefit from their mistakes. If they make an error on the first trial of the item, they are allowed to try again. A child that repeats an error two times in a row may not understand the rules of the task or is exhibiting significant deficits with planning and cognitive flexibility. Performance on this task is also affected by procedural learning such that the child may learn the underlying procedure for determining the correct solution to the problem, especially on the second trial of an item.

The subtest yields a variety of performance indicators designed to enable the clinician to understand the cognitive processes affecting the child's performance. The scaled score is based on accuracy and speed of performance. High scores indicate that the child is able to determine the appropriate combination of dots that do not violate any rules of the task quickly and accurately (i.e., going backward on the path) and the degree to which these skills are automatically invoked and executed. Low scores may occur due to poor planning and impulsive responding. Slow processing or graphomotor speed may also contribute to low scores. Moreover, some obsessive children may perform poorly due to time constraints, mentally attempting all combinations to be assured they are giving the best response. In addition, very low scores may indicate the child does not benefit from seeing their mistakes.

Elithorn Mazes measures only some skills related to executing functioning and adequate performance on this subtest should not be construed as evidence that the child's overall executive functioning is intact. On the same note, low performance on this subtest should not be taken to indicate global impairment in executive abilities. Elithorn Mazes may be best thought of as a brief screener for executive function deficits.

The Elithorn Mazes No Time Bonus score is based on the child's performance on the Elithorn Mazes subtest *without* additional time bonus points for rapid completion of items. The reduced emphasis on speed of performance may be particularly useful when a child's physical limitations, problem-solving strategies, or personality is believed to affect performance on timed tasks. This score does not control for very slow performance speed as time limits are still enforced and the instructions indicate that the child should perform the task as quickly as possible. High scores may indicate good immediate planning and inhibition skills. Low scores may indicate poor planning ability and impulsivity. Very low scores may indicate that the child does not benefit from viewing their mistakes.

Block Design Multiple Choice vs Elithorn Mazes

Comparing these two subtests enables the clinician to rule out deficits in basic visual identification and discrimination that may have an impact on Elithorn Mazes. Low scores on Elithorn Mazes compared to Block Design Multiple Choice indicate that visual–perceptual processes do not account for poor performance on Elithorn Mazes and that poor spatial planning is influencing performance.

Elithorn Mazes is moderately correlated with Block Design Multiple Choice in the standardization sample. This indicates that dissociations between the scores are not rare. For many of the clinical groups, there was low association between these measures and large differences between these scores often occurred. The Autistic group demonstrated large differences in favor of Block Design Multiple Choice, indicating executive functioning problems. The Receptive-Expressive group showed a similar pattern but to a lesser degree. The other groups did not have large differences between the two subtests.

Cancellation vs Elithorn Mazes

The clinician will want to compare Cancellation performance to Elithorn Mazes to determine if motor control, visual scanning, and processing speed have affected performance on Elithorn Mazes. High scores on Cancellation versus Elithorn Mazes indicate that the child has sufficient visual scanning, motor control, and processing speed abilities to perform the Elithorn Mazes subtest but may have specific problems with spatial planning, reasoning, or visual–perceptual skills. Low scores on both tasks may signal more global difficulties with visual scanning, sequencing, and processing skills, as well as higher order planning abilities.

The correlation between Cancellation and Elithorn Mazes (see Table 2) is low in nearly all groups. In the standardization sample, the correlation was quite low and indicates very little overlap in skills being measured. Scanning speed does not play a large role on Elithorn Mazes such that only when the child has extremely poor visual scanning might there be an impact on Elithorn Mazes performance. In the clinical groups, Cancellation tends to be higher than Elithorn Mazes, indicating more difficulty with planning compared to visual scanning. In the ADD and TBI groups, the opposite pattern occurred.

Matrix Reasoning vs Elithorn Mazes

Comparing Elithorn Mazes to Matrix Reasoning provides an indication of the child's capacity to solve visual problems requiring attention to visual detail, understanding the relationship between different visual designs (discrimination and reasoning), and the ability to follow logical sequences to find the correct solution without requiring a significant degree of spatial planning.

The two subtests are moderately correlated in the standardization sample in many of the clinical samples. In general, the clinical groups have more difficulty with Matrix Reasoning than Elithorn Mazes, with the exception being the Autistic group, which consistently demonstrated difficulties with Elithorn Mazes compared to other skills.

Elithorn Mazes vs Elithorn Mazes No Time Bonus

Elithorn Mazes No Time Bonus versus Elithorn Mazes indicates that the child has good planning skills but may need more time to actualize these abilities. The clinician should also consider the preresponse latencies and motor planning when evaluating for slow processing. Impulsive children will have fast response times but inconsistent performance, whereas children with a high degree of preplanning can have slow speed but very accurate performance. Slower speed due to a high degree of motor planning and accurate performance would not be considered a deficiency and would reflect higher order executive functioning skills. Slow speed in the context of poor performance or low motor planning would be considered a deficiency in both poor planning and low processing speed.

Table 2 presents correlations for standard and no bonus point scores. These scores are highly correlated across all groups. Large differences between the bonus and no bonus scores are rare and were not observed to be related to any clinical groups.

INTERPRETING PERCEPTUAL REASONING SCORE DIFFERENCES

When deciding to evaluate and report specific discrepancies, it is important to have a specific hypothesis in mind for completing this comparison. For instance, if the child has obvious motor problems, the hypothesis is that these motor problems have reduced the child's scores on one or more Perceptual Reasoning tasks or the decision to administer Elithorn Mazes was due to overt signs of impulsivity or inability to follow task rules. Having specific a priori hypotheses will reduce the number of type I errors that will occur when completing a large number of statistical comparisons. Alternately, setting a high threshold for interpreting differences may be warranted when completing multiple comparisons. Unlike the verbal domain, procedures in the perceptual domain use more than just multiple-choice procedures. The Block Design Process Approach enables the clinician to break down a child's visual processing into much smaller processes and potentially allows a determination of the source of visual–perceptual problems (i.e., global versus local processing, structure versus unstructured). This subtest was not renormed so direct comparison statistics between the standard version and the Process Approach version cannot be made. The clinician would want to report large differences between the scores.

Interpretation of score comparisons should take into consideration results presented in Table 2. Comparisons of Elithorn Mazes with other subtests result in frequent large discrepancies even among children in the general population; however, very low Elithorn Mazes scores compared to other visual–perceptual processing are indicative of significant problems in executive functioning, as evidenced in the Autism group. In this domain, the Math, Receptive-Expressive Language, and Autism Disorder groups displayed the most variability between subtests. When evaluating children with social, executive, and math impairments, it is important to consider administering additional process procedures.

GOING BEYOND THE NUMBERS

The Perceptual Reasoning subtests provide ample opportunity to observe the child's approach to complex, novel problems. These observations may yield important considerations for intervention or provide a better understanding of the child's cognitive weaknesses. Many key observations have been mentioned already in the Block Design section. Additional considerations are presented here.

A qualitative evaluation of problem-solving strategy can be particularly useful for subtests in the Perceptual domain. The Block Design subtests provide an excellent opportunity to observe the child's problem-solving strategies. The task is novel and difficult, requiring a number of cognitive abilities to complete the task. Some children will obviously use a "trial-and-error" strategy to try to complete the design. They will spin the blocks on the table and put them up against a block while switching colors and orientation with the hopes of stumbling upon the answer. Other children recognize that the designs are made up of four or nine blocks and systematically place the blocks in sequence based on local details that align with the picture. Other children rapidly learn procedural skills such as how to make a diagonal line with two half-colored blocks and quickly identify this pattern within the design. Close observation of the child may reveal important information about their overall problem-solving style, particularly on items that are difficult for them.

Close observation can reveal a child's tendency to construct designs in a disorganized manner or a child's difficulties in accurate perception of abstract, visual stimuli. For example, the examiner may note that the child does not utilize a consistent strategy in assembling designs (i.e., the child constructs designs using a trial-and-error approach). In addition, the practitioner may want to evaluate any differences in the child's performance that may be related to item content. For example, the child may perform better on those items depicting common geometric shapes than those with complex visual patterns or lines or have more difficulty with those items that do not have internal grid lines in the stimulus (Joy, Fein, Kaplan, & Freedman,

2001; Troyer, Cullum, Smernoff, & Kozora, 1994; Wilde, Boake, & Scherer, 2000).

The Elithorn Mazes subtest provided base rate data for key error types. The types of errors are discussed here.

Preresponse Latencies (Planning Time)

This score is the time between the presentation of an item and the child beginning to attempt to complete the item. It is roughly equivalent to the amount of time spent in planning and entails consideration of options, constructing mental representations of alternate routes, and deriving a plan to execute the chosen response. Very fast scores (i.e., low number of seconds) may represent a quick planning ability or indicate an impulsive response style.

An impulsive response style (fast but inaccurate) or a deliberate response style with weak planning skills (slow latency and inaccurate) can be determined by reviewing time and accuracy scores. It is important to consider that the average preresponse time was somewhat longer for children that made errors on the item than for those who responded correctly. Perhaps individuals with longer latency times had difficulty understanding the task or with the task itself. Therefore, slow preresponse latencies may be a sign of difficulty in actualizing planning behavior, whereas very short preresponse latencies indicate difficulties in initiating or engaging in planning behaviors.

Motor Planning

Overt motor planning is evident when the child traces the path in space visually using a finger or a pencil prior to initiating a response to the trial. Evaluate this score in the context of Spatial Span. If the child has low Spatial Span scores, he or she may need to engage in overt motor planning to compensate for weak visual–spatial working memory. If the child has adequate visual–spatial working memory abilities and engages in overt motor planning, they may be using motor planning as an explicit strategy to help with finding the correct solution and identifying the motor program needed to complete the item. Alternatively, motor planning may be a method of trial-and-error problem solving prior to the onset of the actual task.

Motor Imprecision Errors

Motor imprecision errors reflect a rule violation in which the child significantly deviates from the maze pathway due to poor graphomotor control. Poor graphomotor control may be evident on other tasks, such as Coding, Coding Copy, and Written Arithmetic. If the child consistently displays poor graphomotor skills, then errors likely reflect poor motor control. If the child displays good graphomotor control elsewhere but many errors on Elithorn Mazes, errors likely reflect planning problems.

Across and Backward Error Scores

An across error occurs when a child crosses the diamond to go from one track segment to a neighboring track segment. When the child reverses direction on the same path, it is a backward error. These errors occur when the child realizes they cannot complete the number of targets following the current route. These types of errors are considered rule violations. Rule violations occur for a number of reasons. The child could have forgotten the rule or have difficulty monitoring their responses to ensure rule complianace. The child can recall the rule but not realize he or she has violated the rule due to inattention. Frequent rule violations may also indicate an impulsive response style. The child fails to plan the correct path and produces a high rate of errors. Finally, the child can't complete the item without breaking the rule but wanted to comply; therefore, they violate the rule "knowingly" in order to complete the task.

GENERAL OBSERVATIONS/INTERPRETATIONS

Impairments in perceptual reasoning skills are not as readily observable as language impairments. The deficits are most obvious on artistic tasks such as drawing and painting. The child's sense of proportion, perspective, relationship among objects, ability to represent three-dimensional perspective, and integration of details into the overall gestalt of the picture may be inaccurate. A subset of these children may have problems with printing and handwriting due to errors of proportion and spacing. Some of the children may experience figure-ground impairments and have difficulty identifying salient features of pictures. On written projects, they may crowd or poorly plan how they will space their work. In some cases, the nature and severity of the perceptual-reasoning difficulties will affect the child's capacity to create accurate mental maps of places. Others may think that the child gets lost easily or cannot follow directions (i.e., gets lost on the way to the principal's office). The degree that deficits in this domain interfere with overall psychosocial functioning is not clear.

WORKING MEMORY DOMAIN

Low scores in the Working Memory domain can occur for a number of reasons. The primary factors that affect performance are auditory or visual discrimination, attention, mental sequencing, basic automaticity of letter and digit processing, and executive control. In previous versions of the WISC, only auditory working memory measures were provided. In the WISC-IV Integrated, multiple visual working memory tasks have been developed to enable analysis for modality-specific weaknesses in working memory performance. The auditory tasks have been revised to reduce the impact of other cognitive skills.

There is a reciprocal association between working memory skills and other cognitive domains such as language and visual–perceptual processing. Therefore, there will be instances in which significant impairments in one of these domains will limit or reduce the level of performance on the specific working memory tasks. For instance, significant impairments in visual–spatial ability will affect performance on the Spatial Span Task. In some cases, it may be difficult to ascertain if working memory skills are impairing language or visual–perceptual processes or vice versa.

Process analysis of the Working Memory domain includes evaluation of specific aspects of registration and working memory. The specific cognitive components, and corresponding nomenclature, of immediate memory, short-term memory, and working memory are still subjects of theoretical debate (Engle, Tuholski, Laughlin, & Conway, 1999). The working memory tasks selected for the WISC-IV Integrated are best represented by Baddeley and Hitch's (1994) proposed model of a central executive system that controls attention resources for maintaining specific auditory (phonological loop) and visual (visuospatial sketch pad) information in conscious awareness and enabling mental operations to be performed on that information. The nomenclature chosen for the WISC-IV Integrated is designed to differentiate lower level operations that represent integration of a number of early processes, including perceptual decoding, identification, and temporary storage functions, from those that require the simultaneous maintenance of and modification of that information.

A distinction is made between those aspects of working memory that primarily involve registration (taking in) and simple maintenance of that information in conscious awareness from those that emphasize manipulation beyond this basic intake of information. This distinction was predicated on research verifying that different cognitive demands are placed on the child when engaging in registration of information versus working memory tasks (de Jonge & de Jong, 1996; Denckla & Rudel, 1976; Mirsky et al., 1991; Reynolds, 1997). Use of the term "registration" reflects multiple cognitive processes that enable the child to temporarily hold information in conscious awareness in order to execute a response and does not require a significant amount of reprocessing of those stimuli. Certain characteristics of the stimuli must be determined and maintained (i.e., content and sequence) in order for a correct response to be generated. Registration requires multiple processes, including sensory discrimination and storage, brief focused attention, maintenance (i.e., rehearsal or refreshing) of information in conscious memory, and response execution. Long spans may invoke additional strategic cognitive processes such as "chunking" of information that may be invoked routinely by high-ability children.

Mental manipulation is the terminology applied to WISC-IV Integrated measures that require the child to process information before making a response. The processing aspect could be resequencing of items, performing math operations, or processing two types of information simultaneously.

ATTENTION, LETTER–NUMBER KNOWLEDGE, AND EXECUTIVE FUNCTIONING DEMANDS OF WISC-IV INTEGRATED WORKING MEMORY SUBTESTS

The assessment of working memory skills necessarily occurs in the context of other cognitive abilities. By definition, working memory is the conscious manipulation of information (i.e., either previously learned or newly acquired) in order to produce some result (i.e., resequencing, computation). The examinee must attend to this information and process it accurately (i.e., auditory discrimination or visual–spatial decoding) before the information can be manipulated. In some cases, the task requires such low-level processing that the information can be repeated with minimal conscious effort and decoding (i.e., repeating two letters). In most cases, the child will need to have some knowledge or basis on performing the mental operation requested. On Letter–Number Sequencing, the child must know their numbers (one through nine) and know their correct sequence from lowest to highest. Children, especially young children, that have poorly automatized number skills, could potentially struggle with such tasks.

Impairments in attention result in a failure to accurately acquire all information producing inconsistent performance. The demands on sustained attention are minimal but the child must be able to control and focus attention during the administration of each item. Executive functioning deficits will not impact performance directly if the individual has relatively intact working memory skills. Good executive functioning can facilitate performance through clustering of information to be recalled into smaller units. There is likely a reciprocal causation between working memory and executive functioning (i.e., executive functioning skills likely require some degree of working memory and vice versa). The subtests to be reviewed here are Digit Span, Letter–Number Sequencing, Arithmetic, Spatial Span, and Visual Span.

Digit Span

The Digit Span subtest has a long history of use in psychology. The test requires the examinee to repeat a sequence of digits verbatim or in reverse order (reverse from what they were told, not in reverse order according to denomination). The repetition component is referred to as registration, and reverse sequencing is the mental manipulation component. Adequate auditory discrimination and decoding and basic regulation of attention are required. Number knowledge likely facilitates scores on this subtest but is not required. On longer spans, executive control and use of a strategy will facilitate performance. No significant language or visual–perceptual demands should influence performance on this task.

Letter–Number Sequencing and Letter–Number Sequencing Process Approach (Embedded Words)

The Letter–Number Sequencing task is relatively new to the Wechsler scales of intelligence. It was developed to assess mental manipulation without requiring math computation skills. The test measures the child's ability to mentally disassemble a string of numbers and letters, resequence the numbers and letters in their proper order, and then say the numbers and letters back. Auditory discrimination and decoding, attention, letter and number knowledge, and mental sequencing skills are needed to complete this task. Executive regulation of cognitive resources is potentially taxed by this subtest on the difficult items. The embedded words task reduces working memory demands by enabling the examinee to easily chunk the letters into a single unit. In order for this to facilitate performance, the child must recognize that letters spell a word and then be able to take the word apart and resequence the letters.

Letter Span

The Letter Span subtest is an analog to the Digit Span (forward condition only) using letters instead of numbers as stimuli. The subtest uses rhyming versus nonrhyming letters in an effort to understand the impact of auditory discrimination on span performance. Also, the comparison between letters and numbers enables the clinician to test the hypothesis that an underlying knowledge (automaticity of decoding) of letters or numbers is influencing registration performance.

ARITHMETIC, ARITHMETIC PROCESS APPROACH, AND WRITTEN ARITHMETIC

The Arithmetic subtest is a supplemental working memory measure for the WISC-IV Integrated. The subtest requires a number of cognitive skills beyond intact working memory. The child must have adequate auditory discrimination and decoding skills, capacity and speed of language processing (the items are presented verbally), math knowledge, and computational ability. The Process subtests enable the clinician to differentiate the underlying causes of poor performance on this subtest. The Arithmetic Process Approach subtest allows the child to read the problem as the examiner says it (reducing working memory demands). If the child continues to get a problem incorrect, they are allowed to write the problem down and work it out on paper, further reducing working memory demands. The Written Arithmetic subtest presents all the standard Arithmetic items in numeric format. This reduces the language demands required to decode the problem and the working memory demands and focuses solely on math knowledge and computational skill. The child must understand how to apply math symbols correctly to answer the problems correctly. Since the standard items require intact language decoding, deficits in this domain could result in lower scores due to linguistic rather than working memory difficulties.

Spatial Span

The Spatial Span subtest is designed to measure the child's ability to remember a series of visual locations and identify those locations in the same and reverse sequence. This subtest requires intact visual–spatial processing; visual, discrimination, scanning, and attention; and motor execution of the response. This test enables the clinician to determine if deficits in auditory working memory signal more pervasive deficits in working memory or are modality specific. It also enables the clinician to test hypotheses about the impact of working memory skills on perceptual-reasoning abilities.

Visual Digit Span

The Visual Digit Span subtest is a visual analog to the standard Digit Span subtest. Instead of hearing the digits, the examinees see them presented on a page. Unlike with auditory digit span, the examinee is exposed to all the digits at one time rather than in sequence. This may promote the tendency to chunk the numbers for better recall. This test requires intact visual scanning, discrimination and attention, and number knowledge.

REGISTRATION

The registration phase of working memory requires that the child retain information temporarily for the purpose of repeating that information without modification. Although the child may employ such strategies as chunking, visualization, or rehearsal to improve performance on the registration tasks, the level of higher order cognitive processing (i.e., manipulation and transformation) required for effective performance is more limited than that which occurs in tasks that place greater demand on working memory. There are five scaled process scores included in the process analysis of tasks that focus on the registration.

The Digit Span Forward score represents the child's ability to recall numbers presented in an auditory mode. The child must store increasingly longer strings of numbers in short-term memory and repeat them verbatim. Poor performance on this subtest signals capacity limitations for aural information. This may be due to difficulties maintaining attention through rehearsal, difficulties with auditory discrimination, or other central auditory problems (Maerlender, Isquith, & Wallis, 2004). The Visual Digit Span score represents the child's ability to recall numbers presented in a visual mode. However, it is likely that auditory processes are also at work as the child registers the stimuli through language. Visual Digit Span and Digit Span differ in their modality of presentation, visual versus auditory, and also in how the stimulus is presented. For Visual Digit Span, the child is exposed to the entire string of numbers simultaneously, unlike Digit Span, which exposes the child to the digits one at a time. Exposure to the entire number string may facilitate employment of the chunking strategy to a greater degree than exposure to strings of sequentially presented numbers. Low scores on Visual Digit Span may also be related to difficulties with number identification, refreshing visual images in short-term memory, auditory rehearsal (once registered, the visual stimulus may be rehearsed aurally), or sequencing difficulties.

The Spatial Span Forward score is believed to represent the child's visual–spatial registration ability. To perform effectively on this task, the child must track, store, mentally rehearse, and execute a sequence of spatial locations. Poor performance may be related to difficulties with the registration of visual–spatial information, poor sequencing, inattention, visual scanning deficits, or problems executing motor responses accurately.

The Letter Span subtest is a variation of the Digit Span subtest utilizing a series of letters rather than numbers. The subtest is composed of two types of items: those with nonrhyming letters and those with rhyming letters. Low scores on this subtest may occur due to general difficulties with auditory processing, auditory discrimination, poor mental sequencing, inattention, or difficulties registering letters into conscious awareness.

Two scaled scores can be derived from the Letter Span subtest. The Letter Span Nonrhyming score represents the child's ability to recall a series of phonologically distinct letters (i.e., X, L, Q, F, R). Similarly, the Letter Span Rhyming score represents the child's ability to recall phonologically similar, or indistinct, letter series (i.e., Z, B, D, P, V). The rhyming task is more difficult for all children. When registering the nonrhyming letters, most children with effective phonological processing capabilities use the distinct phonological trace of each letter to enhance registration. This type of memory enhancement is not as applicable to items with rhyming series of letters because distinct phonological features are more limited in letters that sound similar.

REGISTRATION COMPARISONS

Comparing performance between specific registration subtests enables the clinician to answer questions regarding specific cognitive weaknesses. These questions relate to modality (i.e., visual versus auditory) and content (i.e., numbers versus letters). Data regarding registration comparisons are presented in Table 3.

Digit Span Forward vs Spatial Span Forward

Comparing these two subtests enables the clinician to answer questions regarding the effect of modality and content. Clinicians will want to report this comparison when the Working Memory Index is significantly lower than other Indices, when Digit Span is low, or when the Perceptual Reasoning Index is significantly lower than other Indices. This comparison is useful for determining the extent (i.e., if it pervades both modalities) of registration deficits.

The correlation between these subtests is low with the only exception being in the Autism group. It would be expected that differences of three points or less will be common and that larger differences such as five or six scaled points may be more meaningful. In the clinical groups, the Expressive Language Disorder group but not the Receptive-Expressive Language Disorder group had lower Digit Span Forward compared to Spatial Span Forward, with the latter group appearing to have more general difficulties registering information. The TBI, ADD, and Math Disorder groups showed the opposite pattern with low scores on Spatial Span Forward. Based on these findings, it may be that Spatial Span Forward is sensitive to difficulties in controlling aspects of visual attention.

Digit Span Forward vs Visual Digit Span

Comparing Digit Span Forward and Visual Digit Span enables the clinician to determine if the "mode of presentation" impacts the child's performance, while holding content constant. High scores in one direction or the other suggest that the child performs better when information is presented visually or aurally. While the mode of stimulus presentation clearly differs between these two tasks, the response processes utilized may not be the same as suggested by the mode of stimulus presentation for all children. Some children will utilize the phonological loop to aurally rehearse digits that were presented visually or visualize the numbers to maintain a memory trace of digits presented orally. Clinicians should pay close attention to the child's behaviors during these tasks to gain insight into the strategies that the child is employing. The clinician should also consider that the tasks differ in how the stimuli are presented: either one number at a time (Digit Span) or all the numbers at once (Visual Digit Span). This difference may affect the degree to which the child is able to chunk the information into smaller bits for easier retention.

There is a moderate correlation between the two subtests in the standardization sample. Differences of two or three points are not unusual in the general population. In the clinical groups, the correlations were similar to

TABLE 3 Correlation coefficients, average differences and rate of discrepancy for WISC-IV Registration Measures

	Digit Span Versus Spatial Span Forward				Digit Span Forward Versus Visual Digit Span			
	r	Mean (SD) Difference	DSF > SSF	DSF < SSF	r	Mean (SD) Difference	DSF > VDS	DSF < VDS
Standardization Sample	0.21	0.05 (3.8)	25.5	25.8	0.46	.14 (3.2)	22.8	18.9
ADD	0.21	1.04 (3.0)	28.3	7.6	−0.10	1.00 (4.0)	43.4	22.6
Autistic	0.59	0.31 (2.6)	18.8	12.5	0.61	1.56 (3.3)	43.8	18.8
Expressive Language Disorder	0.08	−1.90 (3.8)	13.6	52.3	0.15	−.06 (3.9)	18.2	20.4
Receptive-Expressive Language Disorder	−0.15	.09 (4.8)	34.8	40.0	0.44	1.30 (3.7)	34.8	10.9
Math Disorder	0.15	.77 (3.6)	32.6	14.0	0.49	1.58 (2.9)	37.2	4.6
Reading Disorder	0.31	−.42 (3.3)	14.6	11.3	0.27	1.00 (3.4)	33.9	16.1
Traumatic Brain Injury	0.22	1.62 (3.7)	35.9	12.8	0.51	.67 (3.1)	30.8	12.8

	Spatial Span Versus Visual Digit Span				Letter Span Nonrhyming Versus Rhyming			
	r	Mean (SD) Difference	SSF > VDS	VDS < SSF	r	Mean (SD) Difference	LSN > LSR	LSN < LSR
Standardization Sample	0.23	0.9 (3.6)	26.2	23.9	0.60	−.05 (2.7)	14.8	16.4
ADD	0.20	−.04 (3.3)	15.1	16.9	0.50	−.30 (2.9)	17.0	22.6
Autistic	0.58	1.25 (3.4)	37.5	18.8	0.43	−.56 (2.9)	12.5	25.0
Expressive Language Disorder	0.19	1.84 (4.0)	54.5	15.9	0.60	−.45 (2.3)	6.8	20.4
Receptive-Expressive Language Disorder	0.06	1.22 (4.6)	41.3	10.9	0.56	−.76 (2.6)	8.7	34.8
Math Disorder	0.11	.81 (3.4)	27.9	20.9	0.70	−1.40 (2.5)	4.6	37.2
Reading Disorder	0.31	1.42 (3.0)	33.9	9.7	0.52	−.52 (2.3)	4.8	24.2
Traumatic Brain Injury	0.18	−.95 (3.7)	23.1	30.8	0.67	.59 (2.7)	15.4	7.7

(*Continues*)

TABLE 3 (Continued)

| | | **Digit Span Versus Letter Span Nonrhyming** | | |
	r	Mean (SD) Difference	DSF > LSN	DSF < LSN
Standardization Sample	0.55	0.2 (2.9)	19.2	18.6
ADD	0.40	−0.3 (3.0)	18.8	20.8
Autistic	0.63	0.68 (2.4)	18.8	0.0
Expressive Language Disorder	0.66	.03 (2.1)	13.6	15.9
Receptive-Expressive Language Disorder	0.50	.43 (3.1)	21.7	15.2
Math Disorder	0.70	.23 (2.3)	14.0	4.6
Reading Disorder	0.58	.29 (2.5)	19.4	8.1
Traumatic Brain Injury	0.72	.87 (2.4)	23.1	12.8

Note: Listwise deletion used for all measures resulting in the following sample sizes—standardization (725), ADD (53), Autistic (16), Expressive Language Disorder (44), Receptive-Expressive Language Disorder (46), Math Disorder (43), Reading Disorder (62), and Traumatic Brain Injury (39). All comparisons are computed as core or supplemental minus process subtest. *Wechsler Intelligence Scale for Children – Fourth Edition Integrated.* Copyright © 2004 by Harcourt Assessment, Inc. Reproduced with permission. All rights reserved.

the standardization group except for low correlations in the ADD, Reading, and Expressive Language Disorder groups. There is a consistent finding, among clinical groups, of lower Visual Digit Span compared to standard Digit Span Forward, except in the Expressive Language Disorder group. *Large differences between these scores may be a marker for increased risk for learning or developmental difficulties.*

Spatial Span Forward vs Visual Digit Span

This difference score analysis compares the child's registration ability of two types of visually presented information: digits (numbers) and spatial locations. In this comparison the mode of presentation is kept constant while the content to be registered is very different (i.e., spatial locations versus numbers). The clinical question resolved by this comparison is "Are problems with registration for visually presented information restricted to spatial or numeric information or is the problem more pervasive?" Again for Visual Digit Span, it is important to determine if the child is using an auditory rehearsal strategy or trying to maintain the visual trace in conscious awareness. Spatial Span is very difficult to verbalize and is unlikely to be an effective strategy for performing this task.

The correlation between Visual Digit Forward and Spatial Span Forward is low in the standardization sample and in most of the clinical groups. However, the correlation was moderate in the Autistic sample. Despite both tests being presented visually, they do not relate highly and differences between the two measures occur relatively frequently. Auditory Digit Span had a higher correlation with Visual Digit Span, indicating that content may be more important than modality during registration. In general, Spatial Span Forward tends to be higher in nearly all the clinical groups with relatively big differences observed for learning disabled, language disorders, and autistic samples. The opposite profile is observed in children with head injury. Further research focusing on this particular discrepancy may find it useful in differentiating acquired from developmental disorders. *This comparison appears to be a general indicator of a potential developmental disorder.*

Letter Span Nonrhyming vs Letter Span Rhyming

This difference score directly compares registration for nonrhyming and rhyming letters. The distinctiveness of the acoustical content is being compared. The rhyming task has a relatively more restricted range of potential items that could be recalled. The range restriction could serve as a cue to improve recall despite lower auditory distinctiveness. For example, if the series starts with the letter "g," there are only a few other letters that rhyme with "g". If nonrhyming is higher than rhyming, it is likely due to auditory distinctiveness features. If rhyming is higher than nonrhyming, it is likely due to the cueing effect of being able to recall one letter, which restricts the range of the other letters that could have been presented.

The Letter Span Nonrhyming and Letter Span Rhyming tasks are moderately correlated in the standardization sample and moderately to highly correlated in the clinical samples. Large differences in performance are unexpected for this particular comparison. The pattern of scores across clinical groups suggests that the rhyming task was easier for most clinical groups, with the exception of the TBI group. The largest differences occurred in the Math Disorder and Receptive-Expressive Language Disorder groups. The difference is likely attributable to the increased difficulty in the normative sample for the rhyming task. Therefore, having the same span across tasks will appear to be an advantage on the rhyming portion. This difference, though, could be an indicator of a developmental disorder.

Digit Span Forward vs Letter Span Nonrhyming

The Digit Span Forward versus Letter Span Nonrhyming comparison evaluates material-specific differences in the child's registration abilities for numbers and letters. A Digit Span greater than Letter Span difference score suggests that the child is better at registration of numbers than letters. Conversely, a difference score in the other direction would indicate better registration of numbers versus letters. These findings could indicate a relative weakness in the early development of letter or number skills. Assessment of early literacy and math skills could test this hypothesis. This finding may also be observed in specific learning problems observed within the classroom.

Digit Span Forward is moderately correlated with Letter Span Nonrhyming in all the groups presented in Table 3. Scores on Digit Span Forward and Letter Span Nonrhyming were similar for most clinical groups with Digit Span Forward scores being higher in general. The biggest differences were observed in the Autistic and TBI groups. The Math Disorder group did not show a material-specific weakness but performed similarly across tests. These results suggest that Digit Span Forward is not the most sensitive test in identifying registration deficits in children with developmental disorders or acquired neurological impairment.

MENTAL MANIPULATION

The more complex working memory tasks require the child to simultaneously take in information (register) while performing a mental transformation of it. This mental operation requires reversing of sequences, disassociations of integrated information, or performing mental mathematical calculations. Because the child must be able to register the information in order to perform the operations, these subtests assume that deficits in registration contribute to scores on mental manipulation measures. There are eight scaled process scores that focus on the simultaneous storage and manipulation of information in working memory.

For auditory working memory tasks, poor auditory discrimination or executive functioning deficits may contribute to low scores. These auditory problems are likely to affect a number of verbally mediated tasks. Problems with control of focused attention contribute to scores on working memory tasks. Gross inattention, in which the child is obviously unable to listen or attend for even brief periods of time, affects scores, yet more subtle difficulties with sustained attention are not likely to reduce scores substantially.

For visual working memory tasks, difficulties with visual scanning (ability to scan a visual field accurately to identify all salient information), visual tracking (ability to follow a visual object across an area), visual field impairments, gross visual focused attention (ability to maintain periods of brief attention focused on a specific task), and visual discrimination may affect performance.

The Digit Span Backward score measures both auditory registration and working memory. In this task, the child must register the digits as presented, perform a mental operation (i.e., reorder the numbers in reverse sequence), and then execute the new sequence. Children may perform poorly on this task for a variety of reasons, and many of the factors affecting performance on Digit Span Forward (i.e., registering, sequencing, attention, auditory discrimination, chunking, and visualization) also influence performance on Digit Span Backward.

The Spatial Span Backward score assesses the child's ability to track, register, mentally rehearse, reorder, and then execute a sequence of spatial locations. Like on Spatial Span Forward, poor performance on this test may be related to difficulties with registering visual–spatial information, poor sequencing, inattention, visual scanning deficits, or accurate execution of motor responses.

The Letter–Number Sequencing Process Approach subtest is a variation of the core letter–number sequencing subtest in which the scored trials contain embedded words in the presented sequence of letters and numbers. Unlike in the core version of this subtest, the child is asked to repeat the letters first and then the numbers. This difference is designed to cue the child to the presence of the embedded word. Children with well-developed executive control processes and adequate orthographic abilities are likely to perceive the embedded words and use this knowledge to focus additional working memory resources on the sorting and reordering of numbers and letters. Cognitively rigid children may experience difficulty disassociating the letters from the word, which is often required to reorder the letters properly. Low Letter–Number Sequencing Process Approach scores may be related to difficulties with auditory working memory, registration, discrimination, attention, sequencing, spelling ability, or material-specific weaknesses in auditory registration (numeric or alphabetic). For both versions of this task, early items likely represent registration skills more than mental manipulation, as there is little demand made on reorganizing and resequencing of incoming stimuli.

MENTAL MANIPULATION COMPARISONS

Comparing the performance between specific registration subtests enables the clinician to answer questions regarding components of working memory. These questions relate to modality (i.e., visual versus auditory), content (i.e., numbers versus letters), process (i.e., math abilities), and registration load versus manipulation demands. Data regarding registration comparisons are presented in Table 4. The standardization cases are reduced significantly in Table 4. Table 4 is derived from a listwise deletion of cases (i.e., any case without one of the variables in the tables was dropped). The Arithmetic subtest was given to a subset of the standardization cases as it was no longer a core WISC-IV measure.

Digit Span Backward vs Spatial Span Backward

The comparison is designed for the clinician to assess modality-specific deficits in mental manipulation. The tasks differ in content (i.e., spatial versus numeric) and modality (visual versus auditory). The manipulation though is consistent across tasks (i.e., both require the ability to reverse a sequence mentally).

Consistent with Forward Span conditions, the correlation between Spatial Span Backward and Digit Span Backward is low in the standardization sample and for most clinical groups. There were few large effects observed in the clinical groups. The Expressive Language Disorder group had low scores on Digit Span Backward more than Spatial Span Backward, whereas the Receptive-Expressive group had the opposite pattern. Otherwise, the groups had similar performance on both measures.

Letter–Number Sequencing vs Letter–Number Sequencing Process Approach

Embedded words in the Letter–Number Sequencing task were done specifically to reduce the registration load but to keep the level of mental manipulation equivalent across tasks. This comparison is only reported if Letter–Number Sequencing is low. This is not to say that some children will not do worse on the embedded word version, only that the information this lower score provides is ambiguous. It suggests that the embedded word interferes with the manipulation of the letters for some groups of children, thereby impacting performance negatively on the Letter–Number Sequencing Process Approach. In other words, once the child has understood that letters create a word, they are unable to pull the letters apart and sequence them alphabetically and are mentally "stuck" with the mental representation

TABLE 4 Correlation coefficients, average differences and rate of discrepancy for WISC-IV Mental Manipulation Measures

	Digit Span Versus Spatial Span Backward				Letter-Number Sequencing Versus Process Approach			
	r	Mean (SD) Difference	DSB > SSB	DSB < SSB	r	Mean (SD) Difference	LNS > LNS PA	LNS < LNS PA
Standardization Sample	0.23	0.12 (3.7)	27.2	24.0	0.53	.16 (2.8)	16.1	18.4
ADD	0.50	0.37 (2.7)	13.0	30.4	0.33	−.95 (3.0)	13.0	30.4
Autistic	0.71	.09 (3.6)	18.2	18.2	0.64	−1.73 (2.8)	9.1	45.4
Expressive Language Disorder	−0.25	−.83 (3.6)	12.5	29.2	0.27	−.04 (3.0)	12.5	16.7
Receptive-Expressive Language Disorder	0.32	.62 (3.4)	34.3	17.1	0.43	−.97 (3.3)	14.3	22.9
Math Disorder	0.19	.19 (2.9)	21.4	16.7	0.36	.19 (2.7)	19.3	11.9
Reading Disorder	0.22	−.55 (3.5)	19.6	26.8	0.11	−.36 (3.6)	23.2	19.6
Traumatic Brain Injury	0.28	.14 (3.8)	25.7	31.4	0.47	−.60 (3.8)	17.1	25.7

	Digit Span Backward Versus Letter Number Sequencing				Arithmetic Versus Written Arithmetic			
	r	Mean (SD) Difference	DSB > LNS	DSB < LNS	r	Mean (SD) Difference	AR > WA	AR < WA
Standardization Sample	0.45	0.25 (3.0)	21.3	18.8	0.65	−.02 (2.4)	13.6	13.2
ADD	0.31	.65 (3.8)	23.9	21.7	0.51	−.13 (2.6)	15.2	21.7
Autistic	0.16	2.2 (4.6)	27.3	9.1	0.48	.82 (3.8)	27.3	9.1
Expressive Language Disorder	−0.22	1.08 (3.6)	29.2	20.8	0.48	.21 (2.5)	16.7	8.3
Receptive-Expressive Language Disorder	0.42	1.60 (3.4)	31.4	11.4	0.70	.57 (1.8)	14.3	2.9
Math Disorder	0.30	−.28 (2.90)	11.9	16.7	0.56	.19 (1.70)	4.8	4.8
Reading Disorder	0.50	.79 (3.0)	30.4	12.5	0.64	.41 (1.9)	14.3	7.1
Traumatic Brain Injury	0.45	1.46 (3.7)	31.4	5.7	0.61	−.51 (2.7)	14.3	20.0

(Continues)

TABLE 4 (Continued)

	Digit Span Forward Versus Backward				Spatial Span Forward Versus Backward			
	r	Mean (SD) Difference	DSF > DSB	DSB < DSF	Mean (SD) Difference	r	SSF > SSB	SSF < SSB
Standardization Sample	0.37	0.01 (3.4)	21.3	23.6	0.05 (3.2)	0.43	22.0	22.0
ADD	0.14	0.48 (3.4)	30.4	23.9	-.37 (2.4)	0.53	10.9	19.6
Autistic	0.51	.54 (3.1)	27.3	18.2	.27 (3.6)	0.74	27.3	27.3
Expressive Language Disorder	0.09	-.45 (3.1)	20.8	29.2	.33 (2.9)	0.38	20.8	20.8
Receptive-Expressive Language Disorder	0.21	.57 (3.9)	34.3	22.9	.63 (2.8)	0.60	20.0	8.6
Math Disorder	0.14	1.33 (3.6)	38.1	21.4	.74 (2.8)	0.34	16.7	11.9
Reading Disorder	0.55	-.07 (3.3)	21.4	23.2	-.12 (2.8)	0.43	16.1	17.9
Traumatic Brain Injury	0.43	.68 (3.2)	20.0	20.0	-1.08 (3.1)	0.52	11.4	37.1

Note: Listwise deletion used for all measures resulting in the following sample sizes—standardization (441), ADD (46), Autistic (11), Expressive Language Disorder (23), Receptive-Expressive Language Disorder (35), Math Disorder (42), Reading Disorder (56), and Traumatic Brain Injury (36). All comparisons are computed as core or supplemental minus process subtest. *Wechsler Intelligence Scale for Children – Fourth Edition Integrated.* Copyright © 2004 by Harcourt Assessment, Inc. Reproduced with permission. All rights reserved.

of the word itself. They cannot disassociate semantic encoding processes from simple short-term memory processes. This may be evident in the child that repeats the letters back in the word form and not in alphabetical order.

The Letter–Number Sequencing standard and embedded words subtests have a moderate correlation standardization sample and vary from low to moderate in the clinical groups. This suggests that the methodology of using embedded words does have an impact on performance and that the tasks are not equivalent. The embedded words condition is easier for several of the clinical groups, including the ADD, Autistic, Receptive-Expressive Language Disorder and TBI groups. These results indicate that low scores on Letter Number Sequencing are in part related to registration load, particularly letter registration. This is confirmed in the registration analysis, which showed lower Letter Span than Digit Span or Letter Span Rhyming in several clinical groups.

Digit Span Backward vs Letter–Number Sequencing

This comparison evaluates the impact of dual tasking (i.e., managing two sets of stimuli) on resequencing tasks. The resequencing demands are different between the two tasks. The Letter–Number task requires an understanding of order of the stimuli related to previous learning, whereas Digit Span Backward requires only the repetition of the reverse order. The reverse ordering of the sequence is limited in the level of difficulty (i.e., the examinee is aware that the last number heard always comes first when repeating the information). In the Letter–Number sequences, the first stimulus repeated could come from anywhere in the sequence, which may potentially be more difficult. The backward span relies on remembering the sequence exactly, whereas on letter–number series, the child may re-create the correct sequences as long as they know which numbers to recall. The degree of burden on verbatim encoding and repetition is greater in Digit Span Backward. There are a number of reasons why children's scores may disassociate between these two tasks.

Letter–Number Sequencing is moderately correlated with Digit Span Backward in the standardization and from low to moderate in the clinical samples. For most of the clinical groups, Letter–Number Sequencing is more difficult than Digit Span Backward with the largest differences observed in the Autistic, Language Disorder, and TBI groups. *This comparison strongly implicates the presence of cognitive difficulties associated with a variety of clinical groups.*

Arithmetic, ARPA-A, ARPA-B, and Written Arithmetic

These comparisons evaluate degree of working memory problems versus computational impairments affecting performance. Comparing these subtests directly determines the impact of working memory load versus computational ability. The comparison reported here is the Arithmetic versus Written Arithmetic as it directly measures the child's ability to complete the computation aspect of the problems without any working memory versus the full working memory load. The child is provided with the appropriate calculation in written form; there is no requirement for conversion of the word problem into a calculation. When Written Arithmetic is significantly better than Arithmetic, the child has the ability to carry out the relevant numerical operations and their difficulty lies in holding the problem in mind, understanding which operations are appropriate to solve the problem, or carrying out the calculations mentally. In some cases, children will perform better on the standard administration of the Arithmetic subtest relative to their performance on the Written Arithmetic. In this case, the child may have adequate knowledge of mathematical procedures but has less knowledge of mathematical symbols and how they represent the proper sequence of computations, misaligns written problems, or writes the numbers incorrectly. Fine motor control problems might also interfere. This score comparison may have implications for a possible math disability and should be interpreted in the context of scores on a standardized measure of achievement. There are a number of hypotheses related to this difference score that may need further investigation if significant dissociation is reported.

These two measures correlate moderately to highly so large differences should not be observed commonly. For most clinical groups, scores are higher on the standard administration of the Arithmetic compared to the written version. The largest difference was observed in the Autistic and Receptive Expressive-Language Disorder group. These children did not benefit from seeing the problems written on the page. In contrast, the TBI group displayed the opposite profile, although the effects were small. They did benefit from seeing the problem written. This pattern suggests intact knowledge but difficulty completing standard version due to the working memory demands.

REGISTRATION VERSUS MENTAL MANIPULATION

The mental manipulation tasks require that some information is registered and maintained in conscious awareness. Comparing performance on registration tasks to mental manipulation tasks should provide an estimate of the degree to which the child has difficulty with simple storage and maintenance of information in conscious awareness versus their ability to mentally operate on that information. In some cases, the child will approach the mental manipulation task with better preparedness (i.e., better focus, more energy on task), as they are expecting the task to be more challenging and will have better performance on the mental manipulation task compared to the registration task. Alternately, the registration task is always administered first and therefore the child has gained some procedural knowledge regarding the best way to register the information, which potentially helps them perform better on the manipulation task. Data comparing forward and backward performance are presented in Table 4.

Digit Span Forward vs Digit Span Backward

This comparison answers the clinical question regarding the child's ability to register numbers versus their ability to perform verbatim resequencing. If Digit Span Forward is significantly better than Digit Span Backward, it would be interpreted as a deficit in mental manipulation. For some children, the greater difficulty of the Digit Span Backward task may be more engaging than the simple repetition required by the Digit Span Forward task so they will score higher on the backward condition. Maerlender et al. (2004) found that in children referred for central auditory processing disorder with low Digit Span Forward but not Backward displayed deficits in dichotic listening (e.g., selective and divided attention skills).

Digit Span Forward and Digit Span Backward had low to moderate correlations. The two scores measure considerably different mental processes. In most clinical groups, Digit Span Forward was higher than Backward except for the Expressive Language Disorder group. Most of the differences were small, although the Math Disorder group had a much bigger difference.

Spatial Span Forward vs Spatial Span Backward

The difference between Spatial Span Forward and Spatial Span Backward evaluates the hypothesis that the child has difficulty mentally resequencing the spatial locations but does not have difficulty registering spatial information. Unlike the relationship between Digit Span Forward and Digit Span Backward, Spatial Span Backward does not necessarily place greater demands on working memory than Spatial Span Forward. Both tasks require an element of registration and working memory to maintain the visual trace in active memory until the visual-motor sequence may be replicated. When Spatial Span Forward is higher than Spatial Span Backward, it indicates that the child performed better when asked to replicate the visual trace from the point of origin rather than the end point. Conversely, when Spatial Span Backward is higher than Spatial Span Forward, it means the child performed better when asked to replicate a visual trace from the end point rather than the point of origin. In the forward condition, the child must start with the information that was presented the furthest in time from the response, whereas in the backward condition, they start with the most recent information observed.

The Spatial Span Forward and Spatial Span Backward conditions were moderately correlated in the standardization sample and moderate to highly correlated in the clinical groups. This suggests that these processes do not dissociate as readily as Digit Span Forward and Digit Span Backward. Performance on the two measures varied considerably across groups. The ADD and head injury groups displayed higher scores on the backward compared to the forward condition. The other clinical groups showed an advantage for the forward condition. Difficulties associated with attentiveness and executive control may affect performance on the forward condition more than on the backward condition.

LONGEST SPAN MEASURES

The longest span is defined as the highest number of bits of information (i.e., digits in Digit Span) recalled correctly. Some children are inconsistent in their ability to register information or to manipulate information mentally. This may occur for a variety of reasons: they may benefit from anticipatory knowledge (i.e., knowing how many pieces of information to expect) and therefore do better on the second trial of a set of spans; they may be inconsistent in their ability to focus their attention to the task and make simple mistakes; they may have difficulties with interitem perseveration such that recalling an item administered previously interferes with correct recall of later items; or they may have difficulty with learned sequencing and make occasional errors in recall order. The clinician may wish to use longest span data when the child frequently misses one of the trials within a set but appears to have the capability to recall a long span, either forward or backward. The obtained scaled score may be misleading as it suggests that the child has a relatively short span compared to age mates; however, the problem may actually be in the consistency at which the child is able to recall spans. Span length may vary by content, and determining specific areas in which the child displays apparent inconsistency in recall may help the clinician better understand the child's working memory profile. The longest span obtained for each of these conditions may also be compared. This comparison is useful when one or more of the measures have been performed with a high degree of variability at the item-by-item basis. Some children may display very long spans, in either condition, but the difference is masked at the scaled score level due to the variability of performance. Interpretation of the difference must take into consideration both the nature of the task, as described previously, and the inconsistency (i.e., presence in one or both conditions) of performance.

GOING BEYOND THE NUMBERS

Practitioners are encouraged to qualitatively evaluate the child's performance in the Working Memory domain. Such an assessment may yield clinically rich information about how the child perceives and organizes information. This type of analysis is not necessarily diagnostic of particular developmental or acquired disorders, but provides useful insight into the child's strengths and weaknesses that may be useful when developing intervention and accommodation recommendations.

Like the suggested procedures for the qualitative evaluation of the core and supplemental subtests, the qualitative analysis may include an examination of the child's response patterns. The child with an uneven pattern of scores on several subtests may have been fatigued or distracted during administration of the subtest or may have attentional difficulties. As noted earlier, additional raw process scores (i.e., the longest span and sequence scores) and discrepancy comparisons are available for some subtests when an unusual amount of variability in the child's response pattern may affect interpretation of performance.

A qualitative evaluation of the Working Memory domain may also include a content analysis. For example, some children may have more difficulty with those tasks that involve letters than those that involve numbers. Difficulties in sequencing and gross attention are particularly important areas for clinicians to note. Poor sequencing may reflect weak numeric knowledge or difficulties with recalling the specific order of information presented.

Examination of errors can be particularly helpful in this domain. Errors on tasks requiring sequencing or repetition can be characterized as errors of commission, errors of omission, or sequencing errors. Errors of commission occur when a novel response is inserted into the original sequence. For example, the child states 1, 2, 3, 4, 5 in response to a digit span forward item of 1, 2, 3, 4. Errors of omission occur when a portion of the original sequence is deleted in the response; for example, the child states 1, 2, 4 in response to a digit span forward item of 1, 2, 3, 4. Sequencing errors involve reversing or transposing portions of a sequence during a response; for example, the child's response of 1, 3, 2, 4 to a digit span forward item of 1, 2, 3, 4. Each type of error offers different insight into the child's memory difficulties. Helland and Asbjornsen (2004) reported that problems with serial recall in both Digit Span Forward and Digit Span Backward related to poor math skills while low span length was related to language impairments.

Working memory problems may exist for a variety of reasons. If the clinician suspects deficits in the encoding and retrieval of information (i.e., poor incidental learning but adequate working memory), more intensive evaluation of long-term memory function may be warranted. Excellent scores on measures of initial encoding with consistently poor performance on mental manipulation tasks may suggest difficulties in executive functions or attention or could indicate superior echoic memory as in an Autistic Disorder. The clinician's observations regarding the profile of scores and nature of errors are critical components in differentiating the nature of the cognitive problems.

Many of the subtests included in this domain require comprehension of the instructions. This requires a child to attend to the instructions and retain them in memory while completing the task. The Letter Number and Digit Span tasks offer insight into a child's ability to retain the instructions. Failure to follow instructions on these tasks should be noted and interpreted in relation to the child's overall performance.

GENERAL OBSERVATIONS/INTERPRETATIONS

Children that have difficulties in the Working Memory domain will often be described as "forgetful" by people that know the child well. The child may seem forgetful but in other respects they may be perceived as having a good or at least adequate memory. The separation of memory processes into more immediate, active, temporary storage (not trying to remember the information for extended periods) versus storage and retrieval processes for information in long-term memory or episodic memory (i.e., information about self and life events) enables the clinician to understand the nature of the memory problem. This knowledge can be communicated to the child's teacher and parents to help them understand the nature of the problem as well. The child with working memory deficits may forget what they are doing while performing a task or may have difficulty *applying* their knowledge on tests or when writing papers. Working memory skills enable the individual to consciously hold information in their mind long enough to complete an activity.

In developmental disorders, working memory difficulties are pervasive yet mild in severity. It is unlikely that children with a learning disability or Attention Deficit Disorder would perform in the deficient range on these tasks but clearly there is a trend for these scores to be in the lower end of average. Concurrent weaknesses in working memory problems multiply the impact of underlying cognitive problems on academic tasks. For example for children with ADD, the degree of problems with spatial and visual working memory potentially results in problems with academic skills that may not reach threshold for an additional diagnosis of a learning disability (i.e., math and writing).

Observation of the child's performance on working memory tasks yields further insight into the underlying nature of their processing problems. For example, the child that recalls too few items (i.e., recalls five of six digits) may have a capacity deficit, whereas the child that recalls stimuli correctly but in the wrong order may have problems with maintaining sequential processing or with active maintenance of sequences in conscious awareness. Span length scores help differentiate these problems. A child with poor sequencing but intact capacity may have a long span but lose points for stating order incorrectly.

In children with auditory discrimination problems, they may ask for repetitions of stimuli. They may also substitute letters or numbers that have a similar phonological structure. Children with visual discrimination difficulties may not respond or say "don't know" on the Visual Digit Span and Spatial Span subtests. On visual tasks more generally, children with visual discrimination problems may "squint," move closer or away from the page, tilt their head, or attempt to move (i.e., turn the spatial span grid at an angle) stimulus/response materials. Children with discrimination problems will have more global difficulties with auditory or visual subtests.

Executive control problems can be observed in many behaviors. Some children will start responding before all the stimuli have been presented. Others will rush through the repetition, making mental errors (i.e., inconsistent or random errors) and losing points on items within their ability range. On other tasks, evidence of impulsivity or poor mental tracking may be observed.

PROCESSING SPEED DOMAIN

In the processing domain, poor test performance may occur for a number of reasons. The primary hypotheses that need to be explored when low Processing Speed Index scores are obtained include poor visual discrimination, attention and scanning or deficient visuomotor skills. At the subtest level, the demands for specific visual–perceptual skills such as visual discrimination, visual scanning, visuomotor skills (i.e., drawing), working memory, procedural and incidental learning, semantic knowledge, and executive control of visual–perceptual processes vary by test. The subtest content and task demands will affect the degree to which intact visual discrimination and motor skills impact performance. Interpretation of subtest variability should consider the degree to which lower level visual discrimination and motor skills affect performance.

High levels of performance on processing speed tasks require the rapid integration of multiple cognitive skills. For example, Coding requires graphomotor skill and visual scanning, as well as the identification and discrimination of visual-symbolic information. Symbol Search and Cancellation also require these skills, although the demands on graphomotor skill are significantly less than that required for Coding. Joy, Fein, and Kaplan (2003) found that the largest proportion of variance in Coding, in adults, was attributable to processing speed, graphomotor speed, and visual scanning speed, with memory processes contributing only a small degree to the variance in Coding.

Impaired performance on processing speed tasks can be due to many factors, including psychological as well as cognitive reasons, such as anxiety, depression, poor motivation, poor sustained attention, distractibility, impaired perceptual ability, poor motor ability, problems in initiating or maintaining effort, difficulty in maintaining a cognitive set, and lack of graphomotor control. Each subtest requires lower level cognitive functions (i.e., visual discrimination), as well as moderately higher order abilities such as associative learning, object-category decisions, and visual comparative decision making. Specific process measures have been incorporated into the Coding task to determine if superior or deficient incidental/procedural learning skills have influenced the total score.

Incidental learning involves the acquisition of information without explicit instructions to remember that information or without direct effort to encode the information (Lezak, 1995). In many situations, this type of passive learning is viewed as an adaptive mechanism that facilitates performance on other tasks. The process analysis is designed to assist the clinician in evaluating how these skills contribute to performance on processing speed subtests. Executive functioning abilities also play an important facilitative role or, in cases of deficient executive functions, an interfering role in the performance of other cognitive tasks. In the WISC-IV Integrated, the relative facilitative or interfering effects of executive functioning on visuomotor tasks can be estimated by administering the Elithorn Maze subtest. This test assesses the degree to which planning ability, ability to follow rules, and maintaining the cognitive set improve performance on the visuomotor task.

**COGNITIVE DEMANDS OF WISC-IV INTEGRATED
PROCESSING SPEED SUBTESTS**

The WISC-IV Integrated Processing Speed subtests require the rapid identification of visual stimuli and a motor response. Other necessary skills vary with the subtest in question. The Processing Speed subtests on the WISC-IV Integrated include Coding, Coding Copy, Symbol Search, and Cancellation (random and structured conditions).

Coding and Coding Copy

The Coding subtest has a long history of use in the Wechsler scales. The Coding task requires the examinee to rapidly draw symbols based on their association with a specific number. The child sees the association key at all times and does not have to memorize the association; however, learning the association should facilitate performance. The test rewards rapid but accurate performance so the examinee must balance speed and accuracy demands (executive control demands come into play here). Children with poor visual-discrimination skills may be slowed by the need to decode visual stimuli into their correct components. This subtest makes significant demands on rapid visual scanning abilities. The child must constantly refer back to the association key at the top of the page unless they have memorized all the relationships between the numbers and the symbols. Some children will learn the associations without conscious effort, which is referred to as *incidental learning*. Some children will also become more proficient at drawing the designs quickly over the course of the subtest. This is referred to as *procedural learning* (i.e., prolonged exposure to a motor task results in improved performance on that task due to unconscious, fine-tuning processes within the motor system). Changes in performance over the course of the subtest may provide clues to specific difficulties, such as poor sustained effort or limited procedural learning skills (use time segment performance data). The examiner is cautioned when interpreting performance over time on the Coding subtest because the associations are not randomly presented throughout. Some of the associations do not get presented until later, which means that incidental learning of some combinations does not occur during earlier phases of the task. The degree to which incidental or strategic learning of the number–symbol associations has occurred can also be evaluated using data in the manual.

The Coding Copy condition was developed to reduce the impact of competing variables when assessing visual processing speed. The child simply copies the symbols as fast as possible. There is no association required between numbers and letters. Performance is not enhanced by incidental learning or working memory skills. Executive control skills still apply here as the child must balance speed and accuracy demands. The task still requires visual discrimination and visuomotor integration. This subtest is not a substitute for the Coding subtest in the Processing Speed index as its simplicity does not lend itself well as a measure of intelligence.

Symbol Search

The Symbol Search subtest requires the examinee to match visual designs and make a decision if a design matches or does not match. This decision is translated into a verbal representation, which is a "yes" or "no" response. Visual–perceptual discrimination is emphasized, whereas motor skills are not as important as in the Coding subtest. While the final response involves a verbal component, the linguistic demands are quite small and should not detract from overall performance. Any task that requires speed and accuracy will invoke executive control issues as the examinee must balance the desire for quick performance with the need to slow performance down to ensure accuracy. Visual scanning is deemphasized but sustained attention and effort are still important.

Cancellation Random and Structured

The Cancellation subtest is an adaptation of neuropsychological procedures designed to detect visual neglect and visual scanning abilities. In standard

Cancellation tasks, the task is a simple visual matching. The child searches for one or two target stimuli in a visual that contains visual distracters. Cancellation tasks have been used extensively in neuropsychological settings as measures of visual selective attention and focusing, visual neglect, response inhibition, and motor perseveration (Lezak, 1995; Na, Adair, Kang, Chung, Lee, & Heilman, 1999). Unlike some of the previous versions of this task that require the child to identify a simple visual–perceptual match, the Cancellation subtest requires the child to determine if visual stimuli belong to a target category (i.e., animals). Thus, the child may also employ visual–semantic associations to discriminate between target and distracter stimuli.

In the WISC-IV Integrated version, the child is searching for visual representation of a semantic category. The child must find all the animals. This requires accurate visual interpretation and semantic knowledge. The semantic demands are not rigorous but may slow down children with significant semantic impairment. The additional cognitive load is necessary to measure at least a modicum of intellectual ability. Straight scanning tasks will not likely yield a high correlation with intellectual capacity.

The task is composed of two conditions: a random and a structured array of stimuli. The targets are presented in the exact same locations but the distracters are in different locations. For both Random and Structured Cancellation tasks, some children naturally invoke a search strategy to organize their visual scanning of the page. Presumably, an organized strategy allows for more efficient identification of target objects. The structured condition lends itself to an organized search strategy more readily than the random condition. Many children will follow the inherent structure of the rows to search for targets; however, some children will engage in a disorganized search, despite the inherent task structure.

The structured condition facilitates an organized search strategy (i.e., row by row, left to right). An executive functioning element can be determined by evaluating differences in performance between the two versions. Also, data are provided on the frequency with which children use and organize search strategy. In rare instances, a child may exhibit a subtle neglect syndrome, which means they will not attend to stimuli in the left or right visual field. In most cases, children will do poorly due to slow processing speed, weak visual scanning skills, or executive functioning difficulties.

Children with high scores are likely to demonstrate rapid visual scanning ability, effective response inhibition, and organized visual search patterns. Low scores may be related to slow visual scanning or visual-motor abilities, poor response inhibition, disorganized search patterns, or difficulties with visual discrimination. In addition the child's visual–lexical associations (i.e., ability to categorize objects correctly) may be slow or incorrect.

PROCESSING SPEED COMPARISONS

The processing speed comparisons enable the clinician to evaluate hypotheses regarding the impact of incidental learning, visual scanning, procedural learning, and task structure on performance. Data for specific comparisons are provided in Table 5.

Coding vs Coding Copy

The difference between Coding and Coding Copy represents the degree to which the digit-symbol association affects Coding B performance. If Coding Copy is higher than Coding, the child has difficulty encoding visual–symbolic associations or poor visual-motor execution. If the opposite pattern is observed, removal of the paired associates does not improve performance and this learning facilitates performance. Children may have greater motivation to do well on Coding.

Coding and Coding Copy are moderately correlated in the standardization sample and moderately to highly correlated in the clinical samples. Large differences in performance between versions are unusual. For the clinical groups, no specific pattern of performance between versions was observed with most groups exhibiting small differences.

Cancellation Random (CAR) vs Cancellation Structured (CAS)

Comparison of CAR and CAS process scores provides information about how the child's performance on Cancellation varies with the arrangement of visual stimuli. When the structured score is higher than the random score, the child benefited from the structured presentation format. The reverse finding is more difficult to interpret. It may indicate that the child was able to apply a more effective structure to the CAR task than utilized in the CAS task.

The random and structured conditions correlated moderately in the standardization sample and were moderate to high in the clinical sample. Dissociations between the two versions are unusual. In general, in the clinical groups, performance on the random condition was better than on the structured condition. The largest difference in favor of the random condition was observed in the Reading Disorder group, whereas the ADHD and Autistic sample had the opposite profile. The random task pulls for problems in organized behavior, whereas the structured condition only helps performance in children with deficits in organization and planning. Interestingly, the structured tasks seem to highlight difficulties in the linguistic, semantic realm. Controls likely find this an easy task and perform quickly, which may highlight slightly slow performance due to semantic decision making in the reading and language disorder group.

TABLE 5 Correlation coefficients, average differences and rate of discrepancy for WISC-IV Processing Speed Measures

	Coding Versus Coding Copy				Cancellation Random Versus Structured			
	r	Mean (SD) Difference	CD > CDC	CD < CDC	r	Mean (SD) Difference	CAR > CAS	CAR < CAS
Standardization Sample	0.63	−.18 (2.6)	12.7	15.6	0.62	.29 (2.6)	16.4	12.2
ADD	0.56	−.17 (2.4)	7.7	15.4	0.68	−.89 (2.5)	7.7	21.2
Autistic	0.73	0.0 (2.4)	14.3	7.1	0.90	−.57 (1.6)	0	7.1
Expressive Language Disorder	0.56	53 (2.4)	16.7	6.7	0.68	.20 (1.9)	10	10
Receptive-Expressive Language Disorder	0.77	−.22 (2.0)	5.6	8.3	0.70	.36 (2.4)	16.7	11.1
Math Disorder	0.60	−.07 (2.7)	11.6	18.6	0.68	.19 (2.4)	16.3	11.6
Reading Disorder	0.53	.36 (2.5)	18	13.1	0.57	.90 (2.6)	23.2	9.8
Traumatic Brain Injury	0.68	0.0 (2.6)	8.3	11.1	0.78	.05 (2.6)	13.9	16.7

Note: Listwise deletion used for all measures resulting in the following sample sizes—standardization (608), ADD (52), Autistic (14), Expressive Language Disorder (30), Receptive-Expressive Language Disorder (36), Math Disorder (43), Reading Disorder (61), and Traumatic Brain Injury (36). All comparisons are computed as core or supplemental minus process subtest. *Wechsler Intelligence Scale for Children – Fourth Edition Integrated.* Copyright © 2004 by Harcourt Assessment, Inc. Reproduced with permission. All rights reserved.

GOING BEYOND THE NUMBERS

Qualitatively, evaluate the child's performance for obvious signs of motor coordination problems as related to the specific task (i.e., poor pencil grip, poor quality of symbol representation, or weak or tremulous writing) or in general (i.e., history of occupational therapy, frequently dropping of items, or obvious signs of delayed motor development). Errors in drawing symbols occur rarely in both clinical and nonclinical groups (Kaplan et al., 1999). The types of errors (i.e., rotations, missing segments) may provide a clue as to the underlying difficulties producing unusual performance. Children with significant visual–perceptual problems may make rotation errors; impulsive children may make errors due to sloppy handwriting in an effort to achieve a high score by working too fast; and children with motor problems may make errors of construction such that the symbol is drawn inaccurately with missing segments or incorrect representation of segments due to poor drawing abilities. Another error that may be observed is skipped items. If skipped items occur systematically, such as on a particular side of the page, there may be problems with visual attention. If the errors are random, the child may be experiencing a loss of set and the behavior is a failure in self-monitoring for maintenance of the task rules. In other cases, skipped items may be due to general inattention or careless performance. If the child makes frequent errors due to erroneous association between the number and the symbol, then examiners should complete the incidental recall conditions to understand if the source of the memory problem is the association between the symbol and the number or if it is due to a failure to learn the symbols at all. If the child makes frequent rule violations and skips letters or lines, the examiner may wish to check executive functioning by administering Elithorn Mazes.

Cancellation Random and Cancellation Structured Strategy

The child's approach to completing Cancellation may be described using one of four observational codes: the child has a completely organized and systematic method for scanning the page to find the targets; the child may start organized and become disorganized over the course of the task; the child may start disorganized but start to use a systematic and organized search strategy partway through the task; or the child may search haphazardly without any strategy for the entire task. For each score, the clinician assigns a letter (i.e., A, B, C, or D) to describe and classify the child's search strategy into one of four categories. Search strategy A is characterized by a search pattern that remains organized throughout item administration. Search strategy B represents a pattern that began organized but became disorganized as the child progressed. Conversely, a child that began the task using a disorganized search pattern and then adopted an organized pattern would be assigned a search strategy score of C. Visual search patterns that remain disorganized throughout item administration are assigned search strategy D.

While the use of a search strategy A (consistently organized search pattern) increases with age, and a disorganized approach strategy D (consistently disorganized search pattern) decreases with age, many children from the standardization sample use a strategy for only some portion of the task. Also, a relatively high frequency of children from the nonclinical sample do not approach the task in an organized, systematic manner for the entire time of the task. Despite the nonuse of strategy in the standardization sample, it is still important to observe the child's approach to the task as it provides general clues to the nature of the child's problem-solving approach more generally. Consistency in poor planning and organization may be observed across tasks and will help confirm the child's disorganized approach to problem solving.

Incidental and Procedural Learning

The Coding Recall subtest is designed to measure incidental learning that occurs during completion of the Coding subtest (Form B only). Some children may strategically attempt to learn the associations from Coding B, whereas others learn them without cognitive effort through repeated exposure. Following a standard test administration, it may be useful to ask the child if he or she tried to remember the symbols. For those children with relatively good performance on Coding Recall and relatively poor performance on Coding B, a positive response to this question may suggest that the child lost time during performance of Coding B while trying to learn the associations. Some children will do poorly on Coding Recall despite explicitly having tried to learn the associations, indicating the possible existence of deficits in multitrial learning and declarative memory.

Unlike with the other process subtests, no scaled scores are derived from performance on the Coding Recall subtest. The process scores for Coding Recall are reported as base rates and are interpreted in terms of the relative frequency with which the score was obtained in the standardization sample. For example, a base rate of 2–5% indicates that only 2–5% of the children that age in the standardization sample obtained the same or lower score. Problems associated with deficits in visual discrimination and difficulties with procedural learning (i.e., learning of motor routines) may affect performance on this subtest. Because this subtest requires the child to draw symbols and write numbers, children with more serious fine-motor difficulties may also obtain low scores on this subtest.

Process scores are derived for each of the three Coding Recall items: cued symbol recall, free symbol recall, and cued digit recall. The cued symbol recall score represents the child's performance on a task requiring recall of symbols from the paired associates in Coding B. A child that performs well on this task has likely learned, without instruction, which symbol goes with which number. In performing the task, the child has learned both the content (symbol) and the association (the symbol and number pairing) included in the subtest task.

The free symbol recall score represents the child's ability to recall the symbols from Coding B, with no regard to the associated number. Because this task requires only the recall of symbols, the clinician can determine if poor performance on cued symbol recall is related to weaknesses in associative learning. The child may have known the symbols, but was unable to link them consistently with the proper number.

The cued digit recall score represents the child's ability to recall the numbers from the paired associates in Coding B. Similar to cued symbol recall, this task evaluates if the child has been able to encode the association between the symbol and the number. Despite the similar task demands, there are situations in which a child performs differently on cued symbol recall and cued digit recall. This occurrence may suggest that the child has difficulty maintaining consistent access to visualized representations of the associated information. In most cases, performance on cued digit recall is better than performance on cued symbol recall. Numbers are automatized frequently and the child does not need to rely on encoding to recall the digits, whereas the symbols are novel and require significant effort to encode and recall.

Coding and Coding Copy Interval Scores

Coding Copy and Coding interval data provide the clinician with information regarding the child's ability to initiate and sustain rapid processing of visual information. These scores may also provide an indication of efficiency in performance over time and evidence of excess variability that may indicate difficulties with maintaining attention to task. In the standardization sample, the rate of performance tends to decline over the time intervals, suggesting a very mild fatigue effect. Given that the impact of memory is rather small on the test, the learning of the associations may only facilitate performance somewhat over time so that you do not see a large gain in efficiency across intervals. For some individuals that employ a learning strategy actively, a gain in efficiency may be observed over time. Children with difficulties starting tasks may have relatively slow performance during the first interval and show improvement in later intervals. Children that have rather significant problems sustaining their effort over time will demonstrate significant drops in their performance across the intervals.

GENERAL OBSERVATIONS/INTERPRETATIONS

Difficulties in processing speed are readily observable in the classroom and on cognitive tasks in general. Observational data are frequently very important in understanding the underlying problems associated with slow processing speed. Some children perform slowly due to a high need to have errorless performance or perfectly drawn symbols. These children may have anxiety problems or, in many cases, being meticulous is part of their personality style. There may also be cultural differences in the degree to which performing quickly versus accurately may be more highly valued.

While slow processing speed scores in isolation are not diagnostic, they have a high degree of clinical salience. Low scores are frequently associated with developmental or acquired disorders. These children will often display difficulty completing work in a timely fashion. It may appear as if they are off-task or are struggling with the content. While this may be true, these children struggle with completing tasks on time in general. Parents often express frustration as these children take extraordinary amounts of time to complete homework.

Sloppily drawn symbols on Coding should be considered a sign of poor motor control under time constraints. In some cases, the children have normal visuomotor skills as observed on drawing tasks but under time constraints they rush their work and become sloppy. In children with poor motor control more generally, the additional time burden may further reduce the quality of their drawing. These children should be referred for an occupational therapy evaluation to determine if they would benefit from intervention or accommodation (i.e., pencil grips).

SUMMARY

This chapter explored the concept that performance on tests of intellectual functioning is influenced by a number of cognitive skills that do not necessarily represent key intellectual abilities. Intelligence cannot be observed directly and is inferred by the individual's ability to solve problems on many different types of tasks. It is impossible to create a task that does not require other cognitive functions as well as intellectual skill. Furthermore, the design of the task will require more of one underlying skill versus another, even if these tasks on the surface appear to require the same underlying abilities (i.e., language). The assumption that specific cognitive skills such as language have a unitary structure leads to this false premise. Skills such as language or visual–perceptual processing require a number of smaller subsets of abilities that function in an integrated manner. Measures of intellectual functioning in that sense are a good estimate of how the whole cognitive system is functioning as a unit.

This chapter discussed a number of the subcomponent processes required for adequate performance on intellectual measures. This list is by no means comprehensive and not all clinicians would necessarily agree on the specific terminology used here. The point of the chapter though is to emphasize that poor performance on specific skill areas will affect performance and that a change in the content and structure of a task will affect one skill area more than another.

It was emphasized here that it is not possible to interpret a single score without evaluating the entire clinical picture. Close observation of test performance may yield dramatically different interpretations of a single test score. As psychologists, it is our prime directive to aid staff members, teachers, and parents in understanding the nature of their child's problem. At the same time, it is important to not fall into the "fundamental attribution bias" when attributing causal explanations to children's behavior and test performance. This requires a mind-set in which test scores are viewed as providing data for specific hypotheses that may be ruled in or out. Further exploration of test scores and not relying on predetermined interpretations for individual test scores are necessary to accomplish this goal.

Profiles of scores are not diagnostic of specific clinical conditions, but they provide data for further exploration such as in classroom observations, teacher observations, and parent reports. The relative strengths and weaknesses in cognitive performance may be used in treatment planning, developing accommodation strategies, or potentially aid in intervention. Using test scores in this manner requires an understanding of the influence of underlying cognitive profiles, which are elucidated through careful observation and knowledge of the different types of skills needed to complete specific subtests.

REFERENCES

Baddeley, A. D., & Hitch, G. J. (1994). Developments in the concept of working memory. *Neuropsychology, 8,* 485–493.

Barkley, R. A. (1996). Linkages between attention and executive functions. In G.R. Lyon & N. A. Krasnegor (Eds.), *Attention, memory and executive functioning* (pp. 307–325). Baltimore, MD: Paul H. Brookes Publishing Co.

Barkley, R. A. (2003). Issues in the diagnosis of attention deficit/hyperactivity disorder in children. *Brain Development, 25,* 77–83.

Benton, A. L., Hamsher, K., Varney, N. R., & Spreen, O. (1983). *Contribution to neuropsychological assessment.* New York: Oxford University Press.

Budson, A. E., & Proice, B. H. (2005). Memory Dysfunction. *New England Journal of Medicine, 352,* 692–699.

Cytowicz, R. E. (1996). *The neurological side of neuropsychology.* Cambridge, MA: MIT Press.

de Jonge, P., & de Jong, P. F. (1996). Working memory, intelligence and reading ability in children. *Personality and Individual Differences, 21*, 1007–1020.

Denckla, M. B., & Rudel, R. G. (1976). Rapid "automatized" naming (R.A.N.): Dyslexia differentiated from other learning disabilities. *Neuropsychologia, 14*, 471–479.

Engle, R. W., Tuholski, S. W., Laughlin, J. E., & Conway, A. R. A. (1999). Working memory, short-term memory, and general fluid intelligence: A latent-variable approach. *Journal of Experimental Psychology: General, 128*, 309–331.

Feinberg, T. E. & Farah, M. J. (1997). *Behavioral Neurology and Neuropsychology.* New York, NY: McGraw-Hill.

Fiorello, C. A., & Hale, J. B. (2003). *Cognitive hypothesis testing for intervention efficacy.* Presented at the Annual Convention of the National Association of School Psychologists.

Glutting, J. J., McDermott, P. A., Konold, T. R., Snelbaker, A. J., & Watkins, M. W. (1998). More ups and downs of subtest analysis: Criterion validity of the DAS with an unselected cohort. *School Psychology Review, 27*, 599–612.

Hale, J. B., Fiorello, C. A., Kavanagh, J. A., Hoeppner, J. B., & Gaither, R. A. (2001). WISC-III predictors of academic achievement for children with learning disabilities: Are global and factor scores comparable? *School Psychology Quarterly, 16*, 31–55.

Hasher, L., & Zacks, R. T. (1979). Automatic and effortful processes in memory. *Journal of Experimental Psychology: General, 108*, 356–388.

Helland, T., & Asbjornsen, A. (2004). Digit span in dyslexia: Variations according to language comprehension and mathematics skills. *Journal of Clinical and Experimental Neuropsychology, 26*, 31–42.

Joy, S., Fein, D., & Kaplan, E. (2003). Decoding digit symbol: Speed, memory, and visual scanning. *Assessment, 10*, 1–10.

Joy, S., Fein, D., Kaplan, E., & Freedman, M. (2001). Quantifying qualitative features of Block Design performance among healthy older adults. *Archives of Clinical Neuropsychology, 16*, 157–170.

Kaplan, E. (1988). A process approach to neuropsychological assessment. In T. J. Boll & B. K. Bryant (Eds.), *Clinical neuropsychology and brain function: Research measurement and practice* (pp. 129–167). Washington, DC: American Psychological Association.

Kaplan, E., Fein, D., Kramer, J., Delis, D., & Morris, R. (1999). *Wechsler intelligence scales for children-third edition as a process instrument.* San Antonio, TX: The Psychological Corporation.

Kapur, N. (1994). *Memory disorders in clinical practice.* Hove, UK: Lawrence Erlbaum Associates Ltd.

Kaufmann A. S. (1994). *Intelligent testing with the WISC-III.* New York: Wiley.

Kolb, B. & Wishow, I.Q. (1990). *Fundamentals of Human Neuropsychology.* New York, NY: W. H. Freeman and Co.

Lezak, M.D. (1995). *Neuropsychological assessment* (3rd ed.). New York: Oxford Press.

Maerlender, A., Isquith, P., & Wallis, D. (2004). Psychometric and behavioral measures of central auditory function: The relationship of dichotic listening and digit span tasks. *Child Neuropsychology, 10*, 318–327.

McDermott, P. A., Fantuzzo, J. W., & Glutting, J. J. (1990). Just say no to subtest analysis: A critique of Wechsler theory and practice. *Journal of Psychoeducational Assessment, 8*, 290–302.

Mirsky, A. F., Anthony, B. J., Duncan, C. C., Ahearn, M. B., & Kellam, S. G. (1991). Analysis of the elements of attention: A neuropsychological approach. *Neuropsychology Review, 2*, 109–145.

Na, D. L., Adair, J. C., Kang, Y., Chung, C. S., Lee, K. H., & Heilman, K. M. (1999). Motor perseverative behavior on a line cancellation task. *Neurology, 52*, 1569–1576.

Pennington, B. F., Benneto, L. McAleer, O., & Roberts, R. J., Jr. (1996). Executive functions and working memory: Theoretical and measurement issues. In G. R. Lyon & N. A. Krasnegor

(Eds.), *Attention, memory and executive functioning* (pp. 327–348). Baltimore, MD: Paul H. Brookes Publishing Co.

Reynolds, C. R. (1997). Forward and backward memory span should not be combined for clinical analysis. *Archives of Clinical Neuropsychology, 12,* 29–40.

Sattler, J. M. (2001). *Assessment of children: Cognitive applications* (4th ed.). San Diego, CA: Author.

Semel, E., Wiig, E. H., & Secord, W. (2003). *Clinical Evaluation of Language Fundamentals-4th Edition.* San Antonio, TX: Harcourt Assessment, Inc.

Squire, L. R., & Butters, N. (1984). *Neuropsychology of memory.* New York: Guilford Press.

Stringer, A. Y. (1996). *A guide to neuropsychological diagnosis.* Philadephia: F. A. Davis Company.

Troyer, A. K., Cullum, C. M., Smernoff, E. N., & Kozora, E. (1994). Age effects on block design: Qualitative performance features and extended-time effects. *Neuropsychology, 8,* 95–99.

Watkins, M. W., & Glutting, J. J. (2000). Incremental validity of WISC-III profile elevation, scatter, and shape information for predicting reading and math achievement. *Psychological Assessment, 12,* 402–408.

Wechsler, D. (2002). *The Wechsler preschool and primary scale of intelligence.* San Antonio, TX: The Psychological Corporation.

Wechsler, D. (2004). *The Wechsler intelligence scale for children.* San Antonio, TX: Harcourt Assessment, Inc.

7

ADVANCED WISC-IV AND WISC-IV INTEGRATED INTERPRETATION IN CONTEXT WITH OTHER MEASURES

JAMES A. HOLDNACK, LAWRENCE G. WEISS, AND PETER ENTWISTLE

Previous chapters focused on the application and interpretation of the WISC-IV Integrated in isolation from other cognitive measures. Cognitive skills that could impact performance on the WISC-IV Integrated were discussed previously. The current chapter discusses inclusion of tests that measure the skills suggested to affect WISC-IV and WISC-IV Integrated findings. Concurrent validity data demonstrate the association between the WISC-IV Integrated and other tests. Clinical data illustrate the impact of specific cognitive weaknesses on WISC-IV Integrated scores. The purpose of the chapter is to enable the clinician to hypothesize about potential causes of low WISC-IV Integrated scores and provide recommendations for how these skills could be measured. The chapter is organized by cognitive domain: language, executive functioning, memory and learning, and academic achievement.

The decision to use other tests should be made to answer a specific clinical question. The question can be based on presenting information (e.g., inattention, impulsivity), psychosocial history (e.g., head trauma, delayed language, family history of reading disorder), low index scores (e.g., low verbal index), or teacher/parent observations (e.g., slow learning, disruptive). The time available for additional testing is often limited so selecting specific tests or subtests within a larger battery can be the most efficient method for answering clinical questions. The number of published tests within any domain far exceeds the scope of this text; therefore, a few tests are described and some of those have concurrent validity data with WISC-IV Integrated.

Interpreting results of a large number of subtests takes careful thought and consideration as there is substantial variability both within and across measures. Index or subtest differences can be meaningful or can represent differences in reliability, fatigue effects, or chance factors. In some cases, a clear pattern of results will emerge (i.e., all language or all visual memory impaired), while in other cases, the profile may be less overt. The impact of clinically irrelevant subtest variability is minimized when the clinician has a rationale for selecting and interpreting results and has corroboration from other data sources.

GENERAL ISSUES IN COMPARING TESTS

REGRESSION TO THE MEAN EFFECTS

Discrepant scores between tests can be anticipated. For example, comparing IQ tests to measures of more basic cognitive abilities (i.e., not normally distributed or measure one aspect of a specific skill) can frequently result in discrepant scores due to regression to the mean effects. The relationship between an IQ test and a test of a very specific cognitive ability is often predictable. By design, IQ tests assess a large range of cognitive abilities, typically spanning three or more standard deviations above and below the mean. However, most tests measuring specific components of cognition have a more restricted range of scores above the mean (only one to two standard deviations) and are skewed negatively, which results in a greater range of scores below than above the mean.

When comparing an IQ score to another test, the most common pattern is that for IQ scores below 100, scores on the specific measure (i.e., recognition memory or sustained attention) should be about equal or higher than the IQ score. Conversely, when IQ scores are above 100, the distribution of scores on the specific measure will be about equal or lower. The higher the individual's IQ score, the more likely the comparison score on the specific skill will be lower and potentially by what appears to be a large amount. These effects are due to the statistical characteristics of all tests, particularly IQ tests versus specific cognitive skills. It is important to refrain from over-interpreting score differences to be diagnostic of a specific clinical condition or cognitive weakness in high-ability children. By the same token, when children score below the mean on intellectual measures, their score on other measures would generally be expected to be the same or higher than their IQ score. Smaller score differences in which IQ is higher than a specific ability are more meaningful than when IQ is below 100. In many cases, the reason that the IQ scores are low is due to the deficit in a primary area of cognition (i.e., language or memory). The clinician should consider these factors when interpreting test results for higher versus lower ability children.

LOW CORRELATION

When two measures are highly correlated, children have a similar level of performance between the two tests. Base rates of discrepancies confirm this phenomenon. When the correlation between two variables is quite low, small to moderate discrepancies will be common. Frequently, only correlation data are available between two measures (i.e., base rates for discrepancies do not exist). Correlation data can inform the clinician about the degree that the scores are similar. In some cases, the correlation between two measures may not be known and a cautious approach to interpreting difference scores is warranted.

DIFFERENT NORMATIVE SAMPLES

Very few tests are conormed or have a statistical linking sample. When two tests are conormed, the mean standard scores are set to the same value, (i.e., the mean differences of the samples are known). It should not be assumed that two tests will have a mean difference of zero. Again, when data regarding the relative distribution of two scores are unknown, a cautious approach to interpreting difference scores should be utilized. This is particularly true if normative data were collected many years apart. Even in cases where the normative sample was the same, the clinician should never assume that two variables will evidence Flynn effects to the same degree (i.e., VIQ and PIQ) and that profiling tests normed at very different times or profiling tests with dated norms can be misleading.

COGNITIVE REFERENCING

Comparing intellectual ability to performance on specific skill measures is a useful means for understanding weaknesses in cognitive processing. Comparative analysis does not replace the need to describe deficits in problem solving independent of intellectual abilities. By example, in cases where the child has deficient scores on specific language measures, it is important to understand that they will have difficulty processing language regardless of their level of intellectual ability. The presence of such impaired abilities likely contributes to the low scores on measures of intellectual ability. Therefore, both IQ and specific scores will be lowered and a direct comparison may not yield large differences. The clinician needs to look beyond a simple discrepancy and understand that impairments in a specific skill will affect performance on multiple measures. Understanding the child's performance in the context of their overall ability, as well as direct interpretation of specific cognitive measures, can help make diagnostic decisions and inform intervention.

SPECIFIC COGNITIVE SKILLS

LANGUAGE SKILLS

It is important to distinguish between tests of language functioning and measures of verbal intellectual ability. Measures of language functioning test specific language skills relevant to an external criterion (i.e., verb use, grammar development, naming). The specific skills may be distributed normally in the general population. These tests are scored for precision and accuracy of the specific language skill in question (i.e., points are taken off for grammatical errors in sentences). Verbal intellectual tests focus on the use of language to express intelligent behavior to solve complex, abstract problems. Scoring of verbal intelligence tests often ignores errors in language use (i.e., response has syntax errors) if they do not detract from the child's ability to express the appropriate concept. The tests are designed to be distributed normally and therefore will require the integration of multiple cognitive skills, including basic language abilities.

The decision to use additional language measures can frequently be made prior to the evaluation or based on the results of the WISC-IV Integrated. Language testing does not require the administration of an entire battery of language tests unless the goal is to make a diagnosis of a language disorder. The examiner can screen for language problems with a few measures and then recommend the child receive a speech-language evaluation for diagnosis and treatment.

WHEN TO USE ADDITIONAL LANGUAGE MEASURES

Psychosocial History and Prereferral Observations

Language disorders aggregate in families. The risk of developing a language disorder is substantially higher in the presence of a positive family history of language impairment (Choudhury & Benasich, 2003) due to a probable genetic transmission of the disorder [SLI Consortium (SLIC), 2004]. Children whose father had a language disorder or academic difficulties are at higher risk for developing language impairments than if the children's mother had such problems (Tallal, Townsend, Curtiss, & Wulfeck, 1991).

Boys are more likely to have language disorder than girls (Choudhury, 1991). Delayed language development is a risk factor for ongoing language deficits or language disorder (Conti-Ramsden, Botting, Simkin, & Knox, 2001). Parental reports of family history of language disorder or delayed language development indicate a need to assess language skills.

Some types of medical problems may signal potential language difficulties. Children with epilepsy such as temporal lobe epilepsy (TLE), particularly left hemisphere TLE (Thivard, Hombrouck, Te'zenas du Montcel, Delmaire, Cohen, Samson, Dupont, Chiras, Baulac, & Lehe'ricyc, 2005), or benign childhood epilepsy with centrotemporal spikes (BECTS; Monjauzea, Tullera, Hommetb, Barthezc, & Khomsia, 2005; Vinayan, Biji, & Thomas, 2005) are at risk for language processing impairments. Individuals suffering traumatic brain injury, particularly moderate to severe closed head injuries, can have language problems (Catroppa & Anderson, 2004). Numerous medical conditions can impact children's language development. A thorough medical history facilitates a priori hypothesis generation and test selection.

Many referrals do not explicitly identify language impairments as the primary concern. The clinician's awareness that a variety of clinical issues can develop due to underlying problems with language development enables appropriate identification of the potential causes of the observed referral problems. For example, there is considerable overlap between children identified as language disordered and those identified as reading disordered (McArthur, Hogben, Edwards, Heath, & Menger, 2000). Children diagnosed with language disorder as preschoolers have higher rates of academic difficulties such as grade retention, special tutoring, or placement in a learning disabled classroom setting (Aram, Ekelman, & Nation, 1984). Close attention should be paid to Verbal IQ scores when assessing children with Autism and related disorders (Rapin & Dunn, 2003), psychiatric hospitalization (Cohen, Menna, Vallance, Barwick, Im, & Horodezky, 1998), and children with early signs of conduct disorder (Speltz, DeKlyen, Calderon, Greenberg, & Fisher, 1999) to determine the degree that language deficits are present and contributing to observed psychopathology.

In cases of overt language delays, the clinician should assess for expressive and receptive language impairments. If the child's medical history or referral question could implicate language problems, the examiner can screen for language processing difficulties by administering specific language tests. The clinician can also evaluate the results of the WISC-IV Integrated subtests to determine if additional language testing is warranted.

The next section examines WISC-IV Integrated data in clinical groups with varying degrees of language impairment. Data correlating WISC-IV Integrated scores with specific measures of language processing are presented. These results illustrate the degree that language impairments will be evident in WISC-IV scores, providing an indicator that further language assessment is needed.

WISC-IV Integrated Concurrent Validity Data

A number of clinical groups relevant to the current discussion were tested during the standardization of the WISC-IV Integrated. Additional tests were collected to establish convergent–divergent validity. Data are presented for these clinical groups: Attention Deficit Disorder, Autistic Disorder, Expressive Language Disorder, Receptive-Expressive Language Disorder, Math Disorder, Reading Disorder, and Traumatic Brain Injury. The language disorder samples provide important information regarding the impact of language decoding and expression impairments on WISC-IV Integrated subtests. Autistic children exhibit language deficits similar to language disordered children (Rapin & Dunn, 2003) that affect their WISC-IV Integrated scores. The Reading Disorder group has mild language and auditory working memory deficits compared to the two language disorder groups and serves as a dose–response comparison (e.g., mild versus more severe deficits in language). The attention deficit disorder and traumatic brain injury groups provide data regarding impact deficits in executive functioning and processing speed on verbal subtests (Table 1).

A strong diagnosis effect exists; i.e., children with moderate to severe language based disorders (i.e., the Receptive-Expressive Language and Autistic) achieve the lowest scores on the WISC-IV Integrated subtests. Disorders associated with more mild to moderate deficits in language functioning (i.e., Expressive Language Disorder, Reading Disorder and Traumatic Brain Injury) score higher than the moderate to severe group but below those with very mild to no language impairments. Below average scores on Verbal Comprehension subtests indicate that a disturbance in language development is likely present, warranting further assessment of language skills.

Results support the hypothesis that intact language skills are essential to performing well on the Verbal Comprehension subtests. This finding is not restricted to severe language problems but includes circumscribed processing difficulties such as phonological processing and expressive language deficits. The multiple-choice scores are higher than the standard administration of the subtest in some cases. These multiple-choice procedures are useful in assessing intellectual skills in children that do not express language well. WISC-IV Integrated subtests are not diagnostic of specific clinical conditions, however, and additional testing is required to make such a diagnosis.

The number of low scores in the verbal domain obtained by the examinee provides another indication of whether further language testing may be useful. Table 2 presents the percentage of children obtaining multiple low scores in the Verbal domain for the standardization sample and for various clinical groups. The percentage of children having 3 or more verbal subtests at a scaled score of 4 or lower is very rare in the standardization sample and for most clinical groups. This profile likely represents a child with mental retardation. Based on other test scores, the clinician may decide to not

TABLE 1 Clinical Group Performance on WISC-IV Integrated Verbal subtests

Verbal Subtest	Attention Deficit Disorder		Autistic Disorder		Expressive Language Disorder		Receptive-Expressive Language Disorder		Math Disorder		Reading Disorder		Traumatic Brain Injury	
	Mean	SD	Mean	SD	Mean	SD	Mean	SD	Mean	SD	Mean	SD	Mean	SD
Vocabulary	9.5	2.4	6.7	3.1	7.1	2.3	6.1	2.3	8.4	1.9	8.2	2.0	8.5	2.7
Vocabulary Multiple Choice	9.0	2.5	7.0	2.6	7.3	2.9	6.3	3.0	7.9	2.5	7.9	2.8	9.1	2.8
Picture Vocabulary	9.5	2.7	8.2	4.1	7.8	2.8	6.5	2.6	8.5	2.7	8.4	2.2	8.7	3.0
Similarities	9.3	3.0	6.4	3.2	7.6	2.3	6.3	1.9	8.2	2.1	8.6	2.3	9.0	3.1
Similarities Multiple Choice	8.9	3.1	7.8	3.7	7.3	3.0	6.0	2.8	8.4	2.2	8.7	2.8	8.4	3.2
Comprehension	8.9	2.4	5.2	4.0	7.2	3.0	6.1	2.7	8.1	2.1	9.0	1.8	8.7	3.0
Comprehension Multiple Choice	9.0	3.2	4.9	4.1	7.3	3.0	6.2	3.0	7.6	2.6	8.7	2.6	8.1	3.1
Information	9.2	2.4	6.2	3.3	7.4	2.4	6.4	2.2	7.6	1.8	7.9	2.0	8.7	3.0
Information Multiple Choice	9.0	2.4	6.8	3.5	7.3	2.9	6.3	2.7	7.0	2.2	7.6	2.0	8.8	3.0

Note: Data are based on listwise deletion of cases and will vary from published scores for these groups: ADD (n = 49), Autistic Disorder (N = 16), Expressive Language Disorder (n = 46), Receptive-Expressive Language Disorder (n = 46), Math Disorder (n = 62), Reading Disorder (n = 43), Traumatic Brain Injury (n = 38). *Wechsler Intelligence Scale for Children – Fourth Edition Integrated.* Copyright © 2004 by Harcourt Assessment, Inc. Reproduced with permission. All rights reserved.

TABLE 2   Clinical Group Performance on WISC-IV Integrated Verbal Subtests Cumulative Percentages for Multiple Low Scores

Verbal Subtest	Standardization Cases	Mild MR	Attention Deficit Disorder	Autistic Disorder	Expressive Language Disorder	Receptive-Expressive Language Disorder	Math Disorder	Reading Disorder	TBI
3 or more verbal subtests 4 or less	1.8	50	0.0	31.3	2.2	8.7	0.0	0.0	5.3
3 or more verbal subtests 7 or less	11.7	100	22.4	62.5	56.5	56.5	23.3	25.8	29.0
3 or more verbal subtests 9 or less	31.3	100	42.9	75.0	80.5	73.9	76.7	69.4	50.0
3 or more verbal subtests ≥10	52.5	0	40.8	12.5	15.2	2.2	16.3	14.5	31.6
3 or more verbal subtests ≥12	21.9	0	8.2	0.0	2.2	0.0	0.0	3.2	2.6
3 or more multiple choice subtests 4 or less	3.1	60	2.0	12.5	8.7	21.8	2.3	1.6	2.6
3 or more multiple choice subtests 7 or less	14.6	100	28.6	62.5	54.4	73.9	31.9	30.0	34.2
3 or more multiple choice subtests 9 or less	38.9	100	59.2	93.8	80.5	95.6	62.8	77.4	66.8
3 or more multiple choice subtests ≥10	62.1	0	40.8	6.2	19.5	4.4	18.6	9.7	34.2
3 or more multiple choice subtests ≥12	27.5	0	16.3	6.2	4.4	2.2	0.0	3.2	13.2

Note: Data are based on listwise deletion of cases and will vary from published scores for these groups: MR (n = 20), ADD (n = 49), Autistic Disorder (N = 16), Expressive Language Disorder (n = 46), Receptive-Expressive Language Disorder (n = 46), Math Disorder (n = 43), Reading Disorder (n = 62), Traumatic Brain Injury (n = 38), *Wechsler Intelligence Scale for Children – Fourth Edition Integrated.* Copyright © 2004 by Harcourt Assessment, Inc. Reproduced with permission. All rights reserved.

proceed with additional language testing. Likewise, 3 or more scores at 12 or above are very rare among clinical groups, particularly in children with language disorder. In this case, the clinician would not likely administer additional language tests.

Most children with language problems have Verbal domain scores at 9 or below and a large percentage have scores between 5 and 7. Multiple verbal scores in the 5 to 7 range warrant further investigation. If the child has multiple scores below 9, then the decision to test language skills may be more circumscribed, such as a screening or measuring specific language skills. These specific skills could be phonological processing if reading problems are suspected or production measures if poor verbal initiation is observed. The selection of specific language measures should in some way help answer the clinical question.

Clinical Evaluation of Language Fundamentals–4th Edition (CELF-IV)

The CELF-IV is a battery of tests designed to assess the development of language skills in children through young adulthood. The subtests measure language skills, such as the ability to apply English morphological rules; repeat sentences verbatim; generate complete, syntactically and semantically accurate sentences; analyze words for meaning; to understand basic syntactic structure of sentences; follow multistep commands; understand relationships between words; interpret factual and inferential information; and interpret sentences that use a variety of syntactic structures. Additional measures evaluate rapid naming, phonological processing, mental sequencing, and repetition of digits. The CELF-IV explicitly tests hypotheses regarding the integrity of language skills and provides detailed analysis of the nature and severity of the language disorder.

The CELF-IV (Semel, Wiig & Secord, 2003) was administered to children diagnosed with Expressive or Receptive-Expressive Language Disorder as part of the WISC-IV Standardization project. The CELF-IV is composed of subtests that measure specific aspects of language functioning. These subtests differ from WISC-IV subtests in that they require the precise decoding and production of language. Points are deducted if the child makes errors in syntax or semantics. Most of the tasks minimize the degree that abstract reasoning is necessary to achieve a correct result. The subtests do require intact auditory working memory, a skill that overlaps substantially with WISC-IV verbal subtests. Correlations between CELF-IV Indexes/subtests and WISC-IV Verbal Comprehension Index/subtests are presented in Table 3.

A moderate correlation exists between the CELF-IV Total Language Index and the WISC-IV Integrated subtests and a high correlation with the Verbal Comprehension Index. This indicates, at least among children with language impairments, that poor language skills lower their performance on verbal intellectual measures and create a threshold on how well they may achieve on these tests. When interpreting the results of the WISC-IV

TABLE 3 Correlations Statistics for CELF-IV and WISC-IV Integrated Study in Children with Expressive and Receptive-Expressive Language Disorder

CELF-IV Composites

	Total Language	Receptive Language	Expressive Language	Language Content	Language Memory[A]	Language Structure[B]	Working Memory
WISC-IV Integrated Verbal Subtests/Index							
Vocabulary	0.60	0.53	0.54	0.66	0.54	0.49	0.33
Vocabulary Multiple Choice	0.60	0.61	0.53	0.66	0.48	0.63	0.29
Picture Vocabulary	0.37	0.42	0.33	0.42	0.33	0.26	0.03
Similarities	0.56	0.41	0.52	0.55	0.40	0.54	0.38
Similarities Multiple Choice	0.22	0.21	0.19	0.29	0.31	0.14	0.20
Comprehension	0.65	0.55	0.64	0.62	0.61	0.63	0.38
Comprehension Multiple Choice	0.46	0.45	0.42	0.44	0.25	0.58	0.42
Word Reasoning	0.66	0.57	0.60	0.61	0.64	0.58	0.43
Verbal Comprehension Index	0.73	0.61	0.69	0.73	0.63	0.67	0.45

CELF-IV Subtests

	Concepts + Directions[C]	Recalling Sentences	Formulated Sentences	Word Structure[B]	Word Classes-Receptive	Word Classes-Expressive[A]	Word Classes Total	Sentence Structure[B]
WISC-IV Integrated Verbal Subtests/Index								
Vocabulary	0.45	0.43	0.46	0.38	0.46	0.46	0.49	0.39
Vocabulary Multiple Choice	0.50	0.36	0.53	0.37	0.51	0.50	0.54	0.49
Picture Vocabulary	0.20	0.19	0.37	0.07	0.44	0.39	0.43	0.17
Similarities	0.47	0.40	0.43	0.51	0.27	0.30	0.33	0.40
Similarities Multiple Choice	0.30	0.13	0.19	0.10	0.01	0.15	0.10	0.15
Comprehension	0.47	0.56	0.53	0.50	0.39	0.45	0.47	0.56
Comprehension Multiple Choice	0.46	0.36	0.32	0.47	0.30	0.26	0.30	0.48
Word Reasoning	0.59	0.53	0.56	0.34	0.40	0.44	0.45	0.46
Verbal Comprehension Index	0.57	0.56	0.57	0.56	0.46	0.50	0.53	0.55

TABLE 3 (Continued)

	CELF-IV Subtests					
	Expressive Vocabulary	Word Definitions[A]	Understanding Paragraphs[D]	Sentence Assembly[D]	Semantic Relationships[D]	Numbers-Repetition Total	Familiar Sequences[E]
WISC-IV Integrated Verbal Subtests/Index						
Vocabulary	0.72	0.72	0.41	0.58	0.57	0.22	0.36
Vocabulary Multiple Choice	0.55	0.71	0.51	0.44	0.57	0.17	0.34
Picture Vocabulary	0.19	0.48	0.36	0.39	0.53	−0.05	0.10
Similarities	0.47	0.59	0.44	0.54	0.22	0.31	0.35
Similarities Multiple Choice	0.33	0.29	0.29	0.26	0.40	0.16	0.17
Comprehension	0.48	0.64	0.56	0.34	0.33	0.31	0.34
Comprehension Multiple Choice	0.44	0.35	0.35	0.18	0.30	0.34	0.39
Word Reasoning	0.43	0.59	0.58	0.40	0.33	0.30	0.45
Verbal Comprehension Index	0.64	0.77	0.57	0.55	0.47	0.34	0.44

Note: A = 9–12, B = 5–8, C = 9–12, D = 13–21, E = version 1 ages 5–16, version 2 ages 17–21. Data are based on listwise deletion of cases and will vary from published scores for these groups. The expressive and receptive-expressive language disorder groups have been combined here due to small sample sizes of the individual groups. *Wechsler Intelligence Scale for Children – Fourth Edition Integrated.* Copyright © 2004 by Harcourt Assessment, Inc. Reproduced with permission. All rights reserved.

Integrated, the impact of language delays needs to be considered. For instance, if the Verbal Comprehension Index is low, the range of scores on Full-Scale IQ (FSIQ) is truncated. Therefore, FSIQ may not be the best measure of the child's intellectual capacity.

The WISC-IV Integrated Verbal Comprehension Index correlates in the moderate range with most CELF-IV measures. In this sample of children with language disorder, poor language skills impact verbal intellectual skills more than deficits in auditory working memory. Low scores on the Verbal Comprehension Index should prompt the clinician to consider deficits in basic language processing more than attributing low scores to impaired working memory abilities. Of the CELF-IV subtests, Word Definitions and Expressive Vocabulary subtests have the highest correlations with the Verbal Comprehension Index. The lowest correlations are observed on Word Classes Receptive and Semantic Relationships. These subtests require intact semantic knowledge with few demands on language production. This pattern suggests that the Verbal Comprehension Index requires an adequate ability to *communicate* knowledge.

Among the WISC-IV Integrated subtests, the Similarities Multiple Choice and Picture Vocabulary subtests have the lowest correlation with current language functioning. These tasks apparently are not as influenced by the semantic structure and basic auditory working demands as the other WISC-IV Integrated subtests. However, these tasks are reduced when more complex language-based working memory demands require on-line processing, decoding, and production of words and sentences (i.e., Recalling Sentences).

The ability to follow multistep commands of increasing syntactic and semantic complexity (concepts and directions) correlated moderately with most verbal subtests. The Word Reasoning subtest had the highest association with this subtest. Deficits in following directions may particularly affect performance on this subtest.

The ability to repeat sentences verbatim (Recalling Sentences) exhibited a split relationship with WISC-IV subtests. Low correlations were observed with multiple-choice subtests, indicating that these subtests do reduce the demands for on-line linguistic processing compared to the standard administration of these subtests. Among the standard version of the subtests, Comprehension and Word Reasoning made the highest demands on on-line linguistic processing. This subtest is not simply auditory working memory but is a linguistic decoding and production control measure that relates to performance on these WISC-IV subtests.

The Formulated Sentences subtest requires the child to create a semantically and syntactically accurate and complete sentence that is constrained in content by a visually presented scene (e.g., child handing in a homework paper) and the use of a specific word in the sentence (e.g., finally). This subtest is a language production and control task. It correlates lower with the WISC-IV Integrated multiple-choice versions than the standard forms, except for Vocabulary Multiple Choice. In general, the standard WISC-IV

Integrated verbal subtests require, to a small degree, the ability to produce language accurately. The Sentence Assembly task requires the flexible production of language when a limited number of correct solutions are possible. Performance on this subtest relates to the standard versions vocabulary and similarities.

The Word Structure subtest measures the capacity to understand the impact of morphology on semantics (e.g., tense, case, number). This skill relates most to performance on Comprehension and Similarities. Decoding of the syntactic structure at the sentence level (Sentence Structure) had the strongest association with Comprehension performance. The ability to decode semantic relationships between words (Word Classes-Receptive) correlates more with performance on Vocabulary subtests, whereas the ability to communicate those relationships relates to Vocabulary subtests, standard Comprehension, and Word Reasoning. The ability to define words (Word Definitions) and naming ability (Expressive Vocabulary) correlate most highly with vocabulary but affect performance on other standard WISC-IV tasks to a lesser degree.

The ability to decode factual and inferential language (Understanding Paragraphs) related most to performance on the standard Similarities, Comprehension, and Vocabulary multiple-choice tasks. Decoding variations in syntactic structure that impact the meaning of the subtest (Semantic Relationships) had the highest correlations with the Vocabulary subtests.

The concurrent study with CELF-IV revealed that semantic impairments most prominently affect the child's performance on the Verbal Comprehension Index. The Vocabulary subtests are associated with the integrity of the semantic system. Comprehension and Word Reasoning are influenced most by weaknesses in production and controlled use of language. The Similarities Multiple-Choice and Picture Vocabulary subtests have the lowest correlation with current language functioning. Impairments in language functioning differentially affect subtest performance and these findings need to be considered when drawing inferences about profiles of strengths and weaknesses on the WISC-IV Integrated.

LANGUAGE SKILLS CORRELATE WITH VISUAL PERCEPTUAL WISC-IV INTEGRATED SUBTESTS

It is not anticipated that the CELF-IV will have many strong associations with the WISC-IV Integrated Perceptual Reasoning subtests. However, the design of different Perceptual Reasoning tasks could make them more amenable to verbalization. If there are differences, then children without language impairments could use a verbal strategy that enables them to achieve higher scores on these subtests. Therefore, the integrity of language functions may differentially affect performance across the Perceptual-Reasoning subtests. Table 4 provides correlations between CELF-IV and WISC-IV Integrated subtests.

TABLE 4 Correlation Statistics for CELF-IV and WISC-IV Integrated Perceptual Reasoning Tasks in Children with Expressive and Receptive-Expressive Language Disorder

	CELF-IV Composites							CELF-IV Subtests		
	Total Language	Receptive Language	Expressive Language	Language Content	Language Memory[A]	Language Structure[B]	Working Memory	Concepts + Directions[C]	Recalling Sentences	Formulated Sentences
WISC-IV Integrated Verbal Subtests/Index										
Block Design	0.17	0.27	0.11	0.28	0.09	0.14	0.25	0.18	−0.05	0.19
Block Design No Time Bonus	0.15	0.22	0.07	0.22	0.07	0.09	0.26	0.18	−0.09	0.17
Block Design Multiple Choice Time Bonus	0.24	0.27	0.16	0.31	0.07	0.35	0.16	0.27	−0.04	0.30
Block Design Multiple Choice No Time Bonus	0.23	0.21	0.15	0.25	0.06	0.30	0.21	0.22	−0.01	0.22
Matrix Reasoning	0.39	0.39	0.32	0.35	0.53	0.08	0.29	0.45	0.15	0.37
Picture Concepts	0.46	0.51	0.40	0.45	0.29	0.51	0.35	0.47	0.21	0.43
Picture Completion	0.18	0.21	0.09	0.25	0.25	−0.09	0.15	0.19	−0.13	0.26
Elithorn Mazes Time Bonus	0.09	0.21	0.01	0.18	0.16	−0.19	0.18	0.35	−0.11	0.09
Elithorn Mazes No Time Bonus	0.08	0.22	0.00	0.24	0.12	−0.03	0.22	0.37	−0.10	0.06
Perceptual Reasoning Index	0.43	0.50	0.34	0.46	0.39	0.34	0.37	0.49	0.13	0.42

(Continues)

TABLE 4 (Continued)

CELF-IV Subtests

	Word Structure[B]	Word Classes-Receptive[B]	Word Classes-Expressive[A]	Word Classes Total	Sentence Structure[B]	Expressive Vocabulary[B]	Word Definitions[A]	Understanding Paragraphs[D]	Sentence Assembly[D]	Semantic Relationships[D]	Numbers-Repetition Total[D]	Familiar Sequences[E]
WISC-IV Integrated Verbal Subtests/Index												
Block Design	0.06	0.25	0.21	0.23	0.04	0.32	0.30	0.15	0.08	0.25	0.14	0.28
Block Design No Time Bonus	0.05	0.18	0.14	0.16	−0.02	0.26	0.36	0.08	0.08	0.26	0.15	0.30
Block Design Multiple Choice Time Bonus	0.11	0.16	0.15	0.16	0.34	0.33	0.26	0.25	0.06	0.09	0.05	0.22
Block Design Multiple Choice No Time Bonus	0.14	0.10	0.08	0.09	0.27	0.26	0.40	0.13	0.09	0.13	0.11	0.25
Matrix Reasoning	0.07	0.29	0.25	0.27	−0.04	0.37	0.46	0.19	0.17	0.58	0.16	0.34
Picture Concepts	0.30	0.42	0.42	0.47	0.42	0.42	0.30	0.33	0.25	0.41	0.23	0.36
Picture Completion	−0.19	0.18	0.17	0.18	−0.01	0.35	0.46	0.11	0.22	0.29	0.03	0.22
Elithorn Mazes Time Bonus	−0.15	0.06	0.07	0.06	0.06	0.00	0.17	0.17	0.05	0.24	0.01	0.27
Elithorn Mazes No Time Bonus	−0.05	0.11	0.07	0.09	0.07	0.12	0.17	0.17	0.21	0.23	0.10	0.25
Perceptual Reasoning Index	0.18	0.42	0.38	0.42	0.22	0.51	0.42	0.28	0.21	0.52	0.22	0.42

Note: A=9–12, B=5–8, C=9–12, D=13–21, E=version 1 ages 5–16, version 2 ages 17–21. Data are based on listwise deletion of cases and will vary from published scores for these groups. The expressive and receptive-expressive language disorder groups have been combined here due to small sample sizes of the individual groups. *Wechsler Intelligence Scale for Children – Fourth Edition Integrated.* Copyright © 2004 by Harcourt Assessment, Inc. Reproduced with permission. All rights reserved.

The association between Perceptual-Reasoning Index and CELF-IV composite scores was consistently in the low-to-moderate range with the highest correlation observed with the Receptive Language index. Among the WISC-IV Integrated subtests, the Picture Concepts subtest had moderate correlations with most CELF-IV Language Indices except Language and Memory and Working Memory. Matrix Reasoning had the highest correlation with Language and Memory. The specific language skills associated with performance on Picture Concepts are the ability to follow multistep commands and to associate words and constructs. Matrix Reasoning was associated with the ability to follow multistep commands and semantic knowledge. Picture Completion related to semantic knowledge and naming skills.

Perceptual Reasoning scores among the clinical groups revealed that a diagnosed language disorder was associated with some subtests more than others. The degree of impact was less than that observed for verbal subtests. Matrix Reasoning and Picture Concepts were most affected by language impairments. The Autistic group, which benefited the most from multiple-choice language measures (i.e., Picture Vocabulary), did not have unexpectedly low (i.e., from other visual perceptual subtests) Picture Concepts subtests but Matrix Reasoning was low. Elithorn Mazes did not correlate with CELF-IV, yet this subtest was one of the lowest in the Receptive-Expressive and Autistic groups. Perhaps executive control and short-term planning skills are important in these disorders unrelated to apparent language problems (Table 5).

Scores on Matrix Reasoning and Picture Concepts are influenced by impaired language abilities. However, language impairments do not impact these subtests to the same degree as verbal subtests. In children with language disorder, the discrepancy between Verbal Comprehension and the Perceptual Reasoning Index may not be as large as in previous versions of the Wechsler intelligence scales for children. Understanding the impact of language impairments on specific subtests can facilitate the differential diagnosis between language disorders and low average or borderline intellectual ability. Additional language testing should be completed to make a distinction between these deficits in cognition.

A BRIEF LIST OF LANGUAGE MEASURES AND SKILLS ASSESSED

A very large number of published tests of language functioning exist. Not all language tests are developed for the same purpose, subsequently their content will vary considerably. When deciding to use specific language measures, it is essential to determine the intended population of children (i.e., language disorder, learning disabled, or severe aphasia), as the content and nature of the tasks will vary depending on proposed use. This section briefly categorizes subtests from the CELF-IV, NEPSY, Wechsler Individual Achievement Test–2nd Edition, Test of Word Know-

TABLE 5 Clinical Group Performance on WISC-IV Integrated Perceptual Reasoning subtests

Verbal Subtest	Attention Deficit Disorder		Autistic Disorder		Expressive Language Disorder		Receptive-Expressive Language Disorder		Math Disorder		Reading Disorder		Traumatic Brain Injury	
	Mean	SD	Mean	SD	Mean	SD	Mean	SD	Mean	SD	Mean	SD	Mean	SD
Block Design	9.5	2.8	8.1	3.9	9.0	3.0	8.2	3.0	7.4	2.8	9.0	3.0	8.0	2.3
Block Design No Time Bonus	9.5	2.7	7.9	3.9	9.1	3.1	8.3	3.4	7.5	3.1	9.1	3.1	8.1	2.6
Block Design Multiple Choice	9.6	3.3	8.3	4.6	9.2	3.1	8.2	3.2	8.4	3.0	9.2	3.1	8.0	3.1
Block Design Multiple Choice No Time Bonus	10.0	3.0	8.5	4.2	9.4	3.1	8.5	3.7	8.8	3.3	9.4	3.1	9.0	2.8
Matrix Reasoning	9.4	2.7	6.9	3.2	8.6	3.4	7.3	2.9	7.8	2.1	8.6	3.4	8.6	2.7
Picture Concepts	9.8	3.2	8.0	3.9	8.1	2.9	7.5	3.4	8.2	2.6	8.1	2.9	9.3	3.4
Picture Completion	9.7	3.0	6.3	3.5	9.0	2.7	8.2	3.8	8.1	2.7	9.0	2.7	8.7	3.1
Elithorn Mazes	10.0	3.0	6.0	2.6	9.7	3.4	7.4	3.4	8.6	3.5	9.7	3.4	8.4	3.3
Elithorn Mazes No Time Bonus	9.8	2.8	6.1	2.5	9.6	3.1	7.4	3.1	8.4	3.3	9.6	3.1	8.5	3.1

Note: Data are based on listwise deletion of cases and will vary from published scores for these groups: ADD (n = 52), Autistic Disorder (N = 15) Expressive Language Disorder (n = 29), Receptive-Expressive Language Disorder (n = 36), Math Disorder (n = 36), Reading Disorder (n = 43), Traumatic Brain Injury (n = 36). *Wechsler Intelligence Scale for Children – Fourth Edition Integrated.* Copyright © 2004 by Harcourt Assessment, Inc. Reproduced with permission. All rights reserved.

ledge (TOWK), Delis–Kaplan Executive Functioning Scale (D-KEFS), Process Assessment of the Learner (PAL-RW), Early Reading Success Indicator (ERSI), Adaptive Behavioral Assessment Scale–2nd Edition (ABAS-II), and Boston Naming Test (BNT) into specific language functions.

Profiling of language scores can help decision making regarding the severity of language deficits, the nature of the language problems, and diagnostic considerations. The reader is referred to the previous chapter for details regarding the processes measured within the language domain.

1. Phonological processing
   • WIAT-II/PAL-RW/ERSI: Pseudoword Decoding, Word Reading
2. Phonemic/phonological awareness
   • NEPSY: Phonological Processing
   • PAL-RW: Phonemes, Syllables
   • CELF-IV: Phonological Awareness
3. Rapid automatic naming
   • NEPSY: Speeded Naming
   • CELF-IV: Rapid Automatic Naming
   • PAL-RW: Rapid Automatic Naming
   • ERSI: Speeded Naming, Letter Naming
4. Vocabulary/word knowledge
   • WIAT-II Receptive and Expressive Vocabulary
   • WISC-IV Integrated: Vocabulary, Vocabulary Multiple Choice, and Picture Vocabulary
   • TOWK: Expressive and Receptive Vocabulary
   • CELF-IV: Word Definitions
5. Confrontation Naming/Referential Naming
   • Boston Naming Test
   • CELF-IV Expressive Vocabulary
6. Ability to follow multistep commands
   • NEPSY: Comprehension of Instruction
   • WIAT-II: Sentence Comprehension
   • CELF-IV: Concepts and Directions
7. Associative Semantic Knowledge
   • TOWK: Multiple Context, Synonyms, Antonyms (semantic)
   • CELF-IV: Word Classes (semantic)
   • WISC-IV Integrated: Similarities, Similarities Multiple Choice (conceptual)
8. Decoding increasingly complex semantic and syntactic sentences
   • CELF-IV: Understanding paragraphs, semantic relationships
   • WIAT-II: Listening Comprehension

9. Syntactic knowledge
   - CELF-IV: Word Structure, Sentence Structure
   - TOWK: Conjunctions and Transition Words
10. Language Production
    - CELF-IV Formulated Sentences (controlled production requires good control of semantic and syntactic structure)
    - CELF-IV: Sentence Assembly (controlled production with syntactic knowledge important)
    - CELF-IV: Word Associations (production depends on access to semantic knowledge)
    - WIAT-II: Oral Expression (production of organized, cohesive language)
    - WIAT-II: Word Fluency (oral and written versions depend on access to word knowledge in general)
    - PAL: Story Retell (production requiring integrated semantic and syntactic skills)
    - NEPSY: Letter Fluency (access to word knowledge using orthographic prompts)
    - NEPSY: Semantic Fluency (access to word knowledge using semantic prompt)
    - D-KEFS: Letter Fluency (access to word knowledge using orthographic prompts)
    - D-KEFS: Semantic Fluency (access to word knowledge using semantic prompts)
11. Flexibility and abstraction in language production and comprehension
    - TOWK: Figurative Use (concreteness in Comprehension)
    - TOWK: Multiple Meanings (access to multiple meanings of words)
    - CELF-IV Sentence Assembly (requires flexible use of syntax and semantics)
    - D-KEFS: Semantic Switching (requires mental switching between categories)
    - D-KEFS: 20 Questions, Word Context, Sorting Test
    - WISC-IV Integrated: Comprehension, Comprehension Multiple Choice, Word Reasoning
12. Repetition of Language
    - NEPSY: Sentence Repetition
    - CELF-IV: Recalling Sentences
    - WIAT-II: Sentence Repetition (part of oral expression)
13. Social effectiveness of communication and pragmatics
    - CELF-IV: Pragmatics Profile
    - ABAS-II: Communication

INTERPRETATION OF LANGUAGE SCORES VERSUS
VERBAL COMPREHENSION INDEX/SUBTESTS

While WISC-IV Integrated Verbal Comprehension subtests are sensitive to the effects of language dysfunction, they do not measure linguistic skills specifically. WISC-IV Integrated verbal subtests are designed primarily to measure conceptual and abstract reasoning skills. It is important to keep these differences in mind as it impacts the conclusions that can be drawn when performance differences are observed on WISC-IV verbal subtest versus language measures. Interpretation of all possible combinations of scores is beyond the scope of this chapter; however, topical issues are discussed.

At the index level, children having low Verbal Comprehension Index scores but average or better scores on specific language measures have difficulties using language to solve conceptual/abstract reasoning tasks. They may appear rather concrete in their understanding and use of language. However, they do not have a language disorder per se. Children having low VCI scores and even lower language scores have a high probability of language disorder. Deficits in the abstract use of language and poor understanding and production of basic language abilities are present.

Issues of Language Production

Language production refers to the capacity to produce language in different circumstances, incorporating conversational use of language, expression of knowledge, accuracy of production, and simple volume of production. Production deficits can be observed by the classroom teacher and often during the psychoeducational evaluation. The challenge for the clinician is to determine the source of production problems. The most simple language production tasks are those requiring semantic retrieval of common nouns, such as saying as many animal names as possible (NEPSY and D-KEFS category/semantic fluency). Deficits on these tests suggest rather significant problems accessing information. Semantic fluency tasks can also gauge effort level as children with poor verbal IQ or language scores sometimes show average-to-above-average performance on these subtests. This profile can be observed in children demonstrating adequate or better effort but limited knowledge or control of linguistic processes.

Comparing semantic fluency to letter fluency (i.e., word production to a phoneme) informs the clinician if the child has difficulty searching for words using a novel orthographic search compared to a simple categorical strategy. Low letter fluency, in the absence of other types of production deficits, implies problems accessing information during novel problem-solving situations. This problem could affect WISC-IV Integrated standard verbal tasks, particularly on the Similarities subtest, which requires the child to search for information common to two different words. The discrepancy between these two subtests can also be another means of judging effort in verbal production. Children with significantly better semantic fluency than letter fluency are putting forth the effort but do not have the capacity to perform better. The opposite profile is unusual and may suggest deficits in semantic knowledge or an uneven effort on testing.

Tests that mimic conversational language are excellent mechanisms for evaluating the control of language production. Some children are good producers and do well on tasks requiring the production of single words but have poor underlying language. Subsequently, they produce a high quantity of language but the quality is rather poor. On verbal subtests, these children will provide lengthy responses but these may be inaccurate and inconsistent, resulting in spoiled responses. In these cases, the CELF-IV Formulated Sentences subtest and the WIAT-II Oral Expression subtests can provide a good measure of accuracy of production without the demands on conceptual reasoning posed by WISC-IV Integrated subtests. Most WISC-IV Integrated verbal subtests have a moderate correlation with CELF-IV Formulated Sentences with the exception of some of the multiple-choice versions. For children with low scores on verbal subtests, the clinician could use production measures to determine if low scores are due to more basic problems in accessing and using language effectively or if low scores are due to poor intellectual development (i.e., conceptual/abstract reasoning).

Repetition

Some children are able to repeat information accurately but have a limited capacity to understand and use language effectively. On the WISC-IV, this profile is suspected when low VCI scores are accompanied by average or better scores on WMI. Children with language disorders often have concurrent deficits in auditory working memory (Montgomery, 2003), and an absence of lower WMI scores should be followed up with additional testing. There are a number of hypotheses to consider when this profile is obtained.

The clinician will want to compare the child's ability to repeat information verbatim (i.e., NEPSY Sentence Repetition or CELF-IV Recalling Sentences) to tests measuring language comprehension (i.e., NEPSY: Comprehension of Instructions, CELF-IV Concepts and Direction or Semantic Relationships, WIAT-II Listening Comprehension). If the child's language comprehension is good and consistent with their ability to repeat sentences, then the low VCI score indicates poor conceptual reasoning using language or could be due to expressive language problems. If repetition and comprehension are low along with VCI, then the probability of a language disorder is increased and the child may just have strength for repeating simple verbal information.

If language comprehension skills are low, the Verbal Comprehension Index is low but repetition and Working Memory Index are average or better, then a discrepancy between working memory and language use exists. This profile has been associated with nonverbal learning disabilities (Rourke, Del Dotto, Rourke, & Casey, 1990). The most extreme form of repetition without content or appropriate contextual association is *echolalia*. In echolalia, the child repeats words and phrases heard in one context and either says repeatedly what the person has just said or repeats this word, phrase, or sentence in another context. This more rare form of repetition is associated with Autism (Rapin et al., 2003).

In some cases, this profile is associated with the child having an impoverished background. The child does not have a language disorder but has poorly developed linguistic skills due to a lack of appropriate early learning experiences. The cognitive mechanisms needed for language learning are in place but their limited language experiences place them behind peers in comprehension and expression.

Social and Pragmatic Language Issues

Children with Autism Spectrum Disorder have similar linguistic deficits as children identified with specific language impairment (Rapin et al., 2003). Not all children with pragmatic language deficits are autistic (e.g., Semantic-Pragmatic Disorder). The clinician needs to be concerned that an inappropriate social use of language [i.e., not responding directly to questions, speaking out of turn, conversing off-topic, topic perseveration, concreteness in interpreting language, difficulty detecting humor; for review, see Martin & McDonald (2003)] interferes with performance on WISC-IV Integrated verbal subtests. Using the multiple-choice versions of the standard verbal tasks helps structure the task and reduces the impact of pragmatic deficits on verbal performance.

Assessing the social impact of poor language functioning (e.g., ABAS-II communication and CELF-IV Pragmatics Profile) can provide useful diagnostic information. More importantly, the assessment of pragmatic skills informs the clinician to the degree that the social application of language is affecting the child's ability to develop appropriate peer relationships and interferes with psychosocial development. Child–adult interpersonal relationships are affected frequently by language problems, but the quality and character of these relationships depend on a number of factors. These child–adult relationships will depend on the temperament of the adult and their ability to respond to the child in a facilitative rather than punitive manner. Children, however, do not have the cognitive maturity in most cases to understand and facilitate communication with a child with significant pragmatic language problems. Peer relationships can be influenced negatively by the presence of language impairments. The danger for the child with the language impairment is the risk of being isolated, bullied (Knox & Conti-Ramsden, 2003), and having conduct-related problems (Gilmour, Hill, Place, & Skuse, 2004).

Mild Language Deficits

Mild language difficulties place children at risk for academic and potentially long-term psychosocial difficulties. Among the clinical groups presented earlier in this chapter, the Reading and Math Disorder groups, as well as children in the ADD group, were almost three times as likely as children in the standardization sample to have multiple verbal subtests in the low average range. Children with more moderate to severe language problems had five to six times the risk. Children referred for academic problems such as reading, math, or behavioral problems should be screened for possible language difficulties.

Children referred for primarily academic reasons should be evaluated for phonological and rapid naming impairments, as these skills have been linked to reading difficulties (Catts, Fey, Zhang, & Tomblin, 2001; Wolf & Bowers, 1999). Children having normal verbal comprehension and auditory working memory but very poor reading decoding skills may have significant difficulties with phonological awareness and decoding. In children with low verbal comprehension but normal phonological processing, reading decoding can be better than verbal comprehension scores, but reading comprehension scores are likely to be below reading decoding and similar to Verbal Comprehension Index scores. Late onset of reading problems (i.e., fourth grade or later) may be associated with poor verbal reasoning skills more than specific deficits in decoding or phonological processing. Children with lowered scores on Verbal Comprehension and Working Memory (compared to PRI and PSI) may have reading decoding and comprehension scores that are lower than their FSIQ predicted reading scores.

Children with Attention Deficit Disorder do not, in general, manifest overt deficits in language use. However, problems with the executive control and application of language can produce more errors or inconsistent performance in this domain. The clinician and parents may believe that the child is not working up to their potential in the language/written arts. In ADD, problems in language are associated with a control of higher order verbal skills, such as organizing verbal expressions prior to initiating verbal output or slight difficulties applying language flexibly when response options are limited.

SUMMARY

When reporting both verbal IQ scores and specific language measures, there are a few important considerations to keep in mind. Verbal intellectual abilities require considerable expressive and receptive language abilities. Global impairments in language functioning will reduce overall performance on Verbal Comprehension subtests. Process subtests, particularly Similarities Multiple Choice and Picture Vocabulary, make fewer demands on expressive language and verbal working memory skills, yet children with expressive language difficulties still do poorly on these tests. Fluctuations among verbal subtests occur in relationship to the severity of the underlying language problems (i.e., more variability with some subtests average and other lower in mild disorders and consistently low scores in more severe language disorders). Profiles of verbal subtests can provide some information about the specific nature of language deficits but interpretation should be based on specific measures of language functioning.

Language skills are influenced by attention, executive functioning, working memory, and declarative memory functions. When integrating results of WISC-IV Integrated verbal subtests, the role of working memory and executive functioning needs careful consideration when interpreting profiles of verbal comprehension and language subtests. A very poor working memory skill will reduce the capacity to use language and perform intellectual tasks simultaneously. Executive functions play an important role in expressive language skills.

Using a variety of tests, the clinician can hypothesize about the relative influence of different cognitive skills on verbal subtests. Aligning interventions and accommodations with the source of verbal weaknesses may result in better functioning in academic and other psychosocial settings.

A BRIEF KEY FOR HYPOTHESIZING ABOUT VERBAL COMPREHENSION INDEX SUBTESTS

1. Vocabulary significantly lower than Comprehension and Similarities.
   - Vocabulary has a strong association with word knowledge, and a specific deficit on this subtest likely reflects poor semantic development. Administration of measures of confrontation naming and Picture Vocabulary will provide details regarding the extent of vocabulary deficiency.
   - Rule out problems with accessing knowledge for Vocabulary by administering Vocabulary Multiple Choice.
   - Interventions focused on intensive vocabulary development may help academic development in multiple areas.
2. Similarities significantly lower than Comprehension and Vocabulary.
   - Similarities relate to a number of the same language skills as Comprehension so low scores on Similarities in isolation would be unexpected; however, consider assessing cognitive flexibility in using language as well as associative word knowledge (i.e., multiple meanings, multiple contexts, antonyms, and synonyms).
   - Rule out problems with accessing knowledge for Similarities by administering Similarities Multiple Choice.
   - Interventions focused on developing associative knowledge and using language flexibly may be helpful for children with this profile.

3. Comprehension significantly lower than Vocabulary and Similarities.
   - Comprehension scores have a strong association with a number of language skills, such as linguistic working memory, language production, and comprehension. Comprehension appears to be difficult for children with impairments in social/pragmatic aspects of language use. Additional assessment of language-based working memory, language pragmatics, and complex language production may help understand low Comprehension scores.
   - Rule out problems with accessing knowledge for Comprehension by administering Comprehension Multiple Choice.
   - Interventions focusing on language pragmatics and working memory skills (e.g., clustering, chunking, mnemonics) may be helpful.

A BRIEF KEY FOR HYPOTHESIZING ABOUT LANGUAGE EFFECTS ON PRI SUBTESTS

- Block Design is significantly lower than Matrix Reasoning and Picture Completion. This profile is not likely to be associated with specific language problems. Block Design does not correlate highly with language measures and is one of the highest scores in children with language-based disorders.
- Matrix Reasoning is significantly lower than Block Design and Picture Concepts. For children with primary language problems, low scores on Matrix Reasoning would be expected to be accompanied by low scores on Picture Concepts. Children with Autism show a trend to have lower Matrix Reasoning scores, but this is not necessarily due to language impairments but could relate to other aspects of cognition. Matrix Reasoning is associated with linguistic working memory more than Picture Concepts. The hypothesis is that poor working memory for language affecting Matrix Reasoning can be tested using sentence repetition paradigms.
- Picture Concepts significantly lower than Block Design and Matrix Reasoning. Significant problems in language development in the absence of concurrent visual–perceptual deficits can produce this profile. This subtest had higher correlations with a syntactic structure of language. Children having this profile will likely have corresponding low scores on Verbal Comprehension Index subtests, and further assessment of general language skills is warranted.

EXECUTIVE FUNCTIONING

Executive functioning refers to a broad range of higher order cognitive skills that specifically relate to monitoring and self-regulation of cognition and behavior, initiation and modification of behavior based on environmental demands, and the organization of and future orientation of behaviors. Executive functions facilitate performance in other cognitive domains through organization of responses, monitoring behavior for adherence to task rules and erroneous responses, initiation and maintenance of problem solving and information search, abstract and conceptual reasoning, and creative, flexible problem solving. Executive functions are measured within the context of other abilities, such as drawing, verbal search, visual production, and memory.

Given that executive functions influence performance on other cognitive abilities, they will have an influence on intellectual functioning, albeit not to the same degree as language development. Children with very good executive functioning will approach problems in an organized manner. They will plan their response before initiating problem solving. They will actively learn from experience and alter their behavior if they do make an error. Children with poor executive functioning will perform tests haphazardly, making impulsive responses, often repeating mistakes over and over again. They may lose time bonuses or points due to careless, inattentive mistakes, or because their approach to the problem is trial and error rather than systematic, planned, and organized. Executive impairments may produce difficulty initiating behavior or produce poor persistence because they do not know how to search for novel solutions to problems.

The previous chapter described a detailed list of executive skills. This chapter discusses specific tests that measure these skills. Data illustrating the relationship between executive functioning and intellectual test scores are presented for some measures. Clinical groups with potential deficits in executive functioning are also reviewed.

WHEN TO USE EXECUTIVE FUNCTIONING MEASURES

Psychosocial History and Prereferral Observations

The symptoms of Attention Deficit Disorder (ADD) are hypothesized to represent the manifestation of underlying deficits in executive functioning (for review, see Barkley, 1997, 2003). Hallmark symptoms of the disorder, such as disinhibition, poor organization, and problems maintaining consistent effort on tasks, characterize the self-regulatory processes (Barkley, 2003) demarked by the domain of executive functioning. Attention Deficit Disorder is heritable and the presence of a family history of ADD needs to be considered a risk factor in the development of this disorder (Faraone & Biederman, 1998). While ADD has been hypothesized to be a disorder of executive functioning, test results have been mixed and other developmental disorders demonstrate difficulties with executive functioning (Sergeant,

Geurts, & Oosterlaan, 2002) such as Autism (Hill, 2004), Nonverbal Learning Disability (Rourke et al., 1990), and Tourette's Syndrome (Channon, Pratt, & Robertson, 2003). Many children will not have a specific diagnosis prior to testing. Measuring executive functioning should be considered when the primary concerns of the parent or the teacher are behavioral. The behavior problems may be restricted to problems adjusting to the academic environment, such as not remaining seated or calling out during class. The behavior problems may reflect more global issues in behavioral control, such as interpersonal problems (i.e., aggression, arguing with adults, problems following directions and rules), problems regulating activity level (i.e., hyperactive, impulsivity, poor sleep skills), or poor control of emotional responses (i.e., easily angered and frustrated). Parent reports of behavioral control problems, diagnosis of ADD in the family, or the child having a diagnosis of ADD or Autistic Spectrum Disorder warrants investigation of executive functions.

Executive functioning deficits have been associated with a variety of medical conditions. A history of traumatic brain injury either inflicted intentionally (Ewing-Cobbs, Kramer, Prasad, Canales, & Louis, 1998) or occurring accidentally (Ewing-Cobbs, Fletcher, Levin, & Francis, 1997) may result in substantial cognitive impairment. Traumatic brain injury is often associated with diffuse temporal lobe and frontal lobe damage (Wilde, Hunter, Newsome, Scheibel, Bigler, Johnson, Fearing, Cleavinger, Li, Swank, Pedroza, Roberson, Bachevalier, & Levin, 2005), resulting in deficits in executive functioning (Brookshire, Levin, Song, & Zhang, 2004). Prenatal exposure to alcohol with or without a diagnosis of Fetal Alcohol Syndrome affects the development of executive functioning in children (Mattson, Goodman, Caine, Delis, & Riley, 1999). Epilepsy may also produce deficits in executive functioning (Fastenau, Shen, Dunn, Perkins, Hermann, & Austin, 2004). Metabolic disorders, such as phenylketonuria, may (Antshel & Waisbren, 2003) or may not (Channon, German, Cassina, & Lee, 2004) be associated with deficits in executive function, but such a medical history of a metabolic disorder warrants an investigation of these skills. Obtaining the child's medical information prior to initiating testing can provide valuable information regarding potential deficits in executive functioning (for a comprehensive review, see Powell & Voeller, 2004).

Explicit information regarding the probability that an executive functioning impairment exists prior to initiating testing may not exist. Referral information, such as the presence of significant behavioral dyscontrol, impulsivity, emotional outbursts, problems following rules or following instructions without concurrent delays in language development, and inconsistency in academic progress or other cognitive function (i.e., memory), warrants investigation for executive function deficits. During testing, the child that appears impulsive and disorganized, performs inconsistently, or makes errors on items well within their ability range likely has difficulties with cognitive control. In most cases, there will be sufficient reasons to suspect that executive functioning impairments are present and screening for problems in this domain on a routine basis is advisable.

WISC-IV INTEGRATED CONCURRENT VALIDITY DATA

Clinical groups that have been identified as potentially exhibiting deficits in executive functioning were collected as part of the WISC-IV Integrated standardization. WISC-IV Integrated data for Attention Deficit Disorder, Autistic Disorder, and traumatic brain injury groups are reviewed to determine which subtests may be influenced by deficits in executive functioning. The WISC-IV Integrated subtests are reviewed by domain: Verbal, Perceptual, Working Memory, and Processing Speed.

Clinical group data were presented previously for the verbal subtests in Table 2. Among the verbal subtests, Comprehension or Comprehension Multiple Choice was consistently one of the lower scores within the three clinical groups associated with executive functioning deficits. Additionally, Similarities Multiple Choice was lower in these groups, with the exception of the Autistic group in which Similarities was lower than Similarities Multiple Choice. By design, the multiple-choice versions pull for impulsive and overly concrete responses. These measures are an indicator of problems with accuracy of information recall and susceptibility to making false positive errors recognizing information. The differences in verbal subtest scores within a single clinical group are small, although Comprehension is much lower in the Autism group, so it is important to not overinterpret the results as purely an executive function problem. Low scores on either Comprehension or Similarities Multiple Choice warrant further investigation of executive functioning.

Clinical group data for Perceptual Reasoning Index subtests were presented previously in Table 5. Among the perceptual tasks, only the Elithorn Mazes is designed specifically to measure executive functioning. This test requires immediate spatial planning skills, ability to self-monitor performance for rule violations, and a mild degree of inhibitory control. Clinical data find that the Block Design subtest is low in the TBI sample and the Elithorn Mazes is one of the lowest scores in the Autism sample. Elithorn Mazes is performed at a similar level to Block Design in the TBI sample. Not surprisingly, the Block Design subtest has mild executive functioning effects. A systematic, organized approach to this test and the need to execute the motor component quickly and effectively can result in lower, but not impaired, scores by children with moderate executive function deficits. Elithorn Mazes appears to be sensitive to moderate to severe but not mild deficits in executive functioning. Low scores on Elithorn Mazes indicate difficulties with aspects of executive functioning and indicate that a more thorough evaluation of this domain is needed.

Data for Working Memory subtests are presented in Table 6. Results indicate that Letter–Number Sequencing is associated with disorders of executive functioning. Additionally, Spatial Span Forward is low in ADD and TBI groups. The Autism group shows a relatively flat profile of scores with the exception of the low score on Letter–Number Sequencing. Difficulties with Letter–Number Sequencing are not surprising in that it requires both working memory and cognitive flexibility. The latter skill may be accounting for the additional impairment in these groups. Spatial Span Forward is somewhat surprising but perhaps the motor execution component, like that in Block Design, creates the observed effect. Clinicians finding low scores on both of these measures can hypothesize that those executive functioning deficits may be present. In particular, the clinician will want to test the child's cognitive flexibility.

Slow processing speed is commonly observed in ADD and TBI. Low scores in this domain are not unexpected and likely do not relate directly to executive functioning impairment. The exception would be Cancellation Random, which does not provide an obvious structure to facilitate an organized effective response strategy. The results, shown in Table 7, support

TABLE 6   Clinical Group Performance on WISC-IV Integrated Working Memory subtests

Registration Measures	Attention Deficit Disorder		Autistic		Traumatic Brain Injury	
	Mean	SD	Mean	SD	Mean	SD
Digits Forward	9.0	2.6	7.7	2.6	10.2	3.1
Letter Rhyming	9.6	3.1	7.3	3.3	8.8	3.3
Letter Nonrhyming	9.3	3.1	7.0	2.9	9.3	3.3
Spatial Span Forward	7.8	2.1	7.4	2.9	8.3	2.7
Visual Span	7.9	2.8	7.1	3.5	9.5	3.1
Working Memory Measures						
Digits Backward	8.8	2.6	7.2	3.5	9.6	2.8
Letter-Number Sequencing	7.8	3.6	5.0	3.6	8.1	4.0
Letter-Number Embedded Words	8.9	2.7	6.7	2.3	8.7	3.3
Spatial Span Backward	8.4	2.7	7.1	5.2	9.4	3.4
Arithmetic	8.2	2.6	7.4	4.0	8.8	2.8
Arithmetic Process Approach A	8.6	2.4	6.9	3.3	9.4	3.1
Arithmetic Process Approach B	8.3	2.8	6.2	3.1	8.9	2.9
Written Arithmetic	8.6	2.6	6.5	3.4	9.3	3.2

TABLE 7   Clinical Group Performance on WISC-IV Integrated Processing Speed subtests

	Attention Deficit Disorder		Autistic		Traumatic Brain Injury	
	Mean	SD	Mean	SD	Mean	SD
Coding	7.5	2.3	4.0	3.5	6.9	3.0
Coding Copy	7.6	2.7	4.0	3.0	6.9	3.5
Symbol Search	8.7	3.0	4.7	3.6	6.8	3.1
Cancellation Random	8.8	3.2	6.8	3.6	7.9	3.4
Cancellation Structured	9.7	3.1	7.4	3.5	7.8	4.3

Note: Data are based on listwise deletion of cases and will vary from published scores for these groups: ADD (n = 52), Autistic Disorder (N = 14), Traumatic Brain Injury (n = 36). *Wechsler Intelligence Scale for Children – Fourth Edition Integrated.* Copyright © 2004 by Harcourt Assessment, Inc. Reproduced with permission. All rights reserved.

the general processing speed deficit in these disorders. The Cancellation tasks are much easier than the standard Processing Speed subtests. Among the two forms of Cancellation, the random condition was associated with lower performance in the clinical groups.

Executive functioning impairments will affect performance on WISC-IV Integrated subtests to a varying degree. When testing children with potential deficits in executive functioning, specific core subtests, including Comprehension, Similarities, Block Design, and Letter–Number Sequencing, are impacted more than other subtests. This is not to say that the same executive problems are causing these scores to be lower but they can serve as a marker for further investigation.

In addition to identifying subtests that are affected in children with executive functioning deficits, it is helpful to compare performance on measures of executive functioning with WISC-IV Integrated subtest performance. Knowing how or if specific subtests are related to executive function measures will elucidate the types of problems that affect WISC-IV Integrated subtest performance. As part of the WISC-IV Integrated standardization, the D-KEFS was administered to children suffering a traumatic brain injury.

Delis–Kaplan Executive Functioning System

The D-KEFS provides multiple measures of executive functioning. The D-KEFS tests used in this study are the Trail-Making Test, Verbal Fluency, Design Fluency, Color–Word Interference Test, Sorting Test, and the Tower Test. These tests measure components of executive functioning, including behavioral productivity, cognitive flexibility, inhibitory control, maintenance of cognitive set, self-monitoring, planning, and abstract reasoning. The tests measure executive functioning using primarily verbal or visual stimuli or a combination of visual and verbal stimuli. The D-KEFS subtests that are based primarily on verbal responding are Verbal Fluency, Color–Word Interference, and the Sorting Test. Subtests based primarily on visual–perceptual processes are the Trail-Making Test, Design Fluency, and Tower Test.

The Trail-Making Test is composed of five trials. In the first trial, the child is asked to scan the page and mark all the number "3's." This is a simple measure of visual scanning to ensure that the child is able to search the whole visual field. The second trial requires the child to draw a line from numbers 1 to 16 in consecutive order. This determines if the child is able to sequence numbers correctly. The third trial requires the child to connect letters a–p in consecutive order. This allows the examiner to be certain the child has automatized letter knowledge sufficiently to complete the next trial. The fourth trial measures cognitive flexibility at the stimulus level. The child must switch back and forth connecting the numbers and letters in their proper sequence. The task requires mental tracking and the ability to switch between stimulus types. The fifth trial requires the child to follow a path that is equivalent in length and complexity as trial 4 but has no cognitive demands. This is a simple speed check. For the purposes of the chapter, only data on trials 2, 3, and 4 are presented.

The Verbal Fluency test is composed of three trials. In the first trial the examinee must say as many words as they can think of that start with specific letters. In the second trial the examinee says as many words as they can from a specific category (e.g., animals). Finally, the examinee is asked to switch between categories (e.g., fruits and furniture) in the last trial. Total scores reflect the number of words that were stated correctly by the examinee. The set loss score reflects the number of words the examinee said that were errors on that task (e.g., saying ear for "A" words). The repetition score is the number of words the examinee said more than one time (e.g., dog, cat, dog). This task measures verbal productivity to a letter (phonological search) or category cue (semantic search) and cognitive flexibility (category switching). Error scores reflect the examinee's capacity to monitor their own behavior for rule violations and repetitiveness.

The Design Fluency subtest is the visual analog to the Verbal Fluency subtest. In Design Fluency, the child must draw as many unique designs as possible in 1 minute following very specific rules (i.e., use straight lines, must touch another line at a dot, must use four lines, must connect only filled dots or empty dots). The subtest also has a switching condition in which the child must switch back and forth between filled and empty dots. The test measures behavioral productivity in the visual domain. The test also measures cognitive flexibility at the stimulus level (i.e., monitor their switching behavior) and cognitive control (i.e., error scores measure self-monitoring for adherence to task rules and repeated behaviors).

The Color–Word Interference task measures inhibitory control, mental flexibility, and cognitive control for rapid visual–verbal processing. The first two trials are color naming and word reading speed. The third trial measures inhibition, and the fourth trial measures inhibition and switching. Error scores are the total number of incorrectly stated items on the third and fourth trials and provide a good indication of cognitive control and inhibitory control.

The Sorting Test has elements of verbal and visual–perceptual processing embedded in the test. This test measures productivity, conceptual reasoning, abstract thinking, ability to monitor and describe one's own problem solving, mental flexibility, and cognitive control. There are over 30 normed variables for this test; a selected subset of those is presented here. These scores measure production, accuracy, and description errors. There are two conditions: a self-sorting (free sort condition) in which the examinee sorts the cards and describes their rationale for the sort, and a sort recognition condition in which they have to figure out why the examiner sorted the cards in a specific way. Error scores indicate the degree to which the examinee follows the task rules but also to a degree that their verbal descriptions actually match their behavior.

The Tower Test is a measure of immediate spatial planning and self-monitoring. The child must move disks from one peg to another until their tower matches the picture in the stimulus book. In order to complete the task, the child must move away from the final solution in order to complete the design. The test also measures the efficiency of problem solving and the ability to follow task rules.

Executive Functioning and Verbal Comprehension

It was observed previously that some of the Verbal Comprehension subtests were affected by executive functioning deficits more than others. This section analyzes the relationship between executive functioning measures and verbal subtests. Correlation statistics for D-KEFS and WISC-IV Integrated verbal subtests are presented in Table 8.

The Verbal Comprehension Index is related significantly to productivity for letter and category fluency. It is also associated significantly with control/accuracy (error scores) of verbal production. Nearly all the verbal subtests were associated with general verbal productivity, whereas cognitive control over verbal productivity related to Vocabulary, Similarities, and Word Reasoning. Rapid word reading was associated with performance on the Similarities Multiple-Choice test; otherwise, lower level cognitive skills were unrelated to verbal intellectual functioning. The ability to complete the inhibitory and inhibitory-switching tasks quickly was not related to verbal ability either. Cognitive control (Color–Word Interference Test error scores) was associated with overall verbal skills (e.g., Verbal Comprehension Index) for both inhibitory and switching tasks. Similarities, Comprehen-

TABLE 8 Correlations for DKEFS and WISC-IV Integrated Verbal Comprehension Subtests in Children with Open and Closed Head Injury

	Trail Making Test			Verbal Fluency				
	Number Sequencing	Letter Sequencing	Number-Letter Switching	Letter Fluency	Category Fluency	Category Switching	Percent Set-Loss Errors	Percent Repeated Responses
WISC-IV Integrated Verbal Subtests/Index								
Vocabulary	0.03	0.26	0.01	0.53	0.61	0.38	0.54	0.24
Vocabulary Multiple Choice	0.06	0.33	−0.01	0.50	0.50	0.41	0.65	0.33
Picture Vocabulary	0.15	0.24	−0.06	0.68	0.66	0.36	0.60	0.33
Similarities	0.01	0.28	0.00	0.65	0.61	0.38	0.45	0.06
Similarities Multiple Choice	0.07	0.28	0.04	0.51	0.37	0.38	0.53	0.36
Comprehension	0.18	0.31	0.17	0.72	0.68	0.31	0.38	0.26
Comprehension Multiple Choice	−0.06	0.08	−0.14	0.46	0.61	0.37	0.31	0.27
Information	−0.05	0.16	−0.04	0.37	0.63	0.35	0.37	0.23
Information Multiple Choice	−0.09	0.16	−0.08	0.35	0.65	0.38	0.30	0.15
Word Reasoning	0.22	0.37	0.05	0.69	0.72	0.47	0.45	0.10
Verbal Comprehension Index	0.06	0.31	0.05	0.68	0.69	0.39	0.50	0.18

(Continues)

TABLE 8 (Continued)

	Design Fluency					Color-Word Interference					
	Total Designs	Switching Designs	Set Loss Errors	Repeated Responses	Accuracy	Color Patch naming	Word Reading	Inhibition	Inhibition-Switching	Inhibition Errors	Inhibition-Switching Errors
WISC-IV Integrated Verbal Subtests/Index											
Vocabulary	0.15	0.20	0.36	−0.04	0.36	0.07	0.24	0.06	0.24	0.40	0.39
Vocabulary Multiple Choice	0.08	0.26	0.34	−0.06	0.36	−0.19	0.20	−0.14	0.14	0.11	0.25
Picture Vocabulary	0.25	0.36	0.20	−0.13	0.28	−0.01	0.34	−0.04	0.34	0.39	**0.45**
Similarities	0.14	0.22	0.18	−0.03	0.21	0.03	0.36	0.09	0.32	**0.41**	**0.55**
Similarities Multiple Choice	0.27	0.20	0.01	0.02	0.23	0.03	**0.50**	0.10	0.16	0.21	**0.47**
Comprehension	0.33	0.34	0.17	−0.13	0.27	0.11	0.16	0.18	0.28	**0.47**	0.35
Comprehension Multiple Choice	0.12	0.16	0.02	−0.01	0.07	0.22	0.25	0.33	0.12	0.31	**0.43**
Information	−0.09	0.03	0.02	0.09	0.13	0.13	0.05	0.22	0.16	0.34	0.28
Information Multiple Choice	0.06	0.18	0.27	−0.10	0.14	0.28	0.14	0.28	0.14	0.24	0.31
Word Reasoning	0.20	0.27	0.08	−0.23	0.05	0.00	0.16	0.09	0.19	0.28	0.34
Verbal Comprehension Index	0.21	0.27	0.27	−0.06	0.32	0.07	0.29	0.10	0.31	**0.46**	**0.49**

(Continues)

TABLE 8 (Continued)

	Tower Test			Sorting Test					
WISC-IV Integrated Verbal Subtests/Index	Total	Move Accuracy	Rule Violations	Free Sorts	Free Sort Description	Recognition Descriptions	Sorting Accuracy	Free Description Errors	Recognition Errors
Vocabulary	0.26	-0.07	0.25	**0.50**	**0.51**	**0.42**	-0.10	-0.20	0.29
Vocabulary Multiple Choice	0.29	0.01	0.06	0.37	0.39	**0.42**	-0.02	-0.05	0.34
Picture Vocabulary	0.27	-0.08	0.26	**0.55**	**0.58**	**0.57**	0.09	-0.13	**0.42**
Similarities	0.19	-0.17	0.11	**0.59**	**0.62**	**0.66**	0.21	0.14	**0.48**
Similarities Multiple Choice	-0.01	-0.09	-0.03	0.28	0.35	**0.59**	0.28	0.14	0.35
Comprehension	0.21	-0.20	0.32	**0.44**	**0.51**	**0.47**	-0.17	-0.22	0.32
Comprehension Multiple Choice	0.17	-0.15	-0.02	**0.54**	**0.58**	**0.63**	0.17	0.02	0.39
Information	0.21	-0.11	0.15	**0.41**	0.39	0.32	-0.22	-0.21	0.27
Information Multiple Choice	0.17	-0.07	0.12	**0.67**	**0.67**	**0.48**	0.11	-0.14	0.29
Word Reasoning	0.28	-0.15	0.09	**0.48**	**0.53**	**0.58**	0.02	-0.14	0.37
Verbal Comprehension Index	0.22	-0.16	0.25	**0.56**	**0.59**	**0.57**	0.00	-0.07	**0.41**

Note: n = 24-26, based on collapsed open and closed head injury group with listwise deletion of cases. Correlations in bold are statistically significant. *Wechsler Intelligence Scale for Children – Fourth Edition Integrated.* Copyright © 2004 by Harcourt Assessment, Inc. Reproduced with permission. All rights reserved.

sion, and Picture Vocabulary were associated with the cognitive control measures. This result indicates that impulsive responding (self-corrected or not self-corrected) may result in lower scores on some verbal ability measures, particularly Similarities.

Nearly all verbal subtests were correlated significantly with the examinee's total sorting for both free and recognition conditions. The sorting accuracy and free sorting description errors were not associated with verbal intellectual functioning. Recognition of incorrect responses was associated significantly with Similarities and Picture Vocabulary, indicating the ability to self-monitor and control verbalization when trying to figure out how objects relate to one another.

Executive control and self-monitoring of behavior during verbal tasks relate to performance on WISC-IV verbal subtests. In all probability, these skills have a reciprocal influence on one another. Children with better word knowledge and verbal intellectual skills likely have better verbal production, and executive functioning influences verbal intellectual skills. Verbal productivity is particularly salient to verbal intellectual functioning. The inability to initiate and maintain an active mental search for verbal information and to produce even simple verbal output (e.g., single words) predicts verbal intellectual performance. Inhibitory control and conversely impulsivity, particularly when additional switching demands are added, are associated with performance on aspects of verbal intellectual functioning. Similarities, Comprehension, Similarities Multiple Choice, Comprehension Multiple Choice, and Picture Vocabulary are the most susceptible to impulsive responding. Self-monitoring of verbal productions for correctness (e.g., following task rules) was related to performance on all Vocabulary and Similarities subtests as well as Word Reasoning. Monitoring for errors in logic was associated with performance on Similarities and Picture Vocabulary. Overall, Similarities and Picture Vocabulary performance was related to executive control functions more than other WISC-IV Integrated verbal subtests.

Executive Functioning and Perceptual Reasoning Domain

Selected tests from the D-KEFS administered to the head injury sample were correlated with the WISC-IV Integrated Perceptual Reasoning subtests. These tests measure components of executive functioning, including behavioral productivity, cognitive flexibility, inhibitory control, ability to maintain cognitive set, self-monitoring, and abstract reasoning. The correlations are presented in Table 9.

The Tower Test exhibited an unexpected relationship with the WISC-IV Integrated subtests. The move accuracy variable was correlated negatively with the Perceptual Reasoning Index, Picture Concepts, and Block Design No Time Bonus. High scores on the move accuracy variable do not neces-

TABLE 9 Correlations for D-KEFS and WISC-IV Integrated Perceptual Reasoning Subtests in Children with Open and Closed Head Injury

	Trail Making Test			Verbal Fluency				
	Number Sequencing	Letter Sequencing	Number-Letter Switching	Letter Fluency	Category Fluency	Category Switching	Percent Set-Loss Errors	Percent Repeated Responses
WISC-IV Integrated Verbal Subtests/Index								
Block Design	**0.42**	0.25	0.30	**0.47**	**0.39**	0.35	0.33	0.28
Block Design No Time Bonus	0.34	0.21	0.22	**0.51**	**0.40**	0.38	0.36	0.24
Block Design Multiple Choice	0.18	0.07	0.23	**0.44**	0.35	0.27	0.16	0.17
Block Design Multiple Choice No Time Bonus	0.12	−0.05	0.20	0.17	0.09	0.15	0.04	0.21
Matrix Reasoning	0.14	0.27	0.13	**0.49**	**0.39**	0.29	**0.45**	0.34
Picture Concepts	0.25	0.35	0.03	**0.47**	0.21	0.27	**0.45**	0.14
Picture Completion	0.13	0.14	0.24	**0.66**	**0.66**	0.38	0.23	0.18
Elithorn Mazes	0.39	0.13	0.11	0.37	**0.48**	0.36	**0.40**	**0.49**
Elithorn Mazes No Time Bonus	0.32	0.09	0.08	0.25	0.33	0.24	0.34	**0.44**
Perceptual Reasoning Index	0.32	0.38	0.17	**0.59**	**0.39**	0.37	**0.53**	0.31

(Continues)

TABLE 9 (Continued)

	Design Fluency					Color-Word Interference					
	Total Designs	Switching Designs	Set-Loss Errors	Repeated Responses	Accuracy	Color Patch Naming	Word Reading	Inhibition	Inhibition Switching	Inhibition-Errors	Inhibition-Switching Errors
WISC-IV Integrated Verbal Subtests/Index											
Block Design	0.29	0.28	0.00	0.17	0.26	0.35	0.26	0.43	0.38	0.51	0.43
Block Design No Time Bonus	0.20	0.23	0.09	0.29	0.34	0.27	0.27	0.33	0.38	0.42	0.48
Block Design Multiple Choice	0.22	0.14	−0.22	0.30	0.21	0.11	0.19	0.41	0.34	0.34	0.42
Block Design Multiple Choice No Time Bonus	−0.04	−0.20	−0.27	0.21	0.01	0.25	0.09	0.25	0.34	−0.02	0.34
Matrix Reasoning	0.28	0.17	−0.09	−0.05	0.09	0.22	0.32	0.24	0.13	0.17	0.41
Picture Concepts	0.37	0.33	0.14	0.04	0.17	0.19	0.45	0.02	0.32	0.33	0.53
Picture Completion	0.12	0.23	−0.13	0.21	0.13	0.28	0.19	0.40	0.32	0.43	0.32
Elithorn Mazes	0.35	0.18	−0.12	0.05	0.16	0.44	0.57	0.30	0.64	0.47	0.77
Elithorn Mazes No Time Bonus	0.36	0.09	−0.20	−0.07	0.04	0.49	0.50	0.43	0.57	0.51	0.77
Perceptual Reasoning Index	0.40	0.33	0.04	0.06	0.21	0.30	0.46	0.25	0.34	0.40	0.58

(Continues)

TABLE 9 *(Continued)*

	Tower Test			Sorting Test					
	Total	Move Accuracy	Rule Violations	Free Sorts	Free Sort Description	Recognition Descriptions	Sorting Accuracy	Free Description Errors	Recognition Errors
WISC-IV Integrated Verbal Subtests/Index									
Block Design	0.05	−0.38	0.28	**0.40**	**0.42**	0.34	0.27	0.01	0.21
Block Design No Time Bonus	0.03	**−0.46**	0.17	**0.39**	**0.41**	**0.42**	0.32	0.08	0.26
Block Design Multiple Choice	−0.02	−0.27	0.03	0.05	0.14	0.34	0.10	0.17	0.15
Block Design Multiple Choice No Time Bonus	−0.12	−0.24	−0.23	−0.07	−0.02	0.21	−0.06	0.04	−0.04
Matrix Reasoning	−0.01	−0.26	0.05	0.30	0.35	**0.56**	0.28	−0.02	0.29
Picture Concepts	−0.20	**−0.44**	0.04	**0.46**	**0.53**	**0.60**	**0.61**	0.37	**0.56**
Picture Completion	0.36	−0.38	0.30	0.36	**0.39**	**0.39**	0.00	0.03	0.16
Elithorn Mazes	0.14	−0.38	0.27	0.38	**0.43**	**0.64**	0.36	0.28	**0.62**
Elithorn Mazes No Time Bonus	0.06	−0.25	0.25	0.35	**0.42**	**0.58**	**0.41**	0.34	**0.61**
Perceptual Reasoning Index	−0.10	**−0.46**	0.13	**0.49**	**0.55**	**0.66**	**0.53**	0.20	**0.49**

Note: n = 24–26, based on collapsed open and closed head injury group with listwise deletion of cases. *Wechsler Intelligence Scale for Children – Fourth Edition Integrated.* Copyright © 2004 by Harcourt Assessment, Inc. Reproduced with permission. All rights reserved.

sarily indicate superior performance but reflect poor task persistence. Very high scores indicate a lack of sustained effort over time.

Subtests associated with Verbal domain subtests were also significantly related to the WISC-IV Integrated visual–perceptual subtests. On verbal fluency measures, Picture Completion correlated the highest with verbal productivity. Matrix Reasoning, Picture Concepts and Elithorn Mazes related to executive control of verbal search (set maintenance, inhibitory control, self-monitoring for erroneous and repetitive responses). On the Color–Word Interference Test, Elithorn Mazes displayed the highest correlations across measures with the strongest association with inhibition and inhibition/switching errors. These are important cognitive control measures indicating that Elithorn Mazes measures aspects of executive functioning related to the control of automatic responses and rapid switching of cognitive sets. Block Design, Matrix Reasoning, and Picture Concepts had a moderate relationship with cognitive control during inhibition and switching, suggesting that a weakness in complex inhibitory control may affect performance on these tasks.

The Sorting Test has elements of both verbal and visual–perceptual processing embedded within the test. This test measures productivity, conceptual reasoning, abstract thinking, ability to monitor and describe one's own problem solving, mental flexibility, and cognitive control. Picture Concepts and Elithorn Mazes had the highest correlations with the Sorting Test. Both subtests related to the ability to create and explain conceptual relationships and the ability to inhibit incorrect responses.

These results indicate that purely executive functioning on visual–perceptual tasks did not correlate strongly with performance on the WISC-IV Integrated Perceptual subtests. These subtests are associated with an ability to generate words, concepts, and relationships between objects and inhibitory control over behavior. Impulsive, inaccurate, and inattentive children would be expected to obtain lower but not necessarily impaired scores on WISC-IV Integrated subtests. Children who give up easily when confronted with a challenging task would also be expected to have lower scores on the Perceptual-Reasoning subtests.

Executive Functioning and Working Memory

Correlations for the D-KEFS with WISC-IV Integrated Working Memory subtests are presented in Table 10. The Trail-Making Test had low correlations with all the WISC-IV Integrated Working Memory subtests. The Design Fluency total score was associated with a better Spatial Span. In this case, a better spatial working memory probably helps with generating novel designs. The Design Fluency accuracy score, a measure of cognitive control and self-monitoring, was correlated significantly with the Arithmetic

TABLE 10 Correlation Statistics for D-KEFS and WISC-IV Integrated Working Memory Subtests in Children with Open and Closed Head Injury

	Trail Making Test			Verbal Fluency				
	Number Sequencing	Letter Sequencing	Number-Letter Switching	Letter Fluency	Category Fluency	Category Switching	Percent Set-Loss Errors	Percent Repeated Responses
Registration Measures								
Digits Forward	0.34	**0.43**	0.22	0.28	0.26	**0.39**	**0.59**	0.35
Letter Rhyming	−0.09	0.08	−0.01	0.19	**0.44**	**0.47**	0.37	0.21
Letter Nonrhyming	0.12	0.30	0.11	0.24	0.34	**0.45**	**0.45**	0.27
Spatial Span Forward	0.31	0.19	0.26	**0.41**	**0.60**	0.29	0.36	0.26
Visual Span	0.16	0.17	0.04	0.06	0.01	0.25	0.23	0.30
Working Memory Measures								
Digits Backward	0.09	0.34	0.07	**0.55**	**0.52**	0.31	**0.58**	0.28
Letter-Number Sequencing	−0.14	0.02	0.01	**0.40**	**0.49**	0.37	0.38	0.19
Letter-Number Embedded Words	0.03	0.29	0.13	**0.50**	**0.56**	0.37	**0.44**	0.10
Spatial Span Backward	0.17	0.01	0.07	0.26	0.30	−0.11	0.26	0.25
Arithmetic	−0.02	0.13	0.07	**0.39**	**0.53**	**0.41**	**0.42**	0.30
Arithmetic Process Approach A	0.13	0.20	0.22	**0.52**	**0.57**	0.37	**0.56**	**0.53**
Arithmetic Process Approach B	0.04	0.22	0.21	**0.47**	**0.57**	0.32	**0.61**	**0.52**
Written Arithmetic	0.11	0.15	0.10	0.36	**0.52**	**0.43**	**0.43**	0.37

(*Continues*)

TABLE 10 (Continued)

	Design Fluency					Color-Word Interference					
	Total Designs	Switching Designs	Set Loss Errors	Repeated Responses	Accuracy	Color Patch naming	Word Reading	Inhibition	Inhibition-Switching	Inhibition Errors	Inhibition-Switching Errors
Registration Measures											
Digits Forward	0.14	0.33	0.11	−0.09	0.19	−0.06	0.08	−0.06	−0.03	−0.04	0.10
Letter Rhyming	0.09	0.38	0.33	0.10	0.36	0.24	0.17	0.16	0.10	0.02	0.21
Letter Nonrhyming	0.20	0.36	0.36	0.03	0.30	0.27	0.39	0.28	0.13	0.16	0.24
Spatial Span Forward	**0.63**	**0.69**	0.26	−0.19	0.34	0.33	0.33	0.36	**0.57**	**0.48**	**0.51**
Visual Span	0.15	0.16	−0.23	−0.07	−0.19	0.33	0.28	0.28	0.03	−0.06	0.11
Working Memory Measures											
Digits Backward	0.22	0.37	0.18	−0.06	0.28	−0.10	0.12	0.28	0.09	0.38	0.27
Letter-Number Sequencing	0.11	0.13	0.14	0.19	0.32	0.38	**0.40**	0.36	0.39	**0.58**	**0.52**
Letter-Number Embedded Words	0.02	0.21	0.27	0.20	0.33	0.22	0.18	0.37	0.20	0.31	0.37
Spatial Span Backward	**0.44**	**0.50**	0.23	−0.24	0.26	0.02	−0.09	−0.06	0.20	0.29	0.23
Arithmetic	0.08	0.23	0.22	0.20	0.36	0.31	0.25	**0.49**	0.29	0.38	**0.45**
Arithmetic Process Approach A	0.26	0.33	0.26	0.06	**0.46**	0.26	0.22	**0.40**	0.31	**0.49**	**0.47**
Arithmetic Process Approach B	0.25	0.36	0.33	0.08	**0.51**	0.26	0.27	0.36	0.28	**0.50**	**0.51**
Written Arithmetic	0.34	0.29	**0.40**	−0.03	**0.41**	0.39	0.27	**0.44**	0.28	**0.43**	**0.40**

(Continues)

TABLE 10 (Continued)

	Tower Test			Sorting Test					
	Total	Move Accuracy	Rule Violations	Free Sorts	Free Sort Description	Recognition Descriptions	Sorting Accuracy	Free Description Errors	Recognition Errors
Registration Measures									
Digits Forward	0.13	−0.11	−0.07	0.15	0.19	0.25	0.27	0.21	0.23
Letter Rhyming	0.14	−0.12	0.21	0.22	0.25	0.26	**0.40**	**0.48**	0.27
Letter Nonrhyming	0.22	0.01	0.04	**0.44**	**0.46**	0.34	0.36	0.35	0.19
Spatial Span Forward	0.27	−0.18	**0.56**	0.26	0.37	**0.40**	0.22	0.42	**0.47**
Visual Span	−0.16	0.03	−0.23	0.22	0.28	0.26	0.38	0.19	0.01
Working Memory Measures									
Digits Backward	0.34	−0.04	0.14	**0.42**	**0.47**	**0.50**	0.13	−0.03	**0.40**
Letter-Number Sequencing	0.37	−0.06	**0.41**	**0.44**	**0.45**	**0.49**	0.24	0.36	0.33
Letter-Number Embedded Words	0.22	−0.30	0.12	**0.47**	**0.46**	**0.42**	0.17	0.00	0.19
Spatial Span Backward	0.16	−0.17	**0.46**	−0.03	0.04	0.01	−0.19	−0.18	0.06
Arithmetic	0.34	−0.17	0.16	**0.58**	**0.59**	**0.59**	0.39	0.27	0.38
Arithmetic Process Approach A	**0.43**	−0.23	0.28	**0.55**	**0.59**	**0.67**	0.24	0.14	**0.51**
Arithmetic Process Approach B	**0.43**	−0.27	0.37	**0.53**	**0.55**	**0.65**	0.23	0.12	**0.53**
Written Arithmetic	0.27	−0.09	0.38	**0.49**	**0.53**	**0.41**	0.22	0.05	0.29

Note: n = 24–26, based on collapsed open and closed head injury group with listwise deletion of cases. Correlations in bold are statistically significant. *Wechsler Intelligence Scale for Children – Fourth Edition Integrated.* Copyright © 2004 by Harcourt Assessment, Inc. Reproduced with permission. All rights reserved.

Process Approach and Written Arithmetic. Having good executive control appears to help performance on math tasks not heavily affected by working memory demands. On the Tower Test, the total score was related to the Arithmetic Process Approach, indicating that planning and an ability to solve visual–spatial tasks affect math performance. Cognitive control (rule violations) was associated with Letter–Number Sequencing and Spatial Span.

Verbal D-KEFS subtests were associated with performance on measures of auditory working memory. It is likely that children with better auditory working memory are better at producing more words than those with poor auditory working memory. However, cognitive control (set-loss errors) was associated with all of auditory working memory subtests with the exception of Letter–Number Sequencing. Children with poorly controlled linguistic production are likely to do poorly on tasks requiring the verbal recall of information. This relates to self-monitoring aspects of auditory functioning, which means that the child is accurately keeping track of his or her own verbal behaviors. Measures of inhibitory control (color–word errors) were associated with Spatial Span Forward and Letter–Number Sequencing. These WISC-IV Integrated Working Memory measures were by far the most sensitive to the presence of any of the clinical disorders, and perhaps issues related to inhibitory control underlie this finding. Subtests requiring accurate math skills also relate to behavioral control mechanisms.

The Sorting Test correlated moderately with most working memory tasks. This test requires good working memory skills to complete as the child must keep track of the different sorts they have made and they need to mentally analyze and compare ideas. The cognitive control measures on this task were associated with Arithmetic Process Approach subtests, Letter Span Rhyming, Spatial Span Forward, and Digit Span Backward.

There is a high probability of a reciprocal relationship between executive functioning and working memory. However, cognitive control factors such as self-monitoring behavior for adherence to task rules and inhibitory control influence performance on working memory tasks. When low scores on Working Memory subtests occur, the clinician should consider examinee executive functions to determine the impact of poor cognitive control on WISC-IV Integrated performance.

Executive Functioning and Processing Speed Domain

Correlations between D-KEFS and Processing Speed subtests are presented in Table 11. In general, there is little to no correlation between Processing Speed measures and executive functioning. The one exception is Symbol Search. This subtest relates to multiple measures of cognitive flexibility, visual productivity, and cognitive control. Unexpected low scores on

TABLE 11   Correlations for D-KEFS and WISC-IV Integrated Processing Speed in Children with Open and Closed Head Injury

	Trail Making Test			Verbal Fluency				
	Number Sequencing	Letter Sequencing	Number-Letter Switching	Letter Fluency	Category Fluency	Category Switching	Percent Set-Loss Errors	Percent Repeated Responses
Coding	0.66	0.43	0.25	0.35	0.38	0.33	0.44	0.22
Coding Copy	0.51	0.19	0.16	0.04	0.13	0.14	0.09	0.13
Symbol Search	0.58	0.32	0.42	0.35	0.55	0.41	0.24	0.32
Cancellation Random	0.59	0.49	0.32	0.25	0.26	0.39	0.01	0.00
Cancellation Structured	0.55	0.39	0.25	0.03	0.12	0.30	0.11	0.16

	Design Fluency					Color-Word Interference					
	Total Designs	Switching Designs	Set-Loss Errors	Repeated Responses	Accuracy	Color Patch Naming	Word Reading	Inhibition	Inhibition-Switching	Inhibition Errors	Inhibition-Switching Errors
Coding	0.47	0.39	0.01	−0.29	0.08	0.07	0.20	−0.15	0.19	0.19	0.27
Coding Copy	0.55	0.28	0.07	−0.60	−0.11	0.25	0.17	−0.22	0.11	−0.02	0.12
Symbol Search	0.52	0.50	0.00	−0.29	0.05	0.34	0.31	0.15	0.30	0.27	0.31
Cancellation Random	0.34	0.11	−0.15	−0.29	−0.18	0.22	0.30	−0.05	0.22	−0.01	0.22
Cancellation Structured	0.37	0.29	0.02	−0.26	−0.02	0.27	0.37	0.08	0.33	0.07	0.26

(Continues)

TABLE 11 *(Continued)*

	Tower Test			Sorting Test					
	Total	Move Accuracy	Rule Violations	Free Sorts	Free Sort Description	Recognition Descriptions	Sorting Accuracy	Free Description Errors	Recognition Errors
Coding	−0.09	−0.37	0.37	0.07	0.09	0.15	0.19	−0.16	0.28
Coding Copy	−0.17	−0.02	0.26	0.00	0.02	0.12	0.09	−0.19	0.05
Symbol Search	0.21	−0.36	**0.45**	0.13	0.19	0.16	0.05	0.07	0.27
Cancellation Random	−0.38	−0.26	−0.05	0.11	0.15	0.09	0.11	0.02	0.16
Cancellation Structured	−0.31	−0.12	0.23	0.12	0.16	−0.07	0.30	0.20	0.20

Note: n = 24–26, based on collapsed open and closed head injury group with listwise deletion of cases. Correlations in bold are statistically significant. *Wechsler Intelligence Scale for Children – Fourth Edition Integrated.* Copyright © 2004 by Harcourt Assessment, Inc. Reproduced with permission.

this subtest in isolation from other Processing Speed deficits could signal executive functioning problems.

An Executive Index?

Only one subtest, Elithorn Mazes, on the WISC-IV Integrated was designed specifically to assess executive functioning. However, it may be possible to generate an Executive Functioning Index that draws from each domain. The rationale for choosing a measure from each domain is to reduce the possibility that a modality-specific deficit (e.g., language impairment on VCI) causes the score to be low. The subtests should correlate with a measure of executive control and/or be sensitive to disorders associated with weaknesses in executive functioning. Another criterion for choosing a subtest to be included in the Executive Index is that the subtest does not contribute to any other index.

Using these criteria, the following subtests were selected to create an Executive Functioning Index: Comprehension Multiple Choice, Elithorn Mazes, Spatial Span Forward, and Cancellation Random. The clinician is cautioned that this index is designed to provide initial evidence that the child may have difficulties with executive functioning. Additional assessment of executive functioning using tests designed specifically to measure that construct is recommended. Elithorn Mazes was not administered to children ages 6 or 7; the Executive Index may only be applied to children 8 to 16 years of age.

Correlations among the variables in the standardization sample and in the combined Attention Deficit Disorder and head injury are relatively low. This finding is not surprising, as each subtest was drawn from a different domain and that executive function measures often have low intercorrelations. The utility of the index will be how it operates in clinical samples. The composition of the index reflects an empirically keyed rather than factor-derived composite.

As part of the WISC-IV Integrated Standardization, children diagnosed with Asperger's Syndrome were administered the subtests used for the Executive Functioning Index. It would be anticipated that this group would exhibit some impairment in executive functioning and therefore serve as a cross-validation sample. The Appendix provides means and standard deviations for the WISC-IV Integrated Indexes, including the Executive Functioning Index for all the clinical groups, including Asperger's Syndrome.

These groups all demonstrate variability in functioning at the index level with the Processing Speed Index being the lowest or near the lowest score. The Executive Functioning Index was lower than Verbal Comprehension and Perceptual Reasoning in all groups. The Executive Index scores were similar to Processing Speed and Working Memory in the Autism and Asperger's groups, but had slightly less variability than Processing Speed.

In disorders associated with varying degrees of language deficiency, the Executive Functioning Index was higher than Verbal Comprehension and Processing Speed Indexes. This is initial evidence that this index may provide useful information about the child that should be followed up by a more detailed assessment on executive functioning. Reliability, standard error of measurement, norms tables, and discrepancy base rates are provided in the Appendix.

A BRIEF LIST OF EXECUTIVE FUNCTIONING MEASURES AND SKILLS ASSESSED

A large number of published tests of executive functioning exist, although few have large stratified normative samples. Executive functioning measures vary in content and method from one another. They often have low correlation with each other. It is important to recognize that measures that purport to measure similar constructs can give very different results. In the case of executive functioning, the rules of the task are very important. The more rules to follow, the greater the amount of self-monitoring and cognitive control required to complete the task. This section briefly categorizes subtests from the D-KEFS and NEPSY and other executive function measures' general categories.

1. Verbal productivity
   i. D-KEFS Verbal Fluency
   ii. NEPSY Verbal Fluency
   iii. FAS Verbal Fluency
2. Visual productivity
   i. D-KEFS Design Fluency
   ii. NEPSY Design Fluency
   iii. Ruff Figural Fluency
3. Cognitive flexibility
   i. D-KEFS Trail-Making switching
   ii. D-KEFS Design Fluency switching
   iii. D-KEFS Verbal Fluency category switching
   iv. D-KEFS Color–Word Interference switching
   v. D-KEFS Sorting Test
   vi. Wisconsin Card Sorting Test
   vii. CELF-IV Sentence Assembly
4. Inhibitory control
   i. NEPSY: Knock and Tap
   ii. NEPSY: Statue
   iii. D-KEFS Color–Word Interference
   iv. Stroop Test
   v. Go No-Go

5. Planning
   i. D-KEFS Tower Test
   ii. NEPSY Tower Test
   iii. WISC-IV Integrated Elithorn Mazes
6. Organization
   i. Rey-Osterieth Complex Figure (Berstein and Waber scoring)
   ii. California Verbal Learning Test–Children's Edition
7. Conceptual productivity
   i. D-KEFS Sorting Test
8. Abstract/Conceptual Reasoning
   i. D-KEFS Card Sorting
   ii. D-KEFS 20 Questions
   iii. D-KEFS Proverbs
   iv. Children's Category Test
9. Self-monitoring and cognitive control
   i. D-KEFS: Trail Making
   ii. D-KEFS: Verbal Fluency
   iii. D-KEFS: Design Fluency
   iv. D-KEFS: Color–Word Interference
   v. D-KEFS: Sorting Test
   vi. D-KEFS: Tower Test
   vii. California Verbal Learning Test–Children's Edition
   viii. Wisconsin Card Sorting Test

REPORTING EXECUTIVE FUNCTIONING RESULTS

A number of WISC-IV subtests are modestly affected by executive functioning deficits. One or more of these subtests may be lower than expected given the performance on other subtests within the same domain. Completing the four additional subtests required to obtain the Executive Functioning Index can provide further information about the possibility of deficits in this cognitive domain. While subtest profiling enables the clinician to make hypotheses about potential deficits in executive functioning, it cannot identify the nature of the problem or definitively identify the source of the deficits in executive functioning. Subsequently, the clinician will want to administer specific measures in this domain.

The clinician can often make an educated guess about the nature of the problem based on observational data. If the child appeared impulsive, performed tasks haphazardly, or needed to be reminded of task rules frequently, then administering tests that will assess cognitive control is indicated. By the same token, a child providing very little verbal output or sustained effort should be evaluated for impaired initiation and persistence. The most important executive measures when assessing children are cognitive control and productivity (i.e., correlate highly with many skill areas), cognitive flexibility (i.e., understand if the child will have difficulty learning from feedback and experience), and inhibition (i.e., good measure of behavioral control). It is not recommended that clinicians use cognitive referencing for determining if executive functioning deficits are present. When executive functioning deficits are severe, they will likely affect multiple domains of cognitive functioning and suppress the scores on IQ tests. The result is an attenuated comparison. More importantly, there are little data available to determine the relative frequency of such discrepancies so the clinician would not have any data on which to base such a discrepancy. For the purposes of reporting executive functioning scores, the level of performance on the test is important, but in many cases, reporting the error scores provides the most clinically relevant information.

Executive functioning should be reported by skill area (i.e., one single score cannot capture the diversity of this complex cognitive domain). The domains listed earlier are useful as a framework for reporting test results. Descriptions of performance deficits in the executive functioning domain are essential for understanding children's responses to complex social environments. Often, deficits in this domain are interpreted by others as aspects of the child's personality (e.g., poor cognitive flexibility = "always has to have his own way" or poor initiation = "he's lazy"). Careful crafting of the results may have a strong influence on how parents and staff view a child. If the problem appears cognitive, accommodations are often developed to lessen the impact of the specific deficit. If the problem is considered willful, then the child will be treated punitively.

MEMORY SKILLS

The memory skills referenced in this section refer to immediate and delayed episodic, explicit memory functioning. This is differentiated from the registration and mental manipulation skills that comprise the Working Memory domain of the WISC-IV Integrated. To some extent, working memory skills influence declarative memory functioning in that the individual must temporarily hold and operate on information while it is transferred into long-term memory stores. In particular, immediate recall conditions are influenced by working memory as some of the information presented to the examinee may be held in working memory until they respond. Despite the influence of working memory skills on memory functioning, the constructs refer to different neurocognitive systems. This section discusses the differences in memory functions and how they relate to the WISC-IV Integrated.

The decision to use specific memory measures can be more difficult to determine prior to the onset of testing. There are a number of memory batteries and individual memory measures available to the clinician. Selecting a single memory measure or a portion of a memory battery can be an effective means for screening for specific types of memory problems. The WISC-IV Integrated is a useful tool for developing specific hypotheses about memory functioning, which can be tested further using other memory tests, such as the Children's Memory Scale.

WHEN TO USE ADDITIONAL MEMORY MEASURES

The decision to use additional memory measures is more difficult to determine based on psychosocial history or behavioral reports from teachers and parents. Pure amnestic disorders are rare in children, and reports of poor memory functioning by parents and teachers often reflect difficulties with working memory and prospective memory. Forgetfulness is due to immediate mental operations, but in many of these children they remember information adequately or perhaps very well. Prospective memory is a memory difficulty associated with forgetting to do things at a future time, such as remembering that a report is due in 2 weeks. This is a memory skill but it is not assessed frequently in memory batteries. When memory problems exist, they often occur in the context of other impaired cognitive skills, such as language and executive functioning. Often times, memory problems are masked by these other difficulties or are attributed to other cognitive impairments.

Memory problems can occur in many developmental disorders. Children with developmental disorders such as specific Language Impairment and Reading Disorder can have low scores on material specific memory (i.e., verbal memory) tests (Kramer, Knee, & Delis, 2000; Shear, Tallal, & Delis, 1992). In these groups, deficits in verbal memory occur as one in a myriad of weaknesses related to language processing and verbal working memory. While co-occurring with other processing deficits, the presence of memory problems should not be dismissed. Rather, observed memory deficits probably contribute to the child's difficulty developing their knowledge base and general academic skills.

Many medical conditions result in poor memory functioning. A history of moderate to severe traumatic brain injury is associated with symptoms of memory impairment (Hooper, Alexander, Moore, Sasser, Laurent, King, Bartel, & Callahan, 2004), and memory functioning relates to academic development subsequent to TBI (Ewing-Cobbs, Barnes, Fletcher, Levin et al., 2004). Memory functioning impacts academic development in children diagnosed with temporal lobe epilepsy (Fastenau, Shen, Dunn, Perkins et al., 2004). Children receiving lobectomy surgery to control their seizures can experience decreased memory functioning (Lah, 2004). Prenatal exposure to substances of abuse, such as alcohol, impairs memory functions (Willford, Richardson, Leech, & Day, 2004). Memory functioning is susceptible to disturbance due to a number of medical, prenatal, and environmental influences.

When the psychosocial history of the child is not well known, teacher observations may be helpful, specifically, children that appear to lose knowledge after they have gained a new skill or appear to remember information only when prompted or provided a cue or perhaps have inconsistent memory functioning. An observation of "forgetfulness" can implicate a number of cognitive problems so asking more direct questions about information recall is important. Teacher reports may be insufficient for identifying memory problems so the clinician will need to consider including additional memory based observations and test results.

The WISC-IV Integrated is designed to help clinicians hypothesize about possible memory problems. In particular, the multiple-choice subtests help the clinician determine if the child has difficulty retrieving information from remote memory. There are differences between the retrieval processes measured in the WISC-IV Integrated compared to traditional memory measures. The differences are very important as they can lead to different conclusions about memory functioning. On the WISC-IV Integrated, the child is often presented with information that they have encountered previously or can use reasoning skills to derive an answer for. Memory tests rely on providing novel information to the child to determine if they can get information in and out of memory stores efficiently. They cannot rely on previous experience or reasoning to recall the information. The recognition measures on WISC-IV Integrated (i.e., multiple choice subtests) do not ask for "yes" or "no" responses like most memory recognition paradigms. Also, the level of verbal processing and response discrimination is much higher on the Integrated compared to typical memory tests.

The WISC-IV Integrated multiple-choice measures provide information about whether the child recognizes good reasoning about a specific problem or they recognize the meaning of words they are not able to recall freely. What is unknown with the WISC-IV Integrated multiple-choice versions is whether the child was ever exposed to the information and simply can't recall it on demand. Specific memory tests establish that the child is given the same exposure to new information. Their level of recall and recognition is not confounded by previous learning.

WISC-IV INTEGRATED CONCURRENT VALIDITY DATA

Because pure memory disorders are rare in children, no specific clinical groups were collected to assess the degree that memory impairment affects WISC-IV Integrated performance. The TBI group has memory difficulties in the context of other concurrent cognitive impairments. Review of their data indicates a slight benefit on the Vocabulary Multiple Choice versus standard Vocabulary but otherwise the multiple-choice versions were similar or harder than their free recall counterparts. The design of the multiple-choice subtest pulls for impulsive and concrete responses. Concurrent executive functioning deficits will affect the degree the child with memory problems will benefit from the recognition format.

While no clinical data are available to determine the degree to which memory problems impact WISC-IV Integrated performance, a small sample of children completed the entire WISC-IV Integrated and the Children's Memory Scale (CMS). These are not clinical cases but the relationship between the two measures provides initial data for hypothesizing about the effects of memory impairment on intellectual functioning.

CHILDREN'S MEMORY SCALE

The CMS (Cohen, 1997) is a battery of memory tests assessing verbal and visual memory. The test has immediate, learning, delayed, and delayed recognition trials. The design enables clinicians to determine if a child has a material specific deficit (i.e., verbal versus visual), high rate of forgetting or slow consolidation (i.e., immediate versus delayed), and encoding versus retrieval impairments (i.e., recall versus recognition). The CMS subtests are Stories, Word Pairs, Word Lists, Dot Learning, Faces, and Family Pictures. Each subtest measures a different aspect of memory functioning.

The Stories subtest requires the child to listen to and remember two stories. They recall the stories immediately after presentation and after a 20- to 30-minute delay. In the delayed recognition condition, the child is asked multiple questions about story content and must answer "yes" or "no." This subtest measures verbal memory for organized information. On Word Pairs, the child hears one word and a second word that is paired with it. Some of the pairs are related semantically and some are unrelated. This subtest measures verbal association memory. There are four learning, immediate recall, delayed free recall, and delayed recognition trials. The Word List subtest is supplemental and does not contribute to the Verbal Indexes. On Word Lists, the child hears a list of words and must repeat them. They are provided the words they did not remember in subsequent trials, which are referred to as a selective reminding paradigm. The test measures rote verbal memory. There are four learning trials, a free recall trial, a delayed free recall trial, and a delayed recognition trial. The Verbal domain has three indices: verbal immediate, verbal delayed, and delayed recognition.

The Dots subtest requires the child to memorize the location of dots on a grid. This is a visual–spatial memory task. On Dots, there are three learning trials, an immediate recall, and a delayed recall condition. The Faces subtest requires the child to learn new faces after a brief exposure and then they must be able to identify if a face is one they were asked to learn or not. The Faces subtest uses a recognition paradigm for immediate and delayed conditions. The Family Pictures subtest is a visual analog to the story memory subtest. The child sees family members in four different scenes doing various activities. The child must remember which person was in a particular location and recall what they are doing. There are immediate and delayed recall trials for this subtest. Family Pictures is a supplemental subtest and does not contribute to any of the index scores. The Visual domain has two indexes: Visual Immediate and Visual Delayed.

Data comparing Verbal Memory subtests with the Verbal Comprehension subtests are reported in Table 12. Of all the VCI subtests, Vocabulary had the largest and most frequent number of significant correlations of any measure. Picture Vocabulary was moderately correlated with memory functioning. Word Reasoning was associated with memory for conceptually integrated verbal information. The multiple-choice subtests, with the exception of Vocabulary Multiple Choice, were correlated with recognition memory and story memory. This finding supports the recognition aspect of the multiple choice subtests; however, children that have difficulty recalling large amounts of related verbal information after only a single exposure may also have problems performing the multiple-choice subtests. The finding that both recognition and free recall relate to multiple-choice subtests could be the reason why larger performance gains on these subtests were not observed in the clinical groups. The multiple-choice subtests simultaneously reduce the retrieval demands while increasing overall memory load (i.e., remembering multiple sentences from which they need to choose a correct answer). These results indicate that if a child has significant memory problems, they may have unexpectedly lower scores on Vocabulary. It may be that the development of word knowledge is dependent on a strong verbal memory system.

The visual memory measures with Perceptual Reasoning subtests are presented in Table 13. Results suggest that visual–perceptual skills and visual memory as measured by the CMS are not correlated. This may be due to the small sample of cases, due to the nature of the visual memory tasks on the CMS, or due to a low correlation between memory and visual reasoning in general.

Comparing IQ Performance to Memory Functioning

A larger sample of cases comparing the CMS and the standard administration of the WISC-IV was completed as part of the initial Standardization of the WISC-IV. WISC-IV Technical Report #5 (Drozdick, Holdnack, Rolfhus, & Weiss, 2005) provides discrepancy data for WISC-IV Indices and CMS Indices. Consistent with the findings reported here, the correlation between IQ and visual memory was low; therefore, discrepancy data are not provided for these CMS indices. This technical report can be found on the Harcourt Assessment Center Web site.

The psychologist will explore memory functioning in greater detail if a child achieves low scores on the verbal subtests. Memory problems can be pervasive, affecting encoding and retrieval of information. However, in many cases, memory problems relate to the capacity to efficiently organize information and subsequently retrieve that information on demand.

TABLE 12 CMS Verbal Index and Subtest scores with WISC-IV Integrated Verbal Subtests

WISC-IV Integrated Verbal Subtests/Index	CMS Indexes and Subtests						
	General Memory	Verbal Immediate	Verbal Delayed	Delayed Recognition	Story Immediate	Story Delayed	Story Delayed Recognition
Vocabulary	**0.50**	**0.59**	**0.66**	**0.53**	**0.58**	**0.55**	**0.53**
Vocabulary Multiple Choice	0.20	0.35	0.40	0.30	0.30	0.19	0.40
Picture Vocabulary	0.25	0.39	**0.44**	**0.49**	**0.49**	**0.50**	**0.56**
Similarities	0.29	0.23	0.25	0.38	0.38	0.34	0.34
Similarities Multiple Choice	0.28	0.34	0.31	**0.48**	**0.48**	**0.46**	0.40
Comprehension	0.27	0.25	0.25	0.33	0.33	0.34	0.35
Comprehension Multiple Choice	0.28	0.37	**0.41**	**0.44**	**0.44**	**0.50**	**0.55**
Word Reasoning	0.24	**0.42**	**0.53**	0.27	**0.52**	**0.49**	**0.42**
Verbal Comprehension Index	**0.42**	**0.42**	**0.46**	0.36	**0.51**	**0.49**	**0.50**

(*Continues*)

TABLE 12 *(Continued)*

WISC-IV Integrated Verbal Subtests/Index	Word Pairs Learning	Word Pairs Delayed	Word Pairs Delayed Recognition	Word List Learning	Word List Delayed Recall	Word List Delayed Recognition
Vocabulary	0.28	**0.56**	0.30	**0.40**	**0.43**	0.29
Vocabulary Multiple Choice	0.19	**0.49**	0.11	0.30	0.38	0.20
Picture Vocabulary	0.06	0.24	0.09	**0.46**	**0.43**	0.37
Similarities	−0.16	0.06	−0.09	0.27	0.31	0.02
Similarities Multiple Choice	−0.07	0.05	0.06	0.34	0.34	0.15
Comprehension	0.02	0.07	0.03	0.24	0.28	0.15
Comprehension Multiple Choice	0.07	0.18	0.16	0.33	0.35	0.09
Word Reasoning	0.02	0.39	0.05	0.32	**0.57**	0.32
Verbal Comprehension Index	0.06	0.27	0.09	0.37	0.40	0.16

(These indexes and subtests fall under the heading **CMS Indexes and Subtests**.)

TABLE 13   CMS Visual Index and Subtest scores with WISC-IV Integrated Perceptual Reasoning Subtests

				CMS Visual Indexes and Subtests				
	General Memory	Visual Immediate	Visual Delayed	Dots Learning	Dots Delayed	Faces Immediate	Faces Delayed	Family Pictures Immediate	Family Pictures delayed
WISC-IV Integrated Verbal Subtests/Index									
Block Design	-0.29	-0.17	-0.08	0.04	-0.16	-0.24	0.04	-0.15	-0.27
Block Design No Time Bonus	-0.32	-0.24	-0.14	-0.02	-0.20	-0.29	-0.02	-0.23	-0.36
Block Design Multiple Choice	0.13	0.03	0.02	**0.49**	-0.02	-0.31	0.06	-0.10	-0.20
Block Design Multiple Choice No Time Bonus	0.00	-0.15	-0.04	0.20	-0.05	-0.33	-0.01	-0.14	-0.41
Matrix Reasoning	0.06	-0.23	-0.21	0.06	-0.33	-0.31	0.02	-0.28	-0.32
Picture Concepts	-0.08	-0.15	0.02	0.03	-0.07	-0.17	0.12	0.12	-0.36
Picture Completion	0.13	0.07	0.11	0.11	-0.15	0.21	0.37	-0.32	-0.31
Elithorn Mazes	-0.24	-0.07	-0.11	0.34	-0.03	-0.38	-0.17	0.05	0.01
Elithorn Mazes No Time Bonus	-0.19	-0.06	-0.06	0.34	-0.05	-0.38	-0.09	0.10	-0.02

Note: n = 24. Data are based on listwise deletion of cases and will vary from published scores for these groups. *Wechsler Intelligence Scale for Children – Fourth Edition Integrated*.

The clinician can use the WISC-IV Integrated for initial hypothesizing about memory functioning by using the multiple-choice measures. It is strongly recommended that the clinician go beyond the administration of the WISC-IV Integrated to measure specific components of memory functioning.

WISC-IV RECOGNITION INDEXES

Two recognition indexes were developed for the WISC-IV Integrated to facilitate the comparison of multiple-choice versus standard verbal subtest performance. The Verbal Comprehension Index is composed of Vocabulary, Similarities, and Comprehension subtests. The first Recognition Index is composed of Vocabulary Multiple Choice, Similarities Multiple Choice, and Comprehension Multiple Choice. Having the same number of subtests in the indexes facilitates their comparison. Also, composites tend to have higher reliabilities than individual subtests, which increases the stability of the difference scores. Many clinicians will opt to use Picture Vocabulary rather than Vocabulary Multiple Choice. The second Recognition Index is derived using Picture Vocabulary instead of Vocabulary Multiple Choice.

The Appendix at the end of this chapter provides reliabilities, standard errors of measurement, scaled score to standard score conversion, confidence intervals, and directional base rates for VCI versus Recognition Indexes 1 and 2. Performance data for the clinical groups and the additional Asperger's group are presented for both Recognition Indexes in the Appendix. There are no large differences between VCI and RCI for any clinical group except the Asperger's group, which does more poorly on the recognition trials. This discrepancy is not meant to be diagnostic of a specific clinical condition, but it informs the clinician if the individual child has specific problems with retrieving their knowledge or from discriminating between response options effectively.

A BRIEF LIST OF MEMORY MEASURES AND SKILLS ASSESSED

The clinician has a variety of options for measuring memory functioning using standardized batteries. There is considerable overlap between many memory tests although variations in content and administration rules impact the skills that are being measured. For example, there are many list learning tasks, such as the California Verbal Learning Test–Children's Version, Children's Auditory Verbal Learning Test (CAVLT), NEPSY–List Learning Subtests, CMS–List learning subtest and Wide Range Assessment of Memory and Learning–List Learning subtest. The subtests vary considerably in the details of administration, such as using full reminding versus selective reminding, organization of content by semantic category, interference trials, and delayed free, cued, and recognition trials. There are more memory batteries available than can be reported here so a brief list is reviewed by category: Children's Memory Scale (Cohen, 1997), NEPSY Memory subtests (NEPSY: Korkman, Kirk, Kemp, 1997), California Verbal Learning Test–Children's Edition (CVLT: Delis, Kaplan, Kramer, & Ober, 1994), and the Wide Range Assessment of Memory and Learning–2nd edition (Adams & Sheslow, 2003).

1. Memory for organized verbal information
   i. CMS: Stories
   ii. NEPSY: Story
   iii. WRAML: Story Memory
2. Verbal-associative learning (effects of repeated exposure) and memory
   i. CMS: Word Pairs
3. Rote verbal learning (repeated exposure) and memory
   i. CMS: List Learning
   ii. CVLT-C
   iii. NEPSY: List Learning
   iv. WRAML: List Learning
4. Verbal encoding versus retrieval
   i. CMS
   ii. CVLT-C
   iii. WRAML
5. Encoding strategy and organization
   i. CVLT-C
6. Interference effects (proactive and retroactive)
   i. CVLT-C
   ii. NEPSY
7. Verbal recall, self-monitoring control/accuracy of recall, and recognition (intrusions/perseverations/false positives)
   i. CVLT-C
   ii. CMS
   iii. NEPSY
   iv. WRAML
8. Source memory errors
   i. CVLT-C
9. Visual–spatial memory and learning
   i. CMS: Dots
   ii. WRAML: Design and Picture Memory

10. Memory for faces
    i. CMS
    ii. NEPSY
11. Associative verbal–visual memory
    i. CMS: Family Pictures
    ii. WRAML: Sound Symbol
    iii. NEPSY: Memory for Names

Other domains of memory functioning exist that are not covered in the list. The most notable is prospective memory. Prospective memory is the capacity to remember to do a task in the future, such as turning in a project on a specific date or remembering to take out the trash on the correct day. The Rivermead Behavioral Memory Test for Children (Wilson, Ivani-Chalian, & Aldrich, 1991) has an item covering this skill and focuses on daily memory skills.

REPORTING MEMORY SKILLS

It is equally important to use cognitive referencing and level of performance interpretations for memory tests. In adults, it has been demonstrated that pure and severe memory impairment can exist in the absence of concurrent impairments in intelligence. In young children, this dissociation is less likely to occur to the degree observed in adults, as memory functioning is critical for the development of general knowledge in children. As knowledge is established, the potential dissociation is increased. There are a few conditions in childhood that may cause pure amnesia but hypoxic/anoxic events (e.g., near drowning, asphyxiation from carbon monoxide) should be evaluated carefully for significant memory impairment (for review, see Caine & Watson, 2000).

Memory data can be used to answer specific hypotheses raised by performance discrepancies in the WISC-IV Integrated Verbal Comprehension Index and Recognition Indexes or specific subtest differences (i.e., Vocabulary versus Picture Vocabulary). Many times, memory impairment will be observed in the same domain as intellectual impairment. Children having low scores on the Verbal Comprehension Index will similarly do poorly on verbal memory tests. This is not always the case, but in disorders that affect the Verbal Comprehension Index, poor memory skills and working memory skills for the same stimulus domain are often observed. This should not inhibit the clinician from reporting specific aspects of memory performance, as not all components of memory will be affected to the same degree.

When reporting memory scores, it is important to explicitly describe the nature of the memory deficit. Often, single scores such as a global composite will not capture the essence of the memory dysfunction. Memory skills often dissociate from one another, particularly verbal versus visual memory, so reporting a single score will often be misleading. Inconsistency in memory functioning (i.e., better performance on some memory tasks than others such as organized versus unorganized verbal information) is often tremendously helpful for parents and teachers to know. Intervention strategies to minimize memory problems can be developed based on such findings and can explain why a child appears to have a good memory for some information and poor memory for others. Inconsistent memory functioning is often attributed to attention or effort problems.

While it is important to integrate memory findings with intellectual data, it is equally important to determine the effects of executive functioning on memory. Tests that explicitly evaluate the child's ability to organize information to facilitate encoding and retrieval, allow for determination of interference effects, and illustrate self-monitoring and accuracy of recall are extremely helpful in understanding memory problems in children. Often, memory problems are caused or exacerbated by poor executive functioning. Interventions that improve strategic aspects of learning and memory can be devised for the child. Very severe problems with memory and executive functioning may result in "confabulation." The child constructs plausible responses to information requests. This can be interpreted by others as lying or oppositional behavior but true confabulation reflects significant problems in cognition.

Memory data, like executive functioning data, should also be reported separately from IQ data. Using categories, such as those presented earlier, will help structure the reporting of memory data. Structuring data in this manner facilitates the understanding of the child's difficulties and focuses behavior interpretation and intervention appropriately.

ACADEMIC ACHIEVEMENT

Academic skills such as reading, math, and writing are similar to measures of intellectual functioning in that multiple, integrated, cognitive skills are necessary to perform these tasks well. Tests of achievement, for the purpose of psychoeducational assessment, are distributed normally or nearly normally. IQ and achievement data are moderately to highly correlated with one another. In most cases, children with high IQs do equally or nearly as well on academic tests. Both intellectual and academic abilities can be improved through education; however, academic skills are taught explicitly through training and rehearsal, whereas intellectual skills often develop through implicit learning effects.

Numerous children struggle to develop competency in a particular academic domain. Some of these children will have low intellectual abilities concurrent with low academic skills, whereas others have average or even superior intellectual abilities. The cause of learning problems is still poorly understood and is the subject of much controversy and debate. It is beyond the scope of this chapter to provide a comprehensive coverage of the causes and controversies of learning disabilities. One issue in the assessment of learning disabilities in the domains of research and public policy is the use of cognitive referencing to make eligibility determinations for Special Education services. Eligibility determination and identification of relative strengths and weaknesses in cognitive functioning are two different tasks that have unfortunately become inextricably intertwined. There are very good reasons to consider both cognitive referencing and more direct assessment of academic impairment when evaluating children (see Berninger, Hart, Abbott, & Karovsky, 1992; Berninger, 2001b).

In general, considerably more is understood about Reading Disorder than specific learning for math and writing. We have proposed a method for integrating the assessment of intellectual functioning and specific cognitive indicators of reading problems in the early reading success indicator (PsychCorp, 2004). This method is reviewed later in this chapter.

PSYCHOSOCIAL HISTORY AND PREREFERRAL OBSERVATIONS

While academic skills are assessed routinely as part of a comprehensive psychoeducational assessment, the clinician often collects information regarding the child's academic development prior to initiating the assessment process. The teacher is an excellent source of information regarding the particulars of the child's academic problems. Identifying academic problems prior to testing is facilitated (i.e., more complete coverage of academic strengths and weaknesses) using a standardized checklist of academic skills such as academic competence evaluation scale (ACES; DiPerna & Elliott, 2000).

Studies focusing on the social and personal characteristics of youth with reading difficulties and their families yield important information regarding which children may be at increased risk for reading difficulties. Genetic studies indicate a complex locus for component-reading processes and subsequently may be inherited independently or in varying combinations on chromosomes 1p, 6p, and 18: rapid automatic naming (Grigorenko, Wood, Meyer, & Pauls, 2000; Grigorenko, Wood, Meyer, Pauls, Hart, & Pauls, 2001) and single-word decoding (Fisher, Francks, Marlow, MacPhie et al., 2002). A family history of reading difficulties is a risk factor for the child to have reading difficulties themselves. The highest risk for the child occurs when both parents have a history of reading difficulties. The next highest risk level is if the father but not the mother had reading difficulties (Wolff & Melngalis, 1994). When reading difficulties run in families, the children tend to display weak phonological skills (Pennington & Lefly, 2001).

Other individual and psychosocial background factors influence the probability that a child will be identified as learning disabled. Males are identified as learning disabled at a much higher rate than girls (Couthino, Oswald, &

Best, 2002; Wolff & Melngailis, 1994). Children with a history of speech-language delays or a diagnosed language disorder are at increased risk for developing reading difficulties (Aram et al., 1984; Catts et al., 2001; McArthur, Hogben, Edwards, Heath, & Menger, 2000; Scarborough, 1990). Minority youth (except Asian-American) are identified as having learning disabilities at a higher rate than Caucasian children, particularly in higher socioeconomic status school districts (Couthino et al., 2002). Exposure to violence has been associated with an increased risk for reading difficulties (Delaney-Black, Covington, Ondersma, Nordstrom-Klee et al., 2002). Early home environment and socioeconomic status influence early and late developing literacy skills (Molfese, Modglin, & Molfese, 2003). Clinicians will want to investigate reading and related reading skills in children in which there is a family history of Reading Disorder. Environmental and developmental history is important to consider in the decision to use additional prereading and reading measures.

In many instances, prereferral information may be inadequate to determine if reading or other academic difficulties are present. Previous research has indicated that children with reading problems may do more poorly than controls on measures of verbal intellectual functioning (Hatcher & Hulme, 1999), working memory (de Jong, 1998), and processing speed (Willcutt, Pennington, Olson, Chhabildas, & Hulslander, 2003). Slightly lower scores observed on verbal subtests are probably due to subtle language difficulties (Nation, Adams, Bowyer-Crane, Claudine, & Snowling, 2000). Low scores on these indexes or subtests within these indexes should alert the clinician to administer reading and reading-related measures.

CLINICAL GROUPS

Previously, WISC-IV Integrated performance data were provided for children with Reading or Math Disorders. Results indicated a high degree of similarity between children with specific math and specific reading problems on Verbal Comprehension subtests. In the Perceptual-Reasoning domain, the math group had low Block Design scores compared to the Reading Disorder group.

Working memory and processing speed results for these two groups are presented in Table 14. In the Working Memory domain, the Reading Disorder group had low scores at similar levels between registration and manipulation tasks. The Math Disorder group had better auditory registration skills with lower mental manipulation scores and very low scores on arithmetic. These groups have similar deficits in working memory, although auditory registration is better persevered in the math versus reading group. In the Processing Speed domain, the Math group was slower in general and had lower scores on the Cancellation Random measure.

TABLE 14   Learning Disabled Group Performance on WISC-IV Integrated Working Memory and Processing Speed subtests

	Math Disorder		Reading Disorder	
Registration Measures	Mean	SD	Mean	SD
Digits Forward	9.3	3.1	8.4	3.0
Letter Rhyming	10.6	3.5	8.3	2.5
Letter Nonrhyming	9.1	2.9	7.9	2.1
Spatial Span Forward	8.5	2.6	8.8	2.5
Visual Span	7.7	2.7	7.2	2.5
Working Memory Measures				
Digits Backward	8.0	2.4	8.4	2.7
Letter-Number Sequencing	8.3	2.6	7.6	3.1
Letter-Number Embedded Words	8.1	2.2	7.9	2.1
Spatial Span Backward	7.8	2.2	8.9	2.7
Arithmetic	6.6	1.8	7.8	2.3
Arithmetic Process Approach A	6.3	2.2	8.0	2.1
Arithmetic Process Approach B	5.4	2.4	7.4	2.4
Written Arithmetic	6.4	1.8	7.4	2.0
Processing Speed Measures				
Coding	7.6	2.8	8.1	2.3
Coding Copy	7.6	3.2	7.7	2.7
Symbol Search	8.2	3.2	8.9	2.7
Cancellation Random	9.1	2.9	10.3	2.8
Cancellation Structured	8.8	3.1	9.4	2.9

Note: Data are based on listwise deletion of cases by domain and will vary from published scores for these groups: Math Disorder (n = 42, 43), Reading Disorder (n = 55, 61). *Wechsler Intelligence Scale for Children – Fourth Edition Integrated.* Copyright © 2004 by Harcourt Assessment, Inc. Reproduced with permission. All rights reserved.

At the index level (see Appendix), the groups also performed similarly. The Math group had lower scores on the Perceptual Reasoning and Executive Functioning Indices. The degree of difference between the two groups is small. Specific patterns of test scores are not diagnostic of a specific learning problem, but lowered scores in WISC-IV cognitive domains suggest that a learning problem may exist and further assessment of academic and other cognitive skills is warranted.

ABILITY–ACHIEVEMENT DISCREPANCY

The ability–achievement discrepancy has been the standard by which children are deemed eligible for special education services and for diagnosis of specific learning disorders (APA, 1994). The value of assessing intellectual functioning in the assessment of children with learning disabilities has been called into question (Siegel, 1989, 2003). Not only has the value of IQ testing been questioned, but the psychoeducational assessment process has been blamed for the perceived problems of the special education system (Pasternak, 2002). However, the problem of overidentification of children as Learning Disabled is not caused by the use of IQ–achievement discrepancy criteria but relates to the inconsistent use of this as a criterion (Scruggs & Mastropieri, 2001) and the failure of the decision-making process to fully consider psychological test data (MacMillan, 1998). A rigid application of the eligibility process confuses the processes of eligibility decision making and psychological assessment as being one in the same. Psychological testing helps identify the presence or absence of a disorder but does not establish disability.

Critics argue that intellectual functioning does not correlate with academic achievement and therefore cannot create "expectancy" regarding achievement (Siegel, 2003) or that ability–achievement discrepancies are unreliable (Pasternak, 2002). It is also argued that high-ability–low-achieving children do not differ from low ability–low achievers on any cognitive, behavioral, or academic measures (Stuebing, 2002). The definition of these groups is quite variable across studies, and in many cases, the low-ability groups and high-ability groups collected may not differ in intellectual ability at all. Few studies compare children that have a discrepancy (regardless of being identified as learning disabled) versus those who do not have a discrepancy at multiple levels of ability. This type of analysis enables the researcher to determine effects related to ability, discrepancy, and identification.

Relying on single, inflexible, diagnostic criteria, such as IQ–achievement discrepancy, is inadequate for diagnosis of any clinical condition. However, this discrepancy operationalizes the concept of underachievement, which is necessary in establishing the presence of a Learning Disorder. The diagnosis of a Learning Disorder does not mean that the child is "disabled." Disability is a legal term that requires that the identified disorder interfere with the individual's functioning in their current place of education or work. Therefore, it is possible to have a disorder and not be disabled. However, a disorder must be identified to be eligible for disability services. This does not apply only to education settings but also to adult disability claims. The presence of a disorder should transcend the environment of the individual; however, the presence of a "disability" is by definition related to the current psychosocial environment. Greater attention to functioning in the current environment relative to making an accurate assessment of the presence of a disorder may be one reason why eligibility determinations appear more relative than based on specific criteria (Peterson & Shinn, 2002).

The WISC-IV/WIAT-II linking sample was examined to assess the impact of ability, discrepancy, and the eligibility determination of a learning disability in an epidemiological sample (Holdnack, Weiss, & Hale, 2004). The children comprising this sample were referred and nonreferred for special education services. The use of nonreferred children is helpful in understanding if discrepancies occur in nondiagnosed children and how these children compare to those that are identified for special education services. By the same token, evaluating performance in children identified for services from many different regions allows for the identification of common features of being identified whether the child has a discrepancy between ability and achievement or not. For the purposes of these data, a discrepancy was defined as a difference of 15 or more points between FSIQ and the WIAT-II Reading Composite.

The community, unidentified, sample was composed of 880 cases ages 6–16 years. Inclusion/exclusion criteria have been reported in detail elsewhere (Wechlser, 2004). One hundred and twenty-eight children diagnosed with Reading, Reading and Writing, or Reading, Writing, and Math Disorder were collected as part of the WISC-IV validity studies. The children completed the WISC-IV and the WIAT-II. Diagnostic criteria required that a trained professional have made the diagnosis using the eligibility criteria for the state in which the child attended school. The characteristics of the sample include the following: 39.8% have reading only diagnosis, 32.8% have reading and writing diagnosis, and 27.4% have Reading, Writing, and Math Disorder.

Table 15 presents means and standard deviations for WISC-IV indexes. The groups were compared on reading and spelling to assess for differences in academic functioning by ability level. Table 16 displays means and standard deviations for WIAT-II Reading and Spelling subtests. MANOVAs using type III sums of squares were used to test the hypothesis of unique effects of between group factors (ability, discrepancy, and diagnosis) controlling for the overlapping variance among these factors. The multivariate F-statistic is Wilk's lambda. Significant multivariate main effects on WISC-IV indexes (FSIQ was not included) were found for diagnosis [$F(4,926)=3.0$, $p<.01$], discrepancy [$F(4,926)=2.7$, $p<.05$], and ability [$F(8,1852)=66.8$, $p<.0001$]. The only significant interaction was diagnosis by ability [$F(8,1852)=2.3$, $p<.05$]. Not surprisingly, the main effect of ability group was observed for all indexes. Additionally, VCI varied by the interaction of ability by diagnosis and PSI differed for the interaction between ability by discrepancy. Main effects for discrepancy were associated with PRI performance, and the main effect of diagnosis was related to WMI scores.

For the WIAT-II (Reading Composite was not included), significant multivariate main effects were found for diagnosis [$F(4,954)=8.0$, $p<.0001$], discrepancy [$F(4,954)=44.1$, $p<.0001$], and ability [$F(8,1908)=28.8$, $p<.0001$]. Significant interactions were also found for diagnosis by discrepancy [$F(4, 954)=5.0$, $p<.001$] and discrepancy by diagnosis [$F(8,1908)=2.1$, $p<.05$]. Multiple interaction effects were observed at the univariate level. A three-way interaction of ability by diagnosis by discrepancy was significant for spelling. Diagnosis by discrepancy effects were observed for Word Reading, Pseudoword Decoding, and Spelling. An ability by discrepancy interaction was present for Word Reading and Spelling. All academic measures showed main effects for ability, diagnosis, and discrepancy.

TABLE 15 IQ and Index Scores in Ability by Diagnosis by Discrepancy groups

	n	FSIQ		VCI		PRI		WMI		PSI	
		Mean	SD	Mean	SD	Mean	SD	Mean	SD	Mean	SD
High IQ, Not Discrepant, No Diagnosis	388	110.2	7.8	107.6	10.3	107.8	10.2	107.4	11.3	107.1	11.9
High IQ, Discrepant, No Diagnosis	54	113.1	9.7	110.0	10.5	110.4	10.0	108.1	12.7	110.2	11.7
High IQ, Not Discrepant, Diagnosis	8	104.2	3.6	103.1	8.3	107.0	7.5	102.8	8.2	96.8	11.4
High IQ, Discrepant, Diagnosis	15	107.7	6.8	105.1	9.4	110.3	7.4	99.9	13.6	105.4	12.1
Middle IQ, Not Discrepant, No Diagnosis	236	92.7	4.4	93.8	8.2	93.7	8.2	94.3	9.4	96.3	10.6
Middle IQ, Discrepant, No Diagnosis	19	91.8	4.5	87.4	8.7	101.5	11.4	91.3	11.6	95.7	10.5
Middle IQ, Not Discrepant, Diagnosis	35	90.4	4.2	94.6	7.4	93.4	8.5	89.8	10.7	91.6	11.9
Middle IQ, Discrepant, Diagnosis	18	91.6	4.4	92.9	8.9	96.7	6.8	92.7	7.4	92.3	12.0
Low IQ, Not Discrepant, No Diagnosis	142	77.0	6.1	84.2	11.7	85.5	12.4	85.4	12.6	86.3	14.3
Low IQ, Discrepant, No Diagnosis	5	78.8	6.2	83.0	6.8	80.6	8.4	83.8	15.0	86.4	12.3
Low IQ, Not Discrepant, Diagnosis	41	78.2	5.0	84.9	7.3	87.1	11.7	90.4	11.0	84.0	11.2
Low IQ, Discrepant, Diagnosis	11	79.6	3.7	81.0	9.1	87.9	8.8	81.6	7.2	85.9	85.9

TABLE 16 IQ and Index Scores in Ability by Diagnosis by Discrepancy groups

	n	Word Reading		Pseudoword Decoding		Reading Comprehension		Reading Composite		Spelling	
		Mean	SD	Mean	SD	Mean	SD	Mean	SD	Mean	SD
High IQ, Not Discrepant, No Diagnosis	388	109.3	10.7	108.9	10.6	109.7	10.0	110.4	12.2	108.0	12.0
High IQ, Discrepant, No Diagnosis	54	92.1	12.3	93.4	11.6	99.9	11.8	92.8	12.3	95.1	11.5
High IQ, Not Discrepant, Diagnosis	8	91.8	11.2	94.8	11.2	109.6	8.0	96.8	7.8	87.6	10.7
High IQ, Discrepant, Diagnosis	15	85.6	8.9	87.7	8.7	90.1	12.8	85.3	8.6	90.4	14.6
Middle IQ, Not Discrepant, No Diagnosis	236	96.8	10.6	98.3	11.9	96.8	12.2	95.4	10.5	96.6	10.6
Middle IQ, Discrepant, No Diagnosis	19	74.7	5.3	74.8	6.3	77.5	11.0	73.2	5.0	78.3	7.2
Middle IQ, Not Discrepant, Diagnosis	35	84.4	8.5	86.7	11.9	90.5	13.2	84.7	8.2	84.0	8.5
Middle IQ, Discrepant, Diagnosis	18	70.8	6.4	75.4	7.6	72.2	10.4	69.7	8.1	73.6	12.9
Low IQ, Not Discrepant, No Diagnosis	142	88.0	13.6	90.6	13.9	85.7	15.5	86.0	14.0	88.1	14.0
Low IQ, Discrepant, No Diagnosis	5	61.4	6.4	71.6	9.0	61.8	6.8	58.8	3.8	66.8	11.5
Low IQ, Not Discrepant, Diagnosis	41	79.4	11.9	81.7	11.9	78.8	11.6	77.2	10.2	81.0	10.8
Low IQ, Discrepant, Diagnosis	11	61.5	5.0	72.4	4.0	58.6	11.8	57.9	7.1	68.9	7.1

Note: Data presented previously at the International Neuropsychological Society Annual Meeting 2004. *Wechsler Intelligence Scale for Children – Fourth Edition Integrated.* Copyright © 2004 by Harcourt Assessment, Inc. Reproduced with permission. All rights reserved.

The discrepant no diagnosis group performed similarly to the diagnosed but not discrepant group on reading and spelling measures with the exception of Comprehension, which was better in the undiagnosed group. The diagnosed and discrepant group consistently had the lowest achievement scores. Despite having similar levels of single Word Decoding abilities, the community (not diagnosed) discrepant group was not identified as needing additional services. Contextual (relative achievement compared to peers) and individual factors (such as higher ability) appear to play a role in the identification process. Analysis of the diagnosis, discrepancy, and ability groupings indicates that each of these factors differentiates the children as related to specific cognitive processes (e.g., verbal skills and working memory) and academic functioning.

Results implicate that observed differences in intellectual functioning in studies of LD are associated with intellectual deficits rather than the diagnosis per se. However, small differences in specific cognitive skills are associated with both diagnosis and discrepancy. A diagnosis of reading disability was associated with lower verbal skills in the higher and middle ability groups and with lower working memory. Discrepant groups displayed higher perceptual-organization scores compared to nondiscrepant groups.

On academic measures, diagnosis, discrepancy, and ability and the interaction of discrepancy with ability differentiated the groups. Diagnosis did relate to academic functioning beyond the effects of lower ability and discrepancy. The middle and lower ability discrepant groups had the lowest levels of academic functioning, whereas the high-ability discrepant group performed similar to the middle-ability nondiscrepant group.

The manifestation of group differences (diagnosed versus undiagnosed) in reading research relates to the overlap in variance among the constructs being studied, and a failure to control for overlapping variance will result in inconsistent findings across studies. The results presented here suggest that ability, discrepancy, and diagnosis have unique/independent influences on reading scores and when the effects are controlled for, the following conclusions may be ascertained.

Diagnosis is associated with lower Working Memory and Processing Speed scores and lower scores on all reading and spelling measures. Discrepancy is associated with higher scores on Perceptual Reasoning and Processing Speed (this results in a profile that looks like VCI and WMI are low). General ability affected all scores with the impact being largest on Reading Comprehension. The effects of ability on academic achievement are similar to the degree that IQ–achievement discrepancy is related to low academic skills: both effects are larger than the effect of diagnosis.

Results support the use of discrepancy criteria to identify learning disabled children. In all the diagnosed and the undiagnosed discrepant groups, IQ scores were higher than achievement scores. The amount of difference varied depending on if IQ was above or below 100. This supports the use of regression-based difference scores, which adjust for ability above and below the mean. However, use of a single cutoff score will still result in diagnostic errors. It is recommended that a range of discrepancies be considered potentially indicative of a Learning Disorder. A range of 10–20 points in favor of IQ over achievement is considered a risk factor for the presence of a learning disability. Larger discrepancies are likely associated with learning problems when a concurrent restriction is placed on academic ability (e.g., no academic score greater than 105 depending upon the general academic functioning of children in the same grade in that school). Once a discrepancy is identified, the criterion of underachievement has been satisfied (Kavale, Holdnack, & Mostert, 2003). Additional procedures should be employed to confirm if a learning disability is present.

EVALUATING READING PROBLEMS IN CHILDREN

Once underachievement is established, then additional testing may be indicated to determine if a learning disability is present. The following paradigm is a modified version presented in the ERSI. This version is expanded to include additional measures: NEPSY, Process Assessment of the Learner: Reading and Writing (PAL-RW; Berninger, 2001); Early Reading Diagnostic Assessment–Revised (ERDA-R); Wechsler Preschool and Primary Scale of Intelligence–3rd Edition (WPPSI-III; Wechsler, 2002); Differential Ability Scales (DAS; Elliot, 1992); and Wechsler Individual Achievement Test–2nd Edition (The Psychological Corporation, 2000).

1. Evaluate for risk factors
   a. Family history of Reading Disorder—highest risk factor
      i. Biological mother and father both have a history of Reading Disorder—highest genetic risk factor
      ii. Biological father has a history of Reading Disorder—second highest risk factor
      iii. Mother has a history of Reading Disorder—modest risk factor
   b. The child has a history of language disorder
      i. Has the youth received speech-language services?
      ii. Has the child been identified as having delays in Expressive and/or Receptive Language skills?
   c. Family history of language disorder—indirect risk factor
   d. Child has a history of neurological insult or injury such as prenatal exposure to substances of abuse, moderate to severe traumatic brain injury, seizure disorder, etc.
   e. Child comes from an impoverished family with suspected emotional/physical neglect (i.e., early exposure to language and being read to early promote the development of reading skills in children)

2. Teacher- and Parent-based report of academic abilities
   a. Evaluate ACES for reading specific, reading-writing or global academic weaknesses
3. Evaluating young children "at risk" for developing reading difficulties (ages 3–6)
   a. Phonemic awareness
      i. NEPSY: Phonological processing, repetition of nonsense words
      ii. Process assessment of the learner: reading and writing (PAL-RW): Syllables, Phonemes, and Rhyming
      iii. ERDA-R: Rhyming, Syllables
   b. Alphabetics
      i. PAL-RW: Letter Naming, Alphabet Writing, Rapid Automatic Naming-Letters
      ii. WIAT-II: Word/Letter Reading
      iii. ERDA-R: Alphabet Writing, Letter-Naming
   c. Phonological processing
      i. WIAT-II/PAL-RW: Pseudoword Decoding, Word Reading
      ii. ERDA-R: Phonemes and Pseudoword Decoding
   d. Vocabulary/semantic knowledge/processing
      i. WIAT-II: Receptive and Expressive Vocabulary
      ii. WPPSI-III: Verbal Comprehension Index
      iii. WPPSI-III: Language Composite
      iv. WISC-IV: Verbal Comprehension Index
      v. Test of Word Knowledge (TOWK; age 5 and above): Expressive and Receptive Vocabulary (semantic knowledge), Word Definitions, Word Opposites and Synonyms (semantic features and relations—important skills related to vocabulary development and strategy)
      vi. Differential Ability Scales (DAS): Naming Vocabulary
      vii. Clinical Evaluation of Language Fundamentals–4th Edition: Word classes, word definitions
      viii. NEPSY: Body Part Naming
   e. Receptive language skills—comprehension and syntactic
      i. NEPSY: Comprehension of Instruction
      ii. WIAT-II: Sentence Comprehension
      iii. CELF-III (age 6 and above): Sentence Structure (syntactic knowledge), Concepts and Directions, Listening to Paragraphs
      iv. CELF (preschool): Receptive Language Measures
   f. Expressive language skills—comprehension/use of syntax/working memory and language/productivity
      i. NEPSY: Semantic Fluency, Sentence Repetition
      ii. CELF-IV: Word Structure, Formulated Sentences, Recalling Sentences, Word Associations
      iii. WIAT: Sentence Repetition, Word Fluency

    iv. WPPSI-III: Verbal IQ/Verbal Comprehension
    v. WISC-III: Verbal IQ/Verbal Comprehension
  g. Rapid Automatic Naming—automaticity of visual–semantic association
    i. NEPSY: Speeded Naming
    ii. CELF-IV: Rapid Automatic Naming
    iii. PAL-RW: Rapid Automatic Naming
    iv. ERDA-R: Rapid Automatic Naming-Letters
  h. Working Memory
    i. WISC-IV: Working Memory Index
    ii. DAS: Recall of Digits, Recall of Objects
    iii. CMS (ages 5 and above): Numbers, Sequences, picture location
    iv. WISC-IV Integrated: Letter Span, Spatial Span
    v. NEPSY: Auditory Response Test
  i. Visual–perceptual processing and visual processing speed
    i. WISC-IV/WPPSI: Perceptual Organization
    ii. WISC-IV/WPPSI: Processing Speed
4. Evaluating school-age children with suspected Reading Disorder
  a. Phonological Processing
    i. WIAT-II/PAL-RW: Pseudoword Decoding, Word Reading, Reading Comprehension Decoding Process measures
    ii. ERDA-R: Phonemes and Pseudoword Decoding
  b. Phonemic awareness
    i. NEPSY: Phonological Processing
    ii. PAL-RW: Phonemes, Syllables
    iii. ERDA-R: Rhyming, Syllables
  c. Rapid Automatic Naming
    i. NEPSY: Speeded Naming
    ii. CELF-IV: Rapid Automatic Naming
    iii. PAL-RW: Rapid Automatic Naming
  d. Reading Comprehension
    i. WIAT-II: Reading Comprehension with Vocabulary process measure
  e. Vocabulary/semantic knowledge/processing
    i. WIAT-II Receptive and Expressive Vocabulary, Reading Comprehension Vocabulary
    ii. WISC-IV: Verbal Comprehension Index
    iii. WISC-IV: Vocabulary Multiple Choice
    iv. TOWK: Expressive and Receptive Vocabulary (semantic knowledge), Word Definitions, Word Opposites, and Synonyms (semantic features and relations—important skills related to vocabulary development and strategy)
    v. DAS: Word Definitions

      vi. Clinical Evaluation of Language Fundamentals–3rd Edition: Word Classes
- f. Receptive Language Skills—Comprehension and Syntactic
  - i. NEPSY: Comprehension of Instruction
  - ii. WIAT-II: Sentence Comprehension
  - iii. CELF-IV: Concepts and directions, semantic relationships, listening to paragraphs
  - iv. TOWK: Figurative use, Conjunctions and Transition Words
- g. Expressive language skills—comprehension/use of syntax/working memory and language/productivity
  - i. NEPSY: Semantic and Phonemic Fluency, Sentence Repetition
  - ii. CELF-IV: Formulated Sentences, Recalling Sentences, Sentence Assembly, Word Associations
  - iii. WIAT: Sentence Repetition, Word Fluency
  - iv. D-KEFS (Verbal Fluency): 20 Questions (Verbal Concept Formation)
  - v. TOWK: Multiple Contexts
- h. Rapid Automatic Naming
  - i. NEPSY: Speeded Naming
  - ii. D-KEFS: Color Naming and Word Naming
  - iii. CELF-IV: Rapid Automatic Naming
  - iv. PAL-RW: Rapid Automatic Naming
  - v. ERDA-R: Rapid Automatic Naming-Letters
- i. Working Memory
  - i. DAS: Recall of Digits, Recall of Objects
  - ii. CMS: Numbers, Sequences, Picture Location
  - iii. WISC-IV: Working Memory Index
  - iv. WISC-IV Integrated: Letter Span, Spatial Span
  - v. NEPSY: Auditory Response Set
- j. Visual–perceptual processing and speed of visual processing
  - i. WISC-IV: Perceptual Reasoning
  - ii. WISC-IV: Processing Speed Index
  - iii. NEPSY: Arrows
- k. Reading fluency
  - i. WIAT-II Reading Comprehension fluency measures
5. Additional procedures for school-age children with concurrent behavioral disturbance
- a. Executive Functioning
  - i. NEPSY: Tower (statue and knock and tap for younger children), Design Fluency
  - ii. D-KEFS: Design Fluency, Color-Word Interference Test, Trail-Making Test, Tower Test

    iii. California Verbal Learning Test–Children's Edition (process measures–semantic clustering, retrieval deficits, and intrusion/perseverative errors

6. Profiling reading problems
   a. Establish the presence of any predisposing background characteristics and risk factors
      i. A family history of reading difficulties
      ii. Delayed language development, history of language disorder, history of speech language services
      iii. Impoverished developmental environment
      iv. Underachievement (IQ–achievement discrepancy)
   b. Identify core deficits in phonological processing
      i. Using a cutoff scaled score of 7 or less provides good sensitivity and specificity.
      ii. Using multiple criteria enables more robust conclusions regarding weaknesses in phonological abilities (word reading and phonological processing should be below 10 and at least one of the scores is 7 or less). In older children, all 3 subtests should be below 13 and at least 2 of the 3 should be below 10 and one of those 7 or less. The more measures at 7 or below, the more likely there is a core phonological impairment.
      iii. If the profile of phonological tests reveals a significantly low score on phonological processing relative to Word Reading and Pseudoword Decoding (4 or more scaled score points), evaluate the performance of the two tests to determine if relatively good letter identification skills versus poor Phonological Processing is creating a difference (Word Reading > phonological processing). If this is not the case, evaluate the child's performance on the WISC-IV auditory Working Memory Index and Digit Span subtests. If these are also low compared to Word Reading and Pseudoword Decoding, then the core deficit may be auditory working memory and not phonological processing.
      iv. If Word Decoding and Pseudoword Decoding are lower than phonological processing (4 or more points), determine if the child has poor alphabetics. This would be evident in low Letter-Naming versus Speeded Naming and may also be determined by evaluating the item level responses on Word Reading. If there is no apparent deficit in letter knowledge, consider possible deficits in visual working memory compared to auditory working memory (compare WISC-IV Integrated Visual Digits Forward versus auditory Digits Forward).
      v. If all measures of Phonological Processing are 4 or less, consider more in-depth evaluation to rule out more significant developmental difficulties.

c. Evaluate for Rapid Automatic Naming deficits on Speeded Naming and Letter Naming. Apply a multiple cut-score that both subtests should be below 9 and at least one is 7 or less. Rapid Automatic Naming subtests are less sensitive than Phonological Processing measures, and more restrictive criteria for determining difficulty with reading should apply. If the two scores vary considerably (4 or more scaled score points), evaluate client's performance on Word Reading to determine if poor or superior letter knowledge is producing the difference. If both scores are very low (4 or less), evaluate the child for global deficits in processing speed (WISC-IV Processing Speed Index). Also, evaluate the child for visual scanning deficits using WISC-IV Cancellation tasks.

d. Evaluate for "double deficits" (Wolf & Bowers, 1999). All four or five subtests are less than 10; two subtests, 1 measure of Phonological Processing and 1 measure of Rapid Automatic Naming are 7 or less. Subject's meeting criteria for "double deficit" are at high risk for reading difficulties.

e. Evaluate for core working memory deficits
   i. Working Memory Index is less than 90 or Digit Span is 8 or less.
   ii. Working Memory Index and Digit Span subtests differentiate Reading Disordered children from controls but do not have the sensitivity of ERSI variables. The absence of a working memory deficit is not diagnostic, but the presence of working memory problems will have an impact on Comprehension abilities and compensatory functioning.
   iii. Poor working memory in the absence of other deficits will lower but not impair performance on Phonological Processing and the Verbal Comprehension Index.
   iv. Children with poor decoding abilities but average or above average working memory may compensate for poor decoding by making pronunciation corrections after first reading the word incorrectly (refer to WIAT-II error analysis and fluency scores for Word Reading). If this appears to be the case, reading difficulties may be masked as the child does not have decoding mastery to the point of automaticity but may be relying on external correction through auditory working memory channels.

f. Evaluate for deficits in verbal comprehension
   i. Low verbal ability (80 or less) may signal greater developmental difficulties than Reading Disorder, and assessment of language skills would be indicated (CELF-IV or NEPSY-Language Index).
   ii. Children with reading difficulties generally exhibit low average to average verbal abilities. The lower the child's Verbal Comprehension Index, the more likely reading difficulties will be observed, particularly in Reading Comprehension.

    iii. In 85% of children diagnosed with Reading Disorder (WISC-IV/ WIAT-II linking), Verbal Comprehension scores were higher than Word Reading versus 44% of controls.
  g. Evaluate for a "double deficit" in intellectual functioning
    i. If both Digit Span and Vocabulary are 7 or less, the likelihood of having a reading score in the normally developing range is 1%.
    ii. If both Digit Span and Vocabulary are 4 or less, evaluate the child for significant language or developmental difficulties (use FSIQ and possibly additional testing with language measures).
  h. Interpret the child's background and cognitive profile
    i. If the child meets criteria 1a (family history) and 2b, there is a high risk of a genetically predisposed Reading Disorder. Evaluate FSIQ; if above or near 100, the likelihood of a genetically predisposed reading impairment is increased.
    ii. If the child meets criteria 1a (family history) but not any other criteria, the child is at risk but has not manifest the core deficit associated with reading difficulties. This would be a child that would be monitored with reassessment if reading difficulties appear over time.
    iii. If the child meets criteria 1b (delayed language) and meets criteria 2b, 3, or 4 and not 6a or 1e, then the child is likely to be a high risk for reading problems with less risk for more global language impairments.
    iv. If the child meets criteria 1b (delayed language) and meets either criteria for 6a and 1e, then the child is likely to be a high risk for global language problems, including reading difficulties.
    v. If the child meets criteria 1b (delayed language) and meets either criteria for 6a but not 1b, then the child is likely to be a high risk for global language problems but not necessarily word decoding deficits.
    vi. If child meets criteria for 1c but not 1a or 1b
- Child may have reading difficulties due to 2b–due to lack of exposure to early literacy activities.
- Child may have adequate cognitive abilities; Perceptual Reasoning and Working Memory are average or higher but VCI is lower due to lack of exposure to early literacy activities.
- Child may have global low functioning (FSIQ < 80) due to more severe environmental problems.
  i. Evaluate FSIQ
    i. If FSIQ is 75 or below, children may not benefit from standard reading intervention programs if they have significant cognitive limitations (Ehri, Nunes, Stahl, & Willows, 2001).

   ii. If FSIQ is 76–84, child's progress in intervention program will need to be monitored closely to determine if the level of service is adequate to meet the child's needs.

   iii. If FSIQ is 85 or more

- Child may progress rapidly, particularly if poor skills are due to lack of exposure.
- Children that have adequate ability but do not progress may have a more intractable form of reading difficulty that may require more than early intervention (Torgesen, 2000).

   iv. If FSIQ is greater than achievement, the probability that a Reading Disorder exists is increased.

The model presented here is one possible methodology for assessing and identifying Reading Disorders from other common developmental disorders. The key feature of this model is emphasis on the use of multiple criteria set at more moderate cut scores in order to maximize sensitivity and specificity. Further research is necessary to determine if this is the most effective model or if other measures or procedures have greater utility.

CASE VIGNETTES

Jennifer S.

   Jennifer S. is a 14-year-old white female presenting with recent academic and behavior problems. Jennifer's mother sought psychoeducational testing because of lack of progress in Jennifer's new school. The family moved from a lower middle class neighborhood where Jennifer attended public school to an affluent suburban community with academically advanced schools. Prior to moving, Jennifer was getting average grades but her grades dropped precipitously in her new, more challenging school. The family history was notable for parental divorce when Jennifer was 3 years old and for possible Attention Deficit Disorder in the paternal biological family. No significant medical or developmental problems were noted. Jennifer's mom observed that she seems forgetful, daydreams frequently, is inattentive, and frustrates easily. Ms. S fears that Jennifer is depressed because of the move.

   Responses to the Brown Self-Report and the mother's ratings suggest significant difficulty paying attention. Teacher ratings on the Devereaux Scales for Mental Disorders also revealed problems with conduct/attention. Jennifer's responses to the Beck Youth Scales indicated a mild degree of depression and slightly lowered self-esteem. When interviewed, Jennifer denied feeling depressed but frequently feels irritated and gets angry easily. She feels "stupid" since starting at her new school and complained that the work is too difficult. Jennifer says she needs to reread her homework frequently and often is unable to finish all the assignments she is given. She admitted that when she had been learning to be a cheerleader, she had a lot of trouble paying attention to the sequence of steps in the routines. She had also been working part-time after she moved and this impacted her time for homework. She denies substance or alcohol use.

In testing she was very cooperative and very anxious to do her best. She was willing to do any tests given and was eager to please. She put forth good effort but was distracted easily and yawned frequently, despite getting adequate sleep. When directed to the task at hand, she showed adequate attention but she appeared to need external redirection in order to maintain focus. Use of language was age appropriate and normal in level of production.

In the context of low average overall intellectual abilities, Jennifer displayed a weakness in processing speed. Within the Perceptual Reasoning domain, she displayed strength in Picture Concepts. In order to determine the impact of slow processing speed on Block Design, the Block Design Multiple Choice subtest was administered. When both motor and speed components were removed, her performance improved significantly. Also, she showed weaknesses in spatial planning, inhibitory control, and incidental learning (Tables 17 and 18).

The D-KEFS and CMS were administered as part of the evaluation. Results of the D-KEFS indicated very good effort and productivity but poor self-monitoring, and frequent rule violations were evident on visual and verbal tasks. Cognitive flexibility and conceptual reasoning skills were average. On the CMS, Jennifer had average verbal and visual memory skills.

Results of the evaluation indicated symptoms consistent with Attention Deficit Disorder, predominately inattentive type. Her mild symptoms of depression did not account for the observed difficulties in cognitive processing and reflected a mild adjustment disorder with mood and conduct features. Jennifer's behavior, mood, and academic functioning improved somewhat with a combination of stimulant therapy, brief counseling, and tutoring.

TABLE 17   WISC-IV Indexes

Scale	Composite Score	Percentile Rank	95% Confidence Interval	Qualitative Description
Verbal Comprehension (VCI)	93	32	87–100	Average
Perceptual Reasoning (PRI)	88	21	81–97	Low average
Working Memory (WMI)	97	42	90–105	Average
Processing Speed (PSI)	80	9	73–91	Low average
Full Scale IQ (FSIQ)	87	19	82–92	Low average
Executive Functioning (EF)	76	5	71–91	Borderline

TABLE 18 WISC-IV Integrated Subtest Scaled Scores and Standard Error of Measurement

Subtest	Score	Subtest	Score
Similarities (SI)	8	Picture Completion (PCm)	
Vocabulary (VC)	8	Digit Span (DS)	11
Comprehension (CO)	10	Letter–Number Sequencing (LN)	8
Information (IN)	8	Arithmetic (AR)	10
Word Reasoning (WR)	9	Coding (CD)	4
Block Design (BD)	7	Symbol Search (SS)	9
Picture Concepts (PCn)	11	Cancellation Random (CAR)	8
Matrix Reasoning (MR)	6	Cancellation Structured (CAS)	10
Process Score	**Scaled Score**	**Percentile Rank**	
Comprehension Multiple Choice	8	25	
Block Design No Time Bonus (BDN)	7	16	
Block Design Multiple Choice (BDMC)	9	37	
Block Design Multiple Choice No Time Bonus (BDMCN)	11	63	
Elithorn Mazes (EM)	5	5	
Elithorn Mazes No Time Bonus (EMN)	4	2	
Spatial Span Forward	7	16	
Spatial Span Backward	9	37	
Process Score	**Raw Score**	**Base Rate**	
CDR Cued Symbol Recall	1	<2%	
CDR Cued Digit Recall	2	2–5%	

Wechsler Intelligence Scale for Children – Fourth Edition Integrated. Copyright © 2004 by Harcourt Assessment, Inc. Reproduced with permission. All rights reserved.

Marcus C.

Marcus is a 13-year-old African-American male referred for difficulties completing homework. His school grades are below average primarily due to a failure to complete written homework. Marcus's teacher describes him as pleasant and quiet but he does not complete his work. She also noted that Marcus puts forth good effort and that his failure to complete his work is due to slow and labored writing. Mrs. C., Marcus's mother, reports that Marcus is a hard worker and spends several hours a night trying to complete his work. She noted that while he doesn't complain or avoid his work, he gets frustrated because he struggles to finish everything he is assigned. Developmental history is notable for delayed speech, early intervention for language delays, and diagnosis of reading disability in first grade. Marcus had been a special education student from grades 1 to 5 but his progress warranted a return to the regular classroom setting.

While Marcus was able to keep up his grades in sixth and seventh grade, he had slipped considerably in the eighth grade.

Testing completed by the school resulted in a finding of no special needs and his parents felt they needed to do more. Marcus presented as a highly motivated and ambitious youth. He was anxious to complete the testing and show that he was no "dummy." His use of language was age appropriate, although the level of production was somewhat reduced. This was most evident on verbal subtests. He frequently responded with one or two word responses and did not receive full credit. When queried for additional information, he frequently said "I don't know." He had an awkward and unusual pencil grip but maintained it worked for him. Writing was labored but slow and legible.

Results of the WISC-IV Indexes revealed a significant weakness in Verbal Comprehension; however, the Recognition Index was in the average range. These results suggest that a deficit in expressive language, memory retrieval, or verbal initiation may be present. Academic testing with the WIAT-II indicated average reading decoding, low average to average math skills but borderline reading comprehension and deficient writing skills (Tables 19–22).

The D-KEFS, CELF-IV, and CMS were administered as part of this evaluation. The D-KEFS indicated average visual productivity but deficient verbal production to novel prompt and average production to semantic prompt. Cognitive flexibility was within the average range. Measures of inhibitory control were also within the average range. The CELF-IV indexes were average for receptive language but mildly deficient for expressive language functions. Memory assessment revealed retrieval deficits for verbal information with intact visual memory.

While Marcus was raised in a lower income home, his low score on VCI should not be attributed to a lack of learning experiences. This interpretation would miss the clinical issues present. A failure to complete additional testing may have missed the key clinical deficits and a misinterpretation of these findings. Marcus's mother reported that she often read to Marcus when he was a child. She has always stressed the importance of education to her children and has provided them with every educational opportunity available to her.

TABLE 19   WISC-IV Indexes

Scale	Composite Score	Percentile Rank	Confidence Interval	Qualitative Description
Verbal Comprehension (VCI)	77	6	72–85	Borderline
Perceptual Reasoning (PRI)	110	75	102–117	High average
Working Memory (WMI)	102	55	94–109	Average
Processing Speed (PSI)	103	58	94–112	Average
Full Scale IQ (FSIQ)	96	39	91–101	Average
Recognition Index #1	103	58	94–111	Average

TABLE 20   WISC-IV Integrated Subtest Scaled Scores and Standard Error of Measurement

Subtest	Score	Subtest	Score
Similarities (SI)	5	Picture Completion (PCm)	NA
Vocabulary (VC)	6	Digit Span (DS)	11
Comprehension (CO)	7	Letter–Number Sequencing (LN)	10
Information (IN)	NA	Arithmetic (AR)	10
Word Reasoning (WR)	7	Coding (CD)	9
Block Design (BD)	10	Symbol Search (SS)	12
Picture Concepts (PCn)	13	Cancellation (CA)	11
Matrix Reasoning (MR)	12		

Wechsler Intelligence Scale for Children – Fourth Edition Integrated. Copyright © 2004 by Harcourt Assessment, Inc. Reproduced with permission. All rights reserved.

TABLE 21   Verbal Process Subtests

Process Score	Scaled Score	Percentile Rank
Similarities Multiple Choice (SIMC)	9	37
Vocabulary Multiple Choice (VCMC)	13	84
Picture Vocabulary (PVMC)	12	75
Comprehension Multiple Choice (COMC)	10	50

Wechsler Intelligence Scale for Children – Fourth Edition Integrated. Copyright © 2004 by Harcourt Assessment, Inc. Reproduced with permission. All rights reserved.

TABLE 22   Processing Speed Domain Process Score Summary (Total Raw Score to Scaled Score Conversions)

Process Score	Scaled Score	Percentile Rank
Cancellation Random (CAR)	10	50
Cancellation Structured (CAS)	12	75
Coding Copy (CDC)	1	0.1

Wechsler Intelligence Scale for Children – Fourth Edition Integrated. Copyright © 2004 by Harcourt Assessment, Inc. Reproduced with permission. All rights reserved.

Results of the evaluation revealed an Expressive Language and Written Language Disorder. Special education services were reinitiated focusing on written language. Homework accommodations and after-school tutoring were provided. Marcus's grades improved steadily with most being in the low average to average range.

REFERENCES

American Psychiatric Association (1994). *Diagnostic and statistical manual of mental disorders.* Wasington, DC: American Psychiatric Association.

Antshel, K. M., & Waisbren, S. E. (2003). Timing is everything: Executive functions in children exposed to elevated levels of phenylalanine. *Neuropsychology, 17,* 458–468.

Aram, D. M., Ekelman, B. L., & Nation, J. E. (1984). Preschoolers with language disorders: 10 years later. *Journal of Speech and Hearing Research, 27,* 232–244.

Barkley, R. A. (1997). Behavioral inhibition, sustained attention, and executive Functioning: Constructing a unifying theory of ADHD. *Psychological Bulletin, 121,* 65–94.

Barkley, R. A. (2003). Issues in the diagnosis of attention deficit/hyperactivity disorder in children. *Brain and Development, 25,* 77–83.

Berninger, V. W. (2001a). *Process assessment of the learner–Test battery for reading and writing.* San Antonio, TX: The Psychological Corporation.

Berninger, V. W. (2001b). Understanding the lexia in dyslexia: A multidisciplinary team approach to learning disabilities. *Annals of Dyslexia, 51,* 23–48.

Berninger, V. M., Hart, T., Abbott, R., & Karovsky, P. (1992). Defining reading and writing disabilities with and without IQ: A flexible developmental perspective. *Learning Disability Quarterly, 15,* 103–118.

Brookshire, B., Levin, H. S., Song, J., & Zhang, L. (2004). Components of executive function in typically developing and head-injured children. *Developmental Neuropsychology, 25,* 61–83.

Caine, D., & Watson, J. D. (2000). Neuropsychological and neuropathological sequelae of cerebral anoxia: A critical review. *Journal of the International Neuropsychological Society, 6,* 86–99.

Catts, H. W., Fey, M. E., Zhang, X., & Tomblin, J. B. (2001). Estimating the risk of future reading difficulties in kindergarten children: A research-based model and its clinical implementation. *Language, Speech, and Hearing Services in Schools, 32,* 38–50.

Channon, S., German, E., Cassina, C., & Lee P. (2004). Executive functioning, memory, and learning in phenylketonuria. *Neuropsychology, 18,* 613–620.

Channon, S., Pratt, P., & Robertson, M. M. (2003). Executive function, memory, and learning in tourette's syndrome. *Neuropsychology, 17,* 247–254.

Choudhury, N., & Benasich, A. A. (2003). A family aggregation study: The influence of family history and other risk factors on language development. *Journal of Speech, Language, and Hearing Research, 46,* 261–272.

Catroppa, C., & Anderson, V. (2004). Recovery and predictors of language skills two years following pediatric traumatic brain injury. *Brain and Language, 88,* 68–78.

Cohen, M. (1997). *Children's memory scale.* San Antonio, TX: The Psychological Corporation.

Cohen, N. J., Menna, R., Vallance, D. D., Barwick, M. A., Im, N., & Horodezky, N.B. (1998). Language, social cognitive processing, and behavioral characteristics of psychiatrically disturbed children with previously identified and unsuspected language impairments. *Journal of Child Psychology and Psychiatry, 39,* 853–864.

Conti-Ramsden, G., Botting, N., Simkin, Z., & Knox, E. (2001). Follow-up of children attending infant language units: Outcomes at 11 years of age. *International Journal of Language and Communication Disorders, 36,* 207–219.

Couthino, M. J., Oswald, D. P., & Best, A. M. (2002). The influence of sociodemographics and gender on the disproportionate identification of minority students as having learning disabilities. *Remedial and Special Education, 23,* 49–59.

de Jong, P. F. (1998). Working memory deficits of reading disabled children. *Journal of Experimental Child Psychology, 70,* 75–96.

Delaney-Black, V., Covington, C., Ondersma, S. J., Nordstrom-Klee, B., et al. (2002). Violence exposure, trauma, and IQ and/or reading deficits among urban children. *Archives of Pediatric and Adolescent Medicine, 156,* 280–285.

Delis, D. C, Kaplan, E., & Kramer, J. (2001). *Delis-Kaplan executive function system*. San Antonio, TX: The Psychological Corporation.

DiPerna, J. C., & Elliott, S. N. (2000). *Academic competence evaluation scale*. San Antonio, TX: Harcourt Assessment, Inc.

Drozdick, L. W., Holdnack, J. A., Rolfhus, E., & Weiss, L. (2005). WISC-IV and children's memory scale. HTTP://harcourtassessment.com/hai/images/pdf/wisciv/WISCIVTechReports5. pdf

Ehri, L. C. Nunes, S. R., Stahl, S. R., & Willows, D. M. (2001). Systematic phonics instruction helps students learn to read: Evidence from the national reading panel's meta-analysis. *Review of Educational Research, 71*, 393–447.

Elliot, C. (1992). *Differential ability scales*. San Antonio, TX: The Psychological Corporation.

Ewing-Cobbs, L., Barnes, M., Fletcher, J. M., Levin H. S., et al. (2004). Modeling of longitudinal academic achievement scores after pediatric traumatic brain injury. *Developmental Neuropsychology, 25*, 107–133.

Ewing-Cobbs L., Fletcher, J. M., Levin, H. S., Francis, D. J., et al. (1997). Longitudinal neuropsychological outcome in infants and preschoolers with traumatic brain injury. *Journal of the International Neuropsychological Society, 3*, 581–591.

Ewing-Cobbs, L., Kramer, L., Prasad, M., Canales, D.N., Louis, P. T., et al. (1998). Neuroimaging, physical, and developmental findings after inflicted and noninflicted traumatic brain injury in young children. *Pediatrics, 102*, 300–307

Faraone, S. V., & Biederman, J. (1998). Neurobiology of attention-deficit hyperactivity disorder. *Biological Psychiatry, 44*, 951–958.

Fastenau, P. S., Shen, J., Dunn,D. W., Perkins, S. M., Hermann, B. P., & Austin, J. K. Neuropsychological predictors of academic underachievement in pediatric epilepsy: moderating roles of demographic, seizure, and psychosocial variables. *Epilepsia, 45*, 1261–1272.

Fisher, S. E., Francks, C., Marlow, A. J., MacPhie, I. L., et al. (2002). Independent genome-wide scans identify a chromosome 18 quantitative-trait locus influencing dyslexia. *Nature Genetics, 30*, 86–91.

Gilmour, J., Hill, B., Place, M., & Skuse, D. H. (2004). Social communication deficits in conduct disorder: A clinical and community survey. *Journal of Child Psychology and Psychiatr, 45*, 967–978.

Grigorenko, E. L., Wood, F. B., Meyer, M. S., & Pauls, J.E. (2000). Chromosome 6p influences on different dyslexia-related cognitive processes: Further confirmations. *American Journal of Human Genetics, 66*, 715–723   .

Grigorenko, E. L., Wood, F. B., Meyer, M. S., Pauls, J. E., Hart, L. A., & Pauls, D. L. (2001). Linkage studies suggest a possible locus for developmental dyslexia on chromosome 1p. *American Journal of Medical Genetics, 105*, 120–129.

Hatcher, P. J., & Hulme, C. (1999). Phonemes, rhymes, and intelligence as predictors of children's responsiveness to remedial reading instruction: Evidence from a longitudinal intervention study. *Journal of Experimental Child Psychology, 72*, 130–153.

Hill, E. L. (2004). Evaluating the theory of executive dysfunction in autism. *Developmental Review, 24*,189–233.

Holdnack, J. A., Weiss, L., & Hale, J. B. (2004). *Children with Reading Disorder: The Effects of IQ and IQ-achievement discrepancy*. Baltimore, MD:32nd Annual Meeting of the International Neuropsychological Society.

Hooper, S. R., Alexander, J., Moore, D., Sasser, H. C., Laurent, S., King, J., Bartel, S., & Callahan, B. (2004). Caregiver reports of common symptoms in children following a traumatic brain injury. *NeuroRehabilitation, 19*, 175–89.

Kavale, K. A., Holdnack, J. A., & Mostert, M. P. (2003). *The feasibility of a responsiveness to intervention approach for the identification of specific learning disability: A psychometric alternative*. Paper presented at the National Research Center on Learning Disabilities "Responsiveness to Intervention" Symposium, Kansas City, MO.

Knox, E., & Conti-Ramsden, G. (2003). Bullying risks of 11-year-old children with specific language impairment (SLI): Does school placement matter? *International Journal of Language and Communication Disorder, 38*, 1–12.

Korkman, M., Kjirk, U., & Kemp, S. (1997). *NEPSY: A developmental neuropsychological assessment-manual*. San Antonio, TX, The Psychological Corporation.

Kramer, J. H., Knee, K., & Delis, D. C. (2000). Verbal memory impairments in dyslexia. *Archives of Clinical Neuropsychology, 15*, 83–93.

Lah, S. (2004). Neuropsychological outcome following focal cortical removal for intractable epilepsy in children. *Epilepsy Behavior, 5*, 804–817.

Martin, I., & McDonald, S. (2003). Weak coherence, no theory of mind, or executive dysfunction? Solving the puzzle of pragmatic language disorders. *Brain and Language, 85*, 451–466.

McArthur, G. M., Hogben, J. H., Edwards, V. T., Heath, S. M., & Mengler, E. D. (2000). On the specifics of specific reading disability and specific language impairment. *Journal of Child Psychology and Psychiatry, 41*, 869–874.

Molfese, V. J., Modglin, A., & Molfese, D. L. (2003). The role of early environment in the development of reading skills: A longitudinal study of preschool and school-age measures. *Journal of Learning Disabilities, 36*, 59–67.

Monjauzea, C., Tullera, L., Hommetb, C., Barthezc, M., & Khomsia, A. (2005). Language in benign childhood epilepsy with centro-temporal spikes abbreviated form: Rolandic epilepsy and language. *Brain and Language, 92, 300*–308.

Montgomery, J. W. (2003). Working memory and comprehension in children with specific language impairment: What we know so far. *Journal of Communication Disorders, 36*, 221–231.

Nation, K., Adams, J. W., Bowyer-Crane, C. A., & Snowling, M. J. (1999). Working memory deficits in poor comprehenders reflect underlying language impairments. *Journal of Experimental Child Psychology, 73*, 139–158.

Pasternak, R. H. (2002). *The demise of IQ testing for children with learning disabilities*. Presented at the Annual Convention of the National Association of School Psychologists, Chicago, IL.

Pennington, B. F., & Lefly, D. L. (2001). Early reading development in children at family risk for dyslexia. *Child Development, 72*, 816–833.

Peterson, K. M. H., & Shinn, M. R. (2002). Severe discrepancy models: Which best explains school identification practices for learning disabilities. *School Psychology Review, 31*, 459–476.

Powell, K. B., & Voeller, K. K. (2004). Prefrontal executive function syndromes in children. *Journal of Child Neurology, 19*, 785–797.

PsychCorp (2004). *Early reading success indicator*. San Antonio, TX: Harcourt Assessment, Inc.

Rapin, I., & Dunn, M. (2003). Update on the language disorders of individuals on the autistic spectrum. *Brain & Development, 25, 166*–172.

Rourke, B. P., Del Dotto, J. E., Rourke, S. B., & Casey, J.E. (1990). Nonverbal learning disabilities: The syndrome and a case study. *Journal of School Psychology, 28*, 361–385.

Scarborough, H. S. (1990). Very early language deficits in dyslexic children. *Child Development, 61*, 1728–1748.

Semel, E, Wiig, E. H. & Secord, W. A. (2003). *Clinical Evaluation of Language Fundamentals-4th Edition*. San Antonio, TX: Harcourt Assessment, Inc.

Sergeant, J. A., Geurts, H., & Oosterlaan. J. (2002). How specific is a deficit of executive functioning for attention-deficit/hyperactivity disorder? *Behavioural Brain Research, 13*, 3–28.

Siegel, L. S. (1989). IQ is irrelevant to the definition of learning disabilities. *Journal of Learning Disabilities, 22*(8), 469–478.

Siegel L. S. (2003). IQ-discrepancy definitions and the diagnosis of LD: Introduction to the special issue. *Journal of Learning Disabilities, 36*, 2–3.

Shear, P. K., Tallal, P., & Delis, D. C. (1992). Verbal learning and memory in language impaired children. *Neuropsychologia, 30*, 451–458.

Speech Language Impairment Consortium (SLIC) (2004). Highly significant linkage to the SLI1 locus in an expanded sample of individuals affected by specific language impairment. *American Journal of Human Genetics, 74*, 1225–1238

Speltz, M. L., DeKlyen, M., Calderon, R., Greenberg, M. T., & Fisher, P.A. (1999). Neuropsychological characteristics and test behaviors of boys with early onset conduct problems. *Journal of Abnormal Psychology, 108*, 315–325.

Stuebing, K. K., Fletcher, J. M., LeDoux, J. M., Lyon, G. R., et al. (2002). Validity of IQ-discrepancy classification of reading disabilities: A meta-analysis. *American Educational Research Journal, 39*, 469–518.

Tallal, P., Townsend, J., Curtiss, S., & Wulfeck, B. (1991). Phenotypic profiles of language-impaired children based on genetic/family history. *Brain and Language, 41*, 81–95.

Thivard, L., Hombrouck, J., Te'zenas du Montcel, S., Delmaire, C., Cohen, L., Samson, S., Dupont, S., Chiras, J., Baulac, M., & Lehe'ricyc, S. (2005). Productive and perceptive language reorganization in temporal lobe epilepsy. *NeuroImage, 24*, 841–851.

Torgesen, J. K. (2000) Individual differences in response to early interventions in reading: The lingering problem of treatment resisters. *Learning Disabilities Research and Practice, 15*, 55–64.

Vinayan, K. P., Biji, V., & Thomas, S. V. (2005). Educational problems with underlying neuropsychological impairment are common in children with benign epilepsy of childhood with centrotemporal spikes (BECTS). *Seizure, 14*, 207–212

Wechsler, D. (2002). *The Wechsler primary and pre-school scale of intelligence–* Third Edition. San Antonio, TX: Harcourt Assessment, Inc.

Wechsler, D. (2002). *Wechsler individual achievement test-II: Examiner's manual*. San Antonio, TX: Harcourt Assessment, Inc.

Wechsler, D. (2004). *The Wechsler intelligence scale for children–*4th Edition Integrated. San Antonio, TX: Harcourt Assessment, Inc.

Wilde E.A., Hunter J. V., Newsome M.R., Scheibel R. S., Bigler, E. D., Johnson, J. L., Fearing, M. A., Cleavinger, H. B., Li, X., Swank, P. R., Pedroza, C., Roberson, G. S., Bachevalier, J., & Levin, H. S. (2005). Frontal and temporal morphometric findings on MRI in children after moderate to severe traumatic brain injury. *Journal of Neurotrauma, 22*, 333–344.

Willcutt, E. G., Pennington, B. F., Olson, R. K., Chhabildas, N., & Hulslander, J. (2003). Neuropsychological analyses of comorbidity between reading disability and attention deficit hyperactivity disorder: In search of the common deficit. *Developmental Neuropsychology, 27*, 35–78.

Willford, J. A., Richardson, G. A., Leech, S. L., & Day, N. L. (2004). Verbal and visuospatial learning and memory function in children with moderate prenatal alcohol exposure. *Alcohol Clinical and Experimental Research, 28*, 497–507.

Wolf, M., & Bowers, P. G. (1999). The double-deficit hypothesis for the developmental dyslexias. *Journal of Educational Psychology, 91*, 415–438.

Wolff, P. H., & Melngailis, I. (1994). Family patterns of developmental dyslexia: Clinical findings. *American Journal of Medical Genetics, 54*, 122–131.

APPENDIX 1   Clinical Group Performance on all WISC-IV Integrated Indexes including new Executive Functioning and Recognition Indexes

Verbal Subtest	Attention Deficit Disorder		Asperger's Syndrome		Autistic Disorder		Expressive Language Disorder		Receptive-Expressive Language Disorder		Math Disorder		Reading Disorder		Traumatic Brain Injury	
	Mean	SD	Mean	SD	Mean	SD	Mean	SD	Mean	SD	Mean	SD	Mean	SD	Mean	SD
Verbal Comprehension Index	95.0	12.3	108.4	18.5	78.8	16.9	81.1	10.6	78.6	11.8	90.6	8.3	92.1	9.2	93.4	15.0
Perceptual Reasoning Index	97.1	13.8	102.1	19.3	88.3	18.1	91.4	14.9	85.8	16.2	86.9	11.2	94.3	12.8	92.8	13.8
Working Memory Index	90.8	13.1	97.3	13.6	74.2	14.8	83.5	10.9	83.2	13.8	90.6	11.1	86.5	13.7	94.6	15.7
Processing Speed Index	90.6	12.6	89.4	15.6	71.4	19.3	87.0	10.9	79.7	13.7	88.4	15.2	91.4	11.6	83.5	15.6
Executive Functioning Index	91.0	13.4	90.9	15.5	75.1	14.4	90.3	14.4	82.0	12.8	87.4	12.7	93.2	12.1	87.3	14.7
Recognition Index #1	93.4	14.2	102.3	14.8	82.6	13.6	83.3	11.3	80.2	9.9	87.7	8.2	90.6	11.5	92.4	14.1
Recognition Index #2	94.5	14.9	102.8	14.4	84.3	14.3	83.3	11.3	79.5	9.0	88.2	9.3	91.1	11.7	92.0	14.8

Note: Data are based on listwise deletion of cases and will vary from published scores for these groups: ADD (n = 49), Asperger's Syndrome (n = 20), Autistic Disorder (n = 14); Expressive Language Disorder (n = 25), Receptive-Expressive Language Disorder (n = 41), Math Disorder (n = 36), Reading Disorder (n = 34). Traumatic Brain Injury (n = 58). *Wechsler Intelligence Scale for Children – Fourth Edition Integrated.* Copyright © 2004 by Harcourt Assessment, Inc. Reproduced with permission. All rights reserved.

APPENDIX 2 Sum of Scaled Score to Standard Scores for the Executive Functioning Index

Sum Scales Scores	Executive Index	Percentile Rank	90% C.I.	95% C.I.	Sum Scales Scores	Executive Index	Percentile Rank	90% C.I.	95% C.I.
4	48	<0.1	48–65	46–66	40	100	50	92–108	90–110
5	50	<0.1	50–66	48–68	41	102	55	93–110	92–112
6	52	0.1	51–68	50–70	42	104	61	95–112	93–113
7	54	0.1	53–70	51–71	43	107	68	98–114	96–116
8	56	0.2	55–71	53–73	44	108	70	98–115	97–117
9	57	0.2	56–72	54–74	45	110	75	100–117	99–118
10	58	0.3	56–73	55–75	46	112	79	102–118	100–120
11	59	0.3	57–74	56–75	47	115	84	104–121	103–122
12	59	0.3	57–74	56–75	48	118	88	107–123	105–125
13	60	0.4	58–75	57–76	49	120	91	109–125	107–127
14	61	0.5	59–76	57–77	50	122	93	110–127	109–128
15	63	1	61–77	59–79	51	125	95	113–129	111–131
16	64	1	61–78	60–80	52	127	96	114–131	113–133
17	65	1	62–79	61–80	53	129	97	116–133	114–134
18	66	1	63–80	62–81	54	132	98	119–135	117–137
19	67	1	64–81	62–82	55	134	99	120–137	119–138
20	68	2	65–81	63–83	56	136	99	122–139	120–140
21	68	2	65–81	63–83	57	138	99	124–140	122–142
22	69	2	66–82	64–84	58	140	99.6	125–142	124–143
23	70	2	67–83	65–85	59	143	99.8	128–144	126–146
24	71	3	67–84	66–86	60	148	99.9	132–149	130–150

(*Continues*)

Sum Scales Scores	Executive Index	Percentile Rank	90% C.I.	95% C.I.	Sum Scales Scores	Executive Index	Percentile Rank	90% C.I.	95% C.I.
25	72	3	68–85	67–86	61	148	99.9	132–149	130–150
26	73	4	69–86	67–87	62	149	99.9	133–149	131–151
27	74	4	70–86	68–88	63	150	>99.9	134–150	132–152
28	76	5	72–88	70–90	64	152	>99.9	135–152	134–154
29	77	6	72–89	71–91	65	154	>99.9	137–154	135–155
30	79	8	74–91	72–92	66	154	>99.9	137–154	135–155
31	80	9	75–91	73–93	67	154	>99.9	137–154	135–155
32	82	12	77–93	75–95	68	154	>99.9	137–154	135–155
33	84	14	78–95	77–96	69	154	>99.9	137–154	135–155
34	85	16	79–96	78–97	70	154	>99.9	137–154	135–155
35	88	21	82–98	80–100	71	154	>99.9	137–154	135–155
36	90	25	83–100	82–101	72	154	>99.9	137–154	135–155
37	92	30	85–102	83–103	73	154	>99.9	137–154	135–155
38	95	37	88–104	86–106	74	154	>99.9	137–154	135–155
39	97	42	89–106	88–107	75	154	>99.9	137–154	135–155
					76	154	>99.9	137–154	135–155

APPENDIX 3

	8	9	10	11	12	13	14	15	16	Overall
Reliability	0.84	0.81	0.82	0.80	0.86	0.86	0.84	0.83	0.78	0.84
SEM	6	6.54	6.36	6.71	5.61	5.61	6	6.18	7.04	6

Wechsler Intelligence Scale for Children – Fourth Edition Integrated. Copyright © 2004 by Harcourt Assessment, Inc. Reproduced with permission. All rights reserved.

APPENDIX 4   Base Rate of Discrepancies Between the Executive Functioning Index Versus Standard WISC-IV Integrated Index Scores

Amount of Discrepancy	VCI > EFI	VCI < EFI	PRI > EFI	PRI < EFI	WMI > EFI	WMI < EFI	PSI > EFI	EFI < PSI
≥40	0.84	0.34	0.34	0.34	0.51	1.18	0.17	0.34
39	0.84	0.34	0.84	0.34	0.67	1.18	0.17	0.34
38	0.84	0.51	1.01	0.34	0.67	1.52	0.17	0.34
37	0.84	0.67	1.01	0.34	0.67	1.68	0.17	0.34
36	1.01	0.67	1.01	0.51	0.84	1.85	0.34	0.34
35	1.18	0.84	1.01	0.51	1.18	2.69	0.34	0.34
34	1.35	1.52	1.18	0.84	1.52	3.2	0.34	1.01
33	1.52	1.68	1.35	1.01	1.85	3.87	0.84	1.01
32	1.52	2.53	1.35	1.18	2.02	4.38	0.84	1.68
31	2.02	3.03	1.52	2.02	2.36	4.71	0.84	1.68
30	2.36	3.37	1.68	2.86	2.53	4.71	1.35	2.02
29	3.37	4.04	2.53	3.03	2.69	4.88	2.02	2.53
28	3.54	4.38	2.52	4.21	3.87	5.56	2.19	2.69
27	3.70	5.22	3.03	4.38	3.87	5.56	2.69	3.20
26	4.38	5.89	3.87	4.88	4.55	6.06	3.03	3.70
25	4.38	7.07	4.38	5.22	4.55	6.73	3.03	3.70
24	4.88	7.07	5.05	5.72	4.71	7.41	3.54	4.71
23	5.22	8.75	5.56	5.89	5.22	8.25	4.71	5.05
22	7.24	9.43	7.07	7.07	6.90	9.25	5.05	6.40
21	8.08	10.10	7.74	7.58	7.91	11.28	6.57	7.24
20	9.26	11.28	8.92	8.75	9.43	11.62	7.07	8.08
19	10.10	11.95	9.76	9.93	10.44	12.46	7.91	9.26
18	10.61	12.63	11.28	10.44	12.63	15.49	9.60	10.27
17	12.46	14.48	12.12	12.29	13.47	16.50	10.77	12.96
16	14.14	16.16	12.63	13.97	14.81	18.18	11.178	14.31
15	16.50	17.51	15.15	15.15	17.34	18.86	13.30	15.49
14	19.19	19.19	16.16	17.51	18.86	21.38	13.80	17.85

13	20.37	22.05	17.34	19.87	19.87	24.41	14.65	19.36
12	22.22	24.58	19.36	20.54	21.89	25.42	16.67	23.40
11	24.07	25.93	21.21	21.55	23.23	27.44	19.70	24.58
10	26.94	27.61	23.74	23.23	25.25	28.45	21.55	27.44
9	28.45	29.46	26.43	24.41	27.95	29.63	23.40	29.29
8	31.31	31.31	28.96	27.61	28.96	33.16	25.93	30.47
7	33.50	33.16	33	29.80	32.15	35.02	27.78	33.50
6	36.20	35.35	35.02	33	34.18	37.04	31.48	36.36
5	38.22	36.70	37.21	34.85	36.87	42.26	34.34	38.72
4	42.42	39.90	40.57	38.38	38.89	43.60	36.36	43.27
3	44.78	41.58	42.26	41.75	40.57	45.79	40.24	46.13
2	46.80	44.95	45.62	45.45	43.10	48.84	43.43	47.64
1	49.33	47.47	47.98	46.63	44.61	50.84	45.79	50.84
Mean	12.20	13.10	11.70	11.90	12.90	13.50	10.80	11.60
SD	9.10	9.40	8.70	9	9	10.20	8.10	8.60
Median	10	12	9	9	11	11.50	9	10

APPENDIX 5   Sum of Scaled Score to Standard Scores for the Recognition Index #1

Sum Scales Scores	Recognition Index #1	Percentile Rank	90% C.I.	95% C.I.	Sum Scales Scores	Recognition Index #1	Percentile Rank	90% C.I.	95% C.I.
3	59	0.3	56–70	55–71	31	101	53	94–108	93–109
4	63	1	60–74	58–75	32	103	58	96–110	94–111
5	64	1	61–75	59–76	33	106	66	98–112	97–114
6	66	1	62–76	61–78	34	108	70	100–114	99–116
7	66	1	62–76	61–78	35	110	75	102–116	101–117
8	67	1	63–77	62–79	36	112	79	104–118	102–119
9	69	2	65–79	64–80	37	115	84	106–121	105–122
10	69	2	65–79	64–80	38	117	87	108–122	107–124
11	70	2	66–80	65–81	39	119	90	110–124	109–125
12	71	3	67–81	66–82	40	121	92	112–126	111–127
13	72	3	68–82	66–83	41	124	95	115–129	113–130
14	73	3	69–83	67–84	42	127	96	117–131	116–133
15	74	4	70–84	68–85	43	129	97	119–133	118–134
16	75	5	70–85	69–86	44	133	99	123–137	121–138
17	77	6	72–86	71–88	45	137	99	126–140	125–142
18	79	8	74–88	73–89	46	140	99.6	129–143	128–144
19	80	9	75–89	74–90	47	141	99.7	130–144	129–145
20	81	10	76–90	75–91	48	147	99.9	135–149	134–151
21	82	12	77–91	75–92	49	147	99.9	135–149	134–151
22	83	13	78–92	76–93	50	148	99.9	136–150	135–152
23	85	16	79–94	78–95	51	148	99.9	136–150	135–152
24	87	19	81–95	80–97	52	148	99.9	136–150	135–152
25	88	21	82–96	81–98	53	148	99.9	136–150	135–152
26	90	25	84–98	83–99	54	148	99.9	136–150	135–152
27	92	30	86–100	84–101	55	148	99.9	136–150	135–152
28	94	34	88–102	86–103	56	148	99.9	136–150	135–152
29	96	39	89–103	88–105	57	148	99.9	136–150	135–152
30	99	47	92–106	91–107					

APPENDIX 6 Sum of Scaled Score to Standard Scores for the Recognition Index #2

Sum Scales Scores	Recognition Index #2	Percentile Rank	90% C.I.	95% C.I.	Sum Scales Scores	Recognition Index #2	Percentile Rank	90% C.I.	95% C.I.
3	59	0.3	56–70	55–71	31	101	53	94–108	93–109
4	62	1	59–73	57–74	32	103	58	96–110	94–111
5	64	1	61–75	59–76	33	105	63	97–112	96–113
6	65	1	61–76	60–77	34	108	70	100–114	99–116
7	65	1	61–76	60–77	35	110	75	102–116	101–117
8	66	1	62–76	61–78	36	112	79	104–118	102–119
9	67	1	63–77	62–79	37	115	84	106–121	105–122
10	69	2	65–79	64–80	38	117	87	108–122	107–124
11	69	2	65–79	64–80	39	120	91	111–125	110–126
12	70	2	66–80	65–81	40	123	94	114–128	112–129
13	72	3	68–82	66–83	41	126	96	116–130	115–132
14	73	4	69–83	67–84	42	128	97	118–132	117–134
15	74	4	70–84	68–85	43	131	98	121–135	120–136
16	75	5	70–85	69–86	44	134	99	124–138	122–139
17	76	5	71–85	70–87	45	139	99.5	128–142	127–143
18	77	6	72–86	71–88	46	141	99.7	130–144	129–145
19	78	7	73–87	72–89	47	143	99.8	132–146	130–147
20	79	8	74–88	73–89	48	147	99.9	135–149	134–151
21	81	10	76–90	75–91	49	147	99.9	135–149	134–151
22	83	13	78–92	76–93	50	147	99.9	135–149	134–151
23	84	14	79–93	77–94	51	148	99.9	136–150	135–152
24	86	18	80–94	79–96	52	148	99.9	136–150	135–152
25	88	21	82–96	81–98	53	148	99.9	136–150	135–152
26	90	25	84–98	83–99	54	148	99.9	136–150	135–152
27	92	30	86–100	84–101	55	148	99.9	136–150	135–152
28	94	34	88–102	86–103	56	148	99.9	136–150	135–152
29	97	42	90–104	89–106	57	148	99.9	136–150	135–152
30	99	47	92–106	91–107					

APPENDIX 7   Reliability and Standard Errors by Age for the Recognition Indexes 1 and 2

	6	7	8	9	10	11	12	13	14	15	16	Overall
Recognition Index #1												
Reliability	0.92	0.89	0.91	0.89	0.89	0.87	0.89	0.92	0.91	0.92	0.84	0.90
SEM	4.24	4.97	4.50	4.97	4.97	5.41	4.97	4.24	4.50	4.24	6	4.74
Recognition Index #2												
Reliability	0.85	0.88	0.89	0.88	0.88	0.88	0.90	0.93	0.90	0.92	0.85	0.90
SEM	5.81	5.20	4.97	5.20	5.20	5.20	4.74	3.97	4.74	4.24	5.81	4.74

Wechsler Intelligence Scale for Children – Fourth Edition Integrated. Copyright © 2004 by Harcourt Assessment, Inc. Reproduced with permission. All rights reserved.

Amount of Discrepancy	VCI > RCI1	VCI < RCI1	VCI > RCI2	VCI > RCI2
≥40	0	0	0	0
39	0	0	0	0
38	0	0	0	0
37	0	0	0	0
36	0	0	0	0
35	0	0	0	0
34	0	0.14	0	0
33	0	0.14	0	0
32	0	0.14	0	0
31	0	0.14	0	0.14
30	0.14	0.14	0	0.28
29	0.14	0.14	0.28	0.42
28	0.28	0.28	0.42	0.42
27	0.56	0.70	0.70	0.46
26	0.70	0.98	0.84	0.84
25	0.84	1.12	1.40	0.98
24	0.84	1.12	1.68	1.40
23	1.26	1.68	1.96	1.82
22	1.40	2.24	1.96	1.96
21	1.54	3.08	2.24	2.66
20	2.38	3.78	2.38	3.36
19	2.94	4.76	2.52	3.92
18	4.06	5.88	3.08	5.04
17	4.76	7.56	3.92	6.16
16	5.88	8.40	4.90	7.98
15	7.70	9.80	5.74	8.82
14	8.96	11.20	7.98	10.60
13	10.08	13.87	8.96	13.17
12	12.18	15.13	11.76	15.56
11	13.31	17.79	14.01	16.67
10	16.25	20.03	16.53	20.31
9	18.21	22.69	19.48	23.39
8	21.43	26.47	21.71	26.05
7	24.09	28.43	24.93	28.43
6	27.03	32.35	27.59	31.23
5	31.93	34.87	32.07	34.31
4	35.57	38.24	34.41	38.24
3	39.92	42.16	39.78	42.72
2	43.56	45.10	42.02	45.38
1	46.92	49.02	45.80	51.54
Mean	8.20	9.20	8.30	8.60
SD	5.90	6.40	5.90	6.30
Median	7	8	7	8

8

REPORT WRITING: A CHILD-CENTERED APPROACH

VICKI L. SCHWEAN, THOMAS OAKLAND, LAWRENCE
G. WEISS, DONALD H. SAKLOFSKE,
JAMES A. HOLDNACK, AND AURELIO PRIFITERA

This chapter advocates writing psychological reports that communicate a child-centered focus. While clinicians may believe their reports are child centered and communicate fully and effectively, a closer look often reveals that many are written in a routine fashion. Reports may emphasize or even overemphasize test data and psychometric analyses, but fall short in describing a child's important qualities and their history in ways that enhance efforts to promote personal, social, emotional and cognitive development.

In many settings, the psychological report is part of a larger therapeutic process, one in which assessment must be recognized as both an important and ongoing requirement of decision making. Evaluations are requested, and reports written, for the purpose of better understanding the child in order to intervene most effectively. As practitioners adopt a child-centered approach to writing evaluation reports, we move the field away from the unfortunate *test–label–place* description of many practitioners to a newer paradigm that we call the *assess–understand–intervene* model of practice. As shown in the sample reports provided here, this model involves multiple testing sessions to evaluate specific hypotheses, a report that educates readers about how the child's cognitive strengths and weaknesses manifest in the classroom and home, and child-specific intervention recommendations.

When written with a focus on the child, rather than the test scores, and used as one part of an overall approach in which one assesses first to understand and then intervene, psychological reports can become an integral and integrative component of best practice. In fact, it has been shown that providing sensitive feedback about the findings of a psychological assessment can have therapeutic effects in and of itself (Finn & Fischer, 1997). All of the authors have had the rewarding experience of hearing clients (e.g., parents of children, teachers) state how informed, empowered, relieved and otherwise supported they are not only by the results of an assessment but the way in which it was presented by the psychologist. Feedback may be written, oral, or both. Although this chapter focuses on issues important to written reports, oral feedback is likely to be enhanced by using similar methods.

SIX PURPOSES OF REPORTS

Reports generally serve six purposes. Reports address referral issues, educate, integrate information, serve as legal documents, communicate to others, and describe clients (e.g., children)

REPORTS ADDRESS REFERRAL ISSUES

Clinicians typically receive referrals from others who request information on specific issues. For example, teachers may request information as to whether a child's development differs from his or her peers or why a child is having such difficulty in a particular subject area such as reading. A psychologist or rehabilitation specialist may need to know if a child displays changes in affect, social behaviors, and cognitive skills following an accident. A pediatrician may need to know if a child's behaviors at home and school warrant a diagnosis of Attention-Deficit/Hyperactive Disorder. A probation officer or social worker may need to know the likelihood an adolescent, before the court for committing a felony, will benefit from placement in a wilderness program. A judge may need to know the best placement for children involved in a child custody dispute. Each referral asks clinicians to examine different issues. Thus, clinicians tailor their evaluations and reports in light of the specific referral and their intended audiences.

REPORTS EDUCATE

Psychological reports educate the lay reader about the psychological condition of interest and how it manifests in the child's behavior, affect, relations, and/or learning styles. Thoughtfully written, child-centered reports can have a powerful effect on parents and teachers by reframing the child's referral problem in a new light that creates understanding and promotes positive therapeutic relationships between the child and the most influential people in his or her life—parents and teachers. While the recommendations may be the most important part of the report, this educative aspect of the report body prepares the reader to acquire a new understanding of the child, which motivates them to act upon the recommendations in the classroom and home. In the long run of the child's life and progress toward maturity, these two aspects of the assessment (the educative function and the recommendations) are most critical in that they promote an understanding of the child that encourages adults to intervene appropriately.

Reports also educate others by providing information on the conditions that governed an evaluation. Information on the child's test behaviors, modifications that were needed when conducting the appraisal, and other unusual features of the evaluation allow readers to understand the context of the evaluation. Although clinicians attempt to use standardized conditions when administering tests, children's differences often require modifications in the ways an evaluation is conducted. Clinicians should use reports to provide contextual information on administration practices, especially those that are not routine. Chapter 1 was intended to provide further insight into factors that can not only impact a child's WISC-IV (and other) test scores, but that need to be considered when interpreting the results of the assessment.

REPORTS INTEGRATE INFORMATION

Clinicians obtain information from various sources, including existing records, interviews, observations, and testing. Reports that simply recite disparate test scores are inadequate. Reports organize, integrate, and synthesize information in light of referral issues. The referrals received by school psychologists are often initiated and agreed upon by both the home and school. There is a wealth of developmental and other history from the family (e.g., atypical birth history, developmental milestones, frequent moves) that needs to be integrated with information related to both school history (e.g., early screening for reading problems, group ability test results) and current school observations (e.g., acting out and aggressive behaviour, 2 years behind in spelling and reading). As we suggested earlier, many children may earn a WISC-IV FSIQ of 100 but present as very unique children as a function of test scatter and/or many other individual differences factors (e.g., personality, temperament) and factors external to the child (e.g., culture, parenting styles, reading program).

REPORTS SERVE AS LEGAL DOCUMENTS

Legal and ethical principles require professionals to document their work. Work that is undocumented may be seen as work not performed. A clinician may violate legal and ethical standards by failing to record his or her work properly. Reports constitute one means to document who worked with whom; why, when, and where was the work performed and how the work was performed.

REPORTS COMMUNICATE CLEARLY

Psychologists typically conduct evaluations at the request of and to inform others. *Thus, the success of an evaluation requires information to be communicated effectively so as to enable those who receive reports to form a meaningful understanding of the child and to use the information to address referral issues.* Several major problems sometimes encountered by the authors when they read reports prepared by others include: the use of unfamiliar terms and/or abbreviations, vague and non-specific statements, mixing data-based conclusions with hypotheses or guesses, the exclusive use of test-driven computer reports, and statements that are not descriptive of the child or prescriptive (see the next section for further elaboration).

Furthermore, while performing their work, clinicians may uncover information that warrants an extension of their work to issues not identified in the referral (e.g., a child referred due to behavior problems was found to be abused sexually). Thus, reports also clarify referral issues and document extensions of their work.

REPORTS DESCRIBE CHILDREN

Referrals are made for the purpose of assisting others to better understand a child's growth and development, his or her current status, impediments to development, and possible pathways to success. Thus, reports use narratives to describe a child's qualities in light of all information (e.g., existing records, interviews, observations), including test data.

In recent years, there has been a conceptual shift from a focus on numbers and qualitative descriptions of the test themselves to a focus on the person being evaluated and the problem or problems of concern (Kamphaus and Frick, 2002). Kamphaus and Frick argued that the clinician always must keep in mind that the child is the lodestar of the evaluation and the numbers obtained from tests are worthy of emphasis only if they contribute to an understanding of the child. In a similar vein, Lichtenberger, Mather, Kaufman, and Kaufman (2004) contend that *the focus of the report should be upon the person being evaluated and the problem or problems of concern. While data are clearly discussed within a report, they should be presented in such a manner that they contribute to an understanding of the person's responses to specific tasks.*

ADDITIONAL QUALITIES FOUND
IN GOOD REPORTS

Clinicians acquire information initially to facilitate their personal understanding of qualities associated with the referral. However, their ultimate success lies in their ability to convey important information to those who ultimately will use it. Written reports require degrees of precision that exceed that for oral reports. Oral reports enable clinicians to select words likely to be understandable, gauge the extent information is understandable, allow them to repeat and clarify comments, engage in dialogue, to draw diagrams, and in other ways tailor oral reports to promote comprehension. Written reports preclude these opportunities. Thus, considerable care is needed to write reports using methods that communicate as clearly as possible.

The following qualities generally are found in reports that communicate clear and effectively (Sattler, 2002). Paragraphs begin with a strong declarative sentence. Subsequent information within a paragraph explicates and supports the declarative statement. Words are selected for their precision (e.g., use the term *cognitive* only when referring to both achievement and intelligence; the term *environment* is imprecise). Needless words and phrases should be omitted, and the text should avoid a degree of density that diminishes comprehension. Subject and verb tense agree. Avoid redundancies. Information irrelevant to the purpose of the assessment generally is not included. In particular, *it is not necessary to describe every test score in the body of the report*. While all test scores are reported in table format, only those findings that contribute to an understanding of the child need be discussed in the body of the report. Adverbs (e.g., very, greatly) generally should not be used. Words that are uncommon or understood only by members of a profession should be avoided. Test titles are capitalized. Abbreviations are avoided. Reference the source used when making a diagnosis (e.g., state or provincial department of education rules, *Diagnostic and Statistical Manual of Mental Disorders: IV-TM*; *International Classification of Diseases and Related Health Problems, Tenth Edition* (*ICD-10*; World Health Organization, 1992) or when drawing a conclusion based on law (e.g., a judgment of a person's competency to stand trial should reference applicable state or provincial laws and policies).

OTHER QUALITIES THAT IMPACT
REPORTS

LOW OR HIGH STAKES OUTCOMES

The terms *low* and *high stakes* refer to the possible impact testing and evaluation may have on a child's life. Low stakes test use occurs when tests are used routinely, and important decisions rarely are made from them (e.g., teacher-made achievement tests). High stakes test use occurs when tests are used to make decisions that may lead to life-changing conditions. Examples include those that lead to diagnoses, promotion and retention, special class placement, change in one's home or school, and hospitalization. Lower stakes testing requires less knowledge of test use and rarely requires a report. In contrast, higher stakes testing requires greater sophistication in test use and evaluation methods and almost always requires a report.

A REPORT'S CURRENT AND FUTURE FORENSIC VALUE

Professional activities generally are governed by professional and legal standards. Clinicians are knowledgeable of best practices, including desired legal and ethical conduct, and are expected to adhere to them. For example, confidentiality and privilege are acknowledged when preparing and disseminating a report. Moreover, reports that may seem routine while being written later may acquire considerable forensic value. Thus, reports should be prepared with an awareness of their later uses. In addition, lawyers and judges may refer children for assistance during mediation or adjudication. These high stakes activities generally warrant more detailed reports.

A REPORT'S LENGTH AND THOROUGHNESS

Report lengths differ considerably. Some are one page while others may be 20 or more pages. Their length is determined by the complexity and importance of the evaluation (e.g., lower vs higher stakes), quantity of information to be reported, institutional policy, presumptions of professional preference, and other conditions external to the clinician. Some examples follow.

Reports used to qualify a child for a program for gifted and talented students may provide results from one test, together with file data and current teacher observations, and thus be brief. In contrast, reports used to qualify a child for services due to chronic and severe emotional problems, together with additional (comorbid) complex issues, will be longer. Report formats for some health care agencies and school districts are highly structured and require clinicians to do little more than fill in blanks with test data and check boxes to indicate diagnoses and interventions. Reports for physicians may be brief, given the belief physicians have little time to read a long report. In contrast, child-centered reports that are prepared for the parents should be educational in nature and are often more detailed and explanatory. Thus, the desired length of the report should be determined by the nature and complexity of the referral, the report's current and future forensic value, and the recipient's needs.

SECTIONS OF THE REPORT

There is no optimal report format that is suitable for every setting and assessment (Kamphaus & Frick, 2002). The precise nature of the report is dependent on the audience, referral issues, tests administered, and scores obtained. The individualization of a report is best accomplished with these two questions in mind: Who will be responding to the results or implementing the recommendations in the report? What style of report will have the greatest chance of ultimately beneficially impacting the examinee (Gregory, 2000)?

Several formats have been used for report writing: domain by domain, ability by ability, and test by test. Various combinations of these formats also can be used. A report may have as many as 13 sections. Each is described next.

I. *Demographic information.* This section typically provides information on the child's name, birth date, age, sex, and race/ethnicity, together with the names and addresses of the parents, teachers, and school. Dates of testing and the completion of the report are also provided. A title of the report typically is centered across the top of the first pages and a disclaimer is included to protect the individual's privacy, such as "for confidential use only" (Lichtenberger et al., 2004). The title should reflect the specific emphasis of the report.

II. *Documents reviewed.* This section generally lists the documents reviewed (e.g., those from the child's school, medical, and mental heath agencies) by name and date in chronological order.

III. *Assessment methods.* This section typically lists the tests administered, interviews held (by name and date), and observations made (again by name and date).

IV. *Referral issues or questions.* This section briefly states the reasons for the referral and who made the referral. This component of the report is critical as it provides the rationale for the assessment and direction for the design and focus of the report and the assessment protocol that will be selected (Kamphaus & Frick, 2002; Lichtenberger et al., 2004). Ultimately, all other sections of the report should be written with the referral issues or questions in mind.

V. *Background Information.* This section provides a context for understanding the child. The nature of the background information included in the report differs depending on the nature of the referral, its stakes, and the clinician's training, experience, and preferences. This section summarizes prior and current medical, social (including familial), educational, psychological, language, and/or motor qualities. The key word here is *crucial*—information that is included must be relevant. According to Kamphaus and Frick (2004), if information is not relevant to the referral problem, and it is very personal, the clinician should consider carefully the decision to invade a family's privacy by including the information in the report. Other suggestions include incorporating all pertinent information that may affect or provide clarity on the interpretation of a person's scores, specifying sources of information, corroborating sensitive background information corroborating or excluding it if it is inflammatory and cannot be corroborated [see Liehtenberger et al. (2004) for a detailed discussion of material to be included in background information].

VI. *Observations.* This section summarizes observations of a child in their natural environments (e.g., home and school) in both structured and unstructured settings. Clinicians unable to conduct such observations should rely on reports from teachers, parents, and others for this information. This section should also describe the processes the child used to arrive at answers and his/her fears or apprehensions, spontaneous behaviors, and other salient observed behaviors. Clinicians may decide whether to create a separate section on observations or to integrate this information into other sections of their report.

VII. *Test behaviors.* This section describes a child's physical appearance, attitudes, and test behaviors—information that provides a context for the evaluation. A child's test behaviors strongly impact the reliability and validity of test data. Test data on children who do not want to be tested, are uncooperative, and inattentive are likely to be less valid than test data on children who are engaged, enjoy the experience, and are cooperative and attentive. Test behaviors may be evaluated through informal clinical methods or through the use of norm-referenced standardized methods (Oakland, Glutting, & Watkins, 2005). A detailed discussion of how to categorize behaviors you have observed into recurrent themes is included in Liehtenberger et al. (2004).

VIII. *Description of test results.* This section describes children's achievement, intelligence, language, social and emotional qualities, temperament and personality, and may include a description of their motor and sensory-motor skills. Reports define terms readers may not understand and use terms that describe traits more accurately than test titles (e.g., visual conceptual in place of Performance IQ, organized and flexible in place of judging and perceptive). Narrative descriptions often are supplemented by including percentile scores to promote understanding. When reporting results of tests that assess multiple qualities, those that are most highly developed or positive generally are presented first followed by a discussion of personal qualities that are less highly developed or more negative in descending order. *Furthermore, findings should be integrated to build a comprehensive picture of the individual.*

IX. *Summary.* This section integrates important information, especially that which is central to the referral, in an understandable fashion. Some may read only this section. Thus, considerable care is needed when crafting this section.This section relates the diagnostic impression, as well as the recommendations directly to the referral question. Diagnostic impressions about an individual typically are based on multiple pieces of information, including test data. These impressions can be some of the most important information provided by the report because they may help describe and clarify behaviors and explain why an individual exhibits the behaviors or has difficulty performing tasks. When writing diagnostic impressions, a clinician will want to (1) describe data that support the diagnosis, (2) provide enough data to support the conclusion, (3) use diagnostic codes when appropriate, (4) consider the settings of the individual, and (5) consider whether the clinician is qualified to make the diagnosis.

X. *Diagnoses.* This section reports diagnoses and provides supporting evidence for them. Clinicians may or may not provide a diagnosis. Those who do typically rely on state or provincial board of education rules, state or provincial laws and regulations (e.g., those governing insanity or the ability to stand for trial), the *Diagnostic and Statistical Manual of Mental Disorders* (American Psychiatric Association, 2000), *International Classification of Diseases and Related Health Problems, Tenth Edition* (*ICD-10*; World Health Organization, 1992), or the International Classification of Functioning, Disability and Health (World Health Organization, 2001). Support for a diagnosis should be found in prior sections of the report (e.g., description of test results) and summarized here. Institutional policies and practices may not authorize a clinician to offer a diagnosis. For example, the Individuals with Disabilities Education Act reserves this right to a child study team.

XI. *Intervention recommendations.* This section may constitute the *most important section* of the report. The referral source often welcomes recommendations that have the potential to address referral and other issues. Recommendations should be based on best practice documents and tailored to the child's needs, institutional requirements, and environmental resources. They should be specific and clear. Remember the *focus of the recommendations is on the specific person evaluated*; thus, recommendations should be developed on an individualized basis and guided by the specific referral questions (Lichtenberger et al., 2004).

XII. *Signatures.* Those responsible for the report must sign it. Others who may have assisted in obtaining data, such as teachers or research assistants, generally do not need to sign. However, signatures of both the examiner and the supervising psychologist are customary if they differ.

XIII. *Data tables.* All standard and percentile scores typically are provided in a table(s) found at the end of the report. Clinicians also are advised to present data visually, displaying data using a bell curve, when needed.

USE OF COMPUTER-GENERATED
REPORTS

Automated reports generated by computer can be useful and practical when integrated appropriately into overall professional practice. These systems are quite efficient at processing a multitude of score comparisons quickly and accurately. However, the output can be overwhelming and may encourage a data-mining approach in which the examiner searches the tables and graphs for significant score differences that then are interpreted out of context with each other or the referral questions. Thus, practitioners should be cautious when using computer-generated score reports that simply report all possible score comparisons, assuming they are of equal value. In these circumstances, the examiner should generate a priori hypotheses related to the referral question and give them greater weight in the interpretation, without ignoring unexpectedly rare findings.

Many practitioners also use automated narrative reports. The first author of this book, Lawrence G. Weiss, is the senior author of the interpretive reports produced by the WISC-III and WISC-IV writers. The writer logic is written such that each referral question (if entered by the examiner) carries with it a set of hypotheses that are evaluated by the software and either ruled out or supported by the pattern of test scores in order to evaluate particular diagnostic impressions. As the interpretive process unfolds, new findings may prompt another set of related questions and hypotheses that, in turn, are investigated. This is how expert systems are coded into software. These reports can provide an excellent starting point for preparing the written evaluation. However, only the examiner can provide the personalized feel to a report that shows the child as the focal point of the assessment, not the test. The best practice is to consider automated reports as first drafts, to be reviewed and modified as needed. *Never assume the computer knows more than you.* Feel free to edit and modify according to your professional judgment. Further, automated reports that are unsigned should not be accepted as they suggest the examiner did not review and approve the report.

THE CHILD-CENTERED WRITING
STYLE

When evaluating a child, the examiner should mentally separate the investigative process of score interpretation from the exercise of writing the report. Many clinicians learned in graduate school to be *score detectives*, comparing and contrasting various profiles for statistical significance and clinically infrequent base rates. However, a professional's detailed investigative strategies must lead to clear conclusions expressed in written reports received by others. A report should offer concise and informative statements without statistical or clinical jargon, and not simply restate the analytical process used to investigate the data. The following example from another field of science may make it easier to internalize this point. An archeologist examining an ancient bone may go through an analytical process involving a complex series of statistical analyses of shape, structure, function, and carbon dating results to determine the nature and origin of the bone. However, a report that described each of these analyses would not be interpretable by most nonarcheologists.

Teachers and parents may have similar feelings after reading a psychological report that describes the scores and the statistical processes used to analyze them. Thus, the archeologist may state his or her conclusion clearly and succinctly as, "There is a 95% likelihood that this fossil is from the hind leg of a prairie dog between 12,000 and 15,000 years old." Readers of psychological reports desire clear and direct interpretations of this nature. The practice of describing scores and score differences in the report may lead to reports that are statistically correct yet lack meaning and relevance to nontechnical readers. When others for whom reports are written find them to lack clarity, they simply will stop reading them. This deprives parents, teachers, and other professionals of potentially valuable information, wastes professional resources, and does not serve children.

The problem is easily recognizable in reports that spew statistical findings without conclusions. For example,

> The patient scored 80 on the VCI and 100 on the PRI. The 20-point difference between VCI and PRI scores is statistically significant at the $p < .05$ level, and a difference of this magnitude or greater was obtained by 12.3% of the standardization sample.

Reports written in a score-centered style represent correct restatements of the process used by the examiner to analyze the data but do not provide the reader with an appropriate professional interpretation of the scores. The distinction between score analysis and interpretation is important. Score analyses without interpretation are meaningless. Data become information only after they are given meaning. Interpretation adds meaning to score analyses. An examiner using a child-centered report writing style might rewrite the aforementioned statement as follows:

> Jesse's nonverbal reasoning abilities are much better developed than his verbal reasoning abilities. This difference is likely to be obvious to those who know him well. Jesse's reported difficulty in English composition class combined with his expressed interest in math class and his penchant for artistic work at home are but a few examples of how his strengths and weaknesses are being expressed. Such trends are likely to continue and to impact his success as he selects educational opportunities after high school and seeks career opportunities.

A major theme of this book emphasizes meaningful interpretations of WISC-IV scores that also include consideration of the environments within which behaviors are displayed and any individual differences that may influence their expression. Thus, a clinician stretches well beyond simply documenting scores and score differences in narrative form and instead proceeds to explain the meaning of these data for the reader in the context of the child's life.

The following is another example of rewriting a score-based paragraph using a child-centered style. First, the score-based narrative:

> John obtained a WMI of 83, which is in the low average range and the 13th percentile compared to his peers. The difference between his WMI and VCI of 20 points is statistically significant. A difference of this magnitude occurred in only 8.4% of the standardization sample.

Now compare it to the child-centered translation:

> Working memory is the ability to hold information in short-term memory while doing something with it or something else. This ability is an important part of higher level reasoning. John was administered several working memory tasks as part of the WISC-IV evaluation. For example, he was asked to listen to a string of mixed up letters and numbers and then repeat first the letters in alphabetical order and then the numbers in numerical order. The ability to perform this task is important because it shows the extent to which John can divide his attention and concentrate in a sustained manner. These skills are critical to learning new material in school. During this part of the evaluation, John become uncharacteristically silly, laughing, looking away, and attempting to distract attention from his poor performance. At one point, he yelled, "This is dumb, why do I have to do this?" It seemed that he wished to distract attention from his inability to perform the task. John's working memory skills are far below his verbal abilities and better than only 13% of other children his age. John's difficulties in working memory may be seen in the classroom when he is asked to perform two tasks at once, such as copying an assignment from the board while listening to the next set of instructions.

SAMPLE REPORTS

Child-centered reports can take many forms, from those that are largely discourse with no or little mention of the instruments that were used to assess the child to those that provide some background information on the assessment techniques that were used to arrive at conclusions. Regardless of the format that is used, the goal is to describe the *child* rather than a detailed description of the instruments themselves or the scores obtained. Two samples of reports follow. Identifying information has been changed. The first is one written for parents wherein the referral issue was to better understand the child's social, behavioral, and emotional behaviors. The most important task in preparing this report was to ensure it educated and empowered the parents to become collaborators in understanding and advocating for their child. As such, the report describes in detail the tasks that were administered to the child and his responses to those tasks. The psychologist elected to briefly describe approximations of the tasks that were used in the assessment to allow the parents to acquire a better understanding of what their child was asked to do so they could offer their own interpretations of the meaning of his responses. When the psychologist offers interpretations they are supported with multiple sources of data, yet leave room for the parents to form their own conclusions. The language used in this report reflected the parent's educational and literacy levels. In this case, the parents were professionals, with university-level education.

The second report was prepared for a referral agency. The referral issue centers on the need for differential diagnosis and treatment. The audience is professionals with a high degree of familiarity with psychological testing and developmental disabilities. Consequently, the report is succinct.

SAMPLE A: REPORT PREPARED FOR PARENTS

Dr. S. Rutherford, Psychologist
Robertston Child and Youth Assessment Center
Confidential Psychological and Cognitive Evaluation

Name:	Reggie Block	**Parents**:	Mary and Samuel Block
Age:	7 years, 3 months	**Address:**	611 Penny Road
Grade:	2	**City:**	Robertston, DE
School:	Mayfield Elementary	**Telephone:**	966-5246
Assessment Dates:	October 22nd, 24th, 27th – 30th, 2008		
Classroom Observation:	October 30th, 2008		
Evaluators:	S. Rutherford, Ph.D., Licensed Psychologist J. Montgomery, M.A., Certified Psychological Associate		

Reason for Referral

OBSERVE: As you read the reasons for referral, notice the depth and specificity of the referral questions and how they are posed from multiple settings. This psychologist has avoided the simplistic referral questions so often seen such as, "Johnny was referred for a psychoeducational evaluations because of social and learning difficulties in the classroom." The psychologist has taken considerable time to understand the issues the child's parents and teachers are concerned and effectively communicates that to the reader. This section also forms the rationale for specific hypotheses to be tested in the evaluation, as shown in later sections.

Reggie was referred for a psychological evaluation by his parents, Mary and Samuel Block. At our intake interview, the parents expressed concerns about Reggie's social, emotional, and behavioural development. Reggie has marked difficulties when interacting with his peers. It is their observation that, while Reggie has a rich vocabulary, he seems to be very literal in his interpretation of other's verbal communication and has difficulty understanding non-verbal cues. As a result, he frequently responds to others in socially inappropriate ways. Reggie also exhibits significant difficulties with transition and prefers sameness. Shifting attention from one task to another is problematic for him. Further, Reggie is preoccupied with particular subjects of interest (e.g., ducks) and frequently engages in repetitive behaviors (e.g., repeats words in songs and dialogue from television shows, continual throat clearing) and atypical routines that involve hand-flapping and unusual foot movements. Amongst his peers, Reggie is seen as "odd" and is often the victim of teasing and bullying. The parents hoped that an assessment could give them a better understanding of Reggie's condition and help them and the school identify strategies to address his needs.

Background Information

Background information was gathered from a number of sources including Mr. and Mrs. Block; Reggie's classroom teacher, Ms. Jessica Coombs; medical records; and Reggie.

> OBSERVE: As your read the background section of the sample report, notice how the writer emphasizes aspects of the child's background that bear directly on the referral question and demonstrate an in-depth knowledge of the child's history, thus inspiring readers to have confidence that the psychologist has taken the time to understand the uniqueness of this individual child. After reading the background section, these parents are not likely to reject the diagnosis on the grounds that the psychologist "doesn't know my child." Overall, this section communicates relevant background information and predisposes readers to be receptive to the psychologist's subsequent diagnosis and recommendations.

Family Information

Information regarding the Block family was gathered during a structured interview with Mr. and Mrs. Block. Reggie, a 7-year-old English-speaking African American male, is the youngest of three children born to Mary and Samuel Block of Robertston, DE. The family has resided in their current home for the past 18 months. Mr. and Mrs. Block, who have been married for 15 years, describe their relationship as "pretty good," but acknowledged some strains on the marriage due to Reggie's behavior. The couple's two elder daughters, ages 13 and 11, are described by the parents as socially and academically successful. While Reggie feels that his relationships with various family members are good, Mr. and Mrs. Block commented that there often is tension between the children because of Reggie's social insensitivities. For example, when the girls are entertaining friends, Reggie will disrupt their conversations with his inappropriate comments. At other times, he will enter their bedrooms without an invitation. The parents attempt to correct

Reggie's inappropriate behaviors by grounding him; however, they reported that this strategy rarely results in behavioral changes.

Family Psychological or Educational History

Both parents are university graduates and are employed in professional occupations. Neither parent has a history of learning, medical, or psychological problems. Other than anxiety diagnosed in a maternal niece, Mr. and Mrs. Block are not aware of any other member of their extended family being diagnosed or treated for a psychological or learning condition. Asked if Reggie's social and behavioral patterns mirror those of either parent, Mrs. Block commented that, while she is outgoing and extroverted, Mr. Block is extremely introverted and does not enjoy social activities. Mr. Block concurred with this assessment.

Prenatal, Perinatal and Early Developmental History

During our structured interview, Mr. and Mrs. Block provided us with the following information about Reggie's developmental history. Mrs. Block's pregnancy with Reggie was unplanned. Because of complications Mrs. Block experienced during the delivery of her second child (i.e., significant hemorrhaging), she was very apprehensive about a third pregnancy. Throughout her pregnancy with Reggie, she was carefully monitored by a medical specialist. There was no reported use of medications or non-prescription drugs, and Mrs. Block refrained from consuming alcohol or smoking cigarettes. Reggie was born at 41 weeks gestation weighing 7 pounds, 7 ounces following an uncomplicated pregnancy and delivery to the then 38-year-old Mrs. Block. Reggie's APGAR scores following birth were 9 (1 minute) and 9 (5 minutes), indicating normal physical condition. Mother and son were released from the hospital within two days. Relative to his two older siblings, infant Reggie was described as "difficult". Although he was socially responsive to his parents, he was hard to soothe, frequently irritable, strongly reactive to minor changes in his physical and social environment, and easily over stimulated. His crying was loud and intense. Fortunately for the parents, Reggie's eating and sleeping patterns were predictable: it seemed to them that the only time they found respite from his demands was when he was engaged in these activities. Although Reggie met many developmental milestones in a normal temporal sequence (e.g., talking), he was slow to walk.

Reggie's difficult temperament has continued to impact his behavior. He is described as "not being in touch on a social level" and "incapable of conversation," which makes it exceedingly difficult for him to relate to other children and adults. Related to this, Reggie demonstrates limited ability to recognize the feelings or interests of those around him. He frequently changes topics to focus on his interests and never inquires or participates in conversations about the trials and tribulations of others. Further, Reggie is insensitive to the facial expressions and body language of others and manifests significant problems with social problem-solving, hyperactivity, and "telling the truth." Most concerning to the parents is Reggie's inability to handle transitions and changes in his environment. Transitions and changes seem to precipitate angry outbursts. Reggie's outbursts, while brief, occur several times a day and are highly disruptive (e.g., Reggie will shout, stomp his feet, cry, or throw himself on the floor). To minimize these episodes, the parents try throughout the day to prepare Reggie for potential changes to his routines by giving advance preparation and reassurance and through reducing distractions (e.g., turning off the television). Furthermore, Reggie's distinct play patterns distinguish his behavior from that of other same-age children. For example, Reggie seldom uses his toys in creative ways. While he has accumulated a substantial collection of ducks, he never plays with them as 'birds'; rather, he focuses on lining them up in different configurations.

Educational History

We met with Reggie's teacher, Ms. Coombs, who provided the following information and observations on Reggie's performance within the school context. Reggie generally is comparable to his peers in academic abilities, although variability in performance is noted throughout the day. Particular strengths are demonstrated in writing, arts, and singing. The most significant challenges facing Reggie within the school context relate to his social-emotional functioning, lack of flexibility, low frustration level, and inattention. Reggie does not cope successfully with transitions and new experiences and reacts to them with emotional outbursts. While Reggie's outbursts have decreased, considerable energy has been invested in modifying his behavior in stressful situations. Situations likely to precipitate an outburst are those generally perceived by others as relatively innocuous (e.g., not being able to find a pen, not liking the tasks the teacher assigns). Of late, hand-wringing seems to have supplanted outbursts as means of controlling stress. Through trial-and-error, the teacher has found that Reggie seems to be most successful when instruction is highly structured and directions are simplified and minimized. Ms. Coombs also referenced emotional immaturity and poorly developed social skills as areas of additional concern. For example, Reggie has significant difficulty relating to other children; they perceive him as different and react to his atypical behavior either by ignoring or teasing him. He frequently engages in solitary play, which involves talking to himself, repeating lines from movies or television shows, or singing disconnected lyrics to himself. Further, Reggie appears to exhibit motor coordination difficulties and at times has difficulties quickly processing visual information. By way of example, Ms. Coombs noted that Reggie is very slow at tasks such as drawing or copying material. Although he can complete puzzles, it takes him an inordinately long time to do so. Moreover, he appears to be clumsier than other children and as awkward and uncoordinated at sports.

Medical History

Pediatric records revealed that Reggie's medical history is unremarkable. Hearing and vision, assessed by his pediatrician, are normal. There is no history of significant illnesses or injuries, and Reggie has never been hospitalized. The only prescribed medications have been antibiotics used to treat bacterial infections,. The parents describe Reggie as a "picky" eater. He is overly sensitive to particular food textures, tastes, and smells and refuses to eat foods which fall in one of his exclusionary categories. While his current sleep patterns are normal, Reggie has suffered from night terrors in the past. These seemed to occur when he was overtired.

Previous Assessments

Although there have been long-standing concerns about Reggie's behavioral, emotional, and social development, there have been no previous psychological evaluations.

Assessment Methods

Given the referral issues and information obtained through semi-structured interviews, we used assessment methods that allowed us to investigate a number of diagnostic conditions that might be explanatory of Reggie's problems (e.g., Nonverbal Learning Disability (NLD), Autism Spectrum Disorders, and/ or other various conditions of behavior and emotion). Assessment methods we used included:

Semi-Structured Interviews

Mary and Samuel Block, Parents	October 22, 2008
Reggie Block, Client (Also attended by mother)	October 22, 2008
Jessica Coombs, Teacher	October 24, 2008

Observations

Classroom Observation	October 30, 2008

Direct Assessment

Wechsler Intelligence Scale for
  Children-Fourth Edition   (WISC-IV)   October 27, 2008
Children's Memory Scale (CMS)   October 28, 2008
NEPSY: A Developmental Neuropsychological
  Assessment (selected subtests) (NEPSY)   October 29, 2008
Conners' Continuous
  Performance Test   (CCPT-II)   October 29, 2008
Naglieri Nonverbal Analogies Test (NNAT)   October 30, 2008
Woodcock Johnson Tests of
  Cognitive Ability (selected subtests) (WJ-III)   October 31, 2008
Test of Pragmatic Language (TPL)   October 31, 2008

Other Reports

Behavior Assessment for Children (BASC-PR)– Parent Rating Scales (completed by Mary Block)
Behavior Assessment for Children – Teacher Rating Scales (BASC-TR) (completed by Jessica Coombs)
Asperger Syndrome Diagnostic Scale (ASDS) (completed by Mary Block)
Adaptive Behavior Assessment System-II (ABAS-II) (completed by Jessica Coombs)

> OBSERVE: As you read the Assessment Observations section, notice how the writer selects behavioral observations that bear directly on the referral questions posed above. By reporting observations in multiple settings, the psychologist demonstrates again that she knows the child well, which further inspires the reader to have confidence in the report.

Assessment Observations

Interview Observations

At our first meeting with Reggie, which also was attended by his mother, Reggie initially was quiet. However, as he became more comfortable, he began to dominate, the conversation, frequently interrupting his mother or us and responding to our questions with unrelated verbal exchanges. Reggie took advantage of paper and crayons that were in the interview room and proceeded to draw a series of ducks, each essentially the same size and orientation. Throughout the drawing exercise, he repetitively cleared his throat. When his mother indicated that Reggie was very interested in jazz, Reggie immediately responded by humming the theme from Sesame Street. Reggie did not sing the lyrics; rather, his vocalizations were detailed representations of each musical instrument included in the song. For example, he sang the introduction to the song in rhythmic percussive manner, followed by what was obviously the bass guitar line, and next the horn. The song proceeded in this manner until its completion. We observed that Reggie's face and body remained expressionless throughout the song. Reggie also demonstrated an intense interest in game shows. At one point, he drew a cone shaped segment with detailed writing inside it and asked if we knew what it was. When we responded that we did not recognize it, Reggie explained that it was his favorite piece on the Jeopardy board, the one between bankrupt and three thousand dollars. When asked if he enjoyed game shows, Reggie proceeded to talk at great length about all the shows he regularly watches. We found it extremely difficult to redirect his conversation.

Assessment Observations

Reggie's preoccupation with game shows was evident throughout the subsequent assessment appointments. During administration of the WISC-IV, Reggie had to be reminded several times that the activity was not actually a game show. For example, on a number of occasions, his responses to questions, for which he did not know the answers, imitated the lines from a popular game show: "*I think I'll have to go home with the money*" or "*I think I'll ask the audience.*" Further, throughout the assessment, Reggie made beeping sounds when answering questions, as though a clock was timing his response. This was particularly apparent when motor responses were required as part of the answer. During a couple of exchanges, Reggie asked a question when it seemed as though his intention was to make a statement. For example, when entering the clinic one particularly cold day, he exclaimed, "*What is cold?*" When the one of the psychologists attempted to answer, he corrected her by stating "*It changes how you feel. Cold.*" After some thought, the psychologist realized that this unusual pattern of communication also took its direction from a game show. Further observations of Reggie's performance during particular assessment tasks are outlined in the Assessment Findings section.

Classroom Observation

Reggie was observed by us while he and his peers participated in a direct instruction exercise delivered by the classroom teacher. (Reggie's desk and locker were easily identifiable; he had a nameplate on his desk that was decorated with a duck and his locker nameplate was adorned with a sign for *The Price is Right* and the *CBS* television logo.) A specific observation for on-task behavior was conducted during the seatwork portion of the lesson. During this 10-minute observation period, Reggie was noted to be off-task five out of 10 times.

For the most part, his off-task behaviors were not disruptive to others; he simply found items that were of greater interest to him (e.g., drawing on a paper inside his desk; looking at objects on the floor). On three occasions, Reggie responded to teacher questions with comments that were off-topic (e.g., he told a story that was related to a dream he had when the topic introduced by the teacher centered on a written French activity). From time to time, Reggie also blurted out particular phrases (*"I got it"* in reference to an assignment) and was heard to emit a beeping sound as he completed his work. When Reggie was halfway through his assignment, he switched from using a pencil to a crayon. The teacher noticed this and requested that he print with the pencil. While he initially complied, as soon as the teacher turned away, Reggie returned to printing with a crayon.

We also were interested in observing whether Reggie initiated bids for joint attention (i.e., engaged other children's attention to share enjoyment of objects or events) and responded to the joint attention bids of others. To facilitate this, we observed Reggie and his peers during a 15-minute unstructured playground experience. On three occasions, individual classmates approached Reggie to trade equipment; each time, Reggie simply ignored the classmate. While Reggie did approach a classmate, it was for instrumental purposes (i.e., he wanted an object the other student was holding). His communication was brief (i.e., *"give"*); he seemed to be unaware of the social expectations associated with his request (e.g., need for politeness or to provide a rationale for the request).

Assessment Findings

OBSERVE: Notice how the writer now turns from demonstrating knowledge of the child's background and behavior to educating the reader about specific aspects of cognitive functioning. In particular, the role of attentional and executive functions is explained in non-technical language, and the relationship of these behaviors observed in the classroom is spelled out. To explain the constructs being evaluated, the writer uses the technique of describing the task. The writer does not mention test scores in the body of the report. Rather, she reports major findings by describing the child's performance relative to other children of the same age using percentiles. Keep in mind that reporting scores does not constitute reporting findings. They require interpretations and explanations. You will further observe that when the child responds to a task in a way that is highly characteristic of his symptoms, the particular response also is described. Overall, this approach successfully communicates the child's strengths and weaknesses without using statistical jargon.

Within the Assessment Findings section, Reggie's scores have been reported using the percentile rank. When we use the percentile rank (PR), we are comparing Reggie's score on a particular test with the scores of other children similar to him (e.g., age, grade, sex) who have taken the test. This kind of comparison is a normative one. The PR will tell us the percentage of children getting a score that is less or equal to Reggie's score. For example, if

Reggie's score on a particular test placed him in the 72nd percentile, this means that Reggie's score was as high or higher than 72% of the scores of children who took the test. It is important to keep in mind that PRs refer to a percentage of people, not to the percentage of correct items. In addition to comparing Reggie to other children on various tests, we also will discuss Reggie's personal strengths and weaknesses. In this case, we will take Reggie's performance across various tests and compare them against each other. We considered personal strengths to be in areas where test performance was above the 84th percentile. A test score falling between the 25th to 75th percentile rank identified abilities within the average range while test scores between the 1st to 11th percentile rank described areas considered to be weaknesses.

Attention/Executive Functions Attention skills are critical to learning, memory, and complex cognitive skills. Reggie first must pay attention to new information in order to learn, remember, and use information to engage in more complex thought. Various components of attention are involved, including sustained attention (i.e., the ability to stay on task during continuous or repetitive activity), selective attention (i.e., the ability to attend to what is important and ignore other distracting influences), divided attention (i.e., the ability to simultaneously respond to multiple tasks), and alternating attention (i.e., the capacity for mental flexibility which allows one to move between tasks that have different cognitive requirements). The ability to plan, remain flexible, use organized search strategies, monitor and correct performance, inhibit responses while working on a task, and mentally manipulate information (i.e., working memory) are foundational to directing and modulating attention. These abilities are referred to as executive functions. Reggie's teacher described his attention skills as being developmentally immature. To assess Reggie's attention and executive functions, we selected tasks from several measures including the WISC-IV, NEPSY, CMS, WJ-III, and Conners' CPT-II.

A. Divided Attention Imagine Reggie participating in a group activity at school where he and his peers have been asked to identify the five largest populated countries in the world and place them in order of size. There is a lot of verbal interaction within the group, as each of its members spontaneously contributes country names and populations. To be successful at this task, Reggie would need to attend to the potentially overlapping contributions of various group members, hold the information they have offered in his short-term memory, and then redirect his attention to the task of mentally manipulating the material to ensure that the countries are placed in the correct order by population size. This is a task that requires both divided attention and short-term/working memory. To see if Reggie's skills in these areas were comparable to those of his peers, we used a WJ-III test that measured these abilities. For this task, Reggie was asked to reorder information placed in immediate awareness into two discrete categories. For example, he was asked to listen to a series that contained digits and words, such as "*dog, 1, show, 8, 2, apple.*" He then attempted to reorder the information, repeating first the objects in sequential order, and then the digits in sequential order. Reggie scored as well as or better than 26 percent of children who had taken this test. This percentile rank places Reggie within the low average range for this test.

B. Auditory Selective Attention   The classroom environment is one where there is considerable verbal interaction and distractions (e.g., the teacher is presenting a lesson while another class is doing some group work in the hall just outside the class). To learn from the lesson, Reggie would need to selectively direct his attention to the teacher to discriminate what she is saying while ignoring or screening out extraneous auditory information. We used another WJ-III test to see if Reggie could attend to what was important and ignore other distracting influences. Test items were presented from an audio recorder. Reggie was asked to listen to a word while seeing four pictures and then to point to the correct picture for the word. Auditory distractors of increasing intensity were introduced throughout this test. Reggie scored as well as or better than 8 percent of children on this task. During administration of this task, we noted that, as the sound discriminations became more difficult and the background noises increased in intensity, Reggie became visibly agitated as evidenced through hand-wringing and -flapping.

C. Sustained Attention   There are many daily tasks which require that Reggie pay attention to visual material that he might perceive as dull and repetitive. For example, there will be times when Reggie has to perform academic tasks that may not be motivating to him, like completing several pages of arithmetic calculations. To sustain his attention to this activity, he will need to pay close attention to all the arithmetic signs to ensure that he is adding and subtracting at appropriate times; curb the tendency to be distracted by other things; ensure that he does not get over-focused on specific calculation problems or signs (e.g., only doing the calculations that require adding or ignoring subtraction signs and answering all through addition); consistently respond to all the questions from beginning to end rather than just a portion of them; and work in a timely manner. The Conners' Continuous Performance Test allowed us to determine that Reggie displayed average abilities in each of these areas. Moreover, when his pattern was compared to that of normally-developing children, as well as those with clinical attention problems, Reggie's profile on this test very closely approximated the normally developing group.

There also are many activities that require Reggie to sustain his attention to verbal information that he might perceive as boring while remaining responsive and flexible enough to take note of and respond to changes in the verbal information. Imagine Reggie in a social interaction where a peer is verbally articulating some very pedantic game rules. Suddenly, a number of other boys join the interaction and the previously boring rules suddenly change to encompass a much more complex format. Now Reggie must shift his attention from attending to the initial, straightforward presentation to the much more elaborated and detailed one. Moreover, he must ensure that he varies the rules of the game as a function of how many children are involved. The NEPSY has a test that taps these competencies. In Part A of this test, Reggie had to learn to respond to *red*. He was then asked to shift his attention and respond to contrasting stimuli in Part B (*When you hear red, put a yellow square in the box*). Reggie scored as well as or better than 5 percent of children on this task. We noted that while Reggie was successful in attending selectively to the simple auditory material, he encountered difficulty when the task was changed to measure the ability to shift his attention, maintain a complex mental set, and regulate his responses according to both matching and non-matching stimuli. When target stimuli were presented close together, Reggie became frustrated and began grabbing handfuls of the colored squares and dumping them in the box. It appeared to the examiners that complex and multi-task information generated considerable anxiety in Reggie.

D. Auditory Working Memory Whenever Reggie temporarily holds new verbal information (e.g., words, ideas, sentences, or numbers) while he works with it, he is using his auditory working memory. These auditory working memory skills are needed for understanding directions, solving a verbal problem, holding in mind what he wants to say next in a conversation, solving arithmetic problems, and so on. To see how Reggie's auditory working memory skills compared with his peers, we first administered a WISC-IV task that required him to hold verbally presented number sequences in his mind (e.g., 1-5-2-3-9) and then manipulate the sequences by repeating them backwards (e.g., 9-3-2-5-1). Reggie scored as well as or better than 50 percent of children on this test of auditory working memory. He also scored as well as or better than 50 percent of children on another WISC-IV task that measured his ability to focus on verbally presented mathematical material, hold information in working memory, and perform numerical operations on the information (e.g., *If you have nine apples and give three away, how many do you have left?*). Similarly, Reggie scored as well as or better than 50 percent of other children on a WJ-III task that also asked him to hold a sequence of numbers in immediate awareness while performing a mental operation on the information.

E. Executive Functions   To be an effective learner, Reggie must engage in several self-regulated activities that, among others, include goal-setting (i.e., know what he wants to accomplish), planning (i.e., determine how best to use the time and resources he has available for a learning task), controlling attention (i.e., focus his attention on the task at hand), and applying different learning and self-motivational strategies (e.g., use a variety of strategies to keep himself on task). We used a NEPSY task to determine Reggie's competencies in these areas. Reggie was asked to move three colored balls to target positions on three pegs in a prescribed number of moves according to a set of rules. The task was timed. Reggie scored as well as or better than 5 percent of children on this test. Qualitative observation of Reggie's performance indicated that he had difficulty generating new solutions to problems. Moreover, he violated many rules, suggesting potential problems in monitoring performance. Reggie needed to be reminded of the rules (e.g., *move only one ball at a time*) several times during this task. As task complexity increased, rule breaking became more evident.

F. Personal Strengths and Weaknesses in Attention

> OBSERVE: In this section, the writer integrates findings from the assessment of multiple areas of attention. She utilizes easy to understand graphs to better communicate with pictures and words. When describing each major finding, she indicates her relative level of certainty about the finding, and also offers an example of how this characteristic might be observed in the classroom.

Reggie has average abilities to temporarily hold and process a limited amount of verbal information. His competencies in this area suggest that he likely uses various rehearsal strategies, such as repeating or grouping the information, to enhance the capacity of his working memory. In day-to-day functioning, Reggie's skills in auditory working memory will help him achieve success on various learning tasks that involve selecting, comparing, organizing, and processing verbal information (e.g., understanding what he reads, remembering some parts of an arithmetic problem while he is dealing with other parts). Reggie's ability to sustain his attention to visual material that may not be particularly motivating is another area of average development. His success in sustaining his visual attention is facilitated by his abilities to maintain the speed at which he responds to the visual information, curb any tendencies toward responding impulsively, and alter his responses as a function of changes in the visual material. As such, we would expect that Reggie will perform similarly to the majority of his peers on tasks such as learning a spelling list, reading long passages, or paying attention to details in graphs and figures. Reggie also shows low average abilities in dividing his attention (i.e., simultaneously attending to multiple tasks). Taking notes while listening to the teacher present a lecture is one kind of activity that taps these competencies.

   In contrast, Reggie's ability to maintain his attention to continuous and repetitive verbal activities is relatively less developed. Within a classroom context, Reggie may find it difficult to remain attentive to lectures, listen to instructions, or maintain his interest in a documentary, particularly when these activities are not intrinsically motivating to him. Further, Reggie's ability to distinguish the most important or central verbal information from what is irrelevant or less important (i.e., selective auditory attention) is poorly developed. Our observations suggested that, rather than processing too little verbal information, Reggie processes too much, and he finds this overwhelming. Many daily activities will require Reggie to listen selectively (e.g., following a conversation while another one is taking place nearby; listening to directions when a radio or television is playing in the background; focusing on the key purpose of a small group experience when divergent ideas are being expressed). Finally, his ability to regulate his learning, particularly monitoring his progress toward goal achievement and changing his learning strategies or goal if necessary, is less well developed. This weakness limits the attainment of goals that Reggie sets for himself and interferes with his learning and achievement.

Language

> OBSERVE: In this section, the writer introduces the rationale for administering language tasks, ties the rationale to the referral questions, and clearly states what is expected to be learned about the child from the results of these tests. This is core to the *assess-understand-intervene* model of practice. It is the "assess to understand" portion of the model. Here the psychologists is laying out her rationale for what she needs to know about the child and how she will find out. This constitutes an apriori hypothesis, which is always preferred to assessment methods where score differences are "mined" to identify all statistically significant findings.
> In addition, notice that the writer returns to an educative voice in describing the next area of assessment, and how it relates to classroom performance. Your will notice this again in subsequent sections of the report as the writer moves to reporting findings from the visual spatial, processing speed, and memory areas of the evaluation.

   Reggie is perceived by his parents as having difficulty comprehending and producing language in a socially appropriate manner. For Reggie to use language effectively for communicative purposes (as well as for thinking and learning), mastery of its form (e.g., facility at phonological processing and understanding the syntactical structure of language), content (i.e., understand the meaning attached to words and sentences), and function (i.e., use of language appropriately in social contexts) is necessary. Facility with these subcomponents of language will allow him to construct increasingly complex and accurate schemes and ideas about the world, enhance his reading and writing skills, increase his ability to learn abstract ideas and concepts, and regulate his behavior and emotions. Reggie's skills in the form, content, and function of language, as well as his verbal reasoning abilities, were assessed through various tasks from several measures, including the WISC-IV, WJ-III, NEPSY, and Test of Pragmatic Language.

A. Language Form (Phonological Processing; Syntactic Complexity) The ability to deconstruct or break down written language into phonemes (i.e., phonological processing) is an important skill for reading acquisition. For example, to read the word *cat*, Reggie must recognize each of the phonemes (i.e., $c - a - t$). To assess Reggie's phonological processing competencies, we used a WJ-III task that required him to listen to a series of syllables or phonemes and then blend the sounds into a word. Reggie scored as high as or higher than 50 percent of children on this test. On a NEPSY test of phonological processing, Reggie had to identify words from segments and then put them together. In the first segment of this task, Reggie was asked to identify a picture from an orally presented word segment. The second portion assessed phonological segmentation at the level of letter sounds and word segments. Reggie was asked to create a new word by omitting a word segment (syllable) or letter (phoneme) or by substituting one phoneme for another. He scored as high as or higher than 25 percent of other children. We observed that Reggie had success with those components that required him to produce a new word by removing the initial sound but was unsuccessful when he needed to remove a medial or final sound. Finally, we used another NEPSY test to examine Reggie's ability to process and respond to verbal instruction of increasing syntactic complexity. Simple items in this task involved pointing to rabbits of different sizes, colors, and facial expressions. More complex items required Reggie to point to target shapes by color, position, and relationship to other figures in response to verbal instructions. Reggie's skills on this subtest are poorly developed. He scored as well as or better than 5 percent of children on this test. We noted that Reggie was successful only on items that asked for a simple direction to be followed (e.g., *point to the blue and then the yellow one*). He was unable to respond correctly when the directions required him to understand negation (e.g., *is not... but is*), temporal/sequential (e.g., *but first... after*), or spatial (e.g., *underneath/above*) concepts.

B. Language Content Reggie's ability to effectively communicate with others is highly dependent on his expressive word knowledge. To assess this ability, Reggie was administered a subtest from the WISC-IV that required him to give definitions for words that were read aloud to him. Reggie's performance on this subtest was as well as or better than 25 percent of children. He attained a similar score on another task drawn from the WJ-III which also assessed lexical knowledge (i.e., his ability to name pictures of objects), as well as competencies at reasoning using word knowledge

(30th percentile). The latter required that Reggie listen to three words of an analogy and then complete the analogy with an appropriate fourth word. We also were interested in assessing Reggie's ability to access and produce familiar words rapidly (e.g., size, color, and shape words). Reggie excelled on this task; he scored as well as or better than 91 percent of children on this NEPSY test.

C. Language Function (Pragmatics) In light of the interview and observational data indicating Reggie experiences communication and social interaction difficulties, we decided to administer a test of pragmatic language. Pragmatic language is described as language used socially to achieve goals. It involves what is said, why, and for what purpose. Mastery of the pragmatic components of language involves consideration of the physical setting, audience, topic, purpose, visual-gestural cues, and abstraction. On the Test of Pragmatic Language, Reggie scored as well as or better than 4 percent of children. Reggie used formal and rigid language structures as he produced speech responses to pictorially presented situations. He used "polite" words routinely, even when they did not syntactically or contextually make sense. For example, when shown a picture of a boy who had dropped a pin and needed another child to retrieve it, Reggie's suggested request was *"Please may you get some pins."* When asked about what to say at the doctor's office, Reggie responded *"Please may you help me, I'm sick."* Although the meaning and intent were clear, the structure of the sentence was clumsy and unnatural. Additionally, Reggie seemed to have difficulty reasoning with and socially situating many of the questions that were presented. For example, when asked, *"Where might somebody say, 'the swing is broken'?"*, Reggie responded with *"Somebody fix it."*

We also used a WISC-IV task to explore Reggie's knowledge of conventional standards of behavior, social judgment and maturity, and common sense, along with problem-solving abilities. This task required Reggie to answer questions based on his understanding of general principles and social situations. Reggie was unable to respond correctly to any of the questions on this test. His answers were only peripherally or tangentially related to the questions, or he interpreted the question so that it related to his specific interests. For example, Reggie's circumscribed interests in television game shows were reflected in his answers to many questions (*"What should you do if you cut your finger?"* Answer *"I don't know – I'll ask the audience"*). While testing of limits revealed that Reggie often could provide a quasi-appropriate response, redirecting his attention was very time-consuming.

> OBSERVE: Above, the writer describes the child's response to an actual test question because the response is highly characteristic of the child's symptomotology. This can be a powerful communication technique when used properly, however, specific test items should not be revealed to parents and teachers. Both legally and ethically, test items are considered "secure." If intelligence test questions become public

knowledge then children's responses become suspect, and the validity of the testing tool could be compromised for the entire field. For these reasons, you should alter or paraphrase items when using this technique, and use it very infrequently. In this case, the writer may have stated:

> For example, Reggie's circumscribed interests in television game shows was reflected in his answers to many questions *("What should you do if you bruise your knee? Answer 'I don't know' – I'll ask the audience")*.

D. Verbal Reasoning   Many times throughout the day Reggie will need to use his verbal skills to problem-solve or reason. For example, when he is in dispute with his sisters about a particular course of action, Reggie's abilities to use verbal reasoning to solve the problem will determine who wins the argument. To assess these competencies, Reggie was given a WISC-IV task during which he was presented with two words that represent common objects or concepts (e.g., lake and mountain). He then was asked to describe how they are similar. Reggie scored as well as or better than 25 percent of children. We also were interested in determining how Reggie reasons using words. For this WISC-IV task, Reggie was asked to identify the common concept being described in a series of clues. Again, Reggie scored as well as or better than 25 percent of children.

E.   Personal Strengths and Weaknesses in Language

> OBSERVE: The writer uses the term *personal* strengths rather than *intraindividual* or *ipsative* strengths that are commonly used in textbooks on profile interpretation. By avoiding professional jargon, the writer makes the report more readable for teachers and parents.

Reggie demonstrates a strong ability to access and produce familiar words in alternating patterns rapidly, a skill dependent on the retrieval of sound-symbol associations and spoken word-written word connections with ease. This ability is important to reading acquisition. Reggie shows average competencies in a number of other language areas. For example, he has the auditory-phonological perception and analysis skills that are foundational for language comprehension, reading, and spelling. He has difficulty, though, replacing medial or final sounds to form new words. Although not as well developed as his word retrieval and phonological skills, Reggie shows low average abilities in inductive verbal reasoning (i.e., recognizing connections and relationships among verbal concepts), competencies necessary for higher-order learning and problem solving. He also shows low average skills in expressive and receptive vocabulary, important building blocks for the development of verbal reasoning.

In contrast, Reggie has poorly developed skills when he is required to process and comprehend verbal messages that are semantically and syntactically complex. The auditory attention weaknesses identified earlier, in part, may help explain these difficulties. We noted in our interactions with Reggie that he often asked for instructions to be repeated and appeared to be internally distracted (e.g., he would gaze around the room). Spatial problems also would contribute to these difficulties, as the errors that Reggie made often were related to spatial concepts (e.g., behind, beside, over). Further evaluation of Reggie's visual-spatial processing skills will help determine their role in his difficulties with this aspect of language.

Consistent with our classroom observations, as well as those of the teacher and parents, Reggie demonstrates a weakness at using communication functionally and appropriately. For example, we observed that he was unable to vary his language to fit particular purposes and often used formal and rigid language regardless of the goal of the communication. Moreover, Reggie frequently failed to adapt his language according to the needs or expectations of the listener (e.g., he failed to explain to a peer why he needed an object the peer held during our school observation). Further, during our interactions, Reggie demonstrated an inability to follow rules for conversation. He frequently interrupted his conversational partner to pursue a topic of self-interest and repetitively verbalized phrases out of context. Moreover, his ability to socially problem solve is developmentally immature or atypical. For example, when asked questions that assessed his choice of appropriate alternatives with respect to social situations, Reggie gave answers that reflected a lack of depth, social inappropriateness, or tangential relationship to the question. Insofar as verbal communication is the basic medium through which social and academic learning takes place, Reggie's pragmatic and social problem solving deficits will be an impediment to his psychological, social, and school success.

Visual-Spatial Processing and Sensorimotor Skills

Teacher comments indicating that Reggie is slow and clumsy at drawing or copying material, along with assessment findings that indicate difficulties comprehending spatial conceptual terms, led to our assessment of Reggie's visual-spatial and sensorimotor skills. Visual-spatial processing involves a number of interrelated subcomponents including abilities to solve nonverbal problems, synthesize elements into a meaningful whole (visualization), represent objects mentally, discriminate between objects, judge the orientation of lines and angles, distinguish between left and right, understand relationships among objects in space (location and directionality), copy a model or reproduce it using blocks, adopt a variety of perspectives and rotate objects mentally, and understand and interpret symbolic representations of external space (maps and routes). A number of these visual-spatial processing skills were assessed using tasks from the WISC-IV, NEPSY, and WJ-III.

A. Nonverbal Reasoning Nonverbal reasoning is necessary whenever Reggie is required to solve a new problem which involves visual images. For example, nonverbal reasoning skills would be used when Reggie is asked to design and build a model car. To see if Reggie has the nonverbal reasoning skills that would allow him to experience success with this kind of task, we first administered a WISC-IV test that required Reggie to analyze and synthesize abstract visual stimuli. Reggie was required to view a model we constructed out of blocks and then, using similar blocks, recreate the design within a specified time limit. Reggie scored as well as or better than 25 percent of children. As this test placed demands on Reggie's motor abilities and speed of processing visual material, we administered several other tests that reduced these demands. A test, also from the WISC-IV, measured Reggie's ability to categorize (or find what was common among) visual objects. Reggie was presented with two or three rows of pictures and was asked to choose one picture from each row to form a group with a common characteristic. For example,

where the common characteristic is animal. On this task, Reggie scored as well as or better than 37 percent of children. He also completed two matrix reasoning or problem solving tests, one from the WISC-IV and the other a nonverbal problem solving test, the Matrix Analogies Test. These measures required Reggie to look at an incomplete matrix and select the missing portions from among several options. For example,

where the square is the correct answer. On both tests, Reggie scored as well as or better than 50 percent of children.

OBSERVE: The writer uses *simulated* items, rather than real test items, when necessary to effectively communicate critical points.

B. Visual Recognition of Essential and Nonessential Details   The ability to differentiate essential from nonessential visual details is important to facilitate performance of a number of everyday tasks. For example, consider written text that is accompanied by pictorial material introduced to facilitate understanding. If Reggie is alert to the essential visual cues, his comprehension of the text will be enhanced. On the other hand, if nonessential cues capture his attention, his understanding of what he reads may be compromised. To assess this ability, we used a WISC-IV test that required Reggie to view a picture and then point to or name the important part that was missing within a specified time period. Reggie scored as well as or better than 37 percent of children on this test.

OBSERVE: While the WISC-IV is administered in its entirety, specific subtests from other assessment batteries are selected for administration to provide further information about particular clinical questions that remain. Notice that in each case, the writer states why the task is being administered and what she expects to learn from the results. Again, she is *assessing to understand* specific aspects of the child's functioning which are considered critical to differential diagnosis and/or informing intervention strategies.

C. Visual Planning   In social situations, Reggie's success often will depend on his ability to anticipate, judge, and understand the possible antecedents and consequents of events. For example, given all his previous reprimands, does Reggie have the ability to infer cause- and effect-relationships such that he no realizes he should not enter his sister's bedroom unless he is invited? To assess this visual planning ability, we asked Reggie to complete a WISC-III task that required him to place a series of pictures in the logical order so that they tell a story that makes sense. Reggie scored as well as or better than 5 percent of children.

D. Sensorimotor Skills   In assessing Reggie's sensorimotor skills, we first assessed Reggie's finger dexterity, an ability that he will need when he manipulates small objects, transports them through a small space, and places them correctly in a specific location. He will use this ability when he completes a puzzle, assembles a model, or fills a small container with water. Our test required Reggie to tap his fingers sequentially against his thumb from his index to his little finger (complex movement) as quickly as possible. Regardless of whether Reggie used his preferred or non-preferred hand, his performance on both the Repetitions and Sequences was at expected levels. To help us in understanding whether Reggie's slow rate of production on tasks such as handwriting stemmed from poor reception of sensory input, the examiner touched one of two of Reggie's fingers lightly. Reggie then was asked to tell which finger or fingers were touched. Reggie's score on this test was at expected levels, indicating that he was accurately perceiving the sensory information. We then went a step further and explored how well Reggie could integrate what he sees with motor activities (i.e., as in handwriting). We asked him to copy two-dimensional geometric figures on paper. This NEPSY task was not timed. Reggie scored as well as or better than 99 percent of children. We noted that Reggie was deliberate, methodological, and precise when copying the figures. If he perceived discrepancies between his drawing and the model, he attended to them until he thought they were correct. As a result, he took considerable time to complete this task. On a similar timed test where Reggie was required to draw a line inside a track as quickly as possible, he scored as well as or better than 25 percent of children. Reggie's lower score on this test again reflected his tendency toward working slowly to ensure that the line he drew met his perceived standards rather than problems in motor coordination.

E. Summary of Personal Strengths and Weaknesses in Visual-Spatial and Sensorimotor Skills

Reggie's ability to copy visual designs is strong when he is given ample time to complete the task. This ability is dependent on a number of competencies including visual-motor ability, eye-hand coordination, fine motor coordination, and perceptual discrimination. We noted that Reggie works very slowly when he is copying designs, as he is intent on producing the designs exactly as they are depicted. When he perceives that he has made an error, Reggie becomes noticeably frustrated and repeatedly redraws the designs until he determines they are correct. Within a learning context, it will be important to give Reggie sufficient time to complete activities dependent on visual-motor ability or to shorten the task requirements so that he can complete them with minimal anxiety. Reggie's abilities to reason by analogy, serial reasoning, and spatial visualization (i.e., imagining how a figure would look when two or more components are combined) are within the average ranges but not as well developed as his copying skills. Reggie also performs within the average range on activities that require him to focus on the relevant details of visual information. Within his day-to-day performance, we will see these competencies when Reggie is required to recognize objects and details in maps and pictures, identify familiar landmarks that may be important to his ability to find his way home, and proofreading his written products.

In contrast, Reggie's ability to anticipate how people will respond to his behaviors is poorly developed. Given that his abilities in nonverbal reasoning and attention to details are within the average range (skills necessary for successful performance in this area), it is likely that poor social problem solving and planning abilities help explain this weakness.

Processing Speed

Processing speed refers to the ease and speed by which Reggie performs various cognitive tasks. As Reggie increases the speed at which he can process information, his short-term working memory will become more efficient. In turn, that will enhance his ability to engage in higher level thinking. Automatization (i.e., practicing tasks until they no longer require active attention) is one way to enhance processing speed. Reggie was administered several tests, including those from the WISC-IV and WJ-III, designed to measure processing speed.

A. Speed of Processing Visual Symbols   The time it takes for Reggie to process visual symbols will be an important determinant of his success on abilities such as reading comprehension. Quick processing of visual symbols, such as letters, will allow him to redirect his working memory toward understanding the material he reads. Reggie completed timed WISC-IV task on which he was asked to copy symbols that were paired with simple geometric shapes in order to measure how quickly he processes this type of information. Using a key, Reggie was asked to draw each symbol in its corresponding shape or box within a specified time limit. For example,

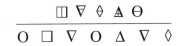

Reggie scored as well as or better than 1 percent of children. As a further check, we had him complete a similar timed WJ-III test. He scored as well as or better than 4 percent of children. Keeping with our earlier observations, we observed that, although Reggie made very few errors, he drew over the same line repeatedly to ensure it was straight. The amount of time he took to complete the task was used to determine his score. His tendency to repeatedly correct his drawing was reflected in his low score. We already have noted that, when time is not a factor in performance on tasks requiring the integration of visual-spatial skills with coordinated activities, Reggie shows an exceptional strength. Results from administration of another WISC-IV test that placed less emphasis on Reggie's handwriting or drawing skills but still assessed the speed at which he processes visual symbols showed that Reggie scored as well as or higher than 25 percent of children.

B. Auditory Processing Speed   We used a WJ-III test to see how quickly Reggie could retrieve verbal information from long-term memory. Reggie's ability to name as many examples as possible from a given category (e.g., things to eat and drink, first names of people, and animals) within a

1-minute time period is poorly developed. He scored as well as or higher than 5 percent of children.

C. Personal Strengths and Weaknesses in Processing Abilities When Reggie is asked to process visual symbols (e.g., letters) quickly and respond to the information he perceives by drawing or writing something, he works very slowly. His slow rate of production is largely related to his extremely cautious approach to drawing or writing material rather than to slow visual processing speed. His rate of retrieving categorical verbal information (i.e., names of things that are related to each other like different kinds of foods or animals) is poorly developed. Keeping with other information we have learned about Reggie, it is likely that the social meaningfulness of this kind of activity may place heavier cognitive demands on Reggie than when unrelated material is involved.

Memory

Memory refers to a person's ability to retain and retrieve information. The Children's Memory Scale along with some tasks from the WJ-III and NEPSY were used to assess Reggie's verbal and visual memory as well as his memory speed. Thus, his immediate (i.e., short-term) and delayed (i.e., long term) memory for meaningful and non-meaningful verbal and nonverbal information was assessed. This evaluation provides information on Reggie's ability to acquire and retain information. Reggie's ability to spontaneously remember information versus his ability to retrieve information when provided with cues also was compared.

A. Immediate Memory

To teach Reggie about numeration systems, his teacher uses concrete materials (i.e., cubes of only one color). For him to benefit from this instruction, Reggie must have competencies in recalling and recognizing visual information. We assessed this ability by having him learn the spatial location of dots. He scored as well as or better than 50 percent of children. Further, he scored as well as or better than 37 percent of children when we asked him to remember and recognize a series of faces.

Reggie demonstrated poorly developed skills when he was asked to retell two stories from memory. He scored as well as or better than 5 percent of children. We were unsure whether Reggie's weakness in recalling meaningful material were caused by poor comprehension of the material or difficulties in organizing and retrieving the information from free recall. To check this out, we had him complete two memory tests from the NEPSY. First, we had him listen to a story and then recall the story. He scored as well as or better than 5 percent of children. While he continued to demonstrate weaknesses, his performance was slightly better when he was given cues to facilitate his recall. On this test, he scored as well as or better than 16 percent of children.

In contrast, Reggie showed average ability to remember the second word in a word pair which he had previously learned. He scored as well as or better than 37 percent of children. It is important to underscore that the word pairs that Reggie learned were not meaningfully connected (e.g., *apple, lamp*). Usually, it is more difficult for a child to remember material that is not meaningful than semantically related material. Reggie showed the opposite pattern.

B. Delayed Memory

Learning ultimately requires new information to be stored in long-term memory. Long-term memory is where Reggie stores such pieces of information as his name, frequently used addresses and telephone numbers, general knowledge about his world, and things he has learned in school. We first examined Reggie's ability to recall visual information to which he had previously been exposed. He scored as well as or better than 37 percent of children when he was asked to recall the dot array that was presented earlier. He also scored as well as or better than 37 percent of children when he was asked to tell us which faces he had previously seen.

Because of Reggie's weakness in immediately recalling meaningful material, we did not anticipate that he would show strong performance when we asked him to retell the stories and answer factual questions about them after a time delay. He scored as well as or better than 1 percent of children. When cues were provided to facilitate Reggie's recall, his performance improved slightly, although his score (he scored as well as or better than 16 percent of children) still suggested a weakness. Again, Reggie's performance was stronger when we assessed his recognition of nonmeaningful word pairs. He scored as well as or better than 37 percent of children.

C. Personal Strengths and Weaknesses in Memory Skills

Reggie's abilities to recall and recognize visual information immediately after he sees it and after a time delay are within average range. These abilities will be important to Reggie when he is asked to work with visual information such as remembering directions, understanding graphs, or recalling people based on facial characteristics. His skill at recognizing unrelated verbal information (e.g., pairs of words that are unrelated such as table/flower) is also similar to that of other children his age, regardless of the length of time that elapses between learning and recognizing. In contrast to this, if Reggie is read a story, a story, he has difficulty recalling the details of the story even after a delay of only a few minutes. If he is given him some cues, his recall improves slightly but still remains a weakness. Being able to remember verbal information that is not meaningfully connected generally is more difficult than recalling material that links to previous social experiences. Reggie's challenges with the latter may relate to weaknesses in social perception and problem solving.

Adaptive and Psychological Functioning

Reggie's social and emotional development was assessed with an adaptive behavior scale completed by his classroom teacher. Adaptive behaviors comprise skills needed for daily living. They include communication skills, use of community resources, functional academics, home living skills, health and safety, use of leisure time, self-care, self-direction, and social relationships. These skills are acquired as one is adapting to his or her surroundings. Reggie's functional academic skills, community use, and school living are in the normal range. In contrast, he shows poorly developed social, communication, and motor skills. For example, he scored as well as or better than 12 percent of children on the socialization and motor skills domains and as well as or better than 7 percent of children on the communication domain.

Reggie's mother and classroom teacher completed a scale that assessed various emotional and social behaviors. The manner in which the teacher and mother characterized him on this scale and during their interviews was consistent. Both respondents rated Reggie within the Clinical range (i.e., T-score of 70 or higher) on scales assessing atypicality, social withdrawal, and depression. In characterizing Reggie as behaving in ways that are immature or "odd," his mother and teacher also observe that he is often preoccupied with particular subjects, prefers sameness in his routines, resists and is unable to adapt to changes. They also describe Reggie as displaying feelings of unhappiness and sadness seen through behaviours such as frequent crying and verbal comments such as "I want to die." Further, Reggie's avoidance of social contact, reluctance to join in group or social activities, failure to establish new friendships, and social rejection by other children are seen by them as an area of significant concern.

Asperger's Syndrome is a developmental disorder that manifests itself through social and language impairments. Individuals with Asperger's Syndrome have a tendency to fixate on limited areas of interest and often demonstrate autistic-like characteristics, such as hand-flapping, sensitivity to noise, lack of flexibility and so on. Deficits in Reggie's pragmatic language, adaptive, behavioral, and emotional qualities together with his perseverant behaviors may characterize a child with Asperger's Syndrome. Thus, Reggie's mother completed a scale that includes items that represent behaviors symptomatic of Asperger's Syndrome. Information on this scale assists us in determining the likelihood that Reggie has Asperger's Syndrome. Reggie's high Asperger's Syndrome Quotient suggested the strong likelihood of this condition. However, this measure should not be used in isolation to diagnose this condition.

Summary of Findings

Mr. and Mrs. Block referred their 7 year old son, Reggie, for an assessment because of concerns centering on his pragmatic competencies, socially inappropriate behaviors, cognitive and behavioral inflexibility, and atypical and repetitive behaviors. Information was acquired through interviews with the parents and Reggie's classroom teacher; observations in clinical, classroom, and playground settings; tests that assess cognitive and language skills directly; and parent and teacher scales of adaptive and social/emotional behaviors.

At home, Reggie's parents describe him as socially insensitive, temperamentally difficult, and sensitive to changes in routines. At school, his teacher characterizes him as demonstrating a lack of flexibility, low frustration tolerance, social immaturity, and developmentally inappropriate attentional skills. Our observations of Reggie within various settings substantiate these descriptions. For example, at school, we observed Reggie to engage in repetitive behaviours, perseverate in chosen activities, demonstrate developmentally immature social and attentional skills, and lack communicative competencies relative to his classmates.

As measured by the WISC-IV, Reggie's current level of intellectual functioning is in the low average range, and above that of only 10% of other children his age. However this single score does not tell the full story because he is able to function commensurate with his peers in some areas but not others. When faced with situations that require him to reason with complex verbal material, Reggie will have noticeable difficulty compared to his friends and classmates. On the other hand, Reggie's ability to reason with complex non-verbal material is almost as good as other children his age. Similarly, his ability to hold verbal information in mind temporarily, correctly rearrange that information in his mind, and produce a meaningful result is equal to most other children. Effective instruction will make use of his strengths to compensate for his weaknesses.

OBSERVE: In the paragraph above the writer describes the major finding from the WISC-IV without citing scores or even naming the indexes. Although there is a 15-point discrepancy between the VCI and the PRI, the writer does not declare the FSIQ "invalid," but simply states that "it does not tell the whole story" and proceeds to give more detailed information about Reggie's strengths and weaknesses. The focus is on what Reggie can and cannot do well rather than his performance on the test.

Our in depth assessment of strengths and weaknesses focused on an examination of Reggie's attention, language, visual-spatial, sensory-motor, processing speed, and memory skills. Reggie displays patterns of strengths and weaknesses. With reference to his attentional skills, Reggie showed average abilities to hold, process, and manipulate limited amounts of verbal information. This ability, called auditory working memory, will help Reggie be successful in situations requiring him to temporarily store verbal information while he works with it (e.g., when he completes arithmetic problems). Reggie's skills also are similar to those of his peers when he has to sustain his attention to visual information that is repetitive and not particularly motivating. His success is facilitated by his abilities to inhibit non-relevant responses, maintain the speed at which he responds to the material throughout the task, and alter his responses as a function of changes in the task demands. However, when Reggie is required to sustain his attention to verbal rather than visual information, he demonstrates a weakness. Listening to detailed instructions or directions or paying attention to a group presentation that is not motivating to him is likely to be difficult due to this weakness. Further, Reggie will find activities that require him to monitor and plan his attention as he works toward goals to be difficult. Activities that require him to sort out the most and least relevant verbal information (e.g., to attend to his mother's talking rather than watch television) also will be challenging.

Reggie's ability to produce familiar words rapidly is strong. He performs as well as the majority of his peers on activities dependent on his knowledge of the sounds of language (e.g., skills needed for spelling), ability to reason with language, and expressive and receptive vocabulary (necessary for communication). On the other hand, Reggie's ability to understand complex verbal messages is poorly developed and, he demonstrates a weakness when using language in contextually appropriate ways. In concert, these weaknesses decrease Reggie's ability to solve social issues through language.

Relative to other children his age, Reggie shows average abilities to reason with things that he sees. He is able to identify those pictures that share common characteristics, determine parts of a puzzle or matrix that are missing, and build a tower after looking at a visual model. His skill at examining common objects and determining what may be missing also is similar to that of the majority of his peers. On the other hand, Reggie shows a weakness when he is asked to infer cause- and effect-relationships from socially meaningful visual material. This poorly developed ability interferes with Reggie's understanding of material such as comics and may signal difficulties with the interpretation of non-verbal expressions of emotion (e.g., anger or sadness signaled by facial expressions). In terms of his sensorimotor skills, Reggie performs at levels expected of children his age when time is not a factor. As previously noted, he is careful and methodological when he draws or writes, a characteristic related more to his psychological profile than to weaknesses in visual-motor coordination.

His rate of processing visual symbols seems exceptionally slow when performing activities that also involve writing or drawing. When these visual-motor demands are not as demanding, his processing speed for this type of material is within the low average range. For example, when Reggie is asked to read, he may slightly require-more time than other children. If we couple the reading task with having to highlight particular text, we would expect that Reggie will require significantly more time than his peers. Further, Reggie's ability to rapidly retrieve meaningful verbal information from long-term memory is poorly developed. This will be evident when he is asked to quickly form verbal connections between particular concepts (e.g., respond quickly to his mother's request to explain elements of his behavior).

Reggie shows average ability to recall and recognize spatial material and faces immediately after he sees them as well as after a time delay. These memory abilities play an important role in his ability to remember information that he acquires as a result of exposure to concrete materials, recalling how to get from one place to another, and recognizing facial characteristics of people he has met. He also performs similarly to other children his age when required to recall unrelated verbal material (e.g., rote facts). However, when the material becomes more meaningful, Reggie's ability to recall the material, even when he is given cues, is poorly developed. This weakness may impair Reggie's ability to use his past experiences to inform his future actions. For example, Reggie will likely have difficulty recalling verbal reprimands and instructions that have used to alter his behavior.

Some of Reggie's adaptive skills are somewhat similar to others his age, including skills needed for daily living (e.g., brushes his teeth; dresses himself), safety (e.g., obeys basic safety rules), and functional academics (e.g., is able to recognize coins). However, he has poorly developed communication (e.g., fails to modify his language to account for listener differences), motor (e.g., is clumsy), and socialization (e.g., fails to show empathy) skills. He is characterized by his mother and teacher as also exhibiting clinical levels of atypicality (e.g., behaviors considered to be immature, deviant, or odd), social withdrawal (e.g., reluctance to join in social activities), and depression (e.g., sadness and unhappiness). Further, Reggie exhibits a range of behaviors that are seen as symptomatic of Asperger' Syndrome (e.g., social and language impairments).

> OBSERVE: In the Diagnosis section of the report, the writer carefully evaluates each differential diagnosis and describes her rationale for ruling them out. Since diagnostic categories often overlap, this approach allows other professionals to evaluate each option, and results in a sense of confidence that this is the correct diagnosis.

Diagnosis

The primary presenting concerns for Reggie centered on impairments in social and emotional behavior, pragmatic deficiencies, poor social problem-solving abilities, inflexible adherence to specific non-functional routines, and stereotyped and repetitive mannerisms.

Because these symptoms could potentially be explained by various conditions that display symptom overlap, including Asperger's Syndrome. High Functioning Autism, and nonverbal learning disability, a comprehensive evaluation was undertaken to assist us with differential diagnosis. We first considered whether Reggie's overall profile could be explained through a diagnosis of High Functioning Autism. Typically, children presenting with this condition demonstrate a social, emotional, and behavioral profile that is consistent with that observed in Reggie. However, children with High Functioning Autism often have delays in the development of spoken language and exhibit language/communicative deviance (i.e., aspects of their language and communication are qualitatively different than that observed in normally-developing children). Information provided by Reggie's mother indicated that Reggie did not demonstrate a developmental delay in language acquisition. Moreover, the current evaluation did not find robust evidence of language deviance.

High Functioning Autism also is frequently defined by significant deficits in auditory perception, expressive vocabulary, verbal memory, and verbal reasoning, while spatial skills are areas of relative strength. While Reggie's profile fits this description in many respects, he demonstrates average abilities in various auditory areas (including auditory working memory, phonological processing, expressive word knowledge, verbal reasoning, and immediate/delayed memory for word pairs) in the context of poorly developed abilities in auditory selective and sustained attention, pragmatics, auditory processing speed, and memory for semantically rich verbal material. In summary, Reggie does not present a classic pattern of High Functioning Autism and consequently, we decided to compare his overall profile with the descriptions of other disorders that may be explanatory.

Nonverbal Learning Disability is defined by a number of specific and potentially debilitating symptoms including neuropsychological deficits, academic deficits, and social-emotional/adaptational symptoms. Neuropsychological deficits include difficulties with tactile and visual perception, psychomotor coordination, tactile and visual attention, nonverbal memory, reasoning, executive functions, and specific aspects of language (e.g., speech prosody, expressing emotional intonation). One of the most debilitating features of nonverbal learning disability is social impairments, which generally involve poor social judgement, problem solving, intimacy, and adaptability. Comparisons between Reggie's profile and that of children with nonverbal learning disability reveal many similarities. For example, evidence of good receptive and expressive vocabulary, rote memory, and attention to detail is common along with deficits in executive functioning, nonverbal aspects of interactions, pragmatic competencies, tactile and haptic discrimination, and gross motor coordination. The social, emotional, and adaptive difficulties also are highly similar although unlike children with nonverbal learning disability who actively seek interpersonal relationships but lack the social competencies to succeed, Reggie does not seem to be strongly motivated to seek and maintain relationships. Most importantly, assessment results did not yield evidence of the most prominent features in nonverbal learning disability (i.e., deficits in visual perception, visual processing, and visual-spatial reasoning). Indeed, Reggie demonstrated average abilities on specific tasks of visual-spatial, fine motor, visual attention, working memory, and spatial memory.

Reggie's profile best fits the pattern defined by Asperger's Syndrome, a neurologically-based disability. Reggie exhibits the constellation of impairments in reciprocal social interaction (e.g., inability to interact with peers, lack of appreciation of social cues, socially and emotionally inappropriate behavior); restricted, repetitive, and stereotyped patterns of behavior, interests, and activities (e.g., preoccupation with or restricted patterns of interest; inflexible adherence to non-functional routines; stereotyped and repetitive motor mannerisms); impairment in imagination and flexible thought processes (e.g., poor understanding of jargon; resistance to change; inability to play creatively; problems in transferring skills from one environment to another); speech and language problems (e.g., superficially, perfect expressive language; formal, pedantic language; odd prosody, peculiar voice characteristics; impairment of comprehension, including misinterpretations of literal/implied meanings); nonverbal communication problems (e.g., limited use of gestures; inappropriate expression; peculiar, stiff gaze); and motor clumsiness (Gillbert, 1989; DSM-IV, 1997 – 299.80 – Asperger's Disorder) characteristic of this condition.

Reggie also appears to exhibit many of the secondary characteristics of Asperger's Syndrome (e.g., is overly sensitive to tastes and smells). However, some discrepancies exist between Reggie's neuropsychological profile and that which research has found to be characteristic of children with Asperger's Syndrome. For example, while Reggie exhibits gross motor deficits, he exhibits normally-developed fine motor skills, and there is little evidence of deficits in visual-motor integration or visual-spatial perception. Visual memory and nonverbal concept formation also are within average ranges. Further multidisciplinary evaluation will be necessary to facilitate differential diagnosis.

Recommendations

OBSERVE: This is the "intervene" part of the *assess-understand-intervene* model. The recommendation section may take the most time and thought to write, and is the most often read section. As your read these recommendations, notice that they are organized by the major problem areas which link back to the referral questions and major findings of the evaluation. Clearly, these are not generic recommendations that have been cut and paste from a computerized bank of standard recommendations. The author of this report has taken the time and care to personalize the recommendations for Reggie. Further, the writer does not stop with high level recommendations such as, "Utilize a cognitive picture rehearsal strategy", but explains in lay terms how to carry out the recommendation. Overall, these are recommendations that have a high likelihood of being carried out because the psychologist has taken the time, effort, and care to prepare a thoughtful report that inspires confidence and creates rapport with the reader by demonstrating an in-depth knowledge of the child's history and behavior in multiple settings, assessing to understand rather than to label and place, and crafting personalized recommendations firmly based on the understanding gained from the assessment. One has the distinct impression that Reggie will be better understood by his parents and teachers, and that he will be better off as a result of this evaluation.

1. Due to the multifaceted nature of Reggie's condition, differential diagnosis can best be accomplished through a thorough and informed evaluation by a multidisciplinary team well versed in the presentation of Asperger's Syndrome and other conditions. We will be referring Reggie to the Blackthorne Children's Center, an interdisciplinary clinic that provides comprehensive assessment, parent support, and treatment programs for children with Autism Spectrum Disorders and other related conditions.

2. The following strategies can be used within both the home and school contexts to enhance Reggie's functioning. The examiners, in collaboration with professionals from the Blackthorne Children's Center, will work with the parents and school to assist in developing an individualized intervention plan for Reggie and implementing those strategies that best fit the home and school environments.

A. Social and Emotional Development   Children who have or display characteristics of Asperger's Syndrome, High Functioning Autism, or nonverbal learning disabilities, benefit from direct training in appropriate ways of interacting socially and expressing emotion. The following strategies are likely to be beneficial to Reggie's social and emotional growth.

- Reggie is likely to benefit from direct and repeated instruction in the areas of social and emotional development. Social Stories and Conversation Comic Strip are two excellent tools created by Carol Gray to assist in direct teaching of social aspects of language and interpretation of the emotions of others. These tools can be applied to teach a wide range of problem solving skills for social environments and can help Reggie to extend learning beyond the immediate situation by practicing application to a variety of situations. This modeling approach will help Reggie to learn appropriate behaviors in a variety of contexts.
- Reggie also is likely to benefit from "incidental teaching." This would involve teaching Reggie about a social situation as it is occurring rather than in a structured lesson. The goal would be to amplify the social environment for Reggie as it is unfolding so that he could pick up on the social cues and rules. Incidental teaching could

be done very concretely for Reggie. One might use visual aids (e.g., using a turn card to denote whose turn it is during a game) or physical prompts (e.g., a tap on the shoulder to indicate Reggie's turn). Alternatively, incidental teaching also can be more conceptual. For example, if Reggie is talking non-stop about some circumscribed interest and his peers are starting to get restless, we might say to Reggie, "Look how the other children are yawning and squirming in their seats. What do you think they are feeling? Why? Can you ask them if they want to hear more?"

- A Cognitive Picture Rehearsal strategy further may be helpful for Reggie. This strategy utilizes cartoon-like drawings combined with positive reinforcement principles. Cognitive picture rehearsal always includes drawings or pictures of three components: the antecedents to a problem situation, the targeted desired behaviour, and a positive reinforcer. The pictures are displayed on index cards. On the back of each card is a script describing the sequence of events. Reggie would be shown the sequence of cards until he can repeat what is happening in each picture. Then the sequence is reviewed just prior to Reggie entering the potentially problematic situation. Unlike social skill picture books, which were designed to model general social skills, cognitive picture rehearsal is used for a specific problem situation. Reggie may benefit from reviewing relevant stories prior to potentially stressful situations or as debriefing after an outburst.

Other strategies for enhancing social and emotional development, including structured learning approaches, transfer and generalization skills, and strategies for expressing emotion, are presented in Appendix B.

B. Anxiety and Transitions   Individuals with Asperger's Syndrome often have difficulty with transitions and change but thrive in structured, predictable environments. As such, the use of techniques to structure the day can help reduce outbursts and stress. However, change and transition are inevitable, and consequently it will be important to provide Reggie with strategies to handle new or unexpected situations. Ideas include the following.

- Use a daily schedule. This may be a pictorial representation of daily events. It can be placed on his desk or laminated in the cover of a notebook. Reggie can cross off each event as it occurs. This will help him to organize his day and feel secure within the routine presented. This schedule also can be used to introduce unexpected changes that may occur throughout the day. Changes should be entered into the daily calendar and be pointed out or highlighted so that Reggie can anticipate them without becoming upset.

- Reggie also may benefit from direct teaching and practice in dealing with unexpected situations. Modeling, role-playing, and using Social Stories may help him learn ways to deal with stress at such times. When a change to his routine arises, Reggie can be prompted to use strategies previously learned.

Other techniques, including coping strategies, the use of verbal explanations, and providing checklists, are included in Appendix B.

C. Pragmatic Language   In addition to the use of Social Stories and Comic Strip Conversations suggested previously, direct teaching and modeling may be effective approaches to help Reggie improve his language in social situations. The following strategies and others listed in Appendix B will facilitate the development of more socially sensitive language skills.

- Take advantage of naturally occurring interactions to increase the use of different language functions. For example, practice greetings at the beginning of a day; have Reggie ask his peers what they want to eat for snacks; have Reggie request necessary materials to complete an art project.
- Role-play conversations that might occur with different people in different contexts. For example, set up a situation (or use one that occurs during the course of Reggie's day) in which Reggie has to explain the same thing to different people. For example, he might be asked to teach the rules of a new game to a younger child and then to an adult. If Reggie's explanations are the same for each listener, model different language patterns for each listener.

D. Attention   Reggie's most significant difficulties revolve around auditory selective and sustained attention. Techniques (e.g., use of self-monitoring techniques) that may help him compensate for weaknesses in these areas are outlined in Appendix B. Other suggestions include the following.

- To ensure Reggie has fully understood instructions, establish eye contact, make directions clear and concise, check for comprehension, encourage Reggie to ask for clarification and assistance, and repeat instructions as needed. Additionally, structured teaching of paraphrasing and self-verbalizing skills may help increase comprehension.
- The use of visual (e.g., a visual chart placed on his desk) and verbal (e.g., "this is really important" or "pay attention to this detail") cues that are paired with positive reinforcement are likely to help Reggie focus on relevant aspects of a task.

E. Memory   Reggie experiences the most significant memory problems when the material presented is semantically and socially rich. His deficits in social knowledge are likely to interfere with his ability to organize and make sense of this material which, in turn, makes spontaneous recall difficult. We have already seen that by providing him with cues to enhance recall, his memory improves. In Appendix B, we have provided a number of suggestions on how Reggie can be helped to better organize and store meaningful material and how both other- and self-generated cues can be employed to facilitate recognition and recall.

We appreciate having this opportunity to work with Reggie, his parents, and teachers. We look forward to further collaborative interactions with your family and professionals at the Black thorne Children's Center.

S. Rutherford, Ph.D.   J. Montgomery, M.A.
Licensed Psychologist   Certified Psychological Associate

APPENDIX A

TEST SCORES

This section should contain all of the needed test score information that makes it possible for the parent or another professional to determine the basis for the descriptions, interpretations, and recommendations contained in the report. This section may vary in detail as a function of who is receiving the report (e.g. parents, other psychologists, teachers, a

Wechsler Intelligence Scale for Children–IV

Index and Subtest Scores	Scaled Score	Percentile Rank
VCI	79	8 (Borderline to low average)
Similarities	8	25
Vocabulary	10	50
Comprehension	1	<1
Word Reasoning	8	25
PRI	94	34 (average range)
Block Design	8	25
Picture Concepts	9	37
Matrix Reasoning	10	50
Picture Completion	9	37
WMI	99	47 (average range)
Digit Span	10	50
Letter-Number	-	n/a
Arithmetic	10	50
PSI	70	2 (borderline to extremely low)
Coding	1	<1
Symbol Search	8	25
FSIQ	81	10 (low average range)

pediatric oncologist, the courts, etc.). The inclusion of a brief description of the tests or other diagnostic procedures to assist those readers who are less familiar with psychological tests and assessment practices may be useful. Graphs as presented in the WISC-IV Writer may also be helpful to readers.

Because this chapter addresses issues important to report writing and not score interpretation, we present only the WISC-IV test results so as not to distract the reader from the organization and flow of the report narrative.

SAME REPORT PREPARED FOR REFERRAL AGENCY

Dr. S. Rutherford, Registered Psychologist
Robertson Child and Youth Assessment Centre
Confidential Psychological and Cognitive Evaluation

Name:	Reggie Block	**Parents**:	Mary and Samuel Block
Age:	7 years, 3 months	**Address:**	611 Penny Road
Grade:	2	**City:**	Robertston, DE
School:	Mayfield Elementary	**Telephone:**	966-5246
Assessment Dates:			October 22nd, 24th, 27th – 31th, 2008
Classroom Observation:			October 30th, 2008
Evaluators:	S. Rutherford, Ph.D., Licensed Psychologist		
	J. Montgomery, Certified Psychological Associate		

Reason for Referral

Mr. and Mrs. Block have consented to have their 7-year-old son, Reggie, referred to the Blackthorne's Children's Center for further evaluation. Findings from our assessment suggest the possible presence of Asperger's Syndrome. However, further differential diagnosis by a multidisciplinary team is needed.

Background Information

Reggie resides with his parents and two elder siblings in what the parents describe as a stable and nurturing environment. Both parents have post-secondary education and are employed; there is no family history of psychological, learning, or medical problems. Mary's pregnancy and delivery with Reggie were uneventful and neonatal health at birth was good. Early infant temperament was described as difficult: Reggie was hard to soothe, frequently irritable, strongly reactive to minor changes, and easily over-stimulated. With the exception of delays in gross motor development, all other milestones were met in a normal temporal sequence. Medical history is unremarkable. Reggie is described as a "picky" eater, who is overly sensitive to particular food textures, tastes, and smells. Reggie has not been previously assessed.

Both Reggie's parents and classroom teacher concur that Reggie presents with significant impairments in: a) social interaction (e.g., interacting with peers, appreciating social cues, socially and emotionally inappropriate behaviour); b) cognitive and behavioural flexibility and adaptability (e.g., Reggie has highly circumscribed interests and routines that involve lining up ducks and repeating phrases associated with television game shows); c) the pragmatic (e.g., impairment in the social comprehension of language; inability to adapt language to fit situational contexts) and non-verbal (e.g., stiff gaze, inappropriate expression) aspects of communication; and, d) social problem solving and imagination (e.g., inability to play creatively or to generate novel solutions to day-to-day problems). In addition, stereotypical behaviors (e.g., hand-flapping) and inattention are observed frequently. According to the parents, Reggie's behavioral profile has been evident throughout his preschool and early school years.

Current Assessment

A. Assessment Methods   Our assessment protocol included semi-structured interviews with the parents, Reggie, and his classroom teacher; observations of Reggie within the classroom and clinical environments; direct assessment of Reggie's attention, language, visual-spatial, sensorimotor, processing speed, memory, and adaptive and psychological skills; and, parent and teacher ratings of his adaptive and behavioral functioning.

B. Summary of Assessment Findings   Our assessment of Reggie's intellectual skills revealed considerable intra/interindividual strengths and weaknesses within and across each of the factors of the WISC-IV. For example, in some areas (auditory working memory), Reggie demonstrated average abilities. In others, his skills were within the borderline or lower ranges (e.g., Social Comprehension subtest). The results from the WISC-IV were used to guide the selection of tasks for a domain-by-domain assessment designed to provide a comprehensive understanding of Reggie's abilities.

Reggie demonstrated average abilities to temporarily hold, process, and mentally manipulate a limited amount of verbal information. Similarly, Reggie was able to sustain his visual attention, curb any impulsive tendencies, maintain a consistent response set, and alter his performance in response to changing task demands. His ability to simultaneously attend to multiple tasks also was within average level. In contrast, Reggie has poorly developed abilities to maintain his attention to continuous and repetitive verbal activities and to distinguish central verbal information from that which is irrelevant. Weaknesses also are noted in Reggie's abilities to self-regulate his attention.

Within the language domain, average competencies were found in phonological processing, although Reggie displays difficulty when required to remove a medial or final sound. Weaknesses further were evident when the syntactic structure of verbal instructions became more complex. Reggie excelled at accessing and producing familiar words rapidly while his expressive vocabulary and verbal reasoning skills were within low average to average ranges. On the other hand, Reggie's pragmatic competencies and understanding of conventional standards of behavior were weak.

Reggie showed low average to average abilities at reasoning with non-verbal material and differentiating essential from nonessential visual details. However, poorly developed abilities to anticipate, judge, and understand the possible antecedents and consequents of socially-laden visual events were evident. In the sensorimotor area, Reggie excelled at copying two-dimensional geometric figures on paper, although we observed that he was extremely methodological and deliberate in his drawings. As a result, he was very slow in completing activities involving drawing or printing. This tendency debilitated his performance on timed tasks. Reggie's finger dexterity and ability to perceive sensory input without the aid of vision were at expected developmental levels.

While Reggie's rate of processing visual symbols was extremely slow, when the visual-motor demands were reduced, his speed of processing increased to within the low average range. He showed poorly developed ability, though, in rapidly retrieving categorical verbal information from long-term memory.

Reggie was able to retrieve and recognize spatial and unrelated word pairs in both immediate and delayed contexts at levels commensurate with the majority of his peers. However, a weakness was evident in recalling semantically complex verbal information. While cues facilitated his recall slightly, Reggie's recall of this material remained weak.

Adaptively, Reggie performs at expected levels in domains such as daily living skills, safety, and self-care. Adaptive skills in communication, motor, and socialization were low. In evaluating Reggie's behaviors and emotions, both his mother and teacher rate him within the clinical range on scales assessing symptoms of atypicality, social withdrawal, and depression. His mother also describes him as presenting with a constellation of symptoms characteristic of Asperger Syndrome.

Diagnostic Interpretations

In evaluating Reggie's overall profile, we considered several explanatory diagnostic categories, including High Functioning Autism (HFA), non-verbal learning disability (NRD), and Asperger's Syndrome (AS). Because

Reggie presents with relative strengths in various areas. (e.g., auditory working memory, phonological processing, expressive word knowledge, verbal reasoning, and immediate and delayed memory for word pairs), did not present with delays in the development of spoken language in his early formative years and currently does not exhibit deviant language patterns, a diagnosis of HFA did not appear to provide the best fit for his profile. We also compared Reggie's profile to that of children presenting with NLD. While there were many similarities, our assessment did not yield evidence of the most prominent features of NLD (i.e., deficits in visual perception, visual processing, and visual-spatial reasoning). We finally considered a diagnosis of Asperger's Syndrome. As with many cases of AS, Reggie did not present completely classic pattern. Assessment data found that Reggie exhibits the constellation of impairments in reciprocal and social interaction; restricted, repetitive, and stereotyped patterns of behavior, interests, and activities; impairment in imagination and flexible thought processes; verbal and nonverbal communicative impairments; and motor clumsiness that is characteristic of this condition. Many of the secondary features of AS also are present (e.g., overly sensitive to smells and tests). However, we note that there are discrepancies between Reggie's neuropsychological profile and that which preliminary research has found in children with AS (e.g., evidence of deficits in visual-spatial perception). As a result, further multidisciplinary evaluation is necessary to facilitate differential diagnosis.

Recommendations

To ensure that there is ongoing support and intervention for Reggie and his family, we request a follow-up interview with the family and your staff when Reggie's assessment has been completed.

S. Rutherford, Ph.D.   J. Montgomery, M.A.
Licensed Psychologist   Certified Psychological Associate

REFERENCES

American Psychiatric Association (1994). *Diagnostic and statistical manual of mental disorders, fourth edition*. Washington, DC: American Psychiatric Association.

American Psychiatric Association (1995). *Diagnostic and statistical manual of mental disorders, fourth edition: International Version with ICD-10 Codes*. Washington, DC: American Psychiatric Association.

American Psychiatric Association (2000). *Diagnostic and statistical manual of mental disorders, fourth edition, text revision*. Washington, DC: American Psychiatric Association.

Finn, S., & Fischer, C. (1997). Therapeutic psychological assessment: illustration and analysis of philosophical assumptions. Presented at annual meeting of the American Psychological Association, August 8, 1997.

Gregory, R. J. (2000). *Psychological testing: History, principles, and applications* (3rd ed.). Needham Heights, MA: Allyn & Bacon.

Kamphaus, R. W., & Frick, P. J. (2002). *Clinical assessment of child and adolescent personality and behavior* (2nd ed.). Boston: Allyn & Bacon.

Lichtenberger, E. O., Mather, N., Kaufman, N. L., & Kaufman, A. S. (2004). *Essentials of assessment report writing*. Hoboken, NJ: John Wiley & Sons.

Oakland, T., Glutting, J., & Watkins, M. (2005). Assessment of test behaviors with the WISC-IV. In A. Prifitera, D. Saklofske, & L. Weiss (Eds.), *WISC-IV: Clinical use and interpretation* (pp. 417–434). New York: Elsevier Academic Press.

Sattler, J. M. (2002). *Assessment of Children: Cognitive applications* (4th ed.). La Mesa, CA: Author.

World Health Organization (1992). *The international classification of diseases and related health problems* (10th ed.). Geneva, Switzerland: Author.

World Health Organization (1992). *International statistical classification of disease and related health problems: Tenth revision*. Geneva: World Health Organization.

World Health Organization (1999). *International classification of functioning and disability*. Geneva, Switzerland: Author.

SUBJECT INDEX